Oracle Press™

W9-AOB-344

Oracle Database 10g
DBA Handbook

About the Authors

Kevin Loney, a senior technical management consultant with TUSC, is an internationally-recognized expert in the design, development, administration, and tuning of Oracle databases. An Oracle developer and DBA since 1987, he has implemented both transaction processing systems and data warehouses. He provides expert assistance to companies for the implementation and tuning of their business-critical Oracle applications.

He is the author of numerous technical articles and the lead author or coauthor of such best-selling books as *Oracle10g: The Complete Reference*. He regularly presents at Oracle user conferences in North America and Europe, and in 2002 was named Consultant of the Year by *ORACLE Magazine*.

Bob Bryla is an Oracle 8, 8*i*, 9*i*, and 10*g* Certified Professional with more than 15 years of experience in database design, database application development, training, and Oracle database administration. He is the primary Internet database designer and an Oracle DBA at Lands' End in Dodgeville, Wisconsin.

In his spare time, he is a technical editor for a number of Oracle Press and Sybex books, in addition to authoring several Sybex certification study guides for both Oracle9*i* and Oracle 10*g*.

ORACLE®

Oracle Press™

Oracle Database 10g DBA Handbook

Kevin Loney
Bob Bryla
and the experts at TUSC

McGraw-Hill/Osborne

New York   Chicago   San Francisco
Lisbon   London   Madrid   Mexico City   Milan
New Delhi   San Juan   Seoul   Singapore   Sydney   Toronto

The McGraw·Hill Companies

McGraw-Hill/Osborne
2100 Powell Street, 10th Floor
Emeryville, California 94608
U.S.A.

To arrange bulk purchase discounts for sales promotions, premiums, or fund-raisers, please contact
McGraw-Hill/Osborne at the above address. For information on translations or book distributors outside the
U.S.A., please see the International Contact Information page immediately following the index of this book.

Oracle Database 10g DBA Handbook

  34567890 CUS CUS 01987

ISBN 0-07-223145-9

Acquisitions Editor
  Lisa McClain

Project Editor
  Lisa Wolters-Broder

Acquisitions Coordinator
  Athena Honore

Technical Editor
  Scott Gossett

Copy Editor
  Bart Reed

Proofreader
  Emily Hsuan

Indexer
  Irv Hershman

Composition
  Apollo Publishing Services

Illustrator
  Melinda Lytle

Series Design
  Jani Beckwith, Peter F. Hancik

Cover Designer
  Damore Johann Design, Inc.

This book was composed with Corel VENTURA™ Publisher.

To Sue, Emily, Rachel, and Jane
for their love and support.

—K. L.

To the gang at home: We finally had enough
snow for the snowman this year...
looking forward to the next one.

—B.B.

Contents at a Glance

PART IV
Networked Oracle

Contents

PART I
Database Architecture

PART II

Database Management

PART III
High Availability

Acknowledgments

This book is the product of two authors, many contributors, and more editors than you can imagine. Special thanks to Bob Bryla in particular—it is largely due to his dedication and knowledge that this project was completed with the quality and timeliness required.

Thanks to the contributors and editors from TUSC, including Brad Brown, Tony Catalano, Mike Killough, Rich Niemiec, Dan Norris, Chris Ostrowski, and Joe Trezzo. Thanks to TUSC for its support during the writing process.

Thanks to the team at McGraw-Hill/Osborne, including Lisa Wolters-Broder and Lisa McClain. Thanks to those readers who suggested topics, changes, or corrections. Thanks to Eyal Aronoff and Rachel Carmichael, among others, for their advice, comments, corrections, and friendship. Thanks to Marlene Theriault for her contributions to the last edition.

Thanks to friends who helped along the way, including Robert Meissner, Br. Declan Kane CFX, Br. William Griffin CFX, Karen Reynolds, Marie Paretti, Jan Riess, Chris O'Neill, Cheryl Bittner, Joann Hanlon, and Bill Fleming.

If you have comments regarding the book or are looking for additional materials related to this book, please go to www.kevinloney.com.

—Kevin Loney

Many technical books need the expertise of more than one author, and this one is no exception. Thanks to Kevin for his flexibility and advice when coming up with a new outline for this book— several times! It was an honor to work with such a seasoned author, and I'm glad I was able to help make this book possible.

Thanks go out to Lisa Wolters-Broder and Lisa McClain for filling in the gaps in my college English courses, and thanks also to Scott Gossett who gave me good advice when the theoretical met the practical.

Many of my professional colleagues at both Lands' End and Greenbrier & Russel were a source of both inspiration and guidance: Joe Johnson, Brook Swenson, Stephen Deutsch, and Julie Krause. In this case, the whole is truly greater than the sum of its parts.

If you have any questions or comments about any part of this book, please do not hesitate to contact me at rjbryla@centurytel.net.

—Bob Bryla

Introduction

hether you're an experienced DBA, a new DBA, or an application developer, you need to understand how Oracle10g's new features can help you best meet your customers' needs. In this book, you will find coverage of the newest features as well as ways of merging those features into the management of an Oracle database. The emphasis throughout is on managing the database's capabilities in an effective, efficient manner to deliver a quality product. The end result will be a database that is dependable, robust, secure, and extensible.

Several components are critical to this goal, and you'll see all of them covered here in depth after we introduce the Oracle Architecture, Oracle 10g upgrade issues, and tablespace planning in Part I; a well-designed logical and physical database architecture will improve performance and ease administration by properly distributing database objects. You'll see appropriate monitoring, security, and tuning strategies for stand-alone and networked databases in Part II of this book. Backup and recovery strategies are provided to help ensure the database's recoverability. Each section focuses on both the features and the proper planning and management techniques for each area.

High availability is covered in all of its flavors: Real Application Clusters (RAC), Recovery Manager (RMAN), and Oracle Data Guard, to name a few of the topics covered in-depth in Part III of this book.

Networking issues and the management of distributed and client/server databases are thoroughly covered. Oracle Net, networking configurations, materialized views, location transparency, and everything else you need to successfully implement a distributed or client/server database are described in detail in Part IV of this book. You'll also find real-world examples for every major configuration.

In addition to the commands needed to perform DBA activities, you will also see the Oracle Enterprise Manager screens from which you can perform similar functions. By following the techniques in this book, your systems can be designed and implemented so well that tuning efforts will be minimal. Administering the database will become easier as the users get a better product, while the database works—and works well.

PART
I

Database
Architecture

CHAPTER
1

Getting Started
with the Oracle
Architecture

racle Database 10*g* is an evolutionary, if not revolutionary, step from the previous release of Oracle9*i*. Not only is Oracle 10*g* more feature rich, it is easier to manage with more tools to help the Oracle DBA "set it and forget it." Part I of this book covers the basics of the Oracle architecture and lays the foundation for deploying a successful Oracle infrastructure by giving practical advice for a new installation or upgrading from a previous release of Oracle. To provide a good foundation for the Oracle 10*g* software, server hardware and operating system configuration issues are covered in the relevant sections.

In Part II of this book, we will cover several areas relevant to the day-to-day maintenance and operation of an Oracle 10*g* database. The first chapter in Part II discusses the requirements that a DBA needs to gather long before the install CD is mounted on the server. Successive chapters deal with ways the DBA can manage disk space, CPU usage, and adjust Oracle parameters to optimize the server's resources, using a variety of tools at the DBA's disposal for monitoring database performance. Transaction management is greatly simplified by Automated Undo Management (AUM), an Oracle Database feature introduced in Oracle9*i* and enhanced in Oracle 10*g*.

Part III of this book focuses on the high availability aspects of Oracle 10*g*. This includes using Oracle's Recovery Manager (RMAN) to perform and automate database backups and recovery, along with other features, such as Oracle Data Guard, to provide a reliable and easy way to recover from a database failure. Last, but certainly not least, we will show how Oracle 10*g* Real Application Clusters (RAC) can at the same time provide extreme scalability and transparent failover capabilities to a database environment.

In Part IV of this book, we will cover a variety of issues revolving around Networked Oracle. Not only will we cover how Oracle Net can be configured in an N-tier environment, but also how we manage large and distributed databases that may reside in neighboring cities or around the world.

In this chapter, we cover the basics of Oracle Database 10*g*, highlighting many of the features we will cover in the rest of the book as well as the basics of installing Oracle 10*g* using Oracle Universal Installer (OUI) and the Database Configuration Assistant (DBCA). We will take a tour of the elements that comprise an instance of Oracle 10*g*, ranging from memory structures to disk structures, initialization parameters, tables, indexes, and PL/SQL. Each of these elements plays a large role in making Oracle 10*g* a highly scalable, available, and secure environment.

An Overview of Databases and Instances

Although the terms "database" and "instance" are often used interchangeably, they are quite different. They are very distinct entities in an Oracle datacenter, as you shall see in the following sections.

Databases

A *database* is a collection of data on disk in one or more files on a database server that collects and maintains related information. The database consists of various physical and logical structures, the table being the most important logical structure in the database. A table consists of rows and columns containing related data. At a minimum, a database must have at least tables to store useful information. Figure 1-1 shows a sample table containing four rows and three columns. The data

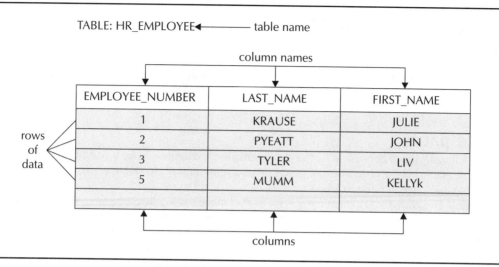

FIGURE 1-1. *Sample database table*

in each row of the table is related: Each row contains information about a particular employee in the company.

In addition, a database provides a level of security to prevent unauthorized access to the data. Oracle Database 10g provides many mechanisms to facilitate the security necessary to keep confidential data confidential. Oracle Security and access control are covered in more detail in Chapter 10.

Files comprising a database fall into two broad categories: database files and non-database files. The distinction lies in what kind of data is stored in each. Database files contain data and metadata; non-database files contain initialization parameters, logging information, and so forth. Database files are critical to the ongoing operation of the database on a moment-by-moment basis. Each of these physical storage structures is discussed later in the section titled "Oracle Physical Storage Structures."

Instances

The main components of a typical enterprise server are one or more CPUs, disk space, and memory. Whereas the Oracle database is stored on a server's disk, an Oracle instance exists in the server's memory. An Oracle *instance* is composed of a large block of memory allocated in an area called the *System Global Area* (*SGA*), along with a number of background processes that interact between the SGA and the database files on disk.

In an Oracle Real Application Cluster (RAC), more than one instance will use the same database. Although the instances that share the database can be on the same server, most likely the instances will be on separate servers that are connected by a high-speed interconnect and access a database that resides on a specialized RAID-enabled disk subsystem. More details on how a RAC installation is configured are provided in Chapter 11.

Oracle Logical Storage Structures

The datafiles in an Oracle database are grouped together into one or more tablespaces. Within each tablespace, the logical database structures, such as tables and indexes, are segments that are further subdivided into extents and blocks. This logical subdivision of storage allows Oracle to have more efficient control over disk space usage. Figure 1-2 shows the relationship between the logical storage structures in a database.

Tablespaces

An Oracle *tablespace* consists of one or more datafiles; a datafile can be a part of one and only one tablespace. For an installation of Oracle 10g, a minimum of two tablespaces are created: the SYSTEM tablespace and the SYSAUX tablespace.

Oracle 10g allows you to create a special kind of tablespace called a *bigfile tablespace,* which can be as large as 8EB (exabytes, or a million terabytes). Using bigfiles makes tablespace management completely transparent to the DBA; in other words, the DBA can manage the tablespace as a unit without worrying about the size and structure of the underlying datafiles.

Using Oracle Managed Files (OMF) can make tablespace datafile management even easier. With OMF, the DBA specifies one or more locations in the file system where datafiles, control files, and redo log files will reside, and Oracle automatically handles the naming and management of these files. We discuss OMF in more detail in Chapter 4.

If a tablespace is *temporary,* the tablespace itself is permanent; only the segments saved in the tablespace are temporary. A temporary tablespace can be used for sorting operations and as a

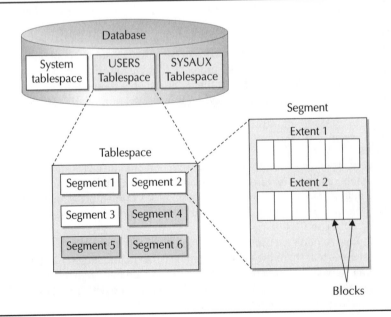

FIGURE 1-2. *Logical storage structures*

working area for building indexes. Dedicating a tablespace for these kinds of operations helps to reduce the I/O contention between temporary segments and permanent segments stored in another tablespace, such as tables.

Tablespaces can be either *dictionary managed* or *locally managed.* In a dictionary-managed tablespace, extent management is recorded in data dictionary tables. Therefore, even if all application tables are in the USERS tablespace, the SYSTEM tablespace will still be accessed for managing DML on application tables. Because all users and applications must use the SYSTEM tablespace for extent management, this creates a potential bottleneck for write-intensive applications. In a locally managed tablespace, Oracle maintains a bitmap in each datafile of the tablespace to track space availability. Only quotas are managed in the data dictionary, dramatically reducing the contention for data dictionary tables.

As of Oracle9*i,* if the SYSTEM tablespace is locally managed, then all other tablespaces must be locally managed if both read and write operations are to be performed on them. Dictionary-managed tablespaces must be read-only in databases with a locally-managed SYSTEM tablespace.

Blocks

A database *block* is the smallest unit of storage in the Oracle database. The size of a block is a specific number of bytes of storage within a given tablespace within the database.

A block is usually a multiple of the operating system block size to facilitate efficient disk I/O. The default block size is specified by the Oracle initialization parameter DB_BLOCK_SIZE. As many as four other block sizes may be defined for other tablespaces in the database, although the blocks in the SYSTEM, SYSAUX, and any temporary tablespaces must be of the size DB_BLOCK_SIZE.

Extents

The *extent* is the next level of logical grouping in the database. An extent consists of one or more database blocks. When a database object is enlarged, the space added to the object is allocated as an extent.

Segments

The next level of logical grouping in a database is the *segment.* A segment is a group of extents that comprise a database object that is treated as a unit, such as a table or index. As a result, this is typically the smallest unit of storage that an end user of the database will deal with. Four types of segments are found in an Oracle database: data segments, index segments, temporary segments, and rollback segments.

Data Segment

Every table in the database resides in a single *data segment,* consisting of one or more extents; more than one segment is allocated for a table if it is a partitioned table or a clustered table. Partitioned and clustered tables are discussed later in this chapter.

Index Segment

Each index is stored in its own *index segment.* As with partitioned tables, each partition of a partitioned index is stored in its own segment.

Temporary Segment

When a user's SQL statement needs disk space to complete an operation, such as a sorting operation that cannot fit in memory, a *temporary segment* is allocated. Temporary segments exist only for the duration of the SQL statement.

Rollback Segment

As of Oracle 10g, rollback segments only exist in the SYSTEM tablespace, and typically the DBA does not need to maintain the SYSTEM rollback segment. In previous Oracle releases, a rollback segment was created to save the previous values of a database DML operation in case the transaction was rolled back, and to maintain the "before" image data to provide read-consistent views of table data for other users accessing the table. Rollback segments were also used during database recovery for rolling back uncommitted transactions that were active when the database instance crashed or terminated unexpectedly.

In Oracle 10g, Automatic Undo Management handles the automatic allocation and management of rollback segments within an undo tablespace. Within an undo tablespace, the undo segments are structured similarly to rollback segments, except that the details of how these segments are managed is under control of Oracle, instead of being managed (often inefficiently) by the DBA. Automatic undo segments were available staring with Oracle9*i*, but manually managed rollback segments are still available in Oracle 10g. However, this functionality is deprecated as of Oracle 10g, and will no longer be available in future releases. Automatic Undo Management is discussed in detail in Chapter 7.

Oracle Logical Database Structures

In this section, we will be covering the highlights of all major logical database structures, starting with tables and indexes. Next, we discuss the variety of datatypes we can use to define the columns of a table. When we create a table with columns, we can place restrictions, or *constraints*, on the columns of the table.

One of the many reasons we use a Relational Database Management System (RDBMS) to manage our data is to leverage the security and auditing features of the Oracle database. We will review the ways we can segregate access to the database by user or by the object being accessed.

We'll also touch upon many other logical structures that can be defined by either the DBA or the user, including synonyms, links to external files, and links to other databases.

Tables

A *table* is the basic unit of storage in an Oracle database. Without any tables, a database has no value to an enterprise. Regardless of the type of table, data in a table is stored in *rows* and *columns*, similar to how data is stored in a spreadsheet. But that is where the similarity ends. The robustness of a database table due to the surrounding reliability, integrity, and scalability of the Oracle database makes a spreadsheet a poor second choice when deciding on a place to store critical information.

In this section, we will review the many different types of tables in the Oracle database and how they can satisfy most every data-storage need for an organization. More details on how to choose between these types of tables for a particular application, and how to manage them, can be found in Chapter 5 and Chapter 8.

Relational Tables

A *relational* table is the most common type of table in a database. A relational table is heap-organized; in other words, the rows in the table are stored in no particular order. In the **create table** command, you can specify the clause **organization heap** to define a heap-organized table, but because this is the default, the clause can be omitted.

Each row of a table contains one or more columns; each column has a datatype and a length. As of Oracle version 8, a column may also contain a user-defined object type, a nested table, or a VARRAY. In addition, a table can be defined as an object table. We will review object tables and objects later in this section.

The built-in Oracle datatypes are presented in Table 1-1.

Oracle Built-in Datatype	Description
VARCHAR2 (*size*) [BYTE | CHAR]	A variable-length character string with a maximum length of 4000 bytes, minimum of 1 byte. CHAR indicates that character semantics are used to size the string; BYTE indicates that byte semantics are used.
NVARCHAR2(*size*)	A variable-length character string with a maximum length of 4000 bytes.
NUMBER(p,s)	A number with a precision *(p)* and scale *(s)*. The precision ranges from 1 to 38, and the scale can be from –84 to 127.
LONG	A variable-length character data with a length up to 2GB ($2^{31}-1$).
DATE	Date values from January 1st, 4712 B.C. to December 31st, 9999 A.D.
BINARY_FLOAT	A 32-bit floating point number.
BINARY_DOUBLE	A 64-bit floating point number.
TIMESTAMP (*fractional_seconds*)	Year, month, day, hour, minute, second, and fractional seconds. Value of *fractional_seconds* can range from 0 to 9; in other words, up to one billionth of a second precision. The default is 6 (one millionth).
TIMESTAMP (*fractional_seconds*) WITH TIME ZONE	Contains a TIMESTAMP value in addition to a time zone displacement value. Time zone displacement can be an offset from UTC (such as '-06:00') or a region name (e.g., 'US/Central').
TIMESTAMP (*fractional_seconds*) WITH LOCAL TIME ZONE	Similar to TIMESTAMP WITH TIMEZONE, except that (1) data is normalized to the database time zone when it is stored and (2) when retrieving columns with this datatype, the user sees the data in the session's time zone.
INTERVAL YEAR (*year_precision*) TO MONTH	Stores a time period in years and months. The value of *year_precision* is the number of digits in the YEAR field.
INTERVAL DAY (*day_precision*) TO SECOND (*fractional_seconds_ precision*)	Stores a period of time as days, hours, minutes, seconds, and fractional seconds. The value for *day_precision* is from 0 to 9, with a default of 2. The value of *fractional_seconds_precision* is similar to the fractional seconds in a TIMESTAMP value; the range is from 0 to 9, with a default of 6.
RAW(*size*)	Raw binary data, with a maximum *size* of 2000 bytes.

TABLE 1-1. *Oracle Built-in Datatypes*

Oracle Built-in Datatype	Description
LONG RAW	Raw binary data, variable length, up to 2GB in size.
ROWID	A base-64 string representing the unique address of a row in its corresponding table. This address is unique throughout the database.
UROWID [(*size*)]	A base-64 string representing the logical address of a row in an index-organized table. The maximum for *size* is 4000 bytes.
CHAR(*size*) [BYTE I CHAR]	A fixed- length character string of length *size*. The minimum size is 1, and the maximum is 2000 bytes. The BYTE and CHAR parameters are BYTE and CHAR semantics, as in VARCHAR2.
NCHAR(*size*)	A fixed-length character string up to 2000 bytes; the maximum *size* depends on the national character set definition for the database. The default *size* is 1.
CLOB	A character large object containing single-byte or multibyte characters; supports both fixed-width or variable-width character sets. The maximum size is (4GB – 1) * DB_BLOCK_SIZE.
NCLOB	Similar to CLOB, except that Unicode characters are stored from either fixed-width and variable-width character sets. The maximum size is (4GB – 1) * DB_BLOCK_SIZE.
BLOB	A binary large object; the maximum size is (4GB – 1) * DB_BLOCK_SIZE.
BFILE	A pointer to a large binary file stored outside the database. Binary files must be accessible from the server running the Oracle instance. The maximum size is 4GB.

TABLE 1-1. *Oracle Built-in Datatypes* (continued)

Oracle also supports ANSI-compatible datatypes; the mapping between the ANSI datatypes and Oracle datatypes is provided in Table 1-2.

Temporary Tables

Temporary tables have been available since Oracle8*i*. They are temporary in the sense of the data that is stored in the table, not in the definition of the table itself. The command **create global temporary table** creates a temporary table.

As long as other users have permissions to the table itself, they may perform **select** statements or Data Manipulation Language Commands (DML), such as **insert**, **update**, or **delete**, on a temporary table. However, each user sees their own and only their own data in the table. When a user truncates a temporary table, only the data that they inserted is removed from the table.

There are two different flavors of temporary data in a temporary table: temporary for the duration of the transaction, and temporary for the duration of the session. The longevity of the temporary data is controlled by the **on commit** clause; **on commit delete rows** removes all rows from the temporary table when a **commit** or **rollback** is issued, and **on commit preserve rows** keeps the rows in the table beyond the transaction boundary. However, when the user's session is terminated, all of the user's rows in the temporary table are removed.

ANSI SQL Datatype	Oracle Datatype
CHARACTER(n) CHAR(n)	CHAR(n)
CHARACTER VARYING(n) CHAR VARYING(n)	VARCHAR(n)
NATIONAL CHARACTER(n) NATIONAL CHAR(n) NCHAR(n)	NCHAR(n)
NATIONAL CHARACTER VARYING(n) NATIONAL CHAR VARYING(n) NCHAR VARYING(n)	NVARCHAR2(n)
NUMERIC(p,s) DECIMAL(p,s)	NUMBER(p,s)
INTEGER INT SMALLINT	NUMBER(38)
FLOAT(b) DOUBLE PRECISION REAL	NUMBER

TABLE 1-2. *ANSI-Equivalent Oracle Datatypes*

There are a few other things to keep in mind when using temporary tables. Although you can create an index on a temporary table, the entries in the index are dropped along with the data rows, as with a regular table. Also, due to the temporary nature of the data in a temporary table, no redo information is generated for DML on temporary tables; however, undo information is created in the undo tablespace.

Index Organized Tables

As you will find out later in the subsection on indexes, creating an index makes finding a particular row in a table more efficient. However, this adds a bit of overhead, because the database must maintain the data rows and the index entries for the table. What if your table does not have many columns, and access to the table occurs primarily on a single column? In this case, an *index organized table (IOT)* might be the right solution. An IOT stores rows of a table in a B-tree index, where each node of the B-tree index contains the keyed (indexed) column along with one or more non-indexed columns.

The most obvious advantage of an IOT is that only one storage structure needs to be maintained instead of two; similarly, the values for the primary key of the table are only stored once in an IOT, versus twice in a regular table.

There are, however, a few disadvantages to using an IOT. Some tables, such as tables for logging events, may not need a primary key, or any keys for that matter; an IOT must have a primary key. Also, IOTs cannot be a member of a cluster. Finally, an IOT might not be the best solution for a table if there are a large number of columns in the table, and many of the columns are frequently accessed when table rows are retrieved.

Object Tables

Since Oracle8, the Oracle Database has supported many object-oriented features in the database. User-defined types, along with any defined methods for these object types, can make an implementation of an object-oriented (OO) development project in Oracle seamless.

Object tables have rows that are themselves objects, or instantiations of type definitions. Rows in an object table can be referenced by object ID (OID), in contrast to a primary key in a relational, or regular, table; however, object tables can still have both primary and unique keys, just as relational tables do.

Let's say, for example, that you are creating a Human Resources (HR) system from scratch, so you have the flexibility to design the database from an entirely OO point of view. The first step is to define an employee object, or type, by creating the type:

```
create type PERS_TYP as object
     (Last_Name        varchar2(45),
      First_Name       varchar2(30),
      Middle_Initial   char(1),
      Surname          varchar2(10),
      SSN              varchar2(15));
```

In this particular case, you're not creating any methods with the PERS_TYP object, but by default Oracle creates a constructor method for the type that has the same name as the type itself (in this case, PERS_TYP). To create an object table as a collection of PERS_TYP objects, you can use the familiar **create table** syntax, as follows:

```
create table pers of pers_typ;
```

To add an instance of an object to the object table, you specify the constructor method in the **insert** command:

```
insert into pers
      values(pers_typ('Judd','Dawn','R','Dr.','123-45-6789'));
```

References to instances of the PERS_TYP object can be stored in other tables as REF objects, and data from the PERS table can be retrieved without a direct reference to the PERS table itself.

More examples of how objects can be used to implement an object-oriented design project can be found in Chapter 5.

External Tables

External tables were introduced in Oracle9*i*. In a nutshell, *external tables* allow a user to access a data source, such as a text file, as if it was a table in the database. The metadata for the table is stored within the Oracle data dictionary, but the contents of the table are stored externally.

The definition for an external table contains two parts. The first and most familiar part is the definition of the table from the database user's point of view. This definition looks like any typical definition that you'd see in a **create table** statement.

The second part, however, is what differentiates an external table from a regular table. This is where the mapping between the database columns and the external data source occurs—what column(s) the data element starts in, how wide the column is, and whether the format of the external column is character or binary. The syntax for the default type of external table,

ORACLE_LOADER, is virtually identical to that of a control file in SQL*Loader. This is one of the advantages of external tables; the user only needs to know how to access a standard database table to get to the external file.

There are a few drawbacks, however, to using external tables. Indexes cannot be created on an external table, and no inserts, updates, or deletes can be performed on external tables. These drawbacks are minor when considering the advantages of using external tables for loading native database tables, for example, in a data warehouse environment.

Clustered Tables

If two or more tables are frequently accessed together (for example, an order table and a line item detail table), then creating a *clustered table* might be a good way to boost the performance of queries that reference those tables. In the case of an order table with an associated line-item detail table, the order header information could be stored in the same block as the line-item detail records, thus reducing the amount of I/O needed to retrieve the order and line-item information.

Clustered tables also reduce the amount of space needed to store the columns the two tables have in common, also known as a *cluster key value*. The cluster key value is also stored in a *cluster index*. The cluster index operates much like a traditional index in that it will improve queries against the clustered tables when accessed by the cluster key value. In our example with orders and line items, the order number is only stored once, instead of repeating for each line-item detail row.

The advantages to clustering a table are reduced if frequent **insert**, **update**, and **delete** operations occur on the table relative to the number of **select** statements against the table. In addition, frequent queries against individual tables in the cluster may also reduce the benefits of clustering the tables in the first place.

Hash Clusters

A special type of clustered table, a *hash cluster,* operates much like a regular clustered table, except that instead of using a cluster index, a hash cluster uses a hashing function to store and retrieve rows in a table. The total estimated amount of space needed for the table is allocated when the table is created, given the number of hash keys specified during the creation of the cluster. In our order-entry example, let's assume that our Oracle database needs to mirror the legacy data-entry system, which reuses order numbers on a periodic basis. Also, the order number is always a six-digit number. We might create the cluster for orders as in the following example:

```
create cluster order_cluster (order_number number(6))
     size 50
     hash is order_number hashkeys 1000000;

create table cust_order (
     order_number      number(6) primary key,
     order_date        date,
     customer_number   number)
cluster order_cluster(order_number);
```

Hash clusters have performance benefits when rows are selected from a table using an equality comparison, as in this example:

```
select order_number, order_date from cust_order
     where order_number = 196811;
```

Typically, this kind of query will retrieve the row with only one I/O if the number of **hashkeys** is high enough and the **hash is** clause, containing the hashing function, produces an evenly distributed hash key.

Sorted Hash Clusters

Sorted hash clusters are new in Oracle 10*g*. They are similar to regular hash clusters in that a hashing function is used to locate a row in a table. However, in addition, sorted hash clusters allow rows in the table to be stored by one or more columns of the table in ascending order. This allows the data to be processed more quickly for applications that lend themselves to First In First Out (FIFO) processing.

You create sorted hash clusters using the same syntax as regular clustered tables, with the addition of the SORT positional parameter after the column definitions within the cluster. Here is an example of creating a table in a sorted hash cluster:

```
create table order_detail (
       order_number        number,
       order_timestamp     timestamp sort,
       customer_number     number)
cluster order_detail_cluster (
       order_number,
       order_timestamp);
```

Due to the FIFO nature of a sorted hash cluster, when orders are accessed by **order_number** the oldest orders are retrieved first based on the value of **order_timestamp**.

Partitioned Tables

Partitioning a table (or index, as you will see in the next section) helps make a large table more manageable. A table may be partitioned, or even subpartitioned, into smaller pieces. From an application point of view, partitioning is transparent (that is, no explicit references to a particular partition are necessary in any end-user SQL). The only effect that a user may notice is that queries against the partitioned table using criteria in the **where** clause that matches the partitioning scheme run a lot faster!

There are many advantages to partitioning from a DBA point of view. If one partition of a table is on a corrupted disk volume, the other partitions in the table are still available for user queries while the damaged volume is being repaired. Similarly, backups of partitions can occur over a period of days, one partition at a time, rather than requiring a single backup of the entire table.

Partitions are one of three types: range partitioned, hash partitioned, or, as of Oracle9*i*, list partitioned. Each row in a partitioned table can exist in one, and only one, partition. The *partition key* directs the row to the proper partition; the partition key can be a composite key of up to 16 columns in the table. There are a few minor restrictions on the types of tables that can be partitioned; for example, a table containing a LONG or LONG RAW column cannot be partitioned.

TIP
Oracle Corporation recommends that any table greater than 2GB in size be seriously considered for partitioning.

No matter what type of partitioning scheme is in use, each member of a partitioned table must have the same logical attributes, such as column names, datatypes, constraints, and so forth. The physical attributes for each partition, however, can be different depending on its size and location on disk. The key is that the partitioned table must be logically consistent from an application or user point of view.

Range Partitions   A *range partition* is a partition whose partition key falls within a certain range. For example, visits to the corporate e-commerce website can be assigned to a partition based on the date of the visit, with one partition per quarter. A website visit on May 25th, 2004 will be recorded in the partition with the name FY2004Q2, whereas a website visit on December 2nd, 2004 will be recorded in the partition with the name FY2004Q4.

List Partitions   A *list partition* is a partition whose partition key falls within groups of distinct values. For example, sales by region of the country may create a partition for NY, CT, MA, and VT, and another partition for IL, WI, IA, and MN. Any sales from elsewhere in the world may be assigned to its own partition when the state code is missing.

Hash Partitions   A *hash partition* assigns a row to a partition based on a hashing function, specifying the column or columns used in the hashing function, but not explicitly assigning the partition, only specifying how many partitions are available. Oracle will assign the row to a partition and ensure a balanced distribution of rows in each partition.

Hash partitions are useful when there is no clear list or range-partitioning scheme given the types of columns in the table, or when the relative sizes of the partitions change frequently, requiring repeated manual adjustments to the partitioning scheme.

Composite Partitions   Even further refinement of the partitioning process is available with *composite partitions*. For example, a table may be partitioned by range, and within each range, subpartitioned by list or by hash.

Partitioned Indexes

The indexes on a table may also be partitioned, either matching the partition scheme of the table being indexed *(local indexes)* or partitioned independently from the partition scheme of the table *(global indexes)*. Local partitioned indexes have the advantage of increased availability of the index when partition operations occur; for example, archiving and dropping the partition FY2002Q4 and its local index will not affect index availability for the other partitions in the table.

Constraints

An Oracle *constraint* is a rule or rules that can be defined on one or more columns in a table to help enforce a business rule. For example, a constraint can enforce the business rule that an employee's starting salary must be at least $25,000.00. Another example of a constraint enforcing a business rule is to require that if a new employee is assigned a department (although they need not be assigned to a particular department right away), the department number must be valid and exist in the DEPT table.

Six types of data integrity rules can be applied to table columns: null rule, unique column values, primary key values, referential integrity values, complex in-line integrity, and trigger-based integrity. We will touch upon each of these briefly in the following sections.

All the constraints on a table are defined either when the table is created or when the table is altered at the column level, except for triggers, which are defined based on which DML operation is being performed on the table. Constraints may be enabled or disabled at creation or at any point of time in the future; when a constraint is either enabled or disabled (using the keyword **enable** or **disable**), existing data in the table may or may not have to be validated (using the keyword **validate** or **novalidate**) against the constraint, depending on the business rules in effect.

For example, a table in an automaker's database named CAR_INFO containing new automobile data needs a new constraint on the AIRBAG_QTY column, where the value of this column must not be NULL and must have a value that is at least 1 for all new vehicles. However, this table contains data for model years before air bags were required, and as a result, this column is either 0 or NULL. One solution, in this case, would be to create a constraint on the AIRBAG_QTY table to enforce the new rule for new rows added to the table, but not to validate the constraint for existing rows.

Here is a table created with all constraint types. Each constraint is reviewed in the following subsections.

```
create table CUST_ORDER
     (Order_Number          NUMBER(6)      PRIMARY KEY,
      Order_Date            DATE           NOT NULL,
      Delivery_Date         DATE,
      Warehouse_Number      NUMBER         DEFAULT 12,
      Customer_Number       NUMBER         NOT NULL,
      Order_Line_Item_Qty   NUMBER         CHECK (Order_Line_Item_Qty < 100),
      UPS_Tracking_Number   VARCHAR2(50)   UNIQUE,
      foreign key (Customer_Number) references CUSTOMER(Customer_Number));
```

Null Rule

The NOT NULL constraint prevents NULL values from being entered into the Order_Date or Customer_Number column. This makes a lot of sense from a business rule point of view: Every order must have an order date, and an order doesn't make any sense unless a customer places it.

Note that a NULL value in a column doesn't mean that the value is blank or zero; rather, the value does not exist. A NULL value is not equal to anything, not even another NULL value. This concept is important when using SQL queries against columns that may have NULL values.

Unique Column Values

The UNIQUE integrity constraint ensures that a column or group of columns (in a composite constraint) is unique throughout the table. In the preceding example, the UPS_Tracking_Number column will not contain duplicate values.

To enforce the constraint, Oracle will create a unique index on the UPS_Tracking_Number column. If there is already a valid unique index on the column, Oracle will use that index to enforce the constraint.

A column with a UNIQUE constraint may also be declared as NOT NULL. If the column is not declared with the NOT NULL constraint, then any number of rows may contain NULL values, as long as the remaining rows have unique values in this column.

In a composite unique constraint that allows NULLs in one or more columns, the columns that are not NULL determine whether the constraint is being satisfied. The NULL column always satisfies the constraint, because a NULL value is not equal to anything.

Primary Key Values

The PRIMARY KEY integrity constraint is the most common type of constraint found in a database table. At most, only one primary key constraint can exist on a table. The column or columns that comprise the primary key cannot have NULL values.

In the preceding example, the Order_Number column is the primary key. A unique index is created to enforce the constraint; if a useable unique index already exists for the column, the primary key constraint uses that index.

Referential Integrity Values

The referential integrity or FOREIGN KEY constraint is more complicated than the others we have covered so far because it relies on another table to restrict what values can be entered into the column with the referential integrity constraint.

In the preceding example, a FOREIGN KEY is declared on the Customer_Number column; any values entered into this column must also exist in the Customer_Number column of another table (in this case, the CUSTOMER table).

As with other constraints that allow NULL values, a column with a referential integrity constraint can be NULL without requiring that the referenced column contain a NULL value.

Furthermore, a FOREIGN KEY constraint can be self-referential. In an EMPLOYEE table whose primary key is Employee_Number, the Manager_Number column can have a FOREIGN KEY declared against the Employee_Number column in the same table. This allows for the creation of a reporting hierarchy within the EMPLOYEE table itself.

Indexes should almost always be declared on a FOREIGN KEY column to improve performance; the only exception to this rule is when the referenced primary or unique key in the parent table is never updated or deleted.

Complex In-Line Integrity

More complex business rules may be enforced at the column level by using a CHECK constraint. In the preceding example, the Order_Line_Item_Qty column must never exceed 99.

A CHECK constraint can use other columns in the row being inserted or updated to evaluate the constraint. For example, a constraint on the STATE_CD column would allow NULL values only if the COUNTRY_CD column is not USA. In addition, the constraint can use literal values and built-in functions such as TO_CHAR or TO_DATE, as long as these functions operate on literals or columns in the table.

Multiple CHECK constraints are allowed on a column. All the CHECK constraints must evaluate to TRUE to allow a value to be entered in the column. For example, we could modify the preceding CHECK constraint to ensure that Order_Line_Item_Qty is greater than 0 in addition to being less than 100.

Trigger-Based Integrity

If the business rules are too complex to implement using unique constraints, a database *trigger* can be created on a table using the **create trigger** command along with a block of PL/SQL code to enforce the business rule.

Triggers are required to enforce referential integrity constraints when the referenced table exists in a different database. Triggers are also useful for many things outside the realm of constraint checking (auditing access to a table, for example).

Database triggers are covered in-depth in Chapter 18.

Indexes

An Oracle *index* allows faster access to rows in a table when a small subset of the rows will be retrieved from the table. An index stores the value of the column or columns being indexed, along with the physical RowID of the row containing the indexed value, except for index organized tables (IOTs), which use the primary key as a logical RowID. Once a match is found in the index, the RowID in the index points to the exact location of the table row: which file, which block within the file, and which row within the block.

Indexes are created on a single column or multiple columns. Index entries are stored in a B-tree structure so that traversing the index to find the key value of the row uses very few I/O operations. An index may serve a dual purpose in the case of a unique index: Not only will it speed the search for the row, but it enforces a unique or primary key constraint on the indexed column. Entries within an index are automatically updated whenever the contents of a table row are inserted, updated, or deleted. When a table is dropped, all indexes created on the table are also automatically dropped.

Several types of indexes are available in Oracle, each suitable for a particular type of table, access method, or application environment. We will present the highlights and features of the most common index types in the following subsections.

Unique Indexes

A *unique index* is the most common form of B*Tree index. It is often used to enforce the primary key constraint of a table. Unique indexes ensure that duplicate values will not exist in the column or columns being indexed. A unique index may be created on a column in the EMPLOYEE table for the Social Security Number because there should not be any duplicates in this column. However, some employees may not have a Social Security Number, so this column would contain a NULL value.

Non-Unique Indexes

A *non-unique* index helps speed access to a table without enforcing uniqueness. For example, we can create a non-unique index on the Last_Name column of the EMPLOYEE table to speed up our searches by last name, but we would certainly have many duplicates for any given last name.

A non-unique B*Tree index is created on a column by default if no other keywords are specified in a CREATE INDEX statement.

Reverse Key Indexes

A *reverse key* index is a special kind of index used typically in an OLTP (online transaction processing) environment. In a reverse key index, all the bytes in each column's key value of the index are reversed. The **reverse** keyword specifies a reverse key index in the **create index** command. Here is an example of creating a reverse key index:

```
create index IE_LINE_ITEM_ORDER_NUMBER
        on LINE_ITEM(Order_Number) REVERSE;
```

If an order number of 123459 is placed, the reverse key index stores the order number as 954321. Inserts into the table are distributed across all leaf keys in the index, reducing the contention among several writers all doing inserts of new rows. A reverse key index also reduces the potential for these "hot spots" in an OLTP environment if orders are queried or modified soon after they are placed.

Function-Based Indexes

A *function-based index* is similar to a standard B*Tree index, except that a transformation of a column or columns, declared as an expression, is stored in the index instead of the columns themselves.

Function-based indexes are useful in cases where names and addresses might be stored in the database as mixed case. A regular index on a column containing the value 'SmiTh' would not return any values if the search criterion was 'Smith'. On the other hand, if the index stored the last names in all uppercase, all searches on last names could use uppercase. Here is an example of creating a function-based index on the Last_Name column of the EMPLOYEE table:

```
create index up_name on employee(upper(Last_Name));
```

As a result, searches using queries such as the following will use the index we just created instead of doing a full table scan:

```
select Employee_Number, Last_Name, First_Name from employee
    where upper(Last_Name) = 'SMITH';
```

Bitmap Indexes

A *bitmap index* has a significantly different structure from a B*Tree index in the leaf node of the index. It stores one string of bits for each possible value (the cardinality) of the column being indexed. The length of the string of bits is the same as the number of rows in the table being indexed.

In addition to saving a tremendous amount of space compared to traditional indexes, a bitmap index can provide dramatic improvements in response time because Oracle can quickly remove potential rows from a query containing multiple **where** clauses long before the table itself needs to be accessed. Multiple bitmaps can use logical **and** and **or** operations to determine which rows to access from the table.

Although a bitmap index can be used on any column in a table, it is most efficient when the column being indexed has a low *cardinality,* or number of distinct values. For example, the Gender column in the PERS table will either be NULL, M, or F. The bitmap index on the Gender column will have only three bitmaps stored in the index. On the other hand, a bitmap index on the Last_Name column will have close to the same number of bitmap strings as rows in the table itself! The queries looking for a particular last name will most likely take less time if a full table scan is performed instead of using an index. In this case, a traditional B*Tree non-unique index makes more sense.

A variation of bitmap indexes called *bitmap join indexes* creates a bitmap index on a table column that is frequently joined with one or more other tables on the same column. This provides tremendous benefits in a data warehouse environment where a bitmap join index is created on a fact table and one or more dimension tables, essentially prejoining those tables and saving CPU and I/O resources when an actual join is performed.

NOTE
Bitmap indexes are only available in the Enterprise Edition of Oracle 10g.

Views

Views allow users to see a customized presentation of the data in a single table or even a join between many tables. A view is also known as a *stored query*—the query details underlying the view are hidden from the user of the view. A regular view does not store any data, only the definition, and the underlying query is run every time the view is accessed. Extensions to a regular view, called a *materialized view,* allows the results of the query to be stored along with the definition of the query to speed processing, among other benefits. Object views, like traditional views, hide the details of the underlying table joins and allow object-oriented development and processing to occur in the database while the underlying tables are still in a relational format.

In the following subsections, we'll review the basics of the types of views a typical user will create and use on a regular basis.

Regular Views

A *regular view,* or more commonly referred to as a *view,* is not allocated any storage; only its definition, a query, is stored in the data dictionary. The tables in the query underlying the view are called *base tables;* each base table in a view can be further defined as a view.

The advantages of a view are many. Views hide data complexity—a senior analyst can define a view containing the EMPLOYEE, DEPARTMENT, and SALARY tables to make it easier for upper management to retrieve information about employee salaries by using a **select** statement against what appears to be a table but is actually a view containing a query that joins the EMPLOYEE, DEPARTMENT, and SALARY tables.

Views can also be used to enforce security. A view on the EMPLOYEE table called EMP_INFO may contain all columns except for salary, and the view can be defined as **read only** to prevent updates to the table:

```
create view EMP_INFO as
      select Employee_Number, Last_Name,
            First_Name, Middle_Initial, Surname
from EMPLOYEE
with READ ONLY;
```

Without the **read only** clause, it is possible to update or add rows to a view, even to a view containing multiple tables. There are some constructs in a view that prevent it from being updatable, such as having a **distinct** operator, an aggregate function, or a **group by** clause.

When Oracle processes a query containing a view, it substitutes the underlying query definition in the user's **select** statement and processes the resulting query as if the view did not exist. As a result, the benefits of any existing indexes on the base tables are not lost when a view is used.

Materialized Views

In some ways, a *materialized view* is very similar to a regular view: The definition of the view is stored in the data dictionary, and the view hides the details of the underlying base query from the user. But that is where the similarities end. A materialized view also allocates space in a database segment to hold the result set from the execution of the base query.

A materialized view can be used to replicate a read-only copy of table to another database, with the same column definitions and data as the base table. This is the simplest implementation of a materialized view. To enhance the response time when a materialized view needs to be refreshed, a *materialized view log* can be created to refresh the materialized view. Otherwise, a full refresh is required when a refresh is required—the results of the base query must be run in their entirety to refresh the materialized view. The materialized view log facilitates incremental updates of the materialized views.

In a data warehouse environment, materialized views can store aggregated data from a **group by rollup** or a **group by cube** query. If the appropriate initialization parameter values are set, such as QUERY_REWRITE_ENABLED, and the query itself allows for query rewrites (with the **query rewrite** clause), then any query that appears to do the same kind of aggregation as the materialized view will automatically use the materialized view instead of running the original query.

Regardless of the type of materialized view, it can be refreshed automatically when a committed transaction occurs in the base table, or it can be refreshed on demand.

Materialized views have many similarities to indexes, in that they are directly tied to a table and take up space, they must be refreshed when the base tables are updated, their existence is virtually transparent to the user, and they can aid in optimizing queries by using an alternate access path to return the results of a query.

More details on how to use materialized views in a distributed environment can be found in Chapter 18.

Object Views

Object-oriented (OO) application development environments are becoming increasingly prevalent, and the Oracle 10*g* database fully supports the implementation of objects and methods natively in the database. However, a migration from a purely relational database environment to a purely OO database environment is not an easy transition to make; few organizations have the time and resources to build a new system from the ground up. Oracle 10*g* makes the transition easier with object views. Object views allow the object-oriented applications to see the data as a collection of objects that have attributes and methods, while the legacy systems can still run batch jobs against the INVENTORY table. Object views can simulate abstract datatypes, object identifiers (OIDs), and references that a purely OO database environment would provide.

As with regular views, you can use **instead of** triggers in the view definition to allow DML against the view by running a block of PL/SQL code instead of the actual DML statement supplied by the user or application.

Users and Schemas

Access to the database is granted to a database account known as a *user*. A user may exist in the database without owning any objects. However, if the user creates and owns objects in the database, those objects are part of a *schema* that has the same name as the database user. A schema can own any type of object in the database: tables, indexes, sequences, views, and so forth. The schema owner or DBA can grant access to these objects to other database users. The user always has full privileges and control over the objects in the user's schema.

When a user is created by the DBA (or by any other user with the **create user** system privilege), a number of other characteristics can be assigned to the user, such as which tablespaces are available to the user for creating objects, and whether the password is preexpired.

Users can be authenticated in the database with three methods: database authentication, operating system authentication, and network authentication. With database authentication, the encrypted password for the user is stored in the database. In contrast, operating system authentication makes an assumption that a user who is already authenticated by an operating system connection has the same privileges as a user with the same or similar name (depending on the value of the

OS_AUTHENT_PREFIX initialization parameter). Network authentication uses solutions based on Public Key Infrastructure (PKI). These network authentication methods require Oracle 10g Enterprise Edition with the Oracle Advanced Security option.

Profiles

Database resources are not unlimited; therefore, a DBA must manage and allocate resources among all database users. Some examples of database resources are CPU time, concurrent sessions, logical reads, and connect time.

A database *profile* is a named set of resource limits that can be assigned to a user. After Oracle is installed, the DEFAULT profile exists and is assigned to any user not explicitly assigned a profile. The DBA can add new profiles or change the DEFAULT profile to suit the needs of the enterprise. The initial values for the DEFAULT profile allow for unlimited use of all database resources.

Sequences

An Oracle *sequence* assigns sequential numbers, guaranteed to be unique unless the sequence is re-created or reset. It produces a series of unique numbers in a multiuser environment without the overhead of disk locking or any special I/O calls, other than what's involved in loading the sequence into the shared pool.

Sequences can generate numbers up to 38 digits in length; the series of numbers can be ascending or descending, the interval can be any user-specified value, and Oracle can cache blocks of numbers from a sequence in memory for even faster performance.

The numbers from sequences are guaranteed to be unique, but not necessarily sequential. If a block of numbers is cached, and the instance is restarted, or a transaction that uses a number from a sequence is rolled back, the next call to retrieve a number from the sequence will not return the number that was not used in the original reference to the sequence.

Synonyms

An Oracle *synonym* is simply an alias to a database object, to simplify references to database objects and to hide the details of the source of the database objects. Synonyms can be assigned to tables, views, materialized views, sequences, procedures, functions, and packages. Like views, a synonym allocates no space in the database, other than its definition in the data dictionary.

Synonyms can be either public or private. A private synonym is defined in the schema of a user and is available only to the user. A public synonym is usually created by a DBA and is automatically available for use by any database user.

TIP
After creating a public synonym, make sure the users of the synonym have the correct privileges to the object referenced by the synonym.

When referencing a database object, Oracle first checks whether the object exists in the user's schema. If no such object exists, Oracle checks for a private synonym. If there is no private synonym, Oracle checks for a public synonym. If there is no public synonym, an error is returned.

PL/SQL

Oracle PL/SQL is Oracle's procedural language extension to SQL. PL/SQL is useful when the standard DML and **select** statements cannot produce the desired results in an easy fashion because of the lack of the procedural elements found in a traditional third-generation language such as C++ and Ada. As of Oracle9*i*, the SQL processing engine is shared between SQL and PL/SQL, which means that all new features added to SQL are automatically available to PL/SQL.

In the next few sections, we'll take a whirlwind tour of the benefits of using Oracle PL/SQL.

Procedures/Functions

PL/SQL procedures and functions are examples of PL/SQL *named blocks.* A PL/SQL block is a sequence of PL/SQL statements treated as a unit for the purposes of execution, and it contains up to three sections: a variable declaration section, an executable section, and an exception section.

The difference between a procedure and function is that a function will return a single value to a calling program such as a SQL **select** statement. A procedure, on the other hand, does not return a value, only a status code. However, procedures may have one or many variables that can be set and returned as part of the argument list to the procedure.

Procedures and functions have many advantages in a database environment. Procedures are compiled and stored in the data dictionary once; when more than one user needs to call the procedure, it is already compiled, and only one copy of the stored procedure exists in the shared pool. In addition, network traffic is reduced, even if the procedural features of PL/SQL are not used. One PL/SQL call uses up much less network bandwidth than several SQL **select** and **insert** statements sent separately over the network, not to mention the reparsing that occurs for each statement sent over the network.

Packages

PL/SQL *packages* group together related functions and procedures, along with common variables and cursors. Packages consist of two parts: a package specification and a package body. In the package specification, the methods and attributes of the package are exposed; the implementation of the methods along with any private methods and attributes are hidden in the package body. Using a package instead of a standalone procedure or function allows the embedded procedure or function to be changed without invalidating any objects that refer to elements of the package specification, thus avoiding recompilation of the objects that reference the package.

Triggers

Triggers are a specialized type of a PL/SQL or Java block of code that is executed, or *triggered,* when a specified event occurs. The types of events can be DML statements on a table or view, DDL statements, and even database events such as startup or shutdown. The specified trigger can be refined to execute on a particular event for a particular user as part of an auditing strategy.

Triggers are extremely useful in a distributed environment to simulate a foreign key relationship between tables that do not exist in the same database. They are also very useful in implementing complex integrity rules that cannot be defined using the built-in Oracle constraint types.

More information on how triggers can be used in a robust distributed environment can be found in Chapter 18.

External File Access

In addition to external tables, there are a number of other ways Oracle can access external files:

- From SQL*Plus, either by accessing an external script containing other SQL commands to be run or by sending the output from a SQL*Plus **spool** command to a file in the operating system's file system.

- Text information can be read or written from a PL/SQL procedure using the UTL_FILE built-in package; similarly, **dbms_output** calls within a PL/SQL procedure can generate text messages and diagnostics that can be captured by another application and saved to a text file.

- External data can be referenced by the BFILE datatype. A BFILE datatype is a pointer to an external binary file. Before BFILEs can be used in a database, a *directory alias* needs to be created with the **create directory** command that specifies a prefix containing the full directory path where the BFILE target is stored.

- DBMS_PIPE can communicate with any 3GL language that Oracle supports, such as C++, Ada, Java, or COBOL, and exchange information.

- UTL_MAIL, a new package in Oracle 10*g*, allows a PL/SQL application to send e-mails without knowing how to use the underlying SMTP protocol stack.

When using an external file as a data source, for either input or output, a number of cautions are in order. The following should be carefully considered before you use an external data source:

- The database data and the external data may be frequently out of synch when one of the data sources changes without synchronizing with the other.

- It is important to make sure that the backups of the two data sources occur at nearly the same time to ensure that the recovery of one data source will keep the two data sources in synch.

- Script files may contain passwords; many organizations forbid the plain-text representation of any user account in a script file. In this situation, operating system validation may be a good alternative for user authentication.

- You should review the security of files located in a directory that is referenced by each DIRECTORY object. Extreme security measures on database objects are mitigated by lax security on referenced operating system files.

Database Links and Remote Databases

Database links allow an Oracle database to reference objects stored outside of the local database. The command **create database link** creates the path to a remote database, which in turn allows access to objects in the remote database. A database link wraps together the name of the remote database, a method for connecting to the remote database, and a username/password combination to authenticate the connection to the remote database. In some ways, a database link is similar to a database synonym: A database link can be public or private, and it provides a convenient shorthand way to access another set of resources. The main difference is that the resource is outside of the database instead of in the same database, and therefore requires more information to resolve the reference. The other difference is that a synonym is a reference to a specific object, whereas a database link is a defined path used to access any number of objects in a remote database.

For links to work between databases in a distributed environment, the global database name of each database in the domain must be different. Therefore, it is important to assign the initialization parameters DB_NAME and DB_DOMAIN correctly.

To make using database links even easier, a synonym can be assigned to a database link, to make the table access even more transparent; the user does not know if the synonym accesses an object locally or on a distributed database. The object can move to a different remote database, or to the local database, and the synonym name can remain the same, making access to the object transparent to users.

How database links to remote databases are leveraged in a distributed environment is covered further in Chapter 18.

Oracle Physical Storage Structures

The Oracle database uses a number of physical storage structures on disk to hold and manage the data from user transactions. Some of these storage structures, such as the datafiles, redo log files, and archived redo log files, hold actual user data; other structures, such as control files, maintain the state of the database objects, and text-based alert and trace files contain logging information for both routine events and error conditions in the database. Figure 1-3 shows the relationship between these physical structures and the logical storage structures we reviewed in the previous section "Oracle Logical Database Structures."

Datafiles

Every Oracle database must contain at least one *datafile*. One Oracle datafile corresponds to one physical operating system file on disk. Each datafile in an Oracle database is a member of one and only one tablespace; a tablespace, however, can consist of many datafiles.

An Oracle datafile may automatically expand when it runs out of space, if the DBA created the datafile with the AUTOEXTEND parameter. The DBA can also limit the amount of expansion for a given datafile by using the MAXSIZE parameter. In any case, the size of the datafile is ultimately limited by the disk volume on which it resides.

TIP
The DBA often has to decide whether to allocate one datafile that can autoextend indefinitely or to allocate many smaller datafiles with a limit to how much each can extend. Although the performance of each solution is likely very similar, it is probably a better idea to stick with more datafiles that are each less than 2GB in size. It is a lot easier to move around relatively smaller files, and some file systems may limit the size of an individual file to 2GB anyway. Also, if you need to temporarily move all the datafiles for a tablespace to another server, it is often easier to find several volumes, each with enough space to hold one of the datafiles, rather than one volume with enough space to hold a single datafile that is 25GB.

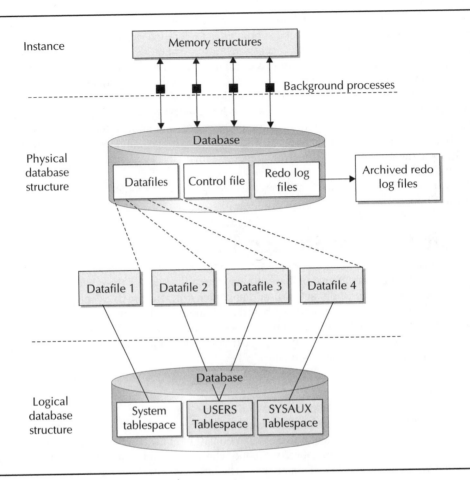

FIGURE 1-3. *Oracle physical storage structures*

The datafile is the ultimate resting place for all data in the database. Frequently accessed blocks in a datafile are cached in memory; similarly, new data blocks are not immediately written out to the datafile but rather are written to the datafile depending on when the database writer process is active. Before a user's transaction is considered complete, however, the transaction's changes are written to the redo log files.

Redo Log Files

Whenever data is added, removed, or changed in a table, index, or other Oracle object, an entry is written to the current *redo log file.* Every Oracle database must have at least two redo log files, because Oracle reuses redo log files in a circular fashion. When one redo log file is filled with *redo log entries,* the current log file is marked as ACTIVE, if it is still needed for instance recovery, or INACTIVE, if it is not needed for instance recovery; the next log file in the sequence is reused from the beginning of the file and is marked as CURRENT.

Ideally, the information in a redo log file is never used. However, when a power failure occurs, or some other server failure causes the Oracle instance to fail, the new or updated data blocks in the database buffer cache may not yet have been written to the datafiles. When the Oracle instance is restarted, the entries in the redo log file are applied to the database datafiles in a *roll forward* operation, to restore the state of the database up to the point where the failure occurred.

To be able to recover from the loss of one redo log file within a redo log group, multiple copies of a redo log file can exist on different physical disks. Later in this chapter, you will see how redo log files, archived log files, and control files can be *multiplexed* to ensure the availability and data integrity of the Oracle database.

Control Files

Every Oracle database has at least one *control file* that maintains the metadata of the database (in other words, data about the physical structure of the database itself). Among other things, it contains the name of the database, when the database was created, and the names and locations of all datafiles and redo log files. In addition, the control file maintains information used by Recovery Manager (RMAN), such as the persistent RMAN settings and the types of backups that have been performed on the database. RMAN is covered in depth in Chapter 13. Whenever any changes are made to the structure of the database, the information about the changes is immediately reflected in the control file.

Because the control file is so critical to the operation of the database, it can also be multiplexed. However, no matter how many copies of the control file are associated with an instance, only one of the control files is designated as primary for purposes of retrieving database metadata.

The **alter database backup controlfile to trace** command is another way to back up the control file. It produces a SQL script that can be used to re-create the database control file in case all multiplexed binary versions of the control file are lost due to a catastrophic failure.

This trace file can also be used, for example, to re-create a control file if the database needs to be renamed, or to change various database limits that could not otherwise be changed without re-creating the entire database.

Archived Log Files

An Oracle database can operate in one of two modes: **archivelog** or **noarchivelog** mode. When the database is in **noarchivelog** mode, the circular reuse of the redo log files (also known as the *online redo log files)* means that redo entries (the contents of previous transactions) are no longer available in case of a failure to a disk drive or another media-related failure. Operating in **noarchivelog** mode does protect the integrity of the database in the event of an instance failure or system crash, because all transactions that are committed but not yet written to the datafiles are available in the online redo log files.

In contrast, **archivelog** mode sends a filled redo log file to one or more specified destinations and can be available to reconstruct the database at any given point in time in the event that a database media failure occurs. For example, if the disk drive containing the datafiles crashes, the contents of the database can be recovered to a point in time before the crash, given a recent backup of the datafiles and the redo log files that were generated since the backup occurred.

The use of multiple archived log destinations for filled redo log files is critical for one of Oracle's high-availability features known as Oracle Data Guard, formerly known as Oracle Standby Database. Oracle Data Guard is covered in detail in Chapter 14.

Initialization Parameter Files

When a database instance starts, the memory for the Oracle instance is allocated, and one of two types of *initialization parameter files* is opened: either a text-based file called init<SID>.ora (known generically as init.ora or a PFILE) or a server parameter file (otherwise known as an SPFILE). The instance first looks for an SPFILE in the default location for the operating system ($ORACLE_HOME/dbs on Unix, for example) as either spfile<SID>.ora or spfile.ora. If neither of these files exists, the instance looks for a PFILE with the name init<SID>.ora. Alternatively, the **startup** command can explicitly specify a PFILE to use for startup.

Initialization parameter files, regardless of the format, specify file locations for trace files, control files, filled redo log files, and so forth. They also set limits on the sizes of the various structures in the System Global Area (SGA) as well as how many users can connect to the database simultaneously.

Until Oracle9*i*, using the init.ora file was the only way to specify initialization parameters for the instance. Although it is easy to edit with a text editor, it has some drawbacks. If a dynamic system parameter is changed at the command line with the **alter system** command, the DBA must remember to change the init.ora file so that the new parameter value will be in effect the next time the instance is restarted.

An SPFILE makes parameter management easier and more effective for the DBA. If an SPFILE is in use for the running instance, any **alter system** command that changes an initialization parameter can change the initialization parameter automatically in the SPFILE, change it only for the running instance, or both. No editing of the SPFILE is necessary, or even possible without corrupting the SPFILE itself.

Although you cannot mirror a parameter file or SPFILE per se, you can back up an SPFILE to an init.ora file, and both the init.ora and the SPFILE for the Oracle instance should be backed up using conventional operating system commands or using Recovery Manager in the case of an SPFILE.

When the DBCA is used to create a database, an SPFILE is created by default.

Alert and Trace Log Files

When things go wrong, Oracle can and often does write messages to the *alert log* and, in the case of background processes or user sessions, *trace log* files.

The alert log file, located in the directory specified by the initialization parameter BACKGROUND_DUMP_DEST, contains both routine status messages as well as error conditions. When the database is started up or shut down, a message is recorded in the alert log, along with a list of initialization parameters that are different from their default values. In addition, any **alter database** or **alter system** commands issued by the DBA are recorded. Operations involving tablespaces and their datafiles are recorded here, too, such as adding a tablespace, dropping a tablespace, and adding a datafile to a tablespace. Error conditions, such as tablespaces running out of space, corrupted redo logs, and so forth, are also recorded here.

The trace files for the Oracle instance background processes are also located in BACKGROUND_DUMP_DEST. For example, the trace files for PMON and SMON contain an entry when an error occurs or when SMON needs to perform instance recovery; the trace files for QMON contain informational messages when it spawns a new process.

Trace files are also created for individual user sessions or connections to the database. These trace files are located in the directory specified by the initialization parameter USER_DUMP_DEST. Trace files for user processes are created in two situations: The first is when some type of error occurs in a user session because of a privilege problem, running out of space, and so forth. In the second situation, a trace file can be created explicitly with the command **alter session set sql_trace=true**. Trace information is generated for each SQL statement that the user executes, which can be helpful when tuning a user's SQL statement.

The alert log file can be deleted or renamed at any time; it is re-created the next time an alert log message is generated. The DBA will often set up a daily batch job (either through an operating system mechanism or using Oracle Enterprise Manager's scheduler) to rename and archive the alert log on a daily basis.

Backup Files

Backup files can originate from a number of sources, such as operating system copy commands or Oracle Recovery Manager (RMAN). If the DBA performs a "cold" backup (see the section titled "Backup/Recovery Overview" for more details on backup types), the backup files are simply operating system copies of the datafiles, redo log files, control files, archived redo log files, and so forth.

In addition to bit-for-bit image copies of datafiles (the default in RMAN), RMAN can generate full and incremental backups of datafiles, control files, redo log files, archived log files, and SPFILEs that are in a special format, called *backupsets,* only readable by RMAN. RMAN backupset backups are generally smaller than the original datafiles because RMAN does not back up unused blocks.

Oracle Managed Files

Oracle Managed Files (OMF), introduced in Oracle version 9*i,* makes the DBA's job easier by automating the creation and removal of the datafiles that comprise the logical structures in the database.

Without OMF, a DBA might drop a tablespace and forget to remove the underlying operating system files. This makes inefficient use of disk resources, and it unnecessarily increases backup time for datafiles that are no longer needed by the database.

OMF is well suited for small databases with a low number of users and a part-time DBA, where optimal configuration of a production database is not necessary.

Password Files

An Oracle *password file* is a file within the Oracle administrative or software directory structure on disk used to authenticate Oracle system administrators for tasks such as creating a database or starting up and shutting down the database. The privileges granted through this file are the SYSDBA and SYSOPER privileges. Authenticating any other type of user is done within the database itself; because the database may be shut down or not mounted, another form of administrator authentication is necessary in these cases.

The Oracle command-line utility **orapwd** creates a password file if one does not exist or is damaged. Because of the extremely high privileges granted via this file, it should be stored in a secure directory location that is not available to anyone except for DBAs and operating system administrators. Once this file is created, the initialization parameter REMOTE_LOGIN_PASSWORDFILE should be set to EXCLUSIVE to allow users other than SYS to use the password file.

TIP
Create at least one user other than SYS or SYSTEM who has DBA privileges for daily administrative tasks. If there is more than one DBA administering a database, each DBA should have their own account with DBA privileges.

Alternatively, authentication for the SYSDBA and SYSOPER privileges can be done with OS authentication; in this case, a password file does not have to be created, and the initialization parameter REMOTE_LOGIN_PASSWORDFILE is set to NONE.

Multiplexing Database Files

To minimize the possibility of losing a control file or a redo log file, multiplexing of database files reduces or eliminates data-loss problems caused by media failures. Multiplexing can be somewhat automated by using an Automatic Storage Management (ASM) instance, available starting in Oracle 10*g*. For a more budget-conscious enterprise, control files and redo log files can be multiplexed manually.

Automatic Storage Management

Using *Automatic Storage Management* is a multiplexing solution that automates the layout of datafiles, control files, and redo log files by distributing them across all available disks. When new disks are added to the ASM cluster, the database files are automatically redistributed across all disk volumes for optimal performance. The multiplexing features of an ASM cluster minimize the possibility of data loss and are generally more effective than a manual scheme that places critical files and backups on different physical drives.

Manual Multiplexing

Without a RAID or ASM solution, you can still provide some safeguards for your critical database files by setting some initialization parameters and providing an additional location for control files, redo log files, and archived redo log files.

Control Files

Control files can be multiplexed immediately when the database is created, or they can be multiplexed at any time later with a few extra steps to manually copy them to multiple destinations. Up to eight copies of a control file can be multiplexed.

Whether you multiplex the control files when the database is created or you multiplex them later, the initialization parameter value for CONTROL_FILES is the same. In the following example, three copies of the control file will be multiplexed:

```
Alter system
    set control_files = '/u01/oracle/whse2/ctrlwhse1.ctl',
                        '/u02/oracle/whse2/ctrlwhse2.ctl',
                        '/u03/oracle/whse2/ctrlwhse3.ctl',
    scope=spfile;
```

If the database is created with this parameter set, the three control files will be created, and there are no additional steps.

If you want to add another multiplexed location, you need to edit the initialization parameter file and add another location to the CONTROL_FILES parameter. If an SPFILE is being used instead of an init.ora file, then use a command similar to the following to change the CONTROL_FILES parameter:

```
alter system
    set control_files = '/u01/oracle/whse2/ctrlwhse1.ctl,
        /u02/oracle/whse2/ctrlwhse2.ctl,
        /u03/oracle/whse2/ctrlwhse3.ctl'
scope=spfile;
```

The other possible values for SCOPE in the **alter system** command are MEMORY and BOTH. Specifying either one of these for SCOPE returns an error, because the CONTROL_FILES parameter cannot be changed for the running instance, only for the next restart of the instance. Therefore, only the SPFILE is changed.

In either case, the next step is to shut down the database. Copy the control file to the new destinations, as specified in CONTROL_FILES, and restart the database. You can always verify the names and locations of the control files by looking in one of the data dictionary views:

```
select value from v$spparameter where name='control_files';
```

This query will return one row for each multiplexed copy of the control file. In addition, the view V$CONTROLFILE contains one row for each copy of the control file along with a status.

Redo Log Files

Redo log files are multiplexed by changing a set of redo log files into a *redo log file group*. In a default Oracle installation, a set of three redo log files is created. As you learned in the previous section on redo log files, after each log file is filled, it starts filling the next in sequence. After the third is filled, the first one is reused. To change the set of three redo log files to a group, we can add one or more identical files as a companion to each of the existing redo log files. After the groups are created, the redo log entries are concurrently written to the group of redo log files. When the group of redo log files is filled, it begins to write redo entries to the next group. Figure 1-4 shows how a set of four redo log files can be multiplexed with four groups, each group containing three members.

Adding a member to a redo log group is very straightforward. In the **alter database** command, we specify the name of the new file and the group to add it to. The new file is created with the same size as the other members in the group:

```
alter database
    add logfile member '/u05/oracle/dc2/log_3d.dbf'
    to group 3;
```

If the redo log files are filling up faster than they can be archived, one possible solution is to add another redo log group. Here is an example of how to add a fifth redo log group to the set of redo log groups in Figure 1-4:

```
alter database
    add logfile group 5
    ('/u02/oracle/dc2/log_3a.dbf',
     '/u03/oracle/dc2/log_3b.dbf',
     '/u04/oracle/dc2/log_3c.dbf') size 10m;
```

All members of a redo log group must be the same size. However, the log file sizes between groups may be different. In addition, redo log groups may have a different number of members. In the preceding example, we started with four redo log groups, added an extra member to redo log group 3 (for a total of four members), and added a fifth redo log group with three members.

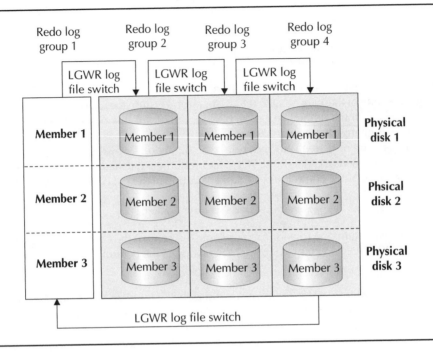

FIGURE 1-4. *Multiplexing redo log files*

As of Oracle 10g, you can use the Redo Logfile Sizing Advisor to assist in determining the optimal size for redo log files to avoid excessive I/O activity or bottlenecks. See Chapter 8 for more information on how to use the Redo Logfile Sizing Advisor.

Archived Redo Log Files
If the database is in **archivelog** mode, redo log files are copied to a specified location before they can be reused in the redo log switch cycle.

Oracle Memory Structures
Oracle uses the server's physical memory to hold many things for an Oracle instance: the Oracle executable code itself, session information, individual processes associated with the database, and information shared between processes (such as locks on database objects). In addition, the memory structures contain user and data dictionary SQL statements, along with cached information that is eventually permanently stored on disk, such as data blocks from database segments and information about completed transactions in the database. The data area allocated for an Oracle instance is called the *System Global Area (SGA)*. The Oracle executables reside in the software code area. In addition, an area called the *Program Global Area (PGA)* is private to each server and background process; one PGA is allocated for each process. Figure 1-5 shows the relationships between these Oracle memory structures.

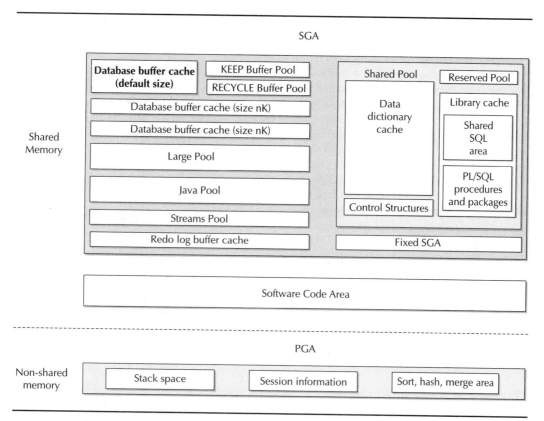

FIGURE 1-5. *Oracle logical memory structures*

System Global Area

The *System Global Area* is a group of shared memory structures for an Oracle instance, shared by the users of the database instance. When an Oracle instance is started, memory is allocated for the SGA based on the values specified in the initialization parameter file or hard-coded in the Oracle software. Many of the parameters that control the size of the various parts of the SGA are dynamic; however, if the parameter SGA_MAX_SIZE is specified, the total size of all SGA areas must not exceed the value of SGA_MAX_SIZE. If SGA_MAX_SIZE is not specified, but the parameter SGA_TARGET is specified, Oracle automatically adjusts the sizes of the SGA components so that the total amount of memory allocated is equal to SGA_TARGET. SGA_TARGET is a dynamic parameter; it can be changed while the instance is running.

Memory in the SGA is allocated in units of *granules*. A granule can be either 4MB or 16MB, depending on the total size of the SGA. If the SGA is less than or equal to 128MB, a granule is 4MB; otherwise, it is 16MB.

In the next few subsections, we will cover the highlights of how Oracle uses each section in the SGA. More information on how to adjust the initialization parameters associated with these areas can be found in Chapter 8.

Buffer Caches

The database *buffer cache* holds blocks of data from disk that have been recently read to satisfy a **select** statement or that contain modified blocks that have been changed or added from a DML statement. As of Oracle9*i*, the memory area in the SGA that holds these data blocks is dynamic. This is a good thing, considering that there may be tablespaces in the database with block sizes other than the default block size; tablespaces with up to five different block sizes (one block size for the default, and up to four others) require their own buffer cache. As the processing and transactional needs change during the day or during the week, the values of DB_CACHE_SIZE and DB_nK_CACHE_SIZE can be dynamically changed without restarting the instance to enhance performance for a tablespace with a given block size.

Oracle can use two additional caches with the same block size as the default (DB_CACHE_SIZE) block size: the KEEP buffer pool and the RECYCLE buffer pool. As of Oracle9*i*, both of these pools allocate memory independently of other caches in the SGA.

When a table is created, you can specify the pool where the table's data blocks will reside by using the BUFFER_POOL KEEP or BUFFER_POOL_RECYCLE clause in the STORAGE clause. For tables that are used frequently throughout the day, it would be advantageous to place this table into the KEEP buffer pool to minimize the I/O needed to retrieve blocks in the table.

Shared Pool

The *shared pool* contains two major subcaches: the library cache and the data dictionary cache. The shared pool is sized by the SHARED_POOL_SIZE initialization parameter. This is another dynamic parameter that can be resized as long as the total SGA size is less than SGA_MAX_SIZE or SGA_TARGET.

Library Cache   The *library cache* holds information about SQL and PL/SQL statements that are run against the database. In the library cache, because it is shared by all users, many different database users can potentially share the same SQL statement.

Along with the SQL statement itself, the execution plan and parse tree of the SQL statement are stored in the library cache. The second time an identical SQL statement is run, by the same user or a different user, the execution plan and parse tree are already computed, improving the execution time of the query or DML statement.

If the library cache is sized too small, the execution plans and parse trees are flushed out of the cache, requiring frequent reloads of SQL statements into the library cache. See Chapter 9 for ways to monitor the efficiency of the library cache.

Data Dictionary Cache   The *data dictionary* is a collection of database tables, owned by the SYS and SYSTEM schemas, that contain the metadata about the database, its structures, and the privileges and roles of database users. The *data dictionary cache* holds cached blocks from the data dictionary. Data blocks from tables in the data dictionary are used continually to assist in processing user queries and other DML commands.

If the data dictionary cache is too small, requests for information from the data dictionary will cause extra I/O to occur; these I/O-bound data dictionary requests are called *recursive calls* and should be avoided by sizing the data dictionary cache correctly.

Redo Log Buffer

The *redo log buffer* holds the most recent changes to the data blocks in the datafiles. When the redo log buffer is one-third full, or every three seconds, redo log records are written to the redo log files. The entries in the redo log buffer, once written to the redo log files, are critical to database recovery if the instance crashes before the changed data blocks are written from the buffer cache to the datafiles. A user's committed transaction is not considered complete until the redo log entries have been successfully written to the redo log files.

Large Pool

The *large pool* is an optional area of the SGA. It is used for transactions that interact with more than one database, message buffers for processes performing parallel queries, and RMAN parallel backup and restore operations. As the name implies, the large pool makes available large blocks of memory for operations that need to allocate large blocks of memory at a time.

The initialization parameter LARGE_POOL_SIZE controls the size of the large pool and is a dynamic parameter as of Oracle9*i* release 2.

Java Pool

The *Java pool* is used by the Oracle JVM (Java Virtual Machine) for all Java code and data within a user session. Storing Java code and data in the Java pool is analogous to SQL and PL/SQL code cached in the shared pool.

Streams Pool

New to Oracle 10*g*, the *streams pool* is sized by using the initialization parameter STREAMS_POOL_SIZE. The streams pool holds data and control structures to support the Oracle Streams feature of Oracle Enterprise Edition. Oracle Streams manages the sharing of data and events in a distributed environment. If the initialization parameter STREAMS_POOL_SIZE is uninitialized or set to zero, the memory used for Streams operations is allocated from the shared pool and may use up to 10 percent of the shared pool. For more information on Oracle Streams, see Chapter 18.

Program Global Area

The *Program Global Area* is an area of memory allocated and private for one process. The configuration of the PGA depends on the connection configuration of the Oracle database: either *shared server* or *dedicated*.

In a shared server configuration, multiple users share a connection to the database, minimizing memory usage on the server, but potentially affecting response time for user requests. In a shared server environment, the SGA holds the session information for a user instead of the PGA. Shared server environments are ideal for a large number of simultaneous connections to the database with infrequent or short-lived requests.

In a dedicated server environment, each user process gets its own connection to the database; the PGA contains the session memory for this configuration.

The PGA also includes a sort area. The sort area is used whenever a user request requires a sort, bitmap merge, or hash join operation.

As of Oracle9*i*, the PGA_AGGREGATE_TARGET parameter, in conjunction with the WORKAREA_SIZE_POLICY initialization parameter, can ease system administration by allowing the DBA to choose a total size for all work areas and let Oracle manage and allocate the memory between all user processes.

Software Code Area

Software code areas store the Oracle executable files that are running as part of an Oracle instance. These code areas are static in nature, and only change when a new release of the software is installed.

Typically, the Oracle software code areas are located in a privileged memory area separate from other user programs.

Oracle software code is strictly read-only and can be installed either shared or non-shared. Installing Oracle software code as sharable saves memory when multiple Oracle instances are running on the same server at the same software release level.

Background Processes

When an Oracle instance starts, multiple background processes start. A *background process* is a block of executable code designed to perform a specific task. Figure 1-6 shows the relationship between the background processes, the database, and the Oracle SGA. In contrast to a foreground

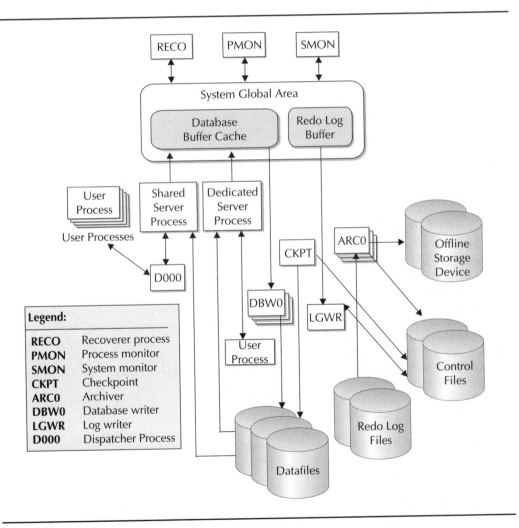

FIGURE 1-6. *Oracle background processes*

process, such as a SQL*Plus session or a web browser, a background process works behind the scenes. Together, the SGA and the background processes comprise an Oracle instance.

SMON

SMON is the *System Monitor* process. In the case of a system crash or instance failure, due to a power outage or CPU failure, the SMON process performs crash recovery by applying the entries in the online redo log files to the datafiles. In addition, temporary segments in all tablespaces are purged during system restart.

One of SMON's routine tasks is to coalesce the free space in tablespaces on a regular basis if the tablespace is dictionary managed.

PMON

If a user connection is dropped, or a user process otherwise fails, PMON, also known as the *Process Monitor,* does the cleanup work. It cleans up the database buffer cache along with any other resources that the user connection was using. For example, a user session may be updating some rows in a table, placing a lock on one or more of the rows. A thunderstorm knocks out the power at the user's desk, and the SQL*Plus session disappears when the workstation is powered off. Within moments, PMON will detect that the connection no longer exists and perform the following tasks:

- Roll back the transaction that was in progress when the power went out
- Mark the transaction's blocks as available in the buffer cache
- Remove the locks on the affected rows in the table
- Remove the process ID of the disconnected process from the list of active processes

PMON will also interact with the listeners by providing information about the status of the instance for incoming connection requests.

DBWn

The *database writer* process, known as DBWR in older versions of Oracle, writes new or changed data blocks (known as *dirty blocks)* in the buffer cache to the datafiles. Using an LRU algorithm, DBWn writes the oldest, least active blocks first. As a result, the most commonly requested blocks, even if they are dirty blocks, are in memory.

Up to 20 DBWn processes can be started, DBW0 through DBW9 and DBWa through DBWj. The number of DBWn processes is controlled by the DB_WRITER_PROCESSES parameter.

LGWR

LGWR, or *Log Writer,* is in charge of redo log buffer management. LGWR is one of the most active processes in an instance with heavy DML activity. A transaction is not considered complete until LGWR successfully writes the redo information, including the commit record, to the redo log files. In addition, the dirty buffers in the buffer cache cannot be written to the datafiles by DBWn until LGWR has written the redo information.

If the redo log files are grouped, and one of the multiplexed redo log files in a group is damaged, LGWR writes to the remaining members of the group, and records an error in the alert log file. If all members of a group are unusable, the LGWR process fails and the entire instance hangs until the problem can be corrected.

ARCn

If the database is in ARCHIVELOG mode, then the *archiver process,* or ARCn, copies redo logs to one or more destination directories, devices, or network locations whenever a redo log fills up and redo information starts to fill the next redo log in sequence. Optimally, the archive process finishes before the filled redo log is needed again; otherwise, serious performance problems occur—users cannot complete their transactions until the entries are written to the redo log files, and the redo log file is not ready to accept new entries because it is still being written to the archive location. There are at least three potential solutions to this problem: make the redo log files larger, increase the number of redo log groups, and increase the number of ARCn processes. Up to ten ARCn processes can be started for each instance by increasing the value of the LOG_ARCHIVE_MAX_PROCESSES initialization parameter.

CKPT

The *checkpoint process,* or CKPT, helps to reduce the amount of time required for instance recovery. During a checkpoint, CKPT updates the header of the control file and the datafiles to reflect the last successful *SCN (System Change Number).* A checkpoint occurs automatically every time a redo log file switch occurs. The DBWn processes routinely write dirty buffers to advance the checkpoint from where instance recovery can begin, thus reducing the *Mean Time to Recovery (MTTR).*

RECO

The RECO, or *recoverer process,* handles failures of distributed transactions (that is, transactions that include changes to tables in more than one database). If a table in the CCTR database is changed along with a table in the WHSE database, and the network connection between the databases fails before the table in the WHSE database can be updated, RECO will roll back the failed transaction.

Backup/Recovery Overview

Oracle supports many different forms of backup and recovery. Some of them can be managed at the user level, such as export and import; most of them are strictly DBA-centric, such as online or offline backups and using operating system commands or the RMAN utility.

Details for configuring and using these backup and recovery methods can be found in Chapter 12 and also in Chapter 13.

Export/Import

The export command is a standalone utility on all Oracle hardware and software platforms, and it's started by running the command **exp** at the operating system command-line prompt or through the Oracle Enterprise Manager console in a GUI environment. Export is considered a *logical* backup, because the underlying storage characteristics of the tables are not recorded, only the table metadata, user privileges, and table data. Depending on the task at hand, and whether you have DBA privileges or not, the **exp** command can either export all tables in the database, all the tables of one or more users, or a specific set of tables.

For restoring from a database export, the import command, started by running the command **imp**, takes a binary format file created by export and imports it into the database with the assumption that the users in the exported database tables exist in the database where the import command is performed.

One advantage to using export and import is that a database power user may be able to manage their own backups and recoveries, especially in a development environment. Also, a binary file generated by export is typically readable across Oracle versions, making a transfer of a small set of tables from an older version to a newer version of Oracle fairly straightforward.

Export and import are inherently "point in time" backups and therefore are not the most robust backup and recovery solutions if the data is volatile.

In Oracle 10g, Oracle Data Pump takes import and export operations to a new performance level. Exports to an external data source can be up to two times faster, and an import operation can be up to 45 times faster because Data Pump Import uses direct path loading, unlike traditional import. In addition, an export from the source database can be simultaneously imported into the target database without an intermediate dump file, saving time and administrative effort. Oracle Data Pump is implemented using the DBMS_DATAPUMP package with the **expdb** and **impdb** commands, and includes numerous other manageability features, such as fine-grained object selection. More information on Oracle Data Pump is provided in Chapter 17.

Offline Backups

One of the ways to make a physical backup of the database is to perform an *offline* backup. To perform an offline backup, the database is shut down and all database-related files, including datafiles, control files, SPFILEs, password files, and so forth, are copied to a second location. Once the copy operation is complete, the database instance can be started.

Offline backups are similar to export backups because they are point-in-time backups and therefore of less value if up-to-the minute recovery of the database is required and the database is not in **archivelog** mode. Another downside to offline backups is the amount of downtime necessary to perform the backup; any multinational company that needs 24/7 database access will most likely not do offline backups very often.

Online Backups

If a database is in **archivelog** mode, it is possible to do *online* backups of the database. The database can be open and available to users even while the backup is in process. The procedure for doing online backups is as easy as placing a tablespace into a backup state by using the **alter tablespace users begin backup** command, backing up the datafiles in the tablespace with operating system commands, and then taking the tablespace out of the backup state with the **alter tablespace users end backup** command.

RMAN

The backup tool Recovery Manager, known more commonly as *RMAN,* has been around since Oracle8. RMAN provides many advantages over other forms of backup. It can perform incremental backups of only changed data blocks in between full database backups while the database remains online throughout the backup.

RMAN keeps track of the backups via one of two methods: through the control file of the database being backed up, or through a recovery catalog stored in another database. Using the target database's control file for RMAN is easy, but it's not the best solution for a robust enterprise backup methodology. Although a recovery catalog requires another database to store the metadata for the target database along with a record of all backups, it is well worth it when all the control files in the target database are lost due to a catastrophic failure. In addition, a recovery catalog retains historical backup information that may be overwritten in the target database's control file if the value of CONTROL_FILE_RECORD_KEEP_TIME is set too low.

RMAN is discussed in detail in Chapter 13.

Security Capabilities

In the next few sections, we'll give a brief overview of the different ways that the Oracle 10*g* Database controls and enforces security in a database. Account security based on user and schema objects was covered in the section on database objects; the other security topics are covered here.

An in-depth look at these and other security capabilities within Oracle is covered in Chapter 10.

Privileges and Roles

In an Oracle database, *privileges* control access to both the actions a user can perform and the objects in the database. Privileges that control access to actions in the database are called *system privileges*, whereas privileges that control access to data and other objects are called *object privileges*.

To make assignment and management of privileges easier for the DBA, a database *role* groups privileges together. To put it another way, a role is a named group of privileges. In addition, a role can itself have roles assigned to it.

Privileges and roles are granted and revoked with the **grant** and **revoke** commands. The user group PUBLIC is neither a user nor a role, nor can it be dropped; however, when privileges are granted to PUBLIC, they are granted to every user of the database, both present and future.

System Privileges

System privileges grant the right to perform a specific type of action in the database, such as creating users, altering tablespaces, or dropping any view. Here is an example of granting a system privilege:

```
grant DROP ANY TABLE to SCOTT WITH ADMIN OPTION;
```

The user SCOTT can drop anyone's table in any schema. The **with grant option** clause allows SCOTT to grant his newly granted privilege to other users.

Object Privileges

Object privileges are granted on a specific object in the database. The most common object privileges are SELECT, UPDATE, DELETE, and INSERT for tables, EXECUTE for a PL/SQL stored object, and INDEX for granting index-creation privileges on a table. In the following example, the user RJB can perform any DML on the JOBS table owned by the HR schema:

```
grant SELECT, UPDATE, INSERT, DELETE on HR.JOBS to RJB;
```

Auditing

To audit access to objects in the database by users, you can set up an audit trail on a specified object or action by using the **audit** command. Both SQL statements and access to a particular database object can be audited; the success or failure of the action (or both) can be recorded in the audit trail table, SYS.AUD$.

For each audited operation, Oracle creates an audit record with the username, the type of operation that was performed, the object involved, and a timestamp. Various data dictionary views, such as DBA_AUDIT_TRAIL and DBA_FGA_AUDIT_TRAIL, make interpreting the results from the raw audit trail table SYS.AUD$ easier.

CAUTION
Excessive auditing on database objects can have an adverse effect on performance. Start out with basic auditing on key privileges and objects, and expand the auditing when the basic auditing has revealed a potential problem.

Fine-grained Auditing

The fine-grained auditing capability has been enhanced in Oracle 10g and takes auditing one step further: Standard auditing can detect when a **select** statement was executed on an EMPLOYEE table; fine-grained auditing will record an audit record containing specific columns accessed in the EMPLOYEE table, such as the SALARY column.

Fine-grained auditing is implemented using the DBMS_FGA package along with the data dictionary view DBA_FGA_AUDIT_TRAIL. The data dictionary view DBA_COMMON_AUDIT_TRAIL combines standard audit records in DBA_AUDIT_TRAIL with fine-grained audit records.

Virtual Private Database

The Virtual Private Database feature of Oracle, first introduced in Oracle8*i*, couples fine-grained access control with a secure application context. The security policies are attached to the data, and not to the application; this ensures that security rules are enforced regardless of how the data is accessed.

For example, a medical application context may return a predicate based on the patient identification number accessing the data; the returned predicate will be used in a WHERE clause to ensure that the data retrieved from the table is only the data associated with the patient.

Label Security

Oracle Label Security provides a "VPD Out-of-the-Box" solution to restrict access to rows in any table based on the label of the user requesting the access and the label on the row of the table itself. Oracle Label Security administrators do not need any special programming skills to assign security policy labels to users and rows in the table.

This highly granular approach to data security can, for example, allow a DBA at an Application Service Provider (ASP) to create only one instance of an accounts receivable application and to use Label Security to restrict rows in each table to an individual company's accounts receivable information.

Real Application Clusters

Oracle's Real Application Clusters (RAC) feature, known in previous Oracle versions as the Oracle Parallel Server option, allows more than one instance, on separate servers, to access the same database files.

A RAC installation can provide extreme high availability for both planned and unplanned outages. One instance can be restarted with new initialization parameters while the other instance is still servicing requests against the database. If one of the hardware servers crashes due to a fault of some type, the Oracle instance on the other server will continue to process transactions, even from users who were connected to the crashed server, transparently and with minimal downtime.

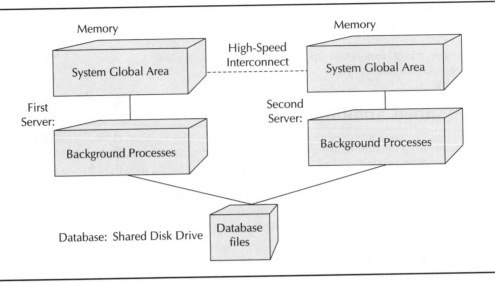

FIGURE 1-7. *A two-node Real Application Clusters (RAC) configuration*

RAC, however, is not a software-only solution: The hardware that implements RAC has special requirements. The shared database should be on a RAID-enabled disk subsystem to ensure that each component of the storage system is fault tolerant. In addition, RAC requires a high-speed interconnect, or a private network, between the nodes in the cluster to support messaging and transfer of blocks from one instance to another using the Cache Fusion mechanism.

The diagram in Figure 1-7 shows a two-node RAC installation. How to set up and configure Real Application Clusters is discussed in depth in Chapter 11.

Oracle Streams

As a component of Oracle Enterprise Edition, *Oracle Streams* is the higher-level component of the Oracle infrastructure that complements Real Application Clusters. Oracle Streams allows the smooth flow and sharing of both data and events within the same database or from one database to another. It is another key piece in Oracle's long list of high-availability solutions, tying together and enhancing Oracle's message queuing, data replication, and event management functions. More information on how to implement Oracle Streams can be found in Chapter 18.

Oracle Enterprise Manager

Oracle Enterprise Manager (OEM) is a valuable set of tools that facilitates the comprehensive management of all components of an Oracle infrastructure, including Oracle database instances, Oracle application servers, and web servers. If a management agent exists for a third-party application, then OEM can manage the third-party application in the same framework as any Oracle-supplied target.

OEM is fully web-enabled via Netscape or Internet Explorer, and as a result any operating system platform that supports Netscape or IE can be used to launch the OEM console.

One of the key decisions to make when using OEM with Oracle Grid Control is the location to store the *management repository*. The OEM management repository is stored in a database separate from the nodes being managed or monitored. The metadata from the nodes and services is centralized and facilitates the administration of these nodes. The management repository database should be backed up often and separately from the databases being managed.

An installation of OEM provides a tremendous amount of value "out of the box." When the OEM installation is complete, e-mail notifications are already set up to send messages to the SYSMAN or any other e-mail account for critical conditions, and the initial target discovery is automatically completed.

Oracle Initialization Parameters

An Oracle database uses *initialization parameters* to configure memory settings, disk locations, and so forth. There are two ways to store initialization parameters: using an editable text file and using a server-side binary file. Regardless of the method used to store the initialization parameters, there is a defined set of basic initialization parameters (as of Oracle 10g) that every DBA should be familiar with when creating a new database.

As of Oracle 10g, initialization parameters fall into two broad categories: basic initialization parameters and advanced initialization parameters. As Oracle becomes more and more self-managing, the number of parameters that a DBA must be familiar with and adjust on a daily basis is reduced.

Basic Initialization Parameters

The list of Oracle 10g basic initialization parameters appears in Table 1-3 along with a brief description of each. In the sections that follow, we will give some further explanation and advice

Initialization Parameter	Description
CLUSTER_DATABASE	Enables this node to be a member of a cluster.
COMPATIBLE	Allows a new database version to be installed while ensuring compatibility with the release specified by this parameter.
CONTROL_FILES	Specifies the location of the control files for this instance.
DB_BLOCK_SIZE	Specifies the size of Oracle blocks. This block size is used for the SYSTEM, SYSAUX, and temporary tablespaces at database creation.
DB_CREATE_FILE_DEST	The default location for OMF datafiles. Also specifies the location of control files and redo log files if DB_CREATE_ONLINE_LOG_DEST_*n* is not set.
DB_CREATE_ONLINE_LOG_DEST_*n*	The default location for OMF control files and online redo log files.
DB_DOMAIN	The logical domain name where the database resides in a distributed database system (for example, us.oracle.com).
DB_NAME	A database identifier of up to eight characters. Prepended to the DB_DOMAIN value for a fully qualified name (for example, marketing.us.oracle.com).

TABLE 1-3. *Basic Initialization Parameters*

Initialization Parameter	Description
DB_RECOVERY_FILE_DEST	The default location for the recovery area. Must be set along with DB_RECOVERY_FILE_DEST_SIZE.
DB_RECOVERY_FILE_DEST_SIZE	The maximum size, in bytes, for the files used for recovery in the recovery area location.
INSTANCE_NUMBER	In a RAC installation, the instance number of this node in the cluster.
JOB_QUEUE_PROCESSES	The maximum number of processes allowed for executing jobs, ranging from 0 to 1000.
LOG_ARCHIVE_DEST_n	For ARCHIVELOG mode, up to ten locations for sending archived log files.
LOG_ARCHIVE_DEST_STATE_n	Sets the availability of the corresponding LOG_ARCHIVE_DEST_n sites.
NLS_LANGUAGE	Specifies the default language of the database, including messages, day and month names, and sorting rules (for example, 'AMERICAN').
NLS_TERRITORY	The territory name used for day and week numbering (for example, 'SWEDEN', 'TURKEY', or 'AMERICA').
OPEN_CURSORS	The maximum number of open cursors per session.
PGA_AGGREGATE_TARGET	The total memory to allocate for all server processes in this instance.
PROCESSES	The maximum number of operating system processes that can connect to Oracle simultaneously. SESSIONS and TRANSACTIONS are derived from this value.
REMOTE_LISTENER	A network name resolving to an Oracle Net remote listener.
REMOTE_LOGIN_PASSWORDFILE	Specifies how Oracle uses password files. Required for RAC.
ROLLBACK_SEGMENTS	Names of private rollback segments to bring online, if undo management is not used for transaction rollback.
SESSIONS	The maximum number of sessions, and therefore simultaneous users, in the instance. Defaults to 1.1*PROCESSES + 5.
SGA_TARGET	Specifies the total size of all SGA components; this parameter automatically determines DB_CACHE_SIZE, SHARED_POOL_SIZE, LARGE_POOL_SIZE, and JAVA_POOL_SIZE.
SHARED_SERVERS	The number of shared server processes to allocate when an instance is started.
STAR_TRANSFORMATION_ENABLED	Controls query optimization when start queries are executed.
UNDO_MANAGEMENT	Specifies whether undo management is automatic (AUTO) or manual (MANUAL). If MANUAL is specified, rollback segments are used for undo management.
UNDO_TABLESPACE	The tablespace to use when UNDO_MANAGEMENT is set to AUTO.

TABLE 1-3.   *Basic Initialization Parameters* (continued)

regarding how some of these parameters should be set, depending on the hardware and software environment, the types of applications, and the number of users in the database.

Some of these parameters will be revisited in the section titled "Software Installation," where we will set the initial parameters for the SGA, file locations, and other limits.

COMPATIBLE

The COMPATIBLE parameter allows a newer version of Oracle to be installed while restricting the feature set of the new version as if an older version of Oracle was installed. This is a good way to move forward with a database upgrade while remaining compatible with an application that may fail when it runs with the new version of the software. The COMPATIBLE parameter can then be bumped up as the applications are reworked or rewritten to work with the new version of the database.

The downside of using this parameter is that none of the new applications for the database can take advantage of new features until the COMPATIBLE parameter is set to the same value as the current release.

DB_NAME

DB_NAME specifies the local portion of the database name. It can be up to eight characters and must begin with an alphanumeric character. Once set, it cannot be changed without re-creating the database; the DB_NAME is recorded in each datafile, redo log file, and control file in the database. At database startup, the value of this parameter must match the value of DB_NAME recorded in the control file.

DB_DOMAIN

DB_DOMAIN specifies the name of the network domain where the database will reside. The combination of DB_NAME and DB_DOMAIN must be unique within a distributed database system.

DB_RECOVERY_FILE_DEST and DB_RECOVERY_FILE_DEST_SIZE

When database recovery operations occur, either due to an instance failure or a media failure, it is convenient to have a *flash recovery area* to store and manage files related to a recovery or backup operation. Starting with Oracle 10g, the parameter DB_RECOVERY_FILE_DEST can be a directory location on the local server, a network directory location, or an ASM (Automatic Storage Management) disk area. The parameter DB_RECOVERY_FILE_DEST_SIZE places a limit on how much space is allowed for the recovery or backup files.

These parameters are optional, but if specified, Recovery Manager (RMAN) can automatically manage the files needed for backup and recovery operations. The size of this recovery area should be large enough to hold two copies of all datafiles, incremental RMAN backups, online redo logs, archived log files not yet backed up to tape, the SPFILE, and the control file.

CONTROL_FILES

The CONTROL_FILES parameter is not required. If it is not specified, Oracle creates one control file in a default location, or if OMF is configured, in the location specified by either DB_CREATE_FILE_DEST or DB_CREATE_ONLINE_LOG_DEST_n.

However, it is strongly recommended that multiple copies of the control file be created on separate physical volumes. Control files are so critical to the database integrity and are so small that at least three multiplexed copies of the control file should be created on separate physical disks. In addition, the command **alter database backup controlfile to trace** should be executed to create a text-format copy of the control file in the event of a major disaster.

The following example specifies three locations for copies of the control file:

```
CONTROL_FILES = (/u01/oracle10g/test/control01.ctl,
                 /u03/oracle10g/test/control02.ctl,
                 /u07/oracle10g/test/control03.ctl)
```

DB_BLOCK_SIZE

The parameter DB_BLOCK_SIZE specifies the size of the default Oracle block in the database. At database creation, the SYSTEM, TEMP, and SYSAUX tablespaces are created with this block size. Ideally, this parameter is the same as or a multiple of the operating system block size for I/O efficiency.

Before Oracle9*i*, you might specify a smaller block size (4KB or 8KB) for OLTP systems and a larger block size (up to 32KB) for DSS systems. However, now that tablespaces with up to five block sizes can coexist in the same database, a smaller value for DB_BLOCK_SIZE is fine. However, 8KB is probably preferable as a minimum for any database, unless it has been rigorously proven in the target environment that a 4KB block size will not cause performance issues.

SGA_TARGET

Another way that Oracle 10*g* can facilitate a "set it and forget it" database is by the ability to specify a total amount of memory for all SGA components. If SGA_TARGET is specified, the parameters DB_CACHE_SIZE, SHARED_POOL_SIZE, LARGE_POOL_SIZE, and JAVA_POOL_SIZE are automatically sized by Automatic Shared Memory Management (ASMM). If any of these four parameters are manually sized when SGA_TARGET is also set, ASMM uses the manually sized parameters as minimums.

Once the instance starts, the automatically sized parameters can by dynamically increased or decreased, as long as the parameter SGA_MAX_SIZE is not exceeded. The parameter SGA_MAX_SIZE specifies a hard upper limit for the entire SGA, and it cannot be exceeded or changed until the instance is restarted.

Regardless of how the SGA is sized, be sure that enough free physical memory is available in the server to hold the components of the SGA and all background processes; otherwise, excessive paging will occur and performance will suffer.

DB_CACHE_SIZE and DB_nK_CACHE_SIZE

The parameter DB_CACHE_SIZE specifies the size of the area in the SGA to hold blocks of the default size, including those from the SYSTEM, TEMP, and SYSAUX tablespaces. Up to four other caches can be defined if there are tablespaces with block sizes other than the SYSTEM and SYSAUX tablespaces. The value of **n** can be 2, 4, 8, 16, or 32; if the value of **n** is the same as the default block size, the corresponding DB_nK_CACHE_SIZE parameter is illegal. Although this parameter is not one of the basic initialization parameters, it becomes very basic when you transport a tablespace from another database with a block size other than DB_BLOCK_SIZE!

There are distinct advantages to a database containing multiple block sizes. The tablespace handling OLTP applications can have a smaller block size, and the tablespace with the data warehouse table can have a larger block size. However, be careful when allocating memory for each of these cache sizes so as not to allocate too much memory for one at the expense of another. As of Oracle9*i*, Oracle's Buffer Cache Advisory feature monitors the cache usage for each cache size in the view V$DB_CACHE_ADVICE to assist the DBA in sizing these memory areas. More information on how to use the Buffer Cache Advisory feature can be found in Chapter 8.

SHARED_POOL_SIZE, LARGE_POOL_SIZE, and JAVA_POOL_SIZE

The parameters SHARED_POOL_SIZE, LARGE_POOL_SIZE, and JAVA_POOL_SIZE, which size the shared pool, large pool, and Java pool, respectively, are automatically sized by Oracle if the SGA_TARGET initialization parameter is specified. More information on manually tuning these areas can be found in Chapter 8.

PROCESSES

The value for the PROCESSES initialization parameter represents the total number of processes that can simultaneously connect to the database. This includes both the background processes and user processes; a good starting point for the PROCESSES parameter would be 15 for the background processes plus the number of expected maximum concurrent users; for a smaller database, 50 is a good starting point, because there is little or no overhead associated with making PROCESSES too big.

UNDO_MANAGEMENT and UNDO_TABLESPACE

Automatic Undo Management, introduced in Oracle9*i*, eliminates or at least greatly reduces the headaches in trying to allocate the right number and size of rollback segments to handle the undo information for transactions. Instead, a single undo tablespace is specified for all undo operations (except for a SYSTEM rollback segment), and all undo management is handled automatically when the UNDO_MANAGEMENT parameter is set to AUTO.

The remaining task for the DBA is sizing the undo tablespace. Data dictionary views such as V$UNDOSTAT and the Undo Advisor can help the DBA adjust the size of the undo tablespace. Multiple undo tablespaces may be created; for example, a smaller undo tablespace is online during the day to handle relatively small transaction volumes, and a larger undo tablespace is brought online overnight to handle batch jobs and long-running queries that load the data warehouse and need transactional consistency. Only one undo tablespace may be active at any given time.

Advanced Initialization Parameters

The advanced initialization parameters include the balance of the initialization parameters not listed here, for a total of 255 of them in Release 1 of Oracle Database 10*g*. Most of these can be automatically set and tuned by the Oracle instance when the basic initialization parameters are set. We will review some of these in the next section, titled "Software Installation."

Software Installation

Although Oracle's installation software becomes easier and easier to use, it is very tempting to open the box of CDs and start the installation right away. Although this is fine if you're going to experiment with some new database features, a lot more planning is required to perform a successful installation without a lot of rework or even reinstallation a month from now. Although the complete details of an Oracle Database 10*g* installation is beyond the scope of this book, we will cover the basics of an Oracle install using the Oracle Universal Installer (OUI) along with a basic template for doing a manual install of the database using the **create database** command. In any case, a thorough review of the installation guide for your specific platform is another key to a successful Oracle database deployment. Here is a checklist of issues that should be addressed or resolved before starting the installation:

- Decide on the local database name and which domain will contain this database. These names are set in the initialization parameters DB_NAME and DB_DOMAIN.

- For the first project to use the database, estimate the number of tables and indexes, as well as their size, to plan for disk space estimates beyond what is required for the Oracle SYSTEM tablespace and the associated Oracle software and tools.

- Plan the locations of the physical datafiles on the server's disk to maximize performance and recoverability. The more physical disks, the better. If a RAID or network attached storage (NAS) area will be used for the datafiles, then consider OMF to manage the placement of the datafiles.

- Review and understand the basic initialization parameters, and plan on using an SPFILE before going live, if not using an SPFILE right away.

- Select the database character set, along with an alternate character set. Although it's easy to let the character sets default on install, you may need to consider where the users of the database are located and their language requirements. Character sets can be changed after installation only if the new character set is a superset of the existing character set.

- Decide on the best default database block size. The default block size defined by DB_BLOCK_SIZE cannot be changed later without reinstalling the database. Although this decision is not critical to future expansion of the database because Oracle can support tablespaces with multiple block sizes, having an incorrectly sized default block size can reduce the performance of operations using the SYSTEM, TEMP, or SYSAUX tablespace.

- Make sure that all non-administrative users are assigned a non-SYSTEM tablespace as their default tablespace. No user objects should ever be stored in the SYSTEM tablespace.

- Automatic Undo Management is a must to ease the administration of transaction undo information. The extra space needed in the undo tablespace is well worth the investment in productivity for both the DBA and users.

- Plan a backup and recovery strategy. Decide how often the database needs to be backed up; use more than one method to back up the database. One of the key questions to ask when selecting a backup strategy is, How long can we afford to have our database down? If the database only processes batch jobs at night, then a full backup every week and daily incremental backups are probably fine. If you're running a website in front of your database that sells widgets to customers all over the world, 24/7, and the cost of being down is six figures a minute, then the investment in an Oracle Real Applications Cluster (RAC) environment along with Data Guard for disaster recovery is probably cost-justified.

Familiarity with a couple key websites is a must. Oracle Technology Network (OTN), at http://otn.oracle.com, has a wealth of information, including white papers, free tools, sample code, and the online version of *Oracle Magazine*. There is no charge for using OTN, other than registering on the site.

Purchasing a license for Oracle database software is a good start, but an Oracle support contract with web support is the key to a successful installation and deployment. Using Oracle's Metalink (http://metalink.oracle.com) means you might never have to leave the friendly confines of your web browser to keep your database up and running. Through Metalink, you can submit a support request, search through other support requests, download patches, download white papers, and search the bug database.

A successful initial software installation is the first step. The database environment grows and evolves with every new business requirement and application that comes your way. For more information on how to successfully plan the implementation of a large database development project, see Chapter 5.

Overview of Licensing and Installation Options

Regardless of the software and hardware platform you're installing Oracle on, the types of installations you can perform are the same:

- **Enterprise Edition**   This is the most feature-laden and extensible version of the Oracle database. It includes features such as Flashback Database and allows you to add additional pieces of licensed functionality, such as Oracle Spatial, Real Application Clusters, Oracle OLAP, Oracle Label Security, and Oracle Data Mining.

- **Standard Edition**   This edition provides a good subset of the features of the Enterprise Edition, including Real Application Clusters for up to four total CPUs, but the additional add-on pieces, such as Oracle Label Security, cannot be added to the Standard Edition.

- **Standard Edition One**   This edition provides the same features of Standard Edition, except for Real Application Clusters, and is limited to a single server with a maximum of two CPUs.

- **Personal Edition**   Allows for the development of applications that will run on either the Standard or Enterprise Edition. This edition cannot be used in a production environment.

As of Oracle 10g, licensing for the Oracle Database is only by named user or CPU, and there is no longer a concurrent user licensing option. Therefore, the DBA should use the initialization parameter LICENSE_MAX_USERS to specify the maximum number of users that can be created in the database. As a result, LICENSE_MAX_SESSIONS and LICENSE_SESSIONS_WARNING are deprecated in Oracle 10g.

Using OUI to Install the Oracle Software

The *Oracle Universal Installer (OUI)* is used to install and manage all Oracle components for both the server-side and client-side components. You can also deinstall any Oracle products from the initial OUI screens.

During the server installation, you will choose the version of Oracle Database 10g from the list in the previous section: Enterprise Edition, Standard Edition, or Personal Edition.

It is strongly recommended that you create a starter database when prompted during the install. Creating the starter database is a good way to make sure the server environment is set up correctly, as well as to review any new features of Oracle 10g. The starter database may also be a good candidate as a Grid Control repository for either Enterprise Manager or Recovery Manager.

At some point in the software installation, the *Database Configuration Assistant (DBCA)* takes over and prompts you for the parameters necessary to size and configure your database. The installation steps in the next session assume you have already completed the software installation and have created a starter database; we will create and configure a second database on the same server with the DBCA.

NOTE
As of Oracle 10g, the DBCA can configure nodes in a Real Application Clusters environment.

Using the DBCA to Create a Database

At the operating system command prompt, launch the DBCA by typing **dbca**. In the subsections that follow, we will provide additional tips and guidance for most of the screens during the creation of the database.

DBCA Options

After an initial welcome screen, you are presented with a choice of four options:

- **Create a Database**   This one is fairly straightforward; you are creating a new database from scratch, using a template as a starting point.

- **Configure Database Options in a Database**   Some of the system parameters for an existing database installation can be changed, such as changing from a dedicated server mode to shared server.

- **Delete a Database**   This one is also straightforward, and very dangerous! It will shut down the database and delete all the datafiles and control files associated with the database. You will need the SYS or SYSTEM password to proceed with this option if you are not using operating system authentication.

- **Manage Templates**   This option allows you to add, modify, or delete templates. During a DBCA session, once all database parameters have been gathered, you have the option to save your settings as a template. In many cases, the predefined templates that Oracle provides are not quite perfect for your environment, and it is a timesaver to be able to save your database options for selection as a template in a future DBCA session.

Selecting a Database Template

In Figure 1-8, you are presented with the list of templates available. If you have created your own templates in previous DBCA sessions, they will appear on this screen also.

The template choices are as follows:

- **Custom Database**   Use this option if you have performed many installations and know ahead of time the values for all the options you need in the database. This option is good if you are creating a new template from scratch or have very specific requirements for the configuration of your database.

■ **Data Warehouse**   This template is for database environments where users are performing numerous, complex queries that join many large tables for reporting, forecasting, and analytics.

■ **General Purpose**   If you are not sure of the intended use of your database yet, or if you need to host users with both analytical and transaction processing requirements, choose this template.

■ **Transaction Processing**   In 24/7 environments where the number of users is high, the transactions are heavy, but short, and the bulk of the activity is creating and updating, use this template.

In this installation, we are choosing the General Purpose template. It combines the features of both a data warehouse and an OLTP environment into a single database; use this option if you must use this database for both environments. Ideally, however, any database you create should be configured and tuned for the types of users and transactions on the database.

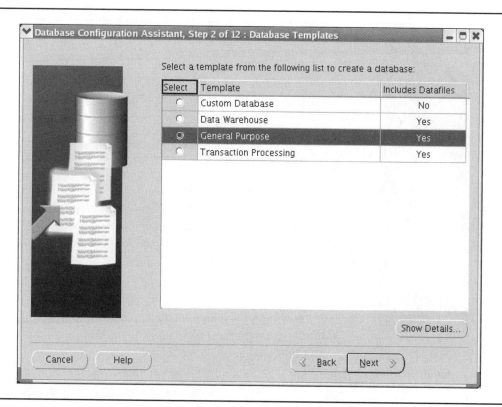

FIGURE 1-8.   *Database template selection*

Database Identification

In step 3 of the DBCA, you will identify the name of the instance along with the global database name; if you type the fully qualified database name, it will use all characters up to the first period as the instance name, or *Oracle System Identifier (SID)*. Figure 1-9 shows the Database Identification screen.

Note the distinction between a SID, an instance name, and a database. You may have one or more databases on a server; each database may have one or more instances opening each database. The instance names that use the same database must be unique. On the server, if there is more than one instance with the same name (but opening different databases), the SID associated with the instance must be unique.

TIP
*If the global database name needs to be changed in the future, you must use the **alter database** command to change it, in addition to changing it in the initialization parameter file. The global database name is stored in the data dictionary when the database is created.*

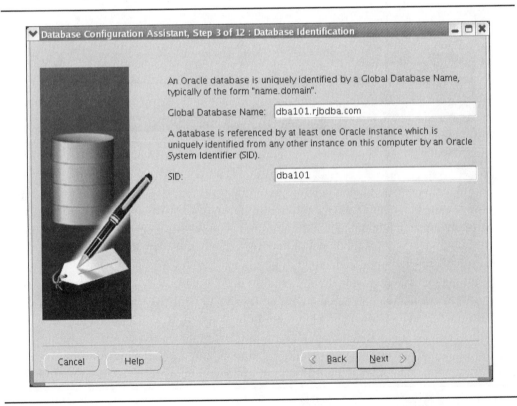

FIGURE 1-9. *Database Identification screen*

Unless you have an existing domain, use the default domain name .world. Check with your system administrator to see if a specific global database name should be used.

Management Options

The next screen, shown in Figure 1-10, specifies the database management options available. If you want to set up web services to control this database with the web-enabled Oracle Enterprise Manager, check the first box. If there is a Grid Control management service running on the network (known as an *Enterprise Manager Repository agent* in previous Oracle versions), you have the option to specify which management service will control this database.

If there is no Grid Control management service available, you can manage the database locally with Database Control. Within the Database Control choice, you can specify where alerts, warnings, and other database notifications are sent by specifying an e-mail address and the mail server name that will forward the e-mail messages. If you want to set up automated daily backups, you can specify the time of day for the backups.

In our example, we don't have any Grid Control management service agents available, so we choose Database Control to manage our Enterprise Manager interface. We also specify the e-mail address where we want our server alerts to be sent (in this case, bob@rjbdba.com).

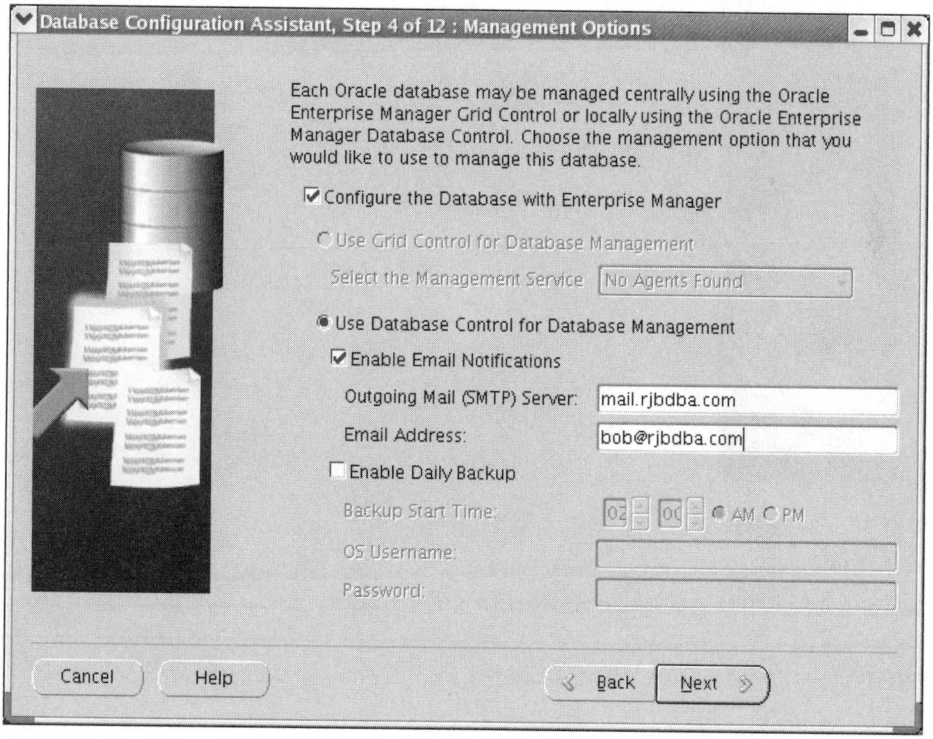

FIGURE 1-10. *Database Management Options screen*

Database Credentials

In Figure 1-11, you provide the initial passwords for the administrative user accounts. After the installation, be sure to create at least one account with DBA privileges to use instead of SYS or SYSTEM for day-to-day administrative tasks.

If you wish to use different passwords for the SYS, SYSTEM, DBSNMP, and SYSMAN accounts, you can do that on this screen; later in the installation, after the database has been created, you will have the opportunity to change the passwords for all of the approximately 30 user accounts created in a typical installation.

Storage Options

The database can use a number of different methods for storing datafiles, control files, and redo log files. If you have the resources to dedicate another database instance for managing disk space, choose ASM. An instance to manage ASM is fairly lightweight; typically, it will use no more than 64MB

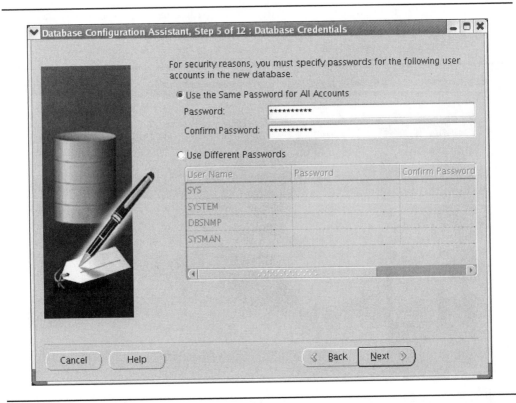

FIGURE 1-11. *Database Credentials screen*

of RAM. If you are in a Real Application Clusters environment and you don't have a cluster file system available (such as OCFS), then choose Raw Devices. Figure 1-12 shows these options on the Storage Options screen.

File Locations

The next screen, shown in Figure 1-13, is where you select the locations for datafiles, control files, and redo log files, as well as the archiving and backup and recovery locations. You can use the locations provided with the template, provide your own single location for all files, or configure OMF (Oracle Managed Files) for this database. In all cases, you will have the option to fine-tune these locations in a later step.

New to Oracle 10g is the concept of a Flash Recovery Area. This is a dedicated location on disk, separate from the location of the database's operational files, containing the backup files from RMAN. It is highly recommended that you use a Flash Recovery Area so that RMAN can more

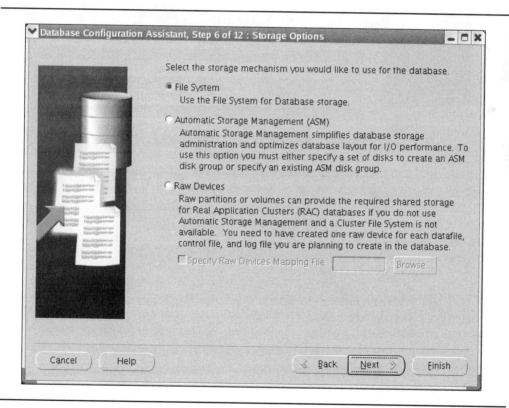

FIGURE 1-12.   *Storage Options screen*

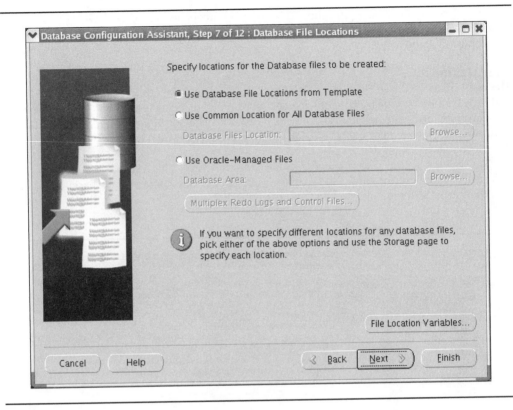

FIGURE 1-13. *Database File Locations screen*

easily manage backup and recovery operations. As mentioned previously in this chapter, be sure that the Flash Recovery Area is large enough to hold at least two copies of all datafiles, incremental backups, control files, SPFILEs, and archived redo log files that are still on disk. Figure 1-14 shows the screen where you specify the location of the Flash Recovery Area, along with its default size.

You can also enable **archivelog** mode, as well as specify the location or locations for the archived redo log files. It is recommended that you leave archiving off until the database is installed, because this will increase the database creation time. The parameters for **archivelog** mode can easily be changed in init.ora or the SPFILE immediately after the database is up and running.

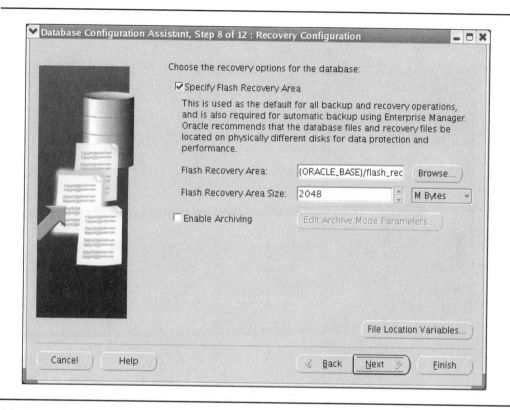

FIGURE 1-14. *Recovery Configuration and Locations screen*

Database Components

In step 9 of the DBCA session, you are asked about installing sample schemas. It is highly recommended that you install the sample schemas; many tutorials and study guides rely on the sample schemas being in the database. They are also useful in that the samples demonstrate nearly all datatypes and constructs available in the database, ranging from bitmapped indexes to clustered tables and object types. The screen shown in Figure 1-15 allows you to specify the installation of the sample schemas. The second tab on this screen gives you the option to specify other scripts that you need to run against this database once it is created, such as scripts to create tablespaces for existing applications, special user accounts, and so forth.

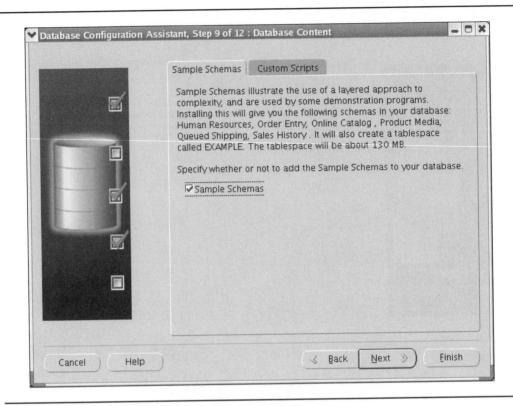

FIGURE 1-15. *Selecting a sample schema installation*

NOTE
Sample schemas should not be installed in a production database for security and performance reasons.

If you choose to not install the sample schemas at this time, they can be created using the scripts in the directory $ORACLE_HOME/demo/schema after the database has been created.

Initialization Parameters

The screens in Figures 1-16 through 1-19 allow the DBA to adjust the key initialization parameters for the database. In previous sections of this chapter, we described many of the basic initialization

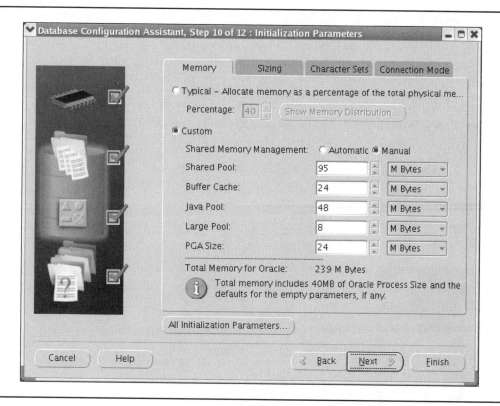

FIGURE 1-16.   *Initialization Parameters, Memory tab*

parameters that a DBA needs to understand. In the next few paragraphs, we will link those parameters with the values you enter on the screens.

Figure 1-16 shows the Memory tab of the Initialization Parameters screen. If you select Typical or select Custom with Shared Memory Management Automatic, Oracle will make assumptions about the memory it can use for the SGA and background processes. Even by defaulting many of the parameters in a Typical configuration, you can still specify how much of the server's physical memory should be used for Oracle, depending on how much memory is used by the operating system, and whether any other applications are going to be running on this server along with Oracle.

Because Java Pool and the Large Pool are optional, you can set these to zero and give more memory to Shared Pool or Buffer Cache; however, even if you only have one Java Stored Procedure in the database, the value for Java Pool must be at least the size of one granule in the database—either 4MB or 16MB, but at least 20MB is recommended.

Figure 1-17 allows you to specify the default block size of the database, as well as the total number of processes that will be simultaneously connecting to Oracle, corresponding to the PROCESSES initialization parameter.

The Block Size parameter should be fine at either 4KB or preferably 8KB, as long as it's a multiple of the operating system block size. Making sure that the database block size is correct is not as critical as it used to be in previous versions of Oracle because other tablespaces in the database can have block sizes different from the default block size.

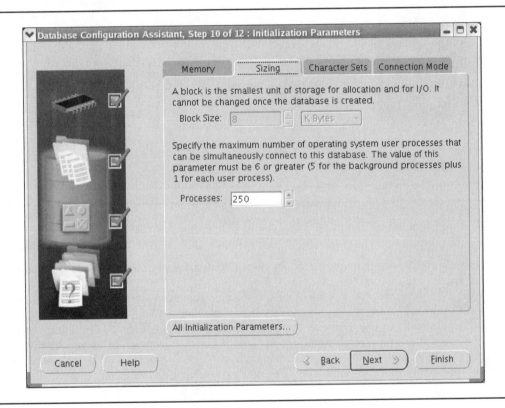

FIGURE 1-17.   *Initialization Parameters, Sizing tab*

If the Oracle Server will not be running in Shared Server mode, and therefore every user connection will be a dedicated connection, be sure to make the Processes setting high enough to include all expected database connections plus at least 15 for background processes.

The next screen in the DBCA specifies the language parameters for the database. Unless you have a multinational organization and have special language requirements for the database end users, the default Database Character Set and National Character Set selections, based on your server settings, should be fine. Figure 1-18 shows the NLS-related parameters.

The next screen allows you to specify how users will connect to the database—via dedicated connections to the database or through a Shared Server environment. If you select Shared Server mode, you can edit some of the specifics of the Shared Server environment, such as what protocols

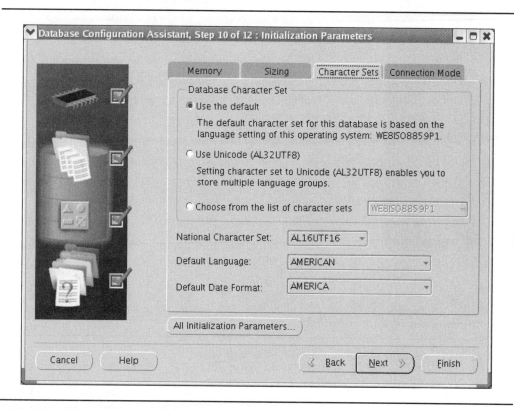

FIGURE 1-18. *Initialization Parameters, Character Sets tab*

are used and how many connections are assigned per dispatcher. In Figure 1-19, we are selecting Shared Server mode, with two Shared Server processes available to handle the connection requests from the dispatchers.

While you are still on the Initialization Parameters screen, you are able to fine-tune the values of initialization parameters by clicking the All Initialization Parameters button. Figure 1-20 shows

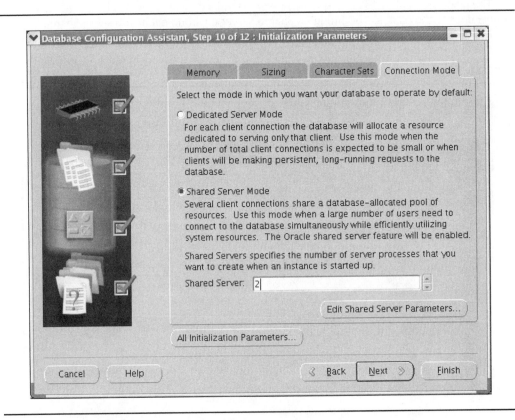

FIGURE 1-19. *Initialization Parameters, Connection Mode tab*

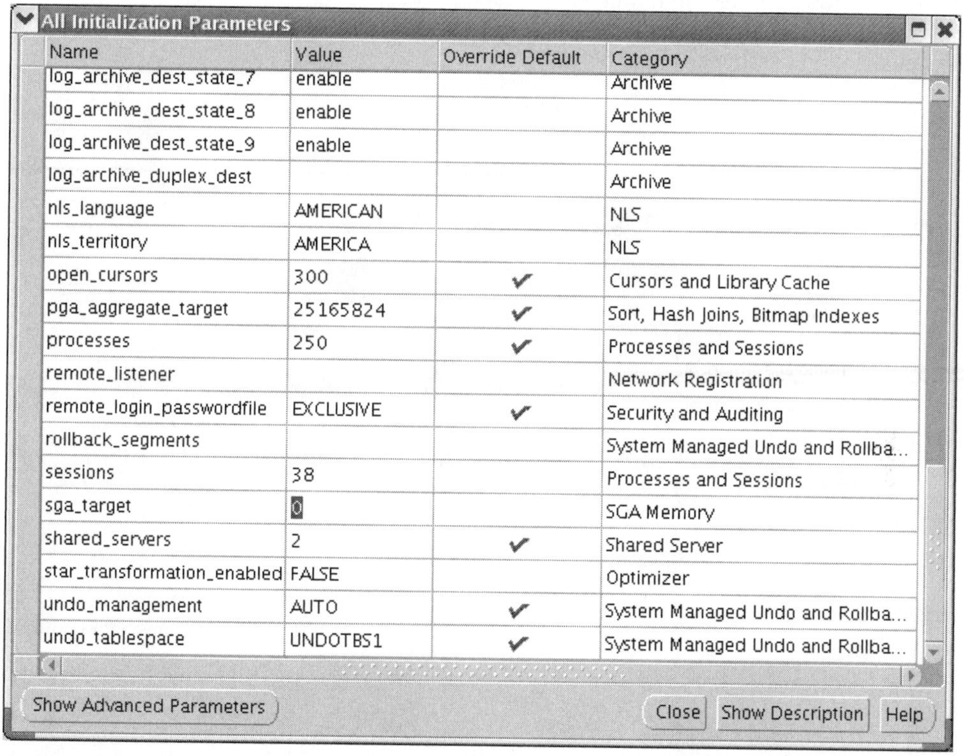

Name	Value	Override Default	Category
log_archive_dest_state_7	enable		Archive
log_archive_dest_state_8	enable		Archive
log_archive_dest_state_9	enable		Archive
log_archive_duplex_dest			Archive
nls_language	AMERICAN		NLS
nls_territory	AMERICA		NLS
open_cursors	300	✔	Cursors and Library Cache
pga_aggregate_target	25165824	✔	Sort, Hash Joins, Bitmap Indexes
processes	250	✔	Processes and Sessions
remote_listener			Network Registration
remote_login_passwordfile	EXCLUSIVE	✔	Security and Auditing
rollback_segments			System Managed Undo and Rollba...
sessions	38		Processes and Sessions
sga_target	0		SGA Memory
shared_servers	2	✔	Shared Server
star_transformation_enabled	FALSE		Optimizer
undo_management	AUTO	✔	System Managed Undo and Rollba...
undo_tablespace	UNDOTBS1	✔	System Managed Undo and Rollba...

Show Advanced Parameters

Close   Show Description   Help

FIGURE 1-20. *Editing the Initialization Parameters list*

how you can modify the value for SGA_TARGET or other parameters, even though you may have already implicitly defined these parameters in previous screens.

Database Storage

On the DBCA Database Storage screen, you can review and revise the locations of the control files, datafiles, and redo log files, as well as multiplex the control files and create redo log file groups.

Figure 1-21 shows how we can multiplex the control files to three different disk locations. The names and locations of the control files on this screen determine the value of CONTROL_FILES in the initialization parameter file or SPFILE.

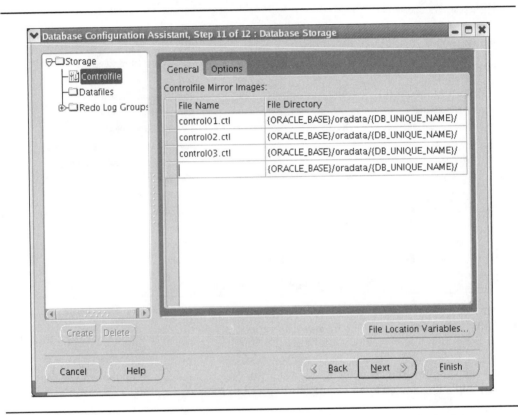

FIGURE 1-21. *Database Storage screen*

Creation Options

In Figure 1-22, we are ready to create the database. In addition, we can use the information we provided in the previous screens and save it to a template. If in doubt, save it as a template; the

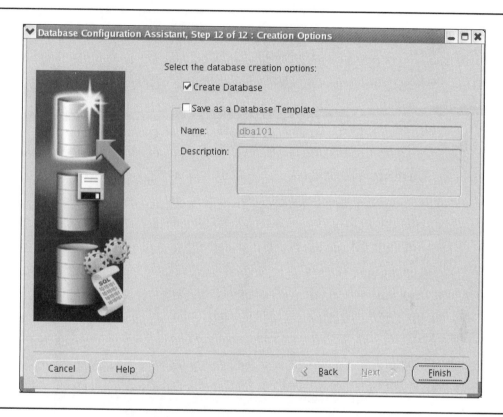

FIGURE 1-22. *Database and template creation options*

storage required to save a template is minimal, and it can easily be deleted later by rerunning the DBCA.

Before the database is created, an HTML summary of your template is presented, as shown in Figure 1-23, and you have the option to save this report as an HTML file for documentation purposes.

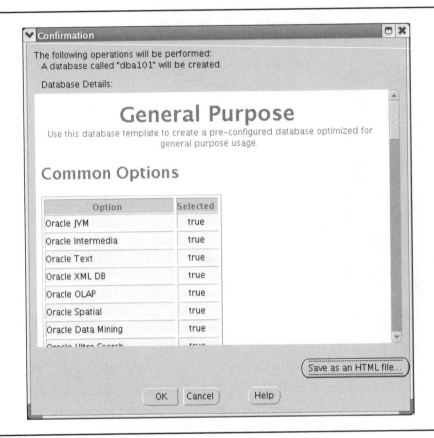

FIGURE 1-23. *HTML installation summary*

Completing the Installation

After clicking OK on the HTML Summary screen, the DBCA performs the tasks to create the database and start the instance. A standard set of scripts is run when the database first starts; this includes the scripts that create the sample schemas, plus any custom scripts you may have specified earlier. Figure 1-24 shows the DBCA performing the initialization tasks.

Once the initialization and creation scripts have completed, a summary screen is presented, as in Figure 1-25, giving the location of the log file for this installation. It is recommended that you review this log file to ensure that there were no unexpected errors during the install. You should also save this log file with the other documentation for this database; it can also be useful for future installations as a baseline.

The Oracle instance you just created is up and running. You have the option to unlock other accounts created during this install and to assign passwords to them.

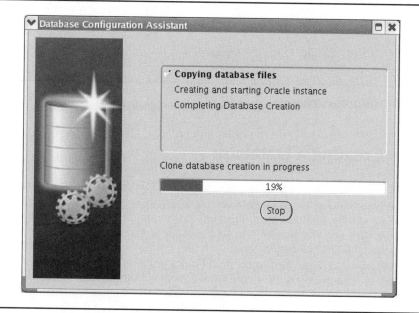

FIGURE 1-24.   *Creating and starting the Oracle instance*

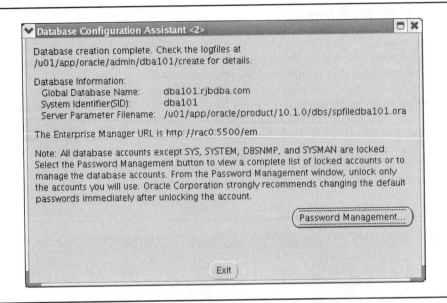

FIGURE 1-25. *DBCA summary*

Manually Creating a Database

In some situations, it is preferable to manually create a database instead of using the DBCA. For example, a DBA may have to create the same database on 20 different servers, or the database may need some parameters in the **create database** command that aren't adjustable using the DBCA. Oracle provides a sample database-creation script that can be customized for a manual install. Alternatively, the DBA can use the DBCA to save a database script to a file, which can be edited later and run at the SQL*Plus command line.

Here are the basic steps needed to create a database manually. Some of these steps are operating system or platform dependent, and we will note the differences. Be sure to review the installation guide for your specific platform before attempting a manual installation. For example, under Windows, you will need to run the utility oradim.exe to create the Oracle background process and to set the relevant Registry values.

1. Decide on a directory structure for the database; it is recommended that you comply with Oracle's Optimal Flexible Architecture (OFA) standards when placing your files on disk. See Chapters 3 and 4 for more information on OFA.

2. Select an Oracle SID to distinguish this instance from any other ones running on this server. Frequently this is the same as the database name specified in the DB_NAME initialization parameter. At a Windows command prompt, you will type the following:

```
set ORACLE_SID=rjbdb
```

Under Unix, you will use either

```
export ORACLE_SID=rjbdb
```

or

```
setenv ORACLE_SID=rjbdb
```

depending on your default command shell.

3. Establish an authentication method for connecting privileged users to the database. Use the orapwd command-line utility to create a password file if you want Oracle to authenticate the privileged users, and you will set the initialization parameter REMOTE_LOGIN_ PASSWORDFILE to EXCLUSIVE. If you are using operating system authentication, there is no need for a password file; set REMOTE_LOGIN_PASSWORDFILE to NONE.

4. Create an initialization parameter file and place it in the default location for your platform, at least initially for the install. Under Unix, the default location is $ORACLE_HOME/dbs; under Windows it is $ORACLE_HOME\database. Here is a sample Oracle-supplied initialization file:

```
# Cache and I/O
DB_BLOCK_SIZE=4096
DB_CACHE_SIZE=20971520

# Cursors and Library Cache
CURSOR_SHARING=SIMILAR
OPEN_CURSORS=300

# Diagnostics and Statistics
BACKGROUND_DUMP_DEST=/u01/oracle10g/admin/rjbdb/bdump
CORE_DUMP_DEST=/u01/oracle10g/admin/rjbdb/cdump
TIMED_STATISTICS=TRUE
USER_DUMP_DEST=/u01/oracle10g/admin/rjbdb/udump

# Control File Configuration
CONTROL_FILES=(/u01/oracle10g/prod/rjbdb/control01.ctl,
               /u02/oracle10g/prod/rjbdb/control02.ctl,
               /u03/oracle10g/prod/rjbdb/control03.ctl)

# Archive
LOG_ARCHIVE_DEST_1='LOCATION=/u06/oracle10g/oradata/rjbdb/archive'
# New log archive format. If compatibility 10.0 and up,
# this is enforced.
LOG_ARCHIVE_FORMAT=%t_%s_%r.dbf
# The following parameter is deprecated in 10iR1
# LOG_ARCHIVE_START=TRUE
```

```
# Shared Server
# Starts shared server if set > 0.
SHARED_SERVERS=2
# Uncomment and use first DISPATCHERS parameter
# below when your listener is
# configured for SSL
# (listener.ora and sqlnet.ora)
# DISPATCHERS = "(PROTOCOL=TCPS)(SER=MODOSE)",
#              "(PROTOCOL=TCPS)(PRE=oracle.aurora.server.SGiopServer)"
DISPATCHERS="(PROTOCOL=TCP)(SER=MODOSE)",
            "(PROTOCOL=TCP)(PRE=oracle.aurora.server.SGiopServer)",
            (PROTOCOL=TCP)

# Miscellaneous
COMPATIBLE=10.0.0
DB_NAME=rjbdb

# Distributed, Replication and Snapshot
DB_DOMAIN=rjbdba.com
REMOTE_LOGIN_PASSWORDFILE=EXCLUSIVE

# Network Registration
INSTANCE_NAME=rjbdb

# Pools
JAVA_POOL_SIZE=31457280
LARGE_POOL_SIZE=1048576
SHARED_POOL_SIZE=52428800

# Processes and Sessions
PROCESSES=150

# Redo Log and Recovery
FAST_START_MTTR_TARGET=300

# Resource Manager
RESOURCE_MANAGER_PLAN=SYSTEM_PLAN

# Sort, Hash Joins, Bitmap Indexes
SORT_AREA_SIZE=524288

# Automatic Undo Management
UNDO_MANAGEMENT=AUTO
UNDO_TABLESPACE=undotbs
```

5. Connect to the instance using SQL*Plus, as shown here:

```
sqlplus /nolog
connect SYS/password as sysdba
```

Note that while the instance itself exists, there is not much that we can do with it because we have not started the database yet.

6. Create a server parameter file (SPFILE). If the initialization file is in the default location, this command will create the SPFILE:

```
create spfile from pfile;
```

7. Start the instance using the following command:

```
startup nomount
```

Note that because we do not have a database created yet, this is the only option we can use with the **startup** command.

8. Issue the **create database** statement. Here is an example:

```
CREATE DATABASE rjbdb
   USER SYS IDENTIFIED BY paris703
   USER SYSTEM IDENTIFIED BY tyler12
   LOGFILE GROUP 1 ('/u02/oracle10g/oradata/rjbdb/redo01.log') SIZE 100M,
           GROUP 2 ('/u04/oracle10g/oradata/rjbdb/redo02.log') SIZE 100M,
           GROUP 3 ('/u06/oracle10g/oradata/rjbdb/redo03.log') SIZE 100M
   MAXLOGFILES 5
   MAXLOGMEMBERS 5
   MAXLOGHISTORY 1
   MAXDATAFILES 100
   MAXINSTANCES 1
   CHARACTER SET US7ASCII
   NATIONAL CHARACTER SET AL16UTF16
   DATAFILE '/u01/oracle10g/oradata/rjbdb/system01.dbf' SIZE 325M REUSE
   EXTENT MANAGEMENT LOCAL
   SYSAUX DATAFILE '/u01/oracle10g/oradata/rjbdb/sysaux01.dbf'
      SIZE 325M REUSE
   DEFAULT TABLESPACE tbs_1
   DEFAULT TEMPORARY TABLESPACE tempts1
      TEMPFILE '/u01/oracle10g/oradata/rjbdb/temp01.dbf'
      SIZE 20M REUSE
   UNDO TABLESPACE undotbs
      DATAFILE '/u02/oracle10g/oradata/rjbdb/undotbs01.dbf'
      SIZE 200M REUSE AUTOEXTEND ON MAXSIZE UNLIMITED;
```

9. A couple of things are worth noting in this example. We are explicitly setting the passwords for SYS and SYSTEM; if we didn't specify them here, they will default to **change_on_install** and **manager**, respectively.

10. The redo log file groups have only one member each; once our database is in production, we should multiplex them. Because we specified an undo tablespace with the UNDO_TABLESPACE parameter in the initialization parameter file, we need to create that tablespace here; otherwise, the instance will not start.

11. After the **create database** command completes successfully, the database is mounted and opened for use.

12. Create additional tablespaces for users, indexes, and applications.

13. Build data dictionary views with the supplied scripts catalog.sql and catproc.sql. The script catalog.sql creates views against the data dictionary tables, dynamic performance views, and public synonyms for most of the views. The group PUBLIC is granted read-only access to the views. The script catproc.sql sets up PL/SQL.

14. Back up the database using either a cold backup or the Recovery Manager. In case of a database failure in the early stages of deployment, you have a complete and running database to fall back on, and most likely you will not have to re-create the database from scratch.

CHAPTER
2

Upgrading to Oracle Database 10g

f you have previously installed an earlier version of the Oracle database server, you can upgrade your database to Oracle Database 10g. Multiple upgrade paths are supported; the right choice for you will depend on factors such as your current Oracle software version and your database size. In this chapter, you will see descriptions of these methods along with guidelines for their use.

If you have not used a version of Oracle prior to Oracle Database 10g, you can skip this chapter for now. However, you will likely need to refer to it when you upgrade from Oracle Database 10g to a later version or when you migrate data from a different database into your database.

Prior to beginning the upgrade, you should read the Oracle Database 10g Installation Guide for your operating system. A successful installation is dependent on a properly configured environment—including operating system patch levels and system parameter settings. Plan to get the installation and upgrade right the first time rather than attempting to restart a partially successful installation. Configure the system to support both the installation of the Oracle software and the creation of a usable starter database.

This chapter assumes that your installation of the Oracle Database 10g software (see Chapter 1) completed successfully and that you have an Oracle database that uses an earlier version of the Oracle software on the same server. To upgrade that database, you have four options:

- **Use the Database Upgrade Assistant to guide and perform the upgrade in place.** The old database will become an Oracle 10g database during this process.

- **Perform a manual upgrade of the database.** The old database will become an Oracle 10g database during this process.

- **Use the Export and Import utilities to move data from an earlier version of Oracle to the Oracle 10g database.** Two separate databases will be used—the old database as the source for the export and the new database as the target for the import.

- **Copy data from an earlier version of Oracle to an Oracle 10g database.** Two separate databases will be used—the old database as the source for the copy and the new database as the target for the copy.

Upgrading a database in place—via either the Database Upgrade Assistant or the manual upgrade path—is called a *direct upgrade.* Because a direct upgrade does not involve creating a second database for the one being upgraded, it may complete faster and require less disk space than an indirect upgrade.

NOTE
Direct upgrade of the database to version 10 is only supported if your present database is using one of these releases of Oracle: 8.0.6, 8.1.7, 9.0.1, or 9.2. If you are using any other release, you will first have to upgrade the database to one of those releases or you will need to use a different upgrade option. Oracle 8.0.6 is only supported for some versions (generally 64-bit), so be sure to check the online certification matrixes at Oracle's Metalink site.

NOTE
Plan your upgrades carefully; you may need to allow time for multiple incremental upgrades (such as from 8.1.6 to 8.1.7) prior to upgrading to Oracle Database 10g.

Choosing an Upgrade Method

As described in the previous section, two direct upgrade and two indirect upgrade paths are available. In this section, you will see a more detailed description of the options, followed by usage descriptions.

In general, the direct upgrade paths will perform the upgrade the fastest because they upgrade the database in place. The other methods involve copying data, either to an Export dump file on the file system or across a database link. For very large databases, the time required to completely re-create the database via the indirect methods may exclude them as viable options.

The first direct method relies on the *Database Upgrade Assistant (DBUA)*. DBUA is an interactive tool that guides you through the upgrade process. DBUA evaluates your present database configuration and recommends modifications that can be implemented during the upgrade process. These recommendations may include the sizing of files and the specifications for the new SYSAUX tablespace. After you accept the recommendations, DBUA performs the upgrade in the background while a progress panel is displayed. DBUA is very similar in approach to the Database Configuration Assistant (DBCA). As discussed in Chapter 1, DBCA is a graphical interface to the steps and parameters required to make the upgrade a success.

The second direct method is called a *manual upgrade.* Whereas DBUA runs scripts in the background, the manual upgrade path involves database administrators running the scripts themselves. The manual upgrade approach gives you a great deal of control, but it also adds to the level of risk in the upgrade because you must perform the steps in the proper order.

You can use Export and Import as an indirect method for upgrading a database. In this method, you export the data from the old version of the database and then import it into a database that uses the new version of the Oracle software. This process may require disk space for multiple copies of the data—in the source database, in the Export dump file, and in the target database. In exchange for these costs, this method gives you great flexibility in choosing which data will be migrated. You can select specific tablespaces, schemas, tables, and rows to be exported.

In the Export/Import method, the original database is not upgraded; its data is extracted and moved, and the database can then either be deleted or be run in parallel with the new database until testing of the new database has been completed. In the process of performing the export/import, you are selecting and reinserting each row of the database. If the database is very large, the import process may take a long time, impacting your ability to provide the upgraded database to your users in a timely fashion. See Chapter 12 for details on the Export and Import utilities.

NOTE
Depending on the version of the source database, you will need to use a specific version of the Export and Import utilities. See "Export and Import Versions to Use" later in this chapter.

In the data-copying method, you issue a series of **create table as select** or **insert as select** commands that cross database links (see Chapter 16) to retrieve the source data. The tables are created in the Oracle 10g database based on queries of data from a separate source database. This method allows you to bring over data incrementally and to limit the rows and columns migrated. However, you will need to be careful that the copied data maintains all the necessary relationships among tables. As with the Export/Import method, this method may require a significant amount of time for large databases.

> **NOTE**
> *If you are changing the operating platform at the same time, you can use transportable tablespaces to move the data from the old database to the new database. For very large databases, this method may be faster than the other data-copying methods. See Chapter 17 for the details on transportable tablespaces.*

Selecting the proper upgrade method requires you to evaluate the technical expertise of your team, the data that is to be migrated, and the allowable downtime for the database during the migration. In general, using DBUA will be the method of choice for very large databases, whereas smaller databases may use an indirect method.

Before Upgrading

Prior to beginning the migration, you should back up the existing database and database software. If the migration fails for some reason and you are unable to revert the database or software to its earlier version, you will be able to restore your backup and re-create your database.

You should develop and test scripts that will allow you to evaluate the performance and functionality of the database following the upgrade. This evaluation may include the performance of specific database operations or the overall performance of the database under a significant user load.

Prior to executing the upgrade process on a production database, you should attempt the upgrade on a test database so any missing components (such as operating system patches) can be identified and the time required for the upgrade can be measured.

Prior to performing a direct upgrade, you should analyze the data dictionary tables. During the upgrade process to Oracle 10g, the data dictionary will be analyzed if it has not been analyzed already, so performing this step in advance will aid the performance of the upgrade.

Using the Database Upgrade Assistant

You can start the Database Upgrade Assistant (DBUA) via the

```
dbua
```

command (in UNIX environments) or by selecting Database Upgrade Assistant from the Oracle Configuration and Migration Tools menu option (in Windows environments). If you are using a UNIX environment, you will need to enable an Xwindows display prior to starting DBUA.

When started, DBUA will display a Welcome screen. At the next screen, select the database you want to upgrade from the list of available databases. You can upgrade only one database at a time.

After you make your selection, the upgrade process begins. DBUA will perform pre-upgrade checks (such as for obsolete initialization parameters or files that are too small). DBUA will then create the SYSAUX tablespace, a standard tablespace in all Oracle 10*g* databases. You can override Oracle's defaults for the location and size parameters for the datafiles used by the SYSAUX tablespace.

DBUA will then prompt you to recompile invalid PL/SQL objects following the upgrade. If you do not recompile these objects after the upgrade, the first user of these objects will be forced to wait while Oracle performs a run-time recompilation.

DBUA will then prompt you to back up the database as part of the upgrade process. If you have already backed up the database prior to starting DBUA, you may elect to skip this step. If you choose to have DBUA back up the database, it will shut down the database and perform an offline backup of the datafiles to the directory location you specify. DBUA will also create a batch file in that directory to automate the restoration of those files to their earlier locations.

The next step is to choose whether to enable Oracle Enterprise Manager (OEM) to manage the database. If you enable the Oracle Management Agent, the upgraded database will automatically be available via OEM.

You will then be asked to finalize the security configuration for the upgraded database. As with the database-creation process, you can specify passwords for each privileged account or you can set a single password to apply to all the OEM user accounts.

Finally, you will be prompted for details on the flash recovery area location (see Chapter 15), the archive log setting, and the network configuration. A final summary screen displays your choices for the upgrade, and the upgrade starts when you accept them. After the upgrade has completed, DBUA will display the Checking Upgrade Results screen, showing the steps performed, the related log files, and the status. The section of the screen titled Password Management allows you to manage the passwords and the locked/unlocked status of accounts in the upgraded database.

If you are not satisfied with the upgrade results, you can choose the Restore option. If you used DBUA to perform the backup, the restoration will be performed automatically; otherwise, you will need to perform the restoration manually.

When you exit DBUA after successfully upgrading the database, DBUA removes the old database's entry in the network listener configuration file, inserts an entry for the upgraded database, and reloads the file.

Performing a Manual Direct Upgrade

In a manual upgrade, you must perform the steps that DBUA performs. The result will be a direct upgrade of the database in which you are responsible for (and control) each step in the upgrade process.

You should use the Pre-Upgrade Information Tool to analyze the database prior to its upgrade. This tool is provided in a SQL script that is installed with the Oracle Database 10*g* software; you will need to run it against the database to be upgraded. The file, named utlu101i.sql, is located in the /rdbms/admin subdirectory under the Oracle 10*g* software home directory. You should run that file *in the database to be upgraded* as a SYSDBA-privileged user, spooling the results to a log file. The results will show potential problems that should be addressed prior to the upgrade.

If there are no issues to resolve prior to the upgrade, you should shut down the database and perform an offline backup before continuing with the upgrade process.

Once you have a backup you can restore if needed, you are ready to proceed with the upgrade process. The process is detailed and script-based, so you should consult with the Oracle installation and upgrade documentation for your environment and version. The steps are as follows:

1. Copy configuration files (init.ora, spfile.ora, password file) from their old location to the new Oracle software home directory. By default, the configuration files are found in the /dbs subdirectory on UNIX platforms and the /database directory on Windows platforms.

2. Remove obsolete and deprecated initialization parameter from the configuration files. Update the COMPATIBLE parameter for Oracle 10. Make sure your SHARED_POOL_ SIZE parameter is set to at least 96MB for 32-bit platforms and at least 144MB for 64-bit platforms. Set PGA_AGGREGATE_TARGET to at least 24MB, LARGE_POOL_SIZE to at least 8MB, and JAVA_POOL_SIZE to at least 48MB. For Windows parameters, set BACKGROUND_DUMP_DEST to \oradata*database_name*\bdump under the Oracle base software directory, and set USER_DUMP_DEST to \oradata*database_name*\udump under the Oracle base software directory. Use full pathnames in the parameter files.

3. If you are upgrading a cluster database, set the CLUSTER_DATABASE initialization parameter to FALSE. After the upgrade, you must set this initialization parameter back to TRUE.

4. Shut down the instance.

5. If you are using Windows, stop the service associated with the instance and delete the Oracle service at the command prompt. For Oracle 8.0, use the command ORADIM80 –DELETE –SID *instance_name*. For Oracle8.1 and higher, use ORADIM –DELETE –SID *instance_name*. Then create the new Oracle Database 10*g* service using ORADIM, as shown here:

```
C:\> ORADIM -NEW -SID SID -INTPWD PASSWORD -MAXUSERS USERS
        -STARTMODE AUTO -PFILE ORACLE_HOME\DATABASE\INITSID.ORA
```

The following variables are available for this command:

Variable	Description
SID	The name of the SID (instance identifier) of the database you are upgrading.
PASSWORD	The password for the new release 10.1 database instance. This is the password for the user connected with SYSDBA privileges. If you do not specify INTPWD, operating system authentication is used and no password is required.
USERS	The maximum number of users who can be granted SYSDBA and SYSOPER privileges.
ORACLE_HOME	The release 10.1 Oracle home directory. Ensure that you specify the full pathname with the -PFILE option, including the drive letter of the Oracle home directory.

6. If your operating system is UNIX, make sure the following environment variables point to the new release 10.1 directories: ORACLE_HOME, PATH, ORA_NLS33, and LD_LIBRARY_PATH.

7. Log into the system as the owner of the Oracle Database 10*g* software.

8. Change your directory to the /rdbms/admin subdirectory under the Oracle software home directory.

9. Connect to SQL*Plus as a user with SYSDBA privileges.

10. Issue the **startup upgrade** command.

11. Use the **spool** command to log the results of the following steps.

12. Create a SYSAUX tablespace via the **create tablespace** command. You should allocate SYSAUX between 500MB and 5GB of disk space, depending on the number of user objects. SYSAUX must be created with the following clauses: **online**, **permanent**, **read write**, **extent management local**, and **segment space management auto**. All those clauses except **segment space management auto** are the defaults. Here's an example:

```
create tablespace SYSAUX
  datafile '/u01/oradata/db1/sysaux01.dbf'
  size 500m reuse
  extent management local
  segment space management auto
  online;
```

13. Run the script for the old release. For example, if you are upgrading from Release 8.0.6, run only the u0800060.sql script and then move on to the next step in the upgrade process. Consult the following table for which script to run.

Upgrading From:	Run Script:
8.0.6	u0800060.sql
8.1.7	u0801070.sql
9.0.1	u0900010.sql
9.2	u0902000.sql

14. Stop spooling (via **spool off**) and review the spool file for errors. Resolve any problems identified there.

15. Run the utlu101s.sql file, with TEXT as the input parameter:

```
@utlu101s TEXT
```

Oracle will then display the status of the upgrade. The upgrade elements should all be listed with a status of "Normal successful completion."

16. Shut down and restart the instance.

17. Run the utlrp.sql script to recompile invalid packages. You can then verify that all packages and classes are valid:

```
select distinct Object_Name from DBA_OBJECTS
 where Status = 'INVALID';
```

18. Exit SQL*Plus.

19. Shut down the database and perform an offline backup of the database; then restart the database. The upgrade is complete.

NOTE
After the upgrade, you should never start your Oracle 10g database with the software from an earlier release.

Using Export and Import

Export and Import provide you with an indirect method for the upgrade. You can create an Oracle 10*g* database alongside your existing database and use Export and Import to move data from the old database to the new database. When the movement of the data is complete, you will need to point your applications to connect to the new database instead of the old database. You will also need to update any configuration files, version-specific scripts, and the networking configuration files (tnsnames.ora and listener.ora) to point to the new database.

Export and Import Versions to Use

When you create an Export dump file via the Export utility, that file can be imported into all later releases of Oracle. Export dump files are not backward compatible, so if you ever need to revert to an earlier version of Oracle, you will need to carefully select the version of Export and Import used. The following table shows the versions of the Export and Import executables you should use when going between versions of Oracle:

Export From:	Import To:	Use Export Utility For:	Use Import Utility For:
Release 9.2	Release 10.1	Release 9.2	Release 10.1
Release 8.1.7	Release 10.1	Release 8.1.7	Release 10.1
Release 8.0.6	Release 10.1	Release 8.0.6	Release 10.1
Release 7.3.4	Release 10.1	Release 7.3.4	Release 10.1
Release 10.1	Release 8.0.6	Release 8.0.6	Release 8.0.6
Release 10.1	Release 8.1.7	Release 8.1.7	Release 8.1.7
Release 10.1	Release 9.0.1	Release 9.0.1	Release 9.0.1
Release 10.1	Release 9.2	Release 9.2	Release 9.2
Release 10.1	Release 10.1	Release 10.1	Release 10.1

Note that when you are exporting in order to downgrade your database release, you should use the older version of the Export utility to minimize compatibility problems. You may still encounter compatibility problems if the newer version of the database uses new features (such as new datatypes) that the old version will not support.

Performing the Upgrade

Export the data from the source database using the version of the Export utility specified in the prior section. Perform a consistent export or perform the export when the database is not available for updates during and after the export.

> **NOTE**
> *If you have little free space available, you may back up and delete the existing database at this point and then install Oracle Database 10g software and create a target database for the import. If at all possible, maintain the source and target databases concurrently during the upgrade. The only benefit of having only one database on the server at a time is that they can share the same database name.*

Install the Oracle Database 10g software and create the target database. In the target database, pre-create the users and tablespaces needed to store the source data. If the source and target databases will coexist on the server, you need to be careful not to overwrite datafiles from one database with datafiles from the other. The Import utility will attempt to execute the **create tablespace** commands found in the Export dump file, and those commands will include the datafile names from the source database. By default, those commands will fail if the files already exist (although this can be overridden via Import's DESTROY parameter). Pre-create the tablespaces with the proper datafile names to avoid this problem.

> **NOTE**
> *You can export specific tablespaces, users, tables, and rows.*

Once the database has been prepared, use Import or Data Pump Import to load the data from the Export dump file into the target database. Review the log file for information about objects that did not import successfully.

Using the Data-Copying Method

The data-copying method requires that the source database and target database coexist. This method is most appropriate when the tables to be migrated are fairly small and few in number. As with the Export/Import method, you must guard against transactions occurring in the source database during and after the extraction of the data. In this method, the data is extracted via queries across database links.

Create the target database using the Oracle Database 10g software and then pre-create the tablespaces, users, and tables to be populated with data from the source database. Create database links (see Chapter 16) in the target database that access accounts in the source database. Use the **insert as select** command to move data from the source database to the target.

The data-copying method allows you to bring over just the rows and columns you need; your queries limit the data migrated. You will need to be careful with the relationships between the tables in the source database so you can re-create them properly in the target database. If you have a long application outage available for performing the upgrade and you need to modify the data structures during the migration, the data-copying method may be appropriate for your needs. Note that this method requires that the data be stored in multiple places at once, thus impacting your storage needs.

To improve the performance of this method, you may consider the following options:

- Disable all indexes and constraints until all the data has been loaded.

- Run multiple data-copying jobs in parallel.

- Use the parallel query option to enhance the performance of individual queries and inserts.

- Use the APPEND hint to enhance the performance of inserts.

As of Oracle 10g, you can use cross-platform transportable tablespaces. When transporting tablespaces, you export and import only the metadata for the tablespace, while the datafiles are physically moved to the new platform. For very large databases, the time required to move the datafiles may be significantly shorter than the time required to reinsert the rows. See Chapter 17 for details on the use of transportable tablespaces.

See Chapter 8 for additional advice on performance tuning.

After Upgrading

Following the upgrade, you should double-check the configuration and parameter files related to the database, particularly if the instance name changed in the migration process. These files include

- The tnsnames.ora file

- The listener.ora file

- Programs that may have hard-coded instance names in them

NOTE
You will need to manually reload the modified listener.ora file if you are not using DBUA to perform the upgrade.

You should review your database initialization parameters to make sure deprecated and obsolete parameters have been removed; these should have been identified during the migration process. Be sure to recompile any programs you have written that rely on the database software libraries.

Once the upgrade has completed, perform the functional and performance tests identified before the upgrade began. If there are issues with the database functionality, attempt to identify any parameter settings or missing objects that may be impacting the test results. If the problem cannot be resolved, you may need to revert to the prior release.

CHAPTER
3

Planning and Managing Tablespaces

ow a DBA configures the layout of the tablespaces in a database directly affects the performance and manageability of the database. In this chapter, we'll review the different types of tablespaces as well as how temporary tablespace usage can drive the size and number of tablespaces in a database leveraging the temporary tablespace group feature new to Oracle 10g.

We'll also show how Oracle's Optimal Flexible Architecture (OFA), supported since Oracle 7, helps to standardize the directory structure for both Oracle executables and the database files themselves.

A default installation of Oracle provides the DBA with a good starting point, not only creating an OFA-compliant directory structure but also segregating segments into a number of tablespaces based on their function. We'll review the space requirements for each of these tablespaces and provide some tips on how to fine-tune the characteristics of these tablespaces.

At the end of the chapter, we'll provide some guidelines to help place segments into different tablespaces based on their type, size, and frequency of access, as well as ways to identify hotspots in one or more tablespaces.

Tablespace Architecture

A prerequisite to competently setting up the tablespaces in your database is understanding the different types of tablespaces and how they are used in an Oracle database. In this section, we'll review the different types of tablespaces and give some examples of how they are managed.

In addition, we'll provide an overview of Oracle's Optimal Flexible Architecture and how it provides a framework for storing tablespace datafiles as well as Oracle executables and other Oracle components, such as redo log files, control files, and so forth. We'll also review the types of tablespaces by category—SYSTEM tablespaces, the SYSAUX tablespace, temporary tablespaces, undo tablespaces, and bigfile tablespaces—and describe their function.

Tablespace Types

The primary types of tablespaces in an Oracle database are permanent, undo, and temporary. Permanent tablespaces contain segments that persist beyond the duration of a session or a transaction.

Although the undo tablespace may have segments that are retained beyond the end of a session or a transaction, it provides read consistency for **select** statements that access tables being modified as well as provides undo data for a number of the flashback features of the database. Primarily, however, undo segments store the previous values of columns being updated or deleted, or to provide an indication that the row did not exist for an insert so that if a user's session fails before the user issues a **commit** or a **rollback**, the updates, inserts, and deletes will be removed. Undo segments are never directly accessible by a user session, and undo tablespaces may only have undo segments.

As the name implies, temporary tablespaces contain transient data that exists only for the duration of the session, such as space to complete a sort operation that will not fit in memory.

Bigfile tablespaces can be used for any of these three types of tablespaces, and they simplify tablespace management by moving the maintenance point from the datafile to the tablespace. Bigfile tablespaces consist of one and only one datafile.

Permanent

The SYSTEM and SYSAUX tablespaces are two examples of permanent tablespaces. In addition, any segments that need to be retained by a user or an application beyond the boundaries of a session or transaction should be stored in a permanent tablespace.

SYSTEM Tablespace   User segments should never reside in the SYSTEM tablespace, period. As of Oracle 10g, we can now specify a default permanent tablespace in addition to the ability to specify a default temporary tablespace in Oracle9i.

If you use the Oracle Universal Installer (OUI) to create a database for you, a separate tablespace other than SYSTEM is created for both permanent and temporary segments. If you create a database manually, be sure to specify both a default permanent tablespace and a default temporary tablespace, as in the sample **create database** command that follows.

```
CREATE DATABASE rjbdb
     USER SYS IDENTIFIED BY paris703
     USER SYSTEM IDENTIFIED BY tyler12
     LOGFILE GROUP 1 ('/u02/oracle10g/oradata/rjbdb/redo01.log') SIZE 100M,
             GROUP 2 ('/u04/oracle10g/oradata/rjbdb/redo02.log') SIZE 100M,
             GROUP 3 ('/u06/oracle10g/oradata/rjbdb/redo03.log') SIZE 100M
     MAXLOGFILES 5
     MAXLOGMEMBERS 5
     MAXLOGHISTORY 1
     MAXDATAFILES 100
     MAXINSTANCES 1
     CHARACTER SET US7ASCII
     NATIONAL CHARACTER SET AL16UTF16
     DATAFILE '/u01/oracle10g/oradata/rjbdb/system01.dbf' SIZE 325M REUSE
     EXTENT MANAGEMENT LOCAL
     SYSAUX DATAFILE '/u01/oracle10g/oradata/rjbdb/sysaux01.dbf'
        SIZE 325M REUSE
DEFAULT TABLESPACE USERS
DATAFILE '/u03/oracle10g/oradata/rjbdb/users01.dbf'
SIZE 50M REUSE
DEFAULT TEMPORARY TABLESPACE tempts1
TEMPFILE '/u01/oracle10g/oradata/rjbdb/temp01.dbf'
SIZE 20M REUSE
     UNDO TABLESPACE undotbs
        DATAFILE '/u02/oracle10g/oradata/rjbdb/undotbs01.dbf'
        SIZE 200M REUSE AUTOEXTEND ON MAXSIZE UNLIMITED;
```

As of Oracle 10g, the SYSTEM tablespace is locally managed by default; in other words, all space usage is managed by a bitmap segment in the first part of the first datafile for the tablespace. In a database where the SYSTEM tablespace is locally managed, the other tablespaces in the database must also be locally managed or they must be read-only. Using locally managed tablespaces takes some of the contention off the SYSTEM tablespace because space allocation and deallocation operations for a tablespace do not need to use data dictionary tables. More details on locally managed tablespaces can be found in Chapter 6.

SYSAUX Tablespace   Like the SYSTEM tablespace, the SYSAUX tablespace should not have any user segments. The contents of the SYSAUX tablespace, broken down by application, can be reviewed using EM Database Control. You can edit the SYSAUX tablespace by clicking the Tablespaces link under the Administration tab. Figure 3-1 shows a graphical representation of the space usage within SYSAUX.

If the space usage for a particular application that resides in the SYSAUX tablespace becomes too high or creates an I/O bottleneck through high contention with other applications that use the SYSAUX tablespace, you can move one or more of these applications to a different tablespace. Scrolling down on the screen shown in Figure 3-1, we can select one of the SYSAUX occupants and move it to another tablespace, as shown in Figure 3-2. An example of moving a SYSAUX occupant to a different tablespace using the command line interface can be found in Chapter 6.

The SYSAUX tablespace can be monitored just like any other tablespace; later in this chapter, we'll show how EM Database Control can help us to identify hotspots in a tablespace.

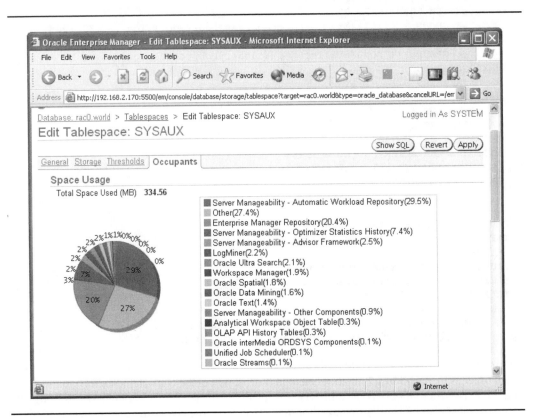

FIGURE 3-1.   *EM Database Control SYSAUX tablespace contents*

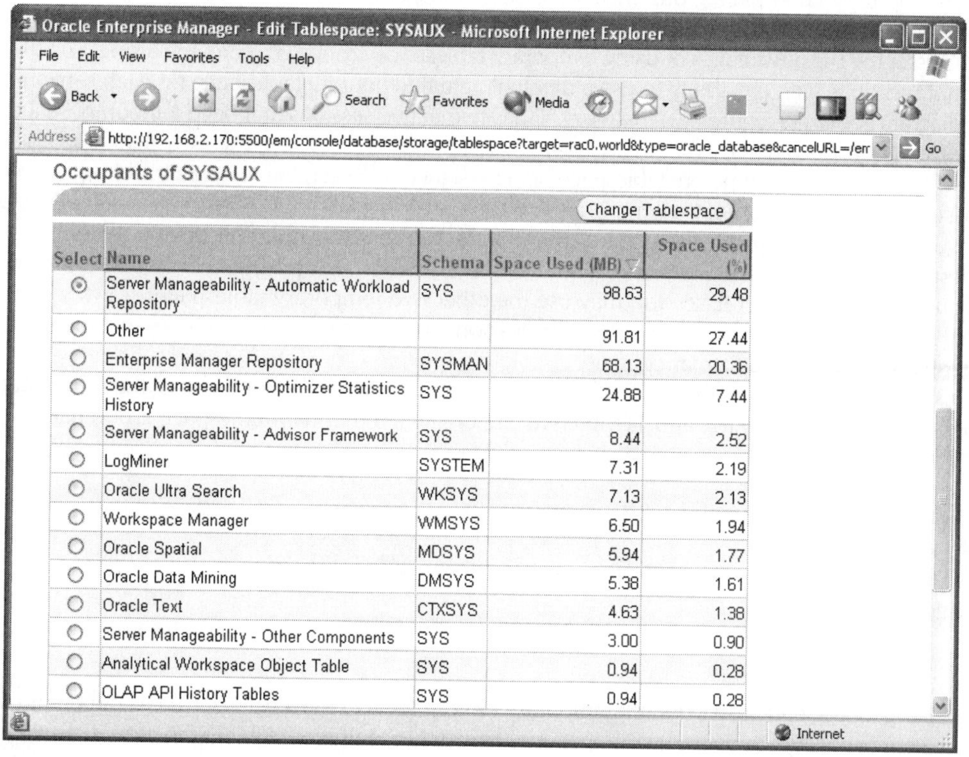

FIGURE 3-2. *Using EM Database Control to move a SYSAUX occupant*

Undo

Multiple undo tablespaces can exist in a database, but only one undo tablespace can be active at any given time. Undo tablespaces are used for rolling back transactions, for providing read consistency for **select** statements that run concurrently with DML statements on the same table or set of tables, and for supporting a number of Oracle Flashback features, such as Flashback Query.

The undo tablespace needs to be sized correctly to prevent "Snapshot too old" errors and to provide enough space to support initialization parameters such as UNDO_RETENTION. More information on how to monitor, size, and create undo tablespaces can be found in Chapter 7.

Temporary

More than one temporary tablespace can be online and active in the database, but until Oracle 10*g*, multiple sessions by the same user would use the same temporary tablespace because only one default temporary tablespace could be assigned to a user. To solve this potential performance bottleneck, Oracle now supports *temporary tablespace groups.* A temporary tablespace group is a synonym for a list of temporary tablespaces.

A temporary tablespace group must consist of at least one temporary tablespace; it cannot be empty. Once a temporary tablespace group has no members, it no longer exists.

One of the big advantages of using temporary tablespace groups is to provide a single user with multiple sessions with the ability to use a different actual temporary tablespace for each session. In the diagram shown in Figure 3-3, the user OE has two active sessions that need temporary space for performing sort operations.

Instead of a single temporary tablespace being assigned to a user, the temporary tablespace group is assigned; in this example, the temporary tablespace group TEMPGRP has been assigned to OE. However, because there are three actual temporary tablespaces within the TEMPGRP temporary tablespace group, the first OE session may use temporary tablespace TEMP1, and the **select** statement executed by the second OE session may use the other two temporary tablespaces, TEMP2 and TEMP3, in parallel. Before Oracle 10g, both sessions would use the same temporary tablespace, potentially causing a performance issue.

Creating a temporary tablespace group is very straightforward. After creating the individual tablespaces TEMP1, TEMP2, and TEMP3, we can create a temporary tablespace group named TEMPGRP as follows:

```
SQL> alter tablespace temp1 tablespace group tempgrp;
Tablespace altered.
SQL> alter tablespace temp2 tablespace group tempgrp;
Tablespace altered.
SQL> alter tablespace temp3 tablespace group tempgrp;
Tablespace altered.
```

Changing the database's default temporary tablespace to TEMPGRP uses the same command as assigning an actual temporary tablespace as the default; temporary tablespace groups are treated logically the same as a temporary tablespace:

```
SQL> alter database default temporary tablespace tempgrp;
Database altered.
```

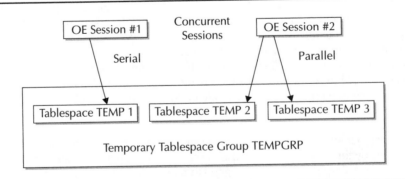

FIGURE 3-3. *Temporary tablespace group TEMPGRP*

To drop a tablespace group, we must first drop all its members. Dropping a member of a tablespace group is accomplished by assigning the temporary tablespace to a group with an empty string (in other words, removing the tablespace from the group):

```
SQL> alter tablespace temp3 tablespace group '';
Tablespace altered.
```

As you might expect, assigning a temporary tablespace group to a user is identical to assigning a temporary tablespace to a user; this assignment can happen either when the user is created or at some point in the future. In the following example, the new user JENWEB is assigned the temporary tablespace TEMPGRP:

```
SQL> create user jenweb identified by pi4001
  2        default tablespace users
  3        temporary tablespace tempgrp;
User created.
```

Note that if we did not assign the tablespace during user creation, the user JENWEB would still be assigned TEMPGRP as the temporary tablespace because it is the database default from our previous **create database** example.

A couple of changes have been made to the data dictionary views to support temporary tablespace groups. The data dictionary view DBA_USERS still has the column TEMPORARY_TABLESPACE, as in previous versions of Oracle, but this column may now contain either the name of the temporary tablespace assigned to the user, or the name of a temporary tablespace group.

```
SQL> select username, default_tablespace, temporary_tablespace
  2        from dba_users where username = 'JENWEB';

USERNAME             DEFAULT_TABLESPACE TEMPORARY_TABLESPACE
-------------------- ------------------ --------------------
JENWEB               USERS              TEMPGRP

1 row selected.
```

The new data dictionary view DBA_TABLESPACE_GROUPS shows the members of each temporary tablespace group:

```
SQL> select group_name, tablespace_name from dba_tablespace_groups;

GROUP_NAME                   TABLESPACE_NAME
---------------------------- ---------------------------
TEMPGRP                      TEMP1
TEMPGRP                      TEMP2
TEMPGRP                      TEMP3

3 rows selected.
```

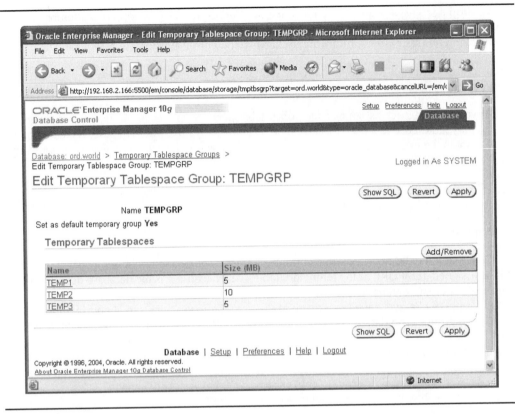

FIGURE 3-4. *Using EM Database Control to edit temporary tablespace groups*

As with most every other feature of Oracle that can be accomplished with the command line, assigning members to temporary tablespace groups or removing members from temporary tablespace groups can be performed using EM Database Control. In Figure 3-4, we can add or remove members from a temporary tablespace group.

Bigfile
A bigfile tablespace eases database administration because it consists of only one datafile. The single datafile can be up to 8EB (exabytes) in size. Many of the commands previously available only for maintaining datafiles can now be used at the tablespace level if the tablespace is a bigfile tablespace. Chapter 6 reviews how bigfile tablespaces are created and maintained.

Optimal Flexible Architecture
Oracle's Optimal Flexible Architecture (OFA) provides guidelines to ease the maintenance of the Oracle software and database files as well as improve the performance of the database by placing the database files such that I/O bottlenecks are minimized.

Although using OFA is not strictly enforced when you're installing or maintaining an Oracle environment, using OFA makes it easy for someone to understand how your database is organized on disk, preventing that phone call in the middle of the night during the week you're on vacation!

OFA is slightly different depending on the type of storage options you use—either an Automatic Storage Management (ASM) environment or a standard operating system file system that may or may not be using a third-party logical volume manager or RAID-enabled disk subsystem.

Non-ASM Environment

In a non-ASM environment on a Unix server, at least three file systems on separate physical devices are required to implement OFA recommendations. Starting at the top, the recommended format for a mount point is */<string const><numeric key>*, where *<string const>* can be one or several letters and *<numeric key>* is either two or three digits. For example, on one system we may have mount points /u01, /u02, /u03, and /u04, with room to expand to an additional 96 mount points without changing the file-naming convention. Figure 3-5 shows a typical Unix file system layout with an OFA-compliant Oracle directory structure.

There are two instances on this server: an ASM instance to manage disk groups and a standard RDBMS instance.

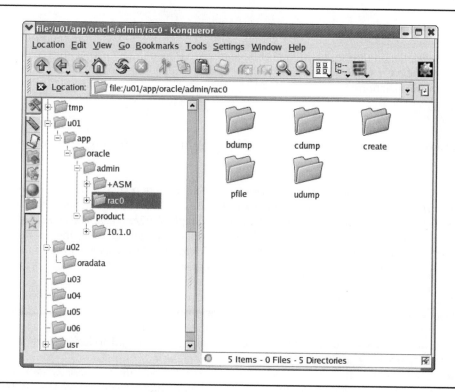

FIGURE 3-5. *OFA-compliant Unix directory structure*

Software Executables The software executables for each distinct product name reside in the directory /*<string const><numeric key>*/*<directory type>*/*<product owner>*, where *<string const>* and *<numeric key>* are defined previously, *<directory type>* implies the type of files installed in this directory, and *<product owner>* is the name of the user that owns and installs the files in this directory. For example, /u01/app/oracle would contain application-related files (executables) installed by the user oracle on the server. The directory /u01/app/apache would contain the executables for the middleware web server installed from a previous version of Oracle.

As of Oracle 10*g*, the OFA standard makes it easy for the DBA to install multiple versions of the database and client software within the same high-level directory. The OFA-compliant Oracle home path, corresponding to the environment variable ORACLE_HOME, contains a suffix that corresponds to the type and incarnation of the installation. For example, two different installations of Oracle 10*g* and one installation of Oracle9*i* may reside in the following three directories:

```
/u01/app/oracle/product/9.2.0.1
/u01/app/oracle/product/10.1.0/db_1
/u01/app/oracle/product/10.1.0/db_2
```

At the same time, the Oracle client executables and configuration may be stored in the same parent directory as the database executables:

```
/u01/app/oracle/product/10.1.0/client_1
```

Some installation directories will never have more than one instance for a given product; for example, Oracle Cluster Ready Services (CRS) will be installed in the following directory given the previous installations:

```
/u01/app/oracle/product/10.1.0/crs
```

Because CRS can only be installed once on a system, it does not have an incrementing numeric suffix.

Database Files Any non-ASM Oracle datafiles reside in /*<mount point>*/oradata/*<database name>*, where *<mount point>* is one of the mount points we discussed earlier, and *<database name>* is the value of the initialization parameter DB_NAME. For example, /u02/oradata/rac0 and /u03/oradata/rac0 would contain the non-ASM control files, redo log files, and datafiles for the instance rac0, whereas /u05/oradata/dev1 would contain the same files for the dev1 instance on the same server. The naming convention for the different file types under the oradata directory are detailed in Table 3-1.

Although Oracle tablespace names can be as long as 30 characters, it is advisable to keep the tablespace names eight characters or less in a Unix environment. Because portable Unix filenames are restricted to 14 characters, and the suffix of an OFA datafile name is *<n>*.dbf, where *n* is two digits, a total of six characters are needed for the suffix in the file system. This leaves eight characters for the tablespace name itself.

Only control files, redo log files, and datafiles associated with the database *<database name>* should be stored in the directory /*<mount point>*/oradata/*<database name>*. For the database ord managed without ASM, the datafile names are as follows:

```
SQL> select file#, name from v$datafile;

     FILE# NAME
---------- -----------------------------------
         1 /u05/oradata/ord/system01.dbf
         2 /u05/oradata/ord/undotbs01.dbf
         3 /u05/oradata/ord/sysaux01.dbf
         4 /u05/oradata/ord/users01.dbf
         5 /u09/oradata/ord/example01.dbf
         6 /u09/oradata/ord/oe_trans01.dbf
         7 /u05/oradata/ord/users02.dbf
         8 /u06/oradata/ord/logmnr_rep01.dbf
         9 /u09/oradata/ord/big_users.dbf
        10 /u08/oradata/ord/idx01.dbf
        11 /u08/oradata/ord/idx02.dbf
        12 /u08/oradata/ord/idx03.dbf
        13 /u08/oradata/ord/idx04.dbf
        14 /u08/oradata/ord/idx05.dbf
        15 /u08/oradata/ord/idx06.dbf
        16 /u08/oradata/ord/idx07.dbf
        17 /u08/oradata/ord/idx08.dbf
17 rows selected.
```

Other than file numbers 8 and 9, all the datafiles in the ord database are OFA compliant and are spread out over four different mount points. The tablespace name in file number 8 is too long, and file number 9 does not have a numeric two-digit counter to represent new datafiles for the same tablespace.

ASM Environment

In an ASM environment, the executables are stored in the directory structure presented previously; however, if you browsed the directory /u02/oradata in Figure 3-5, you would see no files. All the

File Type	Filename Format	Variables
Control files	control.ctl	None.
Redo log files	redo<n>.log	n is a two-digit number.
Datafiles	<tn>.dbf	t is an Oracle tablespace name, and n is a two-digit number.

TABLE 3-1.   *OFA-Compliant Control File, Redo Log File, and Datafile Naming Conventions*

control files, redo log files, and datafiles for the instance rac0 are managed by the ASM instance +ASM on this server.

The actual datafile names are not needed for most administrative functions because ASM files are all Oracle Managed Files (OMF). This eases the overall administrative effort required for the database. Within the ASM storage structure, an OFA-like syntax is used to subdivide the file types even further:

```
SQL> select file#, name from v$datafile;

    FILE# NAME
---------- -----------------------------------
        1 +DATA1/rac0/datafile/system.256.1
        2 +DATA1/rac0/datafile/undotbs1.258.1
        3 +DATA1/rac0/datafile/sysaux.257.1
        4 +DATA1/rac0/datafile/users.259.1
        5 +DATA1/rac0/datafile/example.269.1
        6 +DATA2/rac0/datafile/users3.256.1
6 rows selected.

SQL> select name from v$controlfile;

NAME
----------------------------------------
+DATA1/rac0/controlfile/current.261.3
+DATA1/rac0/controlfile/current.260.3
2 rows selected.

SQL> select member from v$logfile;

MEMBER
----------------------------------------
+DATA1/rac0/onlinelog/group_3.266.1
+DATA1/rac0/onlinelog/group_3.267.1
+DATA1/rac0/onlinelog/group_2.264.1
+DATA1/rac0/onlinelog/group_2.265.1
+DATA1/rac0/onlinelog/group_1.262.1
+DATA1/rac0/onlinelog/group_1.263.1
6 rows selected.
```

Within the disk group +DATA1 and +DATA2, we see that each of the database file types, such as datafiles, control files, and online log files, has its own directory. Fully qualified ASM filenames have the format

```
+<group>/<dbname>/<file type>/<tag>.<file>.<incarnation>
```

where <group> is the disk group name, <dbname> is the database to which the file belongs, <file type> is the Oracle file type, <tag> is information specific to the file type, and the pair <file>.<incarnation> ensures uniqueness within the disk group.

Automatic Storage Management is covered in Chapter 6.

Oracle Installation Tablespaces

Table 3-2 lists the tablespaces created with a standard Oracle installation using the Oracle Universal Installer (OUI).

SYSTEM

As mentioned previously in this chapter, no user segments should ever be stored in the SYSTEM tablespace. The new clause **default tablespace** in the **create database** command helps to prevent this occurrence by automatically assigning a permanent tablespace for all users that have not explicitly been assigned a permanent tablespace. An Oracle installation performed using the Oracle Universal Installer will automatically assign the USERS tablespace as the default permanent tablespace.

The SYSTEM tablespace will grow more quickly the more you use procedural objects such as functions, procedures, triggers, and so forth, because these objects must reside in the data dictionary. This also applies to abstract datatypes and Oracle's other object-oriented features.

SYSAUX

As with the SYSTEM tablespace, user segments should never be stored in the SYSAUX tablespace. If one particular occupant of the SYSAUX tablespace takes up too much of the available space or significantly affects the performance of other applications that use the SYSAUX tablespace, you should consider moving the occupant to another tablespace.

TEMP

Instead of one very large temporary tablespace, consider using several smaller temporary tablespaces and creating a temporary tablespace group to hold them. As you found out earlier in this chapter, this can improve the response time for applications that create many sessions with the same username.

Tablespace	Type	Segment Space Management	Initial Allocated Size (MB)
SYSTEM	Permanent	Auto	450
SYSAUX	Permanent	Auto	350
TEMP	Temporary	Manual	20
UNDOTBS1	Permanent	Manual	30
USERS	Permanent	Auto	5
EXAMPLE	Permanent	Auto	150

TABLE 3-2. *Standard Oracle Installation Tablespaces*

UNDOTBS1

Even though a database may have more than one undo tablespace, only one undo tablespace can be active at any given time. If more space is needed for an undo tablespace, and AUTOEXTEND is not enabled, another datafile can be added. One undo tablespace must be available for each node in a Real Application Clusters (RAC) environment because each instance manages its own undo.

USERS

The USERS tablespace is intended for miscellaneous segments created by each database user, and it's not appropriate for any production applications. A separate tablespace should be created for each application and segment type; later in this chapter we'll present some additional criteria you can use to decide when to segregate segments into their own tablespace.

EXAMPLE

In a production environment, the EXAMPLE tablespace should be dropped; it takes up 150MB of disk space and has examples of all types of Oracle segments and data structures. A separate database should be created for training purposes with these sample schemas; for an existing training database, the sample schemas can be installed by using the scripts in $ORACLE_HOME/demo/schema.

Segment Segregation

As a general rule of thumb, you want to divide segments into different tablespaces based on their type, size, and frequency of access. Furthermore, each of these tablespaces would benefit from being on its own disk group or disk device; in practice, however, most shops will not have the luxury of storing each tablespace on its own device. The following bulleted points identify some of the conditions you might use to determine how segments should be segregated among tablespaces. They are not prioritized here because the priority depends on your particular environment. Using Automatic Storage Management (ASM) eliminates many of the contention issues listed with no additional effort by the DBA. ASM is discussed in detail in Chapter 4.

- Big segments and small segments should be in separate tablespaces.

- Table segments and their corresponding index segments should be in separate tablespaces.

- A separate tablespace should be used for each application.

- Segments with low usage and segments with high usage should be in different tablespaces.

- Static segments should be separated from high DML segments.

- Read-only tables should be in their own tablespace.

- Staging tables for a data warehouse should be in their own tablespace.

- Tablespaces should be created with the appropriate block size, depending on whether segments are accessed row by row or in full table scans.

- Materialized views should be in a separate tablespace from the base table.

- For partitioned tables and indexes, each partition should be in its own tablespace.

Using EM Database Control, you can identify overall contention on any tablespace by identifying hotspots, either at the file level or at the object level. From the home page, click the Performance tab, and select User I/O on the Sessions graph, as shown in Figure 3-6.

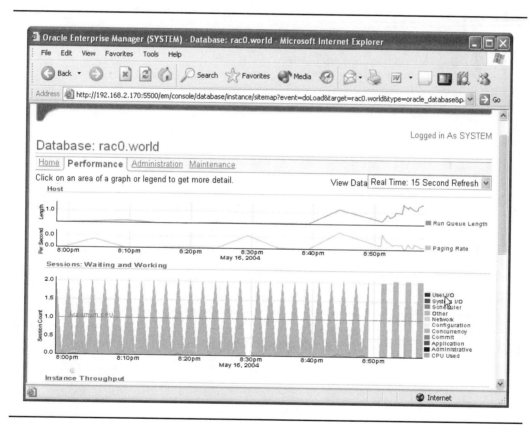

FIGURE 3-6. *EM Database Control Performance page*

In Figure 3-7, we move the slider to the time period that appears to have a high number of waits; in Figure 3-8, we scroll down and select Top Files, giving us the analysis shown in Figure 3-9.

During the analysis time selected, the top two files with the highest amount of contention were the datafiles for the SYSTEM and SYSAUX tablespace. Although it may be difficult to reduce the contention on the SYSTEM tablespace if we are already doing things such as creating all new

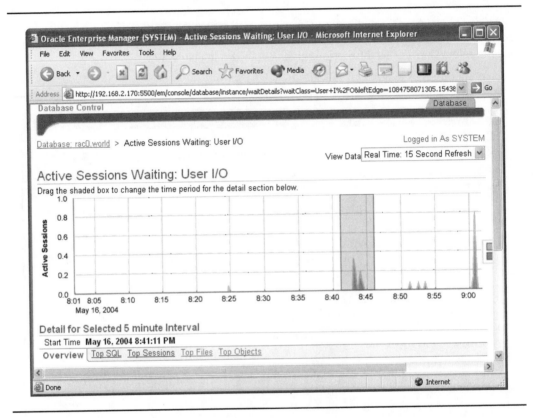

FIGURE 3-7. *EM Database Control: Active Sessions Waiting*

tablespaces with local space management, we may be able to help the SYSAUX tablespace by moving applications that are using the SYSAUX tablespace heavily into their own tablespace. For example, if this database is being used as the repository for all other databases' RMAN recovery catalogs, we may want to consider moving the RMAN metadata out of SYSAUX.

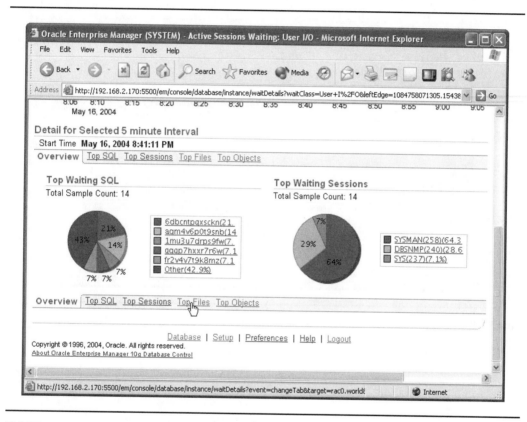

FIGURE 3-8.   *EM Database Control: Top Waiting Overview*

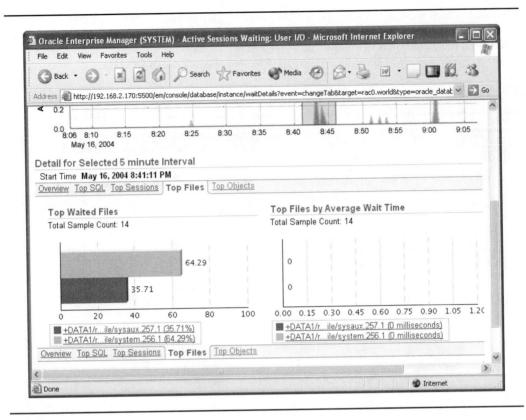

FIGURE 3-9. *EM Database Control: Top Waited Files*

CHAPTER
4

Physical Database
Layouts and
Storage Management

n Chapter 3, we talked about the logical components of the database, tablespaces, and how to not only create the right number and types of tablespaces but also to place table and index segments in the appropriate tablespace based on their usage patterns and function. In this chapter, we'll focus more on the physical aspects of a database, the datafiles, and where to store them to maximize I/O throughput and overall database performance.

The assumption throughout this chapter is that you are using locally managed tablespaces with automatic segment space management. In addition to reducing the load on the SYSTEM tablespace by using bitmaps stored in the tablespace itself instead of freelists stored in the table or index header blocks, automatic segment space management (autoallocated or uniform) makes more efficient use of the space in the tablespace. As of Oracle 10g, the SYSTEM tablespace is created as locally managed. As a result, this requires all read-write tablespaces to also be locally managed.

In the first part of this chapter, we'll review some of the common problems and solutions when using traditional disk space management using a file system on a database server. In the second half of the chapter, we'll present an overview of Automatic Storage Management (ASM), a built-in logical volume manager that eases administration, enhances performance, and improves availability.

Traditional Disk Space Storage

In lieu of using a third-party logical volume or Oracle's Automatic Storage Management (discussed later in this chapter), you must be able to manage the physical datafiles in your database to ensure a high level of performance, availability, and recoverability. In general, this means spreading out your datafiles to different physical disks. In addition to ensuring availability by keeping mirrored copies of redo log files and control files on different disks, I/O performance is improved when users access tables that reside in tablespaces on multiple physical disks instead of one physical disk. Identifying an I/O bottleneck or a storage deficiency on a particular disk volume is only half the battle; once the bottleneck is identified, you need to have the tools and knowledge to move datafiles to different disks. If a datafile has too much space or not enough space, resizing an existing datafile is a common task.

In this section, we'll discuss a number of different ways to resize tablespaces, whether they are smallfile or bigfile tablespaces. In addition, we'll cover the most common ways to move datafiles, online redo log files, and control files to different disks.

Resizing Tablespaces and Datafiles

In an ideal database, all tablespaces and the objects within them are created at their optimal sizes. Resizing a tablespace proactively or setting up a tablespace to automatically extend can potentially avoid a performance hit when the tablespace expands or an application failure occurs if the datafile(s) within the tablespace cannot extend. More details on how to monitor space usage can be found in Chapter 6.

The procedures and methods available for resizing a tablespace are slightly different, depending on whether the tablespace is a *smallfile* or a *bigfile* tablespace. A smallfile tablespace is the only type of tablespace available before Oracle 10g, and can consist of multiple datafiles. A bigfile tablespace, in contrast, can only consist of one datafile, but the datafile can be much larger than a datafile in a smallfile tablespace: A bigfile tablespace with 64K blocks can have a datafile as large as 128TB. In addition, bigfile tablespaces must be locally managed.

Resizing a Smallfile Tablespace Using ALTER DATABASE

In the following examples, we attempt to resize the USERS tablespace, which contains one datafile, starting out at 5MB. First, we make it 15MB, then realize it's too big, and shrink it down to 10MB. Then, we attempt to shrink it too much. Finally, we try to increase its size too much.

```
SQL> alter database
  2       datafile '/u01/app/oracle/oradata/rmanrep/users01.dbf' resize 15m;
   Database altered.
SQL> alter database
  2       datafile '/u01/app/oracle/oradata/rmanrep/users01.dbf' resize 10m;
   Database altered.
SQL> alter database
  2       datafile '/u01/app/oracle/oradata/rmanrep/users01.dbf' resize 1m;
alter database
*
ERROR at line 1:
ORA-03297: file contains used data beyond requested RESIZE value
SQL> alter database
  2       datafile '/u01/app/oracle/oradata/rmanrep/users01.dbf' resize 100t;
alter database
*
ERROR at line 1:
ORA-00740: datafile size of (13421772800) blocks exceeds maximum file size
SQL> alter database
  2       datafile '/u01/app/oracle/oradata/rmanrep/users01.dbf' resize 50g;
alter database
*
ERROR at line 1:
ORA-01144: File size (6553600 blocks) exceeds maximum of 4194303 blocks
```

If the resize request cannot be supported by the free space available, or there is data beyond the requested decreased size, or an Oracle file size limit is exceeded, an error is returned.

To avoid manual resizing of tablespaces reactively, we can instead be proactive and use the **autoextend**, **next**, and **maxsize** clauses when modifying or creating a datafile. Table 4-1 lists the space-related clauses for modifying or creating datafiles in the **alter datafile** and **alter tablespace** commands.

In the following example, we set **autoextend** to ON for the datafile /u01/app/oracle/oradata/rmanrep/users01.dbf, specify that each extension of the datafile is 20MB, and specify that the total size of the datafile cannot exceed 1GB:

```
SQL> alter database
  2       datafile '/u01/app/oracle/oradata/rmanrep/users01.dbf'
  3       autoextend on
```

```
   4      next 20m
   5      maxsize 1g;
Database altered.
```

If the disk volume containing the datafile does not have the disk space available for the expansion of the datafile, we must either move the datafile to another disk volume or create a second datafile for the tablespace on another disk volume. In this example, we're going to add a second datafile to the USERS tablespace on a different disk volume with an initial size of 50MB, allowing for the automatic extension of the datafile, with each extension 10MB and a maximum datafile size of 200MB:

```
SQL> alter tablespace users
   2      add datafile '/u03/oradata/users02.dbf'
   3      size 50m
   4      autoextend on
   5      next 10m
   6      maxsize 200m;
Tablespace altered.
```

Notice that when we modify an existing datafile in a tablespace, we use the **alter database** command, whereas when we add a datafile to a tablespace, we use the **alter tablespace** command. As you will see shortly, using a bigfile tablespace simplifies these types of operations.

Clause	Description
autoextend	When this clause is set to ON, the datafile will be allowed to expand. When it's set to OFF, no expansion is allowed, and the other clauses are set to zero.
next *<size>*	The size, in bytes, of the next amount of disk space to allocate for the datafile when expansion is required; the *<size>* value can be qualified with K, M, G, or T to specify the size in kilobytes, megabytes, gigabytes, or terabytes, respectively.
maxsize *<size>*	When this clause is set to **unlimited**, the size of the datafile is unlimited within Oracle, up to 8EB (otherwise limited by the file system containing the datafile). Otherwise, **maxsize** is set to the maximum number of bytes in the datafile, using the same qualifiers used in the **next** clause: K, M, G, or T.

TABLE 4-1. *Datafile Extension Clauses*

Resizing a Smallfile Tablespace Using EM Database Control

Using EM Database Control, we can use either of the methods described in the previous section: increase the size and turn on autoextend for the tablespace's single datafile, or add a second datafile.

Resizing a Datafile in a Smallfile Tablespace   To resize a datafile in EM Database Control, click the Administration tab from the database home page, then click Tablespaces under the Storage heading. In Figure 4-1, we have selected the EXAMPLE tablespace. Rather than let the tablespace's datafile autoextend, we will change the current size of the datafile to 200MB from 150MB.

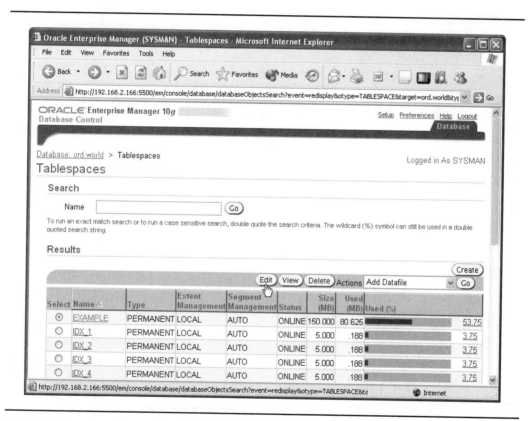

FIGURE 4-1.   Using EM Database Control to edit a tablespace

By clicking the Edit button, you can see the characteristics of the EXAMPLE tablespace, as shown in Figure 4-2. It is locally managed, permanent, and a smallfile tablespace. At the bottom of the page is the single datafile for the EXAMPLE tablespace, /u09/oradata/ord/example01.dbf.

With the only datafile in the EXAMPLE tablespace selected, click the Edit button or the datafile name itself, and you will see the Edit Tablespace: Edit Datafile page, shown in Figure 4-3, where you can change the size of the datafile. On this page, change the file size from 150MB to 200MB and click Continue.

In Figure 4-4, you are back to the Edit Tablespace page. At this point, you can make the changes to the datafile by clicking Apply, cancel the changes by clicking Revert, or show the SQL to be executed by clicking Show SQL.

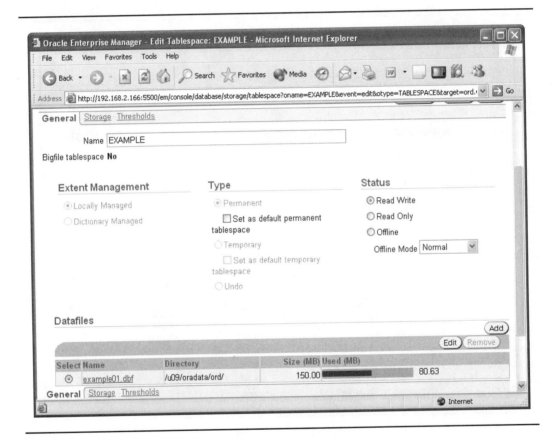

FIGURE 4-2. *Tablespace characteristics*

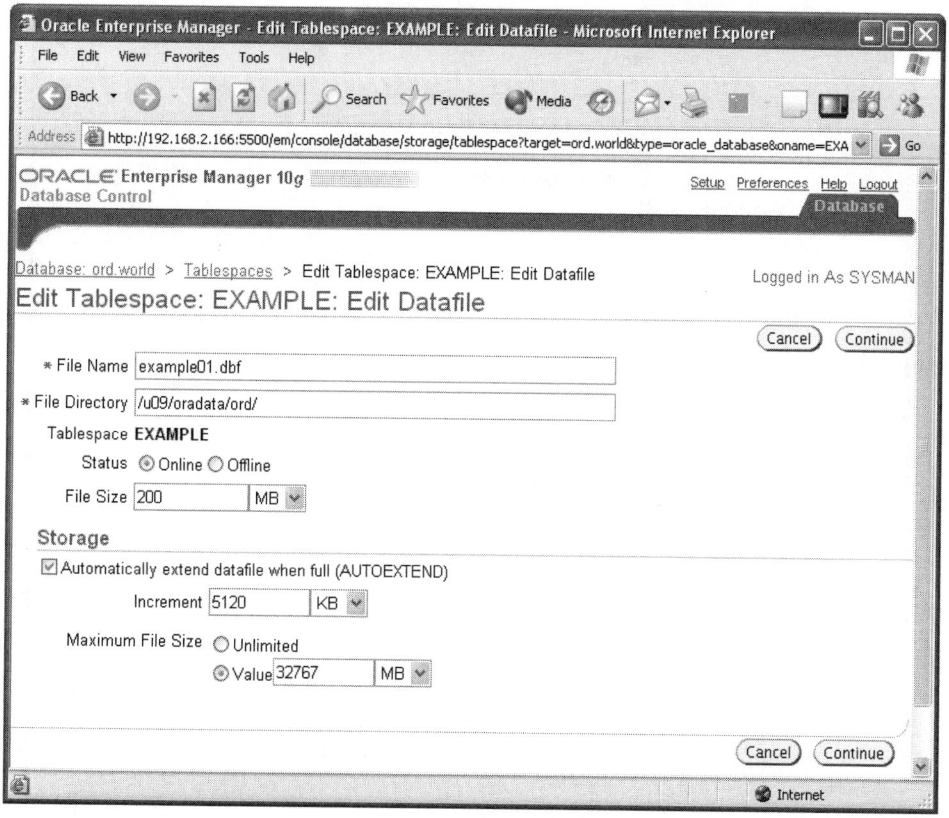

FIGURE 4-3. *Editing a datafile*

Before committing the changes, it is often beneficial to review the SQL commands about to be executed by clicking the Show SQL button—it is a good way to brush up on your SQL command syntax! Here is the command that will be executed when you click Apply:

```
ALTER DATABASE
     DATAFILE '/u09/oradata/ord/example01.dbf'
     RESIZE 200M;
```

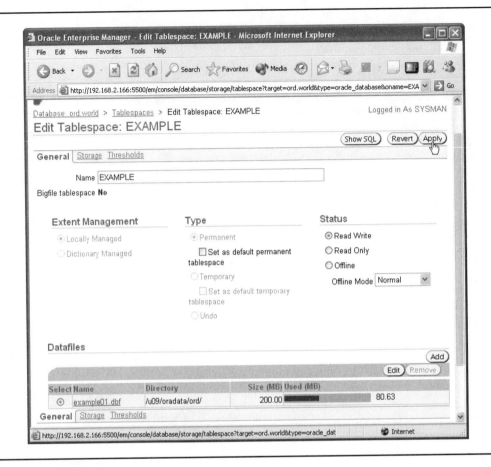

FIGURE 4-4. *Confirming datafile changes*

When you click Apply, the changes are made to the datafile. The Edit Tablespace: EXAMPLE page reflects the successful operation and the new size of the datafile, as you can see in Figure 4-5.

Adding a Datafile to a Smallfile Tablespace   Adding a datafile to a smallfile tablespace is just as easy as resizing a datafile using EM Database Control. In our previous example, we expanded

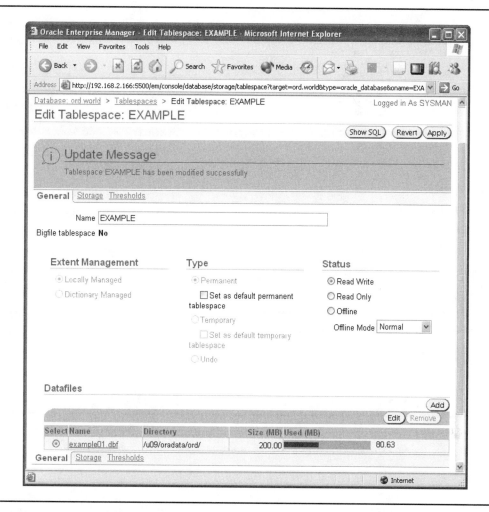

FIGURE 4-5.   *Datafile resizing results*

the datafile for the EXAMPLE tablespace to 200MB. Because the file system (/u09) containing the datafile for the EXAMPLE tablespace is now at capacity, you will have to turn off AUTOEXTEND on the existing datafile and then create a new datafile on a different file system. In Figure 4-6,

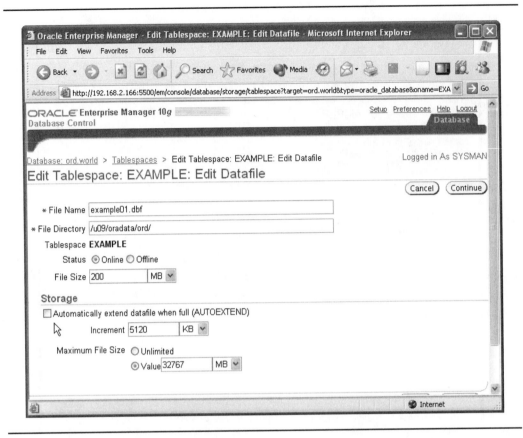

FIGURE 4-6. *Edit Tablespace: edit EXAMPLE tablespace's datafile characteristics*

you turn off AUTOEXTEND for the existing datafile by unchecking the check box in the Storage section. Here is the SQL command that is executed for this operation when you click Continue and then Apply:

```
ALTER DATABASE
     DATAFILE '/u09/oradata/ord/example01.dbf'
     AUTOEXTEND OFF;
```

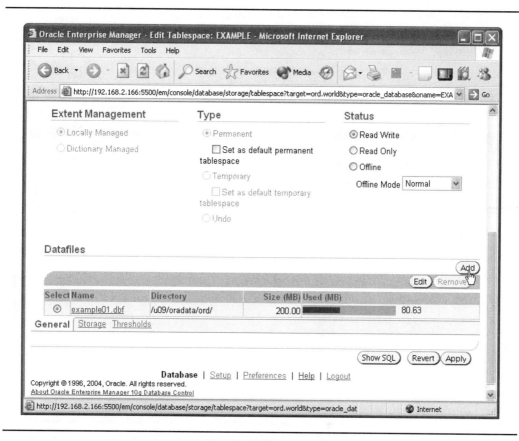

FIGURE 4-7. *Edit Tablespace: EXAMPLE tablespace's datafiles*

On the General tab of the Edit Tablespace screen, the next step is to scroll down to the Datafiles section in Figure 4-7 and click the Add button to add a second datafile.

On the Edit Tablespace: Add Datafile page in Figure 4-8, you specify the filename and directory location for the new datafile. Because you know that the /u06 file system has at least 100MB free, you specify /u06/oradata as the directory and example02.dbf as the filename, although the filename itself need not contain the tablespace name. In addition, you set the file size to 100MB and do not click the check box for AUTOEXTEND.

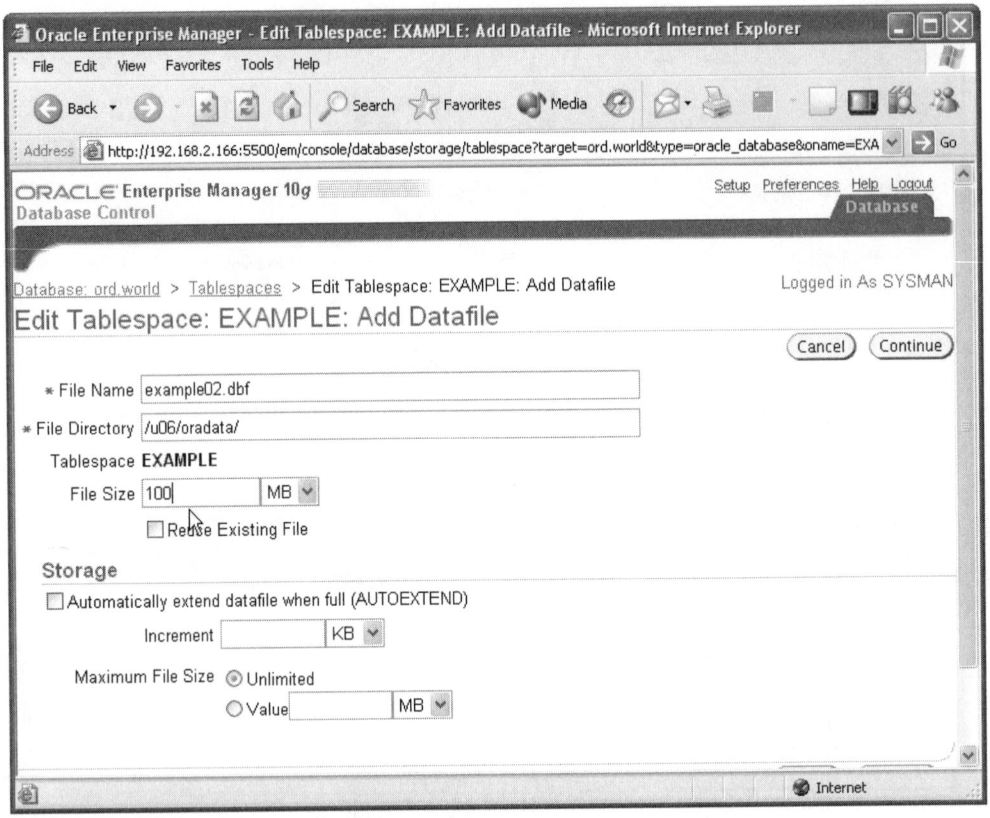

FIGURE 4-8. *Edit Tablespace: EXAMPLE Add Datafile*

After clicking Continue and then Apply, you see the Update Message and the new size of the EXAMPLE tablespace's datafiles, as shown in Figure 4-9.

Dropping a Datafile from a Tablespace

In previous versions of Oracle, dropping a datafile from a tablespace was problematic; there was not a single command you could issue to drop a datafile unless you dropped the entire tablespace. You only had three alternatives:

- Live with it.

- Shrink it and turn off AUTOEXTEND.

- Create a new tablespace, move all the objects to the new tablespace, and drop the original tablespace.

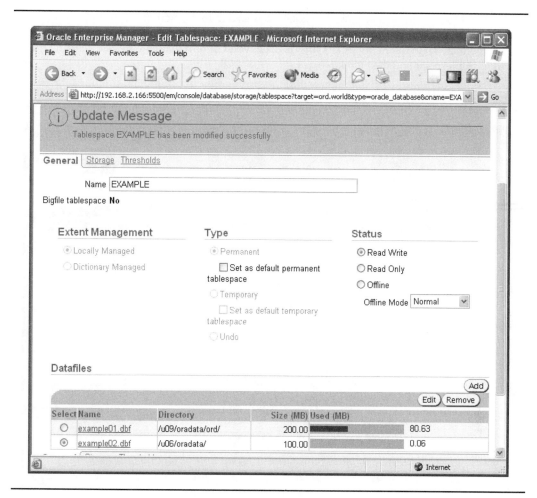

FIGURE 4-9. *Tablespace after a datafile is added*

Although creating a new tablespace was the most ideal from a maintenance and metadata point of view, performing the steps involved was error-prone and involved some amount of downtime for the tablespace, impacting availability.

Using EM Database Control, you can drop a datafile and minimize downtime, and let EM Database Control generate the scripts for you. Following our previous example when we expanded the EXAMPLE tablespace by adding a datafile, we'll step through an example of how you can remove the datafile by reorganizing the tablespace. On the Tablespace page, select the tablespace to be reorganized, choose Reorganize in the Actions drop-down box, and then click Go, as shown in Figure 4-10.

In Figure 4-11, on the Reorganize Objects page, you confirm that you are reorganizing the EXAMPLE tablespace and then click Next.

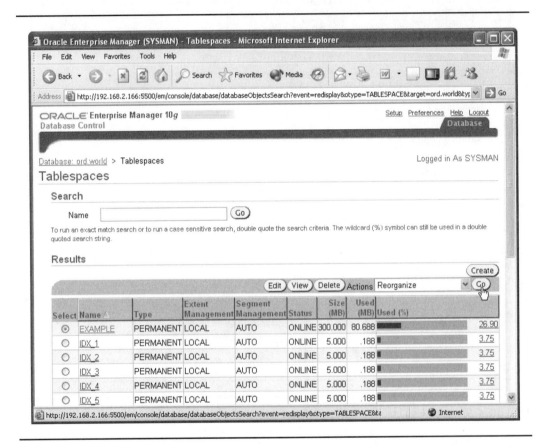

FIGURE 4-10.   *Tablespace: Reorganize*

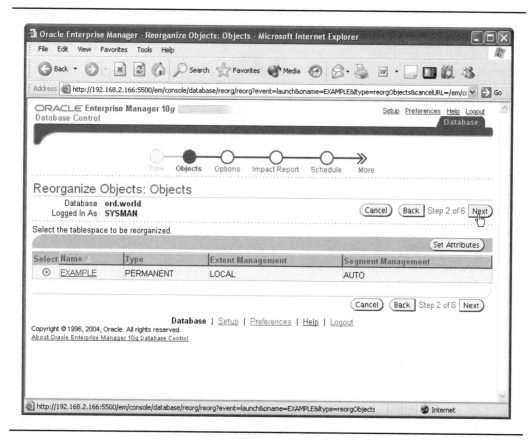

FIGURE 4-11. *Reorganize Objects: Objects*

The next page, as you can see in Figure 4-12, is where you set some of the parameters for the reorganization, such as whether speed of the reorganization or the availability of the tablespace is more important for this reorganization. In addition, you can leverage the tablespace rename feature instead of using a scratch tablespace for a working area, potentially saving disk space or

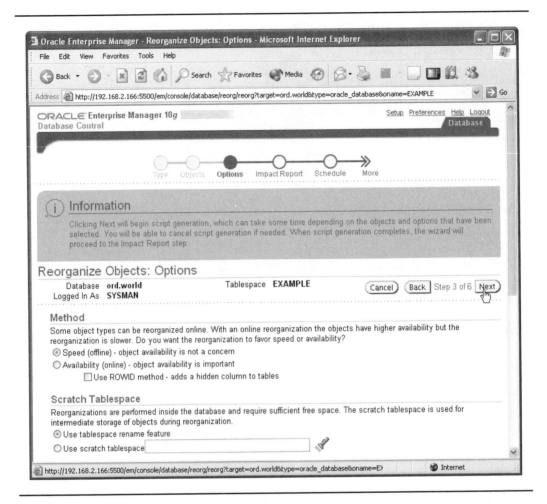

FIGURE 4-12. *Reorganize Objects: Options*

the amount of time it will take for the reorganization. Other parameters on this page include specifying parallel execution, index rebuilds without logging, and what level of statistics gathering is required after the reorganization is complete.

Figure 4-13 shows the status of the script creation. The time it takes to generate the script is roughly proportional to the number of objects in the tablespace.

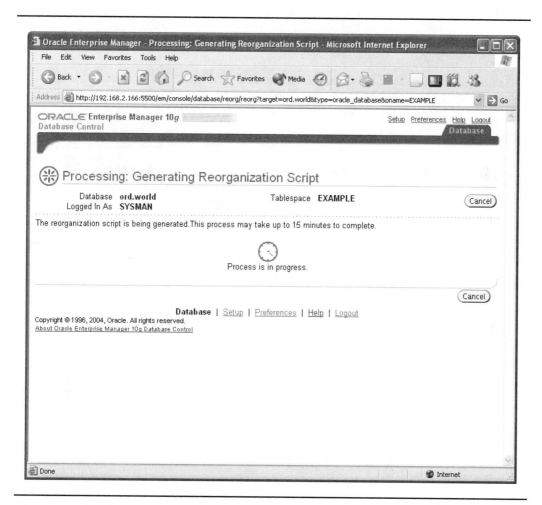

FIGURE 4-13. *Processing: Generating Reorganization Script*

A summary screen is presented with any warnings or errors encountered during script generation, as you can see in Figure 4-14 on the Impact Report.

After clicking Next, you see the Schedule page, as shown in Figure 4-15. In this scenario, go ahead and specify host credentials for the server, but we will not submit the job at the end of the wizard because we need to make one edit to the script.

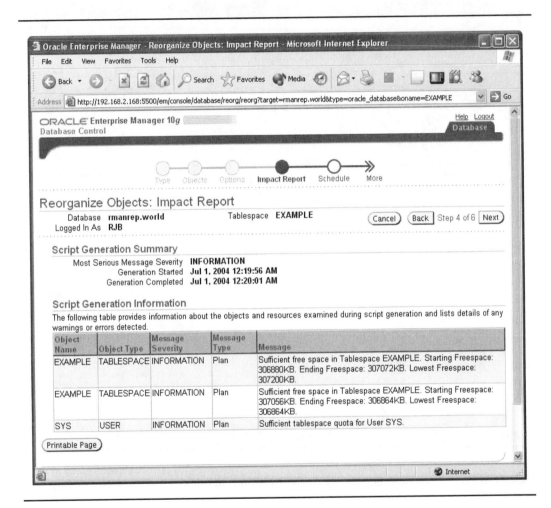

FIGURE 4-14. *Reorganize Objects: Impact Report*

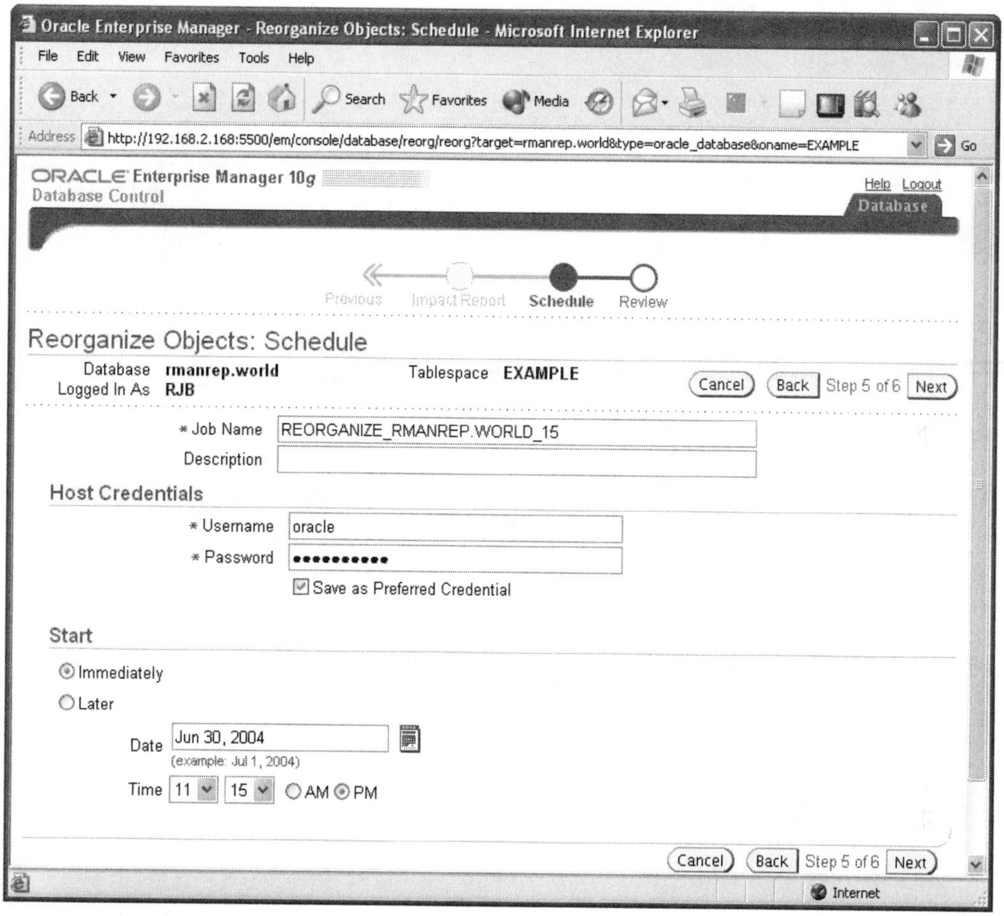

FIGURE 4-15. *Reorganize Objects: Schedule*

Clicking Next, we arrive at the Review page in Figure 4-16. An excerpt of the generated script is presented in the text box. Instead of submitting the job, you will click Save Full Script to make one minor change to the script before you run it.

In Figure 4-17, you specify the location where you want to save the script.

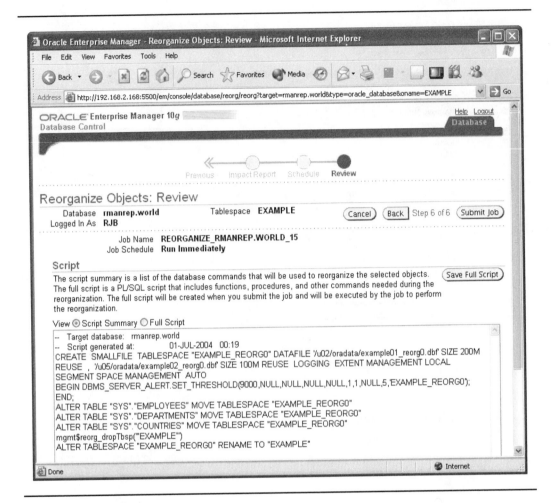

FIGURE 4-16. *Reorganize Objects: Review*

When you edit the full script, locate the **execute immediate** command where the tablespace is created:

```
EXECUTE IMMEDIATE 'CREATE SMALLFILE TABLESPACE "EXAMPLE_REORG0"
     DATAFILE '/u02/oradata/ example01_reorg0.dbf'    SIZE 200M REUSE,
      ''/u06/oradata/example02_reorg0.dbf'' SIZE 100M REUSE
     LOGGING EXTENT MANAGEMENT LOCAL
     SEGMENT SPACE MANAGEMENT AUTO';
```

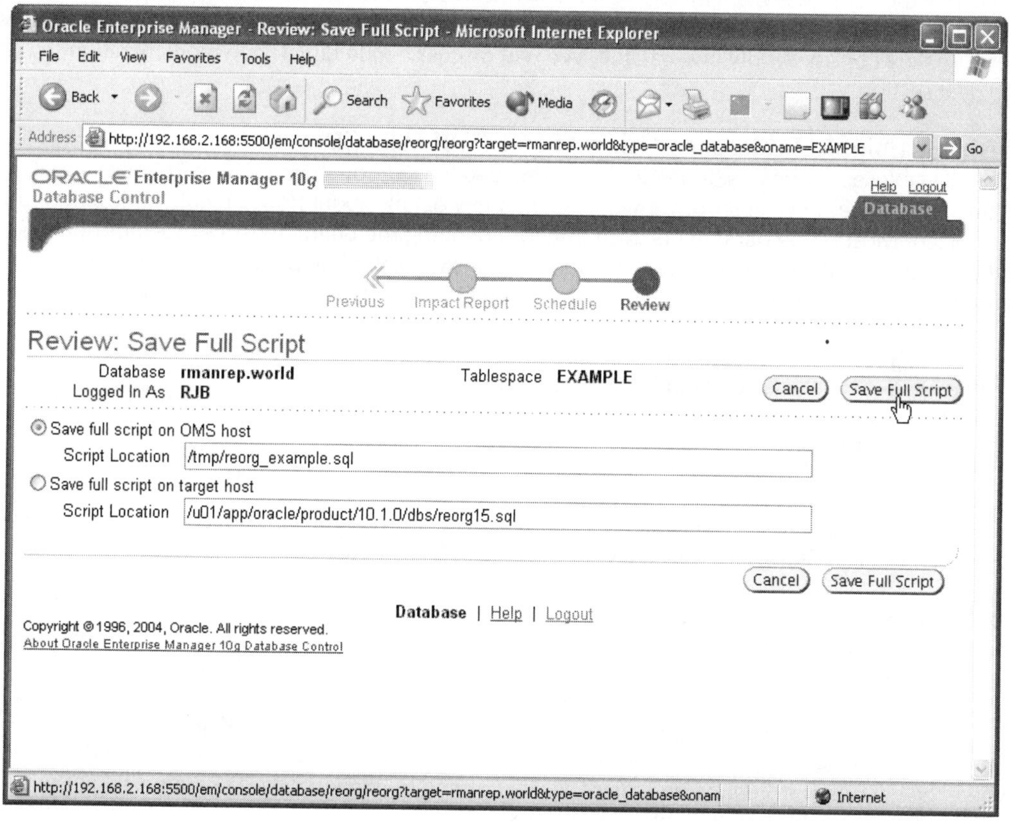

FIGURE 4-17. *Review: Save Full Script*

Because we want to drop a datafile, we want to remove the highlighted datafile clause in the script and then either change the location of the second datafile or re-create the first datafile with a larger size. In this example, you will not only create the new tablespace with a larger size, but also place the new tablespace on a different disk volume:

```
EXECUTE IMMEDIATE 'CREATE SMALLFILE TABLESPACE "EXAMPLE_REORG0"
   DATAFILE ''/u04/oradata/example01.dbf''
      SIZE 300M REUSE
      LOGGING EXTENT MANAGEMENT LOCAL
      SEGMENT SPACE MANAGEMENT AUTO';
```

Once the script has been edited, run the script in SQL*Plus using an account with DBA privileges. You can avoid using reorganization scripts in many cases if you use bigfile tablespaces because they consist of only one datafile. We will discuss bigfile tablespace reorganization in the next section.

Resizing a Bigfile Tablespace Using ALTER TABLESPACE

A bigfile tablespace consists of one and only one datafile. Although you will learn more about bigfile tablespaces in Chapter 6, we will present a few details about how a bigfile tablespace can be resized. Most of the parameters available for changing the characteristics of a tablespace's datafile—such as the maximum size, whether it can extend at all, and the size of the extents—are now modifiable at the tablespace level. Let's start with a bigfile tablespace created as follows:

```
create bigfile tablespace dmarts
    datafile '/u05/oradata/dmarts.dbf' size 250m
    autoextend on next 50m maxsize unlimited
    extent management local
    segment space management auto;
```

Operations that are valid only at the datafile level with smallfile tablespaces can be used with bigfile tablespaces at the tablespace level:

```
SQL> alter tablespace dmarts
  2     resize 1000m;
Tablespace altered.
```

Although using **alter database** with the datafile specification for the DMARTS tablespace will work, the advantage of the **alter tablespace** syntax is obvious: You don't have to or need to know where the datafile is stored. As you might suspect, trying to change datafile parameters at the tablespace level with smallfile tablespaces is not allowed:

```
SQL> alter tablespace users resize 100m;
alter tablespace users resize 100m
*
ERROR at line 1:
ORA-32773: operation not supported for smallfile tablespace USERS
```

If a bigfile tablespace runs out of space because its single datafile cannot extend on the disk, you need to relocate the datafile to another volume, as we will discuss in the "Moving Datafiles" section. Using Automatic Storage Management (ASM), presented later in this chapter, can potentially eliminate the need to manually move datafiles at all: Instead of moving the datafile, you can add another disk volume to the ASM storage group.

Moving Datafiles

To better manage the size of a datafile or improve the overall I/O performance of the database, it may be necessary to move one or more datafiles in a tablespace to a different location. There are three methods for relocating the datafiles: using **alter database**, using **alter tablespace**, and via EM Database Control, although EM Database Control does not provide all the commands necessary to relocate the datafile.

The **alter tablespace** method works for datafiles in all tablespaces except for SYSTEM, SYSAUX, the online undo tablespace, and the temporary tablespace. The **alter database** method works for datafiles in all tablespaces because the instance is shut down when the move operation occurs.

Moving Datafiles with ALTER DATABASE

The steps for moving one or more datafiles with **alter database** are as follows:

1. Connect to the database as SYSDBA and shut down the instance.

2. Use operating system commands to move the datafile(s).

3. Open the database in MOUNT mode.

4. Use **alter database** to change the references to the datafile in the database.

5. Open the database in OPEN mode.

6. Perform an incremental or full backup of the database that includes the control file.

In the following example, we will show you how to move the first datafile of the USERS tablespace to a different disk volume. First, you connect to the database with SYSDBA privileges:

```
[oracle@util oracle]$ sqlplus / as sysdba

SQL*Plus: Release 10.1.0.2.0 - Production on Sun Jun 13 20:40:15 2004
Copyright (c) 1982, 2004, Oracle.  All rights reserved.
Connected to:
Oracle Database 10g Enterprise Edition Release 10.1.0.2.0 - Production
With the Partitioning, OLAP and Data Mining options
SQL>
```

Next, you use a query against the dynamic performance views V$DATAFILE and V$TABLESPACE to confirm the names of the datafiles in the USERS tablespace:

```
SQL> select d.name from
  2     v$datafile d join v$tablespace t using(ts#)
  3     where t.name = 'USERS';

NAME
-------------------------------------------------------------
/u01/app/oracle/oradata/rmanrep/users01.dbf
/u03/oradata/users02.dbf

SQL>
```

To complete step 1, shut down the database:

```
SQL> shutdown immediate;
Database closed.
Database dismounted.
ORACLE instance shut down.
SQL>
```

For step 2, you stay in SQL*Plus and use the "!" escape character to execute the operating system command to move the datafile:

```
SQL> ! mv /u01/app/oracle/oradata/rmanrep/users01.dbf /u02/oradata
```

In step 3, you start up the database in MOUNT mode so that the control file is available without opening the datafiles:

```
SQL> startup mount
ORACLE instance started.

Total System Global Area  188743680 bytes
Fixed Size                   778036 bytes
Variable Size             162537676 bytes
Database Buffers           25165824 bytes
Redo Buffers                 262144 bytes
Database mounted.
```

For step 4, you change the pathname reference in the control file to point to the new location of the datafile:

```
SQL> alter database rename file
  2    '/u01/app/oracle/oradata/rmanrep/users01.dbf' to
  3    '/u02/oradata/users01.dbf';
Database altered.
```

In step 5, you open the database to make it available to users:

```
SQL> alter database open;
Database altered.
```

Finally, in step 6, you can make a backup copy of the updated control file:

```
SQL> alter database backup controlfile to trace;
Database altered.
SQL>
```

Alternatively, you can use RMAN to perform an incremental backup that includes a backup of the control file.

Moving Datafiles with ALTER TABLESPACE

If the datafile you want to move is part of a tablespace other than SYSTEM, SYSAUX, the active undo tablespace, or the temporary tablespace, then it is preferable to use the **alter tablespace** method to move a tablespace for one primary reason: The database, except for the tablespace whose datafile will be moved, remains available to all users during the entire operation.

The steps for moving one or more datafiles with **alter tablespace** are as follows:

1. Using an account with the ALTER TABLESPACE privilege, take the tablespace offline.

2. Use operating system commands to move the datafile(s).

3. Use **alter tablespace** to change the references to the datafile in the database.

4. Bring the tablespace back online.

In the **alter database** example, assume that you moved the second datafile to the wrong file system. In this example, you'll move it from /u02/oradata to /u04/oradata:

```
SQL> alter tablespace users offline;
Tablespace altered.

SQL> ! mv /u02/oradata/users01.dbf /u04/oradata/users01.dbf

SQL> alter tablespace users rename datafile
  2     '/u02/oradata/users01.dbf' to '/u04/oradata/users01.dbf';
Tablespace altered.

SQL> alter tablespace users online;
Tablespace altered.
```

Note how this method is much more straightforward and much less disruptive than the **alter database** method. The only downtime for the USERS tablespace is the amount of time it takes to move the datafile from one disk volume to another.

Moving Datafiles with EM Database Control

In release 1 of Oracle Database 10g, EM Database Control does not have an explicit function for moving a datafile, short of performing a tablespace reorganization, as demonstrated earlier in the chapter. For moving a datafile to another volume, this is overkill. Editing a datafile in EM Database Control and merely changing the File Directory location, as shown in Figure 4-18, produces the following SQL script:

```
ALTER DATABASE RENAME FILE
    '/u01/app/oracle/oradata/rmanrep/users01.dbf' TO
    '/u02/oradata/users01.dbf';
```

The script does not succeed because there are no commands to take the tablespace offline, move the file with operating system commands, and bring the tablespace back online.

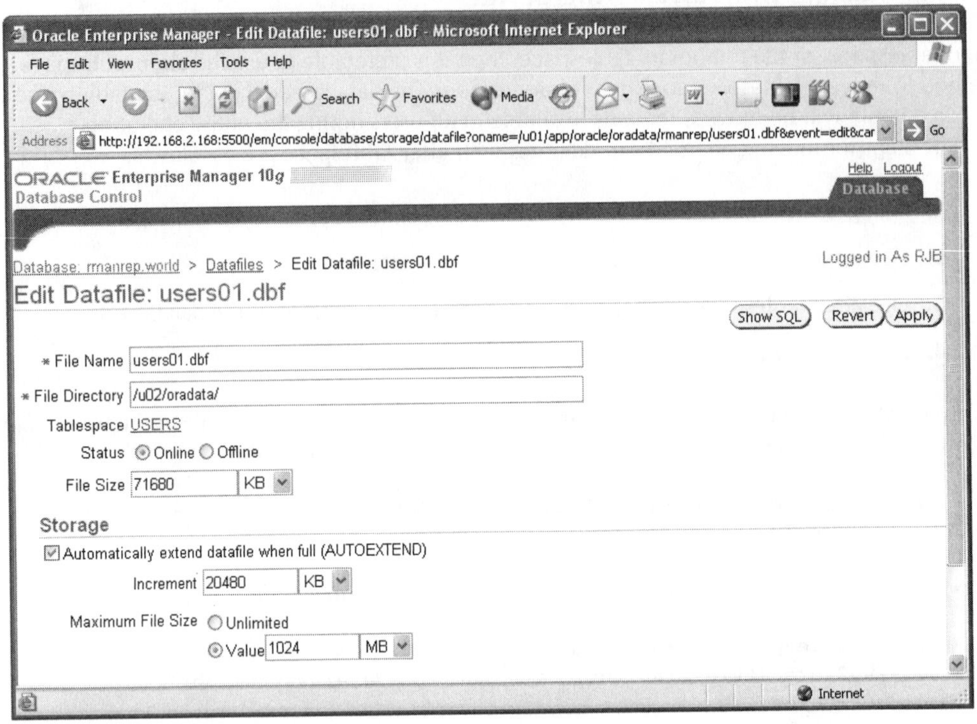

FIGURE 4-18. *EM Database Control: Edit Datafile Location*

Moving Online Redo Log Files

Although it is possible to indirectly move online redo log files by dropping entire redo log groups and re-adding the groups in a different location, this solution will not work if there are only two redo log file groups because a database will not open with only one redo log file group. Temporarily adding a third group and dropping the first or second group is an option if the database must be kept open; alternatively, the method shown here will move the redo log file(s) while the database is shut down.

In the following example, we have three redo log file groups with two members each. One member of each group is on the same volume as the Oracle software and should be moved to a different volume to eliminate any contention between log file filling and accessing Oracle software components. The method you will use here is very similar to the method used to move datafiles with the **alter database** method.

```
SQL> select group#, member from v$logfile
  2      order by group#, member;
```

```
    GROUP# MEMBER
---------- --------------------------------------------
         1 /u01/app/oracle/oradata/rmanrep/redo01.log
         1 /u05/oradata/redo01.log
         2 /u01/app/oracle/oradata/rmanrep/redo02.log
         2 /u05/oradata/redo02.log
         3 /u01/app/oracle/oradata/rmanrep/redo03.log
         3 /u05/oradata/redo03.log
6 rows selected.

SQL> shutdown immediate;
Database closed.
Database dismounted.
ORACLE instance shut down.
SQL> ! mv /u01/app/oracle/oradata/rmanrep/redo0[1-3].log /u04/oradata

SQL> startup mount
ORACLE instance started.

Total System Global Area  188743680 bytes
Fixed Size                   778036 bytes
Variable Size             162537676 bytes
Database Buffers           25165824 bytes

Redo Buffers                 262144 bytes
Database mounted.

SQL> alter database rename file '/u01/app/oracle/oradata/rmanrep/redo01.log'
  2      to '/u04/oradata/redo01.log';
Database altered.

SQL> alter database rename file '/u01/app/oracle/oradata/rmanrep/redo02.log'
  2      to '/u04/oradata/redo02.log';
Database altered.

SQL> alter database rename file '/u01/app/oracle/oradata/rmanrep/redo03.log'
  2      to '/u04/oradata/redo03.log';
Database altered.

SQL> alter database open;
Database altered.

SQL> select group#, member from v$logfile
  2      order by group#, member;

GROUP# MEMBER
---------- --------------------------------------------
         1 /u04/oradata/redo01.log
         1 /u05/oradata/redo01.log
         2 /u04/oradata/redo02.log
```

```
2  /u05/oradata/redo02.log
3  /u04/oradata/redo03.log
3  /u05/oradata/redo03.log
```

```
6 rows selected.
```

```
SQL>
```

The I/O for the redo log files no longer contends with the Oracle software; in addition, the redo log files are multiplexed between two different mount points, /u04 and /u05.

Moving Control Files

Moving a control file when you use an initialization parameter file follows a procedure similar to the one you used for datafiles and redo log files: Shut down the instance, move the file with operating system commands, and restart the instance.

When you use a server parameter file (SPFILE), however, the procedure is a bit different. The initialization file parameter CONTROL_FILES is changed using **alter system ... scope=spfile** when either the instance is running or it's shut down and opened in NOMOUNT mode. Because the CONTROL_FILES parameter is not dynamic, the instance must be shut down and restarted in either case.

In this example, you discover that you have three copies of the control file in your database, but they are not multiplexed on different disks. You will edit the SPFILE with the new locations, shut down the instance so you can move the control files to different disks, and then restart the instance.

```
SQL> select name, value from v$spparameter
  2      where name = 'control_files';
```

```
NAME              VALUE
---------------   --------------------------------------------------
control_files     /u01/app/oracle/oradata/rmanrep/control01.ctl
control_files     /u01/app/oracle/oradata/rmanrep/control02.ctl
control_files     /u01/app/oracle/oradata/rmanrep/control03.ctl
```

```
SQL> show parameter control_files
```

```
NAME              TYPE          VALUE
---------------   -----------   ------------------------------
control_files     string        /u01/app/oracle/oradata/rmanre
                                p/control01.ctl, /u01/app/orac
                                le/oradata/rmanrep/control02.c
                                tl, /u01/app/oracle/oradata/rm
                                anrep/control03.ctl
SQL> alter system set control_files =
  2      '/u02/oradata/control01.ctl',
  3      '/u03/oradata/control02.ctl',
  4      '/u04/oradata/control03.ctl'
  5  scope = spfile;
```

```
System altered.
```

```
SQL> shutdown immediate
Database closed.
Database dismounted.
ORACLE instance shut down.
SQL> ! mv /u01/app/oracle/oradata/rmanrep/control01.ctl /u02/oradata
SQL> ! mv /u01/app/oracle/oradata/rmanrep/control02.ctl /u03/oradata
SQL> ! mv /u01/app/oracle/oradata/rmanrep/control03.ctl /u04/oradata

SQL> startup
ORACLE instance started.

Total System Global Area   188743680 bytes
Fixed Size                    778036 bytes
Variable Size              162537676 bytes
Database Buffers            25165824 bytes
Redo Buffers                  262144 bytes
Database mounted.
Database opened.
SQL> select name, value from v$spparameter
  2  where name = 'control_files';

NAME              VALUE
--------------    ----------------------------------------------------
control_files     /u02/oradata/control01.ctl
control_files     /u03/oradata/control02.ctl
control_files     /u04/oradata/control03.ctl

SQL> show parameter control_files

NAME              TYPE         VALUE
--------------    -----------  -----------------------------
control_files     string       /u02/oradata/control01.ctl, /u
                               03/oradata/control02.ctl, /u04
                               /oradata/control03.ctl
SQL>
```

The three control files have been moved to separate file systems, no longer on the volume with the Oracle software and in a higher availability configuration (if the volume containing one of the control files fails, two other volumes contain up-to-date control files).

Automatic Storage Management

In Chapter 3, we presented some of the file naming conventions used for ASM objects. In this section, we'll delve more deeply into how we can create tablespaces—and ultimately datafiles behind the scenes—in an ASM environment with one or more disk groups.

When creating a new tablespace or other database structure, such as a control file or redo log file, you can specify a disk group as the storage area for the database structure instead of an operating system file. ASM takes the ease of use of Oracle Managed Files (OMF) and combines it with mirroring and striping features to provide a robust file system and logical volume manager that can even support multiple nodes in an Oracle Real Application Cluster (RAC). ASM eliminates the need to purchase a third-party logical volume manager.

ASM not only enhances performance by automatically spreading out database objects over multiple devices, but also increases availability by allowing new disk devices to be added to the database without shutting down the database; ASM automatically rebalances the distribution of files with minimal intervention.

We'll also review the ASM architecture. In addition, we'll show how you create a special type of Oracle instance to support ASM as well as how to start up and shut down an ASM instance. We'll review the new initialization parameters related to ASM and the existing initialization parameters that have new values to support an ASM instance. Finally, we'll use some raw disk devices on a Linux server to demonstrate how disk groups are created and maintained.

ASM Architecture

ASM divides the datafiles and other database structures into extents, and it divides the extents among all the disks in the disk group to enhance both performance and reliability. Instead of mirroring entire disk volumes, ASM mirrors the database objects to provide the flexibility to mirror or stripe the database objects differently depending on their type. Optionally, the objects may not be striped at all if the underlying disk hardware is already RAID enabled, part of a Storage Attached Network (SAN), or part of a Network Attached Storage (NAS) device.

Automatic rebalancing is another key feature of ASM. When an increase in disk space is needed, additional disk devices can be added to a disk group, and ASM moves a proportional number of files from one or more existing disks to the new disks to maintain the overall I/O balance across all disks. This happens in the background while the database objects contained in the disk files are still online and available to users. If the impact to the I/O subsystem is high during a rebalance operation, the speed at which the rebalance occurs can be reduced using an initialization parameter.

ASM requires a special type of Oracle instance to provide the interface between a traditional Oracle instance and the file system; the ASM software components are shipped with the Oracle database software and are always available as a selection when you're selecting the storage type for the SYSTEM, SYSAUX, and other tablespaces when the database is created.

Using ASM does not, however, prevent you from mixing ASM disk groups with manual Oracle datafile management techniques such as those we presented in Chapter 3 and earlier in this chapter. However, the ease of use and performance of ASM makes a strong case for eventually using ASM disk groups for all your storage needs.

Two new Oracle background processes support ASM instances: RBAL and ORB*n*. RBAL coordinates the disk activity for disk groups, whereas ORB*n*, where *n* can be a number from 0 to 9, performs the actual extent movement between disks in the disk groups.

For databases that use ASM disks, there are also two new background processes: OSMB and RBAL. OSMB performs the communication between the database and the ASM instance, whereas RBAL performs the opening and closing of the disks in the disk group on behalf of the database.

Creating an ASM Instance

ASM requires a dedicated Oracle instance to manage the disk groups. An ASM instance generally has a smaller memory footprint, in the range of 60MB to 120MB, and is automatically configured when ASM is specified as the database's file storage option when the Oracle software is installed and an existing ASM instance does not already exist, as you can see in the Oracle Universal Installer screen in Figure 4-19.

As an example of disk devices used to create ASM disk groups, suppose our Linux server has a number of raw disk devices with the capacities listed in Table 4-2.

You configure the first disk group within the Oracle Universal Installer, as shown in Figure 4-20.

The name of the first disk group is DATA1, and you will be using /dev/raw/raw1 and /dev/raw/raw2 to create the normal redundancy disk group. If an insufficient number of raw disks are selected for the desired redundancy level, OUI generates an error message. After the database is created, both the regular instance and the ASM instance are started.

An ASM instance has a few other unique characteristics. Although it does have an initialization parameter file and a password file, it has no data dictionary, and therefore all connections to an ASM instance are via SYS and SYSTEM using operating system authentication only. Disk group commands such as **create diskgroup**, **alter diskgroup**, and **drop diskgroup** are only valid in an ASM instance. Finally, an ASM instance is either in a NOMOUNT or MOUNT state; it is never in an OPEN state.

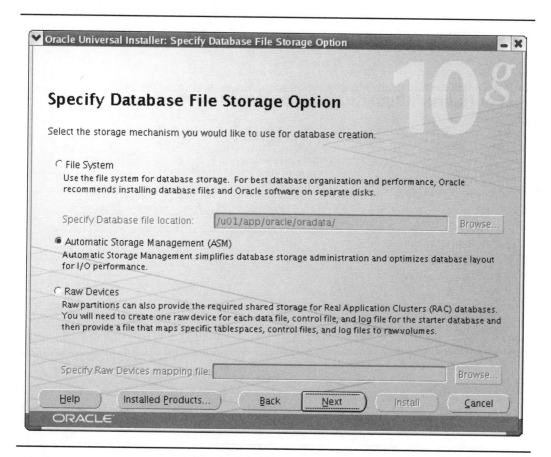

FIGURE 4-19.   *Specifying ASM as the database file storage method*

Device Name	Capacity
/dev/raw/raw1	8GB
/dev/raw/raw2	8GB
/dev/raw/raw3	6GB
/dev/raw/raw4	6GB
/dev/raw/raw5	6GB
/dev/raw/raw6	6GB

TABLE 4-2. *Raw Disks for ASM Disk Groups*

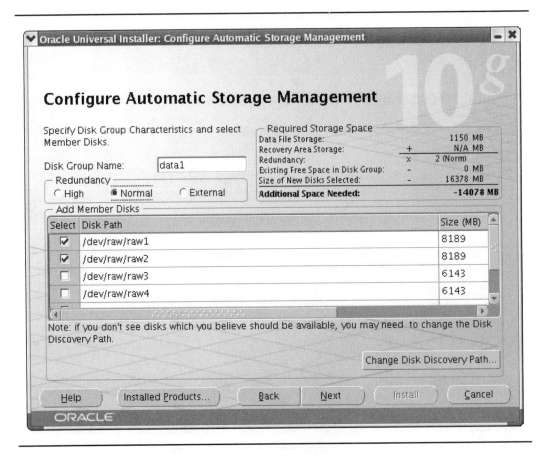

FIGURE 4-20. *Configuring the initial ASM disk group with OUI*

ASM Instance Components

ASM instances cannot be accessed using the variety of methods available with a traditional database. In this section, we'll talk about the privileges available to you that connect with SYSDBA and SYSOPER privileges. We'll also distinguish an ASM instance by the new and expanded initialization parameters available only for an ASM instance. At the end of this section, we'll present the procedures for starting and stopping an ASM instance along with the dependencies between ASM instances and the database instances they serve.

Accessing an ASM Instance

As mentioned earlier in the chapter, an ASM instance does not have a data dictionary, so access to the instance is restricted to users who can authenticate with the operating system—in other words, connecting as SYSDBA or SYSOPER by an operating system user in the dba group.

Users who connect to an ASM instance as SYSDBA can perform all ASM operations, such as creating and deleting disk groups as well as adding and removing disks from disk groups.

The SYSOPER users have a much more limited set of commands available in an ASM instance. In general, the commands available to SYSOPER users give only enough privileges to perform routine operations for an already configured and stable ASM instance. The following list contains the operations available as SYSOPER:

- Starting up and shutting down an ASM instance

- Mounting or dismounting a disk group

- Altering a disk group's disk status from ONLINE to OFFLINE, or vice versa

- Rebalancing a disk group

- Performing an integrity check of a disk group

- Accessing the V$ASM_* dynamic performance views

ASM Initialization Parameters

A number of initialization parameters are either specific to ASM instances or have new values within an ASM instance. An SPFILE is highly recommended instead of an initialization parameter file for an ASM instance. For example, parameters such as ASM_DISKGROUPS will automatically be maintained when a disk group is added or dropped, potentially freeing you from ever having to manually change this value.

We will present the ASM-related initialization parameters in the following sections.

INSTANCE_TYPE   For an ASM instance, the INSTANCE_TYPE parameter has a value of ASM. The default, for a traditional Oracle instance, is RDBMS.

DB_UNIQUE_NAME   The default value for the DB_UNIQUE_NAME parameter is +ASM and is the unique name for a group of ASM instances within a cluster or on a single node; the default value needs to be modified only if you're trying to run multiple ASM instances on a single node.

ASM_POWER_LIMIT   To ensure that rebalancing operations do not interfere with ongoing user I/O, the ASM_POWER_LIMIT parameter controls how fast rebalance operations occur. The values range from 1 to 11, with 11 being the highest possible value; the default value is 1 (low I/O overhead). Because this is a dynamic parameter, you may set this to a low value during the day and set it higher overnight whenever a disk-rebalancing operation must occur.

ASM_DISKSTRING   The ASM_DISKSTRING parameter specifies one or more strings, operating system dependent, to limit the disk devices that can be used to create disk groups. If this value is NULL, all disks visible to the ASM instance are potential candidates for creating disk groups. For the examples in this chapter for our test server, the value of the ASM_DISKSTRING parameter is /dev/raw/*:

```
SQL> select name, type, value from v$parameter
  2       where name = 'asm_diskstring';

NAME                 TYPE VALUE
--------------- ---------- -------------------------
asm_diskstring          2 /dev/raw/*
```

ASM_DISKGROUPS   The ASM_DISKGROUPS parameter specifies a list containing the names of the disk groups to be automatically mounted by the ASM instance at startup or by the **alter diskgroup all mount** command. Even if this list is empty at instance startup, any existing disk group can be manually mounted.

LARGE_POOL_SIZE   The LARGE_POOL_SIZE parameter is useful for both regular and ASM instances; however, this pool is used differently for an ASM instance. All internal ASM packages are executed from this pool, so this parameter should be set to at least 8MB.

ASM Instance Startup and Shutdown

An ASM instance is started much like a database instance, except that the **startup** command defaults to **startup mount**. Because there is no control file, database, or data dictionary to mount, the ASM disk groups are mounted instead of a database. The command **startup nomount** starts up the instance but does not mount any ASM disks. In addition, you can specify **startup restrict** to temporarily prevent database instances from connecting to the ASM instance to mount disk groups.

Performing a **shutdown** command on an ASM instance performs the same **shutdown** command on any database instances using the ASM instance; before the ASM instance finishes a shutdown, it waits for all dependent databases to shut down. The only exception to this is if you use the **shutdown abort** command on the ASM instance, which eventually forces all dependent databases to perform a **shutdown abort**.

For multiple ASM instances sharing disk groups, such as in a Real Application Clusters (RAC) environment, the failure of an ASM instance does not cause the database instances to fail. Instead, another ASM instance performs a recovery operation for the failed instance.

ASM Dynamic Performance Views

A few new dynamic performance views are associated with ASM instances. Table 4-3 contains the common ASM-related dynamic performance views. We'll provide further explanation, where appropriate, later in this chapter for some of these views.

View Name	Used in Standard Database?	Description
V$ASM_DISK	Yes	One row for each disk discovered by an ASM instance, used by a disk group or not. For a database instance, one row for each disk group in use by the instance.
V$ASM_DISKGROUP	Yes	For an ASM instance, one row for each disk group containing general characteristics of the disk group. For a database instance, one row for each disk group in use whether mounted or not.
V$ASM_FILE	No	One row for each file in every mounted disk group.
V$ASM_OPERATION	No	One row for each executing long-running operation in the ASM instance.
V$ASM_TEMPLATE	Yes	One row for each template in each mounted disk group in the ASM instance. For a database instance, one row for each template for each mounted disk group.
V$ASM_CLIENT	Yes	One row for each database using disk groups managed by the ASM instance. For a database instance, one row for the ASM instance if any ASM files are open.
V$ASM_ALIAS	No	One row for every alias in every mounted disk group.

TABLE 4-3.   *ASM-Related Dynamic Performance Views*

ASM Filename Formats

All ASM files are Oracle Managed Files (OMF), so the details of the actual filename within the disk group is not needed for most administrative functions. When an object in an ASM disk group is dropped, the file is automatically deleted. Certain commands will expose the actual filenames, such as **alter database backup controlfile to trace**, as well as some data dictionary and dynamic performance views. For example, the dynamic performance view V$DATAFILE shows the actual filenames within each disk group. Here is an example:

```
SQL> select file#, name, blocks from v$datafile;

    FILE# NAME                                                 BLOCKS
---------- ------------------------------------------------- ----------
        1 +DATA1/rac0/datafile/system.303.1                   57600
        2 +DATA1/rac0/datafile/undotbs1.302.1                  3840
        3 +DATA1/rac0/datafile/sysaux.304.1                   44800
        4 +DATA1/rac0/datafile/users.305.1                      640
        5 +DATA1/rac0/datafile/example.306.1                  19200
        6 +DATA2/rac0/datafile/users3.311.1                   12800

6 rows selected.
```

ASM filenames can be one of six different formats. In the sections that follow, we'll give an overview of the different formats and the context where they can be used—either as a reference to an existing file, during a single-file creation operation, or during a multiple-file creation operation.

Fully Qualified Names
Fully qualified ASM filenames are used only when referencing an existing file. A fully qualified ASM filename has the format

```
+group/dbname/file type/tag.file.incarnation
```

where *group* is the disk group name, *dbname* is the database to which the file belongs, *file type* is the Oracle file type, *tag* is information specific to the file type, and the *file.incarnation* pair ensures uniqueness. Here is an example of an ASM file for the USERS3 tablespace:

```
+DATA2/rac0/datafile/users3.311.1
```

The disk group name is +DATA2, the database name is rac0, it's a datafile for the USERS3 tablespace, and the file number/incarnation pair 311.1 ensures uniqueness if you decide to create another ASM datafile for the USERS3 tablespace.

Numeric Names
Numeric names are used only when referencing an existing ASM file. This allows you to refer to an existing ASM file by only the disk group name and the file number/incarnation pair. The numeric name for the ASM file in the previous section is

```
+DATA2.311.1
```

Alias Names
An alias can be used when either referencing an existing object or creating a single ASM file. Using the **alter diskgroup add alias** command, a more readable name can be created for an existing or a new ASM file, and it's distinguishable from a regular ASM filename because it does not end in a dotted pair of numbers (the file number/incarnation pair), as shown here:

```
SQL> alter diskgroup data2
  2      add directory '+data2/purch';
Diskgroup altered.

SQL> alter diskgroup data2
  2      add alias '+data2/purch/users.dbf'
  3      for '+data2/rac0/datafile/users3.311.1';
Diskgroup altered.

SQL>
```

Alias with Template Names
An alias with a template can only be used when creating a new ASM file. Templates provide a shorthand for specifying a file type and a tag when creating a new ASM file. Here's an example of an alias using a template for a new tablespace in the +DATA2 disk group:

```
SQL> create tablespace users4 datafile '+data2/user_spare(datafile)';
Tablespace created.
```

Incomplete Names

An incomplete filename format can be used either for single-file or multiple-file creation operations. Only the disk group name is specified, and a default template is used depending on the type of file, as shown here:

```
SQL> create tablespace users5 datafile '+data1';
Tablespace created.
```

Incomplete Names with Template

As with incomplete ASM filenames, an incomplete filename with a template can be used either for single-file or multiple-file creation operations. Regardless of the actual file type, the template name determines the characteristics of the file.

Even though we are creating a permanent tablespace in the following example, the characteristics of a tempfile are used instead as the attributes for the datafile:

```
SQL> create tablespace users6 datafile '+data1(tempfile)';
Tablespace created.
```

ASM File Types and Templates

ASM supports all types of files used by the database except for operating system executables. Table 4-4 contains the complete list of ASM file types; the ASM File Type and Tag columns are those presented previously for ASM filenaming conventions.

The default ASM file templates referenced in the last column of Table 4-4 are presented in Table 4-5.

When a new disk group is created, a set of ASM file templates copied from the default templates in Table 4-5 is saved with the disk group; as a result, individual template characteristics can be changed and apply only to the disk group where they reside. In other words, the DATAFILE system template in disk group +DATA1 may have the default coarse striping, but the DATAFILE template in disk group +DATA2 may have fine striping. You can create your own templates in each disk group as needed.

When an ASM datafile is created with the DATAFILE template, by default the datafile is 100MB and autoextensible, and the maximum size is unlimited.

Administering ASM Disk Groups

Using ASM disk groups benefits you in a number of ways: I/O performance is improved, availability is increased, and the ease with which you can add a disk to a disk group or add an entirely new disk group enables you to manage many more databases in the same amount of time. Understanding the components of a disk group as well as correctly configuring a disk group are important goals for a successful DBA.

In this section, we'll delve more deeply into the details of the structure of a disk group. Also, we'll review the different types of administrative tasks related to disk groups and show how disks are assigned to failure groups, how disk groups are mirrored, and how disk groups are created, dropped, and altered. We'll also briefly review the EM Database Control interface to ASM.

Oracle File Type	ASM File Type	Tag	Default Template
Control files	controlfile	cf (control file) or bcf (backup control file)	CONTROLFILE
Data files	datafile	tablespace name.file#	DATAFILE
Online logs	online_log	log_thread#	ONLINELOG
Archive logs	archive_log	parameter	ARCHIVELOG
Temp files	temp	tablespace name.file#	TEMPFILE
RMAN datafile backup piece	backupset	Client specified	BACKUPSET
RMAN incremental backup piece	backupset	Client specified	BACKUPSET
RMAN archive log backup piece	backupset	Client specified	BACKUPSET
RMAN datafile copy	datafile	tablespace name.file#	DATAFILE
Initialization parameters	init	spfile	PARAMETERFILE
Broker config	drc	drc	DATAGUARDCONFIG
Flashback logs	rlog	thread#_log#	FLASHBACK
Change tracking bitmap	ctb	bitmap	CHANGETRACKING
Auto backup	autobackup	Client specified	AUTOBACKUP
Data Pump dumpset	dumpset	dump	DUMPSET
Cross-platform data files			XTRANSPORT

TABLE 4-4. *ASM File Types*

Disk Group Architecture

As defined earlier in this chapter, a disk group is a collection of physical disks managed as a unit. Every ASM disk, as part of a disk group, has an ASM disk name that is either assigned by the DBA or automatically assigned when it is assigned to the disk group.

Files in a disk group are striped on the disks using either coarse striping or fine striping. *Coarse striping* spreads files in units of 1MB each across all disks. Coarse striping is appropriate for a system with a high degree of concurrent small I/O requests, such as an OLTP environment. Alternatively, *fine striping* spreads files in units of 128KB, is appropriate for traditional data warehouse environments or OLTP systems with low concurrency, and maximizes response time for individual I/O requests.

System Template	External Redundancy	Normal Redundancy	High Redundancy	Striping
CONTROLFILE	Unprotected	Two-way mirroring	Three-way mirroring	Fine
DATAFILE	Unprotected	Two-way mirroring	Three-way mirroring	Coarse
ONLINELOG	Unprotected	Two-way mirroring	Three-way mirroring	Fine
ARCHIVELOG	Unprotected	Two-way mirroring	Three-way mirroring	Coarse
TEMPFILE	Unprotected	Two-way mirroring	Three-way mirroring	Coarse
BACKUPSET	Unprotected	Two-way mirroring	Three-way mirroring	Coarse
XTRANSPORT	Unprotected	Two-way mirroring	Three-way mirroring	Coarse
PARAMETERFILE	Unprotected	Two-way mirroring	Three-way mirroring	Coarse
DATAGUARDCONFIG	Unprotected	Two-way mirroring	Three-way mirroring	Coarse
FLASHBACK	Unprotected	Two-way mirroring	Three-way mirroring	Fine
CHANGETRACKING	Unprotected	Two-way mirroring	Three-way mirroring	Coarse
AUTOBACKUP	Unprotected	Two-way mirroring	Three-way mirroring	Coarse
DUMPSET	Unprotected	Two-way mirroring	Three-way mirroring	Coarse

TABLE 4-5.   *ASM File Template Defaults*

Disk Group Mirroring and Failure Groups

Before defining the type of mirroring within a disk group, you must group disks into failure groups. A *failure group* is one or more disks within a disk group that share a common resource, such as a disk controller, whose failure would cause the entire set of disks to be unavailable to the group. In most cases, an ASM instance does not know the hardware and software dependencies for a given disk. Therefore, unless you specifically assign a disk to a failure group, each disk in a disk group is assigned to its own failure group.

Once the failure groups have been defined, you can define the mirroring for the disk group; the number of failure groups available within a disk group can restrict the type of mirroring available for the disk group. There are three types of mirroring available: external redundancy, normal redundancy, and high redundancy.

External Redundancy   External redundancy requires only one failure group and assumes that the disk is not critical to the ongoing operation of the database or that the disk is managed externally with high-availability hardware such as a RAID controller.

Normal Redundancy   Normal redundancy provides two-way mirroring and requires at least two failure groups within a disk group. Failure of one of the disks in a failure group does not cause any downtime for the disk group or any data loss other than a slight performance hit for queries against objects in the disk group.

High Redundancy   High redundancy provides three-way mirroring and requires at least three failure groups within a disk group. The failure of disks in two out of the three failure groups is for the most part transparent to the database users, as in normal redundancy mirroring.

Mirroring is managed at a very low level. Extents, not disks, are mirrored. In addition, each disk will have a mixture of both primary and mirrored (secondary and tertiary) extents on each disk. Although a slight amount of overhead is incurred for managing mirroring at the extent level, it provides the advantage of spreading out the load from the failed disk to all other disks instead of a single disk.

Disk Group Dynamic Rebalancing

Whenever you change the configuration of a disk group—whether you are adding or removing a failure group or a disk within a failure group—dynamic rebalancing occurs automatically to proportionally reallocate data from other members of the disk group to the new member of the disk group. This rebalance occurs while the database is online and available to users; any impact to ongoing database I/O can be controlled by adjusting the value of the initialization parameter ASM_POWER_LIMIT to a lower value.

Not only does dynamic rebalancing free you from the tedious and often error-prone task of identifying hot spots in a disk group, it also provides an automatic way to migrate an entire database from a set of slower disks to a set of faster disks while the entire database remains online. Faster disks are added as a new failure group in the existing disk group with the slower disks and the automatic rebalance occurs. After the rebalance operations complete, the failure groups containing the slower disks are dropped, leaving a disk group with only fast disks. To make this operation even faster, both the **add** and **drop** operations can be initiated within the same **alter diskgroup** command.

As an example, suppose you want to create a new disk group with high redundancy to hold tablespaces for a new credit card authorization. Using the view V$ASM_DISK, you can view all disks discovered using the initialization parameter ASM_DISKSTRING, along with the status of the disk (in other words, whether it is assigned to an existing disk group or is unassigned). Here is the command:

```
SQL> select group_number, disk_number, name,
  2        failgroup, create_date, path from v$asm_disk;

GROUP_NUMBER DISK_NUMBER NAME       FAILGROUP  CREATE_DA PATH
------------ ----------- ---------- ---------- --------- -------------
           0           0                                 /dev/raw/raw6
           0           1                                 /dev/raw/raw5
           0           2                                 /dev/raw/raw4
           0           3                                 /dev/raw/raw3
           1           1 DATA1_0001 DATA1_0001 13-JUN-04 /dev/raw/raw2
           1           0 DATA1_0000 DATA1_0000 13-JUN-04 /dev/raw/raw1

6 rows selected.

SQL>
```

Out of the six disks available for ASM, only two of them are assigned to a single disk group, each in their own failure group. The disk group name can be obtained from the view V$ASM_DISKGROUP:

```
SQL> select group_number, name, type, total_mb, free_mb
  2      from v$asm_diskgroup;

GROUP_NUMBER NAME          TYPE    TOTAL_MB    FREE_MB
------------ ------------ ------ ---------- ----------
           1 DATA1         NORMAL     16378      14024

SQL>
```

Note that if you had a number of ASM disks and disk groups, you could have joined the two views on the GROUP_NUMBER column and filtered the query result by GROUP_NUMBER. Also, you see from V$ASM_DISKGROUP that the disk group DATA1 is a NORMAL REDUNDANCY group consisting of two disks.

Your first step is to create the disk group:

```
SQL> create diskgroup data2 high redundancy
  2        failgroup fg1 disk '/dev/raw/raw3' name d2a
  3        failgroup fg2 disk '/dev/raw/raw4' name d2b
  4        failgroup fg3 disk '/dev/raw/raw5' name d2c
  5        failgroup fg4 disk '/dev/raw/raw6' name d2d;

Diskgroup created.

SQL>
```

Looking at the dynamic performance views, you see the new disk group available in V$ASM_DISKGROUP and the failure groups in V$ASM_DISK:

```
SQL> select group_number, name, type, total_mb, free_mb
  2      from v$asm_diskgroup;

GROUP_NUMBER NAME          TYPE    TOTAL_MB    FREE_MB
------------ ------------ ------ ---------- ----------
           1 DATA1         NORMAL     16378      14024
           2 DATA2         HIGH       24572      24420

SQL> select group_number, disk_number, name,
  2        failgroup, create_date, path from v$asm_disk;

GROUP_NUMBER DISK_NUMBER NAME         FAILGROUP  CREATE_DA PATH
------------ ----------- ----------- ---------- --------- -------------
           2           3 D2D          FG4        14-JUN-04 /dev/raw/raw6
           2           2 D2C          FG3        14-JUN-04 /dev/raw/raw5
```

```
      2          1 D2B          FG2            14-JUN-04 /dev/raw/raw4
      2          0 D2A          FG1            14-JUN-04 /dev/raw/raw3
      1          1 DATA1_0001 DATA1_0001 13-JUN-04 /dev/raw/raw2
      1          0 DATA1_0000 DATA1_0000 13-JUN-04 /dev/raw/raw1

6 rows selected.

SQL>
```

However, if disk space is tight, you don't need four members; for a high-redundancy disk group, only three failure groups are necessary, so you drop the disk group and re-create it with only three members:

```
SQL> drop diskgroup data2;

Diskgroup dropped.
```

If the disk group has any database objects other than disk group metadata, you have to specify **including contents** in the **drop diskgroup** command. This is an extra safeguard to make sure that disk groups with database objects are not accidentally dropped. Here is the command:

```
SQL> create diskgroup data2 high redundancy
  2      failgroup fg1 disk '/dev/raw/raw3' name d2a
  3      failgroup fg2 disk '/dev/raw/raw4' name d2b
  4      failgroup fg3 disk '/dev/raw/raw5' name d2c;

Diskgroup created.

SQL> select group_number, disk_number, name,
  2         failgroup, create_date, path from v$asm_disk;

GROUP_NUMBER DISK_NUMBER NAME       FAILGROUP  CREATE_DA PATH
------------ ----------- ---------- ---------- --------- -------------
           0           3                       15-JUN-04 /dev/raw/raw6
           2           2 D2C        FG3        15-JUN-04 /dev/raw/raw5
           2           1 D2B        FG2        15-JUN-04 /dev/raw/raw4
           2           0 D2A        FG1        15-JUN-04 /dev/raw/raw3
           1           1 DATA1_0001 DATA1_0001 13-JUN-04 /dev/raw/raw2
           1           0 DATA1_0000 DATA1_0000 13-JUN-04 /dev/raw/raw1

6 rows selected.

SQL>
```

Now that the configuration of the new disk group has been completed, you can create a tablespace in the new disk group from the database instance:

```
SQL> create tablespace users3 datafile '+DATA2';
Tablespace created.
```

Because ASM files are Oracle Managed Files (OMF), no other datafile characteristics need to be specified when you create the tablespace.

Altering Disk Groups

Disks can be added and dropped from a disk group; also, most characteristics of a disk group can be altered without re-creating the disk group or impacting user transactions on objects in the disk group.

When a disk is added to a disk group, a rebalance operation is performed in the background after the new disk is formatted for use in the disk group. As mentioned earlier in this chapter, the speed of the rebalance is controlled by the initialization parameter ASM_POWER_LIMIT.

Continuing with our example in the previous section, suppose you decide to improve the I/O characteristics of the disk group DATA1 by adding the last available raw disk to the disk group, as follows:

```
SQL> alter diskgroup data1
  2       add failgroup d1fg3 disk '/dev/raw/raw6' name d1c;

Diskgroup altered.
```

The command returns immediately and the formatting and rebalancing continue in the background. You then check the status of the rebalance operation by checking V$ASM_OPERATION:

```
SQL> select group_number, operation, state, power, actual,
  2       sofar, est_work, est_rate, est_minutes from v$asm_operation;

GROUP_NUMBER OPERA STAT POWER ACTUA SOFAR EST_WORK EST_RATE EST_MINUTES
------------ ----- ---- ----- ----- ----- -------- -------- -----------
           1 REBAL RUN      1     1     3      964       60          16
```

Because the estimate for completing the rebalance operation is 16 minutes, you decide to allocate more resources to the rebalance operation and change the power limit for this particular rebalance operation:

```
SQL> alter diskgroup data1 rebalance power 8;
Diskgroup altered.
```

Checking the status of the rebalance operation confirms that the estimated time to completion has been reduced to four minutes instead of 16:

```
SQL> select group_number, operation, state, power, actual,
  2       sofar, est_work, est_rate, est_minutes from v$asm_operation;

GROUP_NUMBER OPERA STAT POWER ACTUA SOFAR EST_WORK EST_RATE EST_MINUTES
------------ ----- ---- ----- ----- ----- -------- -------- -----------
           1 REBAL RUN      8     8    16      605      118           4
```

About four minutes later, you check the status once more:

```
SQL> /
no rows selected
```

Finally, you can confirm the new disk configuration from the V$ASM_DISK and V$ASM_DISKGROUP views:

```
SQL> select group_number, disk_number, name,
  2    failgroup, create_date, path from v$asm_disk;

GROUP_NUMBER DISK_NUMBER NAME       FAILGROUP  CREATE_DA PATH
------------ ----------- ---------- ---------- --------- -------------
           1           2 D1C        D1FG3      15-JUN-04 /dev/raw/raw6
           2           2 D2C        FG3        15-JUN-04 /dev/raw/raw5
           2           1 D2B        FG2        15-JUN-04 /dev/raw/raw4
           2           0 D2A        FG1        15-JUN-04 /dev/raw/raw3
           1           1 DATA1_0001 DATA1_0001 13-JUN-04 /dev/raw/raw2
           1           0 DATA1_0000 DATA1_0000 13-JUN-04 /dev/raw/raw1

6 rows selected.

SQL> select group_number, name, type, total_mb, free_mb
  2       from v$asm_diskgroup;

GROUP_NUMBER NAME          TYPE    TOTAL_MB   FREE_MB
------------ ------------- ------ ---------- ----------
           1 DATA1         NORMAL      22521     20116
           2 DATA2         HIGH        18429     18279

SQL>
```

Note that the disk group is still normal redundancy, even though it has three failure groups. However, the I/O performance of **select** statements against objects in the disk group is improved due to additional copies of extents available in the disk group.

Other disk group **alter** commands are listed in Table 4-6.

EM Database Control and ASM Disk Groups

The EM Database Control can also be used to administer disk groups. For a database that uses ASM disk groups, the link Disk Groups under the Administration tab brings you to a login page

alter diskgroup command	Description
alter diskgroup ... drop disk	Removes a disk from a failure group within a disk group and performs an automatic rebalance
alter diskgroup ... drop ... add	Drops a disk from a failure group and adds another disk, all in the same command
alter diskgroup ... mount	Makes a disk group available to all instances
alter diskgroup ... dismount	Makes a disk group unavailable to all instances
alter diskgroup ... check all	Verifies the internal consistency of the disk group

TABLE 4-6. *Disk Group ALTER Commands*

for the ASM instance shown in Figure 4-21. Remember that authentication for an ASM instance uses operating system authentication only.

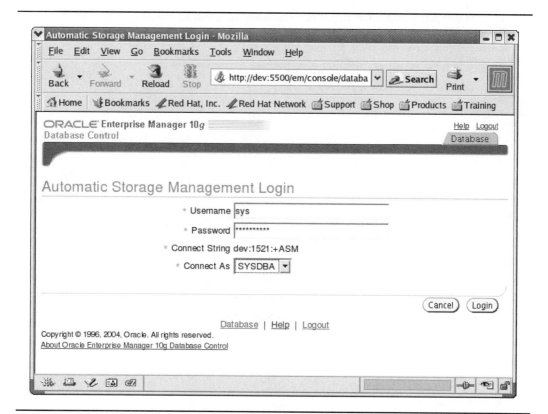

FIGURE 4-21. *EM Database Control ASM instance login page*

After authentication with the ASM instance, you can perform the same operations that you performed earlier in this chapter at the command line—mounting and dismounting disk groups, adding disk groups, adding or deleting disk group members, and so forth. Figure 4-22 shows the ASM administration page, whereas Figure 4-23 shows the statistics and options for the disk group DATA1.

Other EM Database Control ASM–related pages show I/O response time for the disk group, the templates defined for the disk group, the initialization parameters in effect for this ASM instance, and more.

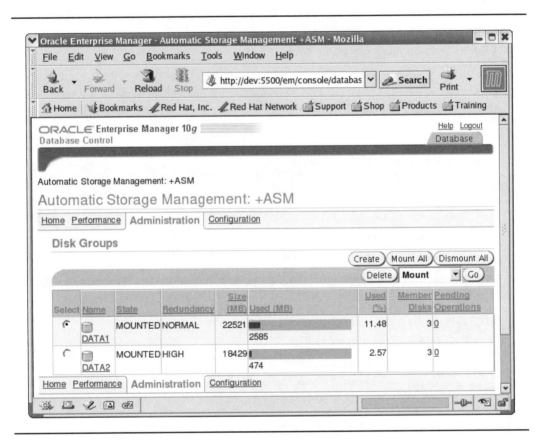

FIGURE 4-22. *EM Database Control ASM administration page*

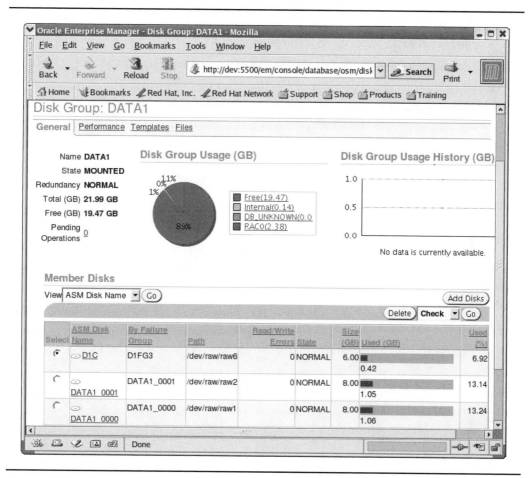

FIGURE 4-23. *EM Database Control ASM disk group statistics*

Migrating a Database to ASM

Because ASM files cannot be accessed via the operating system, Recovery Manager (RMAN) must be used to move database objects from a non-ASM disk location to an ASM disk group. The following steps should be used to move these objects.

1. Note the filenames of the control files and the online redo log files.

2. Shut down the database using NORMAL, IMMEDIATE, or TRANSACTIONAL.

3. Back up the database.

4. Edit the SPFILE to use OMF for all file destinations.

5. Edit the SPFILE to remove the CONTROL_FILES parameter.

6. Run the following RMAN script, substituting your specific filenames as needed:

```
STARTUP NOMOUNT;
RESTORE CONTROLFILE FROM '<controlfile location>';
ALTER DATABASE MOUNT;
BACKUP AS COPY DATABASE FORMAT
    '+<disk group destination>';
SWITCH DATABASE TO COPY;
SQL "ALTER DATABASE RENAME <logfile1>
         TO '+<disk group destination>' ";
# repeat for all log file members
ALTER DATABASE OPEN RESETLOGS;
```

7. Delete or archive the old database files.

Even though all files in this example are now ASM files, you can still create a non-ASM tablespace if, for example, you want to transport a tablespace to a database that does not use ASM.

PART
II
Database Management

CHAPTER
5

Developing and Implementing Applications

anaging application development can be a difficult process. From a DBA's perspective, the best way to manage the development process is to become an integral part of teams involved in the process. In this chapter, you will learn the guidelines for migrating applications into databases and the technical details needed for implementation, including the sizing of database objects.

This chapter focuses on the design and creation of applications that use the database. These activities should be integrated with the database-planning activities described in Chapter 3 and Chapter 4. The following chapters in this part of the book address the monitoring and tuning activities that follow the database creation.

Implementing an application in a database by merely running a series of **create table** commands fails to integrate the creation process with the other major areas (planning, monitoring, and tuning). The DBA must be involved in the application development process in order to correctly design the database that will support the end product. The methods described in this chapter will also provide important information for structuring the database monitoring and tuning efforts.

The first section of this chapter addresses overall design and implementation considerations that directly address performance. The following sections focus on implementation details such as resource management, using stored outlines, sizing tables and indexes, quiescing the database for maintenance activities, and managing packaged applications.

Tuning by Design: Best Practices

At least 50 percent of the time—conservatively—performance problems are designed into an application. During the design of the application and the related database structures, the application architects may not know all the ways in which the business will use the application data over time. As a result, there may be some components whose performance is poor during the initial release, whereas other problems will appear later as the business usage of the application changes.

In some cases, the fix will be relatively straightforward—changing an initialization parameter, adding an index, or rescheduling large operations. In other cases, the problem cannot be fixed without altering the application architecture. For example, an application may be designed to heavily reuse functions for all data access—so that functions call other functions, which call additional functions, even to perform the simplest database actions. As a result, a single database call may result in tens of thousands of function calls and database accesses. Such an application will usually not scale well; as more users are added to the system, the CPU burden of the number of executions per user will slow the performance for the individual users. Tuning the individual SQL statements executed as part of that application may yield little performance benefit; the statements themselves may be well-tuned already. Rather, it is the sheer number of executions that leads to the performance problem.

The following best practices may seem overly simplistic, but they are violated over and over in database applications, and those violations directly result in performance problems. There are always exceptions to the rules—the next change to your software or environment may allow you to violate the rules without affecting your performance. In general, though, following these rules will allow you to meet performance requirements as the application usage increases.

Do As Little As Possible

End users do not care, in general, if the underlying database structures are fully normalized to Third Normal Form or if they are laid out in compliance with object-oriented standards. Users want to perform a business process, and the database application should be a tool that helps that business process complete as quickly as possible. The focus of your design should not be the achievement of theoretical design perfection; it should always be on the end user's ability to do his or her job. Therefore, you should simplify the processes involved at every step in the application.

This can be a difficult point to negotiate with application development teams. If application development teams insist on perfectly normalized data models, DBAs should point out the number of database steps involved in even the simplest transaction. For example, inserts for a complex transaction (such as a line item for an invoice) may involve many code table lookups as well as multiple inserts. For a single user this may not present a problem, but with many concurrent users this design may lead to performance issues or locking issues. From a performance-planning perspective, inserts should involve as few tables as possible, and queries should retrieve data that is already stored in a format that is as close as possible to the final format requested by the users. Fully normalized databases and object-oriented designs tend to require a high number of joins during complex queries. Although you should strive to maintain a manageable data model, the first emphasis should be on the functionality of the application and its ability to meet the business's performance needs.

In Your Application Design, Strive to Eliminate Logical Reads

In the past, there was a heavy focus on eliminating physical reads—and although this is still a good idea, no physical reads occur unless logical reads require them.

Let's take a simple example. Select the current time from DUAL. If you select down to the second level, the value will change 86,400 times per day. Yet there are application designers who repeatedly perform this query, executing it millions of times per day. Such a query likely performs few physical reads throughout the day. Therefore, if you are focused solely on tuning the physical I/O, you would likely disregard it. However, it can significantly impact the performance of the application. How? By using the CPU resources available. Each execution of the query will force Oracle to perform work, using processing power to find and return the correct data. As more and more users execute the command repeatedly, you may find that the number of logical reads used by the query exceeds all other queries. In some cases, multiple processors on the server are dedicated to servicing repeated small queries of this sort. If multiple users need to read the same data, you should store it in a table or in a package variable.

Consider the following real-world example. A programmer wanted to implement a pause in a program, forcing it to wait 30 seconds between the completion of two steps. Because the performance of the environment would not be consistent over time, the programmer coded the routine in the following format (shown in pseudo-code):

```
perform Step 1
select SysDate from DUAL into a StartTime variable
begin loop
    select SysDate from DUAL in a CurrentTime variable;
    Compare CurrentTime with the StartTime variable value.
    If 30 seconds have passed, exit the loop;
        Otherwise repeat the loop, calculating SysDate again.
end loop
Perform Step 2.
```

Is this a reasonable approach? Absolutely not! It will do what the developer wanted, but at a significant cost to the application. What's more, there is nothing a database administrator can do to improve its performance. In this case, the cost will not be due to I/O activity—the DUAL table will stay in the instance's memory area—but rather due to CPU activity. Every time this program is run, by every user, the database will spend 30 seconds consuming as many CPU resources as the system can support. In this particular case the **select SysDate from DUAL** query accounts for over 40 percent of all the CPU time used by the application. All of that CPU time is wasted. Tuning the database initialization parameters will not solve the problem. Tuning the individual SQL statement will not help; the application design must be revised to eliminate the needless execution of commands. For instance, in this case the developer could have used a **sleep** command at the operating system level or within a program to enforce the same behavior without the database accesses.

For those who favor tuning based on the buffer cache hit ratio, this database has a hit ratio of almost 100 percent due to the high number of completely unnecessary logical reads without related physical reads. The buffer cache hit ratio compares the number of logical reads to the number of physical reads; if 10 percent of the logical reads require physical reads, the buffer cache hit ratio is 90 percent. Low hit ratios identify databases that perform a high number of physical reads; extremely high hit ratios such as found in this example may identify databases that perform an excessive number of logical reads. You must look beyond the buffer cache hit ratio to the commands that are generating the logical reads and the physical reads.

In Your Application Design, Strive to Avoid Trips to the Database

Remember that you are tuning an application, not a query. When tuning database operations, you may need to combine multiple queries into a single procedure so that the database can be visited once rather than multiple times for each screen. This bundled-query approach is particularly relevant for "thin-client" applications that rely on multiple application tiers. Look for queries that are interrelated based on the values they return, and see if there are opportunities to transform them into single blocks of code. The goal is not to make a monolithic query that will never complete; the goal is to avoid doing work that does not need to be done. In this case, the constant back-and-forth communication between the database server, the application server, and the end user's computer is targeted for tuning.

This problem is commonly seen on complex data-entry forms in which each field displayed on the screen is populated via a separate query. Each of those queries is a separate trip to the database. As with the example in the previous section, the database is forced to execute large numbers of related queries. Even if each of those queries is tuned, the burden from the number of commands—multiplied by the number of users—will consume the CPU resources available on the server. Such a design may also impact the network usage, but the network is seldom the problem—the issue is the number of times the database is accessed.

Within your packages and procedures, you should strive to eliminate unnecessary database accesses. Store commonly needed values in local variables instead of repeatedly querying the database. If you don't need to make a trip to the database for information, don't make it. That sounds simple, but you would be amazed at how often applications fail to consider this advice.

There is no initialization parameter that can make this change take effect. It is a design issue and requires the active involvement of developers, designers, DBAs, and application users in the application performance planning and tuning process.

For Reporting Systems, Store the Data the Way the Users Will Query It

If you know the queries that will be executed—such as via parameterized reports—you should strive to store the data so that Oracle will do as little work as possible to transform the format of the data in your tables into the format presented to the user. This may require the creation and maintenance of materialized views or reporting tables. That maintenance is, of course, extra work for the database to perform—but it is performed in batch mode and does not directly affect the end user. The end user, on the other hand, benefits from the ability to perform the query faster. The database as a whole will perform fewer logical and physical reads because the accesses to the base tables to populate and refresh the materialized views are performed infrequently when compared to the end-user queries against the views.

Avoid Repeated Connections to the Database

Opening a database connection may take more time than the commands you execute within that connection. If you need to connect to the database, keep the connection open and reuse the connection. Within the database you may be able to use stored procedures, packages, and other methods to maintain connections while you are performing your processing.

One application designer took normalization to the extreme, moving all code tables into their own database. As a result, most operations in the order-processing system repeatedly opened database links to access the code tables, thus severely hampering the performance of the application. Again, tuning the database initialization parameters is not going to lead to the greatest performance benefit; the application is slow by design.

Use the Right Indexes

In an effort to eliminate physical reads, some application developers create numerous indexes on every table. Aside from their impact on data load times, many of the indexes may never be needed to support queries. In OLTP applications, you should not use bitmap indexes; if a column has few distinct values, you should consider leaving it unindexed. The optimizer supports "skip-scan" index accesses, so it may choose an index on a set of columns even if the leading column of the index is not a limiting condition for the query.

Do It As Simply As Possible

Once you have eliminated the performance costs of unnecessary logical reads, unneeded database trips, unmanaged connections, and inappropriate indexes, take a look at the commands that remain.

Go Atomic

You can use SQL to combine many steps into one large query. In some cases, this may benefit your application—you can create stored procedures and reuse the code and thus reduce the number of database trips performed. However, you can take this too far, creating large queries that fail to complete quickly enough. These queries commonly include multiple sets of grouping operations, inline views, and complex multirow calculations against millions of rows.

If you are performing batch operations, you may be able to break such a query into its atomic components, creating temporary tables to store the data from each step. If you have an operation that takes hours to complete, you almost always can find a way to break it into smaller component parts. Divide and conquer the performance problem.

For example, a batch operation may combine data from multiple tables, perform joins and sorts, and then insert the result into a table. On a small scale, this may perform satisfactorily. On a large scale, you may have to divide this operation into multiple steps:

1. Create a work table. Insert rows into it from one of the source tables for the query, selecting only those rows and columns that you care about later in the process.

2. Create a second work table for the columns and rows from the second table.

3. Create any needed indexes on the work tables. Note that all the steps to this point can be parallelized—the inserts, the queries of the source tables, and the creation of the indexes.

4. Perform the join, again parallelized. The join output may go into another work table.

5. Perform any sorts needed. Sort as little data as possible.

6. Insert the data into the target table.

Why go through all these steps? Because you can tune them individually, you may be able to tune them to complete much faster individually than Oracle can complete them as a single command. For batch operations, you should consider making the steps as simple as possible. You will need to manage the space allocated for the work tables, but this approach can generate significant benefits to your batch-processing performance.

Eliminate Unnecessary Sorts

As part of the example in the preceding section, the sort operation was performed last. In general, sort operations are inappropriate for OLTP applications. Sort operations do not return any rows to the user until the entire set of rows is sorted. Row operations, on the other hand, return rows to the user as soon as those rows are available.

Consider the following simple test: Perform a full table scan of a large table. As soon as the query starts to execute, the first rows are displayed. Now, perform the same full table scan but add an **order by** clause on an unindexed column. No rows will be displayed until all the rows have been sorted. Why does this happen? Because for the second query Oracle performs a SORT ORDER BY operation on the results of the full table scan. Because it is a set operation, the set must be completed before the next operation is performed.

Now, imagine an application in which there are many queries executed within a procedure. Each of the queries has an **order by** clause. This turns into a series of nested sorts—no operation can start until the one before it completes.

Note that **union** operations perform sorts. If it is appropriate for the business logic, use a **union all** operation in place of a **union**, because a **union all** does not perform a sort (because it does not eliminate duplicates).

NOTE
*A **union all** operation does not eliminate duplicate rows from the result set, so it may generate different results than a **union**.*

Eliminate the Need to Query Undo Segments

When performing a query, Oracle will need to maintain a read-consistent image of the rows queried. If a row is modified by another user, the database will need to query the undo segment to see the row as it existed at the time your query began. Application designs that call for queries to frequently access data that others may be changing at the same time force the database to do more work—it has to look in multiple locations for one piece of data. Again, this is a design issue. DBAs may be able to configure the undo segment areas to reduce the possibility of queries encountering errors, but correcting the fundamental problem requires a change to the application design.

Tell the Database What It Needs to Know

Oracle's optimizer relies on statistics when it evaluates the thousands of possible paths to take during the execution of a query. How you manage those statistics can significantly impact the performance of your queries.

Keep Your Statistics Updated

How often should you gather statistics? With each major change to the data in your tables, you should reanalyze the tables. If you have partitioned the tables, you can analyze them on a partition-by-partition basis. As of Oracle Database 10g, you can use the Automatic Statistics Gathering feature to automate the collection of statistics. By default, that process gathers statistics during a maintenance window from 10 P.M to 6 A.M. each night and all day on weekends.

Because the analysis job is usually a batch operation performed after hours, you can tune it by improving sort and full table scan performance at the session level. If you are performing the analysis manually, increase the settings for the DB_FILE_MULTIBLOCK_READ_COUNT and PGA_AGGREGATE_TARGET parameters within your session prior to gathering the statistics. If you are not using PGA_AGGREGATE_TARGET, increase SORT_AREA_SIZE instead. The result will be enhanced performance for the sorts and full table scans the analysis performs.

Hint Where Needed

In most cases, the cost-based optimizer (CBO) selects the most efficient execution path for queries. However, you may have information about a better path. You may give Oracle a hint to influence the join operations, the overall query goal, the specific indexes used, or the parallelism of the query.

Maximize the Throughput in the Environment

In an ideal environment, there is never a need to query information outside the buffer cache; all of the data stays in memory all of the time. Unless you are working with a very small database, however, this is not a realistic approach. In this section, you will see guidelines for maximizing the throughput of the environment.

Use Disk Caching

If Oracle cannot find the data it needs in the buffer cache or PGA, it performs a physical read. But how many of the physical reads actually reach the disk? If you use disk caching, you may be able to prevent 90 percent or more of the access requests for the most-needed blocks. If the database buffer cache hit ratio is 90 percent, you are accessing the disks 10 percent of the time—and if the disk cache prevents 90 percent of those requests from reaching the disk, your effective hit ratio is 99 percent. Oracle's internal statistics do not reflect this improvement; you will need to work with your disk administrators to configure and monitor the disk cache.

Use a Larger Database Block Size

There is only one reason not to use the largest block size available in your environment for a new database: if you cannot support a greater number of users performing updates and inserts against a single block. Other than that, increasing the database block size should improve the performance of almost everything in your application. Larger database block sizes help keep indexes from splitting levels and help keep more data in memory longer. If you are experiencing buffer busy waits during inserts, increase the settings for the **freelists** parameter setting at the object level (if you are using Automatic Segment Space Management, the **freelists** parameter does not apply).

Store Data Efficiently at the Block Level

Oracle stores blocks of data in memory. It is in your best interest to make sure those blocks are as densely packed with data as possible. If your data storage is inefficient at the block level, you will not gain as much benefit as you can from the caches available in the database.

By default, the **pctused** parameter is set to 40 for all database blocks, and **pctfree** is set to 10. If you use the defaults, then as rows are added to the table, they will also be added to a block until that block is 90 percent full; at that point the block will be removed from the "freelist" and all new inserts will use other blocks in the table. Updates of the rows in the block will use the space reserved by the **pctfree** setting. Rows may then be deleted from the block, but the block will not be added back to the freelist until the space usage within the block drops below the **pctused** setting. This means that in applications that feature many **delete** and **insert** operations of rows, it is common to find many blocks using just slightly above the **pctused** value of each block. In that case, each block is just over 40 percent used, so each block in the buffer cache is only that full—resulting in a significant increase in the number of blocks requested to complete each command. If your application performs many **delete** and **insert** operations, you should consider increasing **pctused** so the block will be re-added to the freelist as quickly as possible.

NOTE
*If you use Automatic Segment Space Management, the **pctused** setting is managed by the database.*

If the **pctfree** setting is too low, updates may force Oracle to move the row (called a *migrated row*). In some cases, row chaining is inevitable, such as when your row length is greater than your database block size or when you have more than 254 columns in a table. When row chaining and migration occur, each access of a row will require accessing multiple blocks, thus impacting the number of logical reads required for each command. You can detect row chaining by analyzing the table and then checking its statistics via USER_TABLES.

Design to Throughput, Not Disk Space

Take an application that is running on eight 9GB disks and move it to a single 72GB disk. Will the application run faster or slower? In general, it will run slower because the throughput of the single disk is unlikely to be equal to the combined throughput of the eight separate disks. Rather than designing your disk layout based on the space available (a common method), design it based on the throughput of the disks available. You may decide to use only part of each disk. The remaining space on the disk will not be used by the production application unless the throughput available for that disk improves.

Avoid the Use of the Temporary Segments

Whenever possible, perform all sorts in memory. Any operation that writes to the temporary segments is potentially wasting resources. Oracle uses temporary segments when the SORT_AREA_SIZE parameter (or PGA_AGGREGATE_TARGET, if it is used) does not allocate enough memory to support the sorting requirements of operations. Sorting operations include index creations, **order by** clauses, statistics gathering, **group by** operations, and some joins. As noted earlier in this chapter, you should strive to sort as few rows as possible. When performing the sorts that remain, perform them in memory.

Favor Fewer, Faster Processors

Given the choice, use a small number of fast processors in place of a larger number of slower processors. The operating system will have fewer processing queues to manage and will generally perform better.

Divide and Conquer Your Data

If you cannot avoid performing expensive operations on your database, you can attempt to split the work into more manageable chunks. Often you can severely limit the number of rows acted on by your operations, substantially improving performance.

Use Partitions

Partitions can benefit end users, DBAs, and application support personnel. For end users, there are two potential benefits: improved query performance and improved availability for the database. Query performance may improve because of *partition elimination*. The optimizer knows what partitions may contain the data requested by a query. As a result, the partitions that will not participate are eliminated from the query process. Because fewer logical and physical reads are needed, the query should complete faster.

NOTE
The Partitioning Option is an extra-cost option for the Enterprise Edition of the database software.

The availability improves because of the benefits partitions generate for DBAs and application support personnel. Many administrative functions can be performed on single partitions, allowing the rest of the table to be unaffected. For example, you can truncate a single partition of a table. You can split a partition, move it to a different tablespace, or switch it with an existing table (so that the previously independent table is then considered a partition). You can gather statistics on one partition at a time. All these capabilities narrow the scope of administrative functions, reducing their impact on the availability of the database as a whole.

Use Materialized Views

You can use materialized views to divide the types of operations users perform against your tables. When you create a materialized view, you can direct users to query the materialized view directly or you can rely on Oracle's query rewrite capability to redirect queries to the materialized view. As a result, you will have two copies of the data—one that services the input of new transactional data, and a second (the materialized view) that services queries. As a result, you can take one of them offline for maintenance without affecting the availability of the other. Also, the materialized view can pre-join tables and pre-generate aggregations so user queries perform as little work as possible.

Use Parallelism
Almost every major operation can be parallelized—including queries, inserts, object creations, and data loads. The parallel options allow you to involve multiple processors in the execution of a single command, effectively dividing the command into multiple smaller coordinated commands. As a result, the command may perform better. You can specify a degree of parallelism at the object level and can override it via hints in your queries.

Test Correctly
In most development methodologies, application testing has multiple phases, including module testing, full system testing, and performance stress testing. Many times, the full system test and performance stress test are not performed adequately due to time constraints as the application nears its delivery deadline. The result is that applications are released into production without any way to guarantee that the functionality and performance of the application as a whole will meet the needs of the users. This is a serious and significant flaw and should not be tolerated by any user of the application. Users do not need just one component of the application to function properly; they need the entire application to work properly in support of a business process. If they cannot do a day's worth of business in a day, the application fails.

This is a key tenet regarding identifying the need for tuning: *If the application slows the speed of the business process, it should be tuned.* The tests you perform must be able to determine if the application will hinder the speed of the business process under the expected production load.

Test with Large Volumes of Data
As described earlier in this chapter, objects within the database function differently after they have been used for some time. For example, the **pctfree** and **pctused** settings may make it likely that blocks will be only half-used or rows will be chained. Each of these causes performance problems that will only be seen after the application has been used for some time.

A further problem with data volume concerns indexes. As a B*tree index grows in size, it may split internally—the level of entries within the index increases. As a result, you can picture the new level as being an index within the index. The additional level in the index increases the negative effect of the index on data load rates. You will not see this impact until *after* the index is split. Applications that work acceptably for the first week or two in production only to suddenly falter after the data volume reaches critical levels do not support the business needs. In testing, there is no substitute for production data loaded at production rates while the tables already contain a substantial amount of data.

Test with Many Concurrent Users
Testing with a single user does not reflect the expected production usage of most database applications. You must be able to determine if concurrent users will encounter deadlocks, data consistency issues, or performance problems. For example, suppose an application module uses a work table during its processing. Rows are inserted into the table, manipulated, and then queried. A separate application module does similar processing—and uses the same table. When executed at the same time, the two processes attempt to use each other's data. Unless you are testing with

multiple users executing multiple application functions simultaneously, you may not discover this problem and the business data errors it will generate.

Testing with many concurrent users will also help to identify areas in the application where users frequently use undo segments to complete their queries, thus impacting performance.

Test the Impact of Indexes on Your Load Times

Every **insert**, **update**, or **delete** of an indexed column may be slower than the same transaction against an unindexed table. There are some exceptions—sorted data has much less of an impact, for example—but the rule is generally true. The impact is dependent on your operating environment, the data structures involved, and the degree to which the data is sorted.

How many rows per second can you insert in your environment? Perform a series of simple tests. Create a table with no indexes and insert a large number of rows into it. Repeat the tests to reduce the impact of physical reads on the timing results. Calculate the number of rows inserted per second. In most environments you can insert tens of thousands of rows per second into the database. Perform the same test in your other database environments so you can identify any that are significantly different from the others.

Now consider your application. Are you able to insert rows into your tables via your application at anywhere near the rate you just calculated? Many applications run at less than 5 percent of the rate the environment will support. They are bogged down by unneeded indexes or the type of code design issues described earlier in this chapter. If your application's load rate decreases—say, from 40 rows per second to 20 rows per second—your tuning focus should not be solely on how that decrease occurred but also on how the application managed to get only 40 rows per second inserted in an environment that supports thousands of rows inserted per second.

Make All Tests Repeatable

Most regulated industries have standards for tests. Their standards are so reasonable that *all* testing efforts should follow them. Among the standards is that all tests must be repeatable. To be compliant with the standards, you must be able to re-create the data set used, the exact action performed, the exact result expected, and the exact result seen and recorded. Pre-production tests for validation of the application must be performed on the production hardware. Moving the application to different hardware requires retesting the application. The tester and the business users must sign off on all tests.

Most people, on hearing those restrictions, would agree that they are good steps to take in any testing process. Indeed, your business users may be expecting that the people developing the application are following such standards, even if they are not required by the industry. But are they followed? And if not, then why not? The two commonly cited reasons for not following such standards are time and cost. Such tests require planning, personnel resources, business user involvement, and time for execution and documentation. Testing on production-caliber hardware may require the purchase of additional servers. Those are the most evident costs—but what is the business cost of failing to perform such tests? The testing requirements for validated systems in some health industries were implemented because those systems directly impact the integrity of critical products such as the safety of the blood supply. If your business has critical components served by your application (and if it does not, then why are you building the application?), you must consider the costs of insufficient, rushed testing and communicate those potential costs to the business users. The evaluation of the risks of incorrect data or unacceptably slow performance must involve the business users. In turn, that may lead to an extended deadline to support proper testing.

In many cases, the rushed testing cycle occurs because a testing standard was not in place at the start of the project. If there is a consistent, thorough, and well-documented testing standard in place at the enterprise level when the project starts, the testing cycle will be shorter when it is finally executed. Testers will have known long in advance that repeatable data sets will be needed. Templates for tests will be available. If there is an issue with any test result, or if the application needs to be retested following a change, the test can be repeated. Also, the application users will know that the testing is robust enough to simulate the production usage of the application. If the system fails the tests for performance reasons, the problem may be a design issue (as described in the previous sections) or a problem with an individual query.

Standard Deliverables

How do you know if an application is ready to be migrated to a production environment? The application development methodology must clearly define, both in format and in level of detail, the required deliverables for each stage of the life cycle. These should include specifications for each of the following items:

- Entity relationship diagram

- Physical database diagram

- Space requirements

- Tuning goals for queries and transaction processing

- Security requirements

- Data requirements

- Query execution plans

- Acceptance test procedures

In the following sections, you will see descriptions of each of these items.

Entity Relationship Diagram

The *entity relationship (E-R) diagram* illustrates the relationships that have been identified among the entities that make up the application. E-R diagrams are critical for providing an understanding of the goals of the system. They also help to identify interface points with other applications and to ensure consistency in definitions across the enterprise.

Physical Database Diagram

A *physical database diagram* shows the physical tables generated from the entities and the columns generated from the defined attributes in the logical model. A physical database diagramming tool is usually capable of generating the DDL necessary to create the application's objects.

You can use the physical database diagram to identify tables that are most likely to be involved in transactions. You should also be able to identify which tables are commonly used together during a data entry or query operation. You can use this information to effectively plan the distribution of these tables (and their indexes) across the available physical devices to reduce the amount of I/O contention encountered.

In data warehousing applications, the physical database diagram should show the aggregations and materialized views accessed by user queries. Although they contain derived data, they are critical components of the data access path and must be documented.

Space Requirements

The space requirements deliverable should show the initial space requirements for each database table and index. The recommendations for the proper size of tables, clusters, and indexes are shown in the "Sizing Database Objects" section, later in this chapter.

Tuning Goals for Queries and Transaction Processing

Changes to the application design may have significant impact on the application's performance. Application design choices may also directly affect your ability to tune the application. Because application design has such a great effect on the DBA's ability to tune its performance, the DBA must be involved in the design process.

You must identify the performance goals of a system *before* it goes into production. The role of expectation in perception cannot be overemphasized. If the users have an expectation that the system will be at least as fast as an existing system, anything less will be unacceptable. The estimated response time for each of the most-used components of the application must be defined and approved.

It is important during this process to establish two sets of goals: reasonable goals and "stretch" goals. *Stretch goals* represent the results of concentrated efforts to go beyond the hardware and software constraints that limit the system's performance. Maintaining two sets of performance goals helps to focus efforts on those goals that are truly mission-critical versus those that are beyond the scope of the core system deliverables. In terms of the goals, you should establish control boundaries for query and transaction performance; the application performance will be judged to be "out of control" if the control boundaries are crossed.

Security Requirements

The development team must specify the account structure the application will use, including the ownership of all objects in the application and the manner in which privileges will be granted: All roles and privileges must be clearly defined. The deliverables from this section will be used to generate the account and privilege structure of the production application (see Chapter 10 for a full review of Oracle's security capabilities).

Depending on the application, you may need to specify the account usage for batch accounts separately from that of online accounts. For example, the batch accounts may use the database's autologin features, whereas the online users have to manually sign in. Your security plans for the application must support both types of users.

Like the space requirements deliverable, security planning is an area in which the DBA's involvement is critical. The DBA should be able to design an implementation that meets the application's needs while fitting in with the enterprise database security plan.

Data Requirements

The methods for data entry and retrieval must be clearly defined. Data-entry methods must be tested and verified while the application is in the test environment. Any special data-archiving requirements of the application must also be documented because they will be application specific.

You must also describe the backup and recovery requirements for the application. These requirements can then be compared to the enterprise database backup plans (see Chapter 12 for guidelines). Any database recovery requirements that go beyond the site's standard will require modifying the site's backup standard or adding a module to accommodate the application's needs.

Query Execution Plans

Execution plans are the steps that the database will go through while executing queries. They are generated via the **explain plan** or **set autotrace** command, as described in Chapter 8. Recording the execution plans for the most important queries against the database will aid in planning the index usage and tuning goals for the application. Generating them prior to production implementation will simplify tuning efforts and identify potential performance problems before the application is released. Generating the explain plans for your most important queries will also facilitate the process of performing code reviews of the application.

If you are implementing a third-party application, you may not have visibility to all the SQL commands the application is generating. As described in Chapter 9, you can use the STATSPACK utility to monitor the most resource-intensive queries performed between two points in time. You can take STATSPACK "snapshots" before and after a test period and then evaluate the execution paths for the most common or most resource-intensive queries during a test period. See Chapter 9 for details on STATSPACK implementation and the use of the repository introduced with Oracle Database 10g.

Acceptance Test Procedures

Developers and users should very clearly define what functionality and performance goals must be achieved before the application can be migrated to production. These goals will form the foundation of the test procedures that will be executed against the application while it is in the test environment.

The procedures should also describe how to deal with unmet goals. The procedures should very clearly list the functional goals that must be met before the system can move forward. A second list of noncritical functional goals should also be provided. This separation of functional capabilities will aid in both resolving scheduling conflicts and structuring appropriate tests.

NOTE
As part of acceptance testing, all interfaces to the application should be tested and their input and output verified.

Resource Management and Stored Outlines

You can use stored outlines to migrate execution paths between instances, and you can use the Database Resource Manager to control the allocation of system resources among database users. Stored outlines and resource management are important components in a managed development environment. The Database Resource Manager gives DBAs more control over the allocation of system resources than is possible with operating system controls alone.

NOTE
As of Oracle 10g, you can use SQL profiles to further refine the execution path selected.

Implementing the Database Resource Manager

You can use the Database Resource Manager to allocate percentages of system resources to classes of users and jobs. For example, you could allocate 75 percent of the available CPU resources to your online users, leaving 25 percent to your batch users. To use the Database Resource Manager, you will need to create resource plans, resource consumer groups, and resource plan directives.

Prior to using the Database Resource Manager commands, you must create a "pending area" for your work. To create a pending area, use the CREATE_PENDING_AREA procedure of the DBMS_RESOURCE_MANAGER package. When you have completed your changes, use the VALIDATE_PENDING_AREA procedure to check the validity of the new set of plans, subplans, and directives. You can then either submit the changes (via SUBMIT_PENDING_AREA) or clear the changes (via CLEAR_PENDING_AREA). The procedures that manage the pending area do not have any input variables, so a sample creation of a pending area uses the following syntax:

```
execute DBMS_RESOURCE_MANAGER.CREATE_PENDING_AREA();
```

If the pending area is not created, you will receive an error message when you try to create a resource plan.

To create a resource plan, use the CREATE_PLAN procedure of the DBMS_RESOURCE_ MANAGER package. The syntax for the CREATE_PLAN procedure is shown in the following listing:

```
CREATE_PLAN
     (plan                        IN VARCHAR2,
      comment                     IN VARCHAR2,
      cpu_mth                     IN VARCHAR2 DEFAULT
            'EMPHASIS',
      active_sess_pool_mth        IN VARCHAR2 DEFAULT
            'ACTIVE_SESS_POOL_ABSOLUTE',
      parallel_degree_limit_mth   IN VARCHAR2 DEFAULT
            'PARALLEL_DEGREE_LIMIT_ABSOLUTE',
      queueing_mth                IN VARCHAR2 DEFAULT
            'FIFO_TIMEOUT')
```

When you create a plan, give the plan a name (in the *plan* variable) and a comment. By default, the CPU allocation method will use the "emphasis" method, allocating CPU resources based on percentage. The following example shows the creation of a plan called DEVELOPERS:

```
execute DBMS_RESOURCE_MANAGER.CREATE_PLAN -
  (Plan => 'DEVELOPERS', -
   Comment => 'Developers, in Development database');
```

NOTE
The hyphen (-) character is a continuation character in SQL*Plus,
allowing a single command to span multiple lines.

In order to create and manage resource plans and resource consumer groups, you must have the ADMINISTER_RESOURCE_MANAGER system privilege enabled for your session. DBAs have this privilege with the **with admin option**. To grant this privilege to non-DBAs, you must execute the GRANT_SYSTEM_PRIVILEGE procedure of the DBMS_RESOURCE_MANAGER_PRIVS package. The following example grants the user MARTHA the ability to manage the Database Resource Manager:

```
execute DBMS_RESOURCE_MANAGER_PRIVS.GRANT_SYSTEM_PRIVILEGE -
  (grantee_name => 'Martha',   -
  privilege_name => 'ADMINISTER_RESOURCE_MANAGER', -
  admin_option => TRUE);
```

You can revoke MARTHA's privileges via the REVOKE_SYSTEM_PRIVILEGE procedure of the DBMS_RESOURCE_MANAGER package.

With the ADMINISTER_RESOURCE_MANAGER privilege enabled, you can create a resource consumer group using the CREATE_CONSUMER_GROUP procedure within DBMS_RESOURCE_MANAGER. The syntax for the CREATE_CONSUMER_GROUP procedure is shown in the following listing:

```
CREATE_CONSUMER_GROUP
      (consumer_group  IN VARCHAR2,
      comment         IN VARCHAR2,
      cpu_mth         IN VARCHAR2 DEFAULT 'ROUND-ROBIN')
```

You will be assigning users to resource consumer groups, so give the groups names that are based on the logical divisions of your users. The following example creates two groups—one for online developers and a second for batch developers:

```
execute DBMS_RESOURCE_MANAGER.CREATE_CONSUMER_GROUP -
  (Consumer_Group => 'Online_developers', -
  Comment => 'Online developers');

execute DBMS_RESOURCE_MANAGER.CREATE_CONSUMER_GROUP -
  (Consumer_Group => 'Batch_developers', -
  Comment => 'Batch developers');
```

Once the plan and resource consumer groups are established, you need to create resource plan directives and assign users to the resource consumer groups. To assign directives to a plan, use the CREATE_PLAN_DIRECTIVE procedure of the DBMS_RESOURCE_MANAGER package. The syntax for the CREATE_PLAN_DIRECTIVE procedure is shown in the following listing:

```
CREATE_PLAN_DIRECTIVE
      (plan                  IN VARCHAR2,
      group_or_subplan      IN VARCHAR2,
```

```
comment                     IN VARCHAR2,
cpu_p1                      IN NUMBER    DEFAULT NULL,
cpu_p2                      IN NUMBER    DEFAULT NULL,
cpu_p3                      IN NUMBER    DEFAULT NULL,
cpu_p4                      IN NUMBER    DEFAULT NULL,
cpu_p5                      IN NUMBER    DEFAULT NULL,
cpu_p6                      IN NUMBER    DEFAULT NULL,
cpu_p7                      IN NUMBER    DEFAULT NULL,
cpu_p8                      IN NUMBER    DEFAULT NULL,
active_sess_pool_p1         IN NUMBER    DEFAULT UNLIMITED,
queueing_p1                 IN NUMBER    DEFAULT UNLIMITED,
parallel_degree_limit_p1    IN NUMBER    DEFAULT NULL,
switch_group                IN VARCHAR2  DEFAULT NULL,
switch_time                 IN NUMBER    DEFAULT UNLIMITED,
switch_estimate             IN BOOLEAN   DEFAULT FALSE,
max_est_exec_time           IN NUMBER    DEFAULT UNLIMITED,
undo_pool                   IN NUMBER    DEFAULT UNLIMITED,
max_idle_time               IN NUMBER    DEFAULT NULL,
max_idle_time_blocker       IN NUMBER    DEFAULT NULL,
switch_time_in_call         IN NUMBER    DEFAULT NULL);
```

The multiple CPU variables in the CREATE_PLAN_DIRECTIVE procedure support the creation of multiple levels of CPU allocation. For example, you could allocate 75 percent of all your CPU resources (level 1) to your online users. Of the remaining CPU resources (level 2), you could allocate 50 percent to a second set of users. You could split the remaining 50 percent of resources available at level 2 to multiple groups at a third level. The CREATE_PLAN_DIRECTIVE procedure supports up to eight levels of CPU allocations.

The following example shows the creation of the plan directives for the Online_developers and Batch_developers resource consumer groups within the DEVELOPERS resource plan:

```
execute DBMS_RESOURCE_MANAGER.CREATE_PLAN_DIRECTIVE -
  (Plan => 'DEVELOPERS', -
   Group_or_subplan => 'Online_developers', -
   Comment => 'online developers', -
   Cpu_p1 => 75, -
   Cpu_p2=> 0, -
   Parallel_degree_limit_p1 => 12);

execute DBMS_RESOURCE_MANAGER.CREATE_PLAN_DIRECTIVE -
  (Plan => 'DEVELOPERS', -
   Group_or_subplan => 'Batch_developers', -
   Comment => 'Batch developers', -
   Cpu_p1 => 25, -
   Cpu_p2 => 0, -
   Parallel_degree_limit_p1 => 6);
```

In addition to allocating CPU resources, the plan directives restrict the parallelism of operations performed by members of the resource consumer group. In the preceding example, batch developers are limited to a degree of parallelism of 6, reducing their ability to consume system resources. Online developers are limited to a degree of parallelism of 12.

To assign a user to a resource consumer group, use the SET_INITIAL_ CONSUMER_GROUP procedure of the DBMS_RESOURCE_MANAGER package. The syntax for the SET_INITIAL_ CONSUMER_GROUP procedure is shown in the following listing:

```
SET_INITIAL_CONSUMER_GROUP
      (user          IN VARCHAR2,
       consumer_group IN VARCHAR2)
```

If a user has never had an initial consumer group set via the SET_INITIAL_ CONSUMER_ GROUP procedure, the user is automatically enrolled in the resource consumer group named DEFAULT_CONSUMER_GROUP.

To enable the Resource Manager within your database, set the RESOURCE_MANAGER_ PLAN database initialization parameter to the name of the resource plan for the instance. Resource plans can have subplans, so you can create tiers of resource allocations within the instance. If you do not set a value for the RESOURCE_MANAGER_PLAN parameter, resource management is not performed in the instance.

You can dynamically alter the instance to use a different resource allocation plan via the **set initial_consumer_group** clause of the **alter system** command. For example, you could create a resource plan for your daytime users (DAYTIME_USERS) and a second for your batch users (BATCH_USERS). You could create a job that each day executes this command at 6:00 A.M.:

```
alter system set initial_consumer_group = 'DAYTIME_USERS';
```

Then at a set time in the evening, you could change consumer groups to benefit the batch users:

```
alter system set initial_consumer_group = 'BATCH_USERS';
```

The resource allocation plan for the instance will thus be altered without needing to shut down and restart the instance.

When using multiple resource allocation plans in this fashion, you need to make sure you don't accidentally use the wrong plan at the wrong time. For example, if the database is down during a scheduled plan change, your job that changes the plan allocation may not execute. How will that affect your users? If you use multiple resource allocation plans, you need to consider the impact of using the wrong plan at the wrong time. To avoid such problems, you should try to minimize the number of resource allocation plans in use.

In addition to the examples and commands shown in this section, you can update existing resource plans (via the UPDATE_PLAN procedure), delete resource plans (via DELETE_PLAN), and cascade the deletion of a resource plan plus all its subplans and related resource consumer groups (DELETE_PLAN_CASCADE). You can update and delete resource consumer groups via the UPDATE_CONSUMER_GROUP and DELETE_CONSUMER_GROUP procedures, respectively. Resource plan directives may be updated via UPDATE_PLAN_DIRECTIVE and deleted via DELETE_PLAN_DIRECTIVE.

When you are modifying resource plans, resource consumer groups, and resource plan directives, you should test the changes prior to implementing them. To test your changes, create a pending area for your work. To create a pending area, use the CREATE_PENDING_AREA procedure of the DBMS_RESOURCE_MANAGER package. When you have completed your changes, use the VALIDATE_PENDING_AREA procedure to check the validity of the new set of plans, subplans, and directives. You can then either submit the changes (via SUBMIT_PENDING_AREA) or clear the changes (via CLEAR_PENDING_AREA). The procedures that manage the pending area do not have any input variables, so a sample validation and submission of a pending area uses the following syntax:

```
execute DBMS_RESOURCE_MANAGER.VALIDATE_PENDING_AREA();
execute DBMS_RESOURCE_MANAGER.SUBMIT_PENDING_AREA();
```

Switching Consumer Groups

Three of the parameters in the CREATE_PLAN_DIRECTIVE procedure allow sessions to switch consumer groups when resource limits are met. As shown in the previous section, the parameters for CREATE_PLAN_DIRECTIVE include Switch_Group, Switch_Time, and Switch_Estimate.

The Switch_Time value is the time, in seconds, a job can run before it is switched to another consumer group. The default Switch_Time value is NULL (unlimited). You should set the Switch_Group parameter value to the group the session will be switched to once the switch time limit is reached. By default, Switch_Group is NULL. If you set Switch_Group to the value 'CANCEL_SQL', the current call will be cancelled when the switch criteria is met. If the Switch_Group value is 'KILL_SESSION', the session will be killed when the switch criteria is met.

You can use the third parameter, Switch_Estimate, to tell the database to switch the consumer group for a database call before the operation even begins to execute. If you set Switch_Estimate to TRUE, Oracle will use its execution time estimate to automatically switch the consumer group for the operation instead of waiting for it to reach the Switch_Time value.

You can use the group-switching features to minimize the impact of long-running jobs within the database. You can configure consumer groups with different levels of access to the system resources and customize them to support fast jobs as well as long-running jobs—the ones that reach the switch limit will be redirected to the appropriate groups before they even execute.

Implementing Stored Outlines

As you migrate from one database to another, the execution paths for your queries may change. Your execution paths may change for several reasons:

- You may have enabled different optimizer features in the different databases.

- The statistics for the queried tables may differ in the databases.

- The frequency with which statistics are gathered may differ among the databases.

- The databases may be running different versions of the Oracle kernel.

The effects of these differences on your execution paths can be dramatic, and they can have a negative impact on your query performance as you migrate or upgrade your application. To minimize the impact of these differences on your query performance, you can use a feature called a *stored outline*.

A stored outline stores a set of hints for a query. Those hints will be used every time the query is executed. Using the stored hints will increase the likelihood that the query will use the same execution path each time. Hints decrease the impact of database moves on your query performance. You can view the outlines and related hints via the USER_OUTLINES and USER_OUTLINE_HINTS views.

To start creating hints for all queries, create custom categories of outlines and use the category name as a value of the CREATE_STORED_OUTLINES parameter in the database initialization file, as shown here:

```
CREATE_STORED_OUTLINES = development
```

In this example, outlines will be stored for queries within the DEVELOPMENT category.

You must have the CREATE ANY OUTLINE system privilege in order to create an outline. Use the **create outline** command to create an outline for a query, as shown in the following listing:

```
create outline YTD_SALES
    for category DEVELOPMENT
       on
select Year_to_Date_Sales
   from SALES
  where region = 'SOUTH'
    and period = 1;
```

NOTE
If you do not specify a name for your outline, the outline will be given a system-generated name.

If you have set CREATE_STORED_OUTLINES to a category name in your initialization file, Oracle will create stored outlines for your queries; using the **create outline** command gives you more control over the outlines that are created.

NOTE
*You can create outlines for DML commands and for **create table as select** commands.*

Once an outline has been created, you can alter it. For example, you may need to alter the outline to reflect significant changes in data volumes and distribution. You can use the **rebuild** clause of the **alter outline** command to regenerate the hints used during query execution, as shown next:

```
alter outline YTD_SALES rebuild;
```

You can also rename an outline via the **rename** clause of the **alter outline** command, as shown here:

```
alter outline YTD_SALES rename to YTD_SALES_REGION;
```

You can change the category of an outline via the **change category** clause, as shown in the following example:

```
alter outline YTD_SALES_REGION change category to DEFAULT;
```

To manage stored outlines, use the DBMS_OUTLN package, which gives you the following capabilities:

- Drop outlines that have never been used
- Drop outlines within a specific category
- Move outlines from one category to another
- Create outlines for specific statements
- Update outlines to the current version's signature

Each of these capabilities has a corresponding procedure within DBMS_OUTLN. To drop outlines that have never been used, execute the DROP_UNUSED procedure, as shown in the following example:

```
execute DBMS_OUTLN.DROP_UNUSED;
```

You can clear the "used" setting of an outline via the CLEAR_USED procedure. Pass the name of the outline as the input variable to CLEAR_USED:

```
execute DBMS_OUTLN.CLEAR_USED('YTD_SALES_REGION');
```

To drop all the outlines within a category, execute the DROP_BY_CAT procedure. The DROP_BY_CAT procedure has the name of the category as its only input parameter. The following example drops all the outlines within the DEVELOPMENT category:

```
execute DBMS_OUTLN.DROP_BY_CAT('DEVELOPMENT');
```

To reassign outlines from an old category to a new category, use the UPDATE_BY_CAT procedure, as shown in the following example:

```
execute OUTLN_PKG.UPDATE_BY_CAT -
  (oldcat => 'DEVELOPMENT', -
   newcat => 'TEST');
```

To drop a specific outline, use the **drop outline** command.

If you have imported outlines generated in an earlier release, use the UPDATE_SIGNATURES procedure of DBMS_OUTLN to ensure the signatures are compatible with the current release's computation algorithm.

Editing Stored Outlines
You can use DBMS_OUTLN_EDIT to edit the stored outlines. The procedures within DBMS_OUTLN_EDIT are detailed in the following table:

Procedure	Description
CHANGE_JOIN_POS	Changes the join position for the hint identified by outline name and hint number to the position specified. Inputs are *name, hintno,* and *newpos.*
CREATE_EDIT_TABLES	Creates outline editing tables in the user's schema.
DROP_EDIT_TABLES	Drops the outline editing tables in the user's schema.
GENERATE_SIGNATURE	Generates a signature for the specified SQL text.
REFRESH_PRIVATE_OUTLINE	Refreshes the in-memory copy of the outline, synchronizing it with the edits made.

NOTE
As of Oracle 10g, you no longer need to execute the CREATE_EDIT_TABLES procedure because the edit tables are available as temporary tables in the SYSTEM schema. The procedure is still available, however, for backward compatibility.

You can use private outlines, which are seen only within your current session. Changes made to a private outline do not affect any other users. To enable private outline editing, set the USE_PRIVATE_OUTLINES initialization parameter to TRUE. Use the REFRESH_PRIVATE_OUTLINE procedure to have your changes take effect for the in-memory versions of the outlines.

Using SQL Profiles
As of Oracle 10g, you can use SQL profiles to further refine the SQL execution plans chosen by the optimizer. SQL profiles are particularly useful when you are attempting to tune code that you do not have direct access to (for example, within a packaged application). The SQL profile consists of statistics that are specific to the statement, allowing the optimizer to know more about the exact selectivity and cost of the steps in the execution plan.

SQL profiling is part of the automatic tuning capability described in Chapter 8. Once you accept a SQL profile recommendation, it is stored in the data dictionary. As with stored outlines, you can use a category attribute to control its usage. See Chapter 8 for further details on the use of the automatic tools for detection and diagnosis of SQL performance issues.

Sizing Database Objects
Choosing the proper space allocation for database objects is critical. Developers should begin estimating space requirements before the first database objects are created. Afterward, the space requirements can be refined based on the actual usage statistics. In the following sections, you will see the space estimation methods for tables, indexes, and clusters. You'll also see methods for determining the proper settings for **pctfree** and **pctused**.

NOTE
*You can enable Automatic Segment Space Management when you create a tablespace; you cannot enable this feature for existing tablespaces. If you are using Automatic Segment Space Management, Oracle manages the **pctused**, **freelists**, and **freelist groups** parameters.*

Why Size Objects?

You should size your database objects for three reasons:

- To preallocate space in the database, thereby minimizing the amount of future work required to manage objects' space requirements

- To reduce the amount of space wasted due to overallocation of space

- To improve the likelihood of a dropped free extent being reused by another segment

You can accomplish all these goals by following the sizing methodology shown in the following sections. This methodology is based on Oracle's internal methods for allocating space to database objects. Rather than rely on detailed calculations, the methodology relies on approximations that will dramatically simplify the sizing process while simplifying the long-term maintainability of the database.

The Golden Rule for Space Calculations

Keep your space calculations simple, generic, and consistent across databases. There are far more productive ways to spend your work time than performing extremely detailed space calculations that Oracle may ignore anyway. Even if you follow the most rigorous sizing calculations, you cannot be sure how Oracle will load the data into the table or index.

In the following section, you'll see how to simplify the space-estimation process, freeing you to perform much more useful DBA functions. These processes should be followed whether you are generating the **default storage** values for a dictionary managed tablespace or the extent sizes for locally managed tablespaces.

NOTE
In an Oracle 10g database, you should be using locally managed tablespaces. If you have upgraded from a prior release that used dictionary-managed tablespaces, you should replace them with locally managed tablespaces.

The Ground Rules for Space Calculations

Oracle follows a set of internal rules when allocating space:

- Oracle only allocates whole blocks, not parts of blocks.

- Oracle allocates sets of blocks rather than individual blocks.

- Oracle may allocate larger or smaller sets of blocks depending on the available free space in the tablespace.

Your goal should be to work with Oracle's space-allocation methods instead of against them. If you use consistent extent sizes, you can largely delegate the space allocation to Oracle even in a dictionary-managed tablespace.

The Impact of Extent Size on Performance

There is no direct performance benefit gained by reducing the number of extents in a table. In some situations (such as in Parallel Query environments), having multiple extents in a table can significantly reduce I/O contention and enhance your performance. Regardless of the number of extents in your tables, they need to be properly sized.

Oracle reads data from tables in two ways: by RowID (usually immediately following an index access) and via full table scans. If the data is read via RowID, the number of extents in the table is not a factor in the read performance. Oracle will read each row from its physical location (as specified in the RowID) and retrieve the data.

If the data is read via a full table scan, the size of your extents can impact performance to a very small degree. When reading data via a full table scan, Oracle will read multiple blocks at a time. The number of blocks read at a time is set via the DB_FILE_MULTIBLOCK_READ_COUNT database initialization parameter and is limited by the operating system's I/O buffer size. For example, if your database block size is 8KB and your operating system's I/O buffer size is 128KB, you can read up to 16 blocks per read during a full table scan. In that case, setting DB_FILE_MULTIBLOCK_READ_COUNT to a value higher than 16 will not change the performance of the full table scans.

Your extent sizes should take advantage of Oracle's ability to perform multiblock reads during full table scans. For example, if your operating system's I/O buffer is 128KB, your extent sizes should be a multiple of 128KB.

Consider a table that has ten extents, each of which is 128KB in size. For this example, the operating system's I/O buffer size is 128KB. To perform a full table scan, Oracle must perform ten reads (because 128KB is the operating system I/O buffer size). If the data is compressed into a single 1280KB extent, Oracle still must perform ten reads to scan the table. Compressing the extents results in no gain in performance.

If the table's extent size is not a multiple of the I/O buffer size, the number of reads required for full table scans may increase. For the same 1280KB table, you could create eight extents that are 160KB each. To read the first extent, Oracle will perform two reads: one for the first 128KB of the extent, and a second read for the last 32KB of the extent (reads cannot span extents). To read the whole table, Oracle must therefore perform two reads per extent, or 16 reads. Reducing the number of extents from ten to eight increases the number of reads by 60 percent.

To avoid paying a performance penalty for your extent sizes, you must choose from one of the following strategies:

- Create extents that are significantly larger than your I/O size. If the extents are very large, very few additional reads will be necessary even if the extent size is not a multiple of the I/O buffer size.

- Set DB_FILE_MULTIBLOCK_READ_COUNT to take full advantage of the I/O buffer size for your operating system. Note that setting this too high may make the optimizer think that full table scans are more efficient than they actually are, resulting in changes to existing execution plans.

- If you must create small extents, choose extent sizes that are a multiple of the I/O buffer size for your operating system.

If the I/O buffer size for your operating system is 128KB, your pool of extent sizes from which to choose are 128KB, 256KB, 512KB, 1MB, and so on. You can further reduce the pool of extent sizes from which to choose.

Use a pool of extent sizes that meets the following criterion: *Every extent size will hold an integral multiple of every smaller extent size.* The simplest implementation of this rule is to create extent sizes that increase by doubling: 1MB, 2MB, 4MB, 16MB, 32MB. To reduce the number of extent sizes to manage, you can quadruple the values instead of doubling: 1MB, 4MB, 16MB, and so on. Use these values for your locally managed tablespaces or rely on their automatic extent-sizing feature.

Sizing the Objects

To effectively manage your space, all you need to do is select a set of space values that meet the criteria described in the preceding sections. Once the space allocations are finalized, separate them by tablespace. Here's an example:

```
create tablespace DATA_1M
datafile '/u01/oracle/VLDB/data_1m.dbf'
size 100M
extent management local uniform size 1M;

create tablespace DATA_MEDIUM
datafile '/u01/oracle/VLDB/data_4m.dbf'
size 400M
extent management local uniform size 4M;

create tablespace DATA_LARGE
datafile '/u01/oracle/VLDB/data_16m.dbf'
size 16000M
extent management local uniform size 16M;
```

In this example, three separate DATA tablespaces are created, with extent sizes of 1MB, 4MB, and 16MB. If you need to create a table 3MB in size, you can either create it with three 1MB extents in DATA_1M or with one 4MB extent in DATA_4M. A table that will grow to 10MB can be placed in DATA_4M.

As your tables grow in size, your default storage clauses will grow in a consistent fashion, following the space rules and your standards for extent sizes. DATA_64M would be next, followed by DATA_256M and DATA_1G. Use the same extent sizes across your databases to ease space management of your entire database environment.

As the extent sizes grow, the distribution of extent sizes across tablespaces will usually result in a separation of table types—small static tables will be isolated in the tablespaces with small extent sizes. Large transaction-processing tables (or their partitions) will be segregated to the large extent size tables, simplifying later management and tuning activities.

In the following sections you will see guidelines for estimations of the space usage for your objects. Because the target sizes (1MB, 4MB, 16MB, and so on) are not close together, the following estimations do not include highly detailed calculations.

NOTE
You can set the database block size at the tablespace level. You must set the block size during the tablespace creation, and you must have already created a buffer cache for the block size. Be sure the extent sizes you choose account for the largest block size in use in the database. Limiting the usage of nonstandard block sizes in the database will simplify cross-database maintenance and your sizing procedures.

Estimating Space Requirements for Tables

As of Oracle Database 10*g*, you can use the CREATE_TABLE_COST procedure of the DBMS_ SPACE package to estimate the space required by a table. The procedure determines the space required for a table based on attributes such as the tablespace storage parameters, the tablespace block size, the number of rows, and the average row length. The procedure is valid for both dictionary-managed and locally managed tablespaces.

There are two versions of the CREATE_TABLE_COST procedure (it is overloaded so you can use the same procedure both ways). The first version has four input variables: *tablespace_name, avg_row_size, row_count,* and *pct_free.* Its output variables are *used_bytes* and *alloc_bytes.* The second version's input variables are *tablespace_name, colinfos, row_count,* and *pct_free*; its output variables are *used_bytes* and *alloc_bytes.* Descriptions of the variables are provided in the following table:

Parameter	Description
tablespace_name	The tablespace in which the object will be created.
avg_row_size	The average length of a row in the table.
colinfos	The description of the columns.
row_count	The anticipated number of rows in the table.
pct_free	The **pctfree** setting for the table.
used_bytes	The space used by the table's data. This value includes the overhead due to the **pctfree** setting and other block features.
alloc_bytes	The space allocated to the table's data, based on the tablespace characteristics. This value takes the tablespace extent size settings into account.

For example, if you have an existing tablespace named USERS, you can estimate the space required for a new table in that tablespace. In the following example, the CREATE_TABLE_COST procedure is executed with values passed for the average row size, the row count, and the **pctfree** setting. The *used_bytes* and *alloc_bytes* variables are defined and are displayed via the DBMS_ OUTPUT.PUT_LINE procedure:

```
declare
    calc_used_bytes NUMBER;
    calc_alloc_bytes NUMBER;
begin
    DBMS_SPACE.CREATE_TABLE_COST (
        tablespace_name => 'USERS',
```

```
        avg_row_size => 100,
        row_count => 5000,
        pct_free => 10,
        used_bytes => calc_used_bytes,
        alloc_bytes => calc_alloc_bytes
    );
    DBMS_OUTPUT.PUT_LINE('Used bytes: '||calc_used_bytes);
    DBMS_OUTPUT.PUT_LINE('Allocated bytes: '||calc_alloc_bytes);
end;
/
```

The output of this PL/SQL block will display the used and allocated bytes calculated for these variable settings. You can easily calculate the expected space usage for multiple combinations of space settings prior to creating the table.

NOTE
*You must use the **set serveroutput on** command to enable the script's output to be displayed within a SQL*Plus session.*

Estimating Space Requirements for Indexes

As of Oracle Database 10g, you can use the CREATE_INDEX_COST procedure of the DBMS_SPACE package to estimate the space required by an index. The procedure determines the space required for a table based on attributes such as the tablespace storage parameters, the tablespace block size, the number of rows, and the average row length. The procedure is valid for both dictionary-managed and locally managed tablespaces.

For index space estimations, the input variables include the DDL commands executed to create the index and the name of the local plan table (if one exists). The index space estimates rely on the statistics for the related table. You should be sure those statistics are correct before starting the space-estimation process; otherwise, the results will be skewed.

The variables for the CREATE_INDEX_COST procedure are described in the following table:

Parameter	Description
Ddl	The **create index** command
used_bytes	The number of bytes used by the index's data
alloc_bytes	The number of bytes allocated for the index's extents
plan_table	The plan table to use (the default is NULL)

Because the CREATE_INDEX_COST procedure bases its results on the table's statistics, you cannot use this procedure until the table has been created, loaded, and analyzed. The following example estimates the space required for a new index on the BOOKSHELF table. The tablespace designation is part of the **create index** command passed to the CREATE_INDEX_COST procedure as part of the *ddl* variable value.

```
declare
    calc_used_bytes NUMBER;
    calc_alloc_bytes NUMBER;
```

```
begin
   DBMS_SPACE.CREATE_INDEX_COST (
      ddl => 'create index BOOK_CAT on BOOKSHELF '||
        '(CategoryName) tablespace BOOKS_INDEX',
      used_bytes => calc_used_bytes,
      alloc_bytes => calc_alloc_bytes
   );
   DBMS_OUTPUT.PUT_LINE('Used bytes = '||calc_used_bytes);
   DBMS_OUTPUT.PUT_LINE('Allocated bytes = '||calc_alloc_bytes);
end;
/
```

The output of the script will show the used and allocated bytes values for the proposed index.

Estimating the Proper pctfree

The **pctfree** value represents the percentage of *each* data block that is reserved as free space. This space is used when a row that has already been stored in that data block grows in length, either by updates of previously NULL fields or by updates of existing values to longer values.

There is no single value for **pctfree** that will be adequate for all tables in all databases. To simplify space management, choose a consistent set of **pctfree** values:

- For indexes whose key values are rarely changed: 2

- For tables whose rows seldom change: 2

- For tables whose rows frequently change: 10 to 30

Why maintain free space in a table or index even if the rows seldom change? Oracle needs space within blocks to perform block maintenance functions. If there is not enough free space available (for example, to support a large number of transaction headers during concurrent inserts), Oracle will temporarily allocate part of the block's **pctfree** area. You should choose a **pctfree** value that supports this allocation of space. To reserve space for transaction headers in insert-intensive tables, set the **initrans** parameter to a nondefault value. In general, your **pctfree** area should be large enough to hold several rows of data.

> **NOTE**
> *Oracle automatically allows up to 255 concurrent update transactions for any data block, depending on the available space in the block.*

Because **pctfree** is tied to the way in which updates occur in an application, determining the adequacy of its setting is a straightforward process. The **pctfree** setting controls the number of records that are stored in a block in a table. To see if **pctfree** has been set correctly, first determine the number of rows in a block. You can use the DBMS_STATS package to gather statistics. If the **pctfree** setting is too low, the number of chained rows will steadily increase. You can monitor the database's V$SYSSTAT view for increasing values of the "table fetch continued row" action; these indicate the need for the database to access multiple blocks for a single row.

NOTE
*When rows are moved due to inadequate space in the **pctfree** area, the move is called a* row migration. *Row migration will impact the performance of your transactions.*

NOTE
For indexes that will support a large number of inserts, pctfree may need to be as high as 50 percent.

Determining the Proper pctused

The **pctused** value determines when a used block is re-added to the list of blocks into which rows can be inserted. For example, consider a table that has a **pctfree** value of 20 and a **pctused** value of 50. When rows are inserted into the table, Oracle will keep 20 percent of each block free (for use by later updates of the inserted records). If you now begin to delete records from the block, Oracle will not automatically reuse the freed space inside the block. New rows will not be inserted into the block until the block's used space falls below its **pctused** percentage—in this case, 50 percent.

The **pctused** value, by default, is set to 40. If your application features frequent deletions and you use the default value for **pctused**, you may have many blocks in your table that are only 40 percent used.

For most systems, you can set **pctused** so that **pctused** plus **pctfree** equals 80. If your **pctfree** setting is 20 percent, for example, set your **pctused** value to 60 percent. That way, at least 60 percent of each block will be used, saving 20 percent of the block for updates and row extensions.

When creating tablespaces, you can enable Automatic Segment Space Management, in which case Oracle will manage the freelist dynamically. When Automatic Segment Space Management is enabled, you do not set the **pctused** setting.

Reverse Key Indexes

In a reverse key index, the values are stored backward—for example, a value of 2201 is stored as 1022. If you use a standard index, consecutive values are stored near each other. In a reverse key index, consecutive values are not stored near each other. If your queries do not commonly perform range scans and you are concerned about I/O contention in your indexes, reverse key indexes may be a tuning solution to consider. When sizing a reverse key index, follow the same method used to size a standard index, as shown in the prior sections of this chapter.

Sizing Bitmap Indexes

If you create a bitmap index, Oracle will dynamically compress the bitmaps generated. The compression of the bitmap may result in substantial storage savings. To estimate the size of a bitmap index, estimate the size of a standard (B*tree) index on the same columns using the methods provided in the preceding sections of this chapter. After calculating the space requirements for the B*tree index, divide that size by 10 to determine the most likely maximum size of a bitmap index for those columns. In general, bitmap indexes will be between 2 and 10 percent of the size of a comparable B*tree index. The size of the bitmap index will depend on the variability and number of distinct values in the indexed columns.

Sizing Index-Organized Tables

An index-organized table is stored sorted by its primary key. The space requirements of an index-organized table closely mirror those of an index on all of the table's columns. The difference in space estimation comes in calculating the space used per row, because an index-organized table does not have RowIDs.

The following listing gives the calculation for the space requirement per row for an index-organized table (note that this storage estimate is for the entire row, including its out-of-line storage):

```
Row length for sizing = Average row length
                      + number of columns
                      + number of long columns
                      + 2 header bytes
```

Enter this value as the row length when using the CREATE_TABLE_COST procedure for the index-organized table.

Sizing Tables That Contain Large Objects (LOBs)

LOB data (in BLOB or CLOB datatypes) is usually stored apart from the main table. You can use the **lob** clause of the **create table** command to specify the storage for the LOB data. In the main table, Oracle stores a **lob** locator value that points to the LOB data. When the LOB data is stored out of line, between 36 and 86 bytes of control data (the lob locator) remain inline in the row piece.

Oracle does not always store the LOB data apart from the main table. In general, the LOB data is not stored apart from the main table until the LOB data and the **lob** locator value total more than 4000 bytes. Therefore, if you will be storing short LOB values, you need to consider their impact on the storage of your main table. If your LOB values are less than 4000 characters, you may be able to use VARCHAR2 datatypes instead of LOB datatypes for the data storage.

Sizing Partitions

You can create multiple *partitions* of a table. In a partitioned table, multiple separate physical partitions constitute the table. For example, a SALES table may have four partitions: SALES_NORTH, SALES_SOUTH, SALES_EAST, and SALES_WEST. You should size each of those partitions using the table-sizing methods described earlier in this chapter. You should size the partition indexes using the index-sizing methods shown earlier in this chapter.

Using Temporary Tables

You can create temporary tables to hold temporary data during your application processing. The table's data can be specific to a transaction or maintained throughout a user's session. When the transaction or session completes, the data is truncated from the table.

To create a temporary table, use the **create global temporary table** option of the **create table** command. To delete the rows at the end of the transaction, specify **on commit delete rows**, as shown here:

```
create global temporary table MY_TEMP_TABLE
  (Name    VARCHAR2(25),
   Street  VARCHAR2(25),
```

```
City      VARCHAR2(25))
on commit delete rows;
```

You can then insert rows into MY_TEMP_TABLE during your application processing. When you commit, Oracle will truncate MY_TEMP_TABLE. To keep the rows for the duration of your session, specify **on commit preserve rows** instead.

From the DBA perspective, you need to know if your application developers are using this feature. If they are, you need to account for the space required by their temporary tables during their processing. Temporary tables are commonly used to improve processing speeds of complex transactions, so you may need to balance the performance benefit against the space costs. You can create indexes on temporary tables to further improve processing performance, again at the cost of increased space usage.

> **NOTE**
> *Temporary tables and their indexes do not acquire any space until the first **insert** into them occurs. When they are no longer in use, their space is deallocated.*

Supporting Tables Based on Abstract Datatypes

User-defined datatypes, also known as *abstract datatypes,* are a critical part of object-relational database applications. Every abstract datatype has related *constructor methods* users execute to manipulate data in tables. Abstract datatypes define the structure of data—for example, an ADDRESS_ TY datatype may contain attributes for address data, along with methods for manipulating that data. When you create the ADDRESS_TY datatype, Oracle will automatically create a constructor method called ADDRESS_TY. The ADDRESS_TY constructor method contains parameters that match the datatype's attributes, facilitating inserts of new values into the datatype's format. In the following sections, you will see how to create tables that use abstract datatypes, along with information on the sizing and security issues associated with that implementation.

You can create tables that use abstract datatypes for their column definitions. For example, you could create an abstract datatype for addresses, as shown here:

```
create type ADDRESS_TY as object
(Street   VARCHAR2(50),
City      VARCHAR2(25),
State     CHAR(2),
Zip       NUMBER);
/
```

Once the ADDRESS_TY datatype has been created, you can use it as a datatype when creating your tables, as shown in the following listing:

```
create table CUSTOMER
(Name     VARCHAR2(25),
Address   ADDRESS_TY);
```

When you create an abstract datatype, Oracle creates a constructor method for use during inserts. The constructor method has the same name as the datatype, and its parameters are the attributes of the datatype. When you insert records into the CUSTOMER table, you need to use the ADDRESS_TY datatype's constructor method to insert Address values, as shown here:

```
insert into CUSTOMER values
('Joe',ADDRESS_TY('My Street', 'Some City', 'ST', 10001));
```

In this example, the **insert** command calls the ADDRESS_TY constructor method in order to insert values into the attributes of the ADDRESS_TY datatype.

The use of abstract datatypes increases the space requirements of your tables by 8 bytes for each datatype used. If a datatype contains another datatype, you should add 8 bytes for each of the datatypes.

Using Object Views

The use of abstract datatypes may increase the complexity of your development environment. When you query the attributes of an abstract datatype, you must use a syntax that is not used against tables that do not contain abstract datatypes. If you do not implement abstract datatypes in all your tables, you will need to use one syntax for some of your tables and a separate syntax for other tables—and you will need to know ahead of time which queries use abstract datatypes.

For example, the CUSTOMER table uses the ADDRESS_TY datatype described in the previous section:

```
create table CUSTOMER
(Name      VARCHAR2(25),
Address    ADDRESS_TY);
```

The ADDRESS_TY datatype, in turn, has four attributes: Street, City, State, and Zip. If you want to select the Street attribute value from the Address column of the CUSTOMER table, you may write the following query:

```
select Address.Street from CUSTOMER;
```

However, this query will *not* work. When you query the attributes of abstract datatypes, you must use correlation variables for the table names. Otherwise, there may be an ambiguity regarding the object being selected. To query the Street attribute, use a correlation variable (in this case, "C") for the CUSTOMER table, as shown in the following example:

```
select C.Address.Street from CUSTOMER  C;
```

As shown in this example, you need to use correlation variables for queries of abstract datatype attributes *even if the query only accesses one table*. There are therefore two features of queries against abstract datatype attributes: the notation used to access the attributes and the correlation variables requirement. In order to implement abstract datatypes consistently, you may need to alter your SQL standards to support 100-percent usage of correlation variables. Even if you use correlation variables consistently, the notation required to access attribute values may cause problems as well, because you cannot use a similar notation on tables that do not use abstract datatypes.

Object views provide an effective compromise solution to this inconsistency. The CUSTOMER table created in the previous examples assumes that an ADDRESS_TY datatype already exists. But what if your tables already exist? What if you had previously created a relational database application and are trying to implement object-relational concepts in your application without rebuilding and re-creating the entire application? What you would need is the ability to overlay object-oriented (OO) structures such as abstract datatypes on existing relational tables. Oracle provides *object views* as a means for defining objects used by existing relational tables.

If the CUSTOMER table already exists, you could create the ADDRESS_TY datatype and use object views to relate it to the CUSTOMER table. In the following listing, the CUSTOMER table is created as a relational table, using only the normally provided datatypes:

```
create table CUSTOMER
(Name          VARCHAR2(25) primary key,
 Street        VARCHAR2(50),
 City          VARCHAR2(25),
 State         CHAR(2),
 Zip           NUMBER);
```

If you want to create another table or application that stores information about people and addresses, you may choose to create the ADDRESS_TY datatype. However, for consistency, that datatype should be applied to the CUSTOMER table as well. The following examples will use the ADDRESS_TY datatype created in the previous section.

You can create an object view based on the CUSTOMER table, using any datatype you have defined. To create an object view, use the **create view** command. Within the **create view** command, specify the query that will form the basis of the view. The code for creating the CUSTOMER_OV object view is shown in the following listing:

```
create view CUSTOMER_OV (Name, Address) as
select Name,
       ADDRESS_TY(Street, City, State, Zip)
  from CUSTOMER;
```

The CUSTOMER_OV view will have two columns: the Name and the Address columns (the latter is defined by the ADDRESS_TY datatype). Note that you cannot specify **object** as an option within the **create view** command.

Several important syntax issues are presented in this example. When a table is built on existing abstract datatypes, you select column values from the table by referring to the names of the columns (such as Name) instead of their constructor methods. When creating the object view, however, you refer to the names of the constructor methods (such as ADDRESS_TY) instead. Also, you can use **where** clauses in the query that forms the basis of the object view. You can therefore limit the rows that are accessible via the object view.

If you use object views, you as the DBA will administer relational tables the same way as you did before. You will still need to manage the privileges for the datatypes (see the following section of this chapter for information on security management of abstract datatypes), but the table and index structures will be the same as they were before the creation of the abstract datatypes. Using the relational structures will simplify your administration tasks while allowing developers to access objects via the object views of the tables.

You can also use object views to simulate the references used by row objects. Row objects are rows within an object table. To create an object view that supports row objects, you need to first create a datatype that has the same structure as the table, as shown here:

```
create or replace type CUSTOMER_TY as object
(Name           VARCHAR2(25),
 Street         VARCHAR2(50),
 City           VARCHAR2(25),
 State          CHAR(2),
 Zip            NUMBER);
/
```

Next, create an object view based on the CUSTOMER_TY type while assigning OID (object identifier) values to the records in CUSTOMER:

```
create view CUSTOMER_OV of CUSTOMER_TY
    with object identifier (Name) as
select Name, Street, City, State, Zip
    from CUSTOMER;
```

The first part of this **create view** command gives the view its name (CUSTOMER_OV) and tells Oracle that the view's structure is based on the CUSTOMER_TY datatype. An object identifier, also known as an *OID*, identifies the row object. In this object view, the Name column will be used as the OID.

If you have a second table that references CUSTOMER via a foreign key/primary key relationship, you can set up an object view that contains references to CUSTOMER_OV. For example, the CUSTOMER_CALL table contains a foreign key to the CUSTOMER table, as shown here:

```
create table CUSTOMER_CALL
(Name           VARCHAR2(25),
 Call_Number    NUMBER,
 Call_Date      DATE,
 constraint CUSTOMER_CALL_PK
     primary key (Name, Call_Number),
 constraint CUSTOMER_CALL_FK foreign key (Name)
    references CUSTOMER(Name));
```

The Name column of CUSTOMER_CALL references the same column in the CUSTOMER table. Because you have simulated OIDs (called *pkOIDs)* based on the primary key of CUSTOMER, you need to create references to those OIDs. Oracle provides an operator called MAKE_REF that creates the references (called pkREFs). In the following listing, the MAKE_REF operator is used to create references from the object view of CUSTOMER_CALL to the object view of CUSTOMER:

```
create view CUSTOMER_CALL_OV as
select MAKE_REF(CUSTOMER_OV, Name) Name,
        Call_Number,
        Call_Date
    from CUSTOMER_CALL;
```

Within the CUSTOMER_CALL_OV view, you tell Oracle the name of the view to reference and the columns that constitute the pkREF. You could now query CUSTOMER_OV data from within CUSTOMER_CALL_OV by using the DEREF operator on the Customer_ID column:

```
select DEREF(CCOV.Name)
  from CUSTOMER_CALL_OV CCOV
 where Call_Date = TRUNC(SysDate);
```

You can thus return CUSTOMER data from your query without directly querying the CUSTOMER table. In this example, the Call_Date column is used as a limiting condition for the rows returned by the query.

Whether you use row objects or column objects, you can use object views to shield your tables from the object relationships. The tables are not modified; you administer them the way you always did. The difference is that the users can now access the rows of CUSTOMER as if they are row objects.

From a DBA perspective, object views allow you to continue creating and supporting standard tables and indexes while the application developers implement the advanced object-relational features as a layer above those tables.

Security for Abstract Datatypes

The examples in the previous sections assumed that the same user owned the ADDRESS_TY datatype and the CUSTOMER table. What if the owner of the datatype is not the table owner? What if another user wants to create a datatype based on a datatype you have created? In the development environment, you should establish guidelines for the ownership and use of abstract datatypes.

For example, what if the account named DORA owns the ADDRESS_TY datatype, and the user of the account named GEORGE tries to create a PERSON_TY datatype? GEORGE executes the following command:

```
create type PERSON_TY as object
(Name       VARCHAR2(25),
 Address    ADDRESS_TY);
/
```

If GEORGE does not own the ADDRESS_TY abstract datatype, Oracle will respond to this **create type** command with the following message:

```
Warning: Type created with compilation errors.
```

The compilation errors are caused by problems creating the constructor method when the datatype is created. Oracle cannot resolve the reference to the ADDRESS_TY datatype because GEORGE does not own a datatype with that name.

GEORGE will not be able to create the PERSON_TY datatype (which includes the ADDRESS_TY datatype) unless DORA first grants him EXECUTE privilege on her type. The following listing shows this **grant**:

```
grant EXECUTE on ADDRESS_TY to George;
```

NOTE
You must also grant EXECUTE privilege on the type to any user who will perform DML operations on the table.

Now that the proper **grant**s are in place, GEORGE can create a datatype that is based on DORA's ADDRESS_TY datatype:

```
create or replace type PERSON_TY as object
(Name     VARCHAR2(25),
 Address  Dora.ADDRESS_TY);
/
```

GEORGE's PERSON_TY datatype will now be successfully created. However, using datatypes based on another user's datatypes is not trivial. For example, during **insert** operations, you must fully specify the name of the owner of each type. GEORGE can create a table based on his PERSON_TY datatype (which includes DORA's ADDRESS_TY datatype), as shown in the following listing:

```
create table GEORGE_CUSTOMERS
(Customer_ID  NUMBER,
 Person       PERSON_TY);
```

If GEORGE owned the PERSON_TY and ADDRESS_TY datatypes, an **insert** into CUSTOMER would use the following format:

```
insert into GEORGE_CUSTOMERS values
(1,PERSON_TY('SomeName',
   ADDRESS_TY('StreetValue','CityValue','ST',11111)));
```

This command will not work. During the **insert**, the ADDRESS_TY constructor method is used, and DORA owns it. Therefore, the **insert** command must be modified to specify DORA as the owner of ADDRESS_TY. The following example shows the corrected **insert** statement, with the reference to DORA shown in bold:

```
insert into GEORGE_CUSTOMERS values
(1,PERSON_TY('SomeName',
   Dora.ADDRESS_TY('StreetValue','CityValue','ST',11111)));
```

NOTE
In Oracle Database 10g, you can use a synonym for another user's datatype.

Whenever possible, limit the ability to create abstract datatypes to those users who will own the rest of the application schema objects.

NOTE
When you create a synonym, Oracle does not check the validity of the object for which you are creating the synonym. If you use **create synonym x for y**, *for example, Oracle does not check to make sure that "y" is a valid object name or valid object type. The validation of that object's accessibility via synonyms is only checked when the object is accessed via the synonym.*

In a relational-only implementation of Oracle, you grant the EXECUTE privilege on procedural objects, such as procedures and packages. Within the object-relational implementation of Oracle, the EXECUTE privilege is extended to cover abstract datatypes as well. The EXECUTE privilege is used because abstract datatypes can include *methods*—PL/SQL functions and procedures that operate on the datatypes. If you grant someone the privilege to use your datatype, you are granting the user the privilege to execute the methods you have defined on the datatype. Although DORA did not yet define any methods on the ADDRESS_TY datatype, Oracle automatically creates constructor methods that are used to access the data. Any object (such as PERSON_TY) that uses the ADDRESS_TY datatype uses the constructor method associated with ADDRESS_TY.

You cannot create public types, and you cannot create public synonyms for your types. Therefore, you will need to either reference the owner of the type or create the type under each account that can create tables in your database. Neither of these options is a simple solution to the problem of datatype management.

Indexing Abstract Datatype Attributes

In the preceding example, the GEORGE_CUSTOMERS table was created based on a PERSON_TY datatype and an ADDRESS_TY datatype. As shown in the following listing, the GEORGE_ CUSTOMERS table contains a normal column—Customer_ID—and a Person column that is defined by the PERSON_TY abstract datatype:

```
create table GEORGE_CUSTOMERS
(Customer_ID    NUMBER,
 Person         PERSON_TY);
```

From the datatype definitions shown in the previous section of this chapter, you can see that PERSON_TY has one column—Name—followed by an Address column defined by the ADDRESS_ TY datatype.

When referencing columns within the abstract datatypes during queries, updates, and deletes, specify the full path to the datatype attributes. For example, the following query returns the Customer_ ID column along with the Name column. The Name column is an attribute of the datatype that defines the Person column, so you refer to the attribute as Person.Name, as shown here:

```
select C.Customer_ID, C.Person.Name
  from GEORGE_CUSTOMERS C;
```

You can refer to attributes within the ADDRESS_TY datatype by specifying the full path through the related columns. For example, the Street column is referred to as Person.Address.Street, which fully describes its location within the structure of the table. In the following example, the City column is referenced twice—once in the list of columns to select and once within the **where** clause:

```
select C.Person.Name,
       C.Person.Address.City
  from GEORGE_CUSTOMERS C
 where C.Person.Address.City like 'C%';
```

Because the City column is used with a range search in the **where** clause, the optimizer may be able to use an index when resolving the query. If an index is available on the City column, Oracle can quickly find all the rows that have City values starting with the letter *C*, as requested by the query.

To create an index on a column that is part of an abstract datatype, you need to specify the full path to the column as part of the **create index** command. To create an index on the City column (which is part of the Address column), you can execute the following command:

```
create index I_GEORGE_CUSTOMERS$CITY
on GEORGE_CUSTOMERS(Person.Address.City);
```

This command will create an index named I_GEORGE_CUSTOMER$CITY on the Person.Address.City column. Whenever the City column is accessed, the optimizer will evaluate the SQL used to access the data and determine if the new index can be useful to improve the performance of the access.

When creating tables based on abstract datatypes, you should consider how the columns within the abstract datatypes will be accessed. If, like the City column in the previous example, certain columns will commonly be used as part of limiting conditions in queries, they should be indexed. In this regard, the representation of multiple columns in a single abstract datatype may hinder your application performance, because it may obscure the need to index specific columns within the datatype.

When you use abstract datatypes, you become accustomed to treating a group of columns as a single entity, such as the Address columns or the Person columns. It is important to remember that the optimizer, when evaluating query access paths, will consider the columns individually. You therefore need to address the indexing requirements for the columns even when you are using abstract datatypes. In addition, remember that indexing the City column in one table that uses the ADDRESS_TY datatype does not affect the City column in a second table that uses the ADDRESS_TY datatype. If there is a second table named BRANCH that uses the ADDRESS_TY datatype, then *its* City column will not be indexed unless you create an index for it.

Quiescing and Suspending the Database

You can temporarily quiesce or suspend the database during your maintenance operations. Using these options allows you to keep the database open during application maintenance, avoiding the time or availability impact associated with database shutdowns.

While the database is quiesced, no new transactions will be permitted by any accounts other than SYS and SYSTEM. New queries or attempted logins will appear to hang until you unquiesce the database. The quiesce feature is useful when performing table maintenance or complicated data maintenance. To use the quiesce feature, you must first enable the Database Resource Manager, as described earlier in this chapter. In addition, the RESOURCE_MANAGEMENT initialization parameter must have been set to TRUE when the database was started, and it must not have been disabled following database startup.

While logged in as SYS or SYSTEM (other SYSDBA privileged accounts cannot execute these commands), quiesce the database:

```
alter system quiesce restricted;
```

Any non-DBA sessions logged into the database will continue until their current command completes, at which point they will become inactive. In Real Application Clusters configurations, all instances will be quiesced.

To see if the database is in quiesced state, log in as SYS or SYSTEM and execute the following query:

```
select Active_State from V$INSTANCE;
```

The Active_State column value will be either NORMAL (unquiesced), QUIESCING (active non-DBA sessions are still running), or QUIESCED.

To unquiesce the database, use the following command:

```
alter system unquiesce;
```

Instead of quiescing the database, you can suspend it. A suspended database performs no I/O to its datafiles and control files, allowing the database to be backed up without I/O interference. To suspend the database, use the following command:

```
alter system suspend;
```

NOTE
Do not use this command unless you have put the database in hot backup mode.

Although the **alter system suspend** command can be executed from any SYSDBA privileged account, you can only resume normal database operations from the SYS and SYSTEM accounts. Use SYS and SYSTEM to avoid potential errors while resuming the database operations. In Real Application Clusters configurations, all instances will be suspended. To see the current status, use the following command:

```
select Database_Status from V$INSTANCE;
```

The database will be either SUSPENDED or ACTIVE. To resume the database, log in as SYS or SYSTEM and execute the following command:

```
alter system resume;
```

Supporting Iterative Development

Iterative development methodologies typically consist of a series of rapidly developed prototypes. These prototypes are used to define the system requirements as the system is being developed. These methodologies are attractive because of their ability to show the customers something tangible as development is taking place. However, there are a few common pitfalls that occur during iterative development that undermine its effectiveness.

First, effective *versioning* is not always used. Creating multiple versions of an application allows certain features to be "frozen" while others are changed. It also allows different sections of the application to be in development while others are in test. Too often, one version of the application is used for every iteration of every feature, resulting in an end product that is not adequately flexible to handle changing needs (which was the alleged purpose of the iterative development).

Second, the prototypes are not always thrown away. Prototypes are developed to give the customer an idea of what the final product will look like; they should not be intended as the foundation of a finished product. Using them as a foundation will not yield the most stable and flexible system possible. When performing iterative development, treat the prototypes as temporary legacy systems.

Third, the development/test/production divisions are clouded. The methodology for iterative development must very clearly define the conditions that have to be met before an application version can be moved to the next stage. It may be best to keep the prototype development completely separate from the development of the full application.

Finally, unrealistic timelines are often set. The same deliverables that applied to the structured methodology apply to the iterative methodology. The fact that the application is being developed at an accelerated pace does not imply that the deliverables will be any quicker to generate.

Iterative Column Definitions

During the development process, your column definitions may change frequently. You can drop columns from existing tables. You can drop a column immediately, or you can mark it as "unused," to be dropped at a later time. If the column is dropped immediately, the action may impact performance. If the column is marked as unused, there will be no impact on performance. The column can actually be dropped at a later time when the database is less heavily used.

To drop a column, use either the **set unused** clause or the **drop** clause of the **alter table** command. You cannot drop a pseudocolumn, a column of a nested table, or a partition key column.

In the following example, column Col2 is dropped from a table named TABLE1:

```
alter table TABLE1 drop column Col2;
```

You can mark a column as unused, as shown here:

```
alter table TABLE1 set unused column Col3;
```

Marking a column as unused does not release the space previously used by the column. You can also drop any unused columns:

```
alter table TABLE1 drop unused columns;
```

You can query USER_UNUSED_COL_TABS, DBA_UNUSED_COL, and ALL_UNUSED_COL_TABS to see all tables with columns marked as unused.

NOTE
Once you have marked a column as unused, you cannot access that column. If you export the table after designating a column as unused, the column will not be exported.

You can drop multiple columns in a single command, as shown in the following example:

```
alter table TABLE1 drop (Col4, Col5);
```

NOTE
*When dropping multiple columns, you should not use the **column** keyword of the **alter table** command. The multiple column names must be enclosed in parentheses, as shown in the preceding example.*

If the dropped columns are part of primary keys or unique constraints, you will also need to use the **cascade constraints** clause as part of your **alter table** command. If you drop a column that belongs to a primary key, Oracle will drop both the column and the primary key index.

If you cannot immediately arrange for a maintenance period during which you can drop the columns, mark them as unused. During a later maintenance period, you can complete the maintenance from the SYS or SYSTEM account.

Forcing Cursor Sharing

Ideally, application developers should use bind variables in their programs to maximize the reuse of their previously parsed commands in the shared SQL area. If bind variables are not in use, you may see many very similar statements in the library cache—queries that differ only in the literal value in the **where** clause.

Statements that are identical except for their literal value components are called *similar* statements. Similar statements can reuse previously parsed commands in the shared SQL area if the CURSOR_SHARING initialization parameter is set to SIMILAR or FORCE. In general, you should favor using SIMILAR over FORCE, because SIMILAR will allow for a new execution plan to be generated reflecting any histogram data known about the literal value.

Setting CURSOR_SHARING to EXACT (the default setting) reuses previously parsed commands only when the literal values are identical.

To use stored outlines with CURSOR_SHARING set to FORCE or SIMILAR, the outlines must have been generated with that CURSOR_SHARING setting in effect.

NOTE
Dynamic SQL commands are always parsed, essentially bypassing the value of the shared SQL area.

Managing Package Development

Imagine a development environment with the following characteristics:

- None of your standards are enforced.

- Objects are created under the SYS or SYSTEM account.

- Proper distribution and sizing of tables and indexes is only lightly considered.

- Every application is designed as if it were the only application you intend to run in your database.

As undesirable as these conditions are, they are occasionally encountered during the implementation of purchased packaged applications.

Properly managing the implementation of packages involves many of the same issues that were described for the application development processes in the previous sections. This section will provide an overview of how packages should be treated so they will best fit with your development environment.

Generating Diagrams

Most CASE tools have the ability to *reverse engineer* packages into a physical database diagram. Reverse engineering consists of analyzing the table structures and generating a physical database diagram that is consistent with those structures, usually by analyzing column names, constraints, and indexes to identify key columns. However, normally there is no one-to-one correlation between the physical database diagram and the entity relationship diagram. Entity relationship diagrams for packages can usually be obtained from the package vendor; they are helpful in planning interfaces to the package database.

Space Requirements

Most Oracle-based packages provide fairly accurate estimates of their database resource usage during production usage. However, they usually fail to take into account their usage requirements during data loads and software upgrades. You should carefully monitor the package's undo requirements during large data loads. A spare DATA tablespace may be needed as well if the package creates copies of all its tables during upgrade operations.

Tuning Goals

Just as custom applications have tuning goals, packages must be held to tuning goals as well. Establishing and tracking these control values will help to identify areas of the package in need of tuning (see Chapters 8 and 9).

Security Requirements

Unfortunately, many packages that use Oracle databases fall into one of two categories: either they were migrated to Oracle from another database system, or they assume they will have full DBA privileges for their object owner accounts.

If the packages were first created on a different database system, their Oracle port very likely does not take full advantage of Oracle's functional capabilities, such as sequences, triggers, and methods. Tuning such a package to meet your needs may require modifying the source code.

If the package assumes that it has full DBA authority, it must not be stored in the same database as any other critical database application. Most packages that require DBA authority do so in order to add new users to the database. You should determine exactly which system-level privileges the package administrator account actually requires (usually just CREATE SESSION and CREATE USER). You can create a specialized system-level role to provide this limited set of system privileges to the package administrator.

Packages that were first developed on non-Oracle databases may require the use of the same account as another Oracle-ported package. For example, ownership of a database account called SYSADM may be required by multiple applications. The only way to resolve this conflict with full confidence is to create the two packages in separate databases.

Data Requirements

Any processing requirements that the packages have, particularly on the data-entry side, must be clearly defined. These requirements are usually well documented in package documentation.

Version Requirements

Applications you support may have dependencies on specific versions and features of Oracle. If you use packaged applications, you will need to base your kernel version upgrade plans on the vendor's support for the different Oracle versions. Furthermore, the vendor may switch the optimizer features it supports—for example, requiring that your COMPATIBLE parameter be set to a specific value. Your database environment will need to be as flexible as possible in order to support these changes.

Because of these restrictions outside of your control, you should attempt to isolate the packaged application to its own instance. If you frequently query data across applications, the isolation of the application to its own instance will increase your reliance on database links. You need to evaluate the maintenance costs of supporting multiple instances against the maintenance costs of supporting multiple applications in a single instance.

Execution Plans

Generating execution plans requires accessing the SQL statements that are run against the database. The shared SQL area in the SGA maintains the SQL statements that are executed against the database (accessible via the V$SQL_PLAN view). Matching the SQL statements against specific parts of the application is a time-consuming process. You should attempt to identify specific areas whose functionality and performance are critical to the application's success and work with the package's support team to resolve performance issues. You can use the STATSPACK utility or the Automated Workload Repository (see Chapter 9) to gather all the commands generated during testing periods and then determine the explain plans for the most resource-intensive queries in that set. If the commands are still in the shared SQL area, you can see the statistics via V$SQL and the explain plan via V$SQL_PLAN.

Acceptance Test Procedures

Purchased packages should be held to the same functional requirements that custom applications must meet. The acceptance test procedures should be developed before the package has been selected; they can be generated from the package-selection criteria. By testing in this manner, you will be testing for the functionality you need rather than what the package developers thought you wanted.

Be sure to specify what your options are in the event the package fails its acceptance test for functional or performance reasons. Critical success factors for the application should not be overlooked just because it is a purchased application.

The Testing Environment

When establishing a testing environment, follow these guidelines:

- It must be larger than your production environment. You need to be able to forecast future performance.

- It must contain known data sets, explain plans, performance results, and data result sets.

- It must be used for each release of the database and tools, as well as for new features.

- It must support the generation of multiple test conditions to enable the evaluation of the features' business costs. You do not want to have to rely on point analysis of results; ideally, you can determine the cost/benefit curves of a feature as the database grows in size.

- It must be flexible enough to allow you to evaluate different licensing cost options.

- It must be actively used as a part of your technology implementation methodology.

When testing transaction performance, be sure to track the incremental load rate over time. In general, the indexes on a table will slow the performance of loads when they reach a second internal level. See Chapter 8 for details on indexes and load performance.

When testing, your sample queries should represent each of the following groups:

- Queries that perform joins, including merge joins, nested loops, outer joins, and hash joins

- Queries that use database links

- DML that uses database links

- Each type of DML statement (**insert**, **update**, and **delete** statements)

- Each major type of DDL statement, including table creations, index rebuilds, and grants

- Queries that use Parallel Query, if that option is in use in your environment

The sample set should not be fabricated; it should represent your operations, and it must be repeatable. Generating the sample set should involve reviewing your major groups of operations as well as the OLTP operations executed by your users. The result will not reflect every action within the database, but will allow you to be aware of the implications of upgrades and thus allow you to mitigate your risk and make better decisions about implementing new options.

CHAPTER
6

Monitoring
Space Usage

good DBA has a toolset in place to monitor the database, both proactively monitoring various aspects of the database, such as transaction load, security enforcement, space management, and performance monitoring, and effectively reacting to any potentially disastrous system problems. Transaction management, performance tuning, memory management, and database security and auditing are covered in Chapters 7, 8, 9, and 10. In this chapter, we'll address how a DBA can effectively and efficiently manage the disk space used by database objects in the different types of tablespaces: the SYSTEM tablespace, the SYSAUX tablespace, temporary tablespaces, undo tablespaces, and tablespaces of different sizes.

To reduce the amount of time it takes to manages disk space, it is important for the DBA to understand how the applications will be using the database as well as to provide guidance during the design of the database application. Designing and implementing the database application, including tablespace layouts and expected growth of the database, have been covered in Chapters 3, 4, and 5.

In this chapter, we'll also provide some scripts that need not much more than SQL*Plus and the knowledge to interpret the results. These scripts are good for a quick look at the database's health at a given point in time—for example, to see if there is enough disk space to handle a big SQL*Loader job that evening or to diagnose some response-time issues for queries that normally run quickly.

Oracle provides a number of built-in packages to help the busy DBA manage space and diagnose problems. For example, Oracle 10g Segment Advisor helps to determine if a database object has space available for reuse based on how much fragmentation exists in the object. Other features of Oracle, such as Resumable Space Allocation, allow a long-running operation that runs out of disk space to be suspended until the DBA can intervene and allocate enough additional disk space to complete the operation. As a result, the long-running job will not have to be restarted from the beginning.

We'll also cover some of the key data dictionary and dynamic performance views that give us a close look at the structure of the database and a way to optimize space usage. Many of the scripts provided in this chapter use these views.

At the end of this chapter, we'll cover two different methods for automating some of the scripts and Oracle tools: using the Oracle 10g DBMS_SCHEDULER built-in package as well as using the Oracle Enterprise Manager (OEM) infrastructure.

Space usage for tablespaces will be the primary focus in this chapter, along with the objects contained within the tablespaces. Other database files, such as control files and redo log files, take up disk space, but as a percentage of the total space used by a database they are small. We will, however, briefly consider how archived log files are managed because the number of archived log files will increase indefinitely at a pace proportional to how much DML activity occurs in the database. Therefore, a good plan for managing archived log files will help keep disk space usage under control.

Common Space Management Problems

Space management problems generally fall into one of three categories: running out of space in a regular tablespace, not having enough undo space for long-running queries that need a consistent "before" image of the tables, and insufficient space for temporary segments. Although we may still have some fragmentation issues within a database object such as a table or index, locally managed tablespaces solve the problem of tablespace fragmentation.

We will address each of these three problem areas by using the techniques described in the following sections.

Running Out of Free Space in a Tablespace

If a tablespace is not defined with the AUTOEXTEND attribute, then the total amount of space in all the datafiles that comprise the tablespace limits the amount of data that can be stored in the tablespace. If the AUTOEXTEND attribute is defined, then one or more of the datafiles that comprise the tablespace will grow to accommodate the requests for new segments or the growth of existing segments. Even with the AUTOEXTEND attribute, the amount of space in the tablespace is ultimately limited by the amount of disk space on the physical disk drive or storage group.

The conclusion to be reached here is that we want to monitor the free and used space within a tablespace to detect trends in space usage over time, and as a result be proactive in making sure that enough space is available for future space requests.

Insufficient Space for Temporary Segments

A *temporary segment* stores intermediate results for database operations such as sorts, index builds, **distinct** queries, **union** queries, or any other operation that necessitates a sort/merge operation that cannot be performed in memory. Temporary segments should be allocated in a temporary tablespace, which we introduced in Chapter 1. Under no circumstances should the SYSTEM tablespace be used for temporary segments; when the database is created, a non-SYSTEM tablespace should be specified as a default temporary tablespace for users who are not otherwise assigned a temporary tablespace. If the SYSTEM tablespace is locally managed, a separate temporary tablespace must be defined when the database is created.

When there is not enough space available in the user's default temporary tablespace, and either the tablespace cannot be autoextended or AUTOEXTEND is disabled, the user's query or DML statement fails.

Too Much or Too Little Undo Space Allocated

As of Oracle9*i*, undo tablespaces have simplified the management of rollback information by managing undo information automatically within the tablespace. The DBA no longer has to define the number and size of the rollback segments for the kinds of activity occurring in the database. As of Oracle 10*g*, manual rollback management has been deprecated.

Not only does an undo segment allow a rollback of an uncommitted transaction, it provides for read consistency of long-running queries that begin before inserts, updates, and deletes occur on a table. The amount of undo space available for providing read consistency is under the control of the DBA and is specified as the number of seconds that Oracle will attempt to guarantee that "before" image data is available for long-running queries.

As with temporary tablespaces, we want to make sure we have enough space allocated in an undo tablespace for peak demands without allocating more than is needed. As with any tablespace, we can use the AUTOEXTEND option when creating the tablespace to allow for unexpected growth of the tablespace without reserving too much disk space up front.

Undo segment management is discussed in detail in Chapter 7, whereas the tools to help size the undo tablespaces are discussed later in this chapter.

Fragmented Tablespaces and Segments

As of Oracle8*i*, a tablespace that is locally managed uses bitmaps to keep track of free space, which, in addition to eliminating the contention on the data dictionary, eliminates wasted space because all extents are either the same size (with uniform extent allocation) or are multiples of the smallest size (with autoallocation). For migrating from a dictionary managed tablespace, we will review an example that converts a dictionary managed tablespace to a locally managed tablespace. In a default installation of Oracle 10*g* using the Database Creation Assistant (DBCA), all tablespaces, including the SYSTEM and SYSAUX tablespaces, are created as locally managed tablespaces.

Creating a tablespace that is locally managed is as easy as adding a clause to the **create tablespace** statement:

```
SQL> create tablespace USERS2
  2         datafile 'F:\ORACLE\ORADATA\OEMREP\USERS02.DBF'
  3         size 25M autoextend on next 25M maxsize 100M
  4         extent management local uniform size 4M
  5         segment space management auto;
Tablespace created.
```

The tablespace will be created with an initial size of 25MB, and it can grow as large as 100MB; extents will be locally managed with a bitmap, and every extent in this tablespace will be exactly 4MB in size. Space within each segment (table or index) will be managed automatically with a bitmap instead of freelists.

Table and index segments may contain a lot of free space due to update and delete statements. As a result, a lot of unused space can be reclaimed by using some of the scripts we provide later in this chapter, as well as by using the Oracle Segment Advisor.

Oracle Segments, Extents, and Blocks

In Chapter 1, we gave you an overview of tablespaces and the logical structures contained within them. We also briefly presented datafiles, allocated at the operating system level, as the building blocks for tablespaces. Being able to effectively manage disk space in the database requires an in-depth knowledge of tablespaces and datafiles, as well as the components of the segments stored within the tablespaces, such as tables and indexes. At the lowest level, a tablespace segment consists of one or more extents, each extent comprising one or more data blocks. Figure 6.1 shows the relationship between segments, extents, and blocks in an Oracle database.

In the next sections, we'll cover some of the details of data blocks, extents, and segments with the focus on space management.

Data Blocks

A *data block* is the smallest unit of storage in the database. Ideally, an Oracle block is a multiple of the operating system block to ensure efficient I/O operations. The default block size for the database is specified with the DB_BLOCK_SIZE initialization parameter; this block size is used for the SYSTEM, TEMP, and SYSAUX tablespaces at database creation and cannot be changed without re-creating the database.

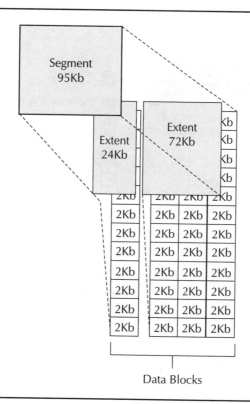

FIGURE 6-1.   *Oracle segments, extents, and blocks*

The format for a data block is presented in Figure 6-2.

Every data block contains a *header* that specifies what kind of data is in the block—data or index. The *table directory* section has information about the table with rows in the block; a block can have rows from only one table or entries from only one index, unless the table is a clustered table, in which case the table directory identifies all the tables with rows in this block. The *row directory* provides details of the specific rows of the table or index entries in the block.

The space for the header, table directory, and row directory is a very small percentage of the space allocated for a block; our focus, then, is on the *free space* and *row data* within the block.

Within a newly allocated block, free space is available for new rows and updates to existing rows; the updates may increase or decrease the space allocated for the row if there are varying-length columns in the row or a non-NULL value is changed to a NULL value, or vice versa. Space is available within a block for new inserts until there is less than a certain percentage of space available in the block defined by the PCTFREE parameter, specified when the segment is created. Once there is less than PCTFREE space in the block, no inserts are allowed. If freelists are used to manage space within the blocks of a segment, then new inserts are allowed on the table when free space within the block falls below PCTUSED.

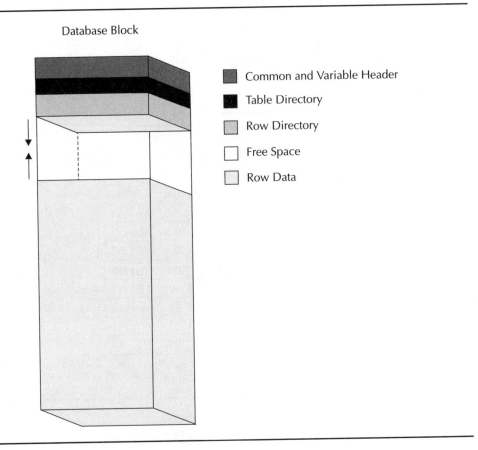

Database Block

- Common and Variable Header
- Table Directory
- Row Directory
- Free Space
- Row Data

FIGURE 6-2. *Contents of an Oracle data block*

A row may span more than one block if the row size is greater than the block size or an updated row no longer fits into the original block. In the first case, a row that is too big for a block is stored in a *chain* of blocks; this may be unavoidable if a row contains columns that exceed even the largest block size allowed, which in Oracle 10*g* is 32KB.

In the second case, an update to a row in a block may no longer fit in the original block, and as a result Oracle will *migrate* the data for the entire row to a new block and leave a pointer in the first block to point to the location in the second block where the updated row is stored. As you may infer, a segment with many migrated rows may cause I/O performance problems because the number of blocks required to satisfy a query can double. In some cases, adjusting the value of PCTFREE or rebuilding the table may result in better space utilization and I/O performance. More tips on how to improve I/O performance can be found in Chapter 8.

Extents

An *extent* is the next level of logical space allocation in a database; it is a specific number of blocks allocated for a specific type of object, such as a table or index. An extent is the minimum number of blocks allocated at one time; when the space in an extent is full, another extent is allocated.

When a table is created, an *initial* extent is allocated. Once the space is used in the initial extent, *incremental* extents are allocated. In a locally managed tablespace, these subsequent extents can either be the same size (using the UNIFORM keyword when the tablespace is created) or optimally sized by Oracle (AUTOALLOCATE). For extents that are optimally sized, Oracle starts with a minimum extent size of 64KB, and increases the size of subsequent extents as multiples of the initial extent as the segment grows. In this way, fragmentation of the tablespace is virtually eliminated.

When the extents are sized automatically by Oracle, the storage parameters INITIAL, NEXT, PCTINCREASE, and MINEXTENTS are used as a guideline, along with Oracle's internal algorithm, to determine the best extent sizes. In the following example, a table created in a tablespace that has AUTOALLOCATE enabled does not use the storage parameters specified in the **create table** statement:

```
SQL> create table aalc (c1 char(2000))
  2  storage (initial 1m next 2m pctincrease 50);

Table created.

SQL> begin
  2      for i in 1..3000 loop
  3          insert into aalc values ('a');
  4      end loop;
  5  end;
  6  /

PL/SQL procedure successfully completed.

SQL>  select segment_name, extent_id, bytes, blocks
  2       from user_extents where segment_name = 'aalc';
```

SEGMENT_NAME	EXTENT_ID	BYTES	BLOCKS
aalc	0	65536	8
aalc	1	65536	8
. . .			
aalc	15	65536	8
aalc	16	1048576	128
. . .			
aalc	22	1048576	128

```
23 rows selected.
```

Unless a table is truncated or the table is dropped, any blocks allocated to an extent remain allocated for the table, even if all rows have been deleted from the table. The maximum number of blocks ever allocated for a table is known as the *high water mark (HWM)*.

Segments

Groups of extents are allocated for a single *segment*. A segment must be wholly contained within one and only one tablespace. Every segment represents one and only one type of database object, such as a table, a partition of a partitioned table, an index, or a temporary segment. For partitioned tables, every partition resides in its own segment; however, a cluster (with two or more tables) resides within a single segment. Similarly, a partitioned index consists of one segment for each index partition.

Temporary segments are allocated in a number of scenarios. When a sort operation cannot fit in memory, such as a **select** statement that needs to sort the data to perform a **distinct**, **group by**, or **union** operation, a temporary segment is allocated to hold the intermediate results of the sort. Index creation also typically requires the creation of a temporary segment. Because allocation and deallocation of temporary segments occurs often, it is highly desirable to create a tablespace specifically to hold temporary segments. This helps to distribute the I/O required for a given operation, and it reduces the possibility that fragmentation may occur in other tablespaces due to the allocation and deallocation of temporary segments. When the database is created, a *default temporary tablespace* can be created for any new users who do not have a specific temporary tablespace assigned; if the SYSTEM tablespace is locally managed, a separate temporary tablespace must be created to hold temporary segments.

How space is managed within a segment depends on how the tablespace containing the block is created. If the tablespace is dictionary managed, the segment uses freelists to manage space within the data blocks; if the tablespace is locally managed, space in segments can be managed with either freelists or bitmaps. Oracle strongly recommends that all new tablespaces be created as locally managed and that free space within segments be managed automatically with bitmaps. Automatic segment space management allows more concurrent access to the bitmap lists in a segment compared to freelists; in addition, tables that have widely varying row sizes make more efficient use of space in segments that are automatically managed.

If a segment is created with automatic segment space management, bitmaps are used to manage the space within the segment. As a result, the **pctused**, **freelist**, and **freelist groups** keywords within a **create table** or **create index** statement are ignored. The three-level bitmap structure within the segment indicates whether blocks below the HWM are full (less than **pctfree**), 0 to 25 percent free, 25 to 50 percent free, 50 to 75 percent free, 75 to 100 percent free, or unformatted.

Data Dictionary Views and Dynamic Performance Views

A number of data dictionary and dynamic performance views are critical in understanding how disk space is being used in your database. The data dictionary views that begin with DBA_ are of a more static nature, whereas the V$ views, as expected, are of a more dynamic nature and give you up-to-date statistics on how space is being used in the database.

In the next few sections, we'll highlight the space management views and provide some quick examples; later in this chapter, we'll see how these views form the basis of Oracle's space management tools.

DBA_TABLESPACES

The view DBA_TABLESPACES contains one row for each tablespace, whether native or currently plugged in from another database. It contains default extent parameters for objects created in the tablespace that don't specify **initial** and **next** values. The EXTENT_MANAGEMENT column indicates whether the tablespace is locally managed or dictionary managed. As of Oracle 10g, the column BIGFILE indicates whether the tablespace is a smallfile or a bigfile tablespace. Bigfile tablespaces are discussed later in this chapter.

In the following query we retrieve the tablespace type and the extent management type for all tablespaces within the database:

```
SQL> select tablespace_name, block_size,
  2              contents, extent_management from dba_tablespaces;

TABLESPACE_NAME                 BLOCK_SIZE CONTENTS  EXTENT_MAN
------------------------------- ---------- --------- ----------
SYSTEM                                8192 PERMANENT DICTIONARY
TOOLS                                 8192 PERMANENT DICTIONARY
TEMP                                  8192 TEMPORARY DICTIONARY
USERS                                 8192 PERMANENT DICTIONARY
DATA01                                8192 PERMANENT DICTIONARY
DATA02                                8192 PERMANENT DICTIONARY
INDX01                                8192 PERMANENT DICTIONARY
INDX02                                8192 PERMANENT DICTIONARY
DATA03                               16384 PERMANENT LOCAL
UNDO                                  8192 UNDO      LOCAL
```

In this example, all the tablespaces except for UNDO and DATA03 are from a previous version of Oracle (before Oracle8*i*) that did not support locally managed tablespaces and were therefore dictionary managed; in addition, the DATA03 tablespace has a larger block size to improve response time for data mart tables.

DBA_SEGMENTS

The data dictionary view DBA_SEGMENTS has one row for each segment in the database. This view is not only good for retrieving the size of the segment, in blocks or bytes, but also for identifying the owner of the object and the tablespace where an object resides:

```
SQL> select tablespace_name, count(*) NUM_OBJECTS,
  2              sum(bytes), sum(blocks), sum(extents) from dba_segments
  3  group by rollup (tablespace_name);
```

TABLESPACE_NAME	NUM_OBJECTS	SUM(BYTES)	SUM(BLOCKS)	SUM(EXTENTS)
DATA01	104	140378112	17136	118
DATA02	70	206045184	25152	79
DATA03	4	41943040	2560	4
INDX01	153	128974848	15744	258
INDX02	158	104071168	12704	331
SYSTEM	961	337141760	41155	2900
TEMP	1	269484032	32896	1028
TOOLS	379	228065280	27840	415
UNDO	10	21151744	2582	39
USERS	172	224395264	27392	466
	2012	1701650432	205161	5638

DBA_EXTENTS

The DBA_EXTENTS view is similar to DBA_SEGMENTS, except that DBA_EXTENTS drills down further into each database object. There is one row in DBA_EXTENTS for each extent of each segment in the database, along with the FILE_ID and BLOCK_ID of the datafile containing the extent:

```
SQL> select owner, segment_name, tablespace_name,
  2          extent_id, file_id, block_id, bytes from dba_extents
  3  where segment_name = 'AUD$';
```

OWNER	SEGMENT_NAM	TABLESPACE	EXTENT_ID	FILE_ID	BLOCK_ID	BYTES
SYS	AUD$	SYSTEM	3	1	32407	196608
SYS	AUD$	SYSTEM	4	1	42169	262144
SYS	AUD$	SYSTEM	5	2	289	393216
SYS	AUD$	SYSTEM	2	1	31455	131072
SYS	AUD$	SYSTEM	1	1	30303	65536
SYS	AUD$	SYSTEM	0	1	261	16384

In this example, the table AUD$ owned by SYS has extents in two different datafiles that comprise the SYSTEM tablespace.

DBA_FREE_SPACE

The view DBA_FREE_SPACE is broken down by datafile number within the tablespace. You can easily compute the amount of free space in each tablespace by using the following query:

```
SQL> select tablespace_name, sum(bytes) from dba_free_space
  2  group by tablespace_name;
```

TABLESPACE_NAME	SUM(BYTES)
DATA01	279044096
DATA02	213377024
DATA03	157286400

```
INDX01                          395304960
INDX02                          420208640
SYSTEM                           14123008
TEMP                           1084219392
TOOLS                           296214528
UNDO                            327876608
USERS                           299884544
```

Note that the free space does not take into account the space that would be available if and when the datafiles in a tablespace are autoextended. Also, any space allocated to a table for rows that are later deleted will be available for future inserts into the table, but it is not counted in the preceding query results as space available for other database objects. When a table is truncated, however, the space is made available for other database objects.

DBA_LMT_FREE_SPACE

The view DBA_LMT_FREE_SPACE provides the amount of free space, in blocks, for all tablespaces that are locally managed, and it must be joined with DBA_DATA_FILES to get the tablespace names.

DBA_THRESHOLDS

New to Oracle 10g, DBA_THRESHOLDS contains the currently active list of the different metrics that gauge the database's health and specify a condition under which an alert will be issued if the metric threshold reaches or exceeds a specified value.

The values in this view are typically maintained via the OEM interface; in addition, the Oracle 10g DBMS_SERVER_ALERT built-in PL/SQL package can set and get the threshold values with the SET_THRESHOLD and GET_THRESHOLD procedures, respectively. To read alert messages in the alert queue, you can use the DBMS_AQ and DBMS_AQADM packages, or OEM can be configured to send a pager or e-mail message when the thresholds have been exceeded.

For a default installation of Oracle 10g, a number of thresholds are configured, including the following:

- At least one user session is blocked every minute for three consecutive minutes.

- Any segments not able to extend for any reason.

- The total number of concurrent processes comes within 80 percent of the PROCESSES initialization parameter value.

- More than two invalid objects for any individual database user.

- The total number of concurrent user sessions comes within 80 percent of the SESSIONS initialization parameter value.

- More than 1200 concurrent open cursors.

- More than 100 logons per second.

- A tablespace is more than 85 percent full (warning) or more than 97 percent full (critical).

- User logon time is greater than 1000 milliseconds (1 second).

DBA_OUTSTANDING_ALERTS

The Oracle 10g view DBA_OUTSTANDING_ALERTS contains one row for each active alert in the database, until the alert is cleared or reset. One of the fields in this view, SUGGESTED_ACTION, contains a recommendation for addressing the alert condition.

DBA_ALERT_HISTORY

After an alert in DBA_OUTSTANDING_ALERTS has been addressed in Oracle 10g and cleared, a record of the cleared alert is available in the Oracle 10g view DBA_ALERT_HISTORY.

V$ALERT_TYPES

The dynamic performance view V$ALERT_TYPES (new to Oracle 10g) lists the 133 alert conditions (as of Oracle 10g, Release 1) that can be monitored. The GROUP_NAME column categorizes the alert conditions by type. For example, for space management issues, we would use alerts with a GROUP_NAME of 'Space':

```
SQL> select reason_id, object_type, scope, internal_metric_category,
  2          internal_metric_name from v$alert_types
  3        where group_name = 'Space';

REASON_ID OBJECT_TYPE        SCOPE    INTERNAL_METRIC_CATE INTERNAL_METRIC_
---------- ------------------ -----    -------------------- ----------------
       11 ROLLBACK SEGMENT    Database Snap_Shot_Too_Old    Rollback_Segment
       13 ROLLBACK SEGMENT    Database Suspended_Session    Rollback_Segment
        0 SYSTEM              Instance
        1 SYSTEM              Instance
        9 TABLESPACE          Database problemTbsp          pctUsed
       10 TABLESPACE          Database Snap_Shot_Too_Old    Tablespace
       12 TABLESPACE          Database Suspended_Session    Tablespace
       14 DATA OBJECT         Database Suspended_Session    Data_Object
       15 QUOTA               Database Suspended_Session    Quota
      123 RECOVERY AREA       Database Recovery_Area        Free_Space
```

Using alert type with REASON_ID=123 as an example, an alert can be initiated when the free space in the database recovery area falls below a specified percentage.

V$UNDOSTAT

Having too much undo space and not enough undo space are both problems. Although an alert can be set up to notify the DBA when the undo space is not sufficient to provide enough transaction history to satisfy Flashback queries or enough "before" image data to prevent "Snapshot Too Old" errors, a DBA can be proactive by monitoring the dynamic performance view V$UNDOSTAT during heavy database usage periods.

V$UNDOSTAT displays historical information about the consumption of undo space for ten-minute intervals. By analyzing the results from this table, a DBA can make informed decisions when adjusting the size of the undo tablespace or changing the value of the UNDO_RETENTION initialization parameter.

V$OBJECT_USAGE

If an index is not being used, it not only takes up space that could be used by other objects, but the overhead of maintaining the index whenever an **insert**, **update**, or **delete** occurs is wasted. By using the **alter index ... monitoring usage** command, the view V$OBJECT_USAGE will be updated when the index has been accessed indirectly because of a **select** statement.

V$SORT_SEGMENT

The view V$SORT_SEGMENT can be used to view the allocation and deallocation of space in a temporary tablespace's sort segment. The column CURRENT_USERS indicates how many distinct users are actively using a given segment. V$SORT_SEGMENT is only populated for temporary tablespaces.

V$TEMPSEG_USAGE

From the perspective of users requesting temporary segments, the view V$TEMPSEG_USAGE identifies the locations, types, and sizes of the temporary segments currently being requested. Unlike V$SORT_SEGMENT, V$TEMPSEG_USAGE will contain information about temporary segments in both temporary and permanent tablespaces.

Space Management Methodologies

In the following sections, we will consider various features of Oracle 10*g* to facilitate the efficient use of disk space in the database. Locally managed tablespaces offer a variety of advantages to the DBA, improving the performance of the objects within the tablespace, as well as easing administration of the tablespace—fragmentation of a tablespace is a thing of the past. Another feature introduced in Oracle9*i*, Oracle Managed Files, eases datafile maintenance by automatically removing files at the operating system level when a tablespace or other database object is dropped. Bigfile tablespaces, introduced in Oracle 10*g*, simplify datafile management because one and only one datafile is associated with a bigfile tablespace. This moves the maintenance point up one level, from the datafile to the tablespace. We'll also review a couple other features introduced in Oracle9*i*—undo tablespaces and multiple block sizes.

Locally Managed Tablespaces

Prior to Oracle8*i*, there was only one way to manage free space within a tablespace—by using data dictionary tables in the SYSTEM tablespace. If a lot of insert, delete, and update activity occurs anywhere in the database, there is the potential for a "hot spot" to occur in the SYSTEM tablespace where the space management occurs. Oracle removed this potential bottleneck by introducing *locally managed tablespaces (LMTs)*. A locally managed tablespace tracks free space in the tablespace with bitmaps, as discussed in Chapter 1. These bitmaps can be managed very efficiently because they are very compact compared to a freelist of available blocks. Because they are stored within the tablespace itself, instead of in the data dictionary tables, contention on the SYSTEM tablespace is reduced.

As of Oracle 10*g*, by default, all tablespaces are created as locally managed tablespaces, including the SYSTEM and SYSAUX tablespaces. When the SYSTEM tablespace is locally managed, you can no longer create any dictionary managed tablespaces in the database that are read/write. A dictionary managed tablespace may still be plugged into the database, but it is read-only.

An LMT can have objects with one of two types of extents: automatically sized or all of a uniform size. If extent allocation is set to UNIFORM when the LMT is created, all extents, as expected, are the same size. Because all extents are the same size, there can be no fragmentation. Gone is the classic example of a 51MB segment that can't be allocated in a tablespace with two free 50MB extents because the two 50MB extents are not adjacent.

On the other hand, automatic segment extent management within a locally managed tablespace allocates space based on the size of the object. Initial extents are small, and if the object stays small, very little space is wasted. If the table grows past the initial extent allocated for the segment, subsequent extents to the segment are larger. Extents in an autoallocated LMT have sizes of 64KB, 1MB, 8MB, and 64MB, and the extent size increases as the size of the segment increases, up to a maximum of 64MB. In other words, Oracle is specifying what the values of INITIAL, NEXT, and PCTINCREASE are automatically, depending on how the object grows. Although it seems like fragmentation can occur in a tablespace with autoallocation, in practice the fragmentation is minimal because a new object with a 64KB initial segment size will fit nicely in a 1MB, 4MB, 8MB, or 64MB block preallocated for all other objects with an initial 64KB extent size.

Given an LMT with either automatically managed extents or uniform extents, the free space within the segment itself can be AUTO or MANUAL. With AUTO segment space management, a bitmap is used to indicate how much space is used in each block. The parameters PCTUSED, FREELISTS, and FREELIST GROUPS no longer need to be specified when the segment is created. In addition, the performance of concurrent DML operations is improved because the segment's bitmap allows concurrent access. In a freelist managed segment, the data block in the segment header that contains the freelist is locked out to all other writers of the block when a single writer is looking for a free block in the segment. Although allocating multiple freelists for very active segments does somewhat solve the problem, it is another structure that the DBA has to manage.

Another advantage of LMTs is that rollback information is reduced or eliminated when any LMT space-related operation is performed. Because the update of a bitmap in a tablespace is not recorded in a data dictionary table, no rollback information is generated for this transaction.

Other than third-party applications, such as SAP, that require dictionary managed tablespaces, there are no other reasons for creating new dictionary managed tablespaces in Oracle 10g. As mentioned earlier, compatibility is provided in part to allow dictionary managed tablespaces from previous versions of Oracle to be "plugged into" an Oracle 10g database, although if the SYSTEM tablespace is locally managed, any dictionary managed tablespaces must be opened read-only. Later in this chapter, you'll see some examples where we can optimize space and performance by moving a tablespace from one database to another and allocating additional data buffers for tablespaces with different sizes.

Migrating a dictionary managed tablespace to a locally managed tablespace is very straightforward using the DBMS_SPACE_ADMIN built-in package:

```
execute sys.dbms_space_admin.tablespace_migrate_to_local('USERS')
```

After upgrading a database to either Oracle9*i* or Oracle 10*g*, you may also want to consider migrating the SYSTEM tablespace to an LMT; if so, a number of prerequisites are in order:

■ Before starting the migration, shut down the database and perform a cold backup of the database.

■ Any non-SYSTEM tablespaces that are to remain read/write should be converted to LMTs.

■ The default temporary tablespace must not be SYSTEM.

■ If automatic undo management is being used, the undo tablespace must be online.

■ For the duration of the conversion, all tablespaces except for the undo tablespace must be set to read-only.

■ The database must be started in RESTRICTED mode for the duration of the conversion.

If any of these conditions are not met, the TABLESPACE_MIGRATE_TO_LOCAL procedure will not perform the migration.

Using OMF to Manage Space

In a nutshell, *Oracle Managed Files (OMF)* simplifies the administration of an Oracle database. At database-creation time, or later by changing a couple parameters in the initialization parameter file, the DBA can specify a number of default locations for database objects such as datafiles, redo log files, and control files. Prior to Oracle9*i*, the DBA had to remember where the existing datafiles were stored by querying the DBA_DATA_FILES and DBA_TEMP_FILES views. On many occasions, a DBA would drop a tablespace, but would forget to delete the underlying datafiles, thus wasting space and the time it took to back up files that were no longer used by the database.

Using OMF, Oracle not only automatically creates and deletes the files in the specified directory location, it ensures that each filename is unique. This avoids corruption and database downtime in a non-OMF environment due to existing files being overwritten by a DBA inadvertently creating a new datafile with the same name as an existing datafile, and using the REUSE clause.

In a test or development environment, OMF reduces the amount of time the DBA must spend on file management and lets them focus on the applications and other aspects of the test database. OMF has an added benefit for packaged Oracle applications that need to create tablespaces: The scripts that create the new tablespaces do not need any modification to include a datafile name, thus increasing the likelihood of a successful application deployment.

Migrating to OMF from a non-OMF environment is easy, and it can be accomplished over a longer time period. Non-OMF files and OMF files can coexist indefinitely in the same database. When the appropriate initialization parameters are set, all new datafiles, control files, and redo log files can be created as OMF files, while the previously existing files can continue to be managed manually until they are converted to OMF, if ever.

The OMF-related initialization parameters are detailed in Table 6-1.

Note that the operating system path specified for any of these initialization parameters must already exist; Oracle will not create the directory. Also, these directories must be writable by the operating system account that owns the Oracle software (which on most platforms is oracle).

Bigfile Tablespaces

Bigfile tablespaces, introduced in Oracle 10*g*, take OMF files to the next level; in a bigfile tablespace, a single datafile is allocated, and it can be up to 8EB (exabytes, a million terabytes) in size.

Initialization Parameter	Description
DB_CREATE_FILE_DEST	The default operating system file directory where datafiles and tempfiles are created if no pathname is specified in the **create tablespace** command. This location is used for redo log files and control files if DB_CREATE_ONLINE_LOG_DEST_*n* is not specified.
DB_CREATE_ONLINE_LOG_DEST_*n*	Specifies the default location to store redo log files and control files when no pathname is specified for redo log files or control files at database-creation time. Up to five destinations can be specified with this parameter, allowing up to five multiplexed control files and five members of each redo log group.
DB_RECOVERY_FILE_DEST	Defines the default pathname in the server's file system where RMAN backups, archived redo logs, and flashback logs are located. Also used for redo log files and control files if neither DB_CREAE_FILE_DEST nor DB_CREATE_ONLINE_LOG_DEST_*n* is specified.

TABLE 6-1. *OMF-Related Initialization Parameters*

Bigfile tablespaces can only be locally managed with automatic segment space management. If a bigfile tablespace is used for automatic undo or for temporary segments, then segment space management must be set to MANUAL.

Bigfile tablespaces can save space in the System Global Area (SGA) and the control file because fewer datafiles need to be tracked; similarly, all **alter tablespace** commands on bigfile tablespaces need not refer to datafiles because one and only one datafile is associated with each bigfile tablespace. This moves the maintenance point from the physical (datafile) level to the logical (tablespace) level, simplifying administration.

Creating a bigfile tablespace is as easy as adding the **bigfile** keyword to the **create tablespace** command:

```
SQL> create bigfile tablespace whs01
  2        datafile 'f:\asm\orcl02.dbf' size 10g;
Tablespace created.
```

If we are using OMF, then the **datafile** clause can be omitted. To resize a bigfile tablespace, we can use the **resize** clause:

```
SQL> alter tablespace whs01 resize 80g;
Tablespace altered.
```

In this scenario, even 80GB is not big enough for this tablespace, so we will let it autoextend 20GB at a time:

```
SQL> alter tablespace whs01 autoextend on next 20g;
Tablespace altered.
```

Notice in both cases that we do not need to refer to a datafile; there is only one datafile, and once the tablespace is created, we no longer need to worry about the details of the underlying datafiles and how they are managed.

Bigfile tablespaces are intended for use with Automatic Storage Management, discussed in the next section.

Automatic Storage Management

Using *Automatic Storage Management (ASM)* can significantly reduce the administrative overhead of managing space in a database because a DBA need only specify an ASM *disk group* when allocating space for a tablespace or other database object. Database files are automatically distributed among all available disks in a disk group, and the distribution is automatically updated whenever the disk configuration changes. For example, when a new disk volume is added to an existing disk group in an ASM instance, all datafiles within the disk group are redistributed to use the new disk volume.

Because ASM automatically places datafiles on multiple disks, performance of queries and DML statements is improved because the I/O is spread out among several disks. Optionally, the disks in an ASM group can be mirrored to provide additional redundancy and performance benefits.

Using ASM provides a number of other benefits. In many cases, an ASM instance with a number of physical disks can be used instead of a third-party volume manager or network attached storage (NAS) subsystem. As an added benefit over volume managers, ASM maintenance operations do not require a shutdown of the database if a disk needs to be added or removed from a disk group.

In the next few sections, we'll delve further into how ASM works, with an example of how to create a database object using ASM.

Disk Group Redundancy

A *disk group* in ASM is a collection of one or more ASM disks managed as a single entity. Disks can be added or removed from a disk group without shutting down the database. Whenever a disk is added or removed, ASM automatically rebalances the datafiles on the disks to maximize redundancy and I/O performance.

In addition to the advantages of high redundancy, a disk group can be used by more than one database. This helps to maximize the investment in physical disk drives by easily reallocating disk space among several databases whose disk space needs may change over the course of a day or the course of a year.

The three types of disk groups are normal redundancy, high redundancy, and external redundancy. The normal redundancy and high redundancy groups require that ASM provide the redundancy for files stored in the group. The difference between normal redundancy and high redundancy is in the number of *failure groups* required: A normal redundancy disk group typically has two failure groups, and a high redundancy disk group will have at least three failure groups. A failure group in ASM would roughly correspond to a redo log file group member using traditional Oracle datafile management. External redundancy requires that the redundancy is provided by a mechanism other than ASM (for example, with a RAID storage array). Alternatively, a disk group might contain a non-mirrored disk volume that is used for a read-only tablespace that can easily be re-created if the disk volume fails.

ASM Instance

ASM requires a dedicated Oracle instance typically on the same node as the database that is using an ASM disk group. In an Oracle Real Application Clusters (RAC) environment, each node in a RAC database has an ASM instance.

An ASM instance never mounts a database; it only coordinates the disk volumes for other database instances. In addition, all database I/O from an instance goes directly to the disks in a disk group. Disk group maintenance, however, is performed in the ASM instance; as a result, the memory footprint needed to support an ASM instance can be as low as 64MB.

For more details on how to configure ASM for use with RAC, see Chapter 11.

Background Processes

Two new Oracle background processes exist in the ASM instance. The RBAL background process coordinates the automatic disk group rebalance activity for a disk group. The other background processes, ORB0 through ORB9, perform the actual rebalance activity in parallel.

Creating Objects Using ASM

Before a database can use an ASM disk group, the group must be created by the ASM instance. In the following example, a new disk group, KJM68, is created to manage the Unix disk volumes /dev/hda1, /dev/hda2, /dev/hdb1, /dev/hdc1, and /dev/hdd4:

```
SQL> create diskgroup kjm68 normal redundancy
  2        failgroup mir1 disk  '/dev/hda1','/dev/hda2',
  3        failgroup mir2 disk  '/dev/hdb1','/dev/hdc1','/dev/hdd4';
```

When normal redundancy is specified, at least two failure groups must be specified to provide two-way mirroring for any datafiles created in the disk group.

In the database instance that is using the disk group, OMF is used in conjunction with ASM to create the datafiles for the logical database structures. In the following example, we set the initialization parameter DB_CREATE_FILE_DEST using a disk group so that any tablespaces created using OMF will automatically be named and placed in the disk group KJM68:

```
db_create_file_dest = '+kjm68'
```

Creating a tablespace in the disk group is straight to the point:

```
SQL> create tablespace lob_video;
```

Once an ASM file is created, the automatically generated filenames can be found in V$DATAFILE and V$LOGFILE, along with manually generated filenames. All typical database files can be created using ASM, except for administrative files, including trace files, alert logs, backup files, export files, and core dump files.

Undo Management Considerations

Creating an undo tablespace provides a number of benefits for both the DBA and a typical database user. For the DBA, the management of rollback segments is a thing of the past—all undo segments are managed automatically by Oracle in the undo tablespace. In addition to providing a read-consistent view of database objects to database readers when a long transaction against an object is in progress, an undo tablespace can provide a mechanism for a user to recover rows from a table.

A big enough undo tablespace will minimize the possibility of getting the classic "Snapshot too old" error message, but how much undo space is enough? If it is undersized, then the availability window for Flashback queries is short; if it is sized too big, disk space is wasted and backup operations may take longer than necessary.

A number of initialization parameter files control the allocation and use of undo tablespaces. The UNDO_MANAGEMENT parameter specifies whether AUTOMATIC undo management is used, and the UNDO_TABLESPACE parameter specifies the undo tablespace itself. To change either of these parameters, the instance must be shut down and restarted for the change to take effect. The UNDO_RETENTION parameter specifies, in seconds, the minimum amount of time that undo information should be retained for Flashback queries. However, with an undersized undo tablespace and heavy DML usage, some undo information may be overwritten before the time period specified in UNDO_RETENTION.

New to Oracle 10g is the RETENTION GUARANTEE clause of the CREATE UNDO TABLESPACE command. In essence, an undo tablespace with a RETENTION GUARANTEE will not overwrite unexpired undo information at the expense of failed DML operations when there is not enough free undo space in the undo tablespace. More details on using this clause can be found in Chapter 7.

The following initialization parameters enable automatic undo management with the undo tablespace UNDO04 using a retention period of at least 24 hours:

```
undo_management = auto
undo_tablespace = undo04
undo_retention = 86400
```

The dynamic performance view V$UNDOSTAT can assist in sizing the undo tablespace correctly for the transaction load during peak processing periods. The rows in V$UNDOSTAT are inserted at ten-minute intervals and give a snapshot of the undo tablespace usage:

```
SQL> select to_char(end_time,'yyyy-mm-dd hh24:mi') end_time,
  2        undoblks, ssolderrcnt from v$undostat;

END_TIME           UNDOBLKS SSOLDERRCNT
------------------ -------- -----------
2004-01-23 10:28        522           0
2004-01-23 10:21       1770           0
2004-01-23 10:11        857           0
2004-01-23 10:01       1605           0
2004-01-23 09:51       2864           3
2004-01-23 09:41        783           0
2004-01-23 09:31       1543           0
2004-01-23 09:21       1789           0
2004-01-23 09:11        890           0
2004-01-23 09:01       1491           0
```

In this example, a peak in undo space usage occurred between 9:41 A.M. and 9:51 A.M., resulting in a "Snapshot too old" error for three queries. To prevent these errors, the undo tablespace should either be manually resized or allowed to autoextend.

SYSAUX Monitoring and Usage

The SYSAUX tablespace, introduced in Oracle 10g, is an auxiliary tablespace to the SYSTEM tablespace, and it houses data for several components of the Oracle database that either required their own tablespace or used the SYSTEM tablespace in previous releases of Oracle. These components include the Enterprise Manager Repository, formerly in the tablespace OEM_ REPOSITORY, as well as LogMiner, Oracle Spatial, and Oracle Text, all of which formerly used the SYSTEM tablespace for storing configuration information. The current occupants of the SYSAUX tablespace can be identified by querying the V$SYSAUX_OCCUPANTS view:

```
SQL> select occupant_name, occupant_desc, space_usage_kbytes
  2       from v$sysaux_occupants;

OCCUPANT_NAME   OCCUPANT_DESC                             SPACE_USAGE_KBYTES
--------------- ----------------------------------------- ------------------
LOGMNR          LogMiner                                                7488
LOGSTDBY        Logical Standby                                            0
STREAMS         Oracle Streams                                           192
AO              Analytical Workspace Object Table                        960
XSOQHIST        OLAP API History Tables                                  960
SM/AWR          Server Manageability - Automatic Workloa               73216
                d Repository
SM/ADVISOR      Server Manageability - Advisor Framework                6144
SM/OPTSTAT      Server Manageability - Optimizer Statist               15808
                ics History
SM/OTHER        Server Manageability - Other Components                 3776
STATSPACK       Statspack Repository                                       0
ODM             Oracle Data Mining                                      5504
SDO             Oracle Spatial                                          6080
WM              Workspace Manager                                       6656
ORDIM           Oracle interMedia ORDSYS Components                      512
ORDIM/PLUGINS   Oracle interMedia ORDPLUGINS Components                    0
ORDIM/SQLMM     Oracle interMedia SI_INFORMTN_SCHEMA Com                   0
                ponents
EM              Enterprise Manager Repository                          61376
TEXT            Oracle Text                                             4736
ULTRASEARCH     Oracle Ultra Search                                     7296
JOB_SCHEDULER   Unified Job Scheduler                                    256

20 rows selected.
```

If the SYSAUX tablespace is taken offline or otherwise becomes corrupted, only these components of the Oracle database will be unavailable; the core functionality of the database will be unaffected. In any case, the SYSAUX tablespace helps to take the load off of the SYSTEM tablespace during normal operation of the database.

To monitor the usage of the SYSAUX tablespace, the column SPACE_USAGE_KBYTES can be queried on a routine basis, and it can alert the DBA when the space usage grows beyond a certain level. If the space usage for a particular component requires a dedicated tablespace to be allocated for the component, such as for the EM Repository, the procedure identified in the

MOVE_PROCEDURE column of the V$SYSAUX_OCCUPANTS view will move the application to another tablespace:

```
SQL> select occupant_name, move_procedure from v$sysaux_occupants
  2      where occupant_name = 'EM';

OCCUPANT_NAME    MOVE_PROCEDURE
---------------  ---------------
EM               emd_maintenance.move_em_tblspc
```

In the following scenario, we know that we will be adding several hundred nodes to our management repository in the near future. Because we want to keep the SYSAUX tablespace from growing too large, we decide to create a new tablespace to hold only the Enterprise Manager data. In the following example, we'll create a new tablespace and move the Enterprise Manager schema into the new tablespace:

```
SQL> create smallfile tablespace EM_REP
  2>      datafile 'f:\oem\orcl05.dbf' size 10g
  3>      autoextend on next 5g;
Tablespace created.
SQL> execute sysman.emd_maintenance.move_em_tblspc('EM_REP');
PL/SQL procedure successfully completed.

SQL> select occupant_name, occupant_desc, space_usage_kbytes
  2>      from v$sysaux_occupants
  3>   where occupant_name = 'EM';

OCCUPANT_NAME   OCCUPANT_DESC                                        SPACE_USAGE_KBYTES
-------------   --------------------------------------------------   ------------------
EM              Enterprise Manager Repository                                         0

1 row selected.
```

Note that the row for Enterprise Manager is still in V$SYSAUX_OCCUPANTS; even though it is not taking up any space in the SYSAUX tablespace, we may want to move its metadata back into SYSAUX at some point in the future. Therefore, we may need to query V$SYSAUX_OCCUPANTS again to retrieve the move procedure. We use the same procedure for moving the application into and out of SYSAUX:

```
SQL> execute sysman.emd_maintenance.move_em_tblspc('SYSAUX');
PL/SQL procedure successfully completed.
```

If a component is not being used in the database at all, such as Ultra Search, a negligible amount of space is used in the SYSAUX tablespace.

Archived Redo Log File Management

It is important to consider space management for objects that exist outside of the database, such as archived redo log files. In ARCHIVELOG mode, an online redo log file is copied to the destination(s) specified by LOG_ARCHIVE_DEST_*n* (where *n* is a number from 1 to 10).

The redo log being copied must be copied successfully to at least one of the destinations before it can be reused by the database. The LOG_ARCHIVE_MIN_SUCCEED_DEST parameter defaults to 1 and must be at least 1. If none of the copy operations are successful, the database will be suspended until at least one of the destinations receives the log file. Running out of disk space is one possible reason for this type of failure.

If the destination for the archived log files is local, an operating system shell script can monitor the space usage of the destination, or it can be scheduled with DBMS_SCHEDULER or with OEM.

Built-in Space Management Tools

Oracle 10g provides a number of built-in tools that a DBA can use on demand to determine if there are any problems with disk space in the database. Most, if not all, of these tools can be manually configured and run by calling the appropriate built-in package. In this section, we'll cover the packages and procedures used to query the database for space problems or advice on space management. Later in this chapter, we'll see how some of these tools can be automated to notify the DBA via e-mail or pager when a problem is imminent.

Segment Advisor

Frequent inserts, updates, and deletes on a table may, over time, leave the space within a table fragmented. Oracle can perform *segment shrink* on a table or index. Shrinking the segment makes the free space in the segment available to other segments in the tablespace, with the potential to improve future DML operations on the segment because fewer blocks may need to be retrieved for the DML operation after the segment shrink. Segment shrink is very similar to online table redefinition in that space in a table is reclaimed. However, segment shrink can be performed in place without the additional space requirements of online table redefinition.

To determine which segments will benefit from segment shrink, you can invoke *Segment Advisor* to perform growth trend analysis on specified segments. In this section, we'll invoke Segment Advisor on some candidate segments that may be vulnerable to fragmentation.

In the example that follows, we'll set up Segment Advisor to monitor the HR.EMPLOYEES table. In recent months, there has been high activity on this table; in addition, a new column, WORK_RECORD, has been added to the table, which HR uses to maintain comments about the employees:

```
SQL> alter table hr.employees add (work_record varchar2(4000));
Table altered.
SQL> alter table hr.employees enable row movement;
Table altered.
```

We have enabled ROW MOVEMENT in the table so that shrink operations can be performed on the table if recommended by Segment Advisor.

After Segment Advisor has been invoked to give recommendations, the findings from Segment Advisor are available in the DBA_ADVISOR_FINDINGS data dictionary view. To show the potential benefits of shrinking segments when Segment Advisor recommends a shrink operation, the view DBA_ADVISOR_RECOMMENDATIONS provides the recommended shrink operation along with the potential savings, in bytes, for the operation.

To set up Segment Advisor to analyze the HR.EMPLOYEES table, we will use an anonymous PL/SQL block, as follows:

```
- begin Segment Advisor analysis for HR.EMPLOYEES
-   rev. 1.0  RJB    1/06/2004
-
- SQL*Plus variable to retrieve the task number from Segment Advisor
variable task_id number
- PL/SQL block follows
```

```
declare
    name varchar2(100);
    descr varchar2(500);
    obj_id number;
begin
    name := ''; - unique name generated from create_task
    descr := 'Check HR.EMPLOYEE';
    dbms_advisor.create_task
        ('Segment Advisor', :task_id, name, descr, NULL);
    dbms_advisor.create_object
        (name, 'TABLE', 'HR', 'EMPLOYEES', NULL, NULL, obj_id);
    dbms_advisor.set_task_parameter(name, 'RECOMMEND_ALL', 'TRUE');
    dbms_advisor.execute_task(name);
end;

PL/SQL procedure successfully completed.

SQL> print task_id

    TASK_ID
----------
         6
SQL>
```

The procedure DBMS_ADVISOR.CREATE_TASK specifies the type of advisor; in this case, it is Segment Advisor. The procedure will return a unique task ID and an automatically generated name to the calling program; we will assign our own description to the task.

Within the task, identified by the uniquely generated name returned from the previous procedure, we identify the object to be analyzed with DBMS_ADVISOR.CREATE_OBJECT. Depending on the type of object, the second through the sixth arguments vary. For tables, we only need to specify the schema name and the table name.

Using DBMS_ADVISOR.SET_TASK_PARAMETER, we tell Segment Advisor to give all possible recommendations about the table. If we want to turn off recommendations for this task, we would specify FALSE instead of TRUE for the last parameter.

Finally, we initiate the Segment Advisor task with the DBMS_ADVISOR.EXECUTE_TASK procedure. Once it is done, we display the identifier for the task so we can query the results in the appropriate data dictionary views.

Now that we have a task number from invoking Segment Advisor, we can query DBA_ ADVISOR_FINDINGS to see what we can do to improve the space utilization of the HR.EMPLOYEES table:

```
SQL> select owner, task_id, task_name, type,
  2        message, more_info from dba_advisor_findings
  3        where task_id = 6;

OWNER      TASK_ID TASK_NAME  TYPE
---------- ------- ---------- ------
RJB              6 TASK_00003 INFORMATION

MESSAGE
--------------------------------------------------
Perform shrink, estimated savings is 107602 bytes.
```

```
MORE_INFO
-----------------------------------------------------------------------
Allocated Space:262144: Used Space:153011: Reclaimable Space :107602:
```

The results are fairly self-explanatory. We can perform a segment shrink operation on the table to reclaim space from numerous insert, delete, and update operations on the HR.EMPLOYEES table. Because the WORK_RECORD column was added to the HR.EMPLOYEES table after the table was already populated, we may have created some chained rows in the table; in addition, since the WORK_RECORD column can be up to 4000 bytes long, updates or deletes of rows with big WORK_RECORD columns may create blocks in the table with free space that can be reclaimed. The view DBA_ADVISOR_RECOMMENDATIONS provides similar information:

```
SQL> select owner, task_id, task_name, benefit_type
  2  from dba_advisor_recommendations
  3  where task_id = 6;

OWNER       TASK_ID TASK_NAME
---------- ------- ---------
RJB              6 TASK_00003

BENEFIT_TYPE
--------------------------------------------------
Perform shrink, estimated savings is 107602 bytes.
```

In any case, we will shrink the segment HR.EMPLOYEES to reclaim the free space. As an added time-saving benefit to the DBA, the SQL needed to perform the shrink is provided in the view DBA_ADVISOR_ACTIONS:

```
SQL> select owner, task_id, task_name, command, attr1
  2         from dba_advisor_actions where task_id = 6;

OWNER       TASK_ID TASK_NAME  COMMAND
---------- ------- --------- --------
RJB              6 TASK_00003 SHRINK SPACE

ATTR1
-------------------------------------
alter table HR.EMPLOYEES shrink space

1 row selected.

SQL> alter table HR.EMPLOYEES shrink space;
Table altered.
```

As mentioned earlier, the shrink operation does not require extra disk space and does not prevent access to the table during the operation, except for a very short period of time at the end of the process to free the unused space. All indexes are maintained on the table during the operation.

In addition to freeing up disk space for other segments, there are other benefits to shrinking a segment. Cache utilization is improved because fewer blocks need to be in the cache to satisfy SELECT or other DML statements against the segment. Also, because the data in the segment is more compact, the performance of full table scans is improved.

There are a couple of caveats and minor restrictions. First, segment shrink will not work on LOB segments. Online table reorganization is a more appropriate method in this case. Also, segment shrink is not allowed on a table that contains any function-based indexes.

Undo Advisor and the Automatic Workload Repository

New to Oracle 10g, the *Undo Advisor* provides tuning information for the undo tablespace, whether it's sized too large, too small, or the undo retention (via the initialization parameter UNDO_RETENTION) is not set optimally for the types of transactions that occur in the database.

Using the Undo Advisor is similar to using the Segment Advisor in that we will call the DBMS_ADVISOR procedures and query the DBA_ADVISOR_* data dictionary views to see the results of the analysis.

The Undo Advisor, however, relies on another feature new to Oracle 10g—the *Automatic Workload Repository (AWR)*. The Automatic Workload Repository, built into every Oracle database, contains snapshots of all key statistics and workloads in the database at 30-minute intervals. The statistics in the AWR are kept for seven days, after which the oldest statistics are dropped. Both the snapshot intervals and the retention period can be adjusted based on your environment, however. The AWR maintains the historical record of how the database is being used over time and helps to diagnose and predict problems long before they can cause a database outage.

To set up Undo Advisor to analyze undo space usage, we will use an anonymous PL/SQL block similar to what we used for Segment Advisor. Before we can use Segment Advisor, however, we need to determine the timeframe to analyze. The data dictionary view DBA_HIST_SNAPSHOT contains the snapshot numbers and date stamps; we will look for the snapshot numbers from 8:00 P.M. Saturday, January 24, 2004 through 9:30 P.M. Saturday, January 24, 2004:

```
SQL> select snap_id, begin_interval_time, end_interval_time
  2        from DBA_HIST_SNAPSHOT
  3  where begin_interval_time > '24-Jan-04 08.00.00 PM' and
  4            end_interval_time < '24-Jan-04 09.31.00 PM'
  5  order by end_interval_time desc;

   SNAP_ID BEGIN_INTERVAL_TIME          END_INTERVAL_TIME
---------- ---------------------------- -------------------
         8 24-JAN-04 09.00.30.828 PM    24-JAN-04 09.30.14.078 PM
         7 24-JAN-04 08.30.41.296 PM    24-JAN-04 09.00.30.828 PM
         6 24-JAN-04 08.00.56.093 PM    24-JAN-04 08.30.41.296 PM
```

Given these results, we will use a SNAP_ID range from 6 to 8 when we invoke Undo Advisor. The PL/SQL anonymous block is as follows:

```
- begin Undo Advisor analysis
- rev. 1.0  RJB    1/09/2004
-
- SQL*Plus variable to retrieve the task number from Segment Advisor
variable task_id number

declare
```

```
        task_id     number;
        name        varchar2(100);
        descr       varchar2(500);
        obj_id      number;
begin
        name := ''; - unique name generated from create_task
        descr := 'Check Undo Tablespace';
        dbms_advisor.create_task
                ('Undo Advisor', :task_id, name, descr);
        dbms_advisor.create_object
                (name, 'UNDO_TBS', NULL, NULL, NULL, 'null', obj_id);
        dbms_advisor.set_task_parameter(name, 'TARGET_OBJECTS', obj_id);
        dbms_advisor.set_task_parameter(name, 'START_SNAPSHOT', 6);
        dbms_advisor.set_task_parameter(name, 'END_SNAPSHOT', 8);
        dbms_advisor.set_task_parameter(name, 'INSTANCE', 1);
        dbms_advisor.execute_task(name);
end;

PL/SQL procedure successfully completed.

SQL> print task_id

TASK_ID
-------
     16
```

As with the Segment Advisor, we can review the DBA_ADVISOR_FINDINGS view to see the problem and the recommendations.

```
SQL> select owner, task_id, task_name, type,
  2      message, more_info from dba_advisor_findings
  3      where task_id = 16;

OWNER       TASK_ID TASK_NAME   TYPE
---------- ------- ---------- -------------
RJB              16 TASK_00003  PROBLEM

MESSAGE
------------------------------------------------------
The undo tablespace is OK.

MORE_INFO
--------------------------------------------------------------------
```

In this particular scenario, Undo Advisor indicates that there is enough space allocated in the undo tablespace to handle the types and volumes of queries run against this database.

To generate a text or HTML report from AWR, you can run the SQL script swrfrpth.sql, which can be found in $ORACLE_HOME/RDBMS/Admin:

```
SQL> @%oracle_home%\rdbms\admin\swrfrpth.sql

Current Instance
~~~~~~~~~~~~~~~~

   DB Id     DB Name      Inst Num Instance
----------- ------------ -------- -----------
 3207671131 OEMREP              1 oemrep

Instances in this Workload Repository schema
~~~~~~~~~~~~~~~~~~~~~~~~~~~~~~~~~~~~~~~~~~~~~~~

   DB Id    Inst Num DB Name      Instance     Host
----------- -------- ------------ ------------ ------------
 3207671131        1 OEMREP       oemrep       ATH2600

Using 3207671131 for database Id
Using           1 for instance number

Specify the number of days of snapshots to choose from
~~~~~~~~~~~~~~~~~~~~~~~~~~~~~~~~~~~~~~~~~~~~~~~~~~~~~~~~~~
Entering the number of days (n) will result in the most recent
(n) days of snapshots being listed.  Pressing <return> without
specifying a number lists all completed snapshots.

Enter value for num_days: 2

Listing the last 2 days of Completed Snapshots

                                                      Snap
Instance     DB Name       Snap Id  Snap Started      Level
------------ ------------- --------- --------------- -----
oemrep       OEMREP              1 24 Jan 2004 18:01   1
                                 2 24 Jan 2004 18:30   1
                                 3 24 Jan 2004 19:00   1
. . .
                                26 25 Jan 2004 06:30   1
                                27 25 Jan 2004 07:00   1
                                28 25 Jan 2004 07:30   1
                                29 25 Jan 2004 08:00   1
                                30 25 Jan 2004 08:30   1
                                31 25 Jan 2004 09:00   1

Specify the Begin and End Snapshot Ids
~~~~~~~~~~~~~~~~~~~~~~~~~~~~~~~~~~~~~~~~
Enter value for begin_snap: 1
Begin Snapshot Id specified: 1

Enter value for end_snap: 29
```

```
End    Snapshot Id specified: 29

Specify the Report Name
~~~~~~~~~~~~~~~~~~~~~~~~
The default report file name is swrf_1_29.html.  To use this name,
press <return> to continue, otherwise enter an alternative.

Enter value for report_name: swrf_1_29.html
```

Figure 6-3 shows an excerpt from the HTML output in swrf_1_29.html.

Note that we're still getting "Snapshot too old" messages, just as we found out earlier in this chapter when we looked at the V$UNDOSTAT view.

Index Usage

Although indexes provide a tremendous benefit by speeding up queries, they can have an impact on space usage in the database. If an index is not being used at all, the space occupied by an index can be better used elsewhere; if we don't need the index, we also can save processing time for insert, update, and delete operations that have an impact on the index. Index usage can be monitored with the dynamic performance view V$OBJECT_USAGE. In our HR schema, we suspect

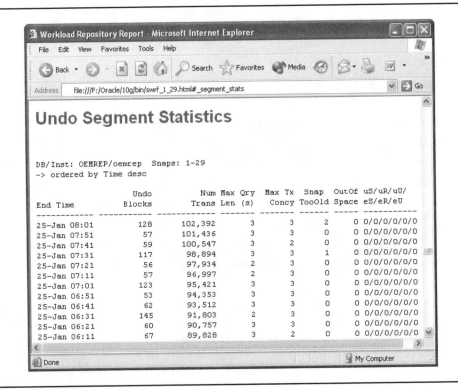

FIGURE 6-3. *HTML report from the Workload Repository*

that the index on the JOB_ID column of the EMPLOYEES table is not being used. We turn on monitoring for this index as follows:

```
SQL> alter index hr.emp_job_ix monitoring usage;
Index altered.
```

We take a quick look at the V$OBJECT_USAGE view to make sure this index is being monitored:

```
SQL> select * from v$object_usage;
INDEX_NAME      TABLE_NAME       MON USED START_MONITORING
--------------- ---------------- --- ---- --------------------
EMP_JOB_IX      EMPLOYEES        YES NO   01/25/2004 10:04:55
```

The column USED will tell us if this index is accessed to satisfy a query. After a full day of typical user activity, we check V$OBJECT_USAGE again and then turn off monitoring:

```
SQL> alter index hr.emp_job_ix nomonitoring usage;
Index altered.
SQL> select * from v$object_usage;
INDEX_NAME  TABLE_NAME       MON USED START_MONITORING     END_MONITORING
----------  ---------------- --- ---- -------------------- ----------------
EMP_JOB_IX  EMPLOYEES        NO  YES  01/25/2004 10:04:55 01/26/2004 11:39:45
```

Sure enough, the index appears to be used at least once during a typical day.

On the other end of the spectrum, an index may be accessed too frequently. If key values are inserted, updated, and deleted frequently, an index can become less efficient in terms of space usage. The following commands can be used as a baseline for an index after it is created, and then run periodically to see if the space usage becomes inefficient:

```
SQL> analyze index hr.emp_job_ix validate structure;
Index analyzed.
SQL> select pct_used from index_stats where name = 'EMP_JOB_IX';
  PCT_USED
  -----
        78
```

The PCT_USED column indicates the percentage of the allocated space for the index in use. Over time, the EMPLOYEES table is heavily used, due to the high turnover rate of employees at the company, and this index, among others, is not using its space efficiently, as indicated by the baseline query, so we decide that a rebuild is in order:

```
SQL> analyze index hr.emp_job_ix validate structure;
Index analyzed.
SQL> select pct_used from index_stats where name = 'EMP_JOB_IX';
  PCT_USED
  ----------
        26
SQL> alter index hr.emp_job_ix rebuild;
Index altered.
```

Space Usage Warning Levels

Earlier in this chapter, we reviewed the data dictionary view DBA_THRESHOLDS, which contains a list of the active metrics to measure a database's health. In a default installation of Oracle 10g, the following thresholds are in place:

```
SQL> select metrics_name, warning_operator, warning_value,
  2      critical_operator, critical_value, consecutive_occurrences
  3      from dba_thresholds;
```

METRICS_NAME	WARNING_OPER	WARNING_VALUE
Blocked User Session Count	GT	11
Process Limit %	GT	80
Session Limit %	GT	90
Tablespace Space Usage	GT	85
User Limit %	GT	90

CRITICAL_OPER	CRITICAL_VALUE	CONSECUTIVE_OCCURRENCES
NONE		3
NONE		3
NONE		3
GT	97	1
NONE		3

In terms of space usage, we see that the warning level for a given tablespace is when the tablespace is 85 percent full, and the space is at a critical level when it reaches 97 percent full. In addition, this condition need only occur during one reporting period, which by default is one minute. For the other conditions in this list, the condition must be true for at least three consecutive reporting periods before an alert is issued.

To change the level at which an alert is generated, we can use the DBMS_SERVER_ALERT.SET_THRESHOLD procedure. In this example, we want to be notified sooner if a tablespace is running out of space, so we will update the warning threshold for alert notification from 85 percent down to 60 percent:

```
--
-- PL/SQL anonymous procedure to update the Tablespace Space Usage threshold
--

declare
     /* OUT */
     warning_operator      number;
     warning_value         varchar2(100);
     critical_operator     number;
     critical_value        varchar2(100);
     observation_period    number;
     consecutive_occurrences number;
     /* IN */
     metrics_id            number;
```

```
     instance_name        varchar2(50);
     object_type          number;
     object_name          varchar2(50);

     new_warning_value varchar2(100) := '60';
begin
     metrics_id := 9000;            /* from V$METRICNAME   */
     object_type := DBMS_SERVER_ALERT.OBJECT_TYPE_TABLESPACE;
     instance_name := 'b2r7seed';   /* from DBA_THRESHOLDS */
     object_name := NULL;

-- retrieve the current values with get_threshold
     dbms_server_alert.get_threshold(
          metrics_id, warning_operator, warning_value,
          critical_operator, critical_value,
          observation_period, consecutive_occurrences,
          instance_name, object_type, object_name);

-- update the warning threshold value from 85 to 60
     dbms_server_alert.set_threshold(
          metrics_id, warning_operator, new_warning_value,
          critical_operator, critical_value,
          observation_period, consecutive_occurrences,
          instance_name, object_type, object_name);

end;

PL/SQL procedure successfully completed.
```

Checking DBA_THRESHOLDS again, we see the warning level has been changed to 60 percent:

```
SQL> select metrics_name, warning_operator, warning_value
  2      from dba_thresholds;
METRICS_NAME                     WARNING_OPER WARNING_VALUE
-------------------------------- ------------ -------------
Blocked User Session Count       GT                11
Process Limit %                  GT                80
Session Limit %                  GT                80
Tablespace Space Usage           GT                60
User Limit %                     GT                90
```

A detailed example of how to use Oracle's Advanced Queuing to subscribe to queue alert messages is beyond the scope of this book. Later in this chapter, we will, however, show some examples of how to use Enterprise Manager to set up asynchronous notification of alert conditions using e-mail, pager, or a PL/SQL procedure.

Resumable Space Allocation

Starting with Oracle9*i*, the Oracle database provides a way to suspend long-running operations in the event of space allocation failures. Once the DBA is notified and the space allocation problem has been corrected, the long-running operation can complete. The long-running operation does not have to be restarted from the beginning.

Three types of space management problems can be addressed with Resumable Space Allocation:

- Out of space in the tablespace
- Maximum extents reached in the segment
- Space quota exceeded for the user

The DBA can automatically make statements resumable by setting the initialization parameter RESUMABLE_TIMEOUT to a value other than 0. This value is specified in seconds. At the session level, a user can enable resumable operations by using the ALTER SESSION ENABLE RESUMABLE command:

```
SQL> alter session enable resumable timeout 3600;
```

In this case, any long-running operation that may run out of space will suspend for up to 3600 seconds (60 minutes) until the space condition is corrected. If it is not corrected within the time limit, the statement fails.

In the scenario that follows, the HR department is trying to add the employees from the branch office EMPLOYEES table to an EMPLOYEE_SEARCH table that contains employees throughout the company. Without Resumable Space Allocation, the HR user receives an error, as follows:

```
SQL> insert into employee_search
2       select * from employees;
insert into employee_search
*
ERROR at line 1:
ORA-01653: unable to extend table HR.EMPLOYEE_SEARCH by 128
          in tablespace USERS9
```

After running into this problem many times, the HR user decides to use Resumable Space Allocation to prevent a lot of rework whenever there are space problems in the database, and tries the operation again:

```
SQL> alter session enable resumable timeout 3600;
Session altered.
SQL> insert into hr.employee_search
2       select * from hr.employees;
```

The user does not receive a message, and it is not clear that the operation has been suspended. However, in the alert log, the message reads as follows:

```
Sun Jan 25 14:44:29 2004
statement in resumable session 'User HR(66), Session 39, Instance 1'
was suspended due to
     ORA-01653: unable to extend table HR.EMPLOYEE_SEARCH by 128
```

```
                  in tablespace USERS9
ORA-12899 encountered when generating server alert SMG-2004
```

The DBA receives a pager alert, set up in OEM, and checks the data dictionary view DBA_RESUMABLE:

```
SQL> select user_id, instance_id, status, name, error_msg
  2  from dba_resumable;

 USER_ID INSTANCE_ID STATUS    NAME                 ERROR_MSG
-------- ----------- --------- -------------------- --------------------
      66           1 SUSPENDED User HR(66), Session ORA-01653: unable to
                               39, Instance 1      extend table HR.EMP
                                                   LOYEE_SEARCH by 128
                                                   in tablespace USERS9
```

The DBA notices that the tablespace USERS9 does not allow autoextend, and modifies the tablespace to allow growth:

```
SQL> alter tablespace users9
  2      add datafile 'F:\OEM\USERS09a.DBF'
  3      size 5M autoextend on;
Tablespace altered.
```

The user session's **insert** completes successfully, and the status of the resumable operation is reflected in the DBA_RESUMABLE view:

```
 USER_ID INSTANCE_ID STATUS    NAME                 ERROR_MSG
----- ------ ----- ---------- ----------
      66           1 NORMAL    User HR(66), Session
                               39, Instance 1
```

The alert log file also indicates a successful resumption of this operation:

```
Sun Jan 25 15:24:32 2004
statement in resumable session 'User  HR(66), Session 39,
      Instance 1' was resumed
```

As far as the user is concerned, the operation took longer than expected, but still completed successfully. Another way to provide more information to the user is to set up a special type of trigger introduced in Oracle9i called a *system trigger*. A system trigger is like any other trigger, except it is based on some type of system event rather than on a DML statement against a table. Here is a template for a system trigger that fires on an AFTER SUSPEND event:

```
create or replace trigger resumable_notify
    after suspend on database  - fired when resumable space event occurs
declare
      -- variables
```

```
begin
    -- give DBA 2 hours to resolve
    dbms_resumable.set_timeout(7200);
    -- check DBA_RESUMABLE for user ID, then send e-mail
    utl_mail.send ('dba@rjb.com', . . . );
end;
```

OS Space Management

Outside of the Oracle environment, space should be monitored by the system administrator with a thorough understanding from the DBA as to the parameters in place for autoextending datafiles. Setting AUTOEXTEND ON with large NEXT values for a tablespace will allow a tablespace to grow and accommodate more inserts and updates, but this will fail if the server's disk volumes do not have the space available.

Space Management Scripts

In this section, we provide a couple scripts you can run on an as-needed basis, or you can schedule them to run on a regular basis to proactively monitor the database.

These scripts take the dictionary views and give a more detailed look at a particular structure. The functionality of some of these scripts might overlap with the results provided by some of the tools we've mentioned earlier in the chapter, but they might be more focused and in some cases provide more detail about the possible space problems in the database.

Segments That Cannot Allocate Additional Extents

In the following script, we want to identify segments (most likely tables or indexes) that cannot allocate additional extents:

```
SQL> select s.tablespace_name, s.segment_name,
  2         s.segment_type, s.owner
  3  from dba_segments s
  4  where s.next_extent >=
  5       (select max(f.bytes)
  6        from dba_free_space f
  7        where f.tablespace_name = s.tablespace_name)
  8  or s.extents = s.max_extents
  9  order by tablespace_name, segment_name;
```

TABLESPACE_NAME	SEGMENT_NAME	SEGMENT_TYPE	OWNER
SYSTEM	SYSTEM	ROLLBACK	SYS
USERS9	EMPLOYEE_SEARCH	TABLE	HR

In this example, we're using a correlated subquery to compare the size of the next extent to the amount of free space left in the tablespace. The other condition we're checking is whether the next extent request will fail because the segment is already at the maximum number of extents.

The reason these objects might be having problems is most likely one of two possibilities: The tablespace does not have room for the next extent for this segment, or the segment has the maximum number of extents allocated. To solve this problem, the DBA can extend the tablespace by adding another datafile or by exporting the data in the segment and re-creating it with storage parameters that more closely match its growth pattern. As of Oracle9*i*, using locally managed tablespaces instead of dictionary managed tablespaces solves this problem when disk space is not the issue—the maximum number of extents in an LMT is unlimited.

Used and Free Space by Tablespace and Datafile

The following SQL*Plus script breaks down the space usage of each tablespace, which is further broken down by datafile within each tablespace. This is a good way to see how space is used and extended within each datafile of a tablespace, and it may be useful for load balancing when you're not using ASM or other high-availability storage.

```
--
-- Free space within non-temporary datafiles, by tablespace.
--
-- No arguments.
-- 1024*1024*1000 = 1048576000 = 1GB to match OEM
--


column free_space_gb  format 9999999.999
column allocated_gb   format 9999999.999
column used_gb        format 9999999.999
column tablespace     format a12
column filename       format a20

select    ts.name tablespace, trim(substr(df.name,1,100)) filename,
          df.bytes/1048576000 allocated_gb,
          ((df.bytes/1048576000) - nvl(sum(dfs.bytes)/1048576000,0)) used_gb,
          nvl(sum(dfs.bytes)/1048576000,0) free_space_gb
      from v$datafile df left outer join dba_free_space dfs
        on df.file# = dfs.file_id join v$tablespace ts
        on df.ts# = ts.ts#
group by ts.name, dfs.file_id, df.name, df.file#, df.bytes
order by filename;


TABLESPACE    FILENAME                 ALLOCATED_GB    USED_GB  FREE_SPACE_GB
----------    --------------------     ------------  ---------  -------------
WHS01         F:\ASM\ORCL02.DBF              10.240       .000         10.240
EM_REP        F:\OEM\ORCL05.DBF              10.240       .000         10.240
USERS9        F:\OEM\USERS10.DBF               .005       .005           .000
EXAMPLE       F:\ORACLE\ORADATA\OE             .150       .079           .071
              MREP\EXAMPLE01.DBF
SYSAUX        F:\ORACLE\ORADATA\OE             .330       .320           .010
              MREP\SYSAUX01.DBF
```

SYSTEM	F:\ORACLE\ORADATA\OE MREP\SYSTEM01.DBF	.440	.439	.001
UNDOTBS1	F:\ORACLE\ORADATA\OE MREP\UNDOTBS01.DBF	.310	.032	.278
USERS	F:\ORACLE\ORADATA\OE MREP\USERS01.DBF	2.265	2.245	.020
USERS	F:\ORACLE\ORADATA\OE MREP\USERS02.DBF	.500	.000	.500

Only the USERS tablespace has more than one datafile, and the space usage has not extended into the second datafile yet. To include temporary tablespaces on this report, you can use a **union** query to combine this query with a similar query based on V$TEMPFILE.

Automating and Streamlining the Notification Process

Although any of the scripts and packages presented earlier in this chapter can be executed on demand, some of them can and should be automated, not only to save time for the DBA but also to be proactive and catch problems long before they cause a system outage.

Two of the primary methods for automating the scripts and packages are DBMS_SCHEDULER and Oracle Enterprise Manager. Each of these methods has its advantages and disadvantages. DBMS_SCHEDULER can provide more control over how the task is scheduled and can be set up using only a command-line interface. Oracle Enterprise Manager, on the other hand, uses a completely web-based environment that allows a DBA to oversee a database environment from wherever there is access to a web browser.

Using DBMS_SCHEDULER

New to Oracle 10*g* is the DBMS_SCHEDULER package. It provides new features and functionality over the previous job scheduler package, DBMS_JOB. Although DBMS_JOB is still available in Oracle 10*g*, it is highly recommended that your jobs convert to DBMS_SCHEDULER because the DBMS_JOB package may be deprecated in a future release.

DBMS_SCHEDULER contains many of the procedures you'd expect from a scheduling package: CREATE_JOB, DROP_JOB, DISABLE, STOP_JOB, and COPY_JOB. In addition, DBMS_SCHEDULER makes it easy to automatically repeat job executions with CREATE_SCHEDULE and to partition jobs into categories based on resource usage with the CREATE_JOB_CLASS procedure.

OEM Job Control and Monitoring

Not only can Oracle Enterprise Manager present most database administration tasks in a graphical, web-based environment, it can automate some of the routine tasks that a DBA might perform on a daily basis. In this section, we'll cover the OEM-equivalent functionality to Segment Advisor and Undo Advisor, covered previously in this chapter.

Segment Advisor

Figure 6-4 shows the home page for OEM. Many of the space management functions are available directly from this home page.

The top portion of the home page lists general availability information of the instance, including the instance name, host name, CPU usage, and session information. The bottom half of the home page lists a number of space management hyperlinks that will help us manage the space in the database. Figure 6-5 shows the bottom half of the home page from Figure 6-4.

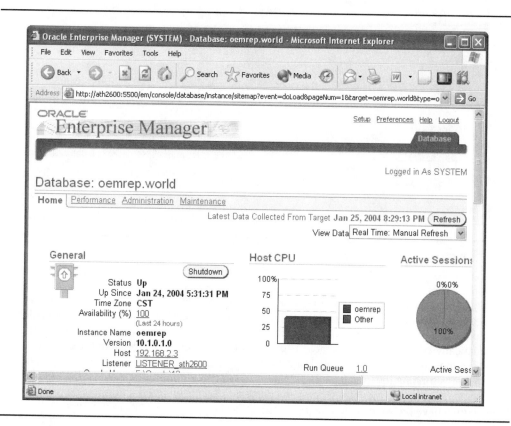

FIGURE 6-4. *Oracle Enterprise Manager home page*

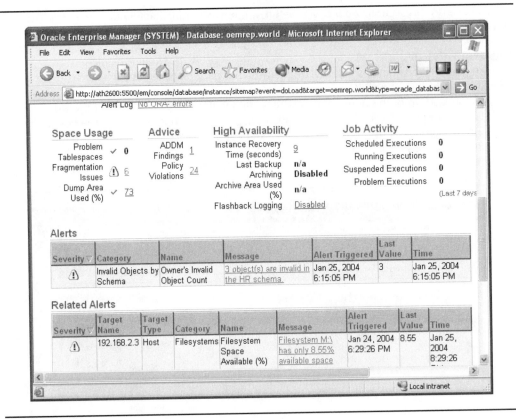

FIGURE 6-5. *Space-related OEM links*

Under the Space Usage column, we don't have any problem tablespaces or fragmentation problems, but the dump area, the dedicated area on disk for RMAN backups and other backup-related files, is at 73 percent capacity and should be reviewed. We have two other alerts (automatically configured when Oracle 10g is installed) that are space-related: three objects in the HR schema that may be corrupted or may be having space problems, as well as a host file system that is running low on space. The Windows system administrator may not be aware of a space problem on the M: volume, and any database objects whose datafiles reside on this volume may have problems when the database objects try to add extents in the future.

To delve deeper into the fragmentation issues, we can click the "6" next to Fragmentation Issues to configure or review the fragmentation analysis. This functionality includes the tools we reviewed previously in this chapter that called DBMS_ADVISOR.CREATE_TASK to set up Segment Advisor. Figure 6-6 shows the first few fragmentation issues that Segment Advisor uncovered.

As an example, the table HR.EMPLOYEES appears to have too many chained rows. By clicking the Reorganize Segment link, we can easily reconfigure the storage characteristics of the HR.EMPLOYEES table as we did manually using the SQL commands from the

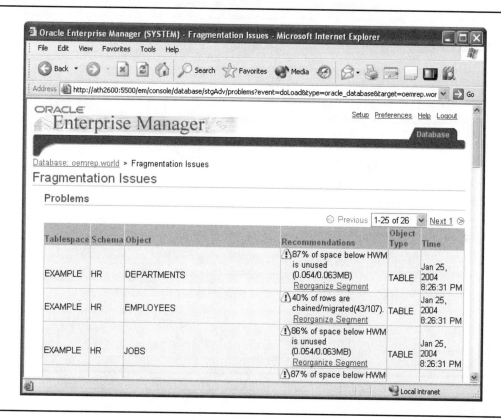

FIGURE 6-6.   *Segment Advisor analysis*

DBA_ADVISOR_ACTIONS view. In Figure 6-7, we start the process of reorganizing the
HR.EMPLOYEES table. We can move it to another tablespace or specify that the object remain
online during the reorganization. An impact report is generated before the actual reorganization
begins, to ensure that we are aware of the impact of the reorganization to the database and its
users. Finally, we have the option to submit the reorganization job to run immediately or to
schedule it for a later time.

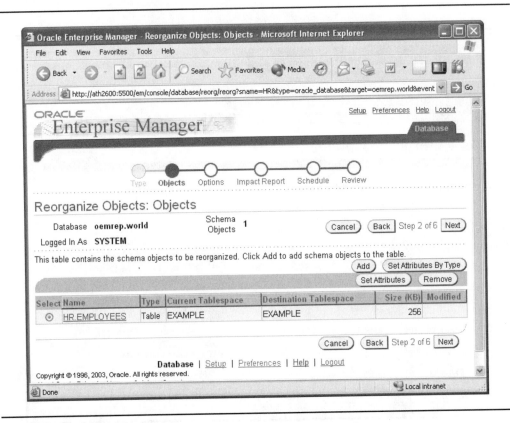

FIGURE 6-7. *Object reorganization*

From the Fragmentation Issues page, we decide that the EXAMPLE tablespace isn't a production tablespace and should probably be dropped at some point in the future. In the mean time, we can remove the tablespace from analysis at the bottom of the page, shown in Figure 6-8. Note that we are analyzing a total of five tablespaces, and we are checking for both wasted space and excessive row chaining.

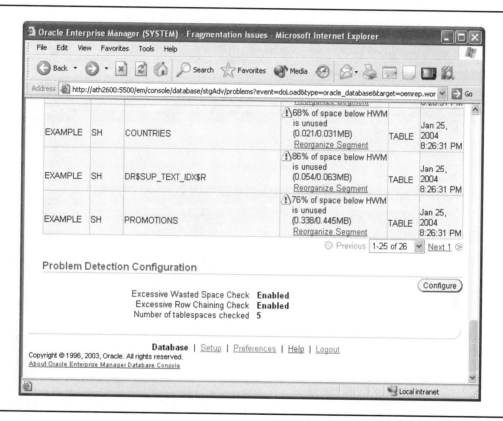

FIGURE 6-8. *Configuring problem detection*

In Figure 6-9, we will remove the EXAMPLE tablespace from our analysis tasks. We select the tablespace and click the Remove button. On the top half of this page, we can also change the types of analyses we are doing on the tablespaces.

Undo Advisor

In Figure 6-10, we have selected the Administration tab on the main OEM page. From here, we will configure Undo Advisor by clicking Undo Management under the Instance column.

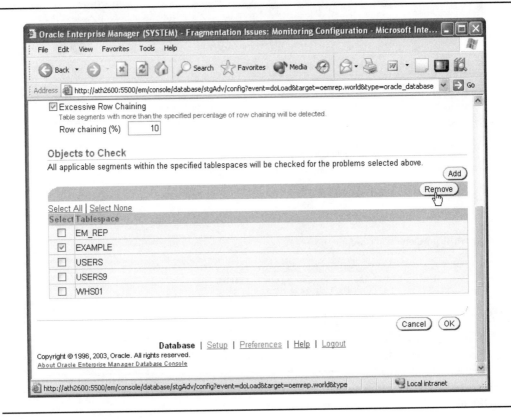

FIGURE 6-9. *Removing tablespaces from analysis*

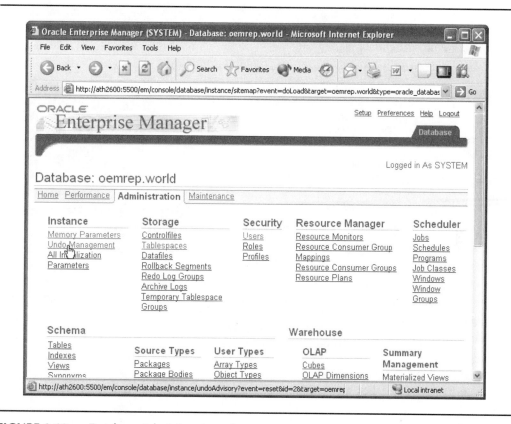

FIGURE 6-10. *Database Administration tab*

The top half of the Undo Management page, shown in Figure 6-11, offers us a number of choices. By default, the amount of undo retained is automatically calculated, but if we want to specify exactly how long we will retain undo information, we can click the hyperlink next to Undo Retention.

In Figure 6-12, we can specify how much undo we will keep in the undo tablespace for long-running queries or to support Flashback queries. Once the proposed retention period is entered, Undo Advisor will provide an analysis showing how much disk space would be required to

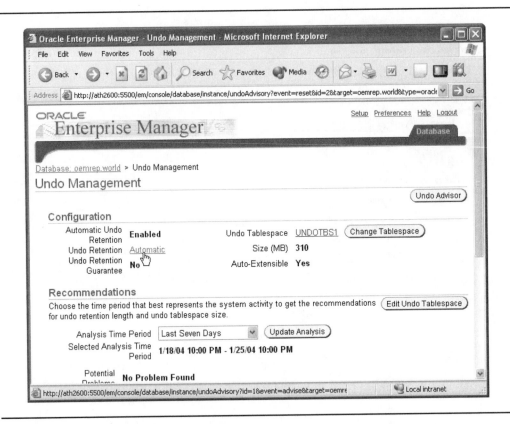

FIGURE 6-11. *Undo Management general configuration*

support the proposed retention period. In addition, a graph displays the relationship between the retention length and the undo tablespace size.

In Figure 6-13, Undo Advisor gives the rationale for the undo recommendations given the system activity and the time period we specified when we configured Undo Advisor; in this case,

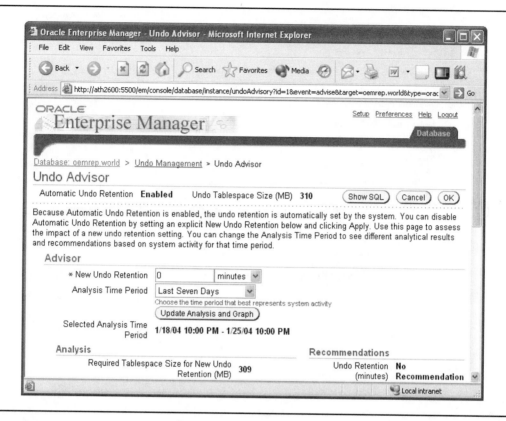

FIGURE 6-12.   *Undo Advisor retention adjustment*

the longest running query ran for over 40 minutes, but the average undo usage was well below the maximum that the current undo tablespace can support. This coincides with the results we received from the DBMS_ADVISOR package example earlier in this chapter.

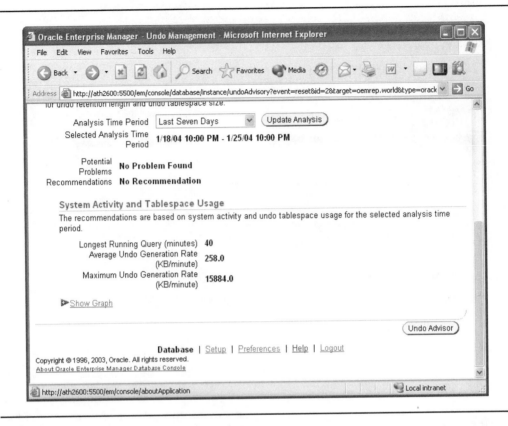

FIGURE 6-13. *Undo Advisor recommendation*

CHAPTER
7

Managing
Transactions with
Undo Tablespaces

I n Chapter 6, we touched briefly on how the space in an undo tablespace is managed, along with views such as V$UNDOSTAT that can help the DBA monitor and size the undo tablespace. In this chapter, we'll delve much more deeply into the configuration and management of the undo tablespace, and how we may resolve the sometimes conflicting requirements of providing enough undo for read consistency while preventing the failure of DML statements because the undo retention parameter is set too high.

To start off this chapter, we'll do a quick review of transactions from a database user's point of view so that you will better understand how to support the user's transactions with the appropriately sized undo tablespace. Next, we'll cover the basics of how to create an undo tablespace, either during database creation or later using the familiar **create tablespace** command. Undo segments fulfill a number of requirements for database users, and we will enumerate and explain each of those requirements in some detail.

Oracle provides a number of ways to monitor and, as a result, more precisely size undo tablespaces. The package **dbms_advisor** can be used to analyze the undo tablespace usage, as we did in Chapter 6; we will investigate this package in more detail, and show how Oracle Enterprise Manager Database Control can make it easy to perform the analysis.

The last major section of this book will review the different types of Oracle Flashback features that rely on an adequately sized undo tablespace to recover from a number of different user error scenarios. All the major Flashback features at the query, table, or transaction level are covered in this section; Flashback Database is covered in Chapter 15.

Rollback segments from previous Oracle releases were hard to manage and were usually sized too large or too small by most DBAs; Oracle strongly recommends that all new databases use Automatic Undo Management and that databases upgraded from a previous version of Oracle be converted to using Automatic Undo Management. We won't cover any aspects of manual undo management here except for how to migrate from rollback segments to automatic undo.

Transaction Basics

A *transaction* is a collection of SQL DML statements that is treated as a logical unit; the failure of any of the statements in the transaction implies that none of the other changes made to the database in the transaction should be permanently saved to the database. Once the DML statements in the transaction have successfully completed, the application or SQL*Plus user will issue a **commit** to make the changes permanent. In the classic banking example, a transaction that transfers a dollar amount from one account to another is successful only if both the debit of one account (an **update** of the savings account balance) and the credit of another account (an **update** of the checking account balance) are both successful. Failure of either or both statements invalidates the entire transaction. When the application or SQL*Plus user issues a **commit**, if only one or the other **update** statement is successful, the bank will have some very unhappy customers!

A transaction is initiated implicitly. After a **commit** of a previous transaction is completed, and at least one row of a table is inserted, updated, or deleted, a new transaction is implicitly created. Also, any DDL commands such as **create table** and **alter index** will commit an active transaction and begin a new transaction. You can name a transaction by using the **set transaction ... name '*transaction_name*'** command; although this provides no direct benefit to the application, the name assigned to the transaction is available in the dynamic performance view V$TRANSACTION and allows a DBA to monitor long-running transactions. The **set transaction** command, if used, must be the first statement within the transaction.

Within a given transaction, you can define a *savepoint*. A savepoint allows the sequence of DML commands within a transaction to be partitioned so that it is possible to roll back one or more of the DML commands after the savepoint, and subsequently submit additional DML commands or commit the DML commands performed before the savepoint. Savepoints are created with the **savepoint** *savepoint_name* command. To undo the DML commands since the last savepoint, you use the command **rollback to savepoint** *savepoint_name*.

A transaction is implicitly committed if a user disconnects from Oracle normally; if the user process terminates abnormally, the most recent transaction is rolled back.

Undo Basics

Undo tablespaces facilitate the rollback of logical transactions. In addition, undo tablespaces support a number of other features, including read consistency, various database-recovery operations, and Flashback functions.

Rollback

As described in the previous section, any DML command within a transaction—whether the transaction is one or one hundred DML commands—may need to be rolled back. When a DML command makes a change to a table, the old data values changed by the DML command are recorded in the undo tablespace within a system-managed undo segment or a rollback segment.

When an entire transaction is rolled back (that is, a transaction without any savepoints), Oracle undoes all the changes made by DML commands since the beginning of the transaction using the corresponding undo records, releases the locks on the affected rows, if any, and the transaction ends.

If part of a transaction is rolled back to a savepoint, Oracle undoes all changes made by DML commands after the savepoint. All subsequent savepoints are lost, all locks obtained after the savepoint are released, and the transaction remains active.

Read Consistency

Undo provides *read consistency* for users who are reading rows that are involved in a DML transaction by another user. In other words, all users who are reading the affected rows will see no changes in the rows until they issue a new query after the DML user commits the transaction. Undo segments are used to reconstruct the datablocks back to a read-consistent version and, as a result, provide the previous values of the rows to any user issuing a **select** statement before the transaction commits.

For example, user CLOLSEN begins a transaction at 10:00 that is expected to commit at 10:15, with various updates and insertions to the EMPLOYEES table. As each **insert**, **update**, and **delete** occurs on the EMPLOYEES table, the old values of the table are saved in the undo tablespace. When the user SUSANP issues a **select** statement against the EMPLOYEES table at 10:08, none of the changes made by CLOLSEN are visible to anyone except CLOLSEN; the undo tablespace provides the previous values of CLOLSEN's changes for SUSANP and all other users. Even if the query from SUSANP does not finish until 10:20, the table still appears to be unchanged until a new query is issued after the changes are committed. Until CLOLSEN performs a **commit** at 10:15, the data in the table appears unchanged as of 10:00.

If there is not enough undo space available to hold the previous values of changed rows, the user issuing the **select** statement may receive an "ORA-01555: Snapshot Too Old" error. Later in this chapter, we will discuss ways in which we can address this issue.

Database Recovery

Undo tablespaces are also a key component of instance recovery. The online redo logs bring both committed and uncommitted transactions forward to the point in time of the instance crash; the undo data is used to roll back any transactions that were not committed at the time of the crash or instance failure.

Flashback Operations

The data in the undo tablespace is used to support the various types of Flashback options: Flashback Table, Flashback Query, and the package DBMS_FLASHBACK. Flashback Table will restore a table as of a point of time in the past, Flashback Query lets you view a table as of an SCN or time in the past, and DBMS_FLASHBACK provides a programmatic interface for Flashback operations. All these Flashback options are covered in more detail at the end of this chapter.

Managing Undo Tablespaces

Creating and maintaining undo tablespaces is a "set it and forget it" operation once the undo requirements of the database are understood. Within the undo tablespace, Oracle automatically creates, sizes, and manages the undo segments, unlike previous versions of Oracle in which the DBA would have to manually size and constantly monitor rollback segments.

In the next couple sections, we'll review the processes used to create and manage undo tablespaces, including the relevant initialization parameters. In addition, we'll review some scenarios where we may create more than one undo tablespace and how to switch between undo tablespaces.

Creating Undo Tablespaces

Undo tablespaces can be created in two ways: at database creation or with the **create tablespace** command after the database is created. As with any other tablespace in Oracle 10g, the undo tablespace can be a bigfile tablespace, further easing the maintenance of undo tablespaces.

Creating an Undo Tablespace with CREATE DATABASE

A database may have more than one undo tablespace, although only one can be active at a time. Here's what creating an undo tablespace at database creation looks like:

```
create database ord
      user sys identified by ds88dkw2
      user system identified by md78s233
      sysaux datafile '/u02/oradata/ord/sysaux001.dbf' size 100m
      default temporary tablespace temp01
          tempfile '/u03/oradata/ord/temp001.dbf' size 25m
      undo tablespace undotbs01
          datafile '/u01/oradata/ord/undo001.dbf' size 50m;
```

If the undo tablespace cannot be successfully created in the **create database** command, the entire operation fails. The error must be corrected, any files remaining from the operation must be deleted, and the command must be reissued.

Although the **undo tablespace** clause in the **create database** command is optional, if it is omitted and Automatic Undo Management is enabled, an undo tablespace is still created with an autoextensible datafile with an initial size of 10MB and the default name SYS_UNDOTBS.

Creating an Undo Tablespace with CREATE TABLESPACE

Any time after the database is created, a new undo tablespace can be created. An undo tablespace is created just as any other tablespace with the addition of the **undo** keyword:

```
create undo tablespace undotbs02
    datafile '/u01/oracle/rbdb1/undo0201.dbf'
    size 25m reuse autoextend on;
```

Depending on the volatility of the database or the expectation that the undo needs of the database may increase dramatically in the future, we start out this tablespace at only 25MB and allow it to grow.

Extents in an undo tablespace must be system managed; in other words, you can only specify **extent management** as **local autoallocate**.

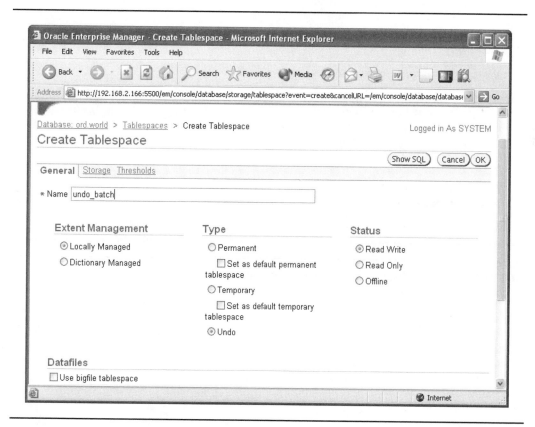

FIGURE 7-1.   *Specifying general undo tablespace characteristics*

Creating an Undo Tablespace Using EM Database Control

Creating an undo tablespace is straightforward using Enterprise Manager Database Control. From the Administration tab, select Tablespaces. You will be presented with a list of existing tablespaces; click on **Create**. In Figure 7-1, we're creating a new undo tablespace named UNDO_BATCH.

At the bottom of the screen, we specify the name of the datafile to use for the undo tablespace, as indicated in Figure 7-2.

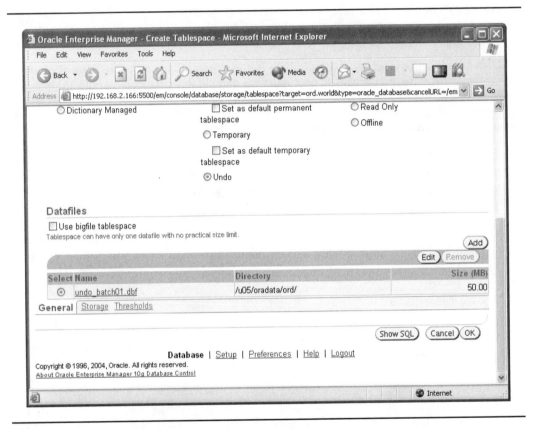

FIGURE 7-2. *Specifying the undo tablespace datafile*

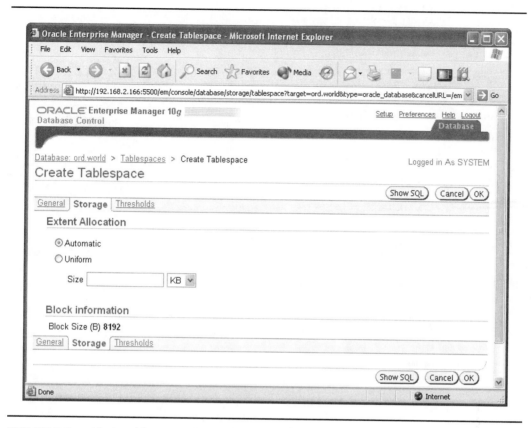

FIGURE 7-3. *Undo tablespace extent allocation and block size*

Clicking on Storage allows us to specify extent allocation, although for an undo tablespace it must be automatic. If we are supporting multiple block sizes, we can specify the block size for the undo tablespace. Figure 7-3 shows that we are specifying automatic extent allocation and a block size of 8192, the default and only block size defined for the database.

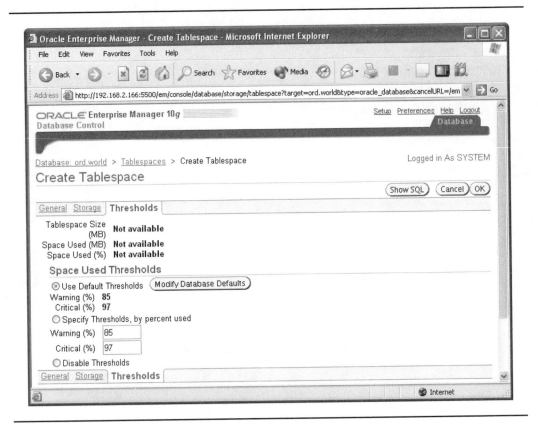

FIGURE 7-4. *Undo tablespace thresholds*

On the third tab, we can set the warning and critical percentages at which the DBA will be notified of a potential space problem with the undo tablespace. We can use the default thresholds of 85 percent for warnings and 97 percent for critical, or we can specify our own values. In Figure 7-4, we accept the default values.

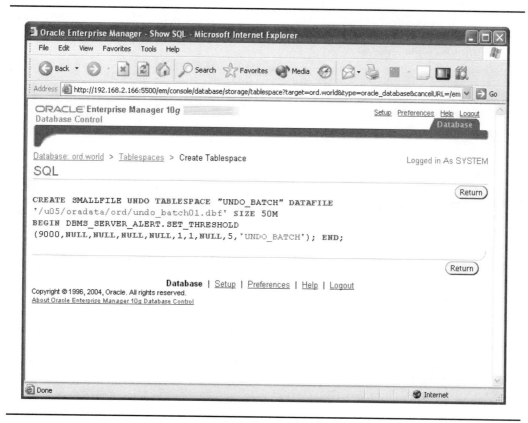

FIGURE 7-5. *Create Undo Tablespace SQL preview*

As with most every EM Database Control maintenance screen, we can view the actual SQL commands that will be executed when we are ready to create the tablespace. In Figure 7-5, we preview the SQL commands used to create the tablespace as well as set up the server alert thresholds for this tablespace.

After we click OK, the new undo tablespace is created successfully in Figure 7-6.

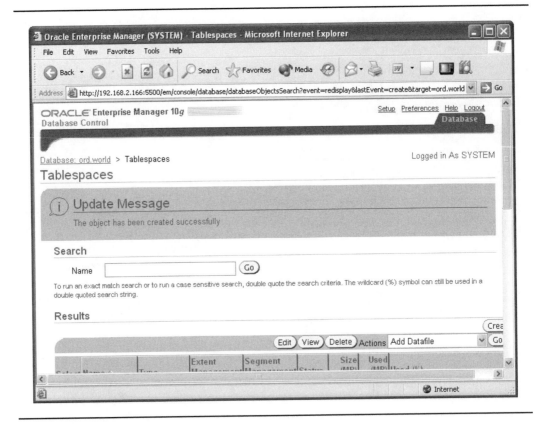

FIGURE 7-6. *Create Undo Tablespace summary*

Note that EM Database Control, although a big timesaver for the DBA, does not cover every possible scenario, nor does it prevent the DBA from trying to create an undo tablespace with the wrong parameters. In Figure 7-3, we could have specified Uniform extent allocation, but when we try to create the tablespace, it fails, as shown in Figure 7-7.

As mentioned earlier in this chapter, undo tablespaces must have automatically allocated extents.

Dropping Undo Tablespaces

Dropping an undo tablespace is similar to dropping any other tablespace; the only restriction is that the undo tablespace being dropped must not be the active undo tablespace or still have undo data for an uncommitted transaction. You may, however, drop an undo tablespace that has unexpired undo information, which may cause a long-running query to fail. To drop the tablespace we created in the previous section, we use the **drop tablespace** command:

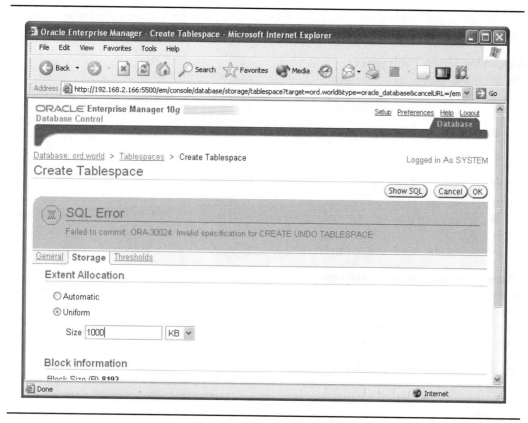

FIGURE 7-7. *Illegal parameters for undo tablespaces*

```
SQL> drop tablespace undo_batch;
Tablespace dropped.
SQL>
```

The clause **including contents** is implied when dropping an undo tablespace. However, to remove the operating system data files when the tablespace is dropped, you must specify **including contents and datafiles**. Trying to drop the active undo tablespace is not allowed:

```
SQL> drop tablespace undotbs1;
drop tablespace undotbs1
*
ERROR at line 1:
ORA-30013: undo tablespace 'UNDOTBS1' is currently in use
SQL>
```

The active undo tablespace must be switched with another undo tablespace before it can be dropped. More information on switching undo tablespaces is covered later in this chapter.

Modifying Undo Tablespaces

The following operations are allowed on undo tablespaces:

- Adding a datafile to an undo tablespace

- Renaming a datafile in an undo tablespace

- Changing an undo tablespace's datafile to online or offline

- Beginning or ending an open tablespace backup (**alter tablespace undotbs begin backup**)

- Enabling or disabling the undo retention guarantee

Everything else is automatically managed by Oracle.

Using OMF for Undo Tablespaces

In addition to using a bigfile tablespace for undo tablespaces, you can also use OMF to automatically name and locate an undo tablespace; the initialization parameter DB_CREATE_FILE_DEST contains the location where an undo tablespace will be created if the **datafile** clause is not specified in the **create undo tablespace** command. In the following example, we create an undo tablespace using OMF:

```
SQL> show parameter db_create_file_dest

NAME                                 TYPE        VALUE
------------------------------------ ----------- ------------------------
db_create_file_dest                  string      /u09/oradata/ord

SQL> create undo tablespace undo_batch;
Tablespace created.

SQL> !ls -l /u09/oradata/ord/ORD/datafile
total 102512
-rw-r-----    1 oracle    oinstall 104865792 Apr 11 21:54
                                        o1_mf_undo_bat_07n16plc_.dbf

SQL>
```

Because we did not specify a datafile size either, the tablespace defaults to a size of 100MB; in addition, the datafile is autoextensible with an unlimited maximum size, limited only by the file system.

Undo Tablespace Dynamic Performance Views

A number of dynamic performance views and data dictionary views contain information about undo tablespaces, user transactions, and undo segments. Table 7-1 contains the view names and their descriptions.

The views in Table 7-1 are described in more detail later in this chapter.

View	Description
DBA_TABLESPACES	Tablespace names and characteristics, including the CONTENTS column, which can be PERMANENT, TEMPORARY, or UNDO; the undo RETENTION column is NOT APPLY, GUARANTEE, or NOGUARANTEE.
DBA_UNDO_EXTENTS	All undo segments in the database, including their size, extents, tablespace where they reside, and current status (EXPIRED or UNEXPIRED).
V$UNDOSTAT	The amount of undo usage for the database at ten-minute intervals; contains at most 1008 rows (7 days).
V$ROLLSTAT	Rollback segment statistics, including size and status.
V$TRANSACTION	Contains one row for each active transaction for the instance.

TABLE 7-1. *Undo Tablespace Views*

Undo Tablespace Initialization Parameters

In the following sections, we'll describe the initialization parameters needed to specify the undo tablespace for the database as well as control how long Oracle will retain undo information in the database.

UNDO_MANAGEMENT

The parameter UNDO_MANAGEMENT defaults to MANUAL. Setting the parameter UNDO_MANAGEMENT to AUTO places the database in Automatic Undo Management mode. At least one undo tablespace must exist in the database for this parameter to be valid, whether UNDO_TABLESPACE is specified or not. UNDO_MANAGEMENT is not a dynamic parameter; therefore, the instance must be restarted whenever UNDO_MANAGEMENT is changed from AUTO to MANUAL, or vice versa.

UNDO_TABLESPACE

The UNDO_TABLESPACE parameter specifies which undo tablespace will be used for Automatic Undo Management. If UNDO_MANAGEMENT is not specified or set to MANUAL, and UNDO_TABLESPACE is specified, the instance will not start.

NOTE
UNDO_TABLESPACE is used in a Real Application Clusters (RAC) environment to assign a particular undo tablespace to an instance, where the total number of undo tablespaces in the database is the same or more than the number of instances in the cluster.

Conversely, if UNDO_MANAGEMENT is set to AUTO and there is no undo tablespace in the database, the instance will start, but then the SYSTEM rollback segment will be used for all undo operations, and a message is written to the alert log. Any user DML that attempts to make changes in non-SYSTEM tablespaces will, in addition, receive the error message "ORA-01552: cannot use system rollback segment for non-system tablespace 'USERS,'" and the statement fails.

UNDO_RETENTION

UNDO_RETENTION specifies a minimum amount of time that undo information is retained for queries. In automatic undo mode, UNDO_RETENTION defaults to 900 seconds. This value is valid only if there is enough space in the undo tablespace to support read-consistent queries; if active transactions require additional undo space, an unexpired undo may be used to satisfy the active transactions and may cause "ORA-01555: Snapshot Too Old" errors.

The column TUNED_UNDORETENTION of the dynamic performance view V$UNDOSTAT gives the tuned undo retention time for each time period; the status of the undo tablespace usage is updated in V$UNDOSTAT every ten minutes:

```
SQL> show parameter undo_retention

NAME                                 TYPE        VALUE
------------------------------------ ----------- ---------------
undo_retention                       integer     43200

SQL> select to_char(begin_time,'yyyy-mm-dd hh24:mi'),
  2   undoblks, txncount, tuned_undoretention
  3   from v$undostat where rownum = 1;

TO_CHAR(BEGIN_TI   UNDOBLKS   TXNCOUNT TUNED_UNDORETENTION
----------------   --------   -------- -------------------
2004-04-11 22:59        206        253               43200
1 row selected.
SQL>
```

Because the transaction load is very light during the most recent time period, and the instance has just recently started up, the tuned undo retention value is the same as the minimum specified in the UNDO_RETENTION initialization parameter: 43200 seconds (12 hours).

TIP
You don't need to specify UNDO_RETENTION unless you have Flashback or LOB retention requirements; the UNDO_RETENTION parameter is not used for managing transaction rollback.

Multiple Undo Tablespaces

As mentioned earlier in this chapter, a database can have multiple undo tablespaces, but only one of them can be active for a given instance at any one time. In this section, we'll show an example of switching to a different undo tablespace while the database is open.

NOTE
*In a Real Application Clusters (RAC) environment, one undo
tablespace is required for each instance in the cluster.*

In our **ord** database, we have two undo tablespaces:

```
SQL> select tablespace_name, status from dba_tablespaces
  2       where contents = 'UNDO';
TABLESPACE_NAME                 STATUS
------------------------------  ---------
UNDOTBS1                        ONLINE
UNDO_BATCH                      ONLINE

2 rows selected.
```

But only one of the undo tablespaces is active:

```
SQL> show parameter undo_tablespace
NAME                            TYPE         VALUE
------------------------------  -----------  ----------------------
undo_tablespace                 string       UNDOTBS1
```

For overnight processing, we change the undo tablespace from UNDOTBS1 to the tablespace
UNDO_BATCH, which is much larger to support higher DML activity. The disk containing the
daytime undo tablespace is much faster, but has a limited amount of space; the disk containing
the overnight undo tablespace is much larger, but slower. As a result, we use the smaller undo
tablespace to support OLTP during the day, and the larger undo tablespace for our data mart and
data warehouse loads, as well as other aggregation activities, at night when response time is not
as big of an issue.

NOTE
*Other than special circumstances described in this section, it is
unlikely that you will be switching undo tablespaces for a given
instance. Oracle's best practices suggest that you create a single
undo tablespace per instance that is large enough to handle all
transaction loads; in other words, "set it and forget it."*

About the time the undo tablespace is going to be switched, the user SCOTT is performing
some maintenance operations on the HR.EMPLOYEES table, and he has an active transaction in
the current undo tablespace:

```
SQL> connect scott/tiger@ord;
Connected.
SQL> set transaction name 'Employee Maintenance';
Transaction set.
```

```
SQL> update hr.employees set commission_pct = commission_pct * 1.1;
107 rows updated.
SQL>
```

Checking V$TRANSACTION, you see SCOTT's uncommitted transaction:

```
SQL> select t.status, t.start_time, t.name
  2     from v$transaction t join v$session s on t.ses_addr = s.saddr
  3     where s.username = 'SCOTT';

STATUS          START_TIME              NAME
-------------   --------------------    -------------------------
ACTIVE          04/12/04 21:56:53       Employee Maintenance

1 row selected.
```

You change the undo tablespace as follows:

```
SQL> alter system set undo_tablespace=undo_batch;
System altered.
```

SCOTT's transaction is still active, and therefore the old undo tablespace still contains the undo information for SCOTT's transaction, leaving the undo segment still available with the following status until the transaction is committed or rolled back:

```
SQL> select r.status
  2     from v$rollstat r join v$transaction t on r.usn=t.xidusn
  3                       join v$session s on t.ses_addr = s.saddr
  4     where s.username = 'SCOTT';

STATUS
---------------
PENDING OFFLINE

1 row selected.
```

Even though the current undo tablespace is UNDO_BATCH, the daytime tablespace UNDOTBS1 cannot be taken offline or dropped until SCOTT's transaction is committed or rolled back:

```
SQL> show parameter undo_tablespace
NAME                            TYPE         VALUE
------------------------------  -----------  ----------------------
undo_tablespace                 string       UNDO_BATCH

SQL> alter tablespace undotbs1 offline;
alter tablespace undotbs1 offline
*
ERROR at line 1:
ORA-30042: Cannot offline the undo tablespace
```

The error message ORA-30042 applies if you try to offline an undo tablespace that is in use—either it is the current undo tablespace or it still has pending transactions. Note that if we switch back to the daytime tablespace before SCOTT commits or rolls back the original transaction, the status of SCOTT's rollback segment reverts back to ONLINE:

```
SQL> alter system set undo_tablespace=undotbs1;
System altered.
SQL> select r.status
  2       from v$rollstat r join v$transaction t on r.usn=t.xidusn
  3                        join v$session s on t.ses_addr = s.saddr
  4       where s.username = 'SCOTT';

STATUS
---------------
ONLINE

1 row selected.
```

Sizing and Monitoring the Undo Tablespace

There are three types of undo data in the undo tablespace: *active* or *unexpired, expired,* and *unused.* Active or unexpired is undo data that is still needed for read consistency, even after a transaction has been committed. Once all queries needing the active undo data have completed and the undo retention period is reached, the active undo data becomes *expired.* Expired undo data may still be used to support other Oracle features, such as the Flashback features, but it is no longer needed to support read consistency for long-running transactions. Unused undo data is space in the undo tablespace that has never been used.

As a result, the minimum size for an undo tablespace is enough space to hold the before-image versions of all data from all active transactions that have not yet been committed or rolled back. If the space allocated to the undo tablespace cannot even support the changes to uncommitted transactions to support a rollback operation, the user will get the error message "ORA-30036: unable to extend segment by *space_qty* in undo tablespace *tablespace_name.*" In this situation, the DBA must increase the size of the undo tablespace, or as a stopgap measure the user can split up a larger transaction into smaller ones while still maintaining any required business rules.

Manual Methods

The DBA can use a number of manual methods to correctly size the undo tablespace. As demonstrated in Chapter 6, we can review the contents of the dynamic performance view V$UNDOSTAT to see the undo segment usage at ten-minute intervals. In addition, the column SSOLDERRCNT indicates how many queries failed with a "Snapshot too old" error:

```
SQL> select to_char(end_time,'yyyy-mm-dd hh24:mi') end_time,
  2>       undoblks, ssolderrcnt from v$undostat;
END_TIME              UNDOBLKS SSOLDERRCNT
----------------      ---------- -----------
2004-04-13 08:12        2114            0
2004-04-13 08:09        4569            0
2004-04-13 07:59        7403            0
```

```
2004-04-13 07:49        2341            0
2004-04-13 07:39        8338            0
2004-04-13 07:29        1483            0
2004-04-13 07:19        1548            0
2004-04-13 07:09       61950            2
2004-04-13 06:59        4433            0
2004-04-13 06:49        5658            0
2004-04-13 06:39         757            0
```

Between 6:59 and 7:09 we have a spike in undo usage, resulting in some failed queries. As a rule of thumb, you can use the following calculations:

```
undo_tablespace_size = UR * UPS + overhead
```

In this formula, UR equals undo retention in seconds (from the initialization parameter UNDO_RETENTION), UPS equals undo blocks used per second (maximum), and overhead equals undo metadata, usually a very small number relative to the overall size. For example, our **ord** database has an 8K block size, and UNDO_RETENTION equals 43200 (12 hours). If we generate 500 undo blocks every second, all of which must be retained for at least 12 hours, our total undo space must be:

```
undo_tablespace_size = 43200 * 500 * 8192 = 176947200000 = 177GB
```

Add about 10 to 20 percent to this calculation to allow for unexpected situations. Alternatively, you can enable autoextend for the datafiles in the undo tablespace. Although this calculation is useful as a starting point, Oracle 10g's built-in advisors, using trending analysis, can give a better overall picture of undo space usage and recommendations.

Undo Advisor

Oracle 10g's Undo Advisor automates a lot of the tasks necessary to fine-tune the amount of space required for an undo tablespace. In Chapter 6, we reviewed two examples of using the Undo Advisor: via the EM Database Control interface and using the PL/SQL DBMS_ADVISOR packages within the Automatic Workload Repository (AWR) to programmatically choose a time period to analyze and perform the analysis.

The Undo Advisor GUI screen is shown in Figure 7-8.

Although we have UNDO_RETENTION set to 43200 (720 minutes), it appears from the Undo Advisor that the autotuned undo retention period does not need to go any higher or lower than 720 minutes to support a read-consistent view of tables being changed, given the current undo segment usage.

When we created our undo tablespace earlier in this chapter (refer back to Figure 7-4), we set some thresholds for the undo tablespace. With these automatic warnings in place, we can proactively resize the undo tablespace if and when the undo tablespace usage goes past our thresholds—before we have any failed DML or queries, and ideally before the phone rings!

Controlling Undo Usage

As of Oracle9i, Oracle's Database Resource Manager can help to control undo space usage by user or by group of users within a resource consumer group via the UNDO_POOL directive. Each consumer group can have its own undo pool; when the total undo generated by a group exceeds

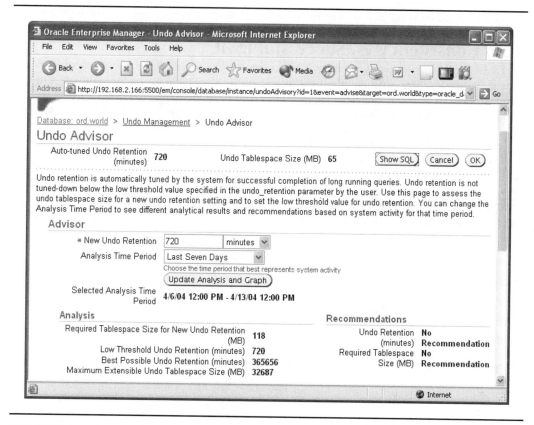

FIGURE 7-8. *EM Database Control Undo Advisor*

the assigned limit, the current transaction generating the undo is terminated and generates the error message "ORA-30027: Undo quota violation—failed to get *number* (bytes)." The session will have to wait until the DBA increases the size of the undo pool or until other transactions from users in the same consumer group complete.

In the following example, we change the default value of UNDO_POOL from NULL (unlimited) to 1000KB for users in the resource consumer group LOW_GROUP:

```
begin
    dbms_resource_manager.create_pending_area();
    dbms_resource_manager.update_plan_directive(
        plan => 'system_plan',
        group_or_subplan => 'low_group',
        new_comment => 'Limit undo space for low priority groups',
        new_undo_pool => 1000);
    dbms_resource_manager.validate_pending_area();
    dbms_resource_manager.submit_pending_area();
end;
```

Oracle Resource Manager and other resource directives are covered in more detail in Chapter 5.

Read Consistency vs. Successful DML

For OLTP databases, generally we want DML commands to succeed at the expense of read-consistent queries. For a DSS environment, however, we may want long-running queries to complete without getting a "Snapshot too old" error. Although increasing the UNDO_RETENTION parameter or increasing the size of the undo tablespace helps to ensure that undo blocks are available for read-consistent queries, undo tablespaces have another characteristic to help ensure that queries will run to completion: the RETENTION GUARANTEE setting.

Undo retention guarantee is set at the tablespace level, and it can be altered at any time. Setting a retention guarantee for an undo tablespace ensures that an unexpired undo within the tablespace should be retained even if it means that DML transactions might not have enough undo space to complete successfully. By default, a tablespace is created with NOGUARANTEE, unless you specify the GUARANTEE keyword, either when the tablespace is created or later with ALTER TABLESPACE:

```
SQL> alter tablespace undotbs1 retention guarantee;
Tablespace altered.

SQL> select tablespace_name, retention
  2    from dba_tablespaces
  3    where tablespace_name = 'UNDOTBS1';

TABLESPACE_NAME                 RETENTION
------------------------------- -----------
UNDOTBS1                        GUARANTEE

1 row selected.
```

For non-undo tablespaces, the value of RETENTION is always NOT APPLY.

Flashback Features

In this section we'll discuss the Flashback features supported by undo tablespaces: Flashback Query, Flashback Table, Flashback Version Query, and Flashback Transaction Query. In addition, we'll cover the highlights of using the DBMS_FLASHBACK package.

Flashback Database and Flashback Drop are covered in Chapter 15. Flashback Database uses Flashback logs in the Flash Recovery Area instead of undo in an undo tablespace to provide the Flashback functionality; Flashback Drop places dropped tables into a virtual recycle bin within the tablespace and they remain there until the user retrieves it with **flashback table ... to before drop**, empties the recycle bin or the space is needed by new permanent objects in the tablespace.

To further extend the self-service capabilities of Oracle10*g*, the DBA can grant system and object privileges to users to allow them to fix their own problems, usually without any DBA intervention. In the following example, we're enabling the user SCOTT to perform Flashback operations on specific tables and to access transaction metadata across the database:

```
SQL> grant insert, update, delete, select on hr.employees to scott;
Grant succeeded.
SQL> grant insert, update, delete, select on hr.departments to scott;
Grant succeeded.
SQL> grant flashback on hr.employees to scott;
Grant succeeded.
SQL> grant flashback on hr.departments to scott;
Grant succeeded.
SQL> grant select any transaction to scott;
Grant succeeded.
```

Flashback Query

Starting with Oracle 9i2, the **as of** clause is available in a **select** query to retrieve the state of a table as of a given timestamp or SCN. You might use this to find out which rows in a table were deleted since midnight, or you might want to just do a comparison of the rows in a table today versus what was in the table yesterday.

In the following example, SCOTT is cleaning up the HR.EMPLOYEES table and deletes two employees who no longer work for the company:

```
SQL> delete from hr.employees
  2  where employee_id in (195,196);
2 rows deleted.

SQL> commit;
Commit complete.

SQL>
```

Normally, SCOTT will copy these rows to the HR.EMPLOYEES_ARCHIVE table first, but forgot to do that this time; he doesn't need to put those rows back into the HR.EMPLOYEES table, but he needs to get the two deleted rows and put them into the archive table. Because SCOTT knows he deleted the rows less than an hour ago, we can use a relative timestamp value with Flashback Query to retrieve the rows:

```
SQL>  insert into hr.employees_archive
  2       select * from hr.employees
  3          as of timestamp systimestamp - interval '60' minute
  4          where hr.employees.employee_id not in
  5             (select employee_id from hr.employees);

2 rows created.

SQL> commit;
Commit complete.
```

Because we know that EMPLOYEE_ID is the primary key of the table, we can use it to retrieve the employee records that existed an hour ago, but do not exist now. Note also that we didn't have to know which records were deleted; we essentially compared the table as it existed now versus an hour ago and inserted the records that no longer exist into the archive table.

TIP
It is preferable to use the SCN for Flashback over a timestamp; SCNs are exact, whereas the timestamp values are only stored every five minutes to support Flashback operations. As a result, enabling Flashback using timestamps may be off by as many as 150 seconds.

Although we could use Flashback Table to get the entire table back, then archive and delete the affected rows, in this case it is much simpler to merely retrieve the deleted rows and insert them directly into the archive table.

Another variation of Flashback Table is to use Create Table As Select (CTAS) with the subquery being a Flashback Query:

```
SQL> delete from hr.employees where employee_id in (195,196);
2 rows deleted.

SQL> commit;
Commit complete.

SQL> create table hr.employees_deleted as
  2       select * from hr.employees
  3           as of timestamp systimestamp - interval '60' minute
  4           where hr.employees.employee_id not in
  5               (select employee_id from hr.employees);
Table created.

SQL> select employee_id, last_name from hr.employees_deleted;

EMPLOYEE_ID LAST_NAME
----------- ------------------------
        195 Jones
        196 Walsh

2 rows selected.
```

This is known as an *out-of-place restore* (in other words, restoring the table or a subset of the table to a different location than the original). This has the advantage of being able to further manipulate the missing rows, if necessary, before placing them back in the table; for example, after reviewing the out-of-place restore, an existing referential integrity constraint may require that you insert a row into a parent table before the restored row can be placed back in the child table.

One of the disadvantages of an out-of-place restore using CTAS is that neither constraints nor indexes are rebuilt automatically.

DBMS_FLASHBACK

An alternative to Flashback Query is the package DBMS_FLASHBACK. One of the key differences between the DBMS_FLASHBACK package and Flashback Query is that DBMS_FLASHBACK operates at the session level, whereas Flashback Query operates at the object level.

Within a PL/SQL procedure or a user session, DBMS_FLASHBACK can be enabled and all subsequent operations, including existing applications, can be carried out without the **as of** clause being added to **select** statements. After DBMS_FLASHBACK is enabled as of a particular timestamp or SCN, the database appears as if the clock was turned back to the timestamp or SCN until DBMS_FLASHBACK is disabled. Although DML is not allowed when DBMS_FLASHBACK is enabled, a cursor can be opened in a PL/SQL procedure before DBMS_FLASHBACK is enabled to allow data from a previous point in time to be inserted or updated in the database as of the current point in time.

Table 7-2 lists the procedures available within DBMS_FLASHBACK.

The procedures that enable and disable Flashback mode are relatively simple to use. The complexity usually lies within a PL/SQL procedure, for example, that creates cursors to support DML commands.

In the following example, we'll revisit SCOTT's deletion of the HR.EMPLOYEES rows and how he can restore those to the table using the DBMS_FLASHBACK package. In this scenario, SCOTT will put the deleted employee rows back into the table and instead add a termination date column to the table to reflect the date at which the employees left the company:

```
SQL> delete from hr.employees where employee_id in (195,196);
2 rows deleted.

SQL> commit;
Commit complete.
```

About 30 minutes later, SCOTT decides to get those rows back using DBMS_FLASHBACK, and enables Flashback for his session:

```
SQL> execute dbms_flashback.enable_at_time(
  2                  to_timestamp(sysdate - interval '45' minute));
PL/SQL procedure successfully completed.
```

Procedure	Description
DISABLE	Disables Flashback mode for the session
ENABLE_AT_SYSTEM_CHANGE_NUMBER	Enables Flashback mode for the session, specifying an SCN
ENABLE_AT_TIME	Enables Flashback mode for the session, using the SCN closest to the TIMESTAMP specified
GET_SYSTEM_CHANGE_NUMBER	Returns the current SCN
SCN_TO_TIMESTAMP	
TIMESTAMP_TO_SCN	Converts an Oracle TIMESTAMP and returns the SCN closest to the TIMESTAMP value

TABLE 7-2. *DBMS_FLASHBACK Procedures*

Next, he verifies that the two deleted rows existed as of 45 minutes ago:

```
SQL> select employee_id, last_name from hr.employees
  2      where employee_id in (195,196);

EMPLOYEE_ID LAST_NAME
----------- ------------------------
        195 Jones
        196 Walsh

SQL>
```

To put the rows back into the HR.EMPLOYEES table, SCOTT writes an anonymous PL/SQL procedure to create a cursor to hold the deleted rows, disable Flashback Query, then reinsert the rows:

```
declare
    -- cursor to hold deleted rows before closing
    cursor del_emp is
        select * from hr.employees where employee_id in (195,196);
    del_emp_rec del_emp%rowtype; -- all columns of the employee row
begin
    -- open the cursor while still in Flashback mode
    open del_emp;
    -- turn off Flashback so we can use DML to put the rows
    -- back into the HR.EMPLOYEES table
    dbms_flashback.disable;
    loop
        fetch del_emp into del_emp_rec;
        exit when del_emp%notfound;
        insert into hr.employees values del_emp_rec;
    end loop;
    commit;
    close del_emp;
end; -- anonymous PL/SQL procedure
```

Note that SCOTT could have enabled Flashback within the procedure; in this case, he enabled it outside of the procedure to run some ad-hoc queries, then used the procedure to create the cursor, turn off Flashback, and reinsert the rows.

Flashback Table

Oracle10*g*'s Flashback Table feature not only restores the state of rows in a table as of a point of time in the past, but it also restores the table's indexes, triggers, and constraints while the database is online, increasing the overall availability of the database. The table can be restored as of a timestamp or an SCN. Flashback Table is preferable to other Flashback methods if the scope of user errors is small and limited to one or very few tables. It's also the most straightforward if you know that you want to restore the table to a point in the past unconditionally. For recovering the state of a larger number of tables, Flashback Database may be a better choice. Flashback Table cannot be used on a standby database and cannot reconstruct all DDL operations, such as adding and dropping columns.

To use Flashback Table on a table or tables, you must enable *row movement* on the table before performing the Flashback operation, although row movement need not be in effect when the user error occurs. Row movement is also required to support Oracle's segment shrink functionality; because row movement will change the ROWID of a table row, do not enable row movement if your applications depend on the ROWID being the same for a given row until the row is deleted. Because none of our applications reference our tables by ROWID, we can safely enable row movement for our tables:

```
SQL> alter table hr.employees enable row movement;
Table altered.
SQL> alter table hr.departments enable row movement;
Table altered.
```

The next day, SCOTT accidentally deletes all the rows in the HR.EMPLOYEES table due to a cut-and-paste error from an existing script:

```
SQL> delete from hr.employees
  2  /
107 rows deleted.

SQL> commit
  2  ;
Commit complete.

SQL> where employee_id = 195
SP2-0734: unknown command beginning "where empl..." - rest of line ignored.
```

Because the undo tablespace is large enough and the retention period is 12 hours, SCOTT can bring back the entire table quickly without calling the DBA:

```
SQL> flashback table hr.employees
  2       to timestamp systimestamp - interval '15' minute;
Flashback complete.

SQL> select count(*) from hr.employees;
  COUNT(*)
----------
       107
```

If two or more tables have a parent/child relationship with foreign key constraints, and rows were inadvertently deleted from both tables, they can be flashed back in the same **Flashback** command:

```
SQL>    flashback table hr.employees, hr.departments
  2          to timestamp systimestamp - interval '15' minute;
Flashback complete.
```

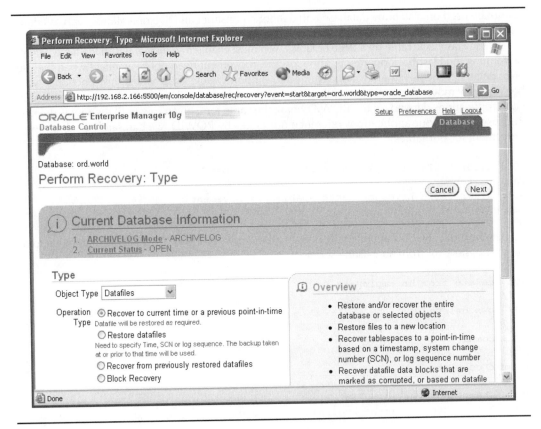

FIGURE 7-9. *EM Database Control Backup/Recovery*

SCOTT can also use EM Database Control to flash back one or more tables. In Figure 7-9, he has selected the Perform Recovery link under the heading Backup/Recovery under the Maintenance tab.

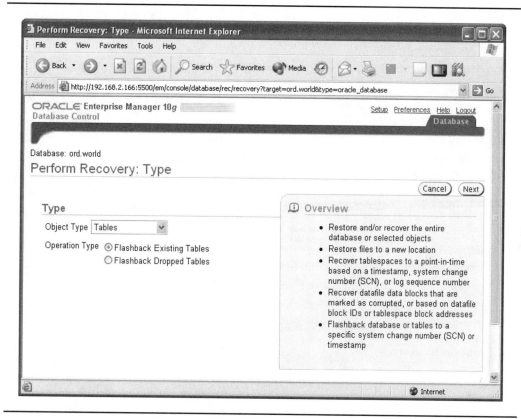

FIGURE 7-10.   *Flashback Existing Tables*

Selecting an object type of Tables, SCOTT have the option to flash back existing tables or dropped tables. In this case, he will be flashing back an existing table, as indicated in Figure 7-10.

After clicking Next, he knows the precise time of day at which the table was valid, so He specifies that on the screen in Figure 7-11.

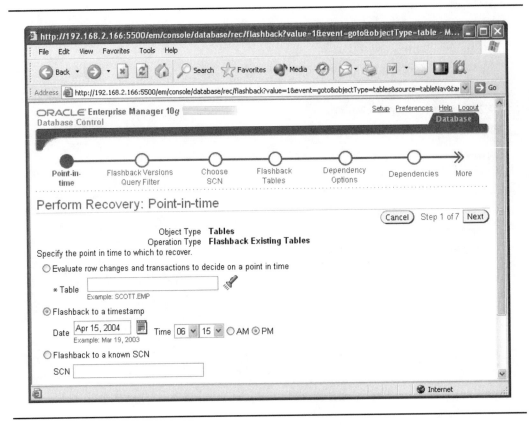

FIGURE 7-11. *Selecting a date and time for Flashback Table*

In Figure 7-12, SCOTT is selecting the table to flash back (in this case, HR.EMPLOYEES). The screen summarizes the timestamp chosen and the equivalent SCN.

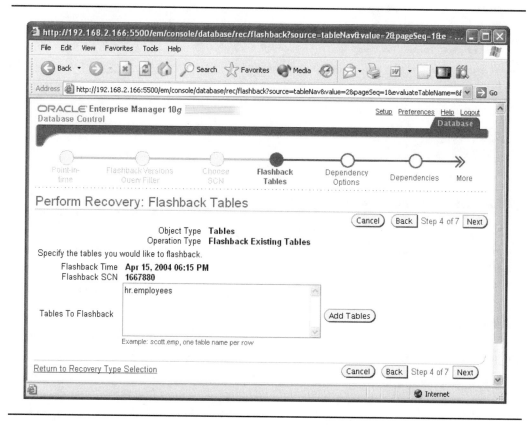

FIGURE 7-12.   *Flashback Table selection*

EM Database Control identifies any dependencies, such as foreign key constraints, and alerts SCOTT in Figure 7-13. Unless there is a good reason to break any parent/child relationships between the tables, leave the default option, Cascade, selected.

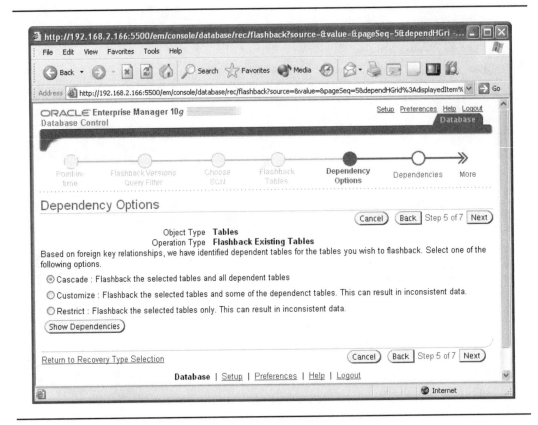

FIGURE 7-13. *EM Database Control Flashback dependency options*

Clicking **Show Dependencies** does just that: It shows the dependencies between the foreign keys in the table to be flashed back and the parent tables. The entire hierarchy of dependencies is shown in Figure 7-14.

In Figure 7-15, SCOTT can take one more look at the options he has selected.

In addition, as with most EM Database Control screens, he can review the SQL commands generated:

```
FLASHBACK TABLE HR.EMPLOYEES, HR.JOBS, HR.DEPARTMENTS TO TIMESTAMP
to_timestamp('2004-04-15 06:15:12 PM', 'YYYY-MM-DD HH:MI:SS AM')
```

Clicking Submit runs the command.

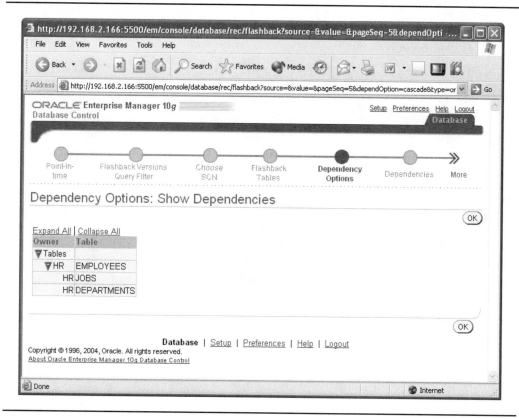

FIGURE 7-14.   *Flashback dependency hierarchy*

Note that in SCOTT's example, using the command line would take less time and is probably more straightforward; however, if you have unknown dependencies or if the command-line syntax is unfamiliar to you, then EM Database Control is a better option.

Flashback Version Query

Flashback Version Query, another Flashback feature that relies on undo data, provides a finer level of detail than an **as of** query: Whereas the Flashback methods we've presented up to now bring back rows of a table or an entire table for a particular point in time, Flashback Version Query will return the entire history of a given row between two SCNs or timestamps.

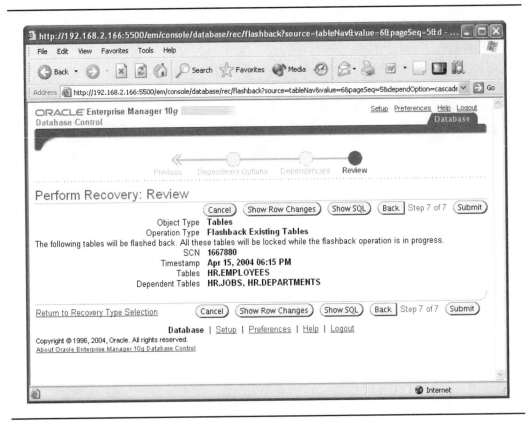

FIGURE 7-15. *Flashback Table Options Review*

For the examples in this and the next section, the user SCOTT makes a number of changes to the HR.EMPLOYEES and HR.DEPARTMENTS tables:

```
SQL> select dbms_flashback.get_system_change_number from dual;
GET_SYSTEM_CHANGE_NUMBER
------------------------
               1673333

SQL> update hr.employees set salary = salary*1.2 where employee_id=195;
1 row updated.

SQL> select dbms_flashback.get_system_change_number from dual;
GET_SYSTEM_CHANGE_NUMBER
------------------------
               1673349

SQL> delete from hr.employees where employee_id = 196;
```

```
1 row deleted.

SQL> select dbms_flashback.get_system_change_number from dual;
GET_SYSTEM_CHANGE_NUMBER
------------------------
                 1673406

SQL> insert into hr.departments values (660,'Security', 100, 1700);
1 row created.

SQL> select dbms_flashback.get_system_change_number from dual;
GET_SYSTEM_CHANGE_NUMBER
------------------------
                 1673433

SQL> update hr.employees set manager_id = 100 where employee_id = 195;
1 row updated.

SQL> commit;
Commit complete.

SQL> select dbms_flashback.get_system_change_number from dual;
GET_SYSTEM_CHANGE_NUMBER
------------------------
                 1673455

SQL> update hr.employees set department_id = 660 where employee_id = 195;
1 row updated.

SQL> select dbms_flashback.get_system_change_number from dual;
GET_SYSTEM_CHANGE_NUMBER
------------------------
                 1673602

SQL> update hr.employees set salary = salary*1.2 where employee_id=195;
1 row updated.

SQL> commit;
Commit complete.

SQL> select dbms_flashback.get_system_change_number from dual;
GET_SYSTEM_CHANGE_NUMBER
------------------------
                 1674188
SQL>
```

The next day, the SCOTT is out of the office, and the HR department wants to know what rows and tables were changed. Using Flashback Version Query, the user HR can see not only the values of a column at a particular time, but the entire history of changes between specified timestamps or SCNs.

A Flashback Version Query uses the **versions between** clause to specify a range of SCNs or timestamps for analysis of a given table (in this case, the HR.EMPLOYEES table). When **versions between** is used in a Flashback Version Query, a number of pseudocolumns are available to help identify the SCN and timestamp of the modifications, as well as the transaction ID and the type of operation performed on the row. Table 7-3 shows the pseudocolumns available with Flashback Version Queries.

The HR user runs a Flashback Version Query to see the changes to any key columns in HR.EMPLOYEES for the two employees with IDs 195 and 196:

```
SQL> select versions_startscn startscn, versions_endscn endscn,
  2       versions_xid xid, versions_operation oper,
  3       employee_id empid, last_name name, manager_id mgrid, salary sal
  4  from hr.employees
  5  versions between scn 1673333 and 1674188
  6  where employee_id in (195,196);
STARTSCN    ENDSCN   XID                OPER EMPID NAME     MGRID      SAL
---------  --------- ----------------   ---- ----- -------- -----   --------
 1674182             0400240098030000 U      195 Jones     100       4032
 1673453   1674182   0400160098030000 U      195 Jones     100       3360
 1673368   1673453   04000F0098030000 U      195 Jones     123       3360
           1673368                            195 Jones     123       2800
 1673368             04000F0098030000 D      196 Walsh     124       3100
           1673368                            196 Walsh     124       3100

6 rows selected.
```

Pseudocolumn	Description
VERSIONS_START{SCN|TIME}	The starting SCN or timestamp when the change was made to the row.
VERSION_END{SCN|TIME}	The ending SCN or timestamp when the change was no longer valid for the row. If this is NULL, either the row version is still current or the row was deleted.
VERSIONS_XID	The transaction ID of the transaction that created the row version.
VERSIONS_OPERATION	The operation performed on the row (I=Insert, D=Delete, U=Update).

TABLE 7-3.   *Flashback Version Query Pseudocolumns*

The rows are presented with the most recent changes first. Alternatively, HR could have filtered the query by TIMESTAMP or displayed the TIMESTAMP values, but either can be used in a Flashback Query or Flashback Table operation, if required later. From this output, we see that one employee was deleted and that another employee received two pay adjustments instead of one. It's also worth noting that some of the transactions contain only one DML command, and others have two.

In the next section, we'll attempt to correct one or more of these problems.

Flashback Transaction Query

Once we have identified any erroneous or incorrect changes to a table, we can use Flashback Transaction Query to identify any other changes that were made by the transaction containing the inappropriate changes. Once identified, all changes within the transaction can be reversed as a group, typically to maintain referential integrity or the business rules used to process the transaction in the first place.

A Flashback Transaction Query, unlike a Flashback Version Query, does not reference the table involved in DML transactions; instead, you query the data dictionary view FLASHBACK_TRANSACTION_QUERY. The columns of FLASHBACK_TRANSACTION_QUERY are summarized in Table 7-4.

Column Name	Description
XID	Transaction ID number
START_SCN	SCN for the first DML in the transaction
START_TIMESTAMP	Timestamp of the first DML in the transaction
COMMIT_SCN	SCN when the transaction was committed
COMMIT_TIMESTAMP	Timestamp when the transaction was committed
LOGON_USER	User who owned the transaction
UNDO_CHANGE#	Undo SCN
OPERATION	DML operation performed: DELETE, INSERT, UPDATE, BEGIN, or UNKNOWN
TABLE_NAME	Table changed by DML
TABLE_OWNER	Owner of the table changed by DML
ROW_ID	ROWID of the row modified by DML
UNDO_SQL	SQL statement to undo the DML operation

TABLE 7-4. *FLASHBACK_TRANSACTION_QUERY Columns*

To further investigate the changes that were made to the HR.EMPLOYEES table, we will query the view FLASHBACK_TRANSACTION_QUERY with the oldest transaction from the query in the previous section:

```
SQL> select start_scn, commit_scn, logon_user,
  2       operation, table_name, undo_sql
  3  from flashback_transaction_query
  4  where xid = hextoraw('04000F0098030000');

START_SCN COMMIT_SCN LOGON_USER OPERATION    TABLE_NAME
--------- ---------- ---------- ------------ ---------------
UNDO_SQL
-----------------------------------------------------------
  1673366    1673368 SCOTT        DELETE       EMPLOYEES
insert into "HR"."EMPLOYEES"("EMPLOYEE_ID","FIRST_NAME","LAS
T_NAME","EMAIL","PHONE_NUMBER","HIRE_DATE","JOB_ID","SALARY"
,"COMMISSION_PCT","MANAGER_ID","DEPARTMENT_ID") values ('196
','Alana','Walsh','AWALSH','650.507.9811',TO_DATE('24-APR-98
', 'DD-MON-RR'),'SH_CLERK','3100',NULL,'124','50');

  1673366    1673368 SCOTT        UPDATE       EMPLOYEES
update "HR"."EMPLOYEES" set "SALARY" = '2800' where ROWID =
'AAAMAeAAFAAAABYABc';

  1673366    1673368 SCOTT        BEGIN

3 rows selected.
```

We confirm what we already expected—that SCOTT made the deletion and salary update. The UNDO_SQL column contains the actual SQL code that can be used to reverse the effect of the transaction. Note, however, that in this example, this is the first transaction to occur between the SCNs of interest. If other transactions made further updates to the same columns, we may want to review the other updates before running this SQL code. Looking at the most recent transaction in the series, we see that there was a more recent update to the SALARY column for the employee:

```
SQL> select start_scn, commit_scn, logon_user,
  2       operation, table_name, undo_sql
  3  from flashback_transaction_query
  4  where xid = hextoraw('04000F0098030000');

START_SCN COMMIT_SCN LOGON_USER OPERATION    TABLE_NAME
--------- ---------- ---------- ------------ ---------------
UNDO_SQL
-----------------------------------------------------------
  1673386    1674182 SCOTT        UPDATE       EMPLOYEES
update "HR"."EMPLOYEES" set "SALARY" = '3360' where ROWID =
'AAAMAeAAFAAAABYABc';

  1673386    1674182 SCOTT        INSERT       JOB_HISTORY
delete from "HR"."JOB_HISTORY" where ROWID = 'AAAMAiAAFAAAAB
tAAB';
```

```
   1673386    1674182 SCOTT       UPDATE        EMPLOYEES
update "HR"."EMPLOYEES" set "DEPARTMENT_ID" = '50' where ROW
ID = 'AAAMAeAAFAAAABYABc';

   1673386    1674182 SCOTT       BEGIN

4 rows selected.
```

The first salary update was valid, whereas the second (most recent) was duplicated and is therefore not valid. During this same transaction, SCOTT also changed the DEPARTMENT_ID of the employee, in addition to an **insert** to the HR.JOB_HISTORY table. The **insert** was not a result of an explicit command, but rather due to a trigger on the HR.EMPLOYEES table that logs changes to HR.EMPLOYEES in HR.JOB_HISTORY when the JOB_ID or DEPARTMENT_ID changes. Only the most recent salary update needs to be reversed:

```
SQL> update "HR"."EMPLOYEES"
  2    set "SALARY" = '3360' where ROWID ='AAAMAeAAFAAAABYABc';
1 row updated.
SQL> commit;
Commit complete.
```

Looking at the second-most-recent transaction, you see the **insert** into the HR.DEPARTMENTS table, plus the reassignment of one employee to that new department:

```
SQL> select start_scn, commit_scn, logon_user,
  2       operation, table_name, undo_sql
  3  from flashback_transaction_query
  4  where xid = hextoraw(' 0400160098030000');

START_SCN COMMIT_SCN LOGON_USER OPERATION     TABLE_NAME
---------- ---------- ---------- ------------ ---------------
UNDO_SQL
-------------------------------------------------------------
   1673449    1673453 SCOTT       UPDATE        EMPLOYEES
update "HR"."EMPLOYEES" set "MANAGER_ID" = '123' where ROWID
 = 'AAAMAeAAFAAAABYABc';

   1673449    1673453 SCOTT       INSERT        DEPARTMENTS
delete from "HR"."DEPARTMENTS" where ROWID = 'AAAMAZAAFAAAAA
1AAB';

   1673449    1673453 SCOTT       BEGIN

3 rows selected.
```

Because you did not include the DEPARTMENT_ID column in the Flashback Versions Query, it was not immediately obvious that there were other changes to other columns of the HR.EMPLOYEES table, in addition to a new row inserted into HR.DEPARTMENTS.

Migrating to Automatic Undo Management

To migrate your environment from manually managed rollback segments to Automatic Undo Management, you need to know one thing: how large to size the undo tablespace based on the usage of the rollback segments in manual undo mode. With all manual rollback segments online, execute the procedure DBMS_UNDO_ADV.RBU_MIGRATION to return the size, in megabytes, of the current rollback segment utilization:

```
SQL> variable undo_size number
SQL> begin
  2        :undo_size := dbms_undo_adv.rbu_migration;
  3  end;
  4  /

PL/SQL procedure successfully completed.

SQL> print :undo_size

 UNDO_SIZE
----------
      2840

SQL>
```

In this example, an undo tablespace created to replace the rollback segments should be at least 2840MB, or 2.84GB, to support the undo requirements currently supported by rollback segments.

CHAPTER
8

Database Tuning

rom a performance perspective, every system is designed to fail at some point. The goal of performance design is to make sure that the physical limitations of the applications—I/O throughput rates, memory sizes, query performance, and so on— do not impact the business performance. If the application performance limits the business process it is supposed to be supporting, the application must be tuned. During the design process, the limits of the application environment—including the hardware and the design of the application's interactions with the database—must be evaluated. No environment provides infinite computing capacity, so every environment is designed to fail at some performance point. In the process of designing the application, you should strive to have your performance needs amply served by the performance capabilities of the environment.

Performance tuning is a part of the life cycle of every database application, and the earlier performance is addressed the more likely it will be successfully resolved. As noted in previous chapters, most performance problems are not isolated symptoms but rather are the result of the system design. Tuning efforts should therefore focus on identifying and fixing the underlying flaws that yield the unacceptable performance.

Tuning is the final step in a four-step process: planning, implementing, and monitoring must precede it. If you tune only for the sake of tuning, you are failing to address the full cycle of activity and will likely never resolve the underlying flaws that caused the performance problem.

Most of the database objects that can be tuned are discussed elsewhere in this book—for example, undo segments are covered thoroughly in Chapter 7. This chapter only discusses the tuning-related activities for such objects, while their own chapters cover planning and monitoring activities.

As of Oracle 10g, you can take advantage of new tuning tools and features, including the Automated Workload Repository. Tools available with earlier versions, such as STATSPACK, have been enhanced. See Chapter 9 for details on the implementation and use of STATSPACK.

In the following sections, you will see tuning activities for the following areas:

- Application design
- SQL
- Memory usage
- Data storage
- Data manipulation
- Physical storage
- Logical storage
- Network traffic

Tuning Application Design

Why should a DBA tuning guide include a section on application design? And why should this section come first? Because nothing you can do as a DBA will have as great an impact on the system performance as the design of the application. The requirements for making the DBA's involvement in application development a reality are described in Chapter 5. In designing an application, you can take several steps to make effective and proper use of the available technology, as described in the following sections.

Effective Table Design

No matter how well designed your database is, poor table design will lead to poor performance. Not only that, but overly rigid adherence to relational table designs will lead to poor performance. That is due to the fact that while fully relational table designs (said to be in the *third normal form*) are logically desirable, they are usually physically undesirable.

The problem with such designs is that although they accurately reflect the ways in which an application's data is related to other data, they do not reflect the normal access paths that users will employ to access that data. Once the user's access requirements are evaluated, the fully relational table design will become unworkable for many large queries. Typically, the first problems will occur with queries that return a large number of columns. These columns are usually scattered among several tables, forcing the tables to be joined together during the query. If one of the joined tables is large, the performance of the whole query may suffer.

In designing the tables for an application, developers should first develop the model in third normal form and then consider denormalizing data to meet specific requirements—for example, creating small summary tables from large, static tables. Can that data be dynamically derived from the large, static tables on demand? Of course. But if the users frequently request it, and the data is largely unchanging, then it makes sense to periodically store that data *in the format in which the users will ask for it.*

For example, some applications store historical data and current data in the same table. Each record may have a timestamp column, so the current record in a set is the one with the most recent timestamp. Every time a user queries the table for a current record, the user will need to perform a subquery, such as the following:

```
where timestamp_col =
    (select max(timestamp_col)
       from table
      where emp_name='some name')
```

If two such tables are joined, there will be two subqueries. In a small database, this may not present a performance problem, but as the number of tables and rows increase, performance problems will follow. Partitioning the historical data away from the current data or storing the historical data in a separate table will involve more work for the DBAs and developers but should improve the long-term performance of the application.

User-centered table design, rather than theory-centered table design, will yield a system that better meets the users' requirements. Design options include separating a single table into multiple tables, and the reverse—combining multiple tables into one. The emphasis should be on providing the users the most direct path possible to the data they want in the format they want.

Distribution of CPU Requirements

When effectively designed and given adequate hardware, an Oracle database application will process I/O requests without excessive waits, will use memory areas without swapping and paging memory to disk, and will use the CPU without generating high load averages. Data that is read into memory by one process will be stored in memory and reused by many processes before it is aged out of memory. SQL commands are reused via the shared SQL area, further reducing the burden on the system.

If the I/O burdens of the system are reduced, the CPU burden may increase. You have several options for managing the CPU resources:

- The CPU load should be scheduled. You should time long-running batch queries or update programs to run at off-peak hours. Rather than run them at lower operating system priority while online users are performing transactions, run them at normal operating system priority at an appropriate time. Maintaining their normal priority level while scheduling the jobs appropriately will minimize potential locking, undo, and CPU conflicts.

- Take advantage of the opportunity to physically shift CPU requirements from one server to another. Wherever possible, isolate the database server from the application's CPU requirements. The data distribution techniques described in the networking chapters of this book will result in data being stored in its most appropriate place, and the CPU requirements of the application may be separated from the I/O requirements against the database.

- Consider using Oracle's Real Application Clusters (RAC) technology to spread the database access requirements for a single database across multiple instances.

- Use the database resource management features. You can use the Database Resource Manager to establish resource allocation plans and resource consumer groups. You can use Oracle's capabilities to change the resource allocations available to the consumer groups. See Chapter 5 for details on creating and implementing resource consumer groups and resource plans via the Database Resource Manager.

- Use Parallel Query to distribute the processing requirements of SQL statements among multiple CPUs. Parallelism can be used by almost every SQL command, including **select**, **create table as select**, **create index**, **recover**, and the SQL*Loader Direct Path loading options.

The degree to which a transaction is parallelized depends on the defined degree of parallelism for the transaction. Each table has a defined degree of parallelism, and a query can override the default degree of parallelism by using the PARALLEL hint. Oracle evaluates the number of CPUs available on the server and the number of disks on which the table's data is stored in order to determine the default degree of parallelism.

The maximum available parallelism is set at the instance level. The PARALLEL_MAX_SERVERS initialization parameter sets the maximum number of parallel query server processes that can be used at any one time by all the processes in the database. For example, if you set PARALLEL_MAX_SERVERS to 32 for your instance, and you run a query that uses 30 parallel query server processes for its query and sorting operations, then only two parallel query server processes are available for all the rest of the users in the database. Therefore, you need to carefully manage the parallelism you allow for your queries and batch operations. The PARALLEL_ADAPTIVE_MULTI_USER parameter, when set to TRUE, enables an adaptive algorithm designed to improve performance in multiuser environments using parallel execution. The algorithm automatically reduces the requested degree of parallelism based on the system load at query startup time. The effective degree of parallelism is based on the default degree of parallelism, or the degree from the table, or hints, divided by a reduction factor.

For each table, you can set a default degree of parallelism via the **parallel** clause of the **create table** and **alter table** commands. The *degree of parallelism* tells Oracle how many parallel query server processes to attempt to use for each part of the operation. For example, if a query that performs both table scanning and data sorting operations has a degree of parallelism of 5, there could be ten parallel query server processes used—five for scanning and five for sorting. You can also specify a degree of parallelism for an index when it is created, via the **parallel** clause of the **create index** command.

The minimum number of parallel query server processes started is set via the PARALLEL_ MIN_SERVERS initialization parameter. In general, you should set this parameter to a very low number (less than 5) unless the system is actively used at all hours of the day. Setting this parameter to a low value will force Oracle to repeatedly start new query server processes, but it will greatly decrease the amount of memory held by idle parallel query server processes during low-use periods. If you set a high value for PARALLEL_MIN_SERVERS, you may frequently have idle parallel query server processes on your server, holding onto the memory they had previously acquired but not performing any functions.

Parallelizing operations distributes their processing requirements across multiple CPUs; however, you should use these features carefully. If you use a degree of parallelism of 5 for a large query, you will have five separate processes accessing the data. If you have that many processes accessing the data, you may create contention for the disks on which the data is stored, thus hurting performance. When using Parallel Query, you should selectively apply it to those tables whose data is well distributed over many physical devices. Also, you should avoid using it for all tables; as noted earlier, a single query may use all the available parallel query server processes, eliminating the parallelism for all the rest of the transactions in your database.

Effective Application Design

In addition to the application design topics described later in this chapter are several general guidelines for Oracle applications.

First, they should minimize the number of times they request data from the database. Options include the use of sequences, PL/SQL blocks, and the denormalization of tables. You can use distributed database objects such as materialized views to help reduce the number of times a database is queried.

NOTE
Even mildly inefficient SQL can impact your database's performance if it is executed frequently enough. SQL that generates few or no physical I/O reads still consumes CPU resources.

Second, different users of the same application should query the database in a very similar fashion. Consistent access paths increase the likelihood that requests may be resolved by information that is already available in the SGA. The sharing of data includes not only the tables and rows retrieved but also the queries that are used. If the queries are identical, a parsed version of a query may already exist in the shared SQL pool, reducing the amount of time needed to process the query. Cursor sharing enhancements in the optimizer increase the likelihood of statement reuse within the shared pool—but the application needs to be designed with statement reuse in mind.

Third, you should restrict the use of dynamic SQL. Dynamic SQL is always reparsed, even if an identical query exists in the shared pool. Dynamic SQL is a useful feature, but it should not be used for the majority of an application's database accesses.

Fourth, you should minimize the number of times you open and close sessions in the database. If the application repeatedly opens a session, executes a small number of commands, and then closes the session, the performance of the SQL may be a minor factor in the overall performance. The session management may cost more than any other step in the application.

When stored procedures are used, the same code may be executed multiple times, taking advantage of the shared pool. You can also manually compile procedures, functions, and packages to avoid run-time compilation. When you create a procedure, Oracle automatically compiles it. If the procedure later becomes invalid, the database must recompile it before executing it. To avoid incurring this compilation cost at run time, use the **alter procedure** command shown here:

```
alter procedure MY_RAISE compile;
```

You can view the SQL text for all procedures in a database via the Text column in the DBA_SOURCE view. The USER_SOURCE view will display the procedures owned by the user performing the query. Text for packages, functions, and package bodies is also accessible via the DBA_SOURCE and USER_SOURCE views, which in turn reference a table named SYS.SOURCE$.

The first two design guidelines discussed—limiting the number of user accesses and coordinating their requests—require the application developer to know as much as possible about how the data is to be used and the access paths involved. For this reason, it is critical that users be as involved in the application design as they are in the table design. If the users spend long hours drawing pictures of tables with the data modelers and little time with the application developers discussing the access paths, the application will most likely not meet the users' needs. The access paths should be discussed as part of the data modeling exercise.

Tuning SQL

As with application design, the tuning of SQL statements seems far removed from a DBA's duties. However, DBAs should be involved in reviewing the SQL that is written as part of the application. A well-designed application may still experience performance problems if the SQL it uses is poorly tuned. Application design and SQL problems cause most of the performance problems in properly designed databases.

The key to tuning SQL is to minimize the search path that the database uses to find the data. In most Oracle tables, each row has a RowID associated with it. The RowID contains information about the physical location of the row—its file, the block within that file, and the row within the database block.

When a query with no **where** clause is executed, the database will usually perform a *full table scan*, reading every block from the table. During a full table scan, the database locates the first block of the table and then reads sequentially through all the other blocks in the table. For large tables, full table scans can be very time-consuming.

When specific rows are queried, the database may use an index to help speed the retrieval of the desired rows. An index maps logical values in a table to their RowIDs—which in turn map them to specific physical locations. Indexes may either be unique—in which case there is no more than one occurrence for each value—or nonunique. Indexes only store RowIDs for NOT NULL values in the indexed columns.

You may index several columns together. This is called a *concatenated* index, and it will be used if its leading column is used in the query's **where** clause. The optimizer can also use a "skip-scan" approach in which a concatenated index is used even if its leading column is not in the query's **where** clause.

Indexes must be tailored to the access path needed. Consider the case of a three-column, concatenated index. As shown in the following listing, this index is created on the City, State, and Zip columns of the EMPLOYEE table:

```
create index CITY_ST_ZIP_NDX
on EMPLOYEE(City, State, Zip)
tablespace INDEXES;
```

If a query of the form

```
select * from EMPLOYEE
  where State='NJ';
```

is executed, then the leading column of the index (City) is not in the **where** clause. Oracle can use two types of index-based accesses to retrieve the rows—a skip-scan of the index or a full scan of the index. The optimizer will select an execution path based on the index's statistics—its size, the size of the table, and the selectivity of the index. If users will frequently run this type of query, the index's columns may need to be reordered with State first in order to reflect the actual usage pattern.

It is critical that the table's data be as ordered as possible. If users are frequently executing *range* queries—selecting those values that are within a specified range—then having the data ordered may require fewer data blocks to be read while resolving the query, thus improving performance. The ordered entries in the index will point to a set of neighboring blocks in the table rather than blocks that are scattered throughout the datafile(s).

For example, consider a range query of the following type:

```
select *
  from EMPLOYEE
where Empno between 1 and 100;
```

This range query will require fewer data blocks to be read if the physical records in the EMPLOYEE table are ordered by the Empno column. To guarantee that the rows are properly ordered in the table, extract the records to a flat file (or another table), sort the records there, and then delete the old records and reload them from the sorted data set.

Impact of Order on Load Rates

Indexes impact the performance of both queries and data loads. During **insert** operations, the rows' order has a significant impact on load performance. Even in heavily indexed environments, properly ordering the rows prior to **insert** may improve load performance by 50 percent.

As an index grows, Oracle allocates new blocks. If a new index entry is added beyond the last previous entry, the new entry will be added to the last block in the index. If the new entry causes Oracle to exceed the space available in that block, the entry will be moved to a new block. There is very little performance impact from this block allocation.

If the inserted rows are not ordered, new index entries will be written to existing index node blocks. If there is no more room in the block where the new value is added, and the block is not the last block in the index, the block's entries will be split in two. Half the index entries will be left in the original block and half will be moved to a new block. As a result, the performance suffers during loads (because of the additional space management activity) and during queries (because the index contains more unused space, requiring more blocks to be read for the same number of entries read).

NOTE
There is a significant drop in load performance when an index increases its number of internal levels. To see the number of levels, analyze an index and then select its B level column value from DBA_INDEXES.

Because of the way Oracle manages its indexes internally, load rates will be affected each time a new index is added (because it is unlikely that inserted rows will be sorted correctly for multiple columns). From a load rate perspective, favor fewer multicolumn indexes over multiple single-column indexes.

Additional Indexing Options

If the data is not very selective, you may consider using *bitmap indexes*. As described in Chapter 17, bitmap indexes are most effective for queries against large, static data sets with few distinct values. You can create both bitmap indexes and normal (B*tree) indexes on the same table, and Oracle will perform any necessary index conversions dynamically during query processing. See Chapter 17 for details on using bitmap indexes.

NOTE
Avoid creating bitmap indexes on tables modified by online transactions.

If two tables are frequently queried together, then *clusters* may be effective in improving performance. Clusters store rows from multiple tables in the same physical data blocks, based on their logical values (the cluster key).

Queries in which a column's value is compared to an exact value (rather than a range of values) are called *equivalence* queries. A *hash cluster* stores a row in a specific location based on its value in the cluster key column. Every time a row is inserted, its cluster key value is used to determine in which block it should be stored; this same logic can be used during queries to quickly find data blocks that are needed for retrieval. Hash clusters are designed to improve the performance of equivalence queries; they will not be as helpful in improving the performance of the range queries discussed earlier.

Reverse indexes provide another tuning solution for equivalence queries. In a reverse index, the bytes of the index are stored in reverse order. In a traditional index, two consecutive values are stored next to each other. In a reverse index, consecutive values are not stored next to each other. For example, the values 2004 and 2005 are stored as 4002 and 5002, respectively, in a reverse index. Although not appropriate for range scans, reverse indexes may reduce contention for index blocks if many equivalence queries are performed.

NOTE
You cannot reverse a bitmap index.

You can create *function-based indexes* on expressions involving columns. This query could not use a B*tree index on the Name column:

```
select * from EMPLOYEE
  where UPPER(Name) = 'JONES';
```

However, the query

```
select * from EMPLOYEE
  where Name = 'JONES';
```

could, because the second query does not perform a function on the Name column. Instead of creating an index on the column Name, you can create an index on the column expression UPPER(Name), as shown in the following example:

```
create index EMP_UPPER_NAME on
EMPLOYEE(UPPER(Name));
```

Although functional indexes can be useful, be sure to consider the following points when creating them:

- Can you restrict the functions that will be used on the column? If so, can you restrict all functions from being performed on the column?

- Do you have adequate storage space for the additional indexes?

- When you drop the table, you will be dropping more indexes (and therefore more extents) than before. How will that impact the time required to drop the table?

Function-based indexes are useful, but you should implement them sparingly. The more indexes you create on a table, the longer all **insert**, **update**, and **delete** operations will take. To create a function-based index, you must have the QUERY REWRITE system privilege, and the following parameters must be set in the initialization parameter file:

```
QUERY_REWRITE_ENABLED=TRUE
QUERY_REWRITE_INTEGRITY=TRUSTED
```

Text indexes use Oracle's text options to create and manage lists of words and their occurrences—similar to the way a book's index works. Text indexes are most often used to support applications that perform searches on portions of words with wildcards.

Partitioned tables can have indexes that span all partitions (global indexes) or indexes that are partitioned along with the table partitions (local indexes). From a query-tuning perspective, local indexes may be preferable because they contain fewer entries than global indexes.

Generating Explain Plans

How can you determine which access path the database will use to perform a query? This information can be viewed via the **explain plan** command. This command will evaluate the execution path for a query and will place its output into a table (named PLAN_TABLE) in the database. A sample **explain plan** command is shown in the following listing:

```
explain plan
  for
select *
  from BOOKSHELF
  where Title like 'M%';
```

The first line of this command tells the database that it is to explain its execution plan for the query without actually executing the query. You can optionally include a **set Statement_ID** clause to label the explain plan in PLAN_TABLE. Following the keyword **for**, the query to be analyzed is listed.

The account that is running this command must have a plan table in its schema. Oracle provides the **create table** commands needed for this table. The file, named utlxplan.sql, is usually located in the /rdbms/admin subdirectory under the Oracle software home directory. Users may run this script to create the table in their schemas.

> **NOTE**
> *You should drop and re-create the plan table following each Oracle upgrade because new columns may be added by the upgrade scripts.*

Query the plan table using the DBMS_XPLAN procedure:

```
select * from table(DBMS_XPLAN.DISPLAY);
```

This query will report on the types of operations the database must perform to resolve the query. The output will show the steps of the query execution in a hierarchical fashion, illustrating the relationships between the steps. For example, you may see an index-based step that has a TABLE ACCESS BY INDEX ROWID step as its parent, indicating that the index step is processed first and the RowIDs returned from the index are used to retrieve specific rows from the table.

You can use the **set autotrace on** command in SQL*Plus to automatically generate the **explain plan** output and trace information for every query you run. The autotrace-generated output will not be displayed until after the query has completed, whereas the **explain plan** output is generated without running the command. To enable autotrace-generated output, a plan table must either be created in the schema in which the autotrace utility will be used or created in the SYSTEM schema with access granted to the schema that will use the autotrace utility. The script plustrce.sql, located in the sqlplus/admin directory under the Oracle software home directory, must also be run as SYS before you can **set autotrace on**. Users must have the PLUSTRACE role enabled prior to executing **set autotrace on**.

NOTE
To show the explain plan output without running the query, use the
set autotrace on trace explain *command.*

If you use the parallel query options or query remote databases, an additional section of the **set autotrace on** output will show the text of the queries executed by the parallel query server processes or the query executed within the remote database.

To disable the autotrace feature, use the **set autotrace off** command.

The following listing shows how to turn on autotrace and the generation of an explain plan:

```
set autotrace on trace explain

select *
  from BOOKSHELF
 where Title like 'M%';

Execution Plan
-------------------------------------------------------------
   0      SELECT STATEMENT Optimizer=ALL_ROWS (Cost=3 Card=2 Bytes=80)
   1    0    TABLE ACCESS (BY INDEX ROWID) OF 'BOOKSHELF' (TABLE) (Cost
          =3 Card=2 Bytes=80)
   2    1      INDEX (RANGE SCAN) OF 'SYS_C004834' (INDEX (UNIQUE)) (Co
          st=1 Card=2)
```

To understand the explain plan, read the order of operations within the hierarchy from inside out, until you come to a set of operations at the same level of indentation; then read from top to bottom. In this example, there are no operations at the same level of indentation; therefore, you read the order of operations from inside out. The first operation is the index range scan, followed by the table access; the SELECT STATEMENT operation displays the output to the user. Each operation has an ID value (the first column) and a parent ID value (the second number; it is blank in the topmost operation). In more complex explain plans, you may need to use the parent ID values to determine the order of operations.

This plan shows that the data returned to the user comes via a TABLE ACCESS BY INDEX ROWID operation. The RowIDs are supplied by an index range scan of a unique index.

Each step is assigned a "cost." The cost is cumulative, reflecting the cost of that step plus the costs of all its child steps. You can use the cost values to identify steps that contribute the greatest amount to the overall cost of the query and then target them for specific tuning efforts.

When evaluating the output of the **explain plan** command, you should make sure that the most selective indexes (that is, the most nearly unique indexes) are used by the query. If a nonselective index is used, you may be forcing the database to perform unnecessary reads to resolve the query. A full discussion of SQL tuning is beyond the scope of this book, but you should focus your tuning efforts on making sure that the most resource-intensive SQL statements are using the most selective indexes possible.

In general, transaction-oriented applications (such as multiuser systems used for data entry) judge performance based on the time it takes to return the first row of a query. For transaction-oriented applications, you should focus your tuning efforts on using indexes to reduce the database's response time to the query.

If the application is batch oriented (with large transactions and reports), you should focus on improving the time it takes to complete the overall transaction instead of the time it takes to return the first row from the transaction. Improving the overall throughput of the transaction may require using full table scans in place of index accesses—and may improve the overall performance of the application.

If the application is distributed across multiple databases, focus on reducing the number of times database links are used in queries. If a remote database is frequently accessed during a query, the cost of accessing that remote database is paid each time the remote data is accessed. Even if the cost of accessing the remote data is low, accessing it thousands of times will eventually place a performance burden on your application. See the "Reducing Network Traffic" section later in this chapter for additional tuning suggestions for distributed databases.

Tuning Memory Usage

As described in Chapter 9, you can use Oracle's STATSPACK toolset to summarize the changes in database statistics for a given period. You can use the STATSPACK utilities and queries of the data dictionary tables to identify problem areas in the database's memory allocation. As of Oracle 10g, you can use the Automatic Workload Repository (AWR) toolset to gather and manage statistical data (as described later in this chapter).

The data block buffer cache and the shared pool are managed via a *least recently used (LRU)* algorithm. A preset area is set aside to hold values; when it fills, the least recently used data is eliminated from memory and written back to disk. An adequately sized memory area keeps the most frequently accessed data in memory; accessing less frequently used data requires physical reads.

You can see the queries performing the logical and physical reads in the database via the V$SQL view. V$SQL reports the cumulative number of logical and physical reads performed for each query currently in the shared pool, as well as the number of times each query was executed. The following script shows the SQL text for the queries in the shared pool, with the most I/O intensive queries listed first. The query also displays the number of logical reads (buffer gets) per execution:

```
select Buffer_Gets,
       Disk_Reads,
       Executions,
       Buffer_Gets/Executions B_E,
       SQL_Text
  from V$SQL
 order by Disk_Reads desc;
```

If the shared pool has been flushed, queries executed prior to the flush will no longer be accessible via V$SQL. However, the impact of those queries can still be seen, provided the users are still logged in. The V$SESS_IO view records the cumulative logical reads and physical reads performed for each user's session. You can query V$SESS_IO for each session's hit ratio, as shown in the following listing:

```
select SESS.Username,
       SESS_IO.Block_Gets,
       SESS_IO.Consistent_Gets,
```

```
        SESS_IO.Physical_Reads,
        round(100*(SESS_IO.Consistent_Gets
           +SESS_IO.Block_Gets-SESS_IO.Physical_Reads)/
           (decode(SESS_IO.Consistent_Gets,0,1,
               SESS_IO.Consistent_Gets+SESS_IO.Block_Gets)),2)
                 session_hit_ratio
   from V$SESS_IO sess_io, V$SESSION sess
 where SESS.Sid = SESS_IO.Sid
   and SESS.Username is not null
 order by Username;
```

To see the objects whose blocks are currently in the data block buffer cache, query the X$BH table in SYS's schema, as shown in the following query (note that the SYS and SYSTEM objects are excluded from the output so the DBA can focus on the application tables and indexes present in the SGA):

```
select Object_Name,
       Object_Type ,
       count(*) Num_Buff
   from X$BH a, SYS.DBA_OBJECTS b
 where A.Obj = B.Object_Id
   and Owner not in ('SYS','SYSTEM')
 group by Object_Name, Object_Type;
```

> **NOTE**
> *You can query the Name and Kind columns from V$CACHE to see similar data.*

There are multiple cache areas within the data block buffer cache:

- **The DEFAULT cache**   This is the standard cache for objects that use the default database block size for the database.

- **The KEEP cache**   This is dedicated to objects you wish to keep in memory at all times. In general, this area is used for small tables with few transactions.

- **The RECYCLE cache**   This is a dedicated to objects you wish to flush from memory quickly. Like the KEEP cache, the RECYCLE cache isolates objects in memory so they do not interfere with the normal functioning of the DEFAULT cache.

- **Block-size-specific caches**   Oracle supports multiple database block sizes within a single database; you must create a cache for each non-default database block size.

With all the areas of the SGA—the data block buffers, the dictionary cache, and the shared pool—the emphasis should be on sharing data among users. Each of these areas should be large enough to hold the most commonly requested data from the database. In the case of the shared pool, it should be large enough to hold the parsed versions of the most commonly used queries. When they are adequately sized, the memory areas in the SGA can dramatically improve the performance of individual queries and of the database as a whole.

The size of the KEEP and RECYCLE buffer pools do not reduce the available space in the data block buffer cache. For a table to use one of the new buffer pools, specify the name of the buffer pool via the **buffer_pool** parameter within the table's **storage** clause. For example, if you want a table to be quickly removed from memory, assign it to the RECYCLE pool. The default pool is named DEFAULT, so you can use the **alter table** command to redirect a table to the DEFAULT pool at a later date.

You can use the LARGE_POOL_SIZE initialization parameter to specify the size of the large pool allocation heap in bytes. The large pool allocation heap is used in shared server systems for session memory, by parallel execution for message buffers, and by backup processes for I/O buffers. By default, the large pool is not created.

As of Oracle Database 10*g*, you can use Automatic Shared Memory Management (ASMM). To activate ASMM, set a nonzero value for the SGA_TARGET database initialization parameter. After you set SGA_TARGET to the size of the SGA you want (that is, all of the caches added together), you can then set the other cache-related parameters (DB_CACHE_SIZE, SHARED_POOL_SIZE, JAVA_POOL_SIZE, and LARGE_POOL_SIZE) each to 0; if you provide values for these parameters, those values will serve as the lower bound for the automatic tuning algorithm. Shut down and restart the database for the changes to take effect; the database will then begin actively managing the size of the different caches. You can monitor the size of the caches at any time via the V$SGASTAT dynamic performance view.

As the workload in the database changes, the database will alter the cache sizes to reflect the needs of the application. For example, if there is a heavy batch-processing load at night and a more intensive online transaction load during the day, the database may alter the cache sizes as the load changes. These changes occur automatically, without DBA intervention. If you specify a value for a pool in your initialization parameter file, Oracle will use that as the minimum value for that pool.

NOTE
DBAs can create KEEP and RECYCLE pools in the buffer cache. KEEP and RECYCLE pools are not affected by the dynamic cache resizing and they are not part of the DEFAULT buffer pool.

From within OEM, you can see if dynamic memory management is enabled by clicking the Memory Parameters option; the Automatic Shared Memory Management button can be set to "Enabled" or "Disabled."

You may wish to selectively "pin" packages in the shared pool. Pinning packages in memory immediately after starting the database will increase the likelihood that a large enough section of contiguous free space is available in memory. As shown in the following listing, the KEEP procedure of the DBMS_SHARED_POOL package designates the packages to pin in the shared pool:

```
execute DBMS_SHARED_POOL.KEEP('APPOWNER.ADD_CLIENT','P');
```

Pinning of packages is more closely related to application management than application tuning, but it can have a performance impact. If you can avoid dynamic management of fragmented memory areas, you minimize the work Oracle has to do when managing the shared pool.

Specifying the Size of the SGA

To enable the automatic management of the caches, set the SGA_TARGET initialization parameter to the size of the SGA.

If you choose to manage the caches manually, you can set the SGA_MAX_SIZE parameter to the size of the SGA. You can then specify the sizes for the individual caches; they can be dynamically altered while the database is running via the **alter system** command.

Parameter	Description
SGA_MAX_SIZE	The maximum size to which the SGA can grow.
SHARED_POOL_SIZE	The size of the shared pool.
DB_BLOCK_SIZE	This will be the default database block size for the database.
DB_CACHE_SIZE	The cache size specified in bytes.
DB_nK_CACHE_SIZE	If you will be using multiple database block sizes within a single database, you must specify at a DB_CACHE_SIZE parameter value and at least one DB_nK_CACHE_SIZE parameter value. For example, if your standard database block size is 4KB, you can also specify a cache for the 8KB block size tablespaces via the DB_8K_CACHE_SIZE parameter.

For example, you may specify the following:

```
SGA_MAX_SIZE=500M
SHARED_POOL_SIZE=80M
DB_BLOCK_SIZE=8192
DB_CACHE_SIZE=160M
DB_4K_BLOCK_SIZE=4M
```

With these parameters, 4MB will be available for data queried from objects in tablespaces with 4KB block sizes. Objects using the standard 8KB block size will use the 160MB cache. While the database is open, you can change the SHARED_POOL_SIZE and DB_CACHE_SIZE parameter values via the **alter system** command.

SGA_TARGET is a dynamic parameter and can be changed through Database Control or with the **alter system** command.

SGA_TARGET can be increased up to the value of SGA_MAX_SIZE. It can be reduced until any one of the auto-tuned components reaches its minimum size—either a user-specified minimum or an internally determined minimum. Both of these parameters can be used to tune the SGA.

Using the Cost-Based Optimizer

With each release of its software, Oracle has added new features to its optimizer and has enhanced existing features. Effective use of the cost-based optimizer requires that the tables and indexes in your application be analyzed regularly. The frequency with which you analyze the objects depends on the rate of change within the objects. For batch transaction applications, you should reanalyze the objects after each large set of batch transactions. For OLTP applications, you should reanalyze the objects on a time-based schedule (such as via a weekly or nightly process).

Statistics on objects are gathered via executions of the DBMS_STATS package's procedures. If you analyze a table, its associated indexes are automatically analyzed as well. You can analyze a schema (via the GATHER_SCHEMA_STATS procedure) or a specific table (via GATHER_TABLE_ STATS). You can also analyze only the indexed columns, thus speeding the analysis process. In general, you should analyze a table's indexes each time you analyze the table. In the following listing, the PRACTICE schema is analyzed:

```
execute DBMS_STATS.GATHER_SCHEMA_STATS('PRACTICE', 'COMPUTE');
```

You can view the statistics on tables and indexes via DBA_TABLES, DBA_TAB_COL_STATISTICS, and DBA_INDEXES. Some column-level statistics are still provided in DBA_TAB_COLUMNS, but they are provided there strictly for backward compatibility. The statistics for the columns of partitioned tables are found in DBA_PART_COL_STATISTICS.

When the command in the preceding listing is executed, all the objects belonging to the PRACTICE schema will be analyzed using the **compute statistics** option. You can also choose to estimate statistics based on a specified percentage of the table's rows.

Implications of the compute statistics Option

In the examples in the preceding section, the **compute statistics** option was used to gather statistics about objects. Oracle also provides the **estimate statistics** option, which bases the object's statistics on a review of a portion of the data. If you choose to use **estimate statistics**, analyze as much of the table as possible. You can specify a percentage of the rows to analyze—analyzing 20 percent is usually sufficient.

Analyzing data can require large amounts of sort space. Because the analysis may include full table scans as well, you should change your session settings immediately prior to starting the analysis. When the analysis completes, either end your session or change your settings back to the database's values. The session settings to change are those for SORT_AREA_SIZE and DB_ FILE_MULTIBLOCK_READ_COUNT. The larger the sort area size is, the less likely you are to need to use the temporary tablespace for sort segments. The higher the multiblock read count is, the more blocks you may be able to read during a single physical read (as limited by the operating system). Use the **alter session** command to increase these values for your session.

Tuning Data Access

Even if your tables are properly configured and indexed, your performance may suffer if there are wait events caused by file accesses. In the following sections, you will see recommendations related to file and tablespace configuration.

In general, you should avoid placing Oracle files on distributed-parity RAID systems such as RAID 5. The overhead generated during writes to such file systems generally presents a performance bottleneck as the system use increases, particularly for sequentially written files such as the online redo log files. Favor the use of RAID 0+1 to support both the mirroring and striping of data without introducing these performance bottlenecks.

Locally Managed Tablespaces

You can use locally managed tablespaces to handle extent management within the tablespaces. Locally managed tablespaces manage their own space by maintaining a bitmap in each datafile of the free and used blocks or sets of blocks in the datafile. Each time an extent is allocated or freed for reuse, the database updates the bitmap to show the new status.

When you use locally managed tablespaces, the data dictionary is not updated and rollback activity is not generated during extent creations. Locally managed tablespaces automatically track adjacent free space, so there is no need to coalesce extents. Within a locally managed tablespace, all extents can have the same size or the system can automatically determine the size of extents.

To use local space management, you can specify the **local** option for the **extent management** clause in the **create tablespace** command. An example of the **create tablespace** command declaring a locally managed tablespace is shown here:

```
create tablespace CODES_TABLES
datafile '/u01/oracle/VLDB/codes_tables.dbf'
size 10M
extent management local uniform size 256K;
```

Assuming that the block size for the database in which this tablespace is created is 8KB, in this example, the tablespace is created with the extent management declared as **local** and with a uniform size of 256KB. Each bit in the bitmap describes 32 blocks (256/8). If the **uniform size** clause is omitted, the default is **autoallocate**. The default **size** for **uniform** is 1MB.

> **NOTE**
> *If you specify **local** in a **create tablespace** command, you cannot specify a **default storage** clause, **minextents**, or **temporary**. If you use the **create temporary tablespace** command to create the tablespace, you can specify **extent_management local**.*

As of Oracle9*i*, tablespaces are locally managed by default, so the **extent management local** clause is optional.

> **NOTE**
> *If you make the SYSTEM tablespace locally managed, you can only create locally managed tablespaces within the database.*

Identifying Chained Rows

When a data segment is created, a **pctfree** value is specified. The **pctfree** parameter tells the database how much space should be kept free in each data block. The free space is used when rows that are already stored in the data block extend in length via **update** operations.

If an **update** to a row causes that row to no longer completely fit in a single data block, that row may be moved to another data block, or the row may be *chained* to another block. If you are storing rows whose length is greater than the Oracle block size, you will automatically have chaining.

Chaining affects performance because it requires Oracle to look in multiple physical locations for data from the same logical row. By eliminating unnecessary chaining, you reduce the number of physical reads needed to return data from a datafile.

You can avoid chaining by setting the proper value for **pctfree** during the creation of data segments. The default value, 10, should be increased if your application will frequently update NULL values to non-NULL values, or if long text values are frequently updated.

You can use the **analyze** command to collect statistics about database objects. The cost-based optimizer can use these statistics to determine the best execution path to use. The **analyze** command has an option that detects and records chained rows in tables. Its syntax is

```
analyze table TABLE_NAME list chained rows into CHAINED_ROWS;
```

The **analyze** command will put the output from this operation into a table called CHAINED_ROWS in your local schema. The SQL to create the CHAINED_ROWS table is in a file named utlchain.sql, in the /rdbms/admin subdirectory under your Oracle software directory. The following query will select the most significant columns from the CHAINED_ROWS table:

```
select
        Owner_Name,       /*Owner of the data segment*/
        Table_Name,       /*Name of the table with the chained rows*/
        Cluster_Name,     /*Name of the cluster, if it is clustered*/
        Head_RowID        /*Rowid of the first part of the row*/
from CHAINED_ROWS;
```

The output will show the RowIDs for all chained rows, allowing you to quickly see how many of the rows in the table are chained. If chaining is prevalent in a table, that table should be rebuilt with a higher value for **pctfree**.

You can see the impact of row chaining by querying V$SYSSTAT. The V$SYSSTAT entry for the "table fetch continued row" statistic will be incremented each time Oracle selects data from a chained row. This statistic will also be incremented when Oracle selects data from a *spanned row*—a row that is chained because it is greater than a block in length. Tables with LONG, BLOB, CLOB, and NCLOB datatypes are likely to have spanned rows.

In addition to chaining rows, Oracle will occasionally move rows. If a row exceeds the space available to its block, the row may be inserted into a different block. The process of moving a row from one block to another is called *row migration,* and the moved row is called a *migrated row.* During row migration, Oracle has to dynamically manage space in multiple blocks and access the freelist (the list of blocks available for **insert** operations). A migrated row does not appear as a chained row, but it does impact the performance of your transactions.

Increasing the Oracle Block Size

The effect of increasing the database block size is significant. Doubling the database block size may improve the performance of query-intensive operations by up to 50 percent.

The performance benefit has few costs. Because there will be more rows per database block, there is a greater likelihood of block-level contention during data manipulation commands. To address the contention problems, increase the settings for **freelists** and **initrans** at the table and index level. In general, setting **freelists** to greater than 4 will not yield much additional benefit. The **initrans** setting should reflect the number of concurrent transactions expected within a block.

NOTE
Oracle now automatically allows up to 255 concurrent update transactions in any data block, depending on the available space in the block.

When you create a tablespace, you can specify a database block size for the tablespace; by default, the tablespace will use the database block size you specify via the DB_BLOCK_SIZE initialization parameter. If you use a non-default database block size for the tablespace, you will need to create a cache for that block size. For example, if your database block size is 8KB and you want to create a 4KB database block size tablespace, you must first set a value for DB_4K_CACHE_SIZE.

To increase the database block size for the entire database, you must rebuild the entire database and delete all the old database files. The new files can be created in the same location as the old files, with the same size, but will be managed more efficiently by the database. The performance savings comes from the way that Oracle manages the block header information. More space is used by data, improving the ability of multiple users to access the same block of data in memory. Doubling the size of the Oracle blocks has little effect on the block header; therefore, a smaller percentage of space is used to store block header information.

To set the block size, modify the DB_BLOCK_SIZE initialization parameter prior to creating a new database.

Using Index-Organized Tables

An index-organized table (IOT) is an index in which an entire row is stored, rather than just the key values for the row. Rather than storing a RowID for the row, the primary key for the row is treated as the row's logical identifier. Rows in IOTs do not have RowIDs.

Within the IOT, the rows are stored sorted by their primary key values. Thus, any range query that is based on the primary key may benefit because the rows are stored near each other (see the "Tuning SQL" section earlier in this chapter for the steps involved in ordering the data within normal tables). Additionally, any equivalence query based on the primary key may benefit because the table's data is all stored in the index. In the traditional table/index combination, an index-based access requires an index access followed by a table access. In an IOT, only the IOT is accessed; there is no companion index.

However, the performance gains from a single index access in place of a normal index/table combination access may be minimal—any index-based access should be fast. To help improve performance further, index-organized tables offer additional features:

- **An overflow area**   By setting the **pctthreshold** parameter when the IOT is created, you can store the primary key data apart from the row data. If the row's data exceeds the threshold of available space in the block, it will dynamically be moved to an overflow area. You can designate the overflow area to be in a separate tablespace, improving your ability to distribute the I/O associated with the table.

- **Secondary indexes**   You can create secondary indexes on the IOT. Oracle will use the primary key values as the logical RowIDs for the rows.

- **Reduced storage requirements**   In a traditional table/index combination, the same key values are stored in two places. In an IOT, they are stored once, reducing the storage requirements.

To create an IOT, use the **organization index** clause of the **create table** command. You must specify a primary key when creating an IOT. Within an IOT, you can drop columns or mark them as inactive via the **set unused** clause of the **alter table** command.

Tuning Issues for Index-Organized Tables

Like indexes, IOTs may become internally fragmented over time, as values are inserted, updated, and deleted. To rebuild an IOT, use the **move** clause of the **alter table** command. In the following example, the EMPLOYEE_IOT table is rebuilt, along with its overflow area:

```
alter table EMPLOYEE_IOT
  move tablespace DATA
overflow tablespace DATA_OVERFLOW;
```

You should avoid storing long rows of data in IOTs. In general, you should avoid using an IOT if the data is longer than 75 percent of the database block size. If the database block size is 4KB, and your rows will exceed 3KB in length, you should investigate the use of normal tables and indexes instead of IOTs. The longer the rows are, and the more transactions are performed against the IOT, the more frequently it will need to be rebuilt.

> **NOTE**
> *You cannot use LONG datatypes in IOTs but you can use LOBs.*

As noted earlier in this chapter, indexes impact data load rates. For best results, the primary key index of an index-organized table should be loaded with sequential values to minimize the costs of index management.

Tuning Data Manipulation

Several data manipulation tasks—usually concerning the manipulation of large quantities of data—may involve the DBA. You have several options when loading and deleting large volumes of data, as described in the following sections.

Bulk Inserts: Using the SQL*Loader Direct Path Option

When used in the Conventional Path mode, SQL*Loader reads records from a file, generates **insert** commands, and passes them to the Oracle kernel. Oracle then finds places for those records in free blocks in the table and updates any associated indexes.

In Direct Path mode, SQL*Loader creates formatted data blocks and writes directly to the datafiles. This requires occasional checks with the database to get new locations for data blocks, but no other I/O with the database kernel is required. The result is a data load process that is dramatically faster than Conventional Path mode.

If the table is indexed, the indexes will be placed in DIRECT PATH state during the load. After the load is complete, the new keys (index column values) will be sorted and merged with the existing keys in the index. To maintain the temporary set of keys, the load will create a temporary index segment that is at least as large as the largest index on the table. The space requirements for this can be minimized by presorting the data and using the SORTED INDEXES clause in the SQL*Loader control file.

To minimize the amount of dynamic space allocation necessary during the load, the data segment that you are loading into should already be created, with all the space it will need already allocated. You should also presort the data on the columns of the largest index in the table. Sorting the data and leaving the indexes on the table during a Direct Path load will usually yield better performance than if you were to drop the indexes before the load and then re-create them after it completed.

To take advantage of the Direct Path option, the table cannot be clustered, and there can be no other active transactions against it. During the load, only NOT NULL, UNIQUE, and PRIMARY KEY constraints will be enforced; after the load has completed, the CHECK and FOREIGN KEY constraints can be automatically reenabled. To force this to occur, use the

```
REENABLE DISABLED_CONSTRAINTS
```

clause in the SQL*Loader control file.

The only exception to this reenabling process is that table insert triggers, when reenabled, are not executed for each of the new rows in the table. A separate process must manually perform whatever commands were to have been performed by this type of trigger.

The SQL*Loader Direct Path loading option provides significant performance improvements over the SQL*Loader Conventional Path loader in loading data into Oracle tables by bypassing SQL processing, buffer cache management, and unnecessary reads for the data blocks. The Parallel Data Loading option of SQL*Loader allows multiple processes to load data into the same table, utilizing spare resources on the system and thereby reducing the overall elapsed times for loading. Given enough CPU and I/O resources, this can significantly reduce the overall loading times.

To use Parallel Data Loading, start multiple SQL*Loader sessions using the **parallel** keyword (otherwise, SQL*Loader puts an exclusive lock on the table). Each session is an independent session requiring its own control file. The following listing shows three separate Direct Path loads, all using the PARALLEL=TRUE parameter on the command line:

```
sqlload USERID=ME/PASS CONTROL=PART1.CTL DIRECT=TRUE PARALLEL=TRUE
sqlload USERID=ME/PASS CONTROL=PART2.CTL DIRECT=TRUE PARALLEL=TRUE
sqlload USERID=ME/PASS CONTROL=PART3.CTL DIRECT=TRUE PARALLEL=TRUE
```

Each session creates its own log, bad, and discard files (part1.log, part2.log, part3.log, part1.bad, part2.bad, and so on) by default. Because you have multiple sessions loading data into the same table, only the APPEND option is allowed for Parallel Data Loading. The SQL*Loader REPLACE, TRUNCATE, and INSERT options are not allowed for Parallel Data Loading. If you need to delete the table's data before starting the load, you must manually delete the data (via **delete** or **truncate** commands). You cannot use SQL*Loader to delete the records automatically if you are using Parallel Data Loading.

NOTE
*If you use Parallel Data Loading, indexes are not maintained by the SQL*Loader session. Before starting the loading process, you must drop all indexes on the table and disable all its PRIMARY KEY and UNIQUE constraints. After the loads complete, you can re-create the table's indexes.*

In serial Direct Path Loading (PARALLEL=FALSE), SQL*Loader loads data into extents in the table. If the load process fails before the load completes, some data could be committed to the table prior to the process failure. In Parallel Data Loading, each load process creates temporary segments for loading the data. The temporary segments are later merged with the table. If a

Parallel Data Loading process fails before the load completes, the temporary segments will not have been merged with the table. If the temporary segments have not been merged with the table being loaded, no data from the load will have been committed to the table.

You can use the SQL*Loader FILE parameter to direct each data loading session to a different datafile. By directing each loading session to its own datafile, you can balance the I/O load of the loading processes. Data loading is very I/O intensive and must be distributed across multiple disks for parallel loading to achieve significant performance improvements over serial loading.

After a Parallel Data Load, each session may attempt to reenable the table's constraints. As long as at least one load session is still underway, attempting to reenable the constraints will fail. The final loading session to complete should attempt to reenable the constraints, and should succeed. You should check the status of your constraints after the load completes. If the table being loaded has PRIMARY KEY and UNIQUE constraints, you can create the associated indexes in parallel prior to enabling the constraints.

Bulk Data Moves—Using External Tables

You can query data from files outside the database via an object called an *external table*. An external table's structure is defined via the **organization external** clause of the **create table** command; its syntax closely resembles the SQL*Loader control file syntax.

You cannot manipulate rows in an external table, and you cannot index it—every access of the table results in a full table scan (that is, a full scan of the file at the operating system level). As a result, the performance of queries against external tables tends to be worse than that of tables stored within the database. However, external tables offer a couple of potential benefits for systems that load large sets of data:

- Because the data is not stored within the database, the data is only stored once (outside the database, rather than both outside and inside the database), thus saving space.

- Because the data is never loaded into the database, the data-loading time is eliminated.

Given that you cannot index external tables, they are most useful for operations in which large volumes of data are accessed by batch programs. For example, many data warehousing environments have a staging area in which data is loaded into temporary tables prior to rows being inserted into the tables users will query. Instead of loading the data into those temporary tables, you can access the operating system files directly via external tables, saving time and space.

From an architectural perspective, external tables allow you to focus your database contents on the objects users will most commonly use—small codes tables, aggregation tables, and transaction tables—while keeping very large data sets outside the database. You can replace the files accessed by the external tables at any time without incurring any transaction overhead within the database.

Bulk Inserts: Common Traps and Successful Tricks

If your data is not being inserted from a flat file, SQL*Loader will not be a useful solution. For example, if you need to move a large set of data from one table to another, you will likely want to avoid having to write the data to a flat file and then read it back into the database. The fastest way to move data in your database is to move it from one table to another without going out to the operating system.

When you're moving data from one table to another, there are several common methods for improving the performance of the data migration:

- Tuning the structures (removing indexes and triggers)

- Disabling constraints during the data migration

- Using hints and options to improve the transaction performance

The first of the tips, tuning the structures, involves disabling any triggers or indexes that are on the table into which data is being loaded. For example, if you have a row-level trigger on the target table, that trigger will be executed for every row inserted into the table. If possible, disable the triggers prior to the data load. If the trigger should be executed for every inserted row, you may be able to do a bulk operation once the rows have been inserted, rather than a repeated operation during each **insert**. If properly tuned, the bulk operation will complete faster than the repeated trigger executions. You will need to be sure that the bulk operations execute for all rows that have not already been processed by the triggers.

In addition to disabling triggers, you should disable the indexes on the target table prior to starting the data load. If the indexes are left on the table, Oracle will dynamically manage the indexes as each row is inserted. Rather than continuously manage the index, drop it prior to the start of the load and re-create it when the load has completed.

NOTE
Disabling indexes and triggers resolves most of the performance problems associated with large table-to-table data migration efforts.

In addition to disabling indexes, you should consider disabling constraints on the table. If the source data is already in a table in the database, you can check that data for its adherence to your constraints (such as foreign keys or CHECK constraints) prior to loading it into your target table. Once the data has been loaded, you can reenable the constraints.

If none of those options gives you adequate performance, you should investigate the options Oracle has introduced for data migration tuning. Those options include the following:

- **The append hint for insert commands**   Like the Direct Path Loader, the APPEND hint loads blocks of data into a table, starting at the high water mark for the table. Use of the APPEND hint may increase your space usage.

- **The nologging option**   If you are performing a **create table as select** command, use the **nologging** option to avoid writing to the redo logs during the operation.

- **The parallel options**   Parallel Query uses multiple processes to accomplish a single task. For a **create table as select**, you can parallelize both the **create table** portion and the query. If you use the parallel options, you should also use the **nologging** option; otherwise, the parallel operations will have to wait due to serialized writes to the online redo log files.

Before using any of these advanced options, you should first investigate the target table's structures to make sure you've avoided the common traps cited earlier in this section.

You can also use programming logic to force **insert**s to be processed in arrays rather than as an entire set. For example, COBOL and C support array **insert**s, thus reducing the size of the transactions required to process a large set of data.

Bulk Deletes: The truncate Command

Occasionally, users attempt to delete all the records from a table at once. When they encounter errors during this process, they complain that the rollback segments are too small, when in fact their transaction is too large.

A second problem occurs once the records have all been deleted. Even though the segment no longer has any records in it, it still maintains all the space that was allocated to it. Therefore, deleting all those records saved not a single byte of allocated space.

The **truncate** command resolves both of these problems. It is a DDL command, not a DML command, *so it cannot be rolled back*. Once you have used the **truncate** command on a table, its records are gone, and none of its **delete** triggers are executed in the process. However, the table retains all its dependent objects—such as grants, indexes, and constraints.

The **truncate** command is the fastest way to delete large volumes of data. Because it will delete all the records in a table, this may force you to alter your application design so that no protected records are stored in the same table as the records to be deleted. If you use partitions, you can truncate one partition of a table without affecting the rest of the table's partitions (see Chapter 17).

A sample **truncate** command for a table is shown here:

```
truncate table EMPLOYEE drop storage;
```

The preceding example, in which the EMPLOYEE table's records are deleted, shows a powerful feature of **truncate**. The **drop storage** clause is used to deallocate the non-**initial** space from the table (this is the default option). Therefore, you can delete all of a table's rows and reclaim all but its initial extent's allocated space, without dropping the table.

The **truncate** command also works for clusters. In this example, the **reuse storage** option is used to leave all allocated space empty within the segment that acquired it:

```
truncate cluster EMP_DEPT reuse storage;
```

When this example command is executed, all the records in the EMP_DEPT cluster will be instantly deleted.

To truncate a partition, you need to know its name. In the following example, the partition named PART3 of the EMPLOYEE table is truncated via the **alter table** command:

```
alter table EMPLOYEE
truncate partition PART3
drop storage;
```

The rest of the partitions of the EMPLOYEE table will be unaffected by the truncation of the PART3 partition. See Chapter 17 for details on creating and managing partitions.

As an alternative, you can create a PL/SQL program that uses dynamic SQL to divide a large **delete** operation into multiple smaller transactions.

Using Partitions

You can use partitions to isolate data physically. For example, you can store each month's transactions in a separate partition of an ORDERS table. If you perform a bulk data load or deletion on the table, you can customize the partitions to tune the data manipulation operation. For example:

- You can truncate a partition and its indexes without affecting the rest of the table.

- You can drop a partition, via the **drop partition** clause of the **alter table** command.

- You can drop a partition's local index.

- You can set a partition to **nologging**, reducing the impact of large transactions.

From a performance perspective, the chief advantage of partitions lies in their ability to be managed apart from the rest of the table. For example, being able to truncate a partition enables you to delete a large amount of data from a table (but not all of the table's data) without generating any redo information. In the short term, the beneficiary of this performance improvement is the DBA; in the longer term, the entire enterprise benefits from the improved availability of the data. See Chapter 17 for details on implementing partitions and subpartitions.

You can use the **exchange partition** option to greatly reduce the impact your data-loading processes have on system availability. Start by creating an empty table that has the same column structure as your partitioned table. Load your data into the new table and then analyze the new table. Create indexes on the new table to match the partitioned table's indexes. When these steps are complete, alter the partitioned table using the **exchange partition** clause to exchange an empty partition with the new table you populated. All the loaded data will now be accessible via the partitioned table. There is little impact to the system availability during this step because it is a DDL operation.

Tuning Physical Storage

Database I/O should be evenly distributed across as many devices as possible. The standard solution is called SAME (which stands for *stripe and mirror everything*). The I/O throughput limits of the disks are the key limits to overcome, so distributing the I/O needs over many disks allows you to take advantage of the combined throughputs of many devices. Striping enhances your throughput, which may improve your performance; mirroring provides support in the case of disk failure.

In addition to that level of physical storage tuning, several other factors should be considered. The following sections address factors that are external to the database but may have a profound impact on its ability to access data quickly.

Using Raw Devices

Raw devices are available with most Unix operating systems. When they are used, Oracle bypasses the Unix buffer cache and eliminates the file system overhead. For I/O-intensive applications, they may result in a performance improvement of around 20 percent over traditional file systems. Recent file system enhancements have largely overcome this performance difference.

Raw devices cannot be managed with the same commands as file systems. For example, the **tar** command cannot be used to back up individual files; instead, the **dd** command must be used. This is a much less flexible command to use and limits your recovery capabilities.

NOTE
Oracle files should not reside on the same physical devices as non-Oracle files, particularly if you use raw devices. Mixing an active Unix file system with an active Oracle raw device will cause I/O performance problems.

Most operating systems that support raw devices also provide a logical volume management layer that allows administrators to perform file system commands for the raw devices. This approach allows you to have the benefits of file system management along with the performance benefits of raw devices. If you are planning to use raw devices, you should use a logical volume management tool to simplify the system management.

NOTE
As of Oracle 10g, you can use Automatic Storage Management to manage your database storage area.

Reducing Network Traffic

As databases and the applications that use them become more distributed, the network that supports the servers may become a bottleneck in the process of delivering data to the users. Because DBAs typically have little control over the network management, it is important to use the database's capabilities to reduce the number of network packets required for the data to be delivered. Reducing network traffic will reduce your reliance on the network, and thus eliminate a potential cause of performance problems.

Replication of Data

You can manipulate and query data from remote databases. However, it is not desirable to have large volumes of data constantly sent from one database to another. To reduce the amount of data being sent across the network, you should consider different data replication options.

In a purely distributed environment, each data element exists in one database. When data is required, it is accessed from remote databases via database links. This purist approach is similar to implementing an application strictly in third normal form—an approach that will not easily support any major production application. Modifying the application's tables to improve data retrieval performance involves denormalizing data. The denormalization process deliberately stores redundant data in order to shorten users' access paths to the data.

In a distributed environment, replicating data accomplishes this goal. Rather than force queries to cross the network to resolve user requests, selected data from remote servers is replicated to the local server. This can be accomplished via a number of means, as described in the following sections.

Replicated data is out of date as soon as it is created. Replicating data for performance purposes is therefore most effective when the source data is very infrequently changed or when the business processes can support the use of old data.

Using Materialized Views/Snapshots to Replicate Data

Oracle's distributed capabilities offer a means of managing the data replication within a database. *Materialized views* replicate data from a master source to multiple targets. Oracle provides tools for refreshing the data and updating the targets at specified time intervals.

Materialized views may be read-only or updatable. The management issues for materialized views are covered in Chapter 18; in this section, you will see their performance-tuning aspects.

Before creating a materialized view for replication, you should first create a database link to the source database. The following example creates a private database link called HR_LINK, using the LOC service name:

```
create database link HR_LINK
connect to HR identified by PUFFINSTUFF
using 'loc';
```

The **create database link** command, as shown in this example, has several parameters:

- The name of the link (HR_LINK, in this case).

- The account to connect to.

- The service name of the remote database (as found in the tnsnames.ora file for the server). In this case, the service name is LOC.

Materialized views automate the data replication and refresh processes. When materialized views are created, a *refresh interval* is established to schedule refreshes of replicated data. Local updates can be prevented, and transaction-based refreshes can be used. Transaction-based refreshes, available for many types of materialized views, send from the master database only those rows that have changed for the materialized view. This capability, described later in this chapter, may significantly improve the performance of your refreshes.

The syntax used to create the materialized view on the local server is shown in the following example, where the materialized view is given a name (LOCAL_EMP) and its storage parameters are specified. Its base query is given as well as its refresh interval. In this case, the materialized view is told to immediately retrieve the master data and then to perform the refresh operation again in seven days (SysDate+7).

```
create materialized view LOCAL_EMP
pctfree 5
tablespace data_2
storage (initial 100K next 100K pctincrease 0)
refresh fast
      start with SysDate
      next SysDate+7
as select * from EMPLOYEE@HR_LINK;
```

The **refresh fast** clause tells the database to use a materialized view log to refresh the local materialized view. The ability to use materialized view logs during refreshes is only available if the materialized view's base query is simple enough that Oracle can determine which row in the materialized view will change when a row changes in the source tables.

When a materialized view log is used, only the changes to the master table are sent to the targets. If you use a complex materialized view, you must use the **refresh complete** clause in place of the **refresh fast** clause. In a complete refresh, the refresh completely replaces the existing data in the materialized view's underlying table.

Materialized view logs must be created in the master database, via the **create materialized view log** command. An example of the **create materialized view log** command is shown here:

```
create materialized view log on EMPLOYEE
tablespace DATA
storage (initial 10K next 10K pctincrease 0);
```

The materialized view log is always created in the same schema as the master table.

You can use simple materialized views with materialized view logs to reduce the amount of network traffic involved in maintaining the replicated data. Because only the changes to the data will be sent via a materialized view log, the maintenance of simple materialized views should use fewer network resources than complex materialized views require, particularly if the master tables are large, fairly static tables. If the master tables are not static, the volume of transactions sent via the materialized view log may not be any less than would be sent to perform a complete refresh. For details on the refresh capabilities of materialized views, see Chapter 18.

Regardless of the refresh option chosen, you should index the materialized view's base table to optimize queries against the materialized view. From a performance perspective, your goal is to present the users with the data they want in the format they want it as quickly as possible. By creating materialized views on remote data, you can avoid traversing database links during queries. By creating materialized views on local data, you can prevent users from repeatedly aggregating large volumes of data, presenting them instead with preaggregated data that answers their most common queries.

Using Remote Procedure Calls

When using procedures in a distributed database environment, you can use one of two options: to create a local procedure that references remote tables or to create a remote procedure that is called by a local application.

The proper location for the procedure depends on the distribution of the data and the way the data is to be used. The emphasis should be on minimizing the amount of data that must be sent through the network in order to resolve the data request. The procedure should reside within the database that contains most of the data used during the procedure's operations.

For example, consider this procedure:

```
create procedure MY_RAISE (My_Emp_No IN NUMBER, Raise IN NUMBER)
as begin
        update EMPLOYEE@HR_LINK
        set Salary = Salary+Raise
        where Empno = My_Emp_No;
end;
/
```

In this case, the procedure only accesses a single table (EMPLOYEE) on a remote node (as indicated by the database link HR_LINK). To reduce the amount of data sent across the network, move this procedure to the remote database identified by the database link HR_LINK and remove the reference to that database link from the **from** clause in the procedure. Then, call the procedure from the local database by using the database link, as shown here:

```
execute MY_RAISE@HR_LINK(1234,2000);
```

In this case, two parameters are passed to the procedure—My_Emp_No is set to 1234, and Raise is set to 2000. The procedure is invoked using a database link to tell the database where to find the procedure.

The tuning benefit of performing a remote procedure call is that all of the procedure's processing is performed in the database where the data resides. The remote procedure call minimizes the amount of network traffic necessary to complete the procedure's processing.

To maintain location transparency, you may create a local synonym that points to the remote procedure. The database link name will be specified in the synonym so that user requests will automatically use the remote database:

```
create synonym MY_RAISE for MY_RAISE@HR_LINK;
```

A user could then enter the command

```
execute MY_RAISE(1234,2000);
```

and it would execute the remote procedure defined by the synonym MY_RAISE.

Using STATSPACK and the Automatic Workload Repository

In Chapter 9, you will see how to use Statspack to gather and report on database statistics. Statspack is useful when you are working with multiple versions of Oracle. As of Oracle 10g, the Automatic Workload Repository (AWR) provides enhancements to the STATSPACK concept.

Like STATSPACK, AWR collects and maintains performance statistics for problem detection and self-tuning purposes. You can generate reports on the AWR data, and you can access it via views. You can report on recent session activity as well as the overall system statistics and SQL usage.

AWR captures the system statistics on an hourly basis (taking "snapshots" of the database) and stores the data in its repository tables. As with STATSPACK, the space requirements of the AWR repository will increase as the historical retention period is increased or the interval between snapshots is decreased. By default, seven days worth of data is maintained in the repository. You can see the snapshots that are stored in the AWR repository via the DBA_HIST_ SNAPSHOT view.

To enable AWR, set the STATISTICS_LEVEL initialization parameter to TYPICAL or ALL. If you set STATISTICS_LEVEL to BASIC, you can take manual snapshots of AWR data, but they will not be as comprehensive as those performed automatically by AWR.

Managing Snapshots

To take a manual snapshot, use the CREATE_SNAPSHOT procedure of the DBMS_WORKLOAD_REPOSITORY package:

```
execute DBMS_WORKLOAD_REPOSITORY.CREATE_SNAPSHOT ();
```

To alter the snapshot settings, use the MODIFY_SNAPSHOT_SETTINGS procedure. You can modify the retention (in minutes) and the interval (in minutes) for snapshots. The following example changes the interval to 30 minutes for the current database:

```
execute  DBMS_WORKLOAD_REPOSITORY.MODIFY_SNAPSHOT_SETTINGS
( interval => 30);
```

To drop a range of snapshots, use the DROP_SNAPSHOT_RANGE procedure, specifying the start and end of the snapshot IDs to drop:

```
execute DBMS_WORKLOAD_REPOSITORY.DROP_SNAPSHOT_RANGE
        (low_snap_id => 1, high_snap_id => 10);
```

Managing Baselines

You can designate a set of snapshots as a baseline for the performance of the system. The baseline data will be retained for later comparisons with snapshots. Use the CREATE_BASELINE procedure to specify the beginning and ending snapshots for the baseline:

```
execute DBMS_WORKLOAD_REPOSITORY.CREATE_BASELINE
    (start_snap_id => 1, end_snap_id => 10,
baseline_name => 'Monday baseline');
```

When you create a baseline, Oracle will assign an ID to the baseline; you can view past baselines via the DBA_HIST_BASELINE view. The snapshots you specify for the beginning and ending of the baseline are maintained until you drop the baseline. To drop the baseline, use the DROP_BASELINE procedure:

```
execute DBMS_WORKLOAD_REPOSITORY.DROP_BASELINE
    (baseline_name => 'Monday baseline', cascade => FALSE);
```

If you set the CASCADE parameter of the DROP_BASELINE procedure to TRUE, the related snapshots will be dropped when the baseline is dropped.

You can see the AWR data via OEM or via the data dictionary views listed earlier in this section. Additional views supporting AWR include V$ACTIVE_SESSION_HISTORY (sampled every second), DBA_HIST_SQL_PLAN (execution plans), and DBA_HIST_WR_CONTROL (for the AWR settings).

Generating AWR Reports

You can generate reports from AWR either via OEM or via the reporting scripts provided. The awrrpt.sql script generates a report based on the differences in statistics between the beginning and ending snapshot. A second report, awrrpti.sql, displays a report based on the beginning and ending snapshot for a specified database and instance.

Both awrrpt.sql and awrrpti.sql are located in the /rdbms/admin subdirectory under the Oracle software home directory. When you execute a report (from any DBA account), you will be prompted for the type of report (HTML or text), the number of days for which snapshots will be listed, the beginning and ending snapshot IDs, and the name for the output file.

Running the Automatic Database Diagnostic Monitor Reports

Rather than relying on manual reporting against the AWR table, you can use the Automatic Database Diagnostic Monitor (ADDM). Because it is based on AWR data, ADDM requires that the STATISTICS_LEVEL parameter be set (either to TYPICAL or ALL, as recommended earlier). You can access ADDM via the Performance Analysis section of OEM or you can run an ADDM report manually.

To run ADDM against a set of snapshots, use the addmrpt.sql script located in the /rdbms/ admin subdirectory under the Oracle software home directory.

NOTE
You must have the ADVISOR system privilege in order to execute this report.

Within SQL*Plus, execute the addmrpt.sql script. You will be prompted for the beginning and ending snapshot IDs for the analysis and a name for the output file.

To view the ADDM data, you can use OEM or the advisor data dictionary views. The advisor views include DBA_ADVISOR_TASKS (existing tasks), DBA_ADVISOR_LOG (status and progress on tasks), DBA_ADVISOR_RECOMMENDATIONS (completed diagnostic tasks plus recommendations), and DBA_ADVISOR_FINDINGS. You can implement the recommendations to address the findings identified via ADDM.

Tuning Solutions

This chapter does not cover every potential tuning solution. However, there is an underlying approach to the techniques and tools presented throughout this chapter. Before spending your time and resources on the implementation of a new feature, you should first stabilize your environment and architecture—the server, the database, and the application. If the environment is stable, you should be able to quickly accomplish two goals:

1. Successfully re-create the performance problem.

2. Successfully isolate the cause of the problem.

To achieve these goals, you may need to have a test environment available for your performance tests. Once the problem has been successfully isolated, you can apply the steps outlined in this chapter to the problem. In general, your tuning approach should mirror the order of the sections of this chapter:

1. Evaluate application design.

2. Tune SQL.

3. Tune memory usage.

4. Tune data storage.

5. Tune data manipulation.

6. Tune physical and logical storage.

7. Tune network traffic.

Depending on the nature of your application, you may choose a different order for the steps, or you may combine steps.

If the application design cannot be altered and the SQL cannot be altered, you can tune the memory and disk areas used by the application. As you alter the memory and disk area settings, you must be sure to revisit the application design and SQL implementation to be sure that your changes do not adversely impact the application. The need to revisit the application design process is particularly important if you choose to use a data replication method, because the timeliness of the replicated data may cause problems within the business process served by the application.

CHAPTER
9

Using STATSPACK

You can use the STATSPACK utility to monitor the performance of your database. In this chapter, you will see how to install STATSPACK, how to manage it, and how to run and interpret the reports generated.

As of Oracle10*g*, you can use the Automatic Workload Repository to gather and analyze statistics. The STATSPACK utility provides an ad hoc capability to analyze database statistics in a similar fashion—by taking snapshots of the database statistics at different times and generating reports based on the differences.

Installing STATSPACK

STATSPACK must be installed in every database to be monitored. The installation script, named spcreate.sql, is found in the /rdbms/admin subdirectory under the Oracle software home directory. The spcreate.sql script creates a user named PERFSTAT and creates a number of objects under that schema.

NOTE
You should allocate at least 100MB for the initial creation of the PERFSTAT schema's objects.

To start the spcreate.sql script, change your directory to the ORACLE_HOME/rdbms/admin directory and log into SQL*Plus using an account with SYSDBA privileges:

```
SQL> connect system/manager as SYSDBA
SQL> @spcreate
```

During the installation process, you will be prompted for a password for the PERFSTAT user and a default tablespace for the PERFSTAT user (a list of available tablespaces will be displayed along with this prompt). You will also be asked to specify a temporary tablespace for the user. Once you have provided the default and temporary tablespaces, the PERFSTAT account will be created, and the installation script will log in as PERFSTAT and continue to create the required objects. If there is not sufficient space to create the PERFSTAT objects in the specified default tablespace, the script will return an error.

NOTE
Although you start the installation script while logged in as a SYSDBA-privileged user, the conclusion of the installation script will leave you logged in as the PERFSTAT user.

If you want to drop the PERFSTAT user at a later date, you can run the spdusr.sql script located in the ORACLE_HOME/rdbms/admin directory.

Security of the PERFSTAT Account

The PERFSTAT account is created with the password you specify during STATSPACK installation. You can change the PERFSTAT account password at any time.

The PERFSTAT account is granted the SELECT_CATALOG_ROLE role and SELECT access on a large number of V$ views, along with several system privileges (CREATE/ALTER SESSION, CREATE TABLE, CREATE/DROP PUBLIC SYNONYM, CREATE SEQUENCE, and CREATE PROCEDURE). Any user who can access your PERFSTAT account can select from all the dictionary views. For example, such a user could query all the database account usernames from DBA_USERS, all the segment owners from DBA_SEGMENTS, and the currently logged-in sessions from V$SESSION. The PERFSTAT account, if left unprotected, provides a security hole that allows intruders to browse through your data dictionary and select targets for further intrusion.

In addition to the privileges it receives during the installation process, the PERFSTAT account will also have any privileges that have been granted to PUBLIC. If you use PUBLIC grants instead of roles for application privileges, you must secure the PERFSTAT account. You can lock database accounts and unlock them as needed; see Chapter 10 for details.

Post-installation

Once the installation process is complete, the PERFSTAT account will own tables, indexes, a sequence, and a package. You will use the package, named STATSPACK, to manage the statistics-collection process and the data in the tables. The collection tables, whose names all begin with "STATS$," will have column definitions based on the V$ view definitions. For example, the columns in STATS$WAITSTAT are the ones found in V$WAITSTAT, with three identification columns added at the top:

```
desc stats$waitstat
```

```
Name                      Null?     Type
----------------------    --------  ------------
SNAP_ID                   NOT NULL  NUMBER(6)
DBID                      NOT NULL  NUMBER
INSTANCE_NUMBER           NOT NULL  NUMBER
CLASS                     NOT NULL  VARCHAR2(18)
WAIT_COUNT                          NUMBER
TIME                                NUMBER
```

The Class, Wait_Count, and Time columns are based on the Class, Count, and Time columns from V$WAITSTAT. STATSPACK has added the following three identification columns:

SNAP_ID	An identification number for the collection. Each collection is called a "snapshot" and is assigned an integer value.
DBID	A numeric identifier for the database.
INSTANCE_NUMBER	A numeric identifier for the instance, for Real Application Clusters (RAC) installations.

Each collection you perform is given a new Snap_ID value that is consistent across the collection tables. When you run a STATSPACK report, you will see a list of all available snapshots.

Gathering Statistics

Each collection of statistics is called a *snapshot*. Snapshots are a point-in-time collection of the statistics available via the V$ views, and they are given a Snap_ID value to identify them. You can generate reports on the changes in the statistics between any two snapshots.

NOTE
As with the UTLBSTAT/UTLESTAT reports, the STATSPACK report will only be valid if the database was not shut down and restarted between the snapshots evaluated.

Between snapshots, STATSPACK performs no processing and adds no burden to your database performance. STATSPACK only impacts performance when you take snapshots and when you generate reports on the changes in statistics between two snapshots.

NOTE
Be sure the TIMED_STATISTICS database initialization parameter is set to TRUE prior to gathering statistics.

To generate a snapshot of the statistics, execute the SNAP procedure of the STATSPACK package, as shown in the following listing. You must be logged in as the PERFSTAT user to execute this procedure.

```
execute STATSPACK.SNAP;

PL/SQL procedure successfully completed.
```

When the SNAP procedure is executed, Oracle populates your SNAP$ tables with the current statistics. You can then query those tables directly, or you can use the standard STATSPACK report (to see the change in statistics between snapshots).

Snapshots should be taken for the following reasons:

- **To evaluate performance during specific tests of the system**   For these tests, you can execute the SNAP procedure manually, as shown in the prior example.

- **To evaluate performance changes over a long period of time**   To establish a baseline of the system performance, you may generate statistics snapshots on a scheduled basis. For these snapshots, you should schedule the SNAP procedure execution via Oracle's internal DBMS_JOB scheduler or via an operating system scheduler. You can use the spauto.sql script in the $ORACLE_HOME/rdbms/admin directory to schedule snapshots.

For the snapshots related to specific tests, you may wish to increase the collection level, which lets you gather more statistics. As noted in the "Managing the STATSPACK Data" section, later in this chapter, each snapshot has a cost in terms of space usage and query performance. Avoid generating thousands of rows of statistical data with each snapshot unless you plan to use them.

To support differing collection levels, STATSPACK provides the **level** parameter. By default, **level** is set to a value of 5. Prior to changing the **level** value, you should generate several snapshots and evaluate the reports generated. The default **level** value is adequate for most reports. Alternative **level** values are listed in the following table:

Level	Description
0	General performance statistics on all memory areas, latches, pools, and events
5	Same statistics from the lower levels, plus high-resource-usage SQL statements
6	Same statistics from the lower levels, plus SQL plan and SQL plan usage data
7	Same statistics from the lower levels, plus segment level statistics, including logical and physical reads, row lock, and buffer-busy waits
10	Same statistics from the lower levels, plus parent/child latch data

The greater the collection level, the longer the snapshot will take. The default value (5) offers a significant degree of flexibility during the queries for the most resource-intensive SQL statements. The parameters used for the resource-intensive SQL portion of the snapshot are stored in a table named STATS$STATSPACK_PARAMETER. You can query STATS$STATSPACK_PARAMETER to see the settings for the different thresholds during the process of SQL statement gathering. Its columns include Snap_Level (the snapshot level), Executions_Th (threshold value for the number of executions), Disk_Reads_Th (threshold value for the number of disk reads), and Buffer_Gets_Th (threshold value for the number of disk reads).

For a level 5 snapshot using the default thresholds, SQL statements are stored if they meet any of the following criteria:

- The SQL statement has been executed at least 100 times.
- The number of disk reads performed by the SQL statement exceeds 1000.
- The number of parse calls performed by the SQL statement exceeds 1000.
- The number of buffer gets performed by the SQL statement exceeds 10,000.
- The sharable memory used by the SQL statement exceeds 1MB.
- The version count for the SQL statement exceeds 20.

When evaluating the snapshot's data and the performance report, keep in mind that the SQL threshold parameter values are cumulative. A very efficient query, if executed enough times, will exceed 10,000 buffer gets. Compare the number of buffer gets and disk reads to the number of executions to determine the activity each time the query is executed.

To modify the default settings for the thresholds, use the MODIFY_STATSPACK_PARAMETER procedure of the STATSPACK package. Specify the snapshot level via the **i_snap_level** parameter, along with the parameters to change. Table 9-1 lists the available parameters for the MODIFY_STATSPACK_PARAMETER procedure.

Parameter Name	Range of Values	Default	Description
i_snap_level	0, 5, 6, 7, 10	5	Snapshot level
i_ucomment	Any text	blank	Comment for the snapshot
i_executions_th	Integer >=0	100	Threshold for the cumulative number of executions
i_disk_reads_th	Integer >=0	1000	Threshold for the cumulative number of disk reads
i_parse_calls_th	Integer >=0	1000	Threshold for the cumulative number of parse calls
i_buffer_gets_th	Integer >=0	10000	Threshold for the cumulative number of buffer gets
i_session_id	Valid SID from V$SESSION	0	Session ID of an Oracle session, if you wish to gather session-level statistics
i_modify_parameter	True or False	False	Set to True if you wish to save your changes for future snapshots

TABLE 9-1. *Modification Parameters*

To increase the Buffer_Gets threshold for a level 5 snapshot to 100,000, issue the following command:

```
STATSPACK.MODIFY_STATSPACK_PARAMETER -
    (i_snap_level=>5, i_buffer_gets_th=>100000);
```

If you plan to run the SNAP procedure more frequently than hourly, you should pin the STATSPACK package in the shared pool following database startup. The following listing shows a trigger that will be executed each time the database is started. The KEEP procedure of the DBMS_SHARED_POOL procedure pins the package in the shared pool.

```
create or replace trigger PIN_ON_STARTUP
after startup on database
begin
    DBMS_SHARED_POOL.KEEP ('PERFSTAT.STATSPACK', 'P');
end;
/
```

Running the Statistics Report

If you have generated more than one snapshot, you can report on the statistics for the period between the two snapshots. The database must not have been shut down between the times the two snapshots were taken. When you execute the report, you will need to know the Snap_ID values for the snapshots. If you run the report interactively, Oracle will provide a list of the available snapshots and the times they were created.

To execute the report, go to the /rdbms/admin directory under the Oracle software home directory. Log into SQL*Plus as the PERFSTAT user and run the spreport.sql file found there, like so:

```
SQL> @spreport
```

Oracle will display the database and instance identification information from V$INSTANCE and V$DATABASE and will then call a second SQL file, sprepins.sql. The sprepins.sql file generates the report of the changes in the statistics during the snapshot time interval. The available snapshots will be listed, and you will be prompted to enter a beginning and ending snapshot ID. Unless you specify otherwise, the output will be written to a file named sp_*beginning_ending*.lst (sp_1_2.lst for a report between the Snap_ID values 1 and 2).

The first portion of the report output provides an overview of the cache areas and their usage. The following listing provides sample output for this section, showing the cache sizes and the load profile:

```
Cache Sizes (end)
~~~~~~~~~~~~~~~~~~
           Buffer Cache:     1,536M      Std Block Size:     8K
       Shared Pool Size:     1,648M      Log Buffer:    10,240K

Load Profile
~~~~~~~~~~~~                    Per Second         Per Transaction
                             ---------------       ---------------
              Redo size:        85,921.59              1,924.45
          Logical reads:        23,431.10                524.80
          Block changes:           520.99                 11.67
         Physical reads:           457.96                 10.26
        Physical writes:            61.19                  1.37
             User calls:         2,000.92                 44.82
                 Parses:           430.78                  9.65
            Hard parses:             0.04                  0.00
                  Sorts:            57.11                  1.28
                 Logons:             0.53                  0.01
               Executes:           699.70                 15.67
           Transactions:            44.65

   % Blocks changed per Read:   2.22      Recursive Call %:  31.02
   Rollback per transaction %:  0.06         Rows per Sort:  64.62
```

The load profile helps to identify the type of activity being performed. In this example, the activity recorded includes both queries and transactions. On average, this database supports 44.65 transactions per second while also supporting logical reads and sort operations. The database is actively performing physical reads and writes. In a read-intensive application, the number of physical writes per second should be far below the number of physical reads per second.

Note that the load profile shows the per-second averages in the database; however, if your STATSPACK reporting interval is too large, there may not be such a thing as an average second. For example, if your interval includes both your data-loading processes and your online user activity, the averages would reflect the combined impact of both types of usage, obscuring the true load profile of each separate activity.

NOTE
When using the load profile statistics, remember that these are presented as "per second" statistics—the rest of the STATSPACK report values are presented as values for the full duration of the snapshot.

The next sections of the report show the instance efficiency percentages (such as the buffer hit ratio and library cache hit ratio) followed by the shared pool statistics. The shared pool statistics show the percentage of the shared pool in use and the percentage of SQL statements that have been executed multiple times (as desired). The following listing shows sample shared pool statistics from the report:

```
Shared Pool Statistics        Begin    End
                              ------   ------
           Memory Usage %:    100.00   100.00
   % SQL with executions>1:    71.68    70.60
   % Memory for SQL w/exec>1:  64.63    62.85
```

Based on the data in the preceding listing, at the time of the second snapshot, 100 percent of the shared pool's memory was in use. Of the statements in the shared pool, only 70 percent had been executed more than once, indicating a potential need to improve cursor sharing in the application. Because the shared pool is completely used, you should consider increasing its size.

The next portion of the generated report shows the top five wait events, the full list of wait events, and the background wait events. Identifying major wait events may help to target your tuning efforts.

Let's consider common wait events: db file scattered reads (waits encountered during multiblock reads such as during full table scans) and db file sequential reads (for single-block reads). For this same database, the statistics (truncated for display here) were as follows:

```
Event                           Waits    Timeouts   Time (s)
----------------------------  ---------  ---------  ---------
db file sequential read       1,410,528          0      3,631
db file scattered read           20,503          0         36
```

Adding them together, we find that for the interval there were a total of 1,431,031 waits during reads from datafiles—single-block reads of indexes, single-block reads of tables, plus multiblock reads. How many waits were there per second? In this report, the time interval was one hour—3600 seconds—so the number of waits per second is

```
1,431,031 waits / 3600 seconds = 397.5 waits per second
```

How does that compare with the number of reads? From the load profile, we already know the number of physical reads per second:

```
~~~~~~~~~~~~~                    Per Second      Per Transaction
                                ------------     ---------------
    Physical reads:                 457.96                10.26
```

So, in an average second, how many waits occur per physical read? To answer this, divide the waits per second by the reads per second:

```
397.5 waits per second / 457.96 physical reads per second = 0.868
```

Based on these statistics, roughly 87 percent of all reads during the interval encountered wait events. That is a very high percentage of waits per read, and you should examine the I/O environment to see if there are opportunities to improve its performance. Don't look for full table scans as the culprits—remember the source of the waits:

```
Event                           Waits    Timeouts   Time (s)
----------------------------  ----------  --------  ----------
db file sequential read       1,410,528         0      3,631
db file scattered read           20,503         0         36
```

Single-block reads accounted for 98.5 percent—that is, 1,410,528/(1,410,528+20,503)—of the waits. Look for inefficient indexes that are being scanned repeatedly. If you eliminate all full table scans in the database, you will reduce the number of physical waits by at most 1.5 percent.

The most resource-intensive SQL statements in the database are listed in the next section of the report, in descending order of buffer gets. Because the buffer gets statistic is cumulative, the query with the most buffer gets may not be the worst-performing query in the database; it may just have been executed enough times to earn the highest ranking. Compare the cumulative number of buffer gets to the cumulative number of disk reads for the queries; if the numbers are close, you should evaluate the explain plan for the query.

NOTE
If the shared pool is flushed between the execution times of the two snapshots, the SQL portion of the output report will not necessarily contain the most resource-intensive SQL executed during the period.

The SQL statements are listed three separate times—ordered by buffer gets, then by physical reads, then by executions. It is common to find resource-intensive SQL commands that show up in only one or two of these three listings. For example, if your application constantly executes a query such as

```
select TRUNC(SYSDATE) from DUAL;
```

then it will not generate many physical reads. However, the number of executions of this command may cause it to be one of the most expensive queries in the database. Some applications run queries like this millions of times per day—to the point at which one or more CPUs are constantly busy doing nothing more than returning the current system date to the user. Even if the commands are efficient in terms of physical I/O by themselves, consider their number of executions and their buffer gets—and the corresponding CPU burdens they incur.

Following the SQL statement listing, you will see the list of changes to statistics from V$SYSSTAT, titled "Instance Activity Stats." The V$SYSSTAT statistics are useful for identifying performance issues not shown in the prior sections. For example, you should compare the number of sorts performed on disk to the number performed in memory; increase the PGA_ AGGREGATE_TARGET value to reduce disk sorts. If there is a significant number of full table scans of large tables, evaluate the most-used queries. The following listing shows four rows from this section of the report:

Statistic	Total	per Second	per Trans
sorts (disk)	13	0.0	0.0
sorts (memory)	205,651	57.1	1.3
table scans (long tables)	23	0.0	0.0
table scans (short tables)	602,813	167.4	3.8

In this case, there are full table scans of long tables (those with more than five blocks), but they are a minority of the full table scans performed. You should check to see if the small tables are being properly cached in memory (such as in the KEEP pool). The sorts to disk are small in number, but every sort to disk is wasted effort. You should increase the sort area size and avoid writing to the temporary tablespace unless absolutely necessary.

The next section of the report provides the I/O statistics by tablespace and by datafile. If the I/O is not properly distributed among your files, you many encounter performance bottlenecks during periods of high activity. You can use this section of the report to identify such bottlenecks and to measure how effectively you have resolved those problems. See Chapter 4 for further details on I/O distribution across files.

Following the I/O statistics, the report lists the buffer cache statistics by pool (DEFAULT, KEEP, and RECYCLE), instance recovery statistics (the number of redo blocks), and the buffer pool advisory. The buffer pool advisory shows an estimated physical read factor so you can judge how much impact increasing the data block buffer cache will have on the number of physical reads required. The buffer pool section is followed by an advisory on the PGA aggregate settings.

The next sections of the report show the buffer statistics related to waits during write events:

Class	Waits	Tot Wait Time (s)	Avg Time (ms)
data block	119	0	1
undo header	86	0	0
undo block	6	0	0

In general, using Automated Undo Management will reduce or eliminate waits for undo headers and undo blocks. Data block waits may be reduced by using asynchronous I/O or by improving the efficiency of the I/O environment. In this example, a few milliseconds are being spent waiting for data blocks.

The next section of the report lists the enqueue waits, including TX locks for individual rows, TC locks for thread checkpoints, and others. Enqueue waits can be caused by application architecture decisions and database configuration issues, so evaluating their cause may require additional testing.

After those sections, the report provides undo segment statistics. First, it lists the activity in the undo segments (writes, wraps, shrinks, extends) and the waits encountered. Following that, the report shows the number of undo blocks written per time interval.

Latch activity and dictionary cache statistics are then presented, followed by the library cache activity. If your "Pct Miss" value is high, you may need to improve cursor sharing in your application or increase the size of the shared pool.

A shared pool advisory is displayed in the next section of the report. In the advisory, Oracle estimates the number of library object hits expected in each incremental increase in the size of the shared pool.

Following an SGA memory summary (from V$SGA) and a listing of the memory changes during the snapshot interval, the report lists the database initialization parameters in use at the beginning and end of the report.

Taken as a whole, the report generates a significant amount of data, allowing you to develop a profile of the database and its usage. Based on the initialization, file I/O, and SGA data, you can develop an understanding of the major components in the database configuration. Because this report generates so much data, you should be careful not to generate more statistics than you plan to use. The next section of this chapter addresses the management of the gathered data.

Managing the STATSPACK Data

You should manage the data generated by STATSPACK to guarantee that the space usage and performance of the STATSPACK application meets your requirements as the application data grows. Managing STATSPACK data includes the following steps:

1. Regularly analyze the STATSPACK data. At a minimum, you should analyze the STATSPACK table prior to running the spreport.sql report:

   ```
   execute DBMS_UTILITY.ANALYZE_SCHEMA('PERFSTAT','COMPUTE');
   ```

2. Purge old data. Because you cannot generate valid interval reports across database shutdown/startup actions, data prior to the last database startup may not be as useful as the most current data. When the data is no longer needed, purge it from the tables. Oracle provides a script, sppurge.sql, to facilitate purges. The sppurge.sql script, located in the /rdbms/admin directory under the Oracle software home directory, lists the currently stored snapshots and prompts you for two input parameters: the beginning and ending snapshot numbers for the purge. The related records in the STATS$ tables will then be deleted. The sppurge script prompts you to back up your old statistics before purging them. You can back up the data by exporting the PERFSTAT schema. You may wish to keep old statistics for baseline measurements.

3. Truncate the STATSPACK tables when the data is not needed. Old statistical data may no longer be relevant, or you may have imported the old statistics during database migrations or creations. To truncate the old tables, execute the sptrunc.sql SQL*Plus script from within the PERFSTAT account. The script is located in the /rdbms/admin directory under the Oracle software home directory.

Deinstalling STATSPACK

Because STATSPACK includes public synonyms as well as private objects, you should remove the application via a SYSDBA privileged account. Oracle provides a script, spdrop.sql, to automate the deinstallation process. From within the /rdbms/admin directory under the Oracle software home directory, log into SQL*Plus and execute the script as shown here:

```
SQL> connect system/manager as SYSDBA
SQL> @spdrop
```

The spdrop.sql script calls the scripts that drop the tables, package, public synonyms, and the PERFSTAT user. To reinstall STATSPACK, execute the spcreate.sql script as shown earlier in the chapter.

CHAPTER
10

Database Security
and Auditing

To protect one of the most vital assets to a company—its data—a DBA must be keenly aware of how Oracle can protect corporate data and the different tools they have at their disposal. The Oracle-provided tools and mechanisms fall into three broad categories: authentication, authorization, and auditing.

Authentication includes methods used to identify who is accessing the database, ensuring that you are who you say you are, regardless of what resources you are requesting of the database. Even if you are merely trying to access the daily lunch menu at the cafeteria, it is important that you identify yourself correctly to the database. If, for example, the web-based database application presents customized content based on the user account, you want to make sure you get the lunch menu for your branch office in Houston, Texas, and not the one for the home office in Buffalo, New York!

Authorization provides access to various objects in the database once you are authenticated by the database. Some users may be authorized to run a report against the daily sales table, some users may be developers and therefore need to create tables and reports, whereas others may only be allowed to see the daily lunch menu. Some users may never log in at all, but their schema may own a number of tables for a particular application, such as payroll or accounts receivable. Additional authorization methods are provided for database administrators, due to the extreme power that a database administrator has. Because a DBA can shut down and start up a database, an additional level of authorization is provided.

Authorization goes well beyond simple access to a table or a report; it also includes the rights to use system resources in the database as well as privileges to perform certain actions in the database. A given database user might only be allowed to use 15 seconds of CPU time per session or can only be idle for five minutes before they are disconnected from the database. Another database user might be granted the privilege to create or drop tables in any other user's schema, but not be able to create synonyms or view data dictionary tables. Fine-grained access control gives the DBA more control over how database objects are accessed. For example, standard object privileges will either give a user access to an entire row of a table or not at all; using fine-grained access control, a DBA can create a policy implemented by a stored procedure that restricts access based on time of day, where the request originates, which column of the table is being accessed, or all three.

At the end of the section on database authorization, we will present a short example of a *Virtual Private Database (VPD)* to provide methods for defining, setting, and accessing application attributes along with the predicates (usually WHERE clauses) to control which data is accessible or returned to the user of the application.

Auditing in an Oracle database encompasses a number of different levels of monitoring in the database. At a high level, auditing can record both successful and unsuccessful attempts to log in, access an object, or perform an action. As of Oracle9*i*, not only can fine-grained auditing (FGA) record what objects are accessed, but what columns of a table are accessed when an insert, update, or delete is being performed on the data in the column. Fine-grained auditing is to auditing what fine-grained access control is to standard authorization: more precise control and information about the objects being accessed or actions being performed.

DBAs must use auditing judiciously so as not to be overwhelmed by audit records or create too much overhead by implementing continuous auditing. On the flip side, auditing can help to protect company assets by monitoring who is using what resource, at what time, and how often, as well as whether the access was successful or not. Therefore, auditing is another tool that the DBA should be using on a continuous basis to monitor the security health of the database.

Non-Database Security

All the methodologies presented later in this chapter are useless if access to the operating system is not secure or the physical hardware is not in a secure location. In this section, we'll discuss a few of the elements outside of the database itself that need to be secure before the database can be considered secure.

In the following list are a few things that need to be considered outside of the database:

- **Operating system security**   Unless the Oracle database is running on its own dedicated hardware with only the **root** and **oracle** user accounts enabled, operating system security must be reviewed and implemented. Ensure that the software is installed with the **oracle** account and not the **root** account. You may also consider using another account instead of **oracle** as the owner of the software and the database files, to eliminate an easy target for a hacker. Ensure that the software and the database files are readable only by the **oracle** account and the group that **oracle** belongs to. Other than the Oracle executables that require it, turn off the SUID (set UID, or running with root privileges) bit on files that don't require it. Don't send passwords (operating system or Oracle) to users via e-mail in plain text. Finally, remove any system services that are not required on the server to support the database, such as telnet and ftp.

- **Securing backup media**   Ensure that the database backup media—whether it be tape, disk, or CD/DVD-ROM—is accessible by a limited number of people. A secure operating system and robust, encrypted passwords on the database are of little value if a hacker can obtain backup copies of the database and load them onto another server. The same applies to any server that contains data replicated from your database.

- **Background security checks**   Screening of employees that deal with sensitive database data—whether it be a DBA, auditor, or operating system administrator—is a must.

- **Security education**   Ensure that all database users understand the security and usage policies of the IT infrastructure. Requiring that users understand and follow the security policies emphasizes the critical nature and value of the data to the company, including the information in the database. A well-educated user will be more likely to resist attempts at system access from a hacker's social-engineering skills.

- **Controlled access to hardware**   All computer hardware that houses the database should be located in a secure environment that is accessible only with badges or security access codes.

Database Authentication Methods

Before the database can allow a person or application access to objects or privileges in the database, the person or application must be authenticated; in other words, the identity of who is attempting access to the database needs to be validated.

In this section, we'll give an overview of the most basic method used to allow access to the database—the user account, otherwise known as *database authentication.* In addition, we'll show how to reduce the number of passwords a user needs to remember by allowing the operating system to authenticate the user and, as a result, automatically connect the user to the database. Using 3-tier authentication via an application server, network authentication, or Oracle's Identity Management can reduce the number of passwords even further. Finally, we'll talk about using a password file to authenticate DBAs when the database is down and cannot provide authentication services.

Database Authentication

In an environment where the network is protected from the outside environment with firewalls and the network traffic between the client and the database server uses some method of encryption, authentication by the database is the most common and easiest method to authenticate the user with the database. All information needed to authenticate the user is stored in a table within the SYSTEM tablespace.

Very special database operations, such as starting up or shutting down the database, require a different and more secure form of authentication, either by using operating system authentication or by using password files.

Network authentication relies on third-party authentication services such as the Distributed Computing Environment (DCE), Kerberos, Public Key Infrastructure (PKI), and Remote Authentication Dial-In User Service (RADIUS). 3-tier authentication, although at first glance appears to be a network authentication method, is different in that a middle tier, such as Oracle Application Server, authenticates the user while maintaining the client's identity on the server. In addition, the middle tier provides connection pooling services as well as implements business logic for the client.

Later in this chapter, in the section titled "User Accounts," we'll go through all the options available to the DBA for setting up accounts in the database for authentication.

Database Administrator Authentication

The database is not always available to authenticate a database administrator, such as when it is down because of an unplanned outage or for an offline database backup. To address this situation, Oracle uses a *password file* to maintain a list of database users who are allowed to perform functions such as starting up and shutting down the database, initiating backups, and so forth.

Alternatively, a database administrator can use operating system authentication, which we discuss in the next section. The flow chart shown in Figure 10-1 identifies the options for a database administrator when deciding what method will work the best in their environment.

For connecting locally to the server, the main consideration is the convenience of using the same account for both the operating system and the Oracle server versus maintaining a password file. For a remote administrator, the security of the connection is the driving factor when choosing an authentication method. Without a secure connection, a hacker could easily impersonate a user with the same account as that of an administrator on the server itself and gain full access to the database with OS authentication.

NOTE
When using a password file for authentication, ensure that the password file itself is in a directory location that is only accessible by the operating system administrators and the user or group that owns the Oracle software installation.

We will discuss system privileges in greater detail later in this chapter. For now, though, you need to know that there are two particular system privileges that give administrators special authentication in the database: SYSDBA and SYSOPER. An administrator with the SYSOPER privilege can start up and shut down the database, perform online or offline backups, archive the current

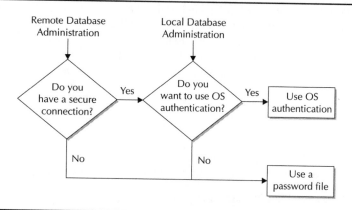

FIGURE 10-1. *Authentication method flowchart*

redo log files, and connect to the database when it is in RESTRICTED SESSION mode. The SYSDBA privilege contains all the rights of SYSOPER, with the addition of being able to create a database and grant the SYSDBA or SYSOPER privilege to other database users.

To connect to the database from a SQL*Plus session, you append AS SYSDBA or AS SYSOPER to your **connect** command. Here's an example:

```
D:\TEMP> sqlplus /nolog

SQL*Plus: Release 10.1.0.1.0 - Production on Sun Feb 15 20:52:10 2004

Copyright (c) 1982, 2004, Oracle Corporation.  All rights reserved.

SQL> connect rjb/rjb999@dw as sysdba
Connected.
SQL>
```

Other than the additional privileges available to the users who connect as SYSDBA or SYSOPER, the default schema is also different for these users when they connect to the database. Users who connect with the SYSDBA privilege connect as the SYS user; the SYSOPER privilege sets the user to PUBLIC:

```
SQL> show user
USER is "SYS"
```

As with any database connection request, you have the option to specify the username and password on the same line as the **sqlplus** command, along with the SYSDBA or SYSOPER keyword:

```
D:\TEMP> sqlplus rjb/rjb999@dw as sysdba
```

Although a default installation of the Oracle Database using the Oracle Universal Installer with a seed database or using the Database Creation Assistant will automatically create a password file, there are occasions when you may need to re-create one if it is accidentally deleted or damaged. The **orapwd** command will create a password file with a single entry for the SYS user and other options, as noted, when you run the **orapwd** command without any options:

```
[oracle@dw10g oracle]$ orapwd
Usage: orapwd file=<fname> password=<password> entries=<users> force=<y/n>
  where
    file - name of password file (mand),
    password - password for SYS (mand),
    entries - maximum number of distinct DBAs and OPERs (opt),
    force - whether to overwrite existing file (opt)
  There are no spaces around the equal-to (=) character.
[oracle@dw10g oracle]$
```

Once you re-create the password file, you will have to grant the SYSDBA and SYSOPER privileges to those database users who previously had those privileges. In addition, if the password you provided in the **orapwd** command is not the same password that the SYS account has in the database, you will have to change the SYS account's password the next time you are connected to the database so that the password in the database and the password in the password file stay in synch.

The system initialization parameter REMOTE_LOGIN_PASSWORDFILE controls how the password file is used for the database instance. It has three possible values: NONE, SHARED, and EXCLUSIVE.

If the value is NONE, then Oracle ignores any password file that exists. Any privileged users must be authenticated by other means, such as by operating system authentication, which is discussed in the next section.

With a value of SHARED, multiple databases can share the same password file, but only the SYS user is authenticated with the password file, and the password for SYS cannot be changed. As a result, this method is not the most secure, but it does allow a DBA to maintain more than one database with a single SYS account.

TIP
If a shared password file must be used, ensure that the password for SYS is at least eight characters long and includes a combination of alphabetic, numeric, and special characters to fend off a brute-force attack.

A value of EXCLUSIVE binds the password file to only one database, and other database user accounts can exist in the password file. As soon as the password file is created, use this value to maximize the security of SYSDBA or SYSOPER connections.

The dynamic performance view V$PWFILE_USERS lists all the database users who have either SYSDBA or SYSOPER privileges, as shown here:

```
SQL> select * from v$pwfile_users;

USERNAME      SYSDBA    SYSOPER
-----------   --------  --------
SYS           TRUE      TRUE
RJB           TRUE      FALSE
SYSTEM        TRUE      FALSE
```

Operating System Authentication

If a DBA chooses to implement *operating system authentication,* a database user is automatically connected to the database when they use the following SQL*Plus syntax:

```
SQL> sqlplus /
```

This method is similar to how an administrator connects to the database, without the **as sysdba** or **as sysoper** clause. The main difference is that the operating system account authorization methods are used instead of an Oracle-generated and maintained password file.

In fact, administrators can also use operating system authentication to connect using **as sysdba** or **as sysoper**. If the administrator's operating system login account is in the Unix group **dba** (or the Windows group ORA_DBA), the administrator can connect to the database using **as sysdba**. Similarly, if the operating system login account is in the Unix group **oper** (or the Windows group ORA_OPER), the administrator can connect to the database using **as sysoper** without the need for an Oracle password file.

The Oracle Server makes the assumption that if the user is authenticated by an operating system account, then the user is also authenticated for the database. With operating system authentication, Oracle does not need to maintain passwords in the database, but it still maintains the usernames. The usernames are still needed to set the default schema and tablespaces in addition to providing information for auditing.

In a default Oracle 10*g* installation, as well as in previous releases of Oracle, operating system authentication is enabled for user accounts if you create database users with the **identified externally** clause. The prefix for the database username must match the value of the initialization parameter OS_AUTHENT_PREFIX; the default value is OPS$. Here's an example:

```
SQL> create user ops$corie identified externally;
```

When the user logs into the operating system with the account CORIE, she is automatically authenticated in the Oracle database as if the account OPS$CORIE was created with database authentication.

Setting the value of OS_AUTHENT_PREFIX to a null string allows the database administrator and the operating system account administrator to use identical usernames when using external authentication.

Using **identified globally** is similar to using **identified externally** in that the authentication is done outside of the database. However, with a globally identified user, authentication is performed by an enterprise directory service such as Oracle Internet Directory (OID). OID facilitates ease of account maintenance for database administrators and the convenience of single sign-on for database users who need to access more than just a single database or service.

Network Authentication

Authentication by a network service is another option available to the DBA to authenticate users in the database. Although a complete treatment is beyond the scope of this book, we will give a brief summary of each method and its components. These components include Secure Sockets Layer (SSL), Distributed Computing Environment (DCE), Kerberos, PKI, RADIUS, and directory-based services.

Secure Sockets Layer Protocol

Secure Sockets Layer (SSL) is a protocol originally developed by Netscape Development Corporation for use in web browsers. Because it is a public standard and open source, it faces continuous scrutiny by the programming community to ensure that there are no holes or "back doors" that can compromise its robustness.

At a minimum, a server-side certificate is required for authentication. Client authentication is also doable with SSL to validate the client, but setting up certificates may become a large administrative effort.

Using SSL over TCP/IP requires only slight changes to the listener configuration by adding another protocol (TCPS) at a different port number in the listener.ora file. In the following excerpt, configured with Oracle Net Configuration Assistant (**netca**), the listener named LISTENER on the server dw10g will accept traffic via TCP on port 1521 and SSL TCP traffic on port 2484:

```
# listener.ora Network Configuration File:
    /u01/app/oracle/product/10.1.0/network/admin/listener.ora
# Generated by Oracle configuration tools.
SID_LIST_LISTENER =
  (SID_LIST =
    (SID_DESC =
      (SID_NAME = PLSExtProc)
      (ORACLE_HOME = /u01/app/oracle/product/10.1.0)
      (PROGRAM = extproc)
    )
    (SID_DESC =
      (GLOBAL_DBNAME = dw.world)
      (ORACLE_HOME = /u01/app/oracle/product/10.1.0)
      (SID_NAME = dw)
    )
  )


LISTENER =
  (DESCRIPTION_LIST =
    (DESCRIPTION =
      (ADDRESS_LIST =
        (ADDRESS = (PROTOCOL = TCP)(HOST = dw10g)(PORT = 1521))
      )
      (ADDRESS_LIST =
        (ADDRESS = (PROTOCOL = TCPS)(HOST = dw10g)(PORT = 2484))
      )
    )
  )
```

Distributed Computing Environment

The Distributed Computing Environment (DCE) provides a number of services, such as remote procedure calls, distributed file services, and distributed time service, in addition to a security service. DCE supports distributed applications in a heterogeneous environment on all major software and hardware platforms.

DCE is one of the protocols that support single sign-on (SSO); once a user authenticates with DCE, they can securely access any Oracle database configured with DCE without specifying a username or password.

Kerberos

Kerberos is another trusted third-party authentication system that, like DCE, provides SSO capabilities. Oracle fully supports Kerberos version 5 with Oracle Advanced Security under the Enterprise Edition of Oracle Database 10*g*.

As with other middleware authentication solutions, the basic premise is that passwords should never be sent across the network; all authentication is brokered by the Kerberos server. In Kerberos terminology, a password is a "shared secret."

Public Key Infrastructure

Public Key Infrastructure (PKI) comprises a number of components. It is implemented using the SSL protocol and is based on the concept of secret private keys and related public keys to facilitate secure communications between the client and server.

To provide identification and authentication services, PKI uses certificates and certificate authorities (CAs). In a nutshell, a certificate is an entity's public key validated by a trusted third party (a certificate authority), and it contains information such as the certificate user's name, an expiration date, the public key, and so forth.

RADIUS

Remote Authentication Dial-In User Service (RADIUS) is a lightweight protocol used for authentication as well as authorization and accounting services. In an Oracle environment, the Oracle Server acts as the client to a RADIUS server when an authorization request is sent from an Oracle client.

Any authentication method that supports the RADIUS standard—whether it be token cards, smart cards, or SecurID ACE—can easily be added to the RADIUS server as a new authentication method without any changes being made on the client or server configuration files, such as sqlnet.ora.

3-Tier Authentication

In a 3-tier or multitier environment, an application server can provide authentication services for a client and provide a common interface to the database server, even if the clients use a variety of different browsers or "thick" client applications. The application server, in turn, is authenticated with the database and demonstrates that the client is allowed to connect to the database, thus preserving the identity of the client in all tiers.

In multitier environments, both users and middle tiers are given the fewest possible privileges necessary to do their jobs. The middle tier is granted permission to perform actions on behalf of a user with a command such as the following:

```
alter user kmourgos
    grant connect through oes_as
    with role all except ordmgmt;
```

In this example, the application server service OES_AS is granted permission to perform actions on behalf of the database user KMOURGOS. The user KMOURGOS has been assigned a number of roles, and they can all be enabled through the application server, except for the ORDMGMT role. As a result, when KMOURGOS connects through the application server, he is permitted to access, via the web, all tables and privileges granted to him via roles, except for the order management functions. Because of the business rules in place at his company, all access to the order management applications must be done via a direct connection to the database. Roles are discussed in detail in the section titled "Creating, Assigning, and Maintaining Roles" later in this chapter.

Client-Side Authentication

Client-side authentication is one way to authenticate users in a multitier environment, but Oracle strongly discourages this method unless all clients are on a secure network, inside a firewall, with no connections allowed to the database from outside the firewall. In addition, users should not have any administrative rights on any workstation that can connect to the database.

If an Oracle user is created with the IDENTIFIED EXTERNALLY attribute, and the initialization parameter REMOTE_OS_AUTHENT is set to TRUE, then an attacker can easily authenticate himself on the workstation with a local user account that matches the Oracle user account, and as a result gain access to the database.

As a result, it is strongly recommended that the REMOTE_OS_AUTHENT parameter be set to FALSE. The database will have to be stopped and restarted for this change to take effect.

Oracle Identity Management

Oracle Identity Management (IM), a component of Oracle Application Server 10*g*, provides a complete end-to-end framework for centrally managing user accounts, from account creation to resource authorization to account deletion. It centralizes the management of accounts along with the devices, applications, web services, or any other networked entity that uses authentication and authorization.

IM saves money and time. Because the user accounts and the associated resources are centralized, administration is the same regardless of the application being maintained.

In addition, IM enhances the security of the enterprise. Because users only use one username and password to access all enterprise resources, they are less prone to write down or forget their password. When a user leaves the company, all access to applications and services can be removed quickly and easily in one place.

Although a complete treatment of Oracle Identity Management is beyond the scope of this book, it's important for the DBA to understand how the components of IM will impact the performance and security of the Oracle database. The user account information and other metadata needs to be stored somewhere, and stored redundantly, in an Oracle database. In addition, the requests for authentication and authorization services must be processed within a reasonable amount of time, defined most likely within the Service Level Agreements (SLAs) in effect for one or more of the applications.

For example, Oracle Internet Directory (OID), one of the major components of Oracle Identity Management, requires database tuning somewhat like tuning for an OLTP system, with many short transactions from a large number of users with widely varying loads depending on the time of day. But that is where the similarity ends! In Table 10-1 are some general guidelines for setting various system-initialization parameters for the database that will be maintaining the Lightweight Directory Access Protocol (LDAP) directory information.

It is assumed that this database's only job is to maintain OID directory information. In addition to tuning basic database parameters, overall throughput will depend on factors such as network

Database Parameter	500 Concurrent Users	2000 Concurrent Users
OPEN_CURSORS	200	200
SESSIONS	445	1655
DB_BLOCK_SIZE	8K	8K
DB_CACHE_SIZE	250MB	250MB
SHARED_POOL_SIZE	40MB	40MB
PROCESSES	400	1500
SORT_AREA_SIZE	256KB	256KB
LOG_BUFFER	512KB	512KB

TABLE 10-1.   *Database Initialization Parameter Sizing for OID*

bandwidth available between the server and the user community, the location of shared disk resources, disk throughput, and so forth. A typical IM deployment with 500,000 directory entries will require approximately 3GB of disk space, and how fast or how slow the entries can be written to or read from disk can easily become the throughput bottleneck.

User Accounts

In order to gain access to the database, a user must provide a *username* to access the resources associated with that account. Each username must have a password and is associated with one and only one schema in the database; some accounts may have no objects in the schema, but instead would have the privileges granted to that account to access objects in other schemas.

In this section, we'll explain the syntax and give examples for creating, altering, and dropping users. In addition, we'll show you how to become another user without explicitly knowing the password for the user.

Creating Users

The **create user** command is fairly straightforward. It has a number of parameters, which are listed in Table 10-2 along with a brief description of each one.

In the following example, we are creating a user (SKING) to correspond with the user Steven King, employee number 100 in the HR.EMPLOYEES table from the sample schemas installed with the database:

```
SQL> create user sking identified by sking901
  2      account unlock
  3      default tablespace users
  4      temporary tablespace temp;
User created.
```

The user SKING is authenticated by the database with an initial password of SKING901. The second line is not required; all accounts are created unlocked by default. Both the default permanent

Parameter	Usage
username	The name of the schema, and therefore the user, to be created. The username can be up to 30 characters long and cannot be a reserved word unless it is quoted (which is not recommended).
IDENTIFIED { BY *password* | EXTERNALLY | GLOBALLY AS '*extname*' }	Specifies how the user will be authenticated: by the database with a password, by the operating system (local or remote), or by a service (such as Oracle Internet Directory).
DEFAULT TABLESPACE *tablespace*	The tablespace where permanent objects are created, unless a tablespace is explicitly specified during creation.
TEMPORARY TABLESPACE *tablespace*	The tablespace where temporary segments are created during sort operations, index creation, and so forth.
QUOTA { *size* | UNLIMITED } ON *tablespace*	The amount of space allowed for objects created on the specified tablespace. Size is in kilobytes (K) or megabytes (M).
PROFILE *profile*	The profile assigned to this user. Profiles are discussed later in this chapter. If a profile is not specified, the DEFAULT profile is used.
PASSWORD EXPIRE	At first logon, the user must change their password.
ACCOUNT {LOCK | UNLOCK}	Specifies whether the account is locked or unlocked. By default, the account is unlocked.

TABLE 10-2. *The Options for the CREATE USER Command*

tablespace and default temporary tablespace are defined at the database level, so the last two lines of the command aren't required unless you want a different default permanent tablespace or a different temporary tablespace for the user.

Even though the user SKING has been either explicitly or implicitly assigned a default permanent tablespace, he cannot create any objects in the database until we provide both a quota and the rights to create objects in their own schema.

A *quota* is simply a space limit, by tablespace, for a given user. Unless a quota is explicitly assigned or the user is granted the UNLIMITED TABLESPACE privilege (privileges are discussed later in this chapter), the user cannot create objects in their own schema. In the following example, we're giving the SKING account a quota of 250MB in the USERS tablespace:

```
SQL> alter user sking quota 250M on users;
User altered.
```

Note that we could have granted this quota at the time the account was created, along with almost every other option in the **create user** command. A default role, however, can only be assigned after the account is created. (Role management is discussed later in this chapter.)

Unless we grant some basic privileges to a new account, the account cannot even log in; therefore, we need to grant at least the CREATE SESSION privilege or the CONNECT role (roles are discussed in detail later in this chapter). The CONNECT role contains the CREATE SESSION privilege, along with other basic privileges, such as CREATE TABLE and ALTER SESSION. In the following example, we grant SKING the CONNECT privilege:

```
SQL> grant connect to sking;
Grant succeeded.
```

Now the user SKING has a quota on the USERS tablespace as well as the privileges to create objects in that tablespace.

All these options for **create user** are available in the web-based Enterprise Manager interface, as demonstrated in Figure 10-2.

As with any Enterprise Manager operation, the Show SQL button shows the actual SQL commands, such as **create** and **grant**, that will be run when the user is created. This is a great way to take advantage of the web interface's ease of use, while at the same time brushing up on your SQL command syntax!

In Figure 10-3, you can see that it's also very easy to pick an existing user and create a new user with the same characteristics except for the password.

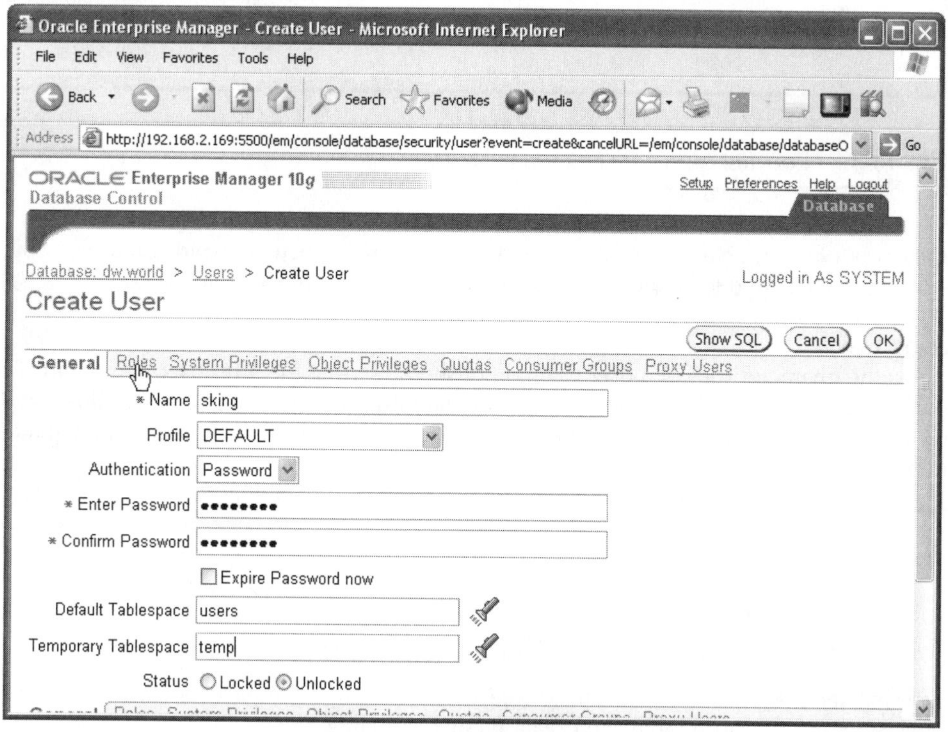

FIGURE 10-2. *Creating users with Enterprise Manager*

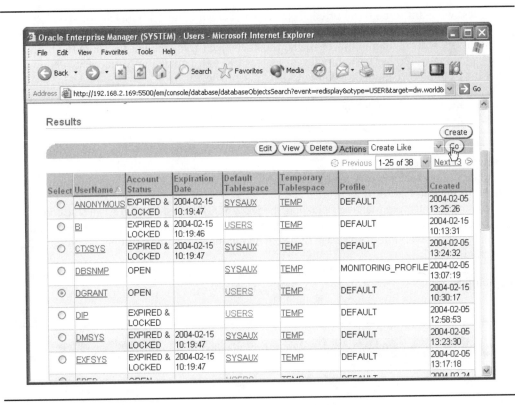

FIGURE 10-3.   *Copying users with Enterprise Manager*

Other options available in the Enterprise Manager interface include expiring a user account, generating the DDL used to create the account, and locking or unlocking the account.

Altering Users
Changing the characteristics of a user is accomplished by using the **alter user** command. The syntax for **alter user** is nearly identical to that of **create user**, except that **alter user** allows you to assign roles as well as grant rights to a middle-tier application to perform functions on behalf of the user.

In this example, we'll change user SKING to use a different default permanent tablespace:

```
SQL> alter user sking
  2         default tablespace users2
  3         quota 500M on users2;
User altered.
```

Note that the user SKING still can create objects in the USERS tablespace, but he must explicitly specify USERS in any **create table** and **create index** commands.

Dropping Users

Dropping users is very straightforward and is accomplished with the **drop user** command. The only parameters are the username to be dropped and the **cascade** option; any objects owned by the user must be explicitly dropped or moved to another schema if the **cascade** option is not used. In the following example, the user QUEENB is dropped, and if there are any objects owned by QUEENB, they are automatically dropped as well:

```
SQL> drop user queenb cascade;
User dropped.
```

If any other schema objects, such as views or packages, rely on objects dropped when the user is dropped, the other schema objects are marked INVALID and must be recoded to use other objects and then recompiled. In addition, any object privileges that were granted by the first user to a second user via the **with grant option** clause are automatically revoked from the second user if the first user is dropped.

Becoming Another User

To debug an application, a DBA sometimes needs to connect as another user to simulate the problem. Without knowing the actual plain-text password of the user, the DBA can retrieve the encrypted password from the database, change the password for the user, connect with the changed password, and then change back the password using an undocumented clause of the **alter user** command. It is assumed that the DBA has access to the DBA_USERS table, along with the ALTER USER privilege. If the DBA has the DBA role, then these two conditions are satisfied.

The first step is to retrieve the encrypted password for the user, which is stored in the table DBA_USERS:

```
SQL> select password from dba_users
  2        where username = 'SKING';

PASSWORD
------------------------------
83C7CBD27A941428

1 row selected.
```

Save this password using cut and paste in a GUI environment, or save it in a text file to retrieve later. The next step is to temporarily change the user's password and then log in using the temporary password:

```
SQL> alter user sking identified by temp_pass;
User altered.
SQL> connect sking/temp_pass@dw;
Connected.
```

At this point, you can debug the application from SKING's point of view. Once you are done debugging, change the password back using the undocumented **by values** clause of **alter user**:

```
SQL> alter user sking identified by values '83C7CBD27A941428';
User altered.
```

Data Dictionary View	Description
DBA_USERS	Contains usernames, encrypted passwords, account status, and default tablespaces.
DBA_TS_QUOTAS	Disk space usage and limits by user and tablespace, for users who have quotas that are not UNLIMITED.
DBA_PROFILES	Profiles that can be assigned to users with resource limits assigned to the profiles.
USER_HISTORY$	Password history with usernames, encrypted passwords, and datestamps. Used to enforce password reuse rules.

TABLE 10-3. *User-Related Data Dictionary Views and Tables*

User-Related Data Dictionary Views

A number of data dictionary views contain information related to users and characteristics of users. Table 10-3 lists the most common views and tables.

Database Authorization Methods

Once a user is authenticated with the database, the next step is to determine what types of objects, privileges, and resources the user is permitted to access or use. In this section, we'll review how profiles can control not only how passwords are managed but also how profiles can put limits on various types of system resources.

In addition, we'll review the two types of privileges in an Oracle database: system privileges and object privileges. Both of these privileges can be assigned directly to users, or indirectly through roles, another mechanism that can make a DBA's job easier when assigning privileges to users.

At the end of this section, we'll cover the Virtual Private Database (VPD) features of Oracle and how it can be used to provide more precise control over what parts of a table can be seen by a user based on a set of DBA-defined credentials assigned to the user. To help make the concepts clearer, we'll step through an implementation of a VPD from beginning to end.

Profile Management

There never seems to be enough CPU power or disk space or I/O bandwidth to run a user's query. Because all these resources are inherently limited, Oracle provides a mechanism to control how much of these resources a user can use. An Oracle *profile* is a named set of resource limits providing this mechanism.

In addition, profiles can be used as an authorization mechanism to control how user passwords are created, reused, and validated. For example, we may wish to enforce a minimum password length, along with a requirement that at least one upper- and lowercase letter appear in the password. In this section, we'll talk about how profiles manage passwords and resources.

The CREATE PROFILE command

The **create profile** command does double duty; we can create a profile to limit the connect time for a user to 120 minutes.

```
create profile lim_connect limit
      connect_time 120;
```

Similarly, we can limit the number of consecutive times a login can fail before the account is locked:

```
create profile lim_fail_login limit
      failed_login_attempts 8;
```

Or, we can combine both types of limits in a single profile:

```
create profile lim_connectime_faillog limit
      connect_time 120
      failed_login_attempts 8;
```

How Oracle responds to one of the resource limits being exceeded depends on the type of limit. When one of the connect time or idle time limits is reached (such as CPU_PER_SESSION), the transaction in progress is rolled back, and the session is disconnected. For most other resource limits (such as PRIVATE_SGA), the current transaction is rolled back, an error is returned to the user, and the user has the option to commit or roll back the transaction. If an operation exceeds a limit for a single call (such as LOGICAL_READS_PER_CALL), the operation is aborted, the current statement is rolled back, and an error is returned to the user. The rest of the transaction remains intact; the user can then roll back, commit, or attempt to complete the transaction without exceeding statement limits.

Oracle provides the DEFAULT profile, which is applied to any new user if no other profile is specified. This query against the data dictionary view DBA_PROFILES reveals the limits for the DEFAULT profile:

```
SQL> select * from dba_profiles
  2         where profile = 'DEFAULT';
```

PROFILE	RESOURCE_NAME	RESOURCE	LIMIT
DEFAULT	COMPOSITE_LIMIT	KERNEL	UNLIMITED
DEFAULT	SESSIONS_PER_USER	KERNEL	UNLIMITED
DEFAULT	CPU_PER_SESSION	KERNEL	UNLIMITED
DEFAULT	CPU_PER_CALL	KERNEL	UNLIMITED
DEFAULT	LOGICAL_READS_PER_SESSION	KERNEL	UNLIMITED
DEFAULT	LOGICAL_READS_PER_CALL	KERNEL	UNLIMITED
DEFAULT	IDLE_TIME	KERNEL	UNLIMITED
DEFAULT	CONNECT_TIME	KERNEL	UNLIMITED
DEFAULT	PRIVATE_SGA	KERNEL	UNLIMITED
DEFAULT	FAILED_LOGIN_ATTEMPTS	PASSWORD	10
DEFAULT	PASSWORD_LIFE_TIME	PASSWORD	UNLIMITED
DEFAULT	PASSWORD_REUSE_TIME	PASSWORD	UNLIMITED
DEFAULT	PASSWORD_REUSE_MAX	PASSWORD	UNLIMITED
DEFAULT	PASSWORD_VERIFY_FUNCTION	PASSWORD	NULL
DEFAULT	PASSWORD_LOCK_TIME	PASSWORD	UNLIMITED
DEFAULT	PASSWORD_GRACE_TIME	PASSWORD	UNLIMITED

```
16 rows selected.
```

The only real restriction in the DEFAULT profile limits the number of consecutive unsuccessful login attempts to ten before the account is locked. In addition, no password verification function is enabled.

Profiles and Password Control

In Table 10-4 are the password-related profile parameters. All units of time are specified in days (to specify any of these parameters in minutes, for example, divide by 1440):

```
SQL> create profile lim_lock limit password_lock_time 5/1440;
Profile created.
```

In this example, an account will only be locked for five minutes after the specified number of login failures.

A parameter value of **unlimited** means that there is no bound on how much of the given resource can be used. **default** means that this parameter takes its values from the DEFAULT profile.

The parameters **password_reuse_time** and **password_reuse_max** must be used together; setting one without the other has no useful effect. In the following example, we create a profile that sets **password_reuse_time** to 20 days and **password_reuse_max** to 5:

```
create profile lim_reuse_pass limit
      password_reuse_time 20
      password_reuse_max 5;
```

For users with this profile, their password can be reused after 20 days if the password has been changed at least five times. If you specify a value for either of these, and UNLIMITED for the other, a user can never reuse a password.

Password Parameter	Description
FAILED_LOGIN_ATTEMPTS	The number of failed login attempts before the account is locked.
PASSWORD_LIFE_TIME	The number of days the password can be used before it must be changed. If it is not changed within PASSWORD_GRACE_TIME, the password must be changed before logins are allowed.
PASSWORD_REUSE_TIME	The number of days a user must wait before reusing a password; this parameter is used in conjunction with PASSWORD_REUSE_MAX.
PASSWORD_REUSE_MAX	The number of password changes that have to occur before a password can be reused; this parameter is used in conjunction with PASSWORD_REUSE_TIME.
PASSWORD_LOCK_TIME	How many days the account is locked after FAILED_LOGIN_ATTEMPTS attempts. After this time period, the account is automatically unlocked.
PASSWORD_GRACE_TIME	The number of days after which an expired password must be changed. If it is not changed within this time period, the account is expired and the password must be changed before the user can log in successfully.
PASSWORD_VERIFY_FUNCTION	A PL/SQL script to provide an advanced password-verification routine. If NULL is specified (the default), no password verification is performed.

TABLE 10-4. *Password-Related Profile Parameters*

As with most other operations, profiles can easily be managed with Oracle Enterprise Manager. Figure 10-4 shows an example of changing the DEFAULT profile to disconnect the user after only 15 minutes of inactivity.

If we wanted to provide tighter control over how passwords are created and reused, such as a mixture of upper- and lowercase characters in every password, we need to enable the PASSWORD_ VERIFY_FUNCTION limit in each applicable profile. Oracle provides a template for enforcing an organization's password policy. It's located in $ORACLE_HOME/rdbms/admin/utlpwdmg.sql. An abbreviated version of this script appears in Appendix A.

The script provides the following functionality for password complexity:

- Ensures that the password is not the same as the username

- Ensures that the password is at least four characters long

- Checks to make sure the password is not a simple, obvious word, such as ORACLE or DATABASE

- Requires that the password contains one letter, one digit, and one punctuation mark

- Ensures that the password is different from the previous password by at least three characters

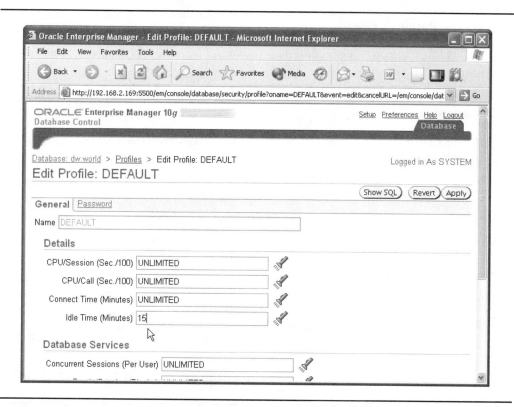

FIGURE 10-4. *Changing password limits with Oracle Enterprise Manager*

To use this policy, the first step is to make your own custom changes to this script. For example, you may wish to have several different verify functions, one for each country or business unit, to match the database password complexity requirements to that of the operating systems in use in a particular country or business unit. Therefore, you can rename this function as VERIFY_FUNCTION_US_MIDWEST, for example. In addition, you might want to change the list of simple words to include names of departments or buildings at your company.

Once the function is successfully compiled, you can either alter an existing profile to use this function with the **alter profile** command, or you can create a new profile that uses this function. In the following example, we're changing the DEFAULT profile to use the function VERIFY_FUNCTION_US_MIDWEST:

```
SQL> alter profile default limit
  2          password_verify_function verify_function_us_midwest;
Profile altered.
```

For all existing users who are using the DEFAULT profile, or for any new users who use the DEFAULT profile, their password will be checked by the function VERIFY_FUNCTION_US_MIDWEST. If the function returns a value other than TRUE, the password is not allowed, and the user must specify a different password. If a user has a current password that does not conform to the rules in this function, it is still valid until the password is changed, at which time the new password must be validated by the function.

Profiles and Resource Control

The list of resource-control profile options that can appear after CREATE PROFILE *profilename* LIMIT are explained in Table 10-5. Each of these parameters can either be an integer, UNLIMITED, or DEFAULT.

Resource Parameter	Description
SESSIONS_PER_USER	The maximum number of sessions a user can simultaneously have
CPU_PER_SESSION	The maximum CPU time allowed per session, in hundredths of a second
CPU_PER_CALL	Maximum CPU time for a statement parse, execute, or fetch operation, in hundredths of a second
CONNECT_TIME	Maximum total elapsed time, in minutes
IDLE_TIME	Maximum continuous inactive time in a session, in minutes, while a query or other operation is not in progress
LOGICAL_READS_PER_SESSION	Total number of data blocks read per session, either from memory or disk
LOGICAL_READS_PER_CALL	Maximum number of data blocks read for a statement parse, execute, or fetch operation
COMPOSITE_LIMIT	Total resource cost, in *service units*, as a composite weighted sum of CPU_PER_SESSION, CONNECT_TIME, LOGICAL_READS_PER_SESSION, and PRIVATE_SGA
PRIVATE_SGA	Maximum amount of memory a session can allocate in the shared pool, in bytes, kilobytes, or megabytes

TABLE 10-5. *Resource-Related Profile Parameters*

As with the password-related parameters, UNLIMITED means that there is no bound on how much of the given resource can be used. DEFAULT means that this parameter takes its values from the DEFAULT profile.

The COMPOSITE_LIMIT parameter allows you to control a group of resource limits when the types of resources typically used varies widely by type; it allows a user to use a lot of CPU time but not much disk I/O during one session, and vice versa during another session, without being disconnected by the policy.

By default, all resource costs are zero:

```
SQL> select * from resource_cost;

RESOURCE_NAME                      UNIT_COST
--------------------------------   ----------
CPU_PER_SESSION                            0
LOGICAL_READS_PER_SESSION                  0
CONNECT_TIME                               0
PRIVATE_SGA                                0

4 rows selected.
```

To adjust the resource cost weights, use the ALTER RESOURCE COST command. In this example, we change the weightings so that CPU_PER_SESSION favors CPU usage over connect time by a factor of 25 to 1; in other words, a user will be disconnected more likely from CPU usage than connect time:

```
SQL> alter resource cost
  2       cpu_per_session 50
  3       connect_time 2;
Resource cost altered.

SQL> select * from resource_cost;

RESOURCE_NAME                      UNIT_COST
--------------------------------   ----------
CPU_PER_SESSION                           50
LOGICAL_READS_PER_SESSION                  0
CONNECT_TIME                               2
PRIVATE_SGA                                0

4 rows selected.
```

The next step is to create a new profile or modify an existing profile to use a composite limit:

```
SQL> create profile lim_comp_cpu_conn limit
  2       composite_limit 250;

Profile created.
```

As a result, users assigned to the profile LIM_COMP_CPU_CONN will have their session resources limited using the following formula to calculate cost:

```
composite_cost = (50 * CPU_PER_SESSION) + (2 * CONNECT_TIME);
```

CPU (Seconds)	Connect (Seconds)	Composite Cost	Exceeded?
0.05	100	$(50*5) + (2*100) = 450$	Yes
0.02	30	$(50*2) + (2*30) = 160$	No
0.01	150	$(50*1) + (2*150) = 350$	Yes
0.02	5	$(50*2) + (2*5) = 110$	No

TABLE 10-6. *Resource Usage Scenarios*

In Table 10-6, we provide some examples of resource usage to see if the composite limit of 250 is exceeded.

The parameters PRIVATE_SGA and LOGICAL_READS_PER_SESSION are not used in this particular example, so unless they are specified otherwise in the profile definition, they default to whatever their value is in the DEFAULT profile. The goal of using composite limits is to give users some leeway in the types of queries or DML they run. On some days, they may run a lot of queries that perform numerous calculations but don't access a lot of table rows; on other days, they may do a lot of full table scans but don't stay connected very long. In these situations, we don't want to limit a user by a single parameter, but instead by total resource usage weighted by the availability of each resource on the server.

System Privileges

A *system privilege* is a right to perform an action on any object in the database, as well as other privileges that do not involve objects at all, but rather things like running batch jobs, altering system parameters, creating roles, and even connecting to the database itself. There are 173 system privileges in Release 1 of Oracle 10g. All of them can be found in the data dictionary table SYSTEM_PRIVILEGE_MAP:

```
SQL> select * from system_privilege_map;

PRIVILEGE   NAME                                                    PROPERTY
---------   -------------------------------------------------   ----------
       -3   ALTER SYSTEM                                                 0
       -4   AUDIT SYSTEM                                                 0
       -5   CREATE SESSION                                               0
       -6   ALTER SESSION                                                0
       -7   RESTRICTED SESSION                                          0
      -10   CREATE TABLESPACE                                          0
      -11   ALTER TABLESPACE                                            0
      -12   MANAGE TABLESPACE                                          0
      -13   DROP TABLESPACE                                            0
      -15   UNLIMITED TABLESPACE                                      0
      -20   CREATE USER                                                  0
      -21   BECOME USER                                                  0
      -22   ALTER USER                                                   0
      -23   DROP USER                                                    0
 . . .
```

```
-271 ALTER ANY SQL PROFILE              0
-272 ADMINISTER SQL TUNING SET          0
-273 ADMINISTER ANY SQL TUNING SET      0
-274 CREATE ANY SQL PROFILE             0
-275 EXEMPT IDENTITY POLICY             0

173 rows selected.
```

Table 10-7 lists some of the more common system privileges, along with a brief description of each.

System Privilege	Capability
ALTER DATABASE	Make changes to the database, such as changing the state of the database from MOUNT to OPEN, or recover a database.
ALTER SYSTEM	Issue ALTER SYSTEM statements: Switch to the next redo log group and change system-initialization parameters in the SPFILE.
AUDIT SYSTEM	Issue AUDIT statements.
CREATE DATABASE LINK	Create database links to remote databases.
CREATE ANY INDEX	Create an index in any schema; CREATE INDEX is granted along with CREATE TABLE for the user's schema.
CREATE PROFILE	Create a resource/password profile.
CREATE PROCEDURE	Create a function, procedure, or package in your own schema.
CREATE ANY PROCEDURE	Create a function, procedure, or package in any schema.
CREATE SESSION	Connect to the database.
CREATE SYNONYM	Create a private synonym in your own schema.
CREATE ANY SYNONYM	Create a private synonym in any schema.
CREATE PUBLIC SYNONYM	Create a public synonym.
DROP ANY SYNONYM	Drop a private synonym in any schema.
DROP PUBLIC SYNONYM	Drop a public synonym.
CREATE TABLE	Create a table in your own schema.
CREATE ANY TABLE	Create a table in any schema.
CREATE TABLESPACE	Create a new tablespace in the database.
CREATE USER	Create a user account/schema.
ALTER USER	Make changes to a user account/schema.
CREATE VIEW	Create a view in your own schema.
SYSDBA	Create an entry in the external password file, if enabled; also, perform startup/shutdown, alter a database, create a database, recover a database, create an SPFILE, and connect when the database is in RESTRICTED SESSION mode.
SYSOPER	Create an entry in the external password file, if enabled; also, perform startup/shutdown, alter a database, recover a database, create an SPFILE, and connect when the database is in RESTRICTED SESSION mode.

TABLE 10-7. *Common System Privileges*

Granting System Privileges

Privileges are granted to a user, role, or PUBLIC using the **grant** command; privileges are revoked using the **revoke** command. PUBLIC is a special group that includes all database users, and it's convenient shorthand for granting privileges to everyone in the database.

To grant the user SCOTT the ability to create stored procedures and synonyms, you can use a command like the following:

```
SQL> grant create procedure, create synonym to scott;
Grant succeeded.
```

Revoking privileges is just as easy:

```
SQL> revoke create synonym from scott;
Revoke succeeded.
```

If you wish to allow grantees the right to grant the same privilege to someone else, you include **with admin option** when you grant the privilege. In the preceding example, we want the user SCOTT to be able to grant the CREATE PROCEDURE privilege to other users. To accomplish this, we need to re-grant the CREATE PROCEDURE privilege:

```
SQL> grant create procedure to scott with admin option;
Grant succeeded.
```

Now Scott may issue the **grant create procedure** command. Note that if Scott's permission to grant his privileges to others is revoked, the users he granted the privileges to retain the privileges.

System Privilege Data Dictionary Views

Table 10-8 contains the data dictionary views related to system privileges.

Object Privileges

In contrast to a system privilege, an *object privilege* is a right to perform a particular type of action on a specific object, such as a table or a sequence, that is not in the user's own schema. As with system privileges, you use the **grant** and **revoke** commands to grant and revoke privileges on objects.

As with system privileges, you can grant object privileges to PUBLIC, and the user with the object privilege may pass it on to others by granting the object privilege with the **with grant option** clause.

Some schema objects, such as clusters and indexes, rely on system privileges to control access. In these cases, the user can change these objects if they own the objects or have the ALTER ANY CLUSTER or ALTER ANY INDEX system privilege.

A user with objects in their own schema automatically has all object privileges on those objects, and can grant any object privilege on these objects to any user or another role, with or without the **grant option** clause.

In Table 10-9 are the object privileges available for different types of objects; some privileges are only applicable to certain types of objects. For example, the INSERT privilege only makes sense with tables, views, and materialized views; the EXECUTE privilege, on the other hand, is applicable to functions, procedures, and packages, but not tables.

Data Dictionary View	Description
DBA_SYS_PRIVS	System privileges assigned to roles and users
SESSION_PRIVS	All system privileges in effect for this user for the session, granted directly or via a role
ROLE_SYS_PRIVS	Current session privileges granted to a user via a role

TABLE 10-8. *System Privilege Data Dictionary Views*

Object Privilege	Capability
ALTER	Can alter a table or sequence definition.
DELETE	Can delete rows from a table, view, or materialized view.
EXECUTE	Can execute a function or procedure, with or without a package.
DEBUG	Allowed to view PL/SQL code in triggers defined on a table, or SQL statements that reference a table. For object types, this privilege allows access to all public and private variables, methods, and types defined on the object type.
FLASHBACK	Allows flashback queries on tables, views, and materialized views using retained undo information.
INDEX	Can create an index on a table.
INSERT	Can insert rows into a table, view, or materialized view.
ON COMMIT REFRESH	Can create a refresh-on-commit materialized view based on a table.
QUERY REWRITE	Can create a materialized view for query rewrite based on a table.
READ	Can read the contents of an operating system directory using an Oracle DIRECTORY definition.
REFERENCES	Can create a foreign key constraint that references another table's primary key or unique key.
SELECT	Can read rows from a table, view, or materialized view, in addition to reading current or next values from a sequence.
UNDER	Can create a view based on an existing view.
UPDATE	Can update rows in a table, view, or materialized view.
WRITE	Can write information to an operating system directory using an Oracle DIRECTORY definition.

TABLE 10-9. *Object Privileges*

It's worth noting that DELETE, UPDATE, and INSERT privileges cannot be granted to materialized views unless they are updatable. Some of these object privileges overlap with system privileges; for example, if you don't have the FLASHBACK object privilege on a table, you can still perform flashback queries if you have the FLASHBACK ANY TABLE system privilege.

In the following example, the DBA grants SCOTT full access to the table HR.EMPLOYEES, but only allows SCOTT to pass on the SELECT object privilege to other users:

```
SQL> grant insert, update, delete on hr.employees to scott;
Grant succeeded.
SQL> grant select on hr.employees to scott with grant option;
Grant succeeded.
```

Note that if the SELECT privilege on the table HR.EMPLOYEES is revoked from SCOTT, the SELECT privilege is also revoked from anyone he granted the privilege.

Table Privileges

The types of privileges that can be granted on a table fall into two broad categories: DML operations and DDL operations. DML operations include **delete**, **insert**, **select**, and **update**, whereas DDL operations include adding, dropping, and changing columns in the table as well as creating indexes on the table.

When granting DML operations on a table, it is possible to restrict those operations only to certain columns. For example, we may want to allow SCOTT to see and update all the rows and columns in the HR.EMPLOYEES table, except for the SALARY column. To do this, we first need to revoke the existing SELECT privilege on the table:

```
SQL> revoke update on hr.employees from scott;
Revoke succeeded.
```

Next, we will let SCOTT update all the columns except for the SALARY column:

```
SQL> grant update (employee_id, first_name, last_name, email,
  2                 phone_number, hire_date, job_id, commission_pct,
  3                 manager_id, department_id)
  4   on hr.employees to scott;

Grant succeeded.
```

SCOTT will be able to update all columns in the HR.EMPLOYEES table except for the SALARY column:

```
SQL> update hr.employees set first_name = 'Stephen' where employee_id = 100;
1 row updated.
SQL> update hr.employees set salary = 50000 where employee_id = 203;
update hr.employees set salary = 50000 where employee_id = 203
                 *
ERROR at line 1:
ORA-01031: insufficient privileges
```

This operation is also easy to perform with the web-based OEM tool, as demonstrated in Figure 10-5.

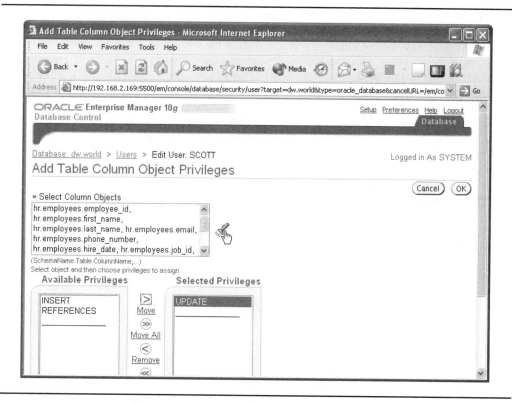

FIGURE 10-5. *Granting column privileges in Oracle Enterprise Manager*

View Privileges

Privileges on views are similar to those granted on tables. Rows in a view can be selected, updated, deleted, or inserted, assuming that the view is updatable. To create a view, first you need either the CREATE VIEW system privilege (to create a view in your own schema) or the CREATE ANY VIEW system privilege (to create a view in any schema). Even to create the view, you must also have at least SELECT object privileges on the underlying tables of the view, along with INSERT, UPDATE, and DELETE, if you wish to perform those operations on the view and the view is updatable. Alternatively, you can have the SELECT ANY TABLE, INSERT ANY TABLE, UPDATE ANY TABLE, or DELETE ANY TABLE privileges if the underlying objects are not in your schema.

To allow others to use your view, you must also have permissions on the view's base tables with the GRANT OPTION, or you must have the system privileges with the ADMIN OPTION. For example, if you are creating a view against the HR.EMPLOYEES table, you must have been granted the SELECT object privilege WITH GRANT OPTION on HR.EMPLOYEES, or you must have the SELECT ANY TABLE system privilege WITH ADMIN OPTION.

Procedure Privileges

For procedures, functions, and the packages that contain procedures and functions, the EXECUTE privilege is the only object privilege that can be applied. As of Oracle8*i*, procedures and functions can be run either from the perspective of the *definer,* the creator of the procedure or function, or from the *invoker,* the user who is running the procedure or function.

A procedure with definer's rights is run as if the definer was running the procedure, with all privileges of the definer in effect against objects referenced in the procedure. This is a good way to enforce restrictions on private database objects: Other users are granted EXECUTE permissions on the procedure and no permissions on the referenced objects. As a result, the definer can control how other users access the objects.

Conversely, an invoker's rights procedure requires that the invoker has direct rights, such as SELECT and UPDATE, to any objects referenced in the procedure. The procedure could reference an unqualified table named ORDERS, and if all users of the database have an ORDERS table, the same procedure could be used by any user who has their own ORDERS table. Another advantage to using invoker's rights procedures is that roles are enabled within them. Roles are discussed in depth later in this chapter.

By default, a procedure is created with definer's rights. To specify that a procedure uses invoker's rights, you must include the keywords **authid current_user** in the procedure definition, as in the following example:

```
create or replace procedure process_orders (order_batch_date   date)
authid current_user as
begin
     -- process user's ORDERS table here using invoker's rights,
     -- all roles are in effect
end;
```

To create a procedure, a user must have either the CREATE PROCEDURE or CREATE ANY PROCEDURE system privilege. For the procedure to compile correctly, the user must have direct privileges against all objects referenced in the procedure, even though roles are enabled at runtime in an invoker's rights procedure to obtain these same privileges. To allow other users to access a procedure, you grant EXECUTE privileges on the procedure or package.

Object Privilege Data Dictionary Views

A number of data dictionary views contain information about object privileges assigned to users. Table 10-10 lists the most important views containing object privilege information.

Data Dictionary View	Description
DBA_TAB_PRIVS	Table privileges granted to roles and users. Includes the user who granted the privilege to the role or user, with or without GRANT OPTION.
DBA_COL_PRIVS	Column privileges granted to roles or users, containing the column name and the type of privilege on the column.
SESSION_PRIVS	All system privileges in effect for this user for the session, granted directly or via a role.
ROLE_TAB_PRIVS	For the current session, privileges granted on tables via roles.

TABLE 10-10. *Object Privilege Data Dictionary Views*

Creating, Assigning, and Maintaining Roles

A *role* is a named group of privileges, either system privileges or object privileges or a combination of the two, that helps to ease the administration of privileges. Rather than granting system or object privileges individually to each user, you can grant the group of system or object privileges to a role, and in turn the role can be granted to the user instead. This reduces tremendously the amount of administrative overhead involved in maintaining privileges for users. Figure 10-6 shows how a role can reduce the number of **grant** commands (and ultimately **revoke** commands) that need to be executed when roles are used to group privileges.

If the privileges for a group of people authorized by a role need to change, only the privileges of the role need to be changed, and the capabilities of the users with that role automatically use the new or changed privileges. Roles may selectively be enabled by a user; some roles may automatically be enabled at login. In addition, passwords can be used to protect a role, adding another level of authentication to the capabilities in the database.

In Table 10-11 are the most common roles that are automatically provided with the database, along with a brief description of what privileges come with each role.

The roles CONNECT, RESOURCE, and DBA are provided mainly for compatibility with previous versions of Oracle; they may not exist in future versions of Oracle. The database administrator should create custom roles using the privileges granted to these roles as a starting point.

Creating or Dropping a Role

To create a role, you use the **create role** command, and you must have the CREATE ROLE system privilege. Typically, this is granted only to database administrators or application administrators. Here's an example:

```
SQL> create role hr_admin not identified;
Role created.
```

By default, no password or authentication is required to enable or use an assigned role; therefore, the **not identified** clause is optional.

As with creating users, you can authorize use of a role by a password (database authorization with **identified by *password***), by the operating system (**identified externally**), or by the network or directory service (**identified globally**).

In addition to these familiar methods, a role can be authorized by the use of a package: This is known as using a *secure application role.* This type of role uses a procedure within the package to enable the role. Typically, the role is enabled only under certain conditions: The user is connecting via a web interface or from a certain IP address, or it's a certain time of day. Here is a role that is enabled using a procedure:

```
SQL> create role hr_clerk identified using hr.clerk_verif;
Role created.
```

The procedure HR.CLERK_VERIF need not exist when the role is created; however, it must be compiled and valid when a user who is granted this role needs to enable it. Typically, with secure application roles, the role is not enabled by default for the user. To specify that all roles are enabled by default, except for the secure application role, use the following command:

```
SQL> alter user wgietz default role all except hr_clerk;
User altered.
```

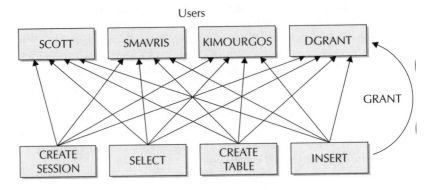

Assigning Privileges Without Roles

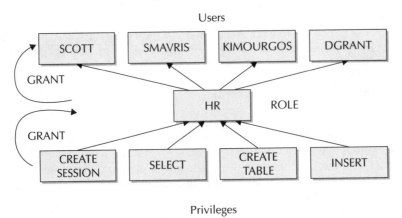

Assigning Privileges With Roles

FIGURE 10-6. *Using roles to manage privileges*

Role Name	Privileges
CONNECT	ALTER SESSION, CREATE CLUSTER, CREATE DATABASE LINK, CREATE SEQUENCE, CREATE SESSION, CREATE SYNONYM, CREATE TABLE, CREATE VIEW. These privileges are typically those given to a general user of the database, allowing them to connect and create tables, indexes, and views.
RESOURCE	CREATE CLUSTER, CREATE INDEXTYPE, CREATE OPERATOR, CREATE PROCEDURE, CREATE SEQUENCE, CREATE TABLE, CREATE TRIGGER, CREATE TYPE. These privileges are typically used for application developers who may be coding PL/SQL procedures and functions.
DBA	All system privileges WITH ADMIN OPTION. Allows a person with the DBA role to grant system privileges to others.
DELETE_CATALOG_ROLE	Does not have any system privileges, but only object privileges (DELETE) on SYS.AUD$ and FGA_LOG$. In other words, this role allows a user to remove audit records from the audit trail for regular or fine-grained auditing.
EXECUTE_CATALOG_ROLE	Execute privileges on various system packages, procedures, and functions, such as DBMS_FGA and DBMS_RLS.
SELECT_CATALOG_ROLE	SELECT object privilege on 1,638 data dictionary tables.
EXP_FULL_DATABASE	EXECUTE_CATALOG_ROLE, SELECT_CATALOG_ROLE, and system privileges such as BACKUP ANY TABLE and RESUMABLE. Allows a user with this role to export all objects in the database.
IMP_FULL_DATABASE	Similar to EXP_FULL_DATABASE, with many more system privileges, such as CREATE ANY TABLE, to allow the import of a previously exported full database.
AQ_USER_ROLE	Execute access for routines needed with Advanced Queuing, such as DBMS_AQ.
AQ_ADMINISTRATOR_ROLE	Manager for Advanced Queuing queues.
SNMPAGENT	Used by the Enterprise Manager Intelligent Agent.
RECOVERY_CATALOG_OWNER	Used to create a user who owns a recovery catalog for RMAN backup and recovery.
HS_ADMIN_ROLE	Provides access to the tables HS_* and the package DBMS_HS for administering Oracle Heterogeneous Services.
SCHEDULER_ADMIN	Provides access to the DBMS_SCHEDULER package, along with privileges to create batch jobs.

TABLE 10-11. *Predefined Oracle Roles*

In this way, when the HR application starts, it can enable the role by performing a **set role hr_clerk** command, thus calling the procedure HR.CLERK_VERIF. The user need not know about the role or the procedure that enables the role; therefore, no access to the objects and privileges provided by the role are available to the user outside of the application.

Dropping a role is just as easy as creating a role:

```
SQL> drop role keypunch_operator;
Role dropped.
```

Any users assigned to this role will lose the privileges assigned to this role the next time they connect to the database. If they are currently logged in, they will retain the privileges until they disconnect from the database.

Granting Privileges to a Role

Assigning a privilege to a role is very straightforward; you use the **grant** command to assign the privilege to a role, just as you would assign a privilege to a user:

```
SQL> grant select on hr.employees to hr_clerk;
Grant succeeded.
SQL> grant create trigger to hr_clerk;
Grant succeeded.
```

In this example, we've assigned an object privilege and a system privilege to the HR_CLERK role. In Figure 10-7, we can use the web-enabled OEM to add more object or system privileges to the role.

Assigning or Revoking Roles

Once we have the desired system and object privileges assigned to the role, we can assign the role to a user, using familiar syntax:

```
SQL> grant hr_clerk to smavris;
Grant succeeded.
```

Any other privileges granted to the HR_CLERK role in the future will automatically be useable by SMAVRIS because SMAVRIS has been granted the role.

Roles may be granted to other roles; this allows a DBA to have a hierarchy of roles, making role administration easier. For example, we may have roles named DEPT30, DEPT50, and DEPT100, each having object privileges to tables owned by each of those departments. An employee in department 30 would be assigned the DEPT30 role, and so forth. The president of the company would like to see tables in all departments; but rather than assigning individual object privileges to the role ALL_DEPTS, we can assign the individual department roles to ALL_DEPTS:

```
SQL> create role all_depts;
Role created.
SQL> grant dept30, dept50, dept100 to all_depts;
Grant succeeded.
SQL> grant all_depts to sking;
Grant succeeded.
```

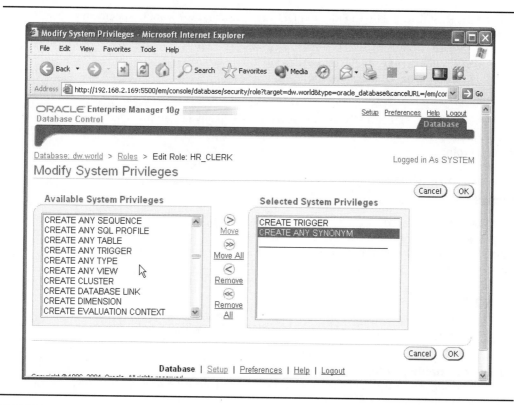

FIGURE 10-7. *Granting privileges to roles with OEM*

The role ALL_DEPTS may also contain individual object and system privileges that do not apply to individual departments, such as object privileges on order entry tables or accounts receivable tables.

Revoking a role from a user is very similar to revoking privileges from a user:

```
SQL> revoke all_depts from sking;
Revoke succeeded.
```

The privileges revoked will no longer be available to the user the next time they connect to the database. However, it is worth noting that if another role contains privileges on the same objects as the dropped role, or privileges on the objects are granted directly, the user retains these privileges on the objects until these and all other grants are explicitly revoked.

Default Roles

By default, all roles granted to a user are enabled when the user connects. If a role is going to be used only within the context of an application, the role can start out disabled when the user is logged in; then it can be enabled and disabled within the application. If the user SCOTT has

CONNECT, RESOURCE, HR_CLERK, and DEPT30 roles, and we want to specify that HR_CLERK and DEPT30 are not enabled by default, we can use something like the following:

```
SQL> alter user scott default role all
  2>      except hr_clerk, dept30;
User altered.
```

When SCOTT connects to the database, he automatically has all privileges granted with all roles except for HR_CLERK and DEPT30. SCOTT may explicitly enable a role in his session by using **set role**:

```
SQL> set role dept30;
Role set.
```

When he's done accessing the tables for department 30, he can disable the role in his session:

```
SQL> set role all except dept30;
Role set.
```

NOTE
The initialization parameter MAX_ENABLED_ROLES is deprecated in Oracle 10g. It is retained for compatibility with previous versions only.

Password-Enabled Roles

To enhance security in the database, the DBA can assign a password to a role. The password is assigned to the role when it's created:

```
SQL> create role dept99 identified by d99secretpw;
Role created.
SQL> grant dept99 to scott;
Grant succeeded.
SQL> alter user scott default role all except hr_clerk, dept30, dept99;
User altered.
```

When the user SCOTT is connected to the database, either the application he is using will provide or prompt for a password, or he can enter the password when he enables the role:

```
SQL> set role dept99 identified by d99secretpw;
Role set.
```

Role Data Dictionary Views

In Table 10-12 are listed the data dictionary views related to roles.

Data Dictionary View	Description
DBA_ROLES	All roles and whether they require a password.
DBA_ROLE_PRIVS	Roles granted to users or other roles.
ROLE_ROLE_PRIVS	Roles granted to other roles.
ROLE_SYS_PRIVS	System privileges that have been granted to roles.
ROLE_TAB_PRIVS	Table and table column privileges that have been granted to roles.
SESSION_ROLES	Roles currently in effect for the session. Available to every user session.

TABLE 10-12. *Role-Related Data Dictionary Views*

The view DBA_ROLE_PRIVS is a good way to find out what roles are granted to a user as well as whether they can pass this role to another user (ADMIN_OPTION) and whether this role is enabled by default (DEFAULT_ROLE):

```
SQL> select * from dba_role_privs
  2          where grantee = 'SCOTT';

GRANTEE      GRANTED_ROLE          ADMIN_OPTION DEFAULT_ROLE
-----------  --------------------  ------------ ------------
SCOTT        DEPT30                NO           NO
SCOTT        DEPT50                NO           YES
SCOTT        DEPT99                NO           YES
SCOTT        CONNECT               NO           YES
SCOTT        HR_CLERK              NO           NO
SCOTT        RESOURCE              NO           YES
SCOTT        ALL_DEPTS             NO           YES
SCOTT        DELETE_CATALOG_ROLE   NO           YES

8 rows selected.
```

Similarly, we can find out which roles we assigned to the ALL_DEPTS role:

```
SQL> select * from dba_role_privs
  2>          where grantee = 'ALL_DEPTS';

GRANTEE      GRANTED_ROLE          ADMIN_OPTION DEFAULT_ROLE
-----------  --------------------  ------------ ------------
ALL_DEPTS    DEPT30                NO           YES
ALL_DEPTS    DEPT50                NO           YES
ALL_DEPTS    DEPT100               NO           YES

3 rows selected.
```

The data dictionary view ROLE_ROLE_PRIVS can also be used to get this information; it only contains information about roles assigned to roles, and it does not have the DEFAULT_ROLE information.

To find out privileges granted to users on a table or table columns, we can write two queries: one to retrieve privileges granted directly, and another to retrieve privileges granted indirectly via a role. Retrieving privileges granted directly is straightforward:

```
SQL> select dtp.grantee, dtp.owner, dtp.table_name,
  2          dtp.grantor, dtp.privilege, dtp.grantable
  3  from dba_tab_privs dtp
  4  where dtp.grantee = 'SCOTT';
```

GRANTEE	OWNER	TABLE_NAME	GRANTOR	PRIVILEGE	GRANTABLE
SCOTT	HR	EMPLOYEES	HR	SELECT	YES
SCOTT	HR	EMPLOYEES	HR	DELETE	NO
SCOTT	HR	EMPLOYEES	HR	INSERT	NO

```
4 rows selected.
```

To retrieve table privileges granted via roles, we need to join DBA_ROLE_PRIVS and ROLE_TAB_PRIVS. DBA_ROLE_PRIVS has the roles assigned to the user, and ROLE_TAB_PRIVS has the privileges assigned to the roles:

```
SQL> select drp.grantee, rtp.owner, rtp.table_name,
  2          rtp.privilege, rtp.grantable, rtp.role
  3  from role_tab_privs rtp
  4          join dba_role_privs drp on rtp.role = drp.granted_role
  5  where drp.grantee = 'SCOTT';
```

GRANTEE	OWNER	TABLE_NAME	PRIVILEGE	GRANTABLE	ROLE
SCOTT	HR	EMPLOYEES	SELECT	NO	HR_CLERK
SCOTT	HR	JOBS	SELECT	NO	JOB_MAINT
SCOTT	HR	JOBS	UPDATE	NO	JOB_MAINT
SCOTT	SYS	AUD$	DELETE	NO	DELETE_CATA LOG_ROLE
SCOTT	SYS	FGA_LOG$	DELETE	NO	DELETE_CATA LOG_ROLE

```
5 rows selected.
```

In the case of SCOTT's privileges, notice that he has the SELECT privilege on the HR.EMPLOYEES table both via a direct **grant** and via a role. Revoking either one of the privileges will still leave him with access to the HR.EMPLOYEES table until both privileges have been removed.

Using a VPD to Implement Application Security Policies

A Virtual Private Database (VPD) combines server-enforced fine-grained access control with a secure application context. The context-aware functions return a predicate—a **where** clause—that is automatically appended to all **select** statements or other DML statements. In other words, a **select** statement on a table, view, or synonym controlled by a VPD will return a subset of rows based on a **where** clause generated automatically by the security policy function in effect by the application context. The major component of a VPD is row-level security (RLS), also known as fine-grained access control (FGAC).

Because a VPD generates the predicates transparently during statement parse, the security policy is enforced consistently regardless of whether the user is running ad-hoc queries, retrieving the data from an application, or viewing the data from Oracle Forms. Because the Oracle Server applies the predicate to the statement at parse time, the application need not use special tables, views, and so forth to implement the policy. As a result, Oracle can optimize the query using indexes, materialized views, and parallel operations where it otherwise might not be able. Therefore, using a VPD may incur less overhead than a query whose results are filtered using applications or other means.

From a maintenance point of view, security policies can be defined within a policy function that would be difficult to create using roles and privileges. Similarly, an Application Server Provider (ASP) may only need to set up one database to service multiple customers for the same application, with a VPD policy to ensure that employees of one customer can see only their data. The DBA can maintain one larger database with a small number of VPD policies instead of an individual database for each customer.   ·

New to Oracle 10*g* are column-level VPD operations. Using column-level VPD, a DBA can restrict access to a particular column or columns in a table. The query returns the same number of rows, but if the user's context does not allow access to the column or columns, NULL values are returned in the restricted column or columns.

VPD policies can be static, context sensitive, or dynamic. Static and context-sensitive policies, new to Oracle 10*g*, can improve performance dramatically because they do not need to call the policy function every time a query is run because it is cached for use later in the session. Before Oracle 10*g*, all policies were dynamic; in other words, the policy function was run every time a SQL statement containing the target VPD table was parsed. Static policies are evaluated once during login and remain cached throughout the session, regardless of application context. With context-sensitive policies, the policy function is called at statement parse time if the application context changes—for example, a policy that enforces the business rule that "employees only see their own salary history, but managers can see all the salaries of their employees." If the employee executing the statement has not changed, the policy function need not be called again, thus reducing the amount of overhead due to VPD policy enforcement.

You create application contexts using the **create context** command, and the package DBMS_ RLS manages VPD policies. The function used to return the predicates to enforce the policy is created like any other function, except that the function has two required parameters and returns a VARCHAR2. Later in this chapter, we'll go into more detail on these functions and we'll step through a VPD example using the sample schemas provided during the installation of the Oracle database.

Application Context

Using the **create context** command, you can create the name of application-defined attributes that will be used to enforce your security policy, along with the package name for the functions and procedures used to set the security context for the user session. Here's an example:

```
create context hr_security using vpd.emp_access;

create or replace package emp_access as
    procedure set_security_parameters;
end;
```

In this example, the context name is HR_SECURITY, and the package used to set up the characteristics or attributes for the user during the session is called EMP_ACCESS. The procedure SET_SECURITY_PARAMETERS will be called in the logon trigger. Because the context HR_SECURITY is bound only to EMP_ACCESS, no other procedures can change the session attributes. This ensures a secure application context that can't be changed by the user or any other process after connecting to the database.

In a typical package used to implement application context, you use the built-in context USERENV to retrieve information about the user session itself. In Table 10-13 are a few of the more common parameters in the USERENV context.

For example, the following calls to SYS_CONTEXT will retrieve the username and IP_ADDRESS of the database session:

```
declare
      username          varchar2(30);
      ip_addr           varchar2(30);
begin
      username := SYS_CONTEXT('USERENV','SESSION_USER');
      ip_addr := SYS_CONTEXT('USERENV','IP_ADDRESS');
      -- other processing here
end;
```

Similarly, the SYS_CONTEXT function can be used within a SQL **select** statement:

```
SQL> select SYS_CONTEXT('USERENV','SESSION_USER') username from dual;

USERNAME
------------------------
SCOTT
```

Using some combination of the USERENV context and authorization information in the database, we use DBMS_SESSION.SET_CONTEXT to assign values to parameters in the application context that we create:

```
dbms_session.set_context('HR_SECURITY','SEC_LEVEL','HIGH');
```

In this example, the application context variable SEC_LEVEL is set to HIGH in the HR_SECURITY context. The value can be assigned based on a number of conditions, including a mapping table that assigns security levels based on user ID.

To ensure that the context variables are set for each session, we can use a logon trigger to call the procedure associated with the context. As mentioned earlier, the variables in the context can only be set or changed within the assigned package. Here is a sample logon trigger that calls the procedure to set up the context:

```
create or replace trigger vpd.set_security_parameters
      after logon on database
begin
    vpd.emp_access.set_security_parameters;
end;
```

Parameter	Return Value
CURRENT_SCHEMA	The default schema for the session
DB_NAME	The name of the database as spescified in the initialization parameter DB_NAME
HOST	The name of the host machine from which the user connected
IP_ADDRESS	The IP address from which the user connected
OS_USER	The operating system account that initiated the database session
SESSION_USER	The authenticated database user's name

TABLE 10-13. *Common USERENV Context Parameters*

In this example, the procedure SET_SECURITY_PARAMETERS would make the necessary calls to DBMS_SESSION.SET_CONTEXT.

Within Oracle Enterprise Manager, you can use Policy Manager to set up contexts and policy groups, as demonstrated in Figure 10-8.

Security Policy Implementation

Once the infrastructure is in place to set up the security environment, the next step is to define the function or functions used to generate the predicate that will be attached to every **select** statement or DML command against the protected tables. The function used to implement the predicate generation has two arguments: the owner of the object being protected, and the name of the object within the owner's schema. One function may handle predicate generation for just one type of operation, such as **select**, or may be applicable to all DML commands, depending on how this function is associated with the protected table. The following example shows a package body containing two functions—one that will be used to control access from **select** statements, and the other for any other DML statements:

```
create or replace package body get_predicates is

    function emp_select_restrict(owner varchar2, object_name varchar2)
        return varchar2 is
      ret_predicate    varchar2(1000);  -- part of WHERE clause
    begin
      -- only allow certain employees to see rows in the table
      -- . . . check context variables and build predicate
      return ret_predicate;
    end emp_select_restrict;

    function emp_dml_restrict(owner varchar2, object_name varchar2)
        return varchar2 is
      ret_predicate    varchar2(1000);  -- part of WHERE clause
    begin
      -- only allow certain employees to make changes to the table
      -- . . . check context variables and build predicate
```

```
      return ret_predicate;
   end emp_dml_restrict;

end; -- package body
```

Each function returns a string containing an expression that is added to a **where** clause for a **select** statement or a DML command. The user or application never sees the value of this WHERE clause; it is automatically added to the command at parse time.

The developer must ensure that the functions always return a valid expression. Otherwise, any access to a protected table will always fail, as in the following example:

```
SQL> select * from hr.employees;
select * from hr.employees
                  *
ERROR at line 1:
ORA-28113: policy predicate has error
```

The error message does not say what the predicate is, and all users are locked out of the table until the predicate function is fixed. Tips on how to debug a predicate function are presented later in this chapter.

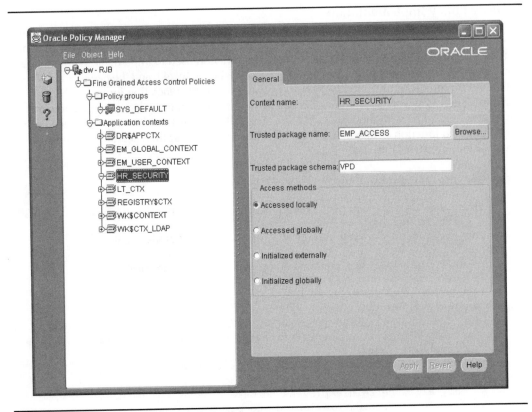

FIGURE 10-8. *Oracle Policy Manager*

Using DBMS_RLS

The built-in package DBMS_RLS contains a number of subprograms that a DBA uses to maintain the security policies associated with tables, views, and synonyms. In Table 10-14 are the subprograms available in the DBMS_RLS package. Any user who needs to create or administer policies must have EXECUTE privileges granted on the package SYS.DBMS_RLS.

   In this chapter, we'll cover the most commonly used subprograms, ADD_POLICY and DROP_POLICY. The syntax of ADD_POLICY follows:

```
DBMS_RLS.ADD_POLICY
(
        object_schema           IN varchar2 null,
        object_name             IN varchar2,
        policy_name             IN varchar2,
        function_schema         IN varchar2 null,
        policy_function         IN varchar2,
        statement_types         IN varchar2 null,
        update_check            IN boolean false,
        enable                  IN boolean true,
        static_policy           IN boolean false,
        policy_type             IN binary_integer null,
        long_predicate          IN in Boolean false,
        sec_relevant_cols       IN varchar2,
        sec_relevant_cols_opt   IN binary_integer null
);
```

Subprogram	Description
ADD_POLICY	Adds a fine-grained access control policy to an object
DROP_POLICY	Drops an FGAC policy from an object
REFRESH_POLICY	Reparses all cached statements associated with the policy
ENABLE_POLICY	Enables or disables an FGAC policy
CREATE_POLICY_GROUP	Creates a policy group
ADD_GROUPED_POLICY	Adds a policy to a policy group
ADD_POLICY_CONTEXT	Adds the context for the current application
DELETE_POLICY_GROUP	Deletes a policy group
DROP_GROUPED_POLICY	Drops a policy from a policy group
DROP_POLICY_CONTEXT	Drops a context for the active application
ENABLE_GROUPED_POLICY	Enables or disables a group policy
DISABLE_GROUPED_POLICY	Disables a group policy
REFRESH_GROUPED_POLICY	Reparses all cached statements associated with the policy group

TABLE 10-14.   *DBMS_RLS Package Subprograms*

Note that some of the parameters have BOOLEAN default values and that the less commonly used parameters are near the end of the argument list. This makes the syntax for any particular call to DBMS_RLS.ADD_POLICY easier to write and understand for the vast majority of cases. The description and usage for each parameter are provided in Table 10-15.

Using the parameter sec_relevant_cols is handy when you don't mind if users see part of a row, just not the columns that might contain confidential information, such as a Social Security Number or a salary. In our example later in this chapter, we'll build on the first security policy we define to filter out sensitive data for most employees of the company.

In the following example, we're applying a policy named EMP_SELECT_RESTRICT to the table HR.EMPLOYEES. The schema VPD owns the policy function get_predicates.emp_select_restrict. The policy explicitly applies to SELECT statements on the table; however, with UPDATE_CHECK set to TRUE, **update** or **delete** commands will also be checked when rows are updated or inserted into the table.

```
dbms_rls.add_policy (
          object_schema =>    'HR',
          object_name =>      'EMPLOYEES',
          policy_name =>      'EMP_SELECT_RESTRICT',
          function_schema =>  'VPD',
          policy_function =>  'get_predicates.emp_select_restrict',
          statement_types =>  'SELECT',
          update_check =>     TRUE,
          enable =>           TRUE
);
```

Because we did not set static_policy, it defaults to FALSE, meaning that the policy is dynamic and is checked every time a **select** statement is parsed. This is the only behavior available before Oracle 10g.

Using the subprogram ENABLE_POLICY is an easy way to disable the policy temporarily without having to rebind the policy to the table later:

```
dbms_rls.enable_policy(
          object_schema =>    'HR',
          object_name =>      'EMPLOYEES',
          policy_name =>      'EMP_SELECT_RESTRICT',
          enable =>           FALSE
);
```

If multiple policies are specified for the same object, an AND condition is added between each predicate. If you need to have an OR condition between predicates for multiple policies instead, the policy most likely needs to be revised. The logic for each policy needs to be combined within a single policy with an OR condition between each part of the predicate.

Creating a VPD

In this section, we'll step through a complete implementation of a VPD from beginning to end. This example relies on the sample schemas installed with Oracle 10g. To be specific, we are going to implement an FGAC policy on the HR.EMPLOYEES table to restrict access based on manager status and the employee's department number. If you are an employee, you can see your own row in HR.EMPLOYEES; if you are a manager, you can see the rows for all the employees who report directly to you.

Parameter	Description
object_schema	The schema containing the table, view, or synonym to be protected by the policy. If this value is NULL, the schema of the user calling the procedure is used.
object_name	The name of the table, view, or synonym to be protected by the policy.
policy_name	The name of the policy to be added to this object. It must be unique for each object being protected.
function_schema	The schema that owns the policy function; if this value is NULL, the schema of the user calling the procedure is used.
policy_function	The name of the function that will generate the predicate for the policy against the object_name. If the function is part of the package, the package name must also be specified here to qualify the policy function name.
statement_types	The statement types to which the policy applies. The allowable values, separated by commas, can be any combination of SELECT, INSERT, UPDATE, DELETE, and INDEX. By default, all types are applied except for INDEX.
update_check	For INSERT or UPDATE types, this parameter is optional, and it defaults to FALSE. If it is TRUE, the policy is also checked for INSERT or UPDATE statements when a SELECT or DELETE operation is being checked.
enable	This parameter defaults to TRUE and indicates if the policy is enabled when it is added.
static_policy	If this parameter is TRUE, the policy produces the same predicate string for anyone accessing the object, except for the SYS user or any user with the EXEMPT ACCESS POLICY privilege. The default is FALSE.
policy_type	Overrides static_policy if this value is not NULL. Allowable values are STATIC, SHARED_STATIC, CONTEXT_SENSITIVE, SHARED_CONTEXT_SENSITIVE, and DYNAMIC.
long_predicate	This parameter defaults to FALSE. If it is TRUE, the predicate string can be up to 32K bytes long. Otherwise, the limit is 4000 bytes.
sec_relevant_cols	Enforces column-level VPD, new to Oracle 10*g*. Applies to tables and views only. Protected columns are specified in a list with either commas or spaces as delimiters. The policy is applied only if the specified sensitive columns are in the query or DML statement. By default, all columns are protected.
sec_relevant_cols_opt	Allows rows in a column-level VPD filtered query to still appear in the result set, with NULL values returned for the sensitive columns. The default for this parameter is NULL; otherwise, you must specify DBMS_RLS.ALL_ROWS to show all columns with NULLs for the sensitive columns.

TABLE 10-15. *DBMS_RLS.ADD_POLICY Parameters*

TIP
*If you do not have the sample schemas installed in your database,
you can create them using the scripts found in $ORACLE_HOME
/demo/schema.*

Once the sample schemas are in place, we need to create some users in the database who
want to see rows from the table HR.EMPLOYEES.

```
create user smavris identified by smavris702;
grant connect, resource to smavris;

create user dgrant identified by dgrant507;
grant connect, resource to dgrant;

create user kmourgos identified by kmourgos622;
grant connect, resource to kmourgos;
```

The user KMOURGOS is the manager for all the stocking clerks, and DGRANT is one of
KMOURGOS's employees. The user SMAVRIS is the HR_REP for the company.

In the following three steps, we will grant SELECT privileges on the HR.EMPLOYEES table
to everyone in the database, and we will create a lookup table that maps employee ID numbers to
their database account. The procedure that sets the context variables for the user session will use
this table to assign the employee ID number to the context variable that will be used in the policy
function to generate the predicate.

```
grant select on hr.employees to public;

create table hr.emp_login_map (employee_id, login_acct)
    as select employee_id, email from hr.employees;

grant select on hr.emp_login_map to public;
```

Next, we will create a user account called VPD that has the privileges to create contexts and
maintains the policy functions:

```
create user vpd identified by vpd439;
grant connect, resource, create any context, create public synonym to vpd;
```

Connecting to the VPD schema, we will create a context called HR_SECURITY and define the
package and procedure used to set the context for the application:

```
connect vpd/vpd439@dw;

create context hr_security using vpd.emp_access;

create or replace package vpd.emp_access as
    procedure set_security_parameters;
end;
```

Remember that the procedures in the package VPD.EMP_ACCESS are the only procedures that can set the context variables. The package body for VPD.EMP_ACCESS follows:

```
create or replace package body vpd.emp_access is

   --
   -- At user login, run set_security_parameters to
   -- retrieve the user login name, which corresponds to the EMAIL
   -- column in the table HR.EMPLOYEES.

   --
   -- context USERENV is pre-defined for user characteristics such
   -- as username, IP address from which the connection is made,
   -- and so forth.
   --
   -- for this procedure, we are only using SESSION_USER
   -- from the USERENV context.
   --

      procedure set_security_parameters is
         emp_id_num      number;
         emp_login       varchar2(50);
      begin

         -- database username corresponds to email address in HR.EMPLOYEES
         emp_login := sys_context('USERENV','SESSION_USER');

         dbms_session.set_context('HR_SECURITY','USERNAME',emp_login);

         -- get employee id number, so manager rights can be established
         -- but don't bomb out other DB users who are not in the
         -- EMPLOYEES table
         begin
            select employee_id into emp_id_num
               from hr.emp_login_map where login_acct = emp_login;

            dbms_session.set_context('HR_SECURITY','EMP_ID',emp_id_num);
         exception
            when no_data_found then
               dbms_session.set_context('HR_SECURITY','EMP_ID',0);
         end;

         -- Future queries will restrict rows based on emp_id

      end; -- procedure

end; -- package body
```

A few things are worth noting about this procedure. We retrieve the user's schema by looking in the USERENV context, which is enabled by default for all users, and assigning it to the variable

USERNAME in the newly created context HR_SECURITY. The other HR_SECURITY context variable EMP_ID is determined by doing a lookup in the mapping table HR.EMP_LOGIN_MAP. We don't want the procedure to terminate with an error if the logged-in user is not in the mapping table; instead, we assign an EMP_ID of 0, which will result in no access to the table HR.EMPLOYEES when the predicate is generated in the policy function.

In the next steps, we grant everyone in the database EXECUTE privileges on the package, and we create a synonym for it to save a few keystrokes any time we need to call it:

```
grant execute on vpd.emp_access to PUBLIC;
create public synonym emp_access for vpd.emp_access;
```

To ensure that the context is defined for each user when they log on, we will connect as SYS and create a logon trigger to set up the variables in the context:

```
connect sys/sys727@dw as sysdba;

create or replace trigger vpd.set_security_parameters
    after logon on database
begin
    vpd.emp_access.set_security_parameters;
end;
```

Because this trigger is fired for every user who connects to the database, it is vitally important that the code be tested for every class of user, if not every user in the database! If the trigger fails with an error, non-SYSDBA users cannot log in.

So far, we have our context defined, the procedure used to set up the context variables, and a trigger that automatically calls the procedure. Logging in as one of our three users defined previously, we can query the contents of the context:

```
SQL> connect smavris/smavris702@dw
Connected.

SQL> select * from session_context;

NAMESPACE                    ATTRIBUTE                    VALUE
--------------------------   ------------------------     --------------------
HR_SECURITY                  USERNAME                     SMAVRIS
HR_SECURITY                  EMP_ID                       203

2 rows selected.
```

Notice what happens when SMAVRIS tries to impersonate another employee:

```
SQL> begin
  2    dbms_session.set_context('HR_SECURITY','EMP_ID',100);
  3  end;

begin
*
```

```
ERROR at line 1:
ORA-01031: insufficient privileges
ORA-06512: at "SYS.DBMS_SESSION", line 82
ORA-06512: at line 2
```

Only the package VPD.EMP_ACCESS is allowed to set or change variables in the context.

The final steps include defining the procedures that will generate the predicate and assigning one or more of these procedures to the HR.EMPLOYEES table. As the user VPD, which already owns the context procedures, we'll set up the package that determines the predicates:

```
connect vpd/vpd439@dw;

create or replace package vpd.get_predicates as

    -- note: security function ALWAYS has two parameters,
    -- table owner name and table name

    function emp_select_restrict
        (owner varchar2, object_name varchar2) return varchar2;

    -- other functions can be written here for INSERT, DELETE, and so forth.

end get_predicates;



create or replace package body vpd.get_predicates is

    function emp_select_restrict
        (owner varchar2, object_name varchar2) return varchar2 is

        ret_predicate    varchar2(1000);   -- part of WHERE clause

    begin
        -- only allow employee to see their row or immediate subordinates
        ret_predicate := 'EMPLOYEE_ID = ' ||
                         sys_context('HR_SECURITY','EMP_ID') ||
                         ' OR MANAGER_ID = ' ||
                         sys_context('HR_SECURITY','EMP_ID');
        return ret_predicate;
    end emp_select_restrict;

end; -- package body
```

Once we attach the function to a table with DBMS_RLS, it will generate a text string that can be used in a WHERE clause every time the table is accessed. The string will always look something like this:

```
EMPLOYEE_ID = 124 OR MANAGER_ID = 124
```

As with the packages that set up the context environment, we need to allow users access to this package:

```
grant execute on vpd.get_predicates to PUBLIC;
create public synonym get_predicates for vpd.get_predicates;
```

Last, but certainly not least, we will attach the policy function to the table using the DBMS_RLS.ADD_POLICY procedure:

```
dbms_rls.add_policy (
          object_schema =>    'HR',
          object_name =>      'EMPLOYEES',
          policy_name =>      'EMP_SELECT_RESTRICT',
          function_schema =>  'VPD',
          policy_function =>  'get_predicates.emp_select_restrict',
          statement_types =>  'SELECT',
          update_check =>     TRUE,
          enable =>           TRUE
);
```

An employee can access the HR.EMPLOYEES table as before, but they will only see their row and the rows of the employees who work for them, if any. Logging in as KMOURGOS, we try to retrieve all the rows of the HR.EMPLOYEES table, but we only see KMOURGOS and the employees who report directly to him:

```
SQL> connect kmourgos/kmourgos622@dw;
Connected.
SQL> select employee_id, first_name, last_name,
  2         email, job_id, salary, manager_id from hr.employees;
```

EMPLOYEE_ID	FIRST_NAME	LAST_NAME	EMAIL	JOB_ID	SALARY	MANAGER_ID
124	Kevin	Mourgos	KMOURGOS	ST_MAN	5800	100
141	Trenna	Rajs	TRAJS	ST_CLERK	3500	124
142	Curtis	Davies	CDAVIES	ST_CLERK	3100	124
143	Randall	Matos	RMATOS	ST_CLERK	2600	124
144	Peter	Vargas	PVARGAS	ST_CLERK	2500	124
196	Alana	Walsh	AWALSH	SH_CLERK	3100	124
197	Kevin	Feeney	KFEENEY	SH_CLERK	3000	124
198	Donald	OConnell	DOCONNEL	SH_CLERK	2600	124
199	Douglas	Grant	DGRANT	SH_CLERK	2600	124

```
9 rows selected.
```

For the user DGRANT, it's a different story:

```
SQL> connect dgrant/dgrant507@dw;
Connected.
SQL> select employee_id, first_name, last_name,
  2         email, job_id, salary, manager_id from hr.employees;
```

EMPLOYEE_ID	FIRST_NAME	LAST_NAME	EMAIL	JOB_ID	SALARY	MANAGER_ID
199 Douglas		Grant	DGRANT	SH_CLERK	2600	124

1 row selected.

DGRANT gets to see only his own row, because he does not manage anyone else in the company.

In the case of SMAVRIS, we see similar results from the query:

```
SQL> connect smavris/smavris702@dw;
Connected.
SQL> select employee_id, first_name, last_name,
  2          email, job_id, salary, manager_id from hr.employees;
```

EMPLOYEE_ID	FIRST_NAME	LAST_NAME	EMAIL	JOB_ID	SALARY	MANAGER_ID
203 Susan		Mavris	SMAVRIS	HR_REP	6500	101

1 row selected.

But wait, SMAVRIS is in the HR department and should be able to see *all* rows from the table. In addition, SMAVRIS should be the only person to see the salary information for all employees. As a result, we need to change our policy function to give SMAVRIS and other employees in the HR department full access to the HR.EMPLOYEES table; in addition, we can use column-level restrictions in the policy assignment to return the same number of rows, but with the sensitive data returned as NULL values.

To facilitate access to the HR.EMPLOYEES table by HR department employees, we first need to change our mapping table to include the JOB_ID column. If the JOB_ID column has a value of HR_REP, the employee is in the HR department. We will first disable the policy in effect and create the new mapping table:

```
SQL> begin
  2      dbms_rls.enable_policy(
  3          object_schema =>    'HR',
  4          object_name =>      'EMPLOYEES',
  5          policy_name =>      'EMP_SELECT_RESTRICT',
  6          enable =>           FALSE
  7      );
  8  end;
PL/SQL procedure successfully completed.

SQL> drop table hr.emp_login_map;
Table dropped.

SQL> create table hr.emp_login_map (employee_id, login_acct, job_id)
  2      as select employee_id, email, job_id from hr.employees;
Table created.

SQL> grant select on hr.emp_login_map to public;
Grant succeeded.
```

The procedure we're using to set up the context variables, VPD.EMP_ACCESS, needs another context variable added that indicates the security level of the user accessing the table. We will change the SELECT statement and make another call to DBMS_SESSION.SET_CONTEXT, as follows:

```
. . .
        emp_job_id        varchar2(50);
. . .
        select employee_id, job_id into emp_id_num, emp_job_id
            from hr.emp_login_map where login_acct = emp_login;

        dbms_session.set_context('HR_SECURITY','SEC_LEVEL',
            case emp_job_id when 'HR_REP' then 'HIGH' else 'NORMAL' end );
. . .
```

Whenever the employee has a job title of HR_REP, the context variable SEC_LEVEL is set to HIGH instead of NORMAL. In our policy function, we need to check for this new condition as follows:

```
create or replace package body vpd.get_predicates is

    function emp_select_restrict
        (owner varchar2, object_name varchar2) return varchar2 is

        ret_predicate    varchar2(1000);   -- part of WHERE clause

    begin
        -- only allow employee to see their row or immediate subordinates,
        -- unless they have high security clearance
        if sys_context('HR_SECURITY','SEC_LEVEL') = 'HIGH' then
            ret_predicate := '';   -- no restrictions in WHERE clause
        else
            ret_predicate := 'EMPLOYEE_ID = ' ||
                                sys_context('HR_SECURITY','EMP_ID') ||
                                ' OR MANAGER_ID = ' ||
                                sys_context('HR_SECURITY','EMP_ID');
        end if;
        return ret_predicate;
    end emp_select_restrict;

end; -- package body
```

Because the policy is dynamic, the predicate is generated each time a SELECT statement is executed, so we don't have to do a policy refresh. When the user SMAVRIS, the HR representative, runs the query now, she sees all rows in the HR.EMPLOYEES table:

```
SQL> connect smavris/smavris702@dw;
Connected.
SQL> select employee_id, first_name, last_name,
  2>        email, job_id, salary, manager_id from hr.employees;
```

```
EMPLOYEE_ID FIRST_NAME  LAST_NAME    EMAIL       JOB_ID      SALARY MANAGER_ID
----------- ----------- -----------  ----------  ----------  ------- ----------
        100 Steven      King         SKING       AD_PRES      24000
        101 Neena       Kochhar      NKOCHHAR    AD_VP        17000        100
. . .
        204 Hermann     Baer         HBAER       PR_REP       10000        101
        205 Shelley     Higgins      SHIGGINS    AC_MGR       12000        101
        206 William     Gietz        WGIETZ      AC_ACCOUNT    8300        205

107 rows selected.
```

However, DGRANT can still only see his row in the table:

```
SQL> connect dgrant/dgrant507@dw;
Connected.
SQL> select employee_id, first_name, last_name,
  2          email, job_id, salary, manager_id from hr.employees;

EMPLOYEE_ID FIRST_NAME LAST_NAME    EMAIL       JOB_ID       SALARY MANAGER_ID
----------- ---------- -----------  ----------  ----------  ------- ----------
        199 Douglas    Grant        DGRANT      SH_CLERK       2600        124

1 row selected.
```

To enforce the requirement that only HR employees can see salary information, we would need to make a slight change to the policy function and enable the policy with column-level restrictions:

```
dbms_rls.add_policy (
           object_schema =>    'HR',
           object_name =>      'EMPLOYEES',
           policy_name =>      'EMP_SELECT_RESTRICT',
           function_schema =>  'VPD',
           policy_function => 'get_predicates.emp_select_restrict',
           statement_types =>  'SELECT',
           update_check =>     TRUE,
           enable =>           TRUE,
           sec_relevant_cols => 'SALARY',
           sec_relevant_cols_opt => dbms_rls.all_rows
);
```

The last parameter, SEC_RELEVANT_COLS_OPT, specifies the package constant DBMS_RLS.ALL_ROWS to indicate that we still want to see all rows in our query results, but with the relevant columns (in this case SALARY) returning NULL values. Otherwise, we would not see any rows from queries that contain the SALARY column.

Debugging a VPD Policy

Even if you're not getting an "ORA-28113: policy predicate has error" or an "ORA-00936: missing expression," it can be very useful to see the actual predicate being generated at statement parse time. There are a couple of ways to debug your predicates, both have their advantages and disadvantages.

The first method uses the dynamic performance views V$SQLAREA and V$VPD_POLICY. As the names imply, V$SQLAREA contains the SQL statements currently in the shared pool, along with current execution statistics. The view V$VPD_POLICY lists all the policies currently being enforced in the database, along with the predicate. Joining the two tables, as in the following example, gives us the information we need to help debug any problems we're having with the query results:

```
SQL> select s.sql_text, v.object_name, v.policy, v.predicate
  2     from v$sqlarea s, v$vpd_policy v
  3     where s.hash_value = v.sql_hash;

SQL_TEXT                OBJECT_NAME   POLICY                 PREDICATE
-------------------     -----------   --------------------   -----------------
select employee_id,     EMPLOYEES     EMP_SELECT_RESTRICT
first_name, last_nam
e,        email, job_i
d, salary, manager_i
d from hr.employees

select employee_id,     EMPLOYEES     EMP_SELECT_RESTRICT    EMPLOYEE_ID = 124
first_name, last_nam                                         OR MANAGER_ID =
e,        email, job_i                                       124
d, salary, manager_i
d from hr.employees

select employee_id,     EMPLOYEES     EMP_SELECT_RESTRICT    EMPLOYEE_ID = 199
first_name, last_nam                                         OR MANAGER_ID =
e,        email, job_i                                       199
d, salary, manager_i
d from hr.employees

3 rows selected.
```

If we add a join to V$SESSION in this query, we can identify which user was running the SQL. There is a downside to this method: If the database is extremely busy, the SQL commands may be flushed from the shared pool for other SQL commands before you get a chance to run this query.

The other method uses the **alter session** command to generate a plain-text trace file containing much of the information from the previous query. Here are the commands to set up tracing:

```
SQL> begin
  2     dbms_rls.refresh_policy;
  3  end;
PL/SQL procedure successfully completed.

SQL> alter session set events '10730 trace name context forever, level 12';
Session altered.
```

Event 10730 is defined for tracing RLS policy predicates. Other common events that can be traced are 10029 and 10030 for session logon/logoff, 10710 to trace bitmap index access, and 10253 for simulating write errors to the redo log, among others. Once the session is altered, the user DGRANT runs his query:

```
SQL> select employee_id, first_name, last_name,
  2       email, job_id, salary, manager_id from hr.employees;

EMPLOYEE_ID FIRST_NAME  LAST_NAME   EMAIL       JOB_ID      SALARY MANAGER_ID
----------- ----------- ----------- ----------- ----------- ------ ----------
        199 Douglas     Grant       DGRANT      SH_CLERK      2600        124

1 row selected.
```

Here's a look at the bottom part of the trace file located in the directory specified by the initialization parameter USER_DUMP_DEST:

```
/u01/app/oracle/admin/dw/udump/dw_ora_32530.trc
. . .
*** MODULE NAME:(SQL*Plus) 2004-02-19 20:50:38.132
*** SERVICE NAME:(SYS$USERS) 2004-02-19 20:50:38.132
*** SESSION ID:(265.44) 2004-02-19 20:50:38.132
-----------------------------------------------------------
Logon user     : DGRANT
Table/View     : HR.EMPLOYEES
Policy name    : EMP_SELECT_RESTRICT
Policy function: VPD.GET_PREDICATES.EMP_SELECT_RESTRICT
RLS view :
SELECT "EMPLOYEE_ID","FIRST_NAME","LAST_NAME","EMAIL",
"PHONE_NUMBER","HIRE_DATE","JOB_ID","SALARY","COMMISSION_PCT",
"MANAGER_ID","DEPARTMENT_ID"
FROM "HR"."EMPLOYEES"  "EMPLOYEES"
WHERE (EMPLOYEE_ID = 199 OR MANAGER_ID = 199)
```

The user's original SQL statement plus the appended predicate are clearly shown in the trace file. The downside to using this method is that while a user may be able to access dynamic performance views, a developer might not normally have access to the user dump directory on the server itself. As a result, the DBA may need to be involved when trying to debug predicate problems.

Be sure to turn off tracing when you're done debugging to reduce the overhead and disk space associated with tracing operations:

```
SQL> alter session set events '10730 trace name context off';
Session altered.
```

Auditing

Oracle uses a number of different auditing methods to monitor what kinds of privileges are being used as well as what objects are being accessed. Auditing does not prevent the use of these privileges, but it can provide useful information to uncover abuse or misuse of privileges.

In Table 10-16, we summarize the different types of auditing in an Oracle database.

Auditing Type	Description
Statement auditing	Audits SQL statements by the type of statement regardless of the specific schema objects being accessed. One or more users can also be specified in the database to be audited for a particular statement.
Privilege auditing	Audits system privileges, such as CREATE TABLE or ALTER INDEX. As with statement auditing, privilege auditing can specify one or more particular users as the target of the audit.
Schema object auditing	Audits specific statements operating on a specific schema object (for example, UPDATE statements on the DEPARTMENTS table). Schema object auditing always applies to all users in the database.
Fine-grained auditing	Audits table access and privileges based on the content of the objects being accessed. Uses the package DBMS_FGA to set up a policy on a particular table.

TABLE 10-16. *Auditing Types*

In the next few sections, we'll review how a DBA can manage audits of both system and object privilege use. When the granularity is required, a DBA can use fine-grained auditing to monitor access to certain rows or columns of a table, not just whether the table was accessed.

Auditing Locations

Audit records can be sent to either the SYS.AUD$ database table or an operating system file. To enable auditing and specify the location where audit records are recorded, the initialization parameter AUDIT_TRAIL is set to one of the following four values:

Parameter Value	Action
NONE, FALSE	Disable auditing.
OS	Enable auditing. Send audit records to an operating system file.
DB, TRUE	Enable auditing. Send audit records to the SYS.AUD$ table.
DB_EXTENDED	Enable auditing. Send audit records to the SYS.AUD$ table, and record additional information in the CLOB columns SQLBIND and SQLTEXT.

The parameter AUDIT_TRAIL is not dynamic; the database must be shut down and restarted for a change in the AUDIT_TRAIL parameter to take effect. When auditing to the SYS.AUD$ table, the size of the table should be carefully monitored so as not to impact the space requirements for other objects in the SYS tablespace. It is recommended that the rows in SYS.AUD$ be periodically archived and the table truncated. Oracle provides the role DELETE_CATALOG_ROLE to use with a special account in a batch job to archive and truncate the audit table.

Statement Auditing

All types of auditing use the **audit** command to turn on auditing and **noaudit** to turn off auditing. For statement auditing, the format of the **audit** command looks something like the following:

```
AUDIT sql_statement_clause BY {SESSION | ACCESS}
    WHENEVER [NOT] SUCCESSFUL;
```

The *sql_statement_clause* contains a number of different pieces of information, such as the type of SQL statement we want to audit and who we are auditing.

In addition, we want to either audit the action every time it happens (**by access**) or only once (**by session**). The default is **by session**.

Sometimes we want to audit successful actions—statements that did not generate an error message. For these statements, we add **whenever successful**. Other times we only care if the commands using the audited statements fail, either due to privilege violations, running out of space in the tablespace, or syntax errors. For these we use **whenever not successful**.

For most categories of auditing methods, we can specify **all** instead of individual statement types or objects if we truly want all types of access to a table or any privileges by a certain user to be audited.

The types of statements we can audit, with a brief description of what statements are covered in each category, are listed in Table 10-17. If **all** is specified, any statement in this list is audited.

Statement Option	SQL Operations
CLUSTER	CREATE, ALTER, DROP, or TRUNCATE a cluster.
CONTEXT	CREATE or DROP a CONTEXT.
DATABASE LINK	CREATE or DROP a database link.
DIMENSION	CREATE, ALTER, or DROP a dimension.
DIRECTORY	CREATE or DROP a dimension.
INDEX	CREATE, ALTER, or DROP an index.
MATERIALIZED VIEW	CREATE, ALTER, or DROP a materialized view.
NOT EXISTS	Failure of SQL statement due to nonexistent referenced objects.
PROCEDURE	CREATE or DROP FUNCTION, LIBRARY, PACKAGE, PACKAGE BODY, or PROCEDURE.
PROFILE	CREATE, ALTER, or DROP a profile.
PUBLIC DATABASE LINK	CREATE or DROP a public database link.
PUBLIC SYNONYM	CREATE or DROP a public synonym.
ROLE	CREATE, ALTER, DROP, or SET a role.
ROLLBACK SEGMENT	CREATE, ALTER, or DROP a rollback segment.
SEQUENCE	CREATE or DROP a sequence.
SESSION	Logons and logoffs.
SYNONYM	CREATE or DROP synonyms.

TABLE 10-17. *Auditable Statements Included in the ALL Category*

Statement Option	SQL Operations
SYSTEM AUDIT	AUDIT or NOAUDIT of system privileges.
SYSTEM GRANT	GRANT or REVOKE system privileges and roles.
TABLE	CREATE, DROP, or TRUNCATE a table.
TABLESPACE	CREATE, ALTER, or DROP a tablespace.
TRIGGER	CREATE, ALTER (enable/disable), DROP triggers; ALTER TABLE with either ENABLE ALL TRIGGERS or DISABLE ALL TRIGGERS.
TYPE	CREATE, ALTER and DROP types and type bodies.
USER	CREATE, ALTER or DROP a user.
VIEW	CREATE or DROP a view.

TABLE 10-17. *Auditable Statements Included in the ALL Category* (continued)

However, the types of statements in Table 10-18 do not fall into the **all** category when enabling auditing; they must be explicitly specified in any **audit** commands.

Some examples will help make all these options a lot clearer. In our sample database, the user SCOTT has all privileges on the tables in the HR schema and other schemas. SCOTT is allowed to create indexes on some of these tables, but we want to know when the indexes are created in case we have some performance issues related to execution plans changing. We can audit index creation by SCOTT with the following command:

```
SQL> audit index by scott whenever successful;
Audit succeeded.
```

Later that day, SCOTT creates an index on the HR.JOBS table:

```
SQL> create index job_title_idx on hr.jobs(job_title);
Index created.
```

Checking the audit trail in the data dictionary view DBA_AUDIT_TRAIL, we see that SCOTT did indeed create an index at 9:21 P.M. on February 24th:

```
SQL> select username, to_char(timestamp,'MM/DD/YY HH24:MI') Timestamp,
  2     obj_name, action_name, sql_text from dba_audit_trail
  3   where username = 'SCOTT';

USERNAME   TIMESTAMP       OBJ_NAME         ACTION_NAME      SQL_TEXT
---------- --------------- ---------------- ---------------- ---------------
SCOTT      02/24/04 21:24  JOB_TITLE_IDX    CREATE INDEX     create index j
                                                             ob_title_idx on
                                                              hr.jobs(job_ti
                                                             tle)

1 row selected.
```

Statement Option	SQL Operations
ALTER SEQUENCE	Any ALTER SEQUENCE command.
ALTER TABLE	Any ALTER TABLE command.
COMMENT TABLE	Add a comment to a table, view, materialized view, or any of their columns.
DELETE TABLE	Delete rows from a table or view.
EXECUTE PROCEDURE	Execute a procedure, function, or any variables or cursors within a package.
GRANT DIRECTORY	GRANT or REVOKE a privilege on a DIRECTORY object.
GRANT PROCEDURE	GRANT or REVOKE a privilege on a procedure, function, or package.
GRANT SEQUENCE	GRANT or REVOKE a privilege on a sequence.
GRANT TABLE	GRANT or REVOKE a privilege on a table, view, or materialized view.
GRANT TYPE	GRANT or REVOKE a privilege on a TYPE.
INSERT TABLE	INSERT INTO a table or view.
LOCK TABLE	LOCK TABLE command on a table or view.
SELECT SEQUENCE	Any command referencing the sequence's CURRVAL or NEXTVAL.
SELECT TABLE	SELECT FROM a table, view, or materialized view.
UPDATE TABLE	Execute UPDATE on a table or view.

TABLE 10-18. *Explicitly Specified Statement Types*

To turn off auditing for SCOTT on the HR.JOBS table, we use the **noaudit** command, as follows:

```
SQL> noaudit index by scott;
Noaudit succeeded.
```

We also may wish to routinely audit both successful and unsuccessful logins. This requires two **audit** commands:

```
SQL> audit session whenever successful;
Audit succeeded.
SQL> audit session whenever not successful;
Audit succeeded.
```

Reviewing the audit trail reveals one failed login attempt by the user RJB:

```
SQL> select username, to_char(timestamp,'MM/DD/YY HH24:MI') Timestamp,
  2        obj_name, returncode, action_name, sql_text from dba_audit_trail
  3  where action_name in ('LOGON','LOGOFF')
  4  order by timestamp desc;
```

USERNAME	TIMESTAMP	OBJ_NAME	RETURNCODE	ACTION_NAME	SQL_TEXT
DBSNMP	02/24/04 21:55		0	LOGOFF	
SYSMAN	02/24/04 21:54		0	LOGOFF	
RJB	02/24/04 21:52		1017	LOGON	
RJB	02/24/04 21:52		0	LOGON	
DBSNMP	02/24/04 21:52		0	LOGOFF	
SCOTT	02/24/04 21:52		0	LOGON	
DBSNMP	02/24/04 21:51		0	LOGOFF	
RJB	02/24/04 21:51		0	LOGOFF	
SCOTT	02/24/04 21:38		0	LOGOFF	
SCOTT	02/24/04 21:24		0	LOGOFF	

```
10 rows selected.
```

The RETURNCODE represents the ORA error message. An ORA-1017 message indicates that an incorrect password was entered. Note that if we are just interested in logons and logoffs, we could use the DBA_AUDIT_SESSION view instead.

Statement auditing also includes startup and shutdown operations. Although we can audit the command **shutdown immediate** in the SYS.AUD$ table, it is not possible to audit the **startup** command in SYS.AUD$ because the database has to be started before rows can be added to this table. For these cases, we can look in $ORACLE_HOME/rdbms/audit to see a record of a startup operation performed by a system administrator. Here is a text file created when the database was started with the **startup** command:

```
Audit file /u01/app/oracle/product/10.1.0/rdbms/audit/ora_2788.aud
Oracle Database 10g Enterprise Edition Release 10.1.0.2.0 - Production
With the Partitioning, OLAP and Data Mining options
ORACLE_HOME = /u01/app/oracle/product/10.1.0
System name: Linux
Node name: dw10g
Release: 2.4.21-9.0.1.EL
Version: #1 Mon Feb 9 22:26:52 EST 2004
Machine: i686
Instance name: dw
Redo thread mounted by this instance: 0 <none>
Oracle process number: 0
2788

Tue Feb 24 17:26:01 2004
ACTION : 'STARTUP'
DATABASE USER: '/'
PRIVILEGE : SYSDBA
CLIENT USER: oracle
CLIENT TERMINAL: Not Available
STATUS: 0
```

In this example, the database was started by a user connected as **oracle** on the host system and connected to the instance with operating system authentication. We will cover additional system administrator auditing issues in the next section.

Privilege Auditing

Auditing system privileges has the same basic syntax as statement auditing, except that system privileges are specified in the *sql_statement_clause* instead of statements.

For example, we may wish to grant the ALTER TABLESPACE privilege to all our DBAs, but we want to generate an audit record when this happens. The command to enable auditing on this privilege looks similar to statement auditing:

```
SQL> audit alter tablespace by access whenever successful;
Audit succeeded.
```

Every time the ALTER TABLESPACE privilege is successfully used, a row is added to SYS.AUD$.

Special auditing is available for system administrators who use the SYSDBA and SYSOPER privileges. To enable this extra level of auditing, set the initialization parameter AUDIT_SYS_OPERATIONS to TRUE. The audit records are sent to the same location as the operating system audit records; therefore, this location is operating system dependent. All SQL statements executed while using one of these privileges, as well as any SQL statements executed as the user SYS, are sent to the operating system audit location.

Schema Object Auditing

Auditing access to various schema objects looks similar to statement and privilege auditing:

```
AUDIT schema_object_clause BY {SESSION | ACCESS}
    WHENEVER [NOT] SUCCESSFUL;
```

The *schema_object_clause* specifies a type of object access and the object being accessed. Thirteen different types of operations on specific objects can be audited; they are listed in Table 10-19.

Object Option	Description
ALTER	Alters a table, sequence, or materialized view
AUDIT	Audits commands on any object
COMMENT	Adds comments to tables, views, or materialized views
DELETE	Deletes rows from a table, view, or materialized view
FLASHBACK	Performs flashback operation on a table or view
GRANT	Grants privileges on any type of object
INDEX	Creates an index on a table or materialized view
INSERT	Inserts rows into a table, view, or materialized view
LOCK	Locks a table, view, or materialized view
READ	Performs a read operation on the contents of a DIRECTORY object
RENAME	Renames a table, view, or procedure
SELECT	Selects rows from a table, view, sequence, or materialized view
UPDATE	Updates a table, view, or materialized view

TABLE 10-19. *Object Auditing Options*

If we wish to audit all **insert** and **update** commands on the HR.JOBS table, regardless of who is doing the update, and every time the action occurs, we can use the **audit** command as follows:

```
SQL> audit insert, update on hr.jobs by access whenever successful;
Audit successful.
```

The user TAMARA decides to add two new rows to the HR.JOBS table:

```
SQL> insert into hr.jobs (job_id, job_title, min_salary, max_salary)
  2  values ('IN_CFO','Internet Chief Fun Officer', 7500, 50000);
1 row created.

SQL> insert into hr.jobs (job_id, job_title, min_salary, max_salary)
  2  values ('OE_VLD','Order Entry CC Validation', 5500, 20000);
1 row created.
```

Looking in the DBA_AUDIT_TRAIL view, we see the two **insert** commands in TAMARA's session:

```
USERNAME    TIMESTAMP       OWNER    OBJ_NAME    ACTION_NAME
SQL_TEXT
---------- --------------- -------- ---------- ---------------
-------------------------------------------------------------
TAMARA     02/24/04 22:54 HR        JOBS        INSERT
insert into hr.jobs (job_id, job_title, min_salary, max_salary)
 values ('IN_CFO','Internet Chief Fun Officer', 7500, 50000);
TAMARA     02/24/04 22:53 HR        JOBS        INSERT
insert into hr.jobs (job_id, job_title, min_salary, max_salary)
 values ('OE_VLD','Order Entry CC Validation', 5500, 20000);
TAMARA     02/24/04 22:51                       LOGON

3 rows selected.
```

Fine-Grained Auditing

Starting with Oracle9*i*, auditing became much more focused and precise with the introduction of fine-grained object auditing, or FGA. FGA is implemented by a PL/SQL package called DBMS_FGA.

With standard auditing, you can easily find out what objects were accessed and by whom, but you don't know which columns or rows were accessed. Fine-grained auditing addresses this problem by not only specifying a predicate, or **where** clause, for which rows need to be accessed, but also by specifying a column or columns in the table being accessed. This can dramatically reduce the number of audit table entries by only auditing access to the table if it accesses certain rows and columns.

The package DBMS_FGA has four procedures:

ADD_POLICY	Adds an audit policy using a predicate and audit column
DROP_POLICY	Drops the audit policy
DISABLE_POLICY	Disables the audit policy but keeps the policy associated with the table or view
ENABLE_POLICY	Enables a policy

The user TAMARA usually accesses the HR.EMPLOYEES table on a daily basis to look up employee e-mail addresses. The system administrators suspect that TAMARA is viewing salary information for managers, so they set up an FGA policy to audit any access to the SALARY column for anyone who is a manager:

```
begin
    dbms_fga.add_policy(
        object_schema =>    'HR',
        object_name =>      'EMPLOYEES',
        policy_name =>      'SAL_SELECT_AUDIT',
        audit_condition =>  'instr(job_id,''_MAN'') > 0',
        audit_column =>     'SALARY'
    );
end;
```

Audit records for fine-grained auditing can be accessed with the data dictionary view DBA_FGA_AUDIT_TRAIL. If you typically need to see both standard audit rows and fine-grained auditing rows, the data dictionary view DBA_COMMON_AUDIT_TRAIL combines rows from both types of audits.

To continue our example, the user TAMARA runs two SQL queries as follows:

```
SQL> select employee_id, first_name, last_name, email from hr.employees
  2      where employee_id = 114;

EMPLOYEE_ID FIRST_NAME           LAST_NAME                   EMAIL
----------- -------------------- --------------------------- --------------
        114 Den                  Raphaely                    DRAPHEAL

1 row selected.

SQL> select employee_id, first_name, last_name, salary from hr.employees
  2      where employee_id = 114;

EMPLOYEE_ID FIRST_NAME           LAST_NAME                   SALARY
----------- -------------------- --------------------------- ----------
        114 Den                  Raphaely                         11000

1 row selected.
```

The first query accesses a manager, but not the SALARY column. The second query is the same as the first, but does access the SALARY column and therefore triggers the FGA policy, thus generating one, and only one, row in the audit trail:

```
SQL> select to_char(timestamp,'mm/dd/yy hh24:mi') timestamp,
  2      object_schema, object_name, policy_name, statement_type
  3  from dba_fga_audit_trail
  4  where db_user = 'TAMARA';

TIMESTAMP       OBJECT_SCHEMA   OBJECT_NAME     POLICY_NAME        STATEMENT_TYPE
--------------- --------------- --------------- ------------------ --------------
02/25/04 00:04  HR              EMPLOYEES       SAL_SELECT_AUDIT   SELECT

1 row selected.
```

Because we set up fine-grained access control in our VPD example earlier in this chapter to prevent unauthorized use of the SALARY column, we need to double-check our policy functions to make sure that SALARY information is still being restricted correctly. Fine-grained auditing, along with standard auditing, is a good way to ensure that our authorization policies are set up correctly in the first place.

Auditing-Related Data Dictionary Views

Table 10-20 contains the data dictionary views related to auditing.

Protecting the Audit Trail

The audit trail itself needs to be protected, especially if non-system users must access the table SYS.AUD$. The built-in role DELETE_ANY_CATALOG is one of the ways that non-SYS users can have access to the audit trail (for example, to archive and truncate the audit trail to ensure that it does not impact the space requirements for other objects in the SYS tablespace).

To set up auditing on the audit trail itself, connect as SYSDBA and run the following command:

```
SQL> audit all on sys.aud$ by access;
Audit succeeded.
```

Now, all actions against the table SYS.AUD$, including **select**, **insert**, **update**, and **delete**, will be recorded in SYS.AUD$ itself. But, you may ask, what if someone deletes the audit records

Data Dictionary View	Description
AUDIT_ACTIONS	Contains descriptions for audit trail action type codes, such as INSERT, DROP VIEW, DELETE, LOGON, and LOCK.
DBA_AUDIT_OBJECT	Audit trail records related to objects in the database.
DBA_AUDIT_POLICIES	Fine-grained auditing policies in the database.
DBA_AUDIT_SESSION	All audit trail records related to CONNECT and DISCONNECT.
DBA_AUDIT_STATEMENT	Audit trail entries related to GRANT, REVOKE, AUDIT, NOAUDIT, and ALTER SYSTEM commands.
DBA_AUDIT_TRAIL	Contains standard audit trail entries. USER_AUDIT_TRAIL contains audit rows for connected user only.
DBA_FGA_AUDIT_TRAIL	Audit trail entries for fine-grained auditing policies.
DBA_COMMON_AUDIT_TRAIL	Combines standard and fine-grained auditing rows into one view.
DBA_OBJ_AUDIT_OPTS	Auditing options in effect for database objects.
DBA_PRIV_AUDIT_OPTS	Auditing options in effect for system privileges.
DBA_STMT_AUDIT_OPTS	Auditing options in effect for statements.

TABLE 10-20. *Auditing-Related Data Dictionary Views*

identifying access to the table SYS.AUD$? The rows in the table are deleted, but then another row is inserted, recording the deletion of the rows. Therefore, there will always be some evidence of activity, intentional or accidental, against the SYS.AUD$ table. In addition, if AUDIT_SYS_OPERATIONS is set to true, any sessions using **as sysdba**, **as sysoper**, or connecting as SYS itself will be logged in the operating system audit location, which presumably even the Oracle DBAs would not have access to. As a result, we have many safeguards in place to ensure that we record all privileged activity in the database, along with any attempts to hide this activity!

Data Encryption Techniques

Data encryption can enhance security both inside and outside the database. A user may have a legitimate need for access to most columns of a table, but if one of the columns is encrypted and the user does not know the encryption key, the information is not usable. The same concern is true for information that needs to be sent securely over a network.

New to Oracle 10g, the package DBMS_CRYPTO replaces the DBMS_OBFUSCATION_TOOLKIT and includes the Advanced Encryption Standard (AES) encryption algorithm, which replaces the Data Encryption Standard (DES).

Procedures within DBMS_CRYPTO can generate private keys for you, or you can specify and store the key yourself. In contrast to DBMS_OBFUSCATION_TOOLKIT, which could only encrypt RAW or VARCHAR2 datatypes, DBMS_CRYPTO can encrypt BLOB and CLOB types.

PART III

High Availability

CHAPTER
11

Real Application
Clusters

n Chapter 4, we presented an overview of Automatic Storage Management (ASM) and Oracle Managed Files (OMF) and how they can ease administration, enhance performance, and improve availability. You can add one or more disk volumes to a rapidly growing VLDB without bringing down the instance.

In Chapter 6, we talked about bigfile tablespaces and how they not only allow the total size of the database to be much larger than in previous versions of Oracle, but also ease administration by moving the maintenance point from the datafile to the tablespace. Chapter 16 will focus on Oracle Net, providing you with the basics for ensuring that your clients can reach the database servers in an efficient and prompt manner. Chapter 17 will expand our coverage of bigfile tablespaces in addition to presenting other tools to make large database management easier, such as partitioned table support, transportable tablespaces, and new to Oracle 10g, Oracle Data Pump.

As your databases get larger, and the number of users increases, the need for availability becomes even more critical. Real Application Clusters (RAC) will tie together OMF, bigfile tablespaces, a robust network infrastructure, and ASM into key elements of the RAC architecture. In this chapter, we will revisit many of these database features, but with an emphasis on how they can be leveraged in a RAC environment.

This chapter focuses on a number of RAC topics, including how to set up your operating system environment—kernel parameters, network configuration, and user accounts. You will perform the requisite installations to support RAC, such as Cluster Ready Services (CRS) for creating a clustered environment, along with the various installation options within the Oracle Universal Installer (OUI) to configure your network, shared storage, and database software installation for both CRS and the Oracle 10g database itself.

During the installation of a RAC, you can configure the Enterprise Manager agent and Enterprise Manager Database Control to manage your cluster. EM Database Control extends the functionality available to manage a single instance by providing a cluster-aware layer; you can manage both the Oracle instances and the underlying cluster configuration from a single web interface.

In subsequent chapters, we will present other ways to ensure high database availability and recoverability: Chapter 14 will give a detailed look at Oracle Data Guard for near-realtime failover capabilities, and Chapter 18 will cover Oracle Streams for advanced replication. In Chapter 15, we'll finish up our discussion on Flashback options started in Chapter 7 by showing you how to perform Flashback Drop and Flashback Database as well as how to use LogMiner to undo individual transactions.

Overview of Real Application Clusters

A Real Application Clusters database is highly available and scalable. The failure of one node in the cluster does not affect client sessions or the availability of the cluster itself until the last node in the cluster fails; the only impact a lost node has on the cluster is a slight degradation in response time, depending on the total number of nodes in the cluster.

A RAC database has a few disadvantages. Licensing costs are higher, because each node in the cluster has to have its own Oracle license. The close physical proximity of the nodes in the cluster due to the high-speed requirements of the cluster interconnect means that a natural disaster can take out the entire cluster; using a remote standby database can help alleviate some of these concerns. You will have to weigh the cost of high availability (or the lack thereof) compared to the increased cost and slight increase in maintenance of a Real Application Cluster database.

In the next few sections, we'll cover some of the hardware and software requirements for a Real Application Cluster database as well as detail the network configuration and disk storage requirements to build a successful Real Application Cluster database.

Hardware Configuration

A complete discussion of all possible Real Application Cluster database hardware configurations is beyond the scope of this book. You want to have at least two and preferably three nodes for a Real Application Cluster database, each with redundant power supplies, network cards, dual CPUs, and error-correcting memory; these are desirable characteristics for any type of server, not just an Oracle server! The higher the number of nodes configured in the cluster, the lower the performance hit you will take when one of the cluster's nodes fails.

The shared disk subsystem should also have hardware redundancy built in—multiple power supplies, RAID-enabled disks, and so forth. You will balance the redundancy built into the shared disk with the types of disk groups you will create for the RAC. The higher redundancy built into the disk subsystem hardware can potentially reduce the amount of software redundancy you specify when you create the database's disk groups.

Software Configuration

Although Oracle clustering solutions have been available since version 6, not until version 10*g* has there been a native clusterware solution that more tightly couples the database to the volume management solution. Cluster Ready Services (CRS) is the clustering solution that can be used on all major platforms instead of an OS vendor or third-party clusterware.

CRS is installed before the RDBMS and must be in its own home directory, referred to as the CRS_HOME. If you are only using a single instance in the near future, but plan to cluster at a later date, it is useful to install CRS first so that the components of CRS that are needed for ASM and RAC are in the RDBMS directory structure. If you do not install CRS first, you will have to perform some extra steps later to remove the CRS-related process executables from the RDBMS home directory.

After CRS is installed, you install the database software in the home directory, referred to as the ORACLE_HOME. On some platforms, such as Microsoft Windows, this directory can be a directory common to all nodes, whereas other platforms, such as Linux, require OCFS version 2.x or later. Otherwise, each node will have its own copy of the binary executables.

Network Configuration

Each node in a RAC has a minimum of three IP addresses: one for the public network, one for the private network interconnect, and a virtual IP address to support faster failover in the event of a node failure. As a result, a minimum of two physical network cards are required to support RAC; additional network cards are used to provide redundancy on the public network and thus an alternate network path for incoming connections. For the private network, additional network cards can boost performance by providing more total bandwidth for interconnect traffic. Figure 11-1 shows a two-node RAC with one network card on each node for the private interconnect and one network card on each node to connect to the public network.

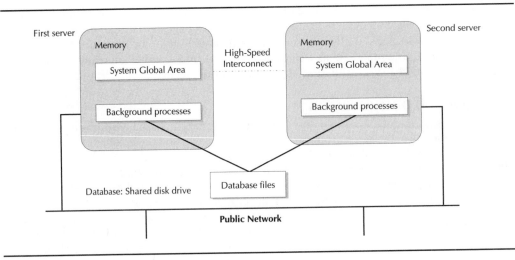

FIGURE 11-1. *RAC network configuration*

The public network is used for all routine connections to and from the server; the interconnect network, or private network, supports communication between the nodes in the cluster, such as node status information and the actual data blocks shared between the nodes. This interface should be as fast as possible, and no other types of communication between the nodes should occur on this interface, otherwise, the performance of the RAC database may suffer.

The virtual IP address is the address assigned to the Oracle listener process and supports *rapid connect-time failover,* which is able to switch the network traffic and Oracle connection to a different instance in the RAC database much faster than a third-party high-availability solution.

Disk Storage

The shared disk drive may or may not be a RAID device to support redundancy; more importantly the disk controllers and connections to the shared storage should be multiplexed to ensure high availability. If the disks in the shared drive are not mirrored, you can use the mirroring capabilities of ASM to provide performance and availability benefits.

For the purposes of the examples in this chapter, we will use a Linux server with the raw device configuration listed in Table 11-1. These raw disks reside on a shared SCSI storage device and have the same device name on each node in the cluster.

The two raw disks that are 100MB in size are reserved for the voting disk and the OCR disk; we will present the uses for these disks in the section "Cluster Ready Services."

Raw Device Name	Physical Device Name	Capacity	Purpose
/dev/raw/raw1	/dev/sda1	10GB	ASM Disk #1: +DATA1
/dev/raw/raw2	/dev/sdb1	10GB	ASM Disk #1: +DATA1
/dev/raw/raw3	/dev/sdc1	10GB	ASM Disk #2: +RECOV1
/dev/raw/raw4	/dev/sdd1	10GB	ASM Disk #2: +RECOV1
/dev/raw/raw5	/dev/sde1	100MB	OCR Disk
/dev/raw/raw6	/dev/sdf1	100MB	Voting Disk

TABLE 11-1. *Raw Disks for ASM Disk Groups, the Voting Disk, and the OCR Disk*

Installation and Setup

For the examples in this chapter, we will use Red Hat Linux to install the RAC database and demonstrate its features. However, most, if not all, the installation tips, techniques and methods presented in this chapter will be applicable to other Unix-like platforms and even Windows-based installations.

We will show you how to set up a three-node RAC database; although a two-node RAC database can demonstrate most the features of a RAC database, you will need a three-node RAC database to see how the remaining nodes in the cluster can still operate as a RAC database and recover from the loss of a single node in the cluster. In practice, the more nodes in the cluster, the less impact there is to throughput when one node in the cluster fails.

On each node, the Oracle software will reside in a local ORACLE_HOME; the database and recovery files will use ASM, and the OCR and voting disks will use raw devices.

NOTE
As an alternative to ASM and raw disks, Oracle Cluster File System (OCFS) version 2.x, available at http://oss.oracle.com, can be used to store both database files and Oracle executables on a common, shared file system.

Finally, we will assume that the shared disk is accessible via the same node name in the /dev directory and that each node in the cluster can access the shared disk simultaneously; the ASM instance on each node will automatically coordinate access to the shared disk.

Operating System Configuration

The first step is to prepare the operating system. Install Red Hat 3.0 ES or AS, and install every option! The small amount of disk space you might save is quickly offset when you are missing a component later and must find the installation CDs to obtain the missing component. Once everything is installed, be sure to apply all patches from Red Hat Network to take advantage of all security and performance enhancements, although Oracle 10g will run as advertised on an unpatched Red Hat 3.0 ES or AS Service Pack 2 installation.

Memory and Disk Requirements

For each node in the cluster, a minimum of 512MB is recommended. The swap space should be at least twice this value, or 1GB. For a successful installation, there should be 400MB free in the /tmp file system.

The Oracle software itself requires approximately 2.5GB of disk space, and the default database files require another 1.2GB; the growth of your database depends, of course, on the application.

On your shared disk subsystem, you need two special partitions: one for a voting disk and one for the Oracle Cluster Registry (OCR). The voting disk is used by Oracle's clustering software, Cluster Ready Services (CRS), to arbitrate ownership of the cluster in case of a private network failure. The OCR disk is used to maintain all metadata about the cluster: the cluster configuration and the cluster database configuration.

Kernel Parameters

Most of the "out of the box" kernel parameters are set correctly for Oracle except a few; ensure that the kernel parameters in Table 11-2 are set to the values provided in the table.

You can confirm that these values are in effect using the following command:

```
[root@rhes30]# /sbin/sysctl -a | egrep 'sem|shm|file-max|ip_local'
net.ipv4.ip_local_port_range = 1024     65000
kernel.sem = 250          32000   100     128
kernel.shmmni = 4096
kernel.shmall = 2097152
kernel.shmmax = 2147483648
fs.file-max = 65536
[root@rhes30]#
```

In a default Red Hat Linux 3.0 installation, some of these parameters are already set. For those values that vary from Table 11-2, simply append the parameter name and the value from the previous sample output to the file /etc/sysctl.conf and then run the **/sbin/sysctl -p** command to change the values immediately. After the next reboot, the values specified in /etc/sysctl.conf will be set automatically.

Kernel Parameter	Value
kernel.shmall	2097152
kernel.shmmax	2147483648
kernel.shmmni	4096
kernel.sem	250 32000 100 128
fs.file-max	65536
net.ipv4.ip_local_port_range	1024 65000

TABLE 11-2.   *Oracle Database 10g Minimum Kernel Parameter Values*

Network Configuration

Each node in a RAC requires at least two network cards; one card is to connect to the public network for client communication, and the other is used for private network traffic between the nodes in the cluster. For the examples in this chapter, we will use the following /etc/hosts file:

```
# Do not remove the following line, or various programs
# that require network functionality will fail.
#
127.0.0.1   localhost.localdomain    localhost

192.168.2.99      rhes30
192.168.2.166     oltp
192.168.2.167     mw

192.168.2.101     oc1     #public1
192.168.1.101     poc1    #private1
192.168.2.176     voc1    #virtual1

192.168.2.102     oc2     #public2
192.168.1.102     poc2    #private2
192.168.2.177     voc2    #virtual2

192.168.2.103     oc3     #public3
192.168.1.103     poc3    #private3
192.168.2.178     voc3    #virtual3
```

If you are using a DNS server, these names and addresses should be hosted there also.

A couple things are worth noting at this point. We only need two network cards on each server; why is there a "virtual" address for each node? The virtual addresses support rapid connect-time failover, a concept we will explore in more detail later in this chapter. All client connections use these virtual addresses for their connections, and each RAC node's listener will be listening on the virtual nodes instead of the public node names. Note also that each virtual address must be on the same subnet as the public address; the private interconnect network, however, is on its own private subnet.

TIP
*Before proceeding with any Oracle software installations, be sure that you can connect from each node in the cluster to every other node using **ssh** without prompts for a password for both the root user and the oracle user.*

User Accounts

Other than the root account, the only other account needed on your Linux server is the oracle account; in fact, in a production environment, you may not want any other user accounts on the server to prevent any inadvertent or intentional access of critical database files, control files, executables, or password files.

The groups oinstall and dba must exist on each node in the cluster, in addition to the oracle user. Use the following commands to create these if they do not already exist, and assign the oracle user to both groups, with oinstall as the primary group:

```
[root@rhes30 root]# /usr/sbin/groupadd oinstall
[root@rhes30 root]# /usr/sbin/groupadd dba
[root@rhes30 root]# /usr/sbin/useradd -g oinstall -G dba oracle
[root@rhes30 root]# passwd oracle
Changing password for user oracle.
New password:
Retype new password:
passwd: all authentication tokens updated successfully.
[root@rhes30 root]#
```

For the oracle user, set up the default environment in the logon script; this sample logon script assumes the bash shell (Bourne Again Shell) on Red Hat:

```
# .bash_profile

# Get the aliases and functions
if [ -f ~/.bashrc ]; then
        . ~/.bashrc
fi


# User specific environment and startup programs
PATH=$PATH:$HOME/bin
export PATH
unset USERNAME
umask 022
ORACLE_BASE=/u01/app/oracle
# ORACLE_HOME is set after installation with OUI.
# ORACLE_HOME=$ORACLE_BASE/product/10.1.0/DB10gHome
# ORACLE_SID different on each node;
# same database, different instance.
ORACLE_SID=rac1
LD_ASSUME_KERNEL=2.4.19
PATH=$ORACLE_HOME/bin:$PATH
export ORACLE_BASE ORACLE_HOME ORACLE_SID PATH LD_ASSUME_KERNEL
```

Make sure that the value for ORACLE_SID is unique on each node! As we install additional products such as CRS and create the RAC instances, we will make changes to this logon script as appropriate. Also, ensure that LD_ASSUME_KERNEL is set to 2.4.19 in root's .bash_profile; this setting is required for Oracle installations on Red Hat 3.0.

NOTE
LD_ASSUME_KERNEL does not need to be set in the login profile if you are using Oracle 10g update 1 or later.

To set up user equivalence between nodes in the cluster, use either the .rhosts or /etc/hosts.equiv file to support the **rsh** and **rcp** commands; better yet, and more secure, ensure that **ssh** and **scp** are configured for all nodes in the cluster. Starting with Oracle 10g, the OUI will use **ssh** and **scp** if possible, and fall back to **rsh** and **rcp** if necessary. Configuring **ssh** using the **ssh-keygen** utility is beyond the scope of this book; consult with your Unix or Linux system administrator to configure **ssh** and **scp**.

Software Directories

Because we are using ASM in these examples for RAC storage, only one directory, /u01/app/oracle, needs to be created on the local storage to hold the Oracle Database and the CRS software. The disk volume on which this directory resides must have at least 2.5GB of space for the database and CRS software. Use these commands to create this directory and assign the correct permissions:

```
[root@rhes30 root]# mkdir -p /u01/app/oracle
[root@rhes30 root]# chown -R oracle:oinstall /u01/app/oracle
[root@rhes30 root]# chmod -R 775 /u01/app/oracle
```

Software Installation

Whether you are creating a two-node or a 16-node cluster, the procedure is the same; if you have configured your servers as detailed in the previous sections, the installations you will perform in the following sections will automatically push to each node you specify in the configuration screens for Cluster Ready Services and the Oracle Database software itself.

Therefore, the following discussion is divided into three parts: CRS to prepare the clustering environment, Oracle Database 10g software installation, and creating an instance of the database on each node in the cluster. As we review each screen of each installation, we will provide background and explanation as required so that you're prepared to make adjustments to your environment once the installations are complete.

In many cases, the installation steps for the database software, the database itself, and ASM are similar or identical to that you've already seen in Chapters 1 and 4; in the following sections, we'll focus on the differences you'll see for a RAC installation.

Cluster Ready Services

As mentioned earlier in this chapter, CRS should be installed in its own home directory called CRS_HOME. As part of the CRS installation, you will have to configure two particular locations that are not specific to any instance, but are used by the cluster itself: the Oracle Cluster Registry and the voting disk. The *Oracle Cluster Registry (OCR)* is the location where the cluster stores its metadata, and 100MB is more than enough disk space to hold the metadata for a very large cluster. The *voting disk* is used by the cluster to resolve situations where one or more nodes in the cluster lose contact with other nodes in the cluster over the private interconnect. In this way, you have a way to shut off one node or one group of nodes from writing to the shared disk files because it assumes it is in control of the shared storage. As with the OCR disk, the voting disk requires no more than 100MB.

The locations of the OCR disk and the voting disk must be on separate raw devices, even when you are using ASM for your other database files; however, if you are using OCFS, the OCR disk and the voting disk can exist as files on an OCFS volume. In the examples that follow, we will use raw devices for the OCR and voting disks; this is the Oracle-recommended method.

The CRS software is provided on a single CD-ROM. After you mount the CD, run the script ./runInstaller as the oracle user. The first screen you will see after the welcome screen and the Oracle inventory location screen is shown in Figure 11-2.

The installation for CRS is similar to that for a database install; you specify a home directory for the executables. In this case, you will use a home directory called CRS10gHome, which must be different from the Oracle Database home.

After selecting the language for the installation, you provide a name for the cluster along with the public and private node names. As you can see in Figure 11-3, you specify the cluster name as lec1 and provide the public and private node names as defined in the /etc/hosts file you defined earlier in this chapter.

On the next installation screen, shown in Figure 11-4, you specify which of your network devices is to be used as the public interface (to connect to the public network) and which will be used for the private interconnect to support cache fusion and the cluster heartbeat. As noted earlier, you can have more than one public and more than one private interface; on this screen you can also mark an interface to not be used at all by CRS.

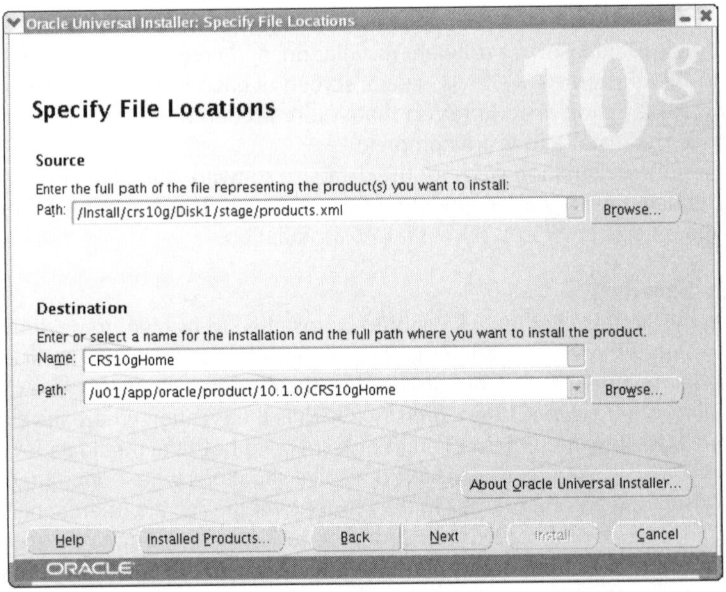

FIGURE 11-2. *Executable file locations*

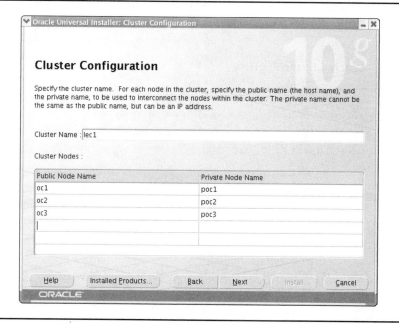

FIGURE 11-3. *Cluster configuration*

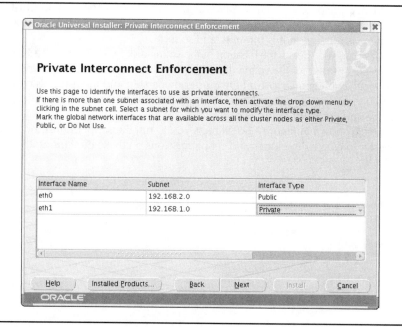

FIGURE 11-4. *Private interconnect enforcement*

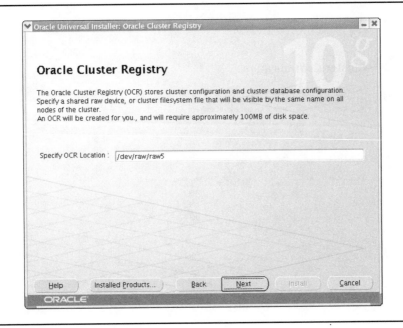

FIGURE 11-5. *Oracle Cluster Registry*

In Figure 11-5, you specify /dev/raw/raw5 as the raw disk for the Oracle Cluster Registry. The OCR is a metadata repository for the cluster configuration, keeping track of things like where a particular service is running, if it is running, and so forth.

In a similar fashion, you specify the location of the voting disk for CRS. In Figure 11-6, you specify /dev/raw/raw6 as the raw disk for the voting disk. The processes known as *Cluster Synchronization Services (CSS)* use the voting disk to arbitrate cluster ownership and interprocess communications in a cluster environment. In a single-instance environment, CSS facilitates communications between the ASM instance and the RDBMS instance.

The next screen, shown in Figure 11-7, directs you to run the script orainstRoot.sh on each node in the cluster to create directories and set permissions on those directories; this script must be run as root.

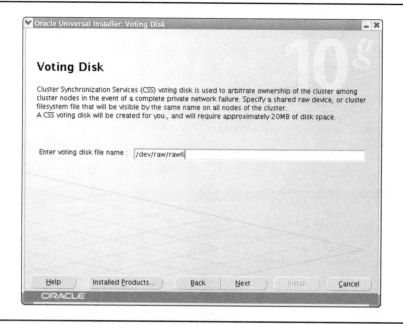

FIGURE 11-6. *Voting Disk location*

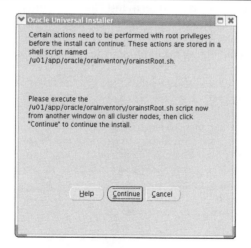

FIGURE 11-7. *Script to run as root*

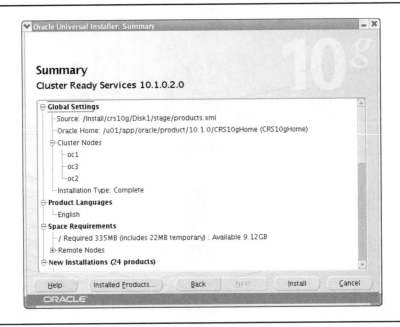

FIGURE 11-8. *Pre-installation summary*

After the pre-installation summary screen shown in Figure 11-8 appears, you click the Install button and the installation begins. In addition to installing the software on the node where you initiated the installation, the installed directory structure is copied to every node on the cluster.

After installation is complete, you are once again prompted to run a script as root on each node of the cluster. Here is the output from running the command on the first node:

```
[root@oc1 mnt]# /u01/app/oracle/product/10.1.0/CRS10gHome/root.sh
Checking to see if Oracle CRS stack is already up...
/etc/oracle does not exist. Creating it now.
Setting the permissions on OCR backup directory
Oracle Cluster Registry configuration upgraded successfully
WARNING: directory '/u01/app/oracle/product/10.1.0' is not owned by root
WARNING: directory '/u01/app/oracle/product' is not owned by root
WARNING: directory '/u01/app/oracle' is not owned by root
assigning default hostname oc1 for node 1.
assigning default hostname oc2 for node 2.
assigning default hostname oc3 for node 3.
Successfully accumulated necessary OCR keys.
Using ports: CSS=49895 CRS=49896 EVMC=49898 and EVMR=49897.
node <nodenumber>: <nodename> <private interconnect name> <hostname>
node 1: oc1 poc1 oc1
node 2: oc2 poc2 oc2
node 3: oc3 poc3 oc3
```

```
Creating OCR keys for user 'root', privgrp 'root'..
Operation successful.
Now formatting voting device: /dev/raw/raw6
Successful in setting block0 for voting disk.
Format complete.
Adding daemons to inittab
Preparing Oracle Cluster Ready Services (CRS):
Expecting the CRS daemons to be up within 600 seconds.
CSS is active on these nodes.
        oc1
CSS is inactive on these nodes.
        oc2
        oc3
Local node checking complete.
Run root.sh on remaining nodes to start CRS daemons.
[root@oc1 mnt]#
```

The voting and OCR disks are initialized the first time this script is run. When you run the script on the other two nodes, you see similar results, except for the voting disk and OCR disk initialization; here is the output for the second node, oc2:

```
[root@oc1 etc]# ssh oc2
Last login: Thu Oct 14 19:32:44 2004 from oc1
[root@oc2 root]# /u01/app/oracle/product/10.1.0/CRS10gHome/root.sh
Checking to see if Oracle CRS stack is already up...
. . .
clscfg: EXISTING configuration version 2 detected.
clscfg: version 2 is 10G Release 1.
assigning default hostname oc1 for node 1.
assigning default hostname oc2 for node 2.
assigning default hostname oc3 for node 3.
Successfully accumulated necessary OCR keys.
Using ports: CSS=49895 CRS=49896 EVMC=49898 and EVMR=49897.
node <nodenumber>: <nodename> <private interconnect name> <hostname>
node 1: oc1 poc1 oc1
node 2: oc2 poc2 oc2
node 3: oc3 poc3 oc3
clscfg: Arguments check out successfully.

NO KEYS WERE WRITTEN. Supply -force parameter to override.
-force is destructive and will destroy any previous cluster
configuration.
Oracle Cluster Registry for cluster has already been initialized
Adding daemons to inittab
Preparing Oracle Cluster Ready Services (CRS):
Expecting the CRS daemons to be up within 600 seconds.
CSS is active on these nodes.
        oc1
        oc2
```

```
CSS is inactive on these nodes.
        oc3
Local node checking complete.
Run root.sh on remaining nodes to start CRS daemons.
[root@oc2 root]#
```

On the third and final node of our three-node cluster, we see similar messages with a confirmation that the CRSD and EVMD processes have started:

```
[root@oc2 root]# ssh oc3
Last login: Thu Oct 14 20:40:15 2004 from oc2
[root@oc3 root]# /u01/app/oracle/product/10.1.0/CRS10gHome/root.sh
Checking to see if Oracle CRS stack is already up...
/etc/oracle does not exist. Creating it now.
. . .
Adding daemons to inittab
Preparing Oracle Cluster Ready Services (CRS):
Expecting the CRS daemons to be up within 600 seconds.
CSS is active on these nodes.
        oc1
        oc2
        oc3
CSS is active on all nodes.
Waiting for the Oracle CRSD and EVMD to start
Oracle CRS stack installed and running under init(1M)
[root@oc3 root]#
```

NOTE
A discussion of CRSD and EVMD is beyond the scope of this book; see the Oracle Press book Oracle Database 10g High Availability with RAC, Flashback & Data Guard, *by Hart and Jesse.*

You can verify that the CRS installation completed successfully by changing to the executable directory for CRS (in CRS10gHome) on any node and then running this command:

```
[oracle@oc1 oracle]$ cd /u01/app/oracle/product/10.1.0/CRS10gHome/bin
[oracle@oc1 bin]$ olsnodes -n
oc1     1
oc2     2
oc3     3
[oracle@oc1 bin]$
```

The output from **olsnodes** shows the node names and node numbers that are running CRS.

Database Software Install
Once you have the cluster software running successfully on each node, you are ready to install the database software into the same directory on each node. In this section, we'll primarily focus on the parts of the database software install that differ from the single-instance installation you performed in Chapter 1.

Although we can create a database at the same time we install the Oracle software, we will only install the software now and run the Database Configuration Assistant later to create the database. From the root directory of the database installation CD, run the script ./runInstaller as the oracle user, just as you did for the CRS install. The first screen you will see after the welcome screen and the Oracle inventory location screen is shown in Figure 11-9.

Although you can install the software in any directory, make sure that this directory is available to the user oracle on all nodes in the cluster. In addition, make sure that this directory is not the same as the CRS installation directory.

As shown in Figure 11-10, if the installer detects clustering software running on the node, it gives you the option to install the software on the entire cluster or to perform a single-instance install. In this case, you select all the nodes you configured earlier as part of the cluster.

As with a single-instance installation, you can select either the Enterprise Edition or the Standard Edition. Choose the edition that is compatible with your site's licensing options. After selecting the edition, the installer confirms that the environment for the Oracle Database software is configured correctly, as you can see in Figure 11-11.

You may get some errors or warnings about modules or products that are missing or the wrong version; in Figure 11-11, the installer did not find the openmotif package at all. You can verify that the package is installed by using a command similar to the following:

```
[root@oc1 root]# rpm -q openmotif
openmotif-2.2.3-3.RHEL3
[root@oc1 root]#
```

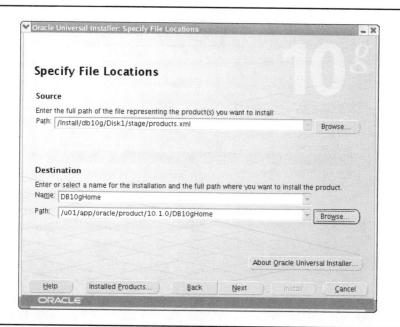

FIGURE 11-9. *Oracle database file locations*

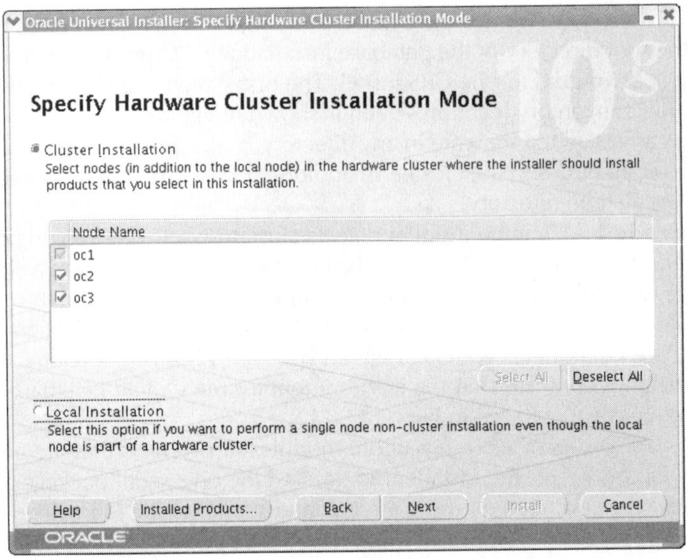

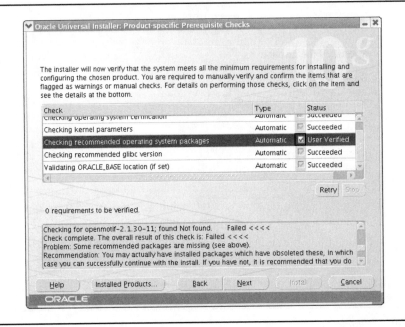

FIGURE 11-10. *Hardware cluster node locations*

FIGURE 11-11. *Platform configuration checks*

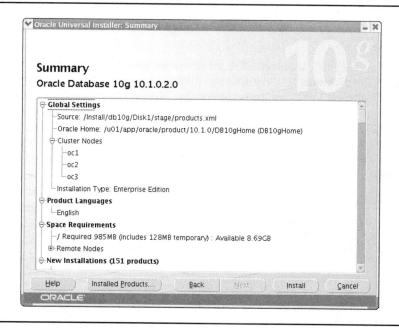

FIGURE 11-12.   *Database pre-installation summary*

Because you have a later version of openmotif on your system, you can safely specify that this package does exist and click Next. On the next screen, you do not specify a starter database; you will create the database with DBCA later.

The summary screen you see in Figure 11-12 is nearly identical to the one you see in a single-instance installation, except that you are installing the software on more than one node in the cluster.

The subsequent screens detail the progress of the installation. Upon completion, you are prompted to run a new root.sh script on each node in the cluster. Here are the results of running the script on the first node (you must be logged on as root to run this script):

```
[root@oc1 root]# /u01/app/oracle/product/10.1.0/DB10gHome/root.sh
Running Oracle10 root.sh script...
\nThe following environment variables are set as:
    ORACLE_OWNER= oracle
    ORACLE_HOME=  /u01/app/oracle/product/10.1.0/DB10gHome
Enter the full pathname of the local bin directory: [/usr/local/bin]:
    Copying dbhome to /usr/local/bin ...
    Copying oraenv to /usr/local/bin ...
    Copying coraenv to /usr/local/bin ...
\nCreating /etc/oratab file...
Adding entry to /etc/oratab file...
Entries will be added to the /etc/oratab file as needed by
Database Configuration Assistant when a database is created
```

```
Finished running generic part of root.sh script.
Now product-specific root actions will be performed.
[root@oc1 root]#
```

For the first node in the cluster only, this script spawns the Virtual IP Configuration Assistant (VIPCA) to configure the virtual IP addresses you will use for application failover and the Enterprise Manager agent. After the VIPCA welcome screen, the Network Interfaces screen, shown in Figure 11-13, provides you with a list of the physical network interfaces available on this server. Choose the public interface and click Next.

In Figure 11-14, you enter one of the virtual IP node names you specified earlier in the /etc/ hosts file (in this case, voc1). The installer automatically fills in the other alias names and addresses from /etc/hosts.

After you see the pre-installation summary screen, click Next; Figure 11-15 shows you the installation progress screen for all three nodes.

After the installation is complete, you open a session on each of the other nodes in the cluster and run root.sh on other nodes. The script produces similar results to those you saw on the first node, but because you already configured with VIPCA, you get the message

```
CRS resources are already configured
```

and the VIPCA is not launched. VIPCA only needs to be configured once per cluster.

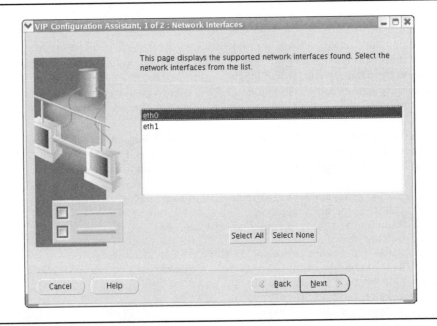

FIGURE 11-13. *VIPCA network interfaces*

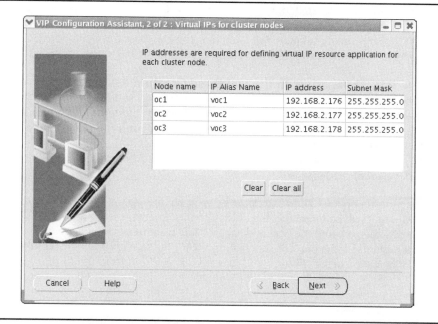

FIGURE 11-14.   *VIPCA addresses for cluster nodes*

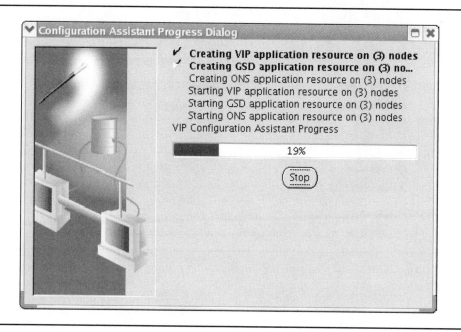

FIGURE 11-15.   *VIPCA installation progress*

Now that the software is installed, you can proceed with creating the database along with one instance per node in the next section. As mentioned earlier, you could have created a starter database with the software installation, but launching the Database Configuration Assistant gives you more options and more flexibility when creating a database and a new instance.

Creating the RAC Database with the Database Creation Assistant

Launching the Database Creation Assistant (DBCA) for installing a RAC database is much the same as launching DBCA for a single instance; if DBCA detects cluster software installed, it gives you the option to install a RAC database or a single instance, as you can see in Figure 11-16, after DBCA is launched:

```
[oracle@oc1 oracle] dbca &
```

After selecting the option to create a database, you see the dialog shown in Figure 11-17; select the nodes that will participate in the cluster. In this case, you select all nodes.

On the next screen, choose the type of database: data warehouse, general purpose, transaction processing, or custom. For the purposes of creating a RAC, the type of database you select will not change the configuration of the cluster.

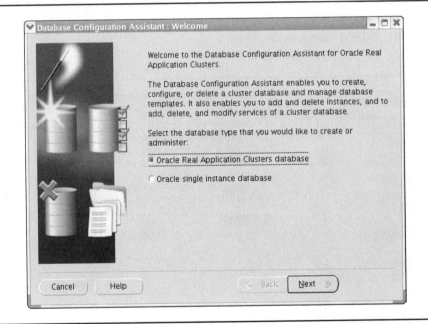

FIGURE 11-16. *DBCA instance type options*

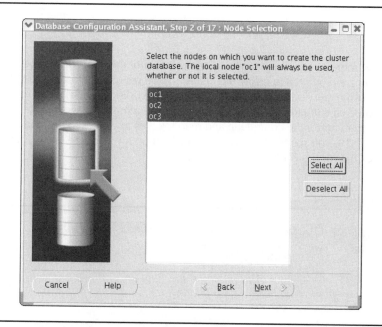

FIGURE 11-17. *Nodes to include for RAC installation*

On step 4 of DBCA, you give the cluster database a name and a SID prefix, just as you would with a standalone database installation. Step 5 asks you if you want to configure your RAC to use EM Database Control, and whether to configure the database with Enterprise Manager or Grid Control. Specify your mail server and e-mail notification address. In step 6, you specify the password for the privileged accounts in the database: SYS, SYSTEM, DBSNMP, and SYSMAN. In step 7, you specify ASM as your database file storage method. Finally, in step 8 you specify the parameters for the ASM instance, as you did in Chapter 4.

Automatic Storage Management (ASM) instances, although available for storage management with standalone Oracle instances, are ideal for use with a RAC database. ASM eliminates both the need for configuring raw devices (raw devices are mapped once within an ASM instance and subsequently are available for all nodes in the cluster) and the need for a cluster file system for database files. Cluster file systems such as Oracle Cluster File System (OCFS) are still available if you want your ORACLE_HOME on a cluster file system instead of a copy on each node in the cluster; Oracle best practices recommends that each node have its own local copy of the Oracle software. More details on how to configure and use ASM can be found in Chapter 4. If you use ASM, it only needs to be configured once, during these steps.

NOTE
OCFS version 2.x supports a shared Oracle Home.

The next few screens track the progress of the creation of the ASM instance. After this process is completed, you are prompted to create the first ASM disk group, as you can see in Figure 11-18. You choose two of the raw devices available to be the DATA1 disk group using normal redundancy. Additionally, you create the RECOV1 disk group using the remaining two disk groups; this disk group will be used to mirror the control file and redo log files as well as to host the Flash Recovery Area. In Figure 11-19, you specify DATA1 as the disk group for database storage. In Figure 11-20, you specify RECOV1 for the Flash Recovery Area.

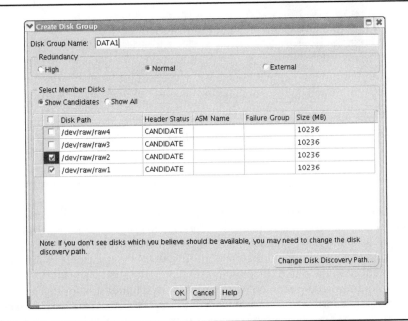

FIGURE 11-18. *Creating ASM raw disk #1*

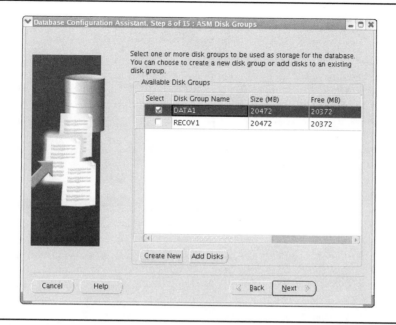

FIGURE 11-19. *Selecting the ASM disk group for storage*

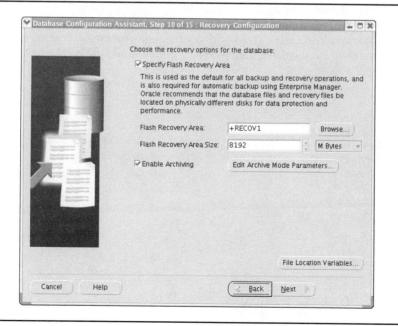

FIGURE 11-20. *Selecting the ASM disk for the Flash Recovery Area*

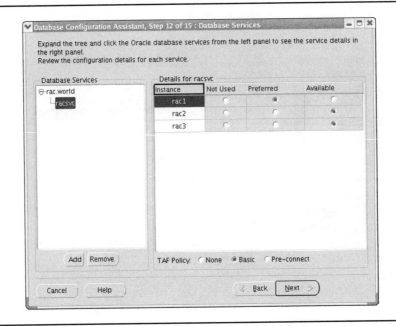

FIGURE 11-21. *Creating a RAC service*

In the next step, shown in Figure 11-21, you will see another option that you did not see in a single-instance install: creating a custom RAC service.

The service you create in Figure 11-21 adds another entry for racsvc in tnsnames.ora, in addition to the standard entry created (rac) when the tnsnames.ora file is created, as you can see in this listing:

```
rac =
  (description =
    (address = (protocol = tcp)(host = voc1)(port = 1521))
    (address = (protocol = tcp)(host = voc2)(port = 1521))
    (address = (protocol = tcp)(host = voc3)(port = 1521))
    (load_balance = yes)
    (connect_data =
      (server = dedicated)
      (service_name = rac.world)
    )
  )

listeners_rac =
  (address_list =
    (address = (protocol = tcp)(host = voc1)(port = 1521))
    (address = (protocol = tcp)(host = voc2)(port = 1521))
    (address = (protocol = tcp)(host = voc3)(port = 1521))
```

```
      )

racsvc =
(description =
    (address = (protocol = tcp)(host = voc1)(port = 1521))
    (address = (protocol = tcp)(host = voc2)(port = 1521))
    (address = (protocol = tcp)(host = voc3)(port = 1521))
    (load_balance = yes)
    (connect_data =
      (server = dedicated)
      (service_name = racsvc.world)
      (failover_mode =
        (type = select)
        (method = basic)
        (retries = 180)
        (delay = 5)
      )
    )
  )

rac3 =
  (description =
    (address = (protocol = tcp)(host = voc3)(port = 1521))
    (connect_data =
      (server = dedicated)
      (service_name = rac.world)
      (instance_name = rac3)
    )
  )

rac2 =
  (description =
    (address = (protocol = tcp)(host = voc2)(port = 1521))
    (connect_data =
      (server = dedicated)
      (service_name = rac.world)
      (instance_name = rac2)
    )
  )

rac1 =
  (description =
    (address = (protocol = tcp)(host = voc1)(port = 1521))
    (connect_data =
      (server = dedicated)
      (service_name = rac.world)
      (instance_name = rac1)
    )
  )
```

Notice also that each node in the RAC has its own entry so that you may connect to a specific node when necessary. Note also that the hostnames for each node are using the virtual node names instead of the physical node names.

The entry for racsvc has a few additional parameters for FAILOVER_MODE; these modes and their values are defined in the following list:

- **type**   The type of failover. Specifying **session** creates a new session for the client, but this does not preserve the position in a cursor when you are running a SELECT statement. Specifying **select** preserves the state of the cursor during a SELECT, but involves extra overhead on the client side. The default, **none**, disables failover functionality.

- **method**   How fast failover occurs. Using a value of **basic** establishes connections when the failover occurs, and this incurs no overhead on the backup server(s). A value of **preconnect** provides faster failover, but as the name implies, it uses resources on the backup server(s) even when no failover scenario is active.

- **retries**   The number of times to attempt to connection after a failover.

- **delay**   The amount of time, in seconds, to wait between connection attempts when a failover scenario is active.

Later in this chapter, we will show you how connecting to the racsvc service ensures high availability for client connections when the client connects to a node and the node fails.

The next few screens are the same as for a single-instance database installation; see Chapter 1 for the options available on these screens. Figure 11-22 summarizes the cluster database installation, which includes the location of the database's SPFILE on the DATA1 disk group.

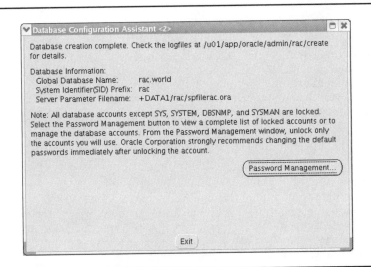

FIGURE 11-22.   *DBCA RAC database creation complete*

Once the installation is complete, EM Database Control is automatically configured and started, just as it is with a single-instance installation; however, you can manage the entire cluster and not just individual nodes.

NOTE
Installing and configuring Enterprise Manager Grid Control 10g is beyond the scope of this book; see the book Oracle Database 10g High Availability with RAC, Flashback & Data Guard *for more information.*

In Figure 11-23, you can see that the EM Database Control login connects you to the entire cluster instead of just a single node.

As with a single-instance database, you can see the status of the database on the database home page; again, the difference is that EM Database Control is cluster-aware. In Figure 11-24, you can see the status of the Oracle instances in the cluster, and in Figure 11-25, you see the status of the cluster itself; remember that CRS is managing the cluster as a separate product from the database.

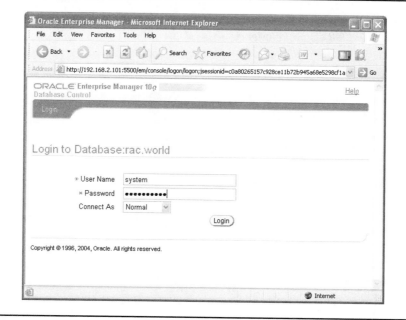

FIGURE 11-23. *EM DB Control cluster login*

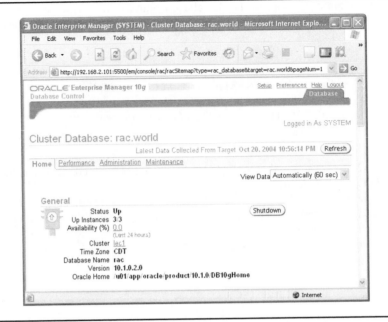

FIGURE 11-24. *EM DB Control cluster database status*

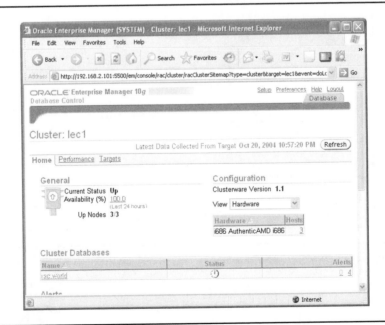

FIGURE 11-25. *EM DB Control cluster hardware status*

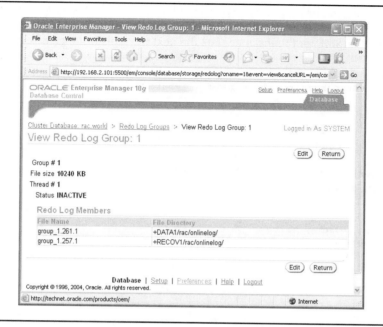

FIGURE 11-26. *EM DB Control RAC redo log group members*

In Figure 11-26, you see the characteristics of one of the redo log members for the cluster; note that we placed one of the group's members on the DATA1 disk group and the other on the RECOV1 disk group. Because each disk group is mirrored on two different raw devices, you have the equivalent of four-way redundancy for the members of your redo log group.

RAC Database Characteristics

A RAC instance is different in many ways from a standalone instance; in this section, we will show you the initialization parameters that are specific to a RAC instance. In addition, we'll show you some of the data dictionary views and dynamic performance views that are either unique to a RAC or have columns that are only populated when the instance is part of a RAC.

Server Parameter File Characteristics

As you saw previously in the section "Creating the RAC Database with the Database Configuration Assistant," the server parameter file (SPFILE) resides on the DATA1 disk group and therefore is shared by each node in the cluster. Within the SPFILE, you can assign different values for given parameters on an instance-by-instance basis; in other words, the value for an initialization parameter can differ between instances. If an initialization parameter is the same for all nodes in the cluster, it is prefixed with "*."; otherwise, it is prefixed with the node name.

In this example, the physical memory on the cluster server oc2 is temporarily reduced. Therefore, to reduce the demands of the instance on the server, you will change the value of SHARED_POOL_SIZE for the instance rac2 the next time this instance is restarted:

```
SQL> select sid, name, value
  2      from v$spparameter where name = 'shared_pool_size';

SID          NAME                  VALUE
----------   --------------------  ---------------
*            shared_pool_size      65614720

SQL> alter system set shared_pool_size=48M
  2      scope=spfile sid='rac2';
System altered.

SQL> select sid, name, value
  2      from v$spparameter where name = 'shared_pool_size';

SID          NAME                  VALUE
----------   --------------------  ---------------
*            shared_pool_size      65614720
rac2         shared_pool_size      50331648
```

Once the memory issue has been resolved, you can restore the size of the shared pool on the rac2 instance as follows:

```
SQL> alter system set shared_pool_size=64M
  2      scope=spfile sid='rac2';
System altered.
SQL>
```

RAC-Related Initialization Parameters

A number of initialization parameters are used only in a RAC environment. Although these initialization parameters exist in any instance, in a single-instance environment they are either null or have a value of 1 (for example, INSTANCE_NUMBER). In Table 11-3, we give you an overview of some of the key RAC-related initialization parameters.

Dynamic Performance Views

In a single-instance environment, all dynamic performance views that begin with V$ have a corresponding view beginning with GV$, with the additional column INST_ID always set to 1. For a RAC environment with two nodes, the GV$ views have twice as many rows as the corresponding V$ views; for a three-node RAC, there are three times as many rows, and so forth. In the sections that follow, we'll review some of the V$ dynamic performance views that show the same contents regardless of the node you are connected to, along with some of the GV$ views that can show you the contents of the V$ views on each node without connecting to each node explicitly.

Initialization Parameter	Description
INSTANCE_NUMBER	Unique number identifying this instance in the cluster.
INSTANCE_NAME	The unique name of this instance within the cluster; typically the cluster name with a numeric suffix.
CLUSTER_DATABASE	This parameter is TRUE if this instance is participating in a RAC environment.
CLUSTER_DATABASE_INSTANCES	The number of instances configured for this cluster, whether each instance is active or not.
ACTIVE_INSTANCE_COUNT	Specifies the primary instance in a two-node cluster; otherwise it is the number of instances in the cluster.
CLUSTER_INTERCONNECTS	Specifies the network used for the cluster's IPC traffic.
MAX_COMMIT_PROPAGATION_DELAY	Controls how fast committed transactions are propagated to other nodes.

TABLE 11-3.   *RAC-Related Initialization Parameters*

Common Database File Views

Some dynamic performance views are the same whether you're in a RAC environment or a single-instance environment; the ASM configuration is a perfect example of this. In this query, you want to verify that all your database files are stored in one of the two ASM disk groups, + DATA1 or +RECOV1:

```
SQL> select name from v$datafile union
  2    select name from v$tempfile union
  3    select member from v$logfile union
  4    select name from v$controlfile union
  5    select name from v$flashback_database_logfile;

NAME
----------------------------------------------------------
+DATA1/rac/controlfile/current.260.3
+DATA1/rac/datafile/example.264.1
+DATA1/rac/datafile/sysaux.257.1
+DATA1/rac/datafile/system.256.1
+DATA1/rac/datafile/undotbs1.258.1
+DATA1/rac/datafile/undotbs2.265.1
+DATA1/rac/datafile/undotbs3.266.1
+DATA1/rac/datafile/users.259.1
+DATA1/rac/onlinelog/group_1.261.1
+DATA1/rac/onlinelog/group_2.262.1
+DATA1/rac/onlinelog/group_3.269.1
```

```
+DATA1/rac/onlinelog/group_4.270.1
+DATA1/rac/onlinelog/group_5.267.1
+DATA1/rac/onlinelog/group_6.268.1
+DATA1/rac/tempfile/temp.263.1
+RECOV1/rac/controlfile/current.256.3
+RECOV1/rac/onlinelog/group_1.257.1
+RECOV1/rac/onlinelog/group_2.258.1
+RECOV1/rac/onlinelog/group_3.261.1
+RECOV1/rac/onlinelog/group_4.262.1
+RECOV1/rac/onlinelog/group_5.259.1
+RECOV1/rac/onlinelog/group_6.260.1
22 rows selected.

SQL> show parameter spfile

NAME                   TYPE         VALUE
-------------------    -----------  --------------------------
spfile                 string       +DATA1/rac/spfilerac.ora
SQL>
```

Cluster-Aware Dynamic Performance Views

The GV$ views make it easy to view each instance's characteristics in a single **select** statement, while at the same time filtering out nodes that you do not want to see; these views also make it easier to aggregate totals from some or all of the nodes in the cluster, as in this example:

```
SQL> select nvl(to_char(inst_id),'TOTAL') INST#,
  2         count(inst_id) sessions from gv$session
  3         group by rollup(inst_id)
  4         order by inst_id;

INST#      SESSIONS
--------   ----------
1                29
2                39
3                26
TOTAL            94

4 rows selected.
```

From this query, you can see the number of sessions per instance and the total number of instances for the cluster using the view GV$SESSION.

RAC Maintenance

Most of the maintenance operations you perform on a single-node instance apply directly to a multiple-node RAC database environment. In this section, we will review the basics for maintaining a RAC database—including starting up a RAC database and discussing how redo logs and undo tablespaces work—and then work through an example of an instance failure scenario using Transparent Application Failover (TAF) as well as rebuilding a failed node and adding it back to the cluster.

Starting Up a RAC Database

Starting up a RAC database is not much different from starting up a standalone instance; the nodes in a RAC database can start up in any order, and they can be shut down and started up at any time with minimal impact to the rest of the cluster. During database startup, first the ASM instance starts and mounts the shared disk groups; next, the RDBMS instance starts and joins the cluster.

On Unix, the file /etc/oratab can be modified to auto-start the instances (both the ASM instance and the RDBMS instance) on each cluster:

```
# This file is used by ORACLE utilities.  It is created by root.sh
# and updated by the Database Configuration Assistant when creating
# a database.
#
# A colon, ':', is used as the field terminator.  A new line terminates
# the entry.  Lines beginning with a pound sign, '#', are comments.
#
# Entries are of the form:
#   $ORACLE_SID:$ORACLE_HOME:<N|Y>:
#
# The first and second fields are the system identifier and home
# directory of the database respectively.  The third filed indicates
# to the dbstart utility that the database should, "Y", or should not,
# "N", be brought up at system boot time.
#
# Multiple entries with the same $ORACLE_SID are not allowed.
#
#*:/u01/app/oracle/product/10.1.0/DB10gHome:N
+ASM1:/u01/app/oracle/product/10.1.0/DB10gHome:Y
rac:/u01/app/oracle/product/10.1.0/DB10gHome:Y
```

Redo Logs in a RAC Environment

As with a single-node instance, online redo logs are used for instance recovery in a RAC environment; each instance in a RAC environment has its own set of online redo log files that are used to roll forward all information in the redo logs and then roll back any uncommitted transactions initiated on that node using the undo tablespace.

Even before the failed instance has restarted, one of the surviving instances detects the instance failure and uses the online redo log files to ensure that no committed transactions are lost; if this process completes before the failed instance restarts, the restarted instance does not need instance recovery. Even if more than one instance fails, all that is required for instance recovery is one remaining node. If all instances in a RAC fail, the first instance that starts up will perform instance recovery for the database using the online redo log files from all instances in the cluster.

If media recovery is required and the entire database must be recovered, all instances except for one must be shut down and media recovery is performed from a single instance. If you are recovering noncritical database files, all nodes may be up as long as the tablespaces containing the files to be recovered are marked as OFFLINE.

Undo Tablespaces in a RAC Environment

As with redo logs, each instance in a RAC environment must have its own undo tablespace on a shared drive or disk group. This undo tablespace is used for rolling back transactions during normal transactional operations or during instance recovery. In addition, the undo tablespace is used by other nodes in the cluster to support read consistency for transactions that are reading rows from a table on node rac2 while a data-entry process on node rac1 makes updates to the same table and has not yet committed the transaction. The user on rac2 needs to see the before-image data stored in rac1's undo tablespace. This is why all undo tablespaces must be visible to all nodes in the cluster.

Failover Scenarios and TAF

If you have configured your client correctly and the instance to which the client is connected to fails, the client connection is rapidly switched to another instance in the cluster and processing can continue with only a slight delay in response time.

Here is the tnsnames entry for the service racsvc we created earlier:

```
racsvc =
  (description =
    (address = (protocol = tcp)(host = voc1)(port = 1521))
    (address = (protocol = tcp)(host = voc2)(port = 1521))
    (address = (protocol = tcp)(host = voc3)(port = 1521))
    (load_balance = yes)
    (connect_data =
      (server = dedicated)
      (service_name = racsvc.world)
      (failover_mode =
        (type = select)
        (method = basic)
        (retries = 180)
        (delay = 5)
      )
    )
  )
```

We will show you what happens and how you will know if a session is connected to the cluster and its instance fails. First, you connect to the cluster via racsvc and find out the node and instance that you are connected to:

```
SQL> connect rjb/rjb@racsvc;
Connected.
SQL> select instance_name, host_name, failover_type,
  2         failover_method, failed_over
  3  from v$instance
  4  cross join
  5  (select failover_type, failover_method, failed_over
```

```
      6    from v$session
      7    where username = 'RJB');


INSTANCE_NAME HOST_NAME FAILOVER_TYPE FAILOVER_METHOD FAILED_OVER
------------- --------- ------------- --------------- -----------
rac1          oc1       SELECT        BASIC           NO

SQL>
```

You are using the columns from V$INSTANCE to give you the instance name and host name that you are connected to and then joining this to V$SESSION and retrieving the columns related to failover, which are only populated in a RAC environment. In this case, the session has not yet failed over, and the failover type is BASIC, as we specified when we created the service.

Next, you will shut down instance rac1 from another session while you are still connected to the first session:

```
SQL> connect system/manager@rac1
Connected.
SQL> shutdown immediate
Database closed.
Database dismounted.
ORACLE instance shut down.
SQL>
```

Back at your user session, you rerun the query to find out what node you are connected to:

```
SQL> select instance_name, host_name, failover_type,
      2        failover_method, failed_over
      3  from v$instance
      4  cross join
      5  (select failover_type, failover_method, failed_over
      6   from v$session
      7   where username = 'RJB');


INSTANCE_NAME HOST_NAME FAILOVER_TYPE FAILOVER_METHOD FAILED_OVER
------------- --------- ------------- --------------- -----------
rac3          oc3       SELECT        BASIC           YES

SQL>
```

If you were running a query at the time the instance was shut down, your query would pause for a second or two and then continue as if nothing happened.

RAC Node Failure Scenario

One of the benefits of a RAC environment is your ability to add or remove nodes to meet changing resource demands. One server that is underutilized in one business unit may be needed in another business unit that is entering its peak processing period. Adding or removing a node in a RAC environment may also be driven by a failure of a node; while the remaining nodes in the cluster service ongoing requests, you will have to repair or replace the missing node and add it back to the cluster without bringing down the rest of the cluster.

In this section, we'll show you the steps required to remove a node's metadata from the cluster registry and then rebuild a node and add it back to the cluster. The assumption in this scenario is that the local hard disk of the third cluster node is damaged beyond repair; therefore, you will rebuild the node from scratch and add it to the cluster registry. After this step, you will reinstall the Oracle software and create the instance as part of the database cluster.

Remove the Instance

Even if the instance on the failed server is not available, you still want to remove any traces of the instance from the remaining nodes in the cluster. You can use the **srvctl** command to remove the instance from the cluster, as in this example:

```
[oracle@oc1 oracle]$ srvctl remove instance -d rac -i rac3
Remove instance rac3 for the database rac? (y/[n]) y
[oracle@oc1 oracle]$
```

The parameter **-d rac** specifies the RAC to be modified, and **-i rac3** specifies the instance to be removed from the RAC.

Remove the Node from the Cluster

To remove the server itself from the cluster, execute the **rootdeletenode.sh** command from the CRS10gHome directory, specifying both the node name and the CRS-assigned node number, as in the following example:

```
[root@oc1 root] # cd /u01/app/oracle/product/10.1.0/CRS10gHome/bin
[root@oc1 bin]# ./olsnodes -n
oc1      1
oc2      2
oc3      3
[root@oc1 bin]# cd ../install
[root@oc1 install]# ./rootdeletenode.sh oc3,3
clscfg: EXISTING configuration version 2 detected.
clscfg: version 2 is 10G Release 1.
Successfully deleted 13 values from OCR.
Key SYSTEM.css.interfaces.nodeoc3 marked for deletion is not there.
Ignoring.
Successfully deleted 5 keys from OCR.
Node deletion operation successful.
'oc3,3' deleted successfully
[root@oc1 install]# cd ../bin
```

```
[root@oc1 bin]# ./olsnodes -n
oc1      1
oc2      2
[root@oc1 bin]#
```

You also need to remove the node from the list of node locations maintained by the Oracle Universal Installer (OUI); in the directory $ORACLE_BASE/oraInventory/ContentsXML, identify any files that reference the deleted node, such as this example in the file inventory.xml:

```
<HOME NAME="CRS10gHome"
    LOC="/u01/app/oracle/product/10.1.0/CRS10gHome"
    TYPE="O" IDX="1" CRS="true">
    <NODE_LIST>
       <NODE NAME="oc1"/>
       <NODE NAME="oc3"/>
       <NODE NAME="oc2"/>
    </NODE_LIST>
</HOME>
```

> **NOTE**
> *See MetaLink Note 269320.1 for other procedures specific to your environment that may need to be performed to remove a node from a cluster.*

Note that you have specified the node name of the server that hosts the instance. There are now only two nodes in your CRS clusterware environment.

Install Operating System Software
The next step is to reinstall the server software and prepare the environment as you did in the examples earlier in this chapter in the section "Operating System Configuration." At the end of this process, you will have the Oracle directories created along with the oracle user account, but without the CRS and database software installed. You will also assign the public, private, and virtual IP addresses using the same addresses you used when this node was first created. As a result, you will not have to change the /etc/hosts file on the remaining nodes in the cluster.

Add the Node to the Cluster with CRS
The node is ready to add to the cluster at the clusterware layer so that the other nodes in the cluster consider it to be a part of the cluster again. From one of the remaining nodes in the cluster, change to $CRS_HOME/oui/bin and run the **addNode.sh** command, which launches OUI and prompts you for the new node, as you can see in Figure 11-27.

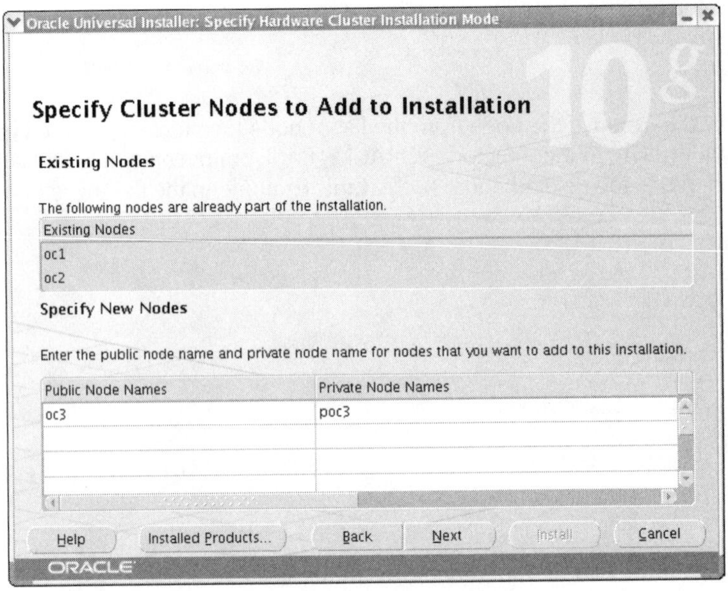

FIGURE 11-27. *Specifying the node to add using OUI*

After presenting a summary of the existing nodes and the node to be added, you click Next and the CRS files are copied to the new node. To start the services on the new node, you are prompted to run **rootaddnode.sh** on the active node and root.sh on the new node, as you can see in this example:

```
[root@oc1 oraInventory]#
    /u01/app/oracle/product/10.1.0/CRS10gHome/rootaddnode.sh
clscfg: EXISTING configuration version 2 detected.
clscfg: version 2 is 10G Release 1.
Attempting to add 1 new nodes to the configuration
Using ports: CSS=49895 CRS=49896 EVMC=49898 and EVMR=49897.
node <nodenumber>: <nodename> <private interconnect name> <hostname>
node 3: oc3 poc3 oc3
Creating OCR keys for user 'root', privgrp 'root'..
Operation successful.
[root@oc1 oraInventory]# ssh oc3
Last login: Sun Oct 31 21:12:08 2004 from oc2
[root@oc3 root]# /u01/app/oracle/product/10.1.0/CRS10gHome/root.sh
Checking to see if Oracle CRS stack is already up...
/etc/oracle does not exist. Creating it now.
Setting the permissions on OCR backup directory
```

```
Oracle Cluster Registry configuration upgraded successfully
WARNING: directory '/u01/app/oracle/product/10.1.0' is not owned by root
WARNING: directory '/u01/app/oracle/product' is not owned by root
WARNING: directory '/u01/app/oracle' is not owned by root
clscfg: EXISTING configuration version 2 detected.
clscfg: version 2 is 10G Release 1.
assigning default hostname oc1 for node 1.
assigning default hostname oc2 for node 2.
assigning default hostname oc3 for node 3.
Successfully accumulated necessary OCR keys.
Using ports: CSS=49895 CRS=49896 EVMC=49898 and EVMR=49897.
node <nodenumber>: <nodename> <private interconnect name> <hostname>
node 1: oc1 poc1 oc1
node 2: oc2 poc2 oc2
node 3: oc3 poc3 oc3
clscfg: Arguments check out successfully.

NO KEYS WERE WRITTEN. Supply -force parameter to override.
-force is destructive and will destroy any previous cluster
configuration.
Oracle Cluster Registry for cluster has already been initialized
Adding daemons to inittab
Preparing Oracle Cluster Ready Services (CRS):
Expecting the CRS daemons to be up within 600 seconds.
CSS is active on these nodes.
        oc1
        oc2
        oc3
CSS is active on all nodes.
Waiting for the Oracle CRSD and EVMD to start
Waiting for the Oracle CRSD and EVMD to start
Oracle CRS stack installed and running under init(1M)
[root@oc3 root]#
```

For release 10.1.0.2.0, you may have to use the racgons utility in the CRS_HOME directory to configure the Oracle Notification Services (ONS) port number, as follows:

```
[root@oc3 root]# $CRS_HOME/bin/racgons add_config oc3:4948
```

If the port is already configured, you will receive this message:

```
WARNING: oc3:4948 already configured.
```

Install Oracle Software on the New Node

In this step, you will copy the Oracle software from one of the existing nodes in the cluster to the new node. From $ORACLE_HOME/oui/bin run the **addNode.sh** script. Make sure you are in $ORACLE_HOME and not $CRS_HOME.

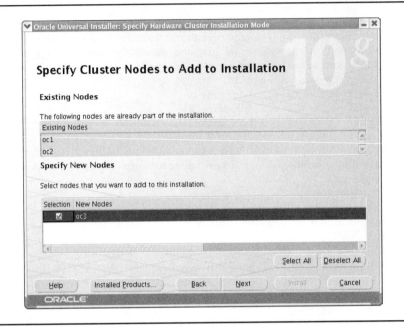

FIGURE 11-28. *Specifying the cluster node to add to the installation*

The OUI will start in Add Node mode, and after the startup screens, you will see the Specify Cluster Nodes screen, as shown in Figure 11-28. On this screen, you add the new node oc3.

After you see the summary screen, similar to the screen you saw for the CRS install, click Next to copy the Oracle software to the new node. After this step completes, you will be prompted to run the root.sh script on the new node. In the final step of the procedure, the updated cluster information is saved to the OCR disk.

Create a New Oracle Instance

To create the Oracle instance on the new node, run DBCA from an existing node and choose a RAC database. On a subsequent screen, choose Instance Management and then add an instance to the existing cluster, as you can see in Figure 11-29.

On the next screen, you are prompted for the new instance name; to be consistent with your previous naming convention, choose rac3 and click Next. In step 6, you will see the existing cluster services; update the services with the new node name as appropriate. On the last step, step 7, you specify the tablespaces, datafiles, and redo log groups that will be added for this instance; in this case, an undo tablespace, the datafile for the tablespace, and two redo log groups, as you can see in Figure 11-30.

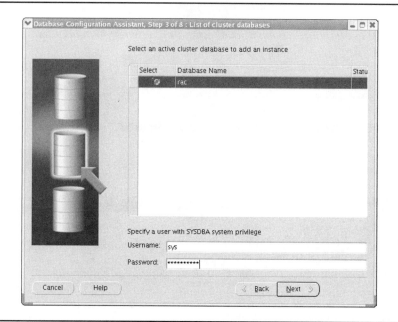

FIGURE 11-29. *Adding an instance to an existing cluster*

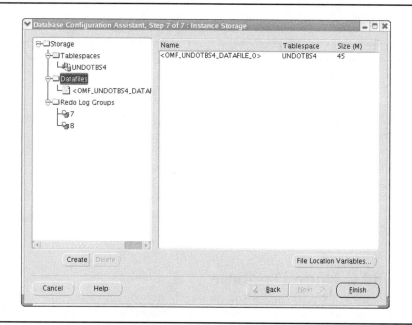

FIGURE 11-30. *Specifying storage for the new instance*

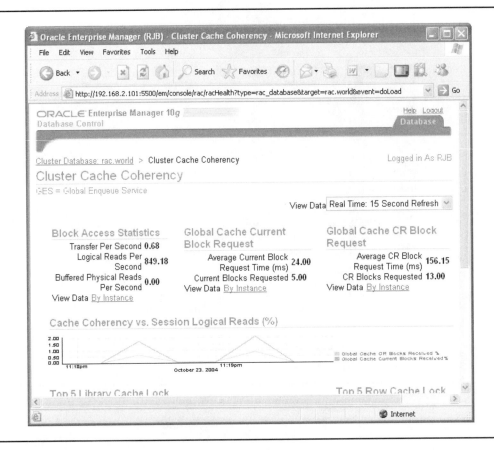

FIGURE 11-31.   *EM Database Control RAC cache statistics*

A confirmation screen appears when the instance is up and running; the cluster once again has three nodes:

```
SQL> select inst_id from gv$instance;

INST_ID
-------
      1
      2
      3
```

Tuning a RAC Node Database

The first step in tuning a RAC database is to tune each individual instance first. If an individual instance is not tuned correctly, the performance of the entire cluster will not be optimal. You can use the Automatic Workload Repository (AWR) to tune an instance as if it was not part of a cluster.

Using EM Database Control, you can further leverage the statistics from the AWR to produce reports on a cluster-wide basis. In Figure 11-31, you can see how EM Database Control makes it easy to analyze the performance of the shared global cache as well as the cache performance on an instance-by-instance basis.

Tablespace Management

In a RAC environment, tablespace management is much the same as in a single-instance environment. There is still only one database and one set of tablespaces to manage; it's just that there is more than one instance accessing the tablespaces.

Automatic Segment Space Management (ASSM), introduced in Oracle9*i*, enhances the usability of tablespaces in a RAC environment. Because you no longer have to worry about more freelists and freelist groups to support multiple instances, and therefore more concurrent writers to a table, adding more instances to the cluster does not necessarily require table reorganizations.

CHAPTER
12

Backup and Recovery Options

racle provides a variety of backup procedures and options that help protect an Oracle database. If they are properly implemented, these options will allow you to effectively back up your databases and recover them easily and efficiently.

Oracle's backup capabilities include logical and physical backups, both of which have a number of options available. This chapter will not detail every possible option and recovery scenario; rather, the focus in this chapter is on using the best options in the most effective manner possible. You will see how to best integrate the available backup procedures with each other and with the operating system backups. You will also see details on the options for Data Pump Export and Import, both introduced in Oracle Database 10*g*.

Capabilities

There are three standard methods of backing up an Oracle database: exports, offline backups, and online backups. An export is a *logical* backup of the database; the other two backup methods are *physical* file backups. In the following sections, you will see each of these options described. The standard tool for physical backups is Oracle's Recovery Manager (RMAN) utility; see Chapter 13 for details on the implementation and usage of RMAN.

A robust backup strategy includes both physical and logical backups. In general, production databases rely on physical backups as their primary backup method, and logical backups serve as the secondary method. For development databases and for some small data movement processing, logical backups offer a viable solution. You should understand the implications and uses of both physical and logical backups in order to develop the most appropriate solution for your applications.

Logical Backups

A *logical backup* of a database involves reading a set of database records and writing them to a file. These records are read independently of their physical location. In Oracle, the Data Pump Export utility performs this type of database backup. To recover using the file generated from a Data Pump Export, use Data Pump Import.

NOTE
Oracle's Import and Export utilities, available prior to Oracle Database 10g, are still provided as part of the Oracle 10g installation. Users of the old Export and Import utilities are encouraged to replace their usage with Data Pump Export and Data Pump Import.

The Data Pump Export/Import Process

Oracle's Data Pump Export utility queries the database, including the data dictionary, and writes the output to an XML file called an *export dump file*. You can export the full database, specific users, tablespaces, or specific tables. During exports, you may choose whether or not to export the data dictionary information associated with tables, such as grants, indexes, and constraints. The file written by Data Pump Export will contain the commands necessary to completely re-create all the chosen objects and data.

Once data has been exported via Data Pump Export, it may be imported via the Data Pump Import utility. Data Pump Import reads the dump file created by Data Pump Export and executes the commands found there. For example, these commands may include a **create table** command, followed by an **insert** command to load data into the table.

The data that has been exported does not have to be imported into the same database, or the same schema, as was used to generate the export dump file. You may use the export dump file to create a duplicate set of the exported objects under a different schema or in a separate database.

You can import either all or part of the exported data. If you import the entire export dump file from a full export, then all the database objects—including tablespaces, datafiles, and users—will be created during the import. However, it is often useful to precreate tablespaces and users in order to specify the physical distribution of objects in the database.

If you are only going to import part of the data from the export dump file, the tablespaces, datafiles, and users that will own and store that data should be set up prior to the import.

Physical Backups

Physical backups involve copying the files that constitute the database. These backups are also referred to as *file system backups* because they involve using operating system file backup commands. Oracle supports two different types of physical file backups: *offline backups* and the *online backups* (also known as *cold* and *hot backups*, respectively). You can use the RMAN utility (see Chapter 13) to perform all physical backups. You may optionally choose to write your own scripts to perform physical backups, but doing so will prevent you from obtaining many of the benefits of the RMAN approach.

Offline Backups

Consistent offline backups occur when the database has been shut down normally (that is, not due to instance failure). While the database is "offline," the following files should be backed up:

- All datafiles
- All controlfiles
- All online redo logs
- The init.ora file (optional) and server parameter file (spfile), if used

It is easiest to back up the datafiles if the database file architecture uses a consistent directory structure.

Having all these files backed up while the database is closed provides a complete image of the database as it existed at the time it was closed. The full set of these files could be retrieved from the backups at a later date, and the database would be able to function. It is *not* valid to perform a file system backup of the database while it is open unless an online backup is being performed. Offline backups that occur following database aborts will also be considered inconsistent and may require more effort to use during recoveries—if they are usable.

Online Backups

You can use online backups for any database that is running in ARCHIVELOG mode. In this mode, the online redo logs are archived, creating a log of all transactions within the database.

Oracle writes to the online redo log files in a cyclical fashion: After filling the first log file, it begins writing to the second, until that one fills, and then it begins writing to the third. Once the last online redo log file is filled, the LGWR (Log Writer) background process begins to overwrite the contents of the first redo log file.

When Oracle is run in ARCHIVELOG mode, the ARCH (Archiver) background process makes a copy of each redo log file before overwriting it. These archived redo log files are usually written to a disk device. The archived redo log files may also be written directly to a tape device, but this tends to be very operator-intensive.

> **NOTE**
> *Most production databases, particularly those that support transaction-processing applications, must be run in ARCHIVELOG mode.*

You can perform file system backups of a database while that database is open, provided the database is running in ARCHIVELOG mode. An online backup involves setting each tablespace into a backup state, backing up its datafiles, and then restoring the tablespace to its normal state.

> **NOTE**
> *When using the Oracle-supplied Recovery Manager (RMAN) utility, you do not have to manually place each tablespace into a backup state. RMAN reads the data blocks in the same manner Oracle uses for queries.*

The database can be fully recovered from an online backup, and it can, via the archived redo logs, be rolled forward to any point in time. When the database is then opened, any committed transactions that were in the database at that time will have been restored, and any uncommitted transactions will have been rolled back.

While the database is open, the following files can be backed up:

- All datafiles
- All archived redo log files
- One controlfile, via the **alter database** command

Online backup procedures are very powerful for two reasons. First, they provide full point-in-time recovery. Second, they allow the database to remain open during the file system backup. Even databases that cannot be shut down due to user requirements can still have file-system backups. Keeping the database open also keeps the System Global Area (SGA) of the database instance from being reset during database startups. Keeping the memory from being reset will improve the database's performance because it will reduce the number of physical I/Os required by the database.

NOTE
*You can use the **flashback database** option, introduced in Oracle Database 10g, to roll the database backward in time without relying on physical backups. To use the **flashback database** command, you must be running in ARCHIVELOG mode and must have issued the **alter database flashback on** command while the database was mounted but not open. Logs written to the Flashback Recovery Area are used by Oracle during the **flashback database** operation.*

Using Data Pump Export and Import

Introduced with Oracle Database 10g, Data Pump provides a server-based data-extraction and data-import utility. Its features include significant architectural and functional enhancements over the original Import and Export utilities. Data Pump allows you to stop and restart jobs, see the status of running jobs, and restrict the data that is exported and imported.

NOTE
Data Pump files are incompatible with those generated from the original Export utility.

Data Pump runs as a server process, benefiting users in multiple ways. The client process that starts the job can disconnect and later reattach to the job. Performance is enhanced (as compared to Export/Import) because the data no longer has to be processed by a client program. Data Pump extractions and loads can be parallelized, further enhancing performance.

In this chapter, you will see how to use Data Pump, along with descriptions and examples of its major options.

Creating a Directory

Data Pump requires you to create directories for the datafiles and log files it will create and read. Use the **create directory** command to create the directory pointer within Oracle to the external directory you will use. Users who will access the Data Pump files must have the READ and WRITE privileges on the directory.

NOTE
*Before you start, verify that the external directory exists and that the user who will be issuing the **create directory** command has the CREATE ANY DIRECTORY system privilege.*

The following example creates a directory named DTPUMP and grants READ and WRITE access to the Practice schema:

```
create directory dtpump as 'e:\dtpump';
grant read on directory DTPUMP to practice, system;
grant write on directory DTPUMP to practice, system;
```

The PRACTICE and SYSTEM schemas can now use the DTPUMP directory for Data Pump jobs.

Data Pump Export Options

Oracle provides a utility called expdp that serves as the interface to Data Pump. If you have previous experience with the Export utility, some of the options will be familiar. However, some significant features are available only via Data Pump. Table 12-1 shows the command-line input parameters for expdp when a job is created.

As shown in Table 12-1, five modes of Data Pump exports are supported. Full exports extract all the database's data and metadata. Schema exports extract the data and metadata for specific user schemas. Tablespace exports extract the data and metadata for tablespaces, and Table exports

Parameter	Description
ATTACH	Connects a client session to a currently running Data Pump Export job.
CONTENT	Filters what is exported: DATA_ONLY, METADATA_ONLY, or ALL.
DIRECTORY	Specifies the destination directory for the log file and the dump file set.
DUMPFILE	Specifies the names and directories for dump files.
ESTIMATE	Determines the method used to estimate the dump file size (BLOCKS or STATISTICS).
ESTIMATE_ONLY	A Y/N flag is used to instruct Data Pump whether the data should be exported or just estimated.
EXCLUDE	Specifies the criteria for excluding objects and data from being exported.
FILESIZE	Specifies the maximum file size of each export dump file.
FLASHBACK_SCN	The SCN for the database to flash back to during the export.
FLASHBACK_TIME	The timestamp for the database to flash back to during the export.
FULL	Tells Data Pump to export all data and metadata in a Full mode export.
HELP	Displays a list of available commands and options.
INCLUDE	Specifies the criteria for which objects and data will be exported.
JOB_NAME	Specifies a name for the job; the default is system-generated.
LOGFILE	The name and optional directory name for the export log.
NETWORK_LINK	Specifies the source database link for a Data Pump job exporting a remote database.
NOLOGFILE	A Y/N flag is used to suppress log file creation.
PARALLEL	Sets the number of workers for the Data Pump Export job.
PARFILE	Names the parameter file to use, if any.
QUERY	Filters rows from tables during the export.
SCHEMAS	Names the schemas to be exported for a Schema mode export.
STATUS	Displays detailed status of the Data Pump job.

TABLE 12-1. *Command-Line Input Parameters for expdp*

Parameter	Description
TABLES	Lists the tables and partitions to be exported for a Table mode export.
TABLESPACES	Lists the tablespaces to be exported.
TRANSPORT_FULL_CHECK	Specifies whether the tablespaces being exported should first be verified as a self-contained set.
TRANSPORT_TABLESPACES	Specifies a Transportable Tablespace mode export.
VERSION	Specifies the version of database objects to be created so the dump file set may be compatible with earlier releases of Oracle. The options are COMPATIBLE, LATEST, and database version numbers (not lower than 10.0.0).

TABLE 12-1. *Command-Line Input Parameters for expdp* (continued)

extract data and metadata for tables and their partitions. As described in Chapter 17, Transportable Tablespace exports extract metadata for specific tablespaces.

NOTE
You must have the EXP_FULL_DATABASE system privilege in order to perform a Full export or a Transportable Tablespace export.

When you submit a job, Oracle will give the job a system-generated name. If you specify a name for the job via the JOB_NAME parameter, you must be certain the job name will not conflict with the name of any table or view in your schema. During Data Pump jobs, Oracle will create and maintain a master table for the duration of the job. The master table will have the same name as the Data Pump job, so its name cannot conflict with existing objects.

While a job is running, you can execute the commands listed in Table 12-2 via Data Pump's interface.

Parameter	Description
ADD_FILE	Add dump files.
CONTINUE_CLIENT	Exit the interactive mode and enter logging mode.
EXIT_CLIENT	Exit the client session, but leave the server Data Pump Export job running.
HELP	Display online help for the import.
KILL_JOB	Kill the current job and detach related client sessions.
PARALLEL	Alter the number of workers for the Data Pump Export job.
START_JOB	Restart the attached job.
STATUS	Display a detailed status of the Data Pump job.
STOP_JOB	Stop the job for later restart.

TABLE 12-2. *Parameters for Interactive Mode Data Pump Export*

As the entries in Table 12-2 imply, you can change many features of a running Data Pump Export job via the interactive command mode. If the dump area runs out of space, you can attach to the job, add files, and restart the job at that point; there is no need to kill the job or to reexecute it from the start. You can display the job status at any time, either via the STATUS parameter or via the USER_DATAPUMP_JOBS and DBA_DATAPUMP_JOBS data dictionary views or the V$SESSION_LONGOPS view.

Starting a Data Pump Export Job

You can store your job parameters in a parameter file, referenced via the PARFILE parameter of expdp. For example, you can create a file named dp1.par with the following entries:

```
DIRECTORY=dtpump
DUMPFILE=metadataonly.dmp
CONTENT=METADATA_ONLY
```

You can then start the Data Pump Export job:

```
expdp practice/practice PARFILE=dp1.par
```

Oracle will then pass the dp1.par entries to the Data Pump Export job. A Schema-type Data Pump Export (the default type) will be executed, and the output (the metadata listings, but no data) will be written to a file in the dtpump directory previously defined. When you execute the **expdp** command, the output will be in the following format (there will be separate lines for each major object type—tables, grants, indexes, and so on):

```
Export: Release 10.1.0.1.0 on Wednesday, 26 May, 2004 17:29
Copyright (c) 2003, Oracle.  All rights reserved.

Connected to: Oracle10i Enterprise Edition Release 10.1.0.1.0
With the Partitioning, OLAP and Data Mining options
FLASHBACK automatically enabled to preserve database integrity.
Starting "PRACTICE"."SYS_EXPORT_SCHEMA_01":  practice/******** parfile=dp1.par
Processing object type SCHEMA_EXPORT/SE_PRE_SCHEMA_PROCOBJACT/PROCACT_SCHEMA
Processing object type SCHEMA_EXPORT/TYPE/TYPE_SPEC
Processing object type SCHEMA_EXPORT/TABLE/TABLE
Processing object type SCHEMA_EXPORT/TABLE/GRANT/OBJECT_GRANT
Processing object type SCHEMA_EXPORT/TABLE/INDEX/INDEX
Processing object type SCHEMA_EXPORT/TABLE/CONSTRAINT/CONSTRAINT
Processing object type SCHEMA_EXPORT/TABLE/COMMENT
Processing object type SCHEMA_EXPORT/VIEW/VIEW
Processing object type SCHEMA_EXPORT/PACKAGE/PACKAGE_SPEC
Processing object type SCHEMA_EXPORT/PACKAGE/PACKAGE_BODY
Processing object type SCHEMA_EXPORT/PACKAGE/GRANT/OBJECT_GRANT
Processing object type SCHEMA_EXPORT/TABLE/CONSTRAINT/REF_CONSTRAINT
Processing object type SCHEMA_EXPORT/SE_EV_TRIGGER/TRIGGER
Master table "PRACTICE"."SYS_EXPORT_SCHEMA_01" successfully loaded/unloaded
******************************************************************************
Dump file set for PRACTICE.SYS_EXPORT_SCHEMA_01 is:
  E:\DTPUMP\METADATAONLY.DMP
Job "PRACTICE"."SYS_EXPORT_SCHEMA_01" successfully completed at 17:30
```

The output file, as shown in the listing, is named METADATAONLY.DMP. The output dump file contains XML entries for re-creating the structures for the Practice schema. During the export, Data Pump created and used an external table named SYS_EXPORT_SCHEMA_01.

NOTE
Dump files will not overwrite previously existing dump files in the same directory.

You can use multiple directories and dump files for a single Data Pump Export. Within the DUMPFILE parameter setting, list the directory along with the filename, in this format:

```
DUMPFILE=directory1:file1.dmp,
         directory2:file2.dmp
```

Stopping and Restarting Running Jobs

After you have started a Data Pump Export job, you can close the client window you used to start the job. Because it is server based, the export will continue to run. You can then attach to the job, check its status, and alter it. For example, you can start the job via expdp:

```
expdp practice/practice PARFILE=dp1.par
```

Press CTRL-C to leave the log display, and Data Pump will return you to the export prompt:

```
Export>
```

Exit to the operating system via the EXIT_CLIENT command:

```
Export> EXIT_CLIENT
```

You can then restart the client and attach to the currently running job under your schema:

```
expdp practice/practice attach
```

If you gave a name to your Data Pump Export job, specify the name as part of the ATTACH parameter call. For example, if you had named the job PRACTICE_JOB, attach to the job by name:

```
expdp practice/practice attach=PRACTICE_JOB
```

When you attach to a running job, Data Pump will display the status of the job—its basic configuration parameters and its current status. You can then issue the CONTINUE_CLIENT command to see the log entries as they are generated, or you can alter the running job:

```
Export> CONTINUE_CLIENT
```

You can stop a job via the STOP_JOB option:

```
Export> STOP_JOB
```

With the job stopped, you can then add additional dump files in new directories, via the ADD_FILE option. You can then restart the job:

```
Export> START_JOB
```

You can specify a log file location for the export log via the LOGFILE parameter. If you do not specify a LOGFILE value, the log file will be written to the same directory as the dump file.

Exporting from Another Database

You can use the NETWORK_LINK parameter to export data from a different database. If you are logged into the HQ database and you have a database link to a separate database, Data Pump can use that link to connect to the database and extract its data.

> **NOTE**
> *If the source database is read-only, the user on the source database must have a locally managed tablespace assigned as the temporary tablespace; otherwise, the job will fail.*

In your parameter file (or on the expdp command line), set the NETWORK_LINK parameter equal to the name of your database link. The Data Pump Export will write the data from the remote database to the directory defined in your local database.

Using EXCLUDE, INCLUDE, and QUERY

You can exclude or include sets of tables from the Data Pump Export via the EXCLUDE and INCLUDE options. You can exclude objects by type and by name. If an object is excluded, all its dependent objects are also excluded. The format for the EXCLUDE option is

```
EXCLUDE=object_type[:name_clause] [, ...]
```

> **NOTE**
> *You cannot specify EXCLUDE if you specify CONTENT=DATA_ONLY.*

For example, to exclude the PRACTICE schema from a full export, the format for the EXCLUDE option would be

```
EXCLUDE=SCHEMA:"='PRACTICE'"
```

> **NOTE**
> *You can specify more than one EXCLUDE option within the same Data Pump Export job.*

The EXCLUDE option in the preceding example contains a limiting condition (='PRACTICE') within a set of double quotes. The *object_type* variable can be any Oracle object type, including a grant, index, or table. The *name_clause* variable restricts the values returned. For example, to exclude from the export all tables whose names contain begin with "TEMP," you could specify the following:

```
EXCLUDE=TABLE:"LIKE 'TEMP%'"
```

When you enter this at the command line, you may need to use escape characters so the quotation marks and other special characters are properly passed to Oracle. Your **expdp** command will be in the following format:

```
expdp practice/practice EXCLUDE=TABLE:\"LIKE \'TEMP%\'\"
```

NOTE
This example shows part of the syntax, not the full syntax for the command.

If no *name_clause* value is provided, all objects of the specified type are excluded. To exclude all indexes, for example, you would specify the following:

```
expdp practice/practice EXCLUDE=INDEX
```

For a listing of the objects you can filter, query the DATABASE_EXPORT_OBJECTS, SCHEMA_EXPORT_OBJECTS, and TABLE_EXPORT_OBJECTS data dictionary views. If the *object_type* value is CONSTRAINT, NOT NULL constraints will not be excluded. Additionally, constraints needed for a table to be created successfully (such as primary key constraints for index-organized tables) cannot be excluded. If the *object_type* value is USER, the user definitions are excluded, but the objects within the user schemas will still be exported. Use the SCHEMA *object_type*, as shown in the previous example, to exclude a user and all of the user's objects. If the *object_type* value is GRANT, all object grants and system privilege grants are excluded.

A second option, INCLUDE, is also available. When you use INCLUDE, only those objects that pass the criteria are exported; all others are excluded. INCLUDE and EXCLUDE are mutually exclusive. The format for INCLUDE is

```
INCLUDE = object_type[:name_clause] [, ...]
```

NOTE
You cannot specify INCLUDE if you specify CONTENT=DATA_ONLY.

For example, to export two tables and all procedures, your parameter file may include these two lines:

```
INCLUDE=TABLE:"IN ('BOOKSHELF','BOOKSHELF_AUTHOR')"
INCLUDE=PROCEDURE
```

What rows will be exported for the objects that meet the EXCLUDE or INCLUDE criteria? By default, all rows are exported for each table. You can use the QUERY option to limit the rows returned. The format for the QUERY option is

```
QUERY = [schema.][table_name:] query_clause
```

If you do not specify values for the *schema* and *table_name* variables, the *query_clause* will be applied to all the exported tables. Because *query_clause* will usually include specific column names, you should be very careful when selecting the tables to include in the export.

You can specify a QUERY value for a single table, as shown in the following example:

```
QUERY=BOOKSHELF:'"WHERE Rating > 2"'
```

As a result, the dump file will only contain rows that meet the QUERY criteria as well as the INCLUDE or EXCLUDE criteria. You can also apply these restrictions during the subsequent Data Pump Import, as described in the next section of this chapter.

Data Pump Import Options

To import a dump file exported via Data Pump Export, use Data Pump Import. As with the export process, the import process runs as a server-based job you can manage as it executes. You can interact with Data Pump Import via the command-line interface, a parameter file, and an interactive interface. Table 12-3 lists the parameters for the command-line interface.

Parameter	Description
ATTACH	Attaches the client to a server session and places you in interactive mode.
CONTENT	Filters what is imported: ALL, DATA_ONLY, or METADATA_ONLY.
DIRECTORY	Specifies the location of the dump file set and the destination directory for the log and SQL files.
DUMPFILE	Specifies the names and, optionally, the directories for the dump file set.
ESTIMATE	Determines the method used to estimate the dump file size (BLOCKS or STATISTICS).
EXCLUDE	Excludes objects and data from being exported.
FLASHBACK_SCN	The SCN for the database to flash back to during the import.
FLASHBACK_TIME	The timestamp for the database to flash back to during the import.
FULL	A Y/N flag is used to specify that you want to import the full dump file.
HELP	Displays online help for the import.
INCLUDE	Specifies the criteria for objects to be imported.
JOB_NAME	Specifies a name for the job; the default is system-generated.
LOGFILE	The name and optional directory name for the import log.
NETWORK_LINK	Specifies the source database link for a Data Pump job importing a remote database.

TABLE 12-3.   *Data Pump Import Command-Line Parameters*

Parameter	Description
NOLOGFILE	A Y/N flag is used to suppress log file creation.
PARALLEL	Sets the number of workers for the Data Pump Import job.
PARFILE	Names the parameter file to use, if any.
QUERY	Filters rows from tables during the import.
REMAP_DATAFILE	Changes the name of the source datafile to the target datafile in **create library**, **create tablespace**, and **create directory** commands during the import.
REMAP_SCHEMA	Imports data exported from the source schema into the target schema.
REMAP_TABLESPACE	Imports data exported from the source tablespace into the target tablespace.
REUSE_DATAFILES	Specifies whether existing datafiles should be reused by **create tablespace** commands during Full mode imports.
SCHEMAS	Names the schemas to be exported for a Schema mode import.
SKIP_UNUSABLE_INDEXES	A Y/N flag. If set to Y, the import does not load data into tables whose indexes are set to the Index Unusable state.
SQLFILE	Names the file to which the DDL for the import will be written. The data and metadata will not be loaded into the target database.
STATUS	Displays a detailed status of the Data Pump job.
STREAMS_CONFIGURATION	A Y/N flag is used to specify whether Streams configuration information should be imported.
TABLE_EXISTS_ACTION	Instructs Import how to proceed if the table being imported already exists. Values include SKIP, APPEND, TRUNCATE, and REPLACE. The default is APPEND if CONTENT=DATA_ONLY; otherwise, the default is SKIP.
TABLES	Lists tables for a Table mode import.
TABLESPACES	Lists tablespaces for a Tablespace mode import.
TRANSFORM	Directs changes to the segment attributes or storage during import.
TRANSPORT_DATAFILES	Lists the datafiles to be imported during a Transportable Tablespace mode import.
TRANSPORT_FULL_CHECK	Specifies whether the tablespaces being imported should first be verified as a self-contained set.
TRANSPORT_TABLESPACES	Lists the tablespaces to be imported during a Transportable Tablespace mode import.
VERSION	Specifies the version of database objects to be created so the dump file set may be compatible with earlier releases of Oracle. The options are COMPATIBLE, LATEST, and database version numbers (not lower than 10.0.0). Only valid for NETWORK_LINK and SQLFILE.

TABLE 12-3. *Data Pump Import Command-Line Parameters* (continued)

NOTE
The directory for the dump file and log file must already exist; see the prior section on the create directory command.

As with Data Pump Export, five modes are supported in Data Pump Import: Full, Schema, Table, Tablespace, and Transportable Tablespace. If no mode is specified, Data Pump Import attempts to load the entire dump file.

Table 12-4 lists the parameters that are valid in the interactive mode of Data Pump Import.

Many of the Data Pump Import parameters are the same as those available for Data Pump Export. In the following sections, you will see how to start an import job, along with descriptions of the major options unique to Data Pump Import.

Starting a Data Pump Import Job

You can start a Data Pump Import job via the impdp executable provided with Oracle Database 10g. Use the command-line parameters to specify the import mode and the locations for all the files. You can store the parameter values in a parameter file and then reference the file via the PARFILE option.

In the first export example of this chapter, the parameter file named dp1.par contained the following entries:

```
DIRECTORY=dtpump
DUMPFILE=metadataonly.dmp
CONTENT=METADATA_ONLY
```

The import will create the PRACTICE schema's objects in a different schema. The REMAP_SCHEMA option allows you to import objects into a different schema than was used for the export.

Parameter	Description
CONTINUE_CLIENT	Exit the interactive mode and enter logging mode. The job will be restarted if idle.
EXIT_CLIENT	Exit the client session, but leave the server Data Pump Import job running.
HELP	Display online help for the import.
KILL_JOB	Kill the current job and detach related client sessions.
PARALLEL	Alter the number of workers for the Data Pump Import job.
START_JOB	Restart the attached job.
STATUS	Display detailed status of the Data Pump job.
STOP_JOB	Stop the job for later restart.

TABLE 12-4. *Interactive Parameters for Data Pump Import*

If you want to change the tablespace assignments for the objects at the same time, use the REMAP_ TABLESPACE option. The format for REMAP_SCHEMA is

```
REMAP_SCHEMA=source_schema:target_schema
```

Next, create a new user account to hold the objects:

```
create user Newpractice identified by newp;
grant CREATE SESSION to Newpractice;
grant CREATE SESSION to Newpractice;
grant CREATE TABLE to Newpractice;
grant CREATE INDEX to Newpractice;
```

You can now add the REMAP_SCHEMA line to the dp1.par parameter file:

```
DIRECTORY=dtpump
DUMPFILE=metadataonly.dmp
CONTENT=METADATA_ONLY
REMAP_SCHEMA=Practice:Newpractice
```

You can now start the import job. Because you are changing the owning schema for the data, you must have the IMP_FULL_DATABASE system privilege. Data Pump Import jobs are started via the impdp executable. The following example shows the creation of a Data Pump Import job using the dp1.par parameter file:

NOTE
All dump files must be specified at the time the job is started.

```
impdp system/passwd parfile=dp1.par
```

Oracle will then perform the import and display its progress. Because the NOLOGFILE option was not specified, the log file for the import will be placed in the same directory as the dump file and will be given the name import.log. You can verify the success of the import by logging into the Newpractice schema. The Newpractice schema should have a copy of all the valid objects that had previously been created in the Practice schema.

What if a table being imported already exists? In this example, with the CONTENT option set to METADATA_ONLY, the table would be skipped by default. If the CONTENT option was set to DATA_ONLY, the new data would be appended to the existing table data. To alter this behavior, use the TABLE_EXISTS_ACTION option. Valid values for TABLE_EXISTS_OPTION are SKIP, APPEND, TRUNCATE, and REPLACE.

Stopping and Restarting Running Jobs
After you have started a Data Pump Import job, you can close the client window you used to start the job. Because it is server based, the import will continue to run. You can then attach to the job, check its status, and alter it:

```
impdp system/passwd PARFILE=dp1.par
```

Press CTRL-C to leave the log display, and Data Pump will return you to the import prompt:

```
Import>
```

Exit to the operating system via the EXIT_CLIENT command:

```
Import> EXIT_CLIENT
```

You can then restart the client and attach to the currently running job under your schema:

```
impdp system/passwd attach
```

If you gave a name to your Data Pump Import job, specify the name as part of the ATTACH parameter call. When you attach to a running job, Data Pump will display the status of the job— its basic configuration parameters and its current status. You can then issue the CONTINUE_ CLIENT command to see the log entries as they are generated, or you can alter the running job:

```
Import> CONTINUE_CLIENT
```

You can stop a job via the STOP_JOB option:

```
Import> STOP_JOB
```

While the job is stopped, you can increase its parallelism via the PARALLEL option. You can then restart the job:

```
Import> START_JOB
```

EXCLUDE, INCLUDE, and QUERY

Data Pump Import, like Data Pump Export, allows you to restrict the data processed via the use of the EXCLUDE, INCLUDE, and QUERY options, as described earlier in this chapter. Because you can use these options on both the export and the import, you can be very flexible in your imports. For example, you may choose to export an entire table but only import part of it—the rows that match your QUERY criteria. You could choose to export an entire schema but when recovering the database via import include only the most necessary tables so the application downtime can be minimized. EXCLUDE, INCLUDE, and QUERY provide powerful capabilities to developers and database administrators during both export and import jobs.

Transforming Imported Objects

In addition to changing or selecting schemas, tablespaces, datafiles, and rows during the import, you can change the segment attributes and storage requirements during import via the TRANSFORM option. The format for TRANSFORM is

```
TRANSFORM = transform_name:value[:object_type]
```

The *transform_name* variable can have a value of SEGMENT_ATTRIBUTES or STORAGE. You can use the *value* variable to include or exclude segment attributes (physical attributes, storage attributes, tablespaces, and logging). The *object_type* variable is optional and, if specified, must be either TABLE or INDEX.

For example, object storage requirements may change during an export/import—you may be using the QUERY option to limit the rows imported or you may be importing only the metadata without the table data. To eliminate the exported storage clauses from the imported tables, add the following to the parameter file:

```
TRANSFORM=STORAGE:n:table
```

To eliminate the exported tablespace and storage clauses from all tables and indexes, use the following:

```
TRANSFORM=SEGMENT_ATTRIBUTES:n
```

When the objects are imported, they will be assigned to the user's default tablespace and will have used that tablespace's default storage parameters.

Generating SQL

Instead of importing the data and objects, you can generate the SQL for the objects (not the data) and store it in a file on your operating system. The file will be written to the directory and filename specified via the SQLFILE option. The SQLFILE option format is

```
SQLFILE=[directory_object:]file_name
```

NOTE
If you do not specify a value for the directory_object *variable, the file will be created in the dump file directory.*

The following listing shows a sample parameter file for an import using the SQLFILE option. Note that the CONTENT option is not specified. The output will be written to the DTPUMP directory.

```
DIRECTORY=dtpump
DUMPFILE=metadataonly.dmp
SQLFILE=sql.txt
```

You can then run the import to populate the sql.txt file:

```
impdp practice/practice parfile=dp1.par
```

In the sql.txt file the import creates, you will see entries for each of the object types within the schema. The format for the output file will be similar to the following listing, although the object IDs and SCNs will be specific to your environment. For brevity, not all entries in the file are shown here.

```
-- CONNECT PRACTICE
-- new object type path is: SCHEMA_EXPORT/
```

```
SE_PRE_SCHEMA_PROCOBJACT/PROCACT_SCHEMA

BEGIN
sys.dbms_logrep_imp.instantiate_schema(schema_name=>'PRACTICE',
export_db_name=>'ORCL', inst_scn=>'3377908');
COMMIT;
END;
/


-- new object type path is: SCHEMA_EXPORT/TABLE/TABLE
 CREATE TABLE "PRACTICE"."STOCK_TRX"
    (  "ACCOUNT" NUMBER(10,0),
        "SYMBOL" VARCHAR2(20),
        "PRICE" NUMBER(6,2),
        "QUANTITY" NUMBER(6,0),
        "TRX_FLAG" VARCHAR2(1)
   ) PCTFREE 10 PCTUSED 40 INITRANS 1 MAXTRANS 255 NOCOMPRESS LOGGING
STORAGE(INITIAL 65536 NEXT 1048576 MINEXTENTS 1 MAXEXTENTS 2147483645
PCTINCREASE 0 FREELISTS 1 FREELIST GROUPS 1 BUFFER_POOL DEFAULT)
   TABLESPACE "USERS" ;

CREATE TABLE "PRACTICE"."STOCK_ACCOUNT"
    (  "ACCOUNT" NUMBER(10,0),
        "ACCOUNTLONGNAME" VARCHAR2(50)
   ) PCTFREE 10 PCTUSED 40 INITRANS 1 MAXTRANS 255 NOCOMPRESS LOGGING
STORAGE(INITIAL 65536 NEXT 1048576 MINEXTENTS 1 MAXEXTENTS 2147483645
PCTINCREASE 0 FREELISTS 1 FREELIST GROUPS 1 BUFFER_POOL DEFAULT)
   TABLESPACE "USERS" ;

-- new object type path is: SCHEMA_EXPORT/TABLE/GRANT/OBJECT_GRANT
GRANT SELECT ON "PRACTICE"."STOCK_TRX" TO "ADAMS";
GRANT SELECT ON "PRACTICE"."STOCK_TRX" TO "BURLINGTON";
GRANT SELECT ON "PRACTICE"."STOCK_ACCOUNT" TO "ADAMS";
GRANT SELECT ON "PRACTICE"."STOCK_ACCOUNT" TO "BURLINGTON";
GRANT INSERT ON "PRACTICE"."STOCK_TRX" TO "ADAMS";
```

The SQLFILE output is a plain-text file, so you can edit the file, use it within SQL*Plus, or keep it as documentation of your application's database structures.

Comparing Data Pump Export/Import to Export/Import

The original Export and Import utilities are still available via the exp and imp executables. As shown in this chapter, there are many ways in which Data Pump Export and Import offer superior capabilities over the original Export and Import utilities. Data Pump's server-based architecture leads to performance gains and improved manageability. However, Data Pump does not support the incremental commit capability offered by the COMMIT and BUFFER parameters in the original Import. Also, Data Pump will not automatically merge multiple extents into a single extent during the Data Pump Export/Import process; the original Export/Import offer this functionality via the COMPRESS parameter. In Data Pump, you can use the TRANSFORM option to suppress the storage attributes during the import—an option that many users of the original Export/Import may prefer over the COMPRESS functionality.

If you are importing data via Data Pump into an existing table using either the APPEND or TRUNCATE settings of the TABLE_EXISTS_ACTION option and a row violates an active constraint, the load is discontinued and no data is loaded. In the original Import, the load would have continued.

Implementing Offline Backups

An offline backup is a physical backup of the database files made after the database has been shut down via either a **shutdown normal**, a **shutdown immediate**, or a **shutdown transactional** command. While the database is shut down, each of the files that is actively used by the database is backed up. These files provide a complete image of the database as it existed at the moment it was shut down.

NOTE
You should not rely on an offline backup performed following a **shutdown abort**, *because it may be inconsistent. If you must perform a* **shutdown abort**, *you should restart the database and perform a normal* **shutdown** *or a* **shutdown immediate** *or a* **shutdown transactional** *prior to beginning your offline backup.*

The following files should be backed up during cold backups:

- All datafiles
- All controlfiles
- All online redo logs

You may optionally choose to back up the database initialization parameter file and the password file, particularly if the backup will serve as the basis for a disaster recovery process.

To simplify the backup process, use a consistent directory structure for your datafiles. All your datafiles should be located in directories at the same level on each device. The following listing shows a sample directory tree for a data disk named /db01:

```
/db01
        /oracle
                /CASE
                        control1.dbf
                        sys01.dbf
                        tools.dbf
                /CC1
                        control1.dbf
                        sys01.dbf
                        tools.dbf
                /DEMO
                        control1.dbf
                        sys01.dbf
```

In the sample directory tree, all database files are stored in an instance-specific subdirectory under an /oracle directory for the device. Directories such as these should contain all the datafiles, redo log files, and controlfiles for a database.

If you use the directory structure in the prior example, your backup commands are greatly simplified. The following listing shows a sample Unix **tar** command, which is used here to back up files to a tape drive called /dev/rmt/0hc. Because the directory structure is consistent and the drives are named /db01 through /db09, the following command will back up all the CC1 database's datafiles, redo log files, and controlfiles:

```
> tar -cvf /dev/rmt/0hc /db0[1-9]/oracle/CC1
```

NOTE
Oracle's RMAN utility simplifies the backup process. See Chapter 13 for details on RMAN. The examples in this chapter feature user-managed backup procedures.

The **-cvf** flag creates a new **tar** saveset. In many production systems, the database backup writes files to a separate file system area, and the database is then restarted. The disk-to-disk backup method is significantly faster than the disk-to-tape method, allowing the database to be shut down for a shorter period of time. After the database has been restarted, the backup copies of the files may be written to tape without impacting the availability of the database.

NOTE
If you use disk-to-disk backups as part of your backup strategy, the backup disks must be separate from the production disks. Otherwise, a failure of your production database disks may also affect your most recent backups.

Because offline backups involve changes to the database's availability, they are usually scheduled to occur at night.

During a recovery, an offline backup can restore the database to the point in time at which the database was shut down. Offline backups commonly play a part in disaster recovery planning, because they are self-contained and may be simpler to restore on a disaster recovery server than other types of backups. If the database is running in ARCHIVELOG mode, you can apply archived redo logs to the restored offline backup.

Implementing Online Backups

Consistent offline backups can only be performed while the database is shut down. However, you can perform physical file backups of a database while the database is open—provided the database is running in ARCHIVELOG mode and the backup is performed correctly. These backups are referred to as *online backups.*

Oracle writes to the online redo log files in a cyclical fashion: After filling the first log file, it begins writing to the second, until that one fills, and it then begins writing to the third. Once the last online redo log file is filled, the LGWR (Log Writer) background process begins to overwrite the contents of the first redo log file.

When Oracle is run in ARCHIVELOG mode, the ARCH background process makes a copy of each redo log file after the LGWR process finishes writing to it. These archived redo log files are usually written to a disk device. They may instead be written directly to a tape device, but this tends to be very operator intensive.

Getting Started

To make use of the ARCHIVELOG capability, you must first place the database in ARCHIVELOG mode. The following listing shows the steps needed to place a database in ARCHIVELOG mode:

```
SQL> connect internal as sysdba
SQL> startup mount cc1;
SQL> alter database archivelog;
SQL> alter database open;
```

NOTE
To see the currently active online redo log and its sequence number, query the V$LOG dynamic view.

To change a database back to NOARCHIVELOG mode, use the following set of commands after shutting down the database:

```
SQL> connect / as sysdba
SQL> startup mount cc1;
SQL> alter database noarchivelog;
SQL> alter database open;
```

A database that has been placed in ARCHIVELOG mode will remain in that mode until it is placed in NOARCHIVELOG mode.

The location of the archived redo log files is determined by the settings in the database's parameter file. The parameters to note include the following (with sample values):

```
log_archive_dest_1          = 'LOCATION="/db01/oracle/arch/CC1/arch"',
log_archive_dest_state_1    = ENABLE
log_archive_start           = TRUE
```

In this example, the archived redo log files are being written to the directory /db01/oracle/arch/CC1/arch.

Each of the archived redo log files contains the data from a single online redo log. They are numbered sequentially, in the order in which they were created. The size of the archived redo log files varies, but it does not exceed the size of the online redo log files.

If the destination directory of the archived redo log files runs out of space, ARCH will stop processing the online redo log data and the database will stop itself. This situation can be resolved by adding more space to the archived redo log file destination disk or by backing up the archived redo log files and then removing them from this directory.

NOTE
Never delete archived redo log files until you have backed them up and verified that you can restore them successfully.

In a database that is currently running, you can query the parameter settings from the V$PARAMETER dynamic performance view:

```
select Name,
       Value
  from V$PARAMETER
 where Name like 'log_archive%';
```

Although the LOG_ARCHIVE_START parameter may be set to TRUE, the database will *not* be in ARCHIVELOG mode unless you have executed the **alter database archivelog** command shown earlier in this section. Once the database is in ARCHIVELOG mode, it will remain in that mode through subsequent database shutdowns and startups until you explicitly place it in NOARCHIVELOG mode via the **alter database noarchivelog** command.

NOTE
To see if the database is in ARCHIVELOG mode from within Oracle Enterprise Manager (OEM), view the General portion of the Instance Manager screen.

Automating Multiplexing of Archived Redo Log Files

You can instruct the database to write to multiple separate archived redo log file destination areas simultaneously. Writing to separate destination areas allows you to recover in the event that one of those destination disks fails. The archiving process must be able to write to at least one location in order for the database to continue functioning; you can specify the number of writes that must succeed.

NOTE
Oracle writes to multiple archived redo log file destination areas simultaneously, not consecutively.

You can use the LOG_ARCHIVE_DEST_*n* parameter to specify up to 10 locations for your archived redo log files (LOG_ARCHIVE_DEST_1, LOG_ARCHIVE_DEST_2, and so on). The ARCH process will write files to all the specified locations simultaneously. Each of the archive destinations has a corresponding "state" set via the LOG_ARCHIVE_DEST_STATE_*n* parameter. An archive destination's state may be either ENABLED, in which case files are written there, or DEFER, in which case the destination is not presently active. You should create a LOG_ARCHIVE_DEST_STATE_*n* entry (such as LOG_ARCHIVE_DEST_STATE_1, LOG_ARCHIVE_DEST_STATE_2, and so on) for each LOG_ARCHIVE_DEST_*n* entry in your init.ora file.

Performing Online Database Backups

Once a database is running in ARCHIVELOG mode, you can back it up while it is open and available to users. This capability allows round-the-clock database availability to be achieved while still guaranteeing the recoverability of the database.

Although online backups can be performed during normal working hours, they should be scheduled for the times of the least user activity for several reasons. First, the online backups will use operating system commands to back up the physical files, and these commands will use the available I/O resources in the system (impacting the system performance for interactive users). Second, while the tablespaces are being backed up, the manner in which transactions are written to the archived redo log files changes. When you put a tablespace in "online backup" mode, the DBWR process writes all the blocks in the buffer cache that belong to any file that is part of the tablespace back to disk. When the blocks are read back into memory and then changed, they will be copied to the log buffer the first time that a change is made to them. As long as they stay in the buffer cache, they will not be recopied to the online redo log file. This will use a great deal more space in the archived redo log file destination directory.

NOTE
You can create a command file to perform your online backups, but using RMAN is preferred for several reasons: RMAN maintains a catalog of your backups, allows you to manage your backup repository, and allows you to perform incremental backups of the database.

If you wish to create your own command file to perform online backups, the command file should follow these steps:

1. Set the database into backup state (prior to Oracle 10g, this can be done on a tablespace-by-tablespace basis).

2. Back up the datafiles.

3. Set the database back to its normal state.

4. Back up the archived redo log files. If necessary, compress or delete the backed-up archived redo log files to free space on disk.

5. Back up the controlfile.

NOTE
See Chapter 13 for details on RMAN's automation of this process.

Ideally, you should maintain enough free space in your archive destination area to store enough compressed archived redo logs to enable you to perform a recovery without needing to recover archived redo log files from tape.

Integration of Backup Procedures

Because there are multiple methods for backing up the Oracle database, there is no need to have a single point of failure in your backup strategy. Depending on your database's characteristics, one method should be chosen, and at least one of the remaining methods should be used as a backup to your primary backup method.

NOTE
When considering physical backups, you should also evaluate the use of RMAN to perform incremental physical backups.

In the following sections, you will see how to choose the primary backup method for your database, how to integrate logical and physical backups, and how to integrate database backups with file system backups.

For backup strategies specific to very large databases, see Chapter 17. For details on RMAN, see Chapter 13.

Integration of Logical and Physical Backups

Which backup method is appropriate to use as the primary backup method for your database? When deciding, you should take into account the characteristics of each method:

Method	Type	Recovery Characteristics
Data Pump Export	Logical	Can recover any database object to its status as of the moment it was exported.
Offline backups	Physical	Can recover the database to its status as of the moment it was shut down; if the database is run in ARCHIVELOG mode, you can recover the database to its status at any point in time.
Online backups	Physical	Can recover the database to its status at any point in time.

Offline backups are the least flexible method of backing up the database if the database is running in NOARCHIVELOG mode. Offline backups are a point-in-time snapshot of the database. Also, because they are a physical backup, DBAs cannot selectively recover logical objects (such as tables) from them. Although there are times when they are appropriate (such as for disaster recovery), offline backups should normally be used as a fallback position in the event that the primary backup method fails. If you are running the database in ARCHIVELOG mode, you can use the offline backups as the basis for a media recovery, but an online backup would normally be more appropriate for that situation.

Of the two remaining methods, which one is more appropriate? For production environments, the answer is almost always online backups. Online backups, with the database running in ARCHIVELOG mode, allow you to recover the database to the point in time immediately preceding a system fault or a user error. Using a Data Pump Export–based strategy would limit you to only being able to go back to the data as it existed the last time the data was exported.

Consider the size of the database and what objects you will likely be recovering. Given a standard recovery scenario—such as the loss of a disk—how long will it take for the data to be recovered? If a file is lost, the quickest way to recover it is usually via a physical backup, which again favors online backups over exports.

If the database is small, transaction volume is very low, and availability is not a concern, then offline backups may serve your needs. If you are only concerned about one or two tables, you could use Data Pump Export to selectively back them up. However, if the database is large, the recovery time needed for Data Pump Export/Import may be prohibitive. For large, low-transaction environments, offline backups may be appropriate.

Regardless of your choice for primary backup method, the final implementation should include a physical backup and some sort of logical backup, either via Data Pump Export or via replication. This redundancy is necessary because these methods validate different aspects of the database:

Data Pump Export validates that the data is logically sound, and physical backups that it is physically sound. A good database backup strategy integrates logical and physical backups. The frequency and type of backup performed will vary based on the database's usage characteristics.

Other database activities may call for ad hoc backups. Ad hoc backups may include offline backups before performing database upgrades and exports during application migration between databases.

Integration of Database and Operating System Backups

As described in this chapter, the DBA's backup activities involve a number of tasks normally assigned to a systems management group: monitoring disk usage, maintaining tapes, and so on. Rather than duplicate these efforts, it is best to integrate them; focus on a process-based alignment of your organization. The database backup strategy should be modified so that the systems management personnel's file system backups will take care of all tape handling, allowing you to centralize the production control processes in your environment.

Centralization of production control processes is usually accomplished by dedicating disk drives as destination locations for physical file backups. Instead of files being backed up to tape drives, the backups will instead be written to other disks on the same server. Those disks should be targeted for backups by the systems management personnel's regular file system backups. The DBA does not have to run a separate tape backup job. However, the DBA does need to verify that the systems management team's backup procedures executed correctly and completed successfully.

If your database environment includes files outside the database—such as datafiles for external tables or files accessed by BFILE datatypes—then you must determine how you are going to back those files up in a way that will provide consistent data in the event of a recovery. The backups of these flat files should be coordinated with your database backups and should also be integrated into any disaster recovery planning.

CHAPTER
13

Using Recovery
Manager (RMAN)

I n Chapter 12, we discussed a number of different ways in which we can back up our data and protect the database from accidental, inadvertent, or deliberate corruption. Physical backups of the database ensure that no committed transaction is lost, and we can restore the database from any previous backup to the current point in time or any point in between; logical backups allow the DBA or a user to capture the contents of individual database objects at a particular point in time, providing an alternative recovery option when a complete database-restoration operation would have too big an impact on the rest of the database.

Oracle's Recovery Manager (RMAN) takes backup and recovery to a new level of protection and ease of use. Since RMAN's appearance in Oracle version 8, there have been a number of major improvements and enhancements that can make RMAN a "one-stop shopping" solution for nearly every database environment. In addition to the RMAN command line interface improvements in Oracle 10g, all the RMAN functionality has been included in the web-based Oracle Enterprise Manager (OEM) interface as well, allowing a DBA to monitor and perform backup operations when only a web browser connection is available.

In this chapter, we'll use a number of examples of RMAN operations, both using command line syntax and the OEM web interface. The examples will run the gamut from RMAN environment setup to backup, and the recovery and validation of the backup itself. We'll go into some detail about how RMAN manages the metadata associated with the database and its backups. Finally, we'll cover a number of miscellaneous topics, such as using RMAN to catalog backups made outside of the RMAN environment.

Due to the wide variety of tape backup management systems available, discussing any particular hardware configuration would be beyond the scope of this book. Instead, the focus in this chapter will be on using the Flash Recovery Area, a dedicated area allocated on disk to store disk-based copies of all types of objects that RMAN can back up. The Flash Recovery Area is new to Oracle 10g.

For all the examples in this chapter, we will use a recovery catalog with RMAN. Although most of the functionality of RMAN is available by only using the control file of the target database, benefits such as being able to store RMAN scripts and additional recovery capabilities far outweigh the relatively low cost of maintaining an RMAN user account and repository in a different database.

RMAN Features and Components

RMAN is more than just a client-side executable that can be used with a web interface. It comprises a number of other components, including the database to be backed up (the target database), an optional recovery catalog, an optional Flash Recovery Area, and media management software to support tape backup systems. We will review each of these briefly in this section.

Many features of RMAN do not have equivalents in the backup methods presented in Chapter 12. We'll contrast the advantages and disadvantages of using RMAN versus the more traditional methods of backups.

RMAN Components

The first, and minimal, component in the RMAN environment is the RMAN executable. It is available along with the other Oracle utilities in the directory $ORACLE_HOME/bin, and it's installed by default with both the Standard and Enterprise Editions of Oracle 10g. From a command line prompt, you can invoke RMAN with or without command line arguments; in the following example, we're starting up RMAN using operating system authentication without connecting to a recovery catalog:

```
oltp [oracle]$ rman target /
RMAN>
```

The command line arguments are optional; we can specify our target database and a recovery catalog from the **RMAN>** prompt also. In Figure 13-1, you can see how to access RMAN features from Oracle Enterprise Manager.

RMAN would not be of much use unless we have a database to back up. One or more target databases can be cataloged in the recovery catalog; in addition, the control file of the database being backed up contains information about backups performed by RMAN. From within the RMAN client, you can also issue SQL commands for those operations you cannot perform with native RMAN commands.

The RMAN recovery catalog, whether using the target database control file or a dedicated repository in a separate database, contains the location of recovery data, its own configuration settings, and the target database schema. At a minimum, the target database control file contains

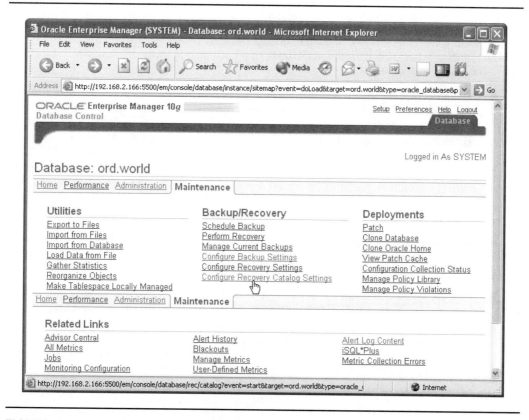

FIGURE 13-1.   *Accessing RMAN functionality from OEM*

this data; to be able to store scripts and to maintain a copy of the target database control file, a recovery catalog is highly recommended. In this chapter, all examples will use a recovery catalog.

As of Oracle 10g, the *Flash Recovery Area* simplifies disk-based backup and recovery by defining a location on disk to hold all RMAN backups. Along with the location, the DBA can also specify an upper limit to the amount of disk space used in the Flash Recovery Area. Once a retention policy is defined within RMAN, RMAN will automatically manage the backup files by deleting obsolete backups from both disk and tape. The initialization parameters related to the Flash Recovery Area are covered in the next section.

To access all non-disk-based media, such as tape and DVD-ROM, RMAN utilizes third-party media management software to move backup files to and from these offline and near-line devices, automatically requesting the mount and dismount of the appropriate media to support backup and restore operations. Most major media management software and hardware vendors have device drivers that directly support RMAN.

RMAN vs. Traditional Backup Methods

There are very few reasons not to use RMAN as your main tool for managing backups. Here are some of the major features of RMAN that are either not available with traditional backup methods or have significant restrictions using traditional backup methods:

- **Skip unused blocks**   Blocks that have never been written to, such as blocks above the high water mark (HWM) in a table, are not backed up by RMAN when the backup is an RMAN backupset. Traditional backup methods have no way to know which blocks have been used.

- **Backup compression**   In addition to skipping blocks that have never been used, RMAN can also use an Oracle-specific binary compression mode to save space on the backup device. Although operating-system specific compression techniques are available with traditional backup methods, the compression algorithm used by RMAN is customized to maximize the compression for the typical kinds of data found in Oracle data blocks. Although there is a slight increase in CPU time during an RMAN compressed backup or recovery operation, the amount of media used for backup may be significantly reduced, as well as network bandwidth if the backup is performed over the network. Multiple CPUs can be configured for an RMAN backup to help alleviate the compression overhead.

- **Open database backups**   Tablespace backups can be performed in RMAN without using the **begin/end backup** clause with **alter tablespace**. Whether using RMAN or a traditional backup method, however, the database must be in ARCHIVELOG mode.

- **True incremental backups**   For any RMAN incremental backup, unchanged blocks since the last backup will not be written to the backup file. This saves a significant amount of disk space, I/O time, and CPU time. For restore and recovery operations, RMAN supports *incrementally updated backups*. Data blocks from an incremental backup are applied to a previous backup to potentially reduce the amount of time and number of files that need to be accessed to perform a recovery operation. We will cover an example of an incrementally updated backup later in this chapter.

- **Block-level recovery**   To potentially avoid downtime during a recovery operation, RMAN supports *block-level recovery* for recovery operations that only need to restore or repair a small number of blocks identified as being corrupt during the backup operation. The rest of the tablespace and the objects within the tablespace can remain online while RMAN repairs the damaged blocks. The rows of a table not being repaired by RMAN are even available to applications and users.

■ **Multiple I/O channels**   During a backup or recovery operation, RMAN can utilize many I/O channels, via separate operating system processes, to perform concurrent I/O. Traditional backup methods, such as a Unix **cp** command or an Oracle **export**, are typically single-threaded operations.

■ **Platform independence**   Backups written with RMAN commands will be syntactically identical regardless of the hardware or software platform used, with the only difference being the media management channel configuration. On the other hand, a Unix script with lots of **cp** commands will not run very well if the backup script is migrated to a Windows platform!

■ **Tape manager support**   All major enterprise backup systems are supported within RMAN by a third-party media management driver provided by a tape backup vendor.

■ **Cataloging**   A record of all RMAN backups is recorded in the target database control file, and optionally in a recovery catalog stored in a different database. This makes restore and recovery operations relatively simple compared to manually tracking operating system–level backups using "copy" commands.

■ **Scripting capabilities**   RMAN scripts can be saved in a recovery catalog for retrieval during a backup session. The tight integration of the scripting language, the ease of maintaining scripts in RMAN, and the Oracle scheduling facility make it a better choice than storing traditional operating system scripts in an operating system directory with the operating system's native scheduling mechanisms.

In a few limited cases, a traditional backup method may have an advantage over RMAN; for example, RMAN does not support the backup of password files and other non-database files such as tnsnames.ora, listener.ora, and sqlnet.ora. However, these files are relatively static in nature, and they can easily be backed up and restored using a traditional backup method such as the Unix **cp** command.

Backup Types

RMAN supports a number of different backup methods, depending on your availability needs, the desired size of your recovery window, and the amount of downtime you can endure while the database or a part of the database is involved in a recovery operation.

Consistent and Inconsistent Backups

A physical backup can be classified by being a *consistent* or an *inconsistent* backup. In a consistent backup, all datafiles have the same SCN; in other words, all changes in the redo logs have been applied to the datafiles. Because an open database with no uncommitted transactions may have some dirty blocks in the buffer cache, it is rare that an open database backup can be considered consistent. As a result, consistent backups are taken when the database is shut down normally or in a MOUNT state.

In contrast, an inconsistent backup is performed while the database is open and users are accessing the database. Because the SCNs of the datafiles typically do not match when an inconsistent backup is taking place, a recovery operation performed using an inconsistent backup must rely on both archived and online redo log files to bring the database into a consistent state before it is opened. As a result, a database must be in ARCHIVELOG mode to use an inconsistent backup method.

Full and Incremental Backups

Full backups include all blocks of every datafile within a tablespace or a database; it is essentially a bit-for-bit copy of one or more datafiles in the database. Either RMAN or an operating system command can be used to perform a full backup, although backups performed outside of RMAN must be cataloged with RMAN before they can be used in an RMAN recovery operation.

In Oracle 10g, incremental backups can be level 0 or level 1. A level 0 backup is a full backup of all blocks in the database that can be used in conjunction with differential, incremental, or cumulative incremental level 1 backups in a database recovery operation. A distinct advantage to using an incremental backup in a recovery strategy is that archived and online redo log files may not be necessary to restore a database or tablespace to a consistent state; the incremental backups may have some or all of the blocks needed. An example of using level 0 and level 1 incremental backups is presented later in this chapter. Incremental backups can only be performed within RMAN.

Image Copies

Image copies are full backups created by operating system commands or RMAN **backup as copy** commands. Although a full backup created with a Unix **cp** command can be later registered in the RMAN catalog as a database backup, doing the same image copy backup in RMAN has the advantage of checking for corrupt blocks as they are being read by RMAN and recording the information about the bad blocks in the data dictionary. Image copies are the default backup file format in RMAN.

This is a great feature of Oracle 10g for the following reason: If you add another datafile to a tablespace, you need to also remember to add the new datafile to your Unix script **cp** command. By creating image copies using RMAN, all datafiles will automatically be included in the backup. Forgetting to add the new datafile to a Unix script will make a recovery situation extremely inconvenient at best and a disaster at worst.

Backupsets and Backup Pieces

In contrast to image copies, which can be created in most any backup environment, backupsets can be created and restored only with RMAN. A *backupset* is an RMAN backup of part or all of a database, consisting of one or more *backup pieces*. Each backup piece belongs to only one backupset, and can contain backups of one or many datafiles in the database. All backupsets and pieces are recorded in the RMAN repository, the same as any other RMAN-initiated backup.

Compressed Backups

For any Oracle10g RMAN backup creating a backupset, compression is available to reduce the amount of disk space or tape needed to store the backup. Compressed backups are only usable by RMAN, and they need no special processing when used in a recovery operation; RMAN automatically decompresses the backup. Creating compressed backups is as easy as specifying **as compressed backupset** in the RMAN **backup** command.

Overview of RMAN Commands and Options

In the next few sections, we'll review the basic set of commands you'll use on a regular basis. We'll show you how to make your job even easier by persisting some of the settings in an RMAN session; in addition, we'll set up the retention policy and the repository we'll use to store RMAN metadata.

At the end of this section, we'll review the initialization parameters related to RMAN backups and the Flash Recovery Area.

Frequently Used Commands

Table 13-1 provides a list of the most common RMAN commands you'll use on a regular basis, along with some common options and caveats for each command. For the complete list of all RMAN commands and their syntax, see the *Oracle Database Recovery Manager Reference, 10g Release 1.*

RMAN Command	Description
@	Runs an RMAN command script at the pathname specified after the @. If no path is specified, the path is assumed to be the directory from which RMAN was invoked.
BACKUP	Performs an RMAN backup, with or without archived redo logs. Backs up datafiles, datafile copies, or performs an incremental level 0 or level 1 backup. Backs up an entire database, or a single tablespace or datafile. Validates the blocks to be backed up with the VALIDATE clause.
CHANGE	Changes the status of a backup in the RMAN repository. Useful for explicitly excluding a backup from a restore or recovery operation, or to notify RMAN that a backup file was inadvertently or deliberately removed by an operating system command outside of RMAN.
CONFIGURE	Configures the persistent parameters for RMAN. The parameters configured are available during every subsequent RMAN session unless they are explicitly cleared or modified.
CREATE CATALOG	Creates the repository catalog containing RMAN metadata for one or more target databases. It is strongly recommended that this catalog not be stored in one of the target databases.
CROSSCHECK	Checks the record of backups in the RMAN repository against the actual files on disk or tape. Objects are flagged as EXPIRED, AVAILABLE, UNAVAILABLE, or OBSOLETE. If the object is not available to RMAN, it is marked UNAVAILABLE.

TABLE 13-1. *Common RMAN Commands*

RMAN Command	Description
DELETE	Deletes backup files or copies and marks them as DELETED in the target database control file. If a repository is used, the record of the backup file is removed.
FLASHBACK	Performs a Flashback Database operation, new to Oracle 10g. The database is restored to a point in the past by SCN or log sequence number using flashback logs to undo changes before the SCN or log sequence number, then archived redo logs are applied to bring the database forward to a consistent state.
LIST	Displays information about backupsets and image copies recorded in the target database control file or repository. See REPORT for identifying complex relationships between backupsets.
RECOVER	Performs a complete or incomplete recovery on a datafile, a tablespace, or the entire database. Can also apply incremental backups to a datafile image copy to roll it forward in time.
REGISTER DATABASE	Registers a target database in the RMAN repository.
REPORT	Performs a detailed analysis of the RMAN repository. For example, this command can identify which files need a backup to meet the retention policy or which backup files can be deleted.
RESTORE	Restores files from image copies or backupsets to disk, typically after a media failure. Can be used to validate a restore operation without actually performing the restore by specifying the PREVIEW option.
RUN	Runs a sequence of RMAN statements as a group between { and }. Allows you to override default RMAN parameters for the duration of the execution of the group.
SET	Sets RMAN configuration settings for the duration of the RMAN session, such as allocated disk or tape channels. Persistent settings are assigned with CONFIGURE.
SHOW	Shows all or individual RMAN configured settings.
SHUTDOWN	Shuts down the target database from within RMAN. Identical to the SHUTDOWN command within SQL*Plus.
STARTUP	Starts up the target database. This command has the same options and function as the SQL*Plus STARTUP command.
SQL	Runs SQL commands that cannot be accomplished directly or indirectly using standard RMAN commands; for example, it can run **sql 'alter tablespace users offline immediate';** before restoring and recovering the USERS tablespace.

TABLE 13-1. *Common RMAN Commands* (continued)

If backups use a Flash Recovery Area, you can back up the database without any other explicit RMAN configuration by running the following command:

```
RMAN> backup database;
```

Setting Up a Repository

Whether you use a repository for the metadata from one database or a hundred, the repository setup is very straightforward and needs to be done only once. The examples that follow assume that we have a default installation of an Oracle 10*g* database; the repository database itself can be used for other applications if there is no significant performance degradation when RMAN needs to update metadata in the repository.

CAUTION
Using an RMAN target database for the repository is strongly discouraged. Loss of the target database prevents any chance of a successful recovery of the database using RMAN because the repository metadata is lost along with the target database.

The following sequence of commands creates a tablespace and a user to maintain the metadata in the repository database. In this and all subsequent examples, a database with a SID of **rmanrep** is used for all repository operations.

```
SQL> create tablespace rman
  2      datafile '/u01/app/oracle/oradata/rmanrep/rman01.dbf'
  3      size 10m autoextend on next 5m;
Tablespace created.

SQL> create user rman identified by rman001
  2      default tablespace rman;
User created.

SQL> grant resource, connect, recovery_catalog_owner to rman;
Grant succeeded.
```

Now that the RMAN user account exists in the repository database, we can start RMAN, connect to the catalog, and initialize the repository with the **create catalog** command:

```
[oracle@oltp oracle]$ rman catalog rman/rman001@rmanrep

Recovery Manager: Release 10.1.0.2.0 - Production

Copyright (c) 1995, 2004, Oracle.  All rights reserved.

connected to recovery catalog database
recovery catalog is not installed
```

```
RMAN> create catalog;
recovery catalog created
RMAN>
```

From this point on, using a repository is as easy as specifying the repository username and password on the RMAN command line with the **catalog** parameter or using the **connect catalog** command in an RMAN session. Within Oracle Enterprise Manager, the repository credentials can be persisted as demonstrated in Figure 13-2.

In future OEM sessions, any RMAN backup or recovery operations will automatically use the recovery catalog.

Registering a Database

For each database for which RMAN will perform a backup or recovery, we must *register* the database in the RMAN repository; this operation records information such as the target database

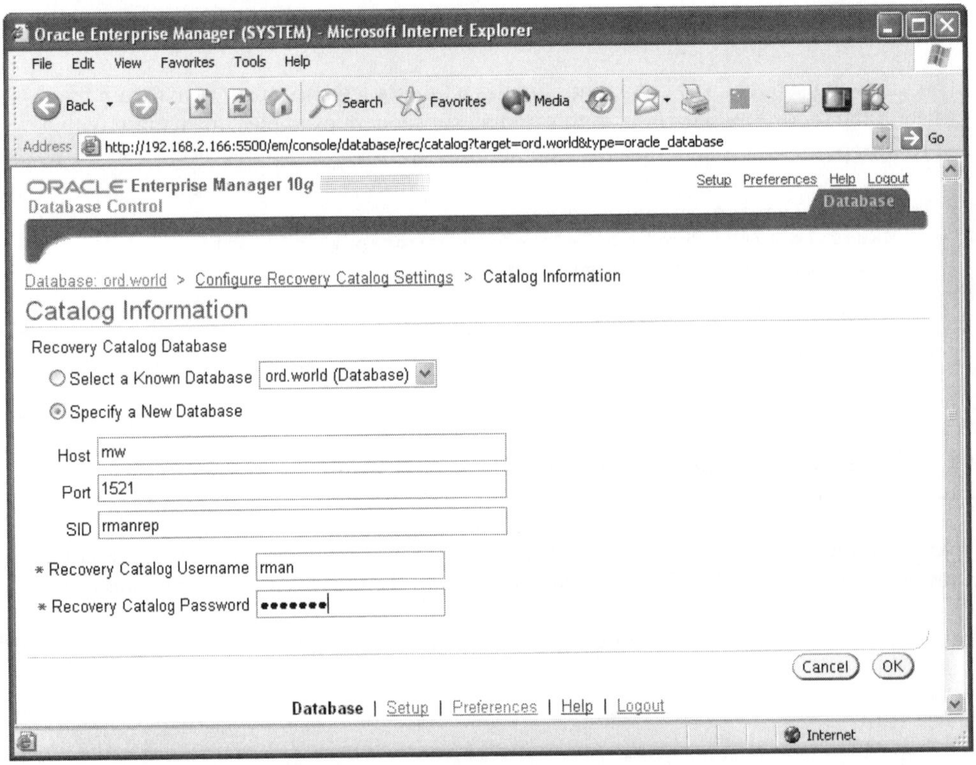

FIGURE 13-2. *Persisting RMAN repository credentials*

schema and the unique database ID (DBID) of the target database. The target database need only be registered once; subsequent RMAN sessions that connect to the target database will automatically reference the correct metadata in the repository.

```
[oracle@oltp oracle]$ rman target / catalog rman@rmanrep

Recovery Manager: Release 10.1.0.2.0 - Production

Copyright (c) 1995, 2004, Oracle.  All rights reserved.

connected to target database: ORD (DBID=1387044942)
recovery catalog database Password: xxxxxxxxx
connected to recovery catalog database

RMAN> register database;

database registered in recovery catalog
starting full resync of recovery catalog
full resync complete

RMAN>
```

In the preceding example, we connect to the target database using operating system authentication and to the repository with password authentication. All databases registered with the repository must have unique DBIDs; trying to register the database again yields the following error message:

```
RMAN> register database;

RMAN-00571: ===========================================================
RMAN-00569: =============== ERROR MESSAGE STACK FOLLOWS ===============
RMAN-00571: ===========================================================
RMAN-03009: failure of register command on default channel
            at 03/15/2004 20:58:56
RMAN-20002: target database already registered in recovery catalog

RMAN>
```

Registering a database using OEM is straightforward, as demonstrated in Figure 13-3.

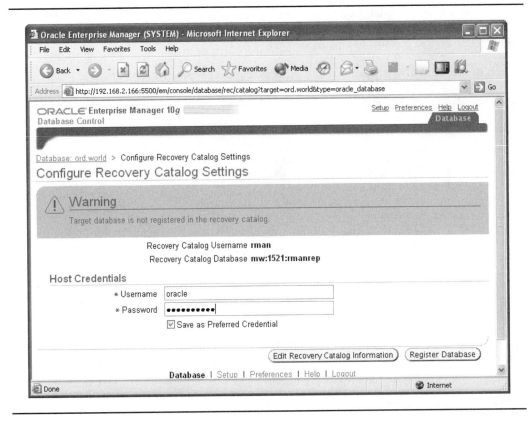

FIGURE 13-3. *Registering a database using OEM*

Persisting RMAN Settings

To make the DBA's job easier, a number of RMAN settings can be *persisted*. In other words, these settings will stay in effect between RMAN sessions. In the example that follows, we use the **show** command to display the default RMAN settings:

```
RMAN> show all;

RMAN configuration parameters are:
CONFIGURE RETENTION POLICY TO REDUNDANCY 1; # default
CONFIGURE BACKUP OPTIMIZATION OFF; # default
CONFIGURE DEFAULT DEVICE TYPE TO DISK; # default
CONFIGURE CONTROLFILE AUTOBACKUP OFF; # default
CONFIGURE CONTROLFILE AUTOBACKUP FORMAT FOR DEVICE TYPE DISK TO '%F';
        # default
CONFIGURE DEVICE TYPE DISK PARALLELISM 1 BACKUP TYPE TO BACKUPSET; # default
```

```
CONFIGURE DATAFILE BACKUP COPIES FOR DEVICE TYPE DISK TO 1; # default
CONFIGURE ARCHIVELOG BACKUP COPIES FOR DEVICE TYPE DISK TO 1; # default
CONFIGURE MAXSETSIZE TO UNLIMITED; # default
CONFIGURE ARCHIVELOG DELETION POLICY TO NONE; # default
CONFIGURE SNAPSHOT CONTROLFILE NAME TO
        '/u01/app/oracle/product/10.1.0/dbs/snapcf_ord.f'; # default

RMAN>
```

Any parameters that are set to their default values have **# default** at the end of the configuration setting. These parameters are easy to review and change using OEM, as demonstrated in Figure 13-4.

In the next few sections, we'll review a few of the more common RMAN persistent settings.

Retention Policy

Backups can be automatically retained and managed using one of two methods: by a *recovery window* or by *redundancy*. Using a recovery window, RMAN will retain as many backups as

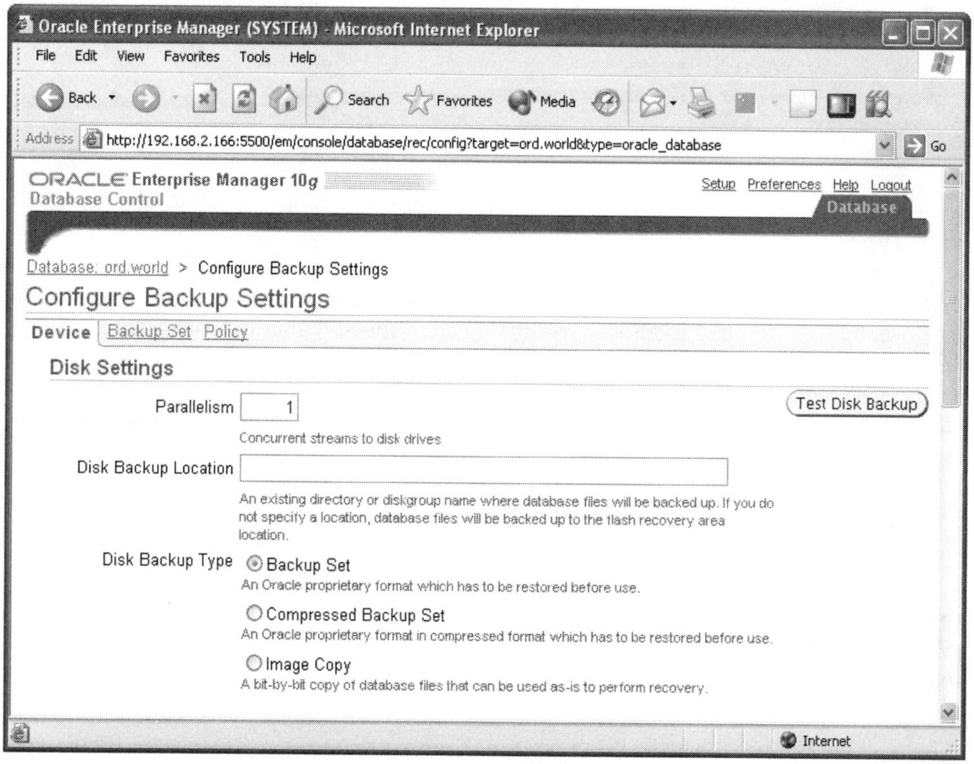

FIGURE 13-4. *RMAN persistent parameters in OEM*

necessary to bring the database to any point in time within the recovery window. For example, with a recovery window of seven days, RMAN will maintain enough image copies, incremental backups, and archived redo logs to ensure that the database can be restored and recovered to any point in time within the last seven days. Any backups that are not needed to support this recovery window are marked as OBSOLETE, and are automatically removed by RMAN if a Flash Recovery Area is used and disk space is needed for new backups.

In contrast, a redundancy retention policy directs RMAN to retain the specified number of backups or copies of each datafile and control file. Any extra copies or backups beyond the number specified in the redundancy policy are marked as OBSOLETE. As with a recovery window, obsolete backups are automatically removed if disk space is needed and a Flash Recovery Area is used. Otherwise, you can use the **delete obsolete** command to remove the backup files and update the catalog.

If the retention policy is set to NONE, no backups or copies are ever considered obsolete, and the DBA must manually remove unneeded backups from the catalog and from disk.

In the following example, we will set the retention policy to a recovery window of four days:

```
RMAN> configure retention policy to recovery window of 4 days;

new RMAN configuration parameters:
CONFIGURE RETENTION POLICY TO RECOVERY WINDOW OF 4 DAYS;
new RMAN configuration parameters are successfully stored
starting full resync of recovery catalog
full resync complete

RMAN>
```

Device Type

If the default device type is set to DISK and no pathname parameter is specified, RMAN uses the Flash Recovery Area for all backups. As with many of the simplified administration tasks from Oracle 10g, there is no need to allocate or deallocate a specific channel for backups unless you're using a tape device or sending the disk backup to a specific location outside of the Flash Recovery Area.

Although configuring a tape device is specific to your installation, in general terms we configure a tape device as follows:

```
RMAN> configure channel device type sbt
2>    parms='ENV=(<vendor specific arguments>)';
```

NOTE
sbt is the device type used for any tape backup subsystem, regardless of vendor.

Although we can use the Flash Recovery Area to restore and recover our database entirely from disk, at some point it becomes inefficient to keep all our backups on disk, especially if we have a large recovery window. As a result, we can make copies of our backup files to tape, and RMAN will dutifully keep track of where the backups are in case we need to restore or recover the database from tape, or restore archived redo logs to roll forward an image copy in the Flash Recovery Area.

Control File Autobackup

Because of the importance of the control file, we want to back it up at least as often as it changes due to modifications in the structure of the database. RMAN can be configured to back up the control file automatically, either any time a successful backup must be recorded in the repository or when a structural change affects the contents of the control file (in other words, cases when a control file backup must occur to ensure a successful recovery if and when a recovery operation is required).

```
RMAN> configure controlfile autobackup on;

new RMAN configuration parameters:
CONFIGURE CONTROLFILE AUTOBACKUP ON;
new RMAN configuration parameters are successfully stored
starting full resync of recovery catalog
full resync complete

RMAN>
```

Every RMAN backup from this point on will automatically include a copy of the control file.

Backup Compression

If disk space is at a premium, and you have some extra CPU capacity, it makes sense to compress the backups to save space. The files are decompressed automatically during a restore or recovery operation.

```
RMAN> configure device type disk backup type to compressed backupset;

new RMAN configuration parameters:
CONFIGURE DEVICE TYPE DISK BACKUP TYPE TO
        COMPRESSED BACKUPSET PARALLELISM 1;
new RMAN configuration parameters are successfully stored
starting full resync of recovery catalog
full resync complete

RMAN>
```

Compressing backupsets may not be necessary if the operating system's file system has compression enabled or if the tape device hardware automatically compresses backups; however, RMAN's compression algorithm is tuned to efficiently back up Oracle data blocks, and as a result it may do a better job of compressing the backupsets.

Initialization Parameters

A number of initialization parameters are used to control RMAN backups. We'll cover some of the more important parameters in this section.

CONTROL_FILE_RECORD_KEEP_TIME

A record of all RMAN backups is kept in the target control file. This parameter specifies the number of days that RMAN will attempt to keep a record of backups in the target control file. After this time, RMAN will begin to reuse records older than this retention period. If RMAN needs to write a new backup record, and the retention period has not been reached, RMAN will attempt to expand the size of the control file. Usually, this is successful because the size of the control file is relatively small compared to other database objects. However, if space is not available for the expansion of the control file, RMAN will reuse the oldest record in the control file and write a message to the alert log.

As a rule of thumb, you should set CONTROL_FILE_RECORD_KEEP_TIME to several days beyond your actual recovery window to ensure that backup records are retained in the control file.

DB_RECOVERY_FILE_DEST

This parameter specifies the location of the Flash Recovery Area. It should be located on a file system different from any database datafiles, control files, or redo log files, online or archived. If you lose the disk with the datafiles, the Flash Recovery Area is gone too, mitigating the advantages of using a Flash Recovery Area.

DB_RECOVERY_FILE_DEST_SIZE

The parameter DB_RECOVERY_FILE_DEST_SIZE specifies an upper limit to the amount of space used for the Flash Recovery Area. The underlying file system may have less or more than this amount of space; the DBA should ensure that at least this amount of space is available for backups.

In our order entry database, **ord**, a Flash Recovery Area is defined in the directory **/OraFlash** with a maximum size of 15GB. As this limit is reached, RMAN will automatically remove obsolete backups and generate an alert in the alert log when the amount of space occupied by nonobsolete backups is within 10 percent of the value specified in DB_RECOVERY_FILE_DEST_SIZE.

The parameters DB_RECOVERY_FILE_DEST and DB_RECOVERY_FILE_DEST_SIZE are both dynamic; they can be changed on the fly while the instance is running to respond to changes in disk space availability.

Data Dictionary and Dynamic Performance Views

A number of Oracle data dictionary and dynamic performance views contain information specific to RMAN operations, on both the target database and the catalog database. In Table 13-2 are the key views related to RMAN. Each of these views will be covered in more detail later in this chapter.

View	Description
RC_*	RMAN Recovery Catalog views. Only exist in the RMAN repository database and contain recovery information for all target databases.
V$RMAN_STATUS	Displays finished and in-progress RMAN jobs.
V$RMAN_OUTPUT	Contains messages generated by RMAN sessions and each RMAN command executed within the session.
V$SESSION_LONGOPS	Contains the status of long-running administrative operations that run for more than six seconds; includes statistics gathering and long-running queries, in addition to RMAN recovery and backup operations.
V$DATABASE_BLOCK_CORRUPTION	Corrupted blocks detected during an RMAN session.
V$RECOVERY_FILE_DEST	The number of files, space used, space that can be reclaimed, and space limit for the Flash Recovery Area.
V$RMAN_CONFIGURATION	RMAN configuration parameters with non-default values for this database.

TABLE 13-2.   *RMAN Data Dictionary and Dynamic Performance Views*

The RC_* views only exist in a database that is used as an RMAN repository; the V$ views exist and have rows in any database that is backed up using RMAN. To highlight this difference, we'll look at the view V$RMAN_CONFIGURATION in the target database:

```
SQL> connect system/manager@ord
Connected.
SQL> select * from v$rman_configuration;
CONF#    NAME                      VALUE
-----    --------------------      --------------------------
    1    CONTROLFILE AUTOBACKUP    ON
    2    RETENTION POLICY          TO RECOVERY WINDOW O
                                   F 4 DAYS
    3    DEVICE TYPE               DISK BACKUP TYPE TO
                                   COMPRESSED BACKUPSET
                                      PARALLELISM 1
    4    BACKUP OPTIMIZATION       ON

4 rows selected.
```

Note that these are the four RMAN persistent parameters that we changed earlier. The recovery catalog database keeps these non-default values in the view RC_RMAN_CONFIGURATION for all databases registered with RMAN:

```
SQL> connect rman/rman001@rmanrep
Connected.
SQL> select db_key, db_unique_name, name, value
  2       from rman.rc_rman_configuration;

  DB_KEY  DB_UNIQUE_NAME   NAME                   VALUE
  ------  --------------   ----------------------  --------------------
       1  ord              CONTROLFILE AUTOBACKUP  ON
       1                   RETENTION POLICY        TO RECOVERY WINDOW O
                                                   F 4 DAYS
       1  ord              DEVICE TYPE             DISK BACKUP TYPE TO
                                                   COMPRESSED BACKUPSET
                                                   PARALLELISM 1
       1  ord              BACKUP OPTIMIZATION     ON

4 rows selected.
```

If we were using RMAN to back up another database, this view would contain other values for DB_KEY and DB_UNIQUE_NAME for other target databases with non-default RMAN parameters.

Because we are not using RMAN to back up the **rmanrep** database, the views V$RMAN_* are empty.

Backup Operations

In this section, we'll run through some examples to back up the target database in a variety of ways: We'll perform two kinds of full backups, create image copies of selected database files, investigate how incremental backups work, and delve further into backup compression, incremental backup optimization, and the Flash Recovery Area.

We'll continue to use our order entry database, **ord**, as the target database, with the database **rmanrep** as the RMAN repository.

Full Database Backups

In our first example of a full database backup, we'll use backupsets to copy all database files, including the SPFILE, to the Flash Recovery Area:

```
RMAN> backup as backupset database spfile;
Starting backup at 15-MAR-04
allocated channel: ORA_DISK_1
channel ORA_DISK_1: sid=235 devtype=DISK
channel ORA_DISK_1: starting full datafile backupset
channel ORA_DISK_1: specifying datafile(s) in backupset
input datafile fno=00001 name=/u05/oradata/ord/system01.dbf
input datafile fno=00003 name=/u05/oradata/ord/sysaux01.dbf
```

```
input datafile fno=00005 name=/u05/oradata/ord/example01.dbf
input datafile fno=00002 name=/u05/oradata/ord/undotbs01.dbf
input datafile fno=00004 name=/u05/oradata/ord/users01.dbf
channel ORA_DISK_1: starting piece 1 at 15-MAR-04
channel ORA_DISK_1: finished piece 1 at 15-MAR-04
piece handle=/OraFlash/ORD/backupset/2004_03_15/
    o1_mf_nnndf_TAG20040315T221256_05dzp9nz_.bkp comment=NONE
channel ORA_DISK_1: backup set complete, elapsed time: 00:03:44
channel ORA_DISK_1: starting full datafile backupset
channel ORA_DISK_1: specifying datafile(s) in backupset
including current SPFILE in backupset
channel ORA_DISK_1: starting piece 1 at 15-MAR-04
channel ORA_DISK_1: finished piece 1 at 15-MAR-04
piece handle=/OraFlash/ORD/backupset/2004_03_15/
    o1_mf_nnsnf_TAG20040315T221256_05dzxg62_.bkp comment=NONE
channel ORA_DISK_1: backup set complete, elapsed time: 00:00:02
Finished backup at 15-MAR-04

Starting Control File and SPFILE Autobackup at 15-MAR-04
piece handle=/OraFlash/ORD/autobackup/2004_03_15/
    o1_mf_s_520899415_05dzxsnn_.bkp comment=NONE
Finished Control File and SPFILE Autobackup at 15-MAR-04

RMAN> sql 'alter system archive log current';
sql statement: alter system archive log current
RMAN>
```

The **alter system** command ensures that we have archived logs for all transactions, including those that occurred while the backup was taking place; this ensures that we can perform media recovery after restoring this backup.

Note that the SPFILE is backed up twice, the second time along with the control file. Because we set **configure controlfile autobackup** to **on**, we automatically back up the control file and SPFILE whenever we do any other kind of backup or the structure of the database changes. As a result, we don't need to specify SPFILE in the **backup** command.

Taking a peek into the Flash Recovery Area, we see a lot of cryptic filenames for the recent archived redo logs and the full database backup we just performed:

```
SQL> connect system/manager@ord
Connected.
SQL> show parameter db_recovery_file_dest
NAME                             TYPE          VALUE
-------------------------------  -----------   -----------
db_recovery_file_dest            string        /OraFlash
db_recovery_file_dest_size       big integer   15728640000

SQL> select name from v$database;
NAME
----
ORD
1 row selected.
```

```
SQL> exit
[oracle@oltp bdump]# cd /OraFlash/ORD
[oracle@oltp ORD]# ls
archivelog  autobackup  backupset
[oracle@oltp ORD]# find . -print
.
./archivelog
./archivelog/2004_03_14
./archivelog/2004_03_14/o1_mf_1_180_059dscwh_.arc
./archivelog/2004_03_14/o1_mf_1_181_059dshjx_.arc
./archivelog/2004_03_14/o1_mf_1_182_059ntxyc_.arc
. . .
./archivelog/2004_03_14/o1_mf_1_188_05b7kx3j_.arc
./archivelog/2004_03_14/o1_mf_1_189_05bfflq9_.arc
./archivelog/2004_03_15
./archivelog/2004_03_15/o1_mf_1_190_05bkt6rf_.arc
./archivelog/2004_03_15/o1_mf_1_191_05br7onw_.arc
./archivelog/2004_03_15/o1_mf_1_192_05bwyd93_.arc
./archivelog/2004_03_15/o1_mf_1_193_05c2sssw_.arc
. . .
./archivelog/2004_03_15/o1_mf_1_207_05f1nktm_.arc
./archivelog/2004_03_15/o1_mf_1_208_05f5wk22_.arc
./archivelog/2004_03_16
./archivelog/2004_03_16/o1_mf_1_209_05f60xlh_.arc
./archivelog/2004_03_16/o1_mf_1_210_05f62opo_.arc
. . .
./archivelog/2004_03_16/o1_mf_1_216_05fvwyrb_.arc
./archivelog/2004_03_16/o1_mf_1_217_05g0h4o1_.arc
./backupset
./backupset/2004_03_15
./backupset/2004_03_15/o1_mf_nnndf_TAG20040315T221256_05dzp9nz_.bkp
./backupset/2004_03_15/o1_mf_nnsnf_TAG20040315T221256_05dzxg62_.bkp
./autobackup
./autobackup/2004_03_15
./autobackup/2004_03_15/o1_mf_s_520899415_05dzxsnn_.bkp
[oracle@oltp ORD]#
```

Using RMAN's **list** command, we see these backups as they are cataloged in the target database control file and the RMAN repository. There are three backupsets: one containing the datafiles themselves, one for the explicit SPFILE backup, and one for the implicit SPFILE and control file backup.

```
RMAN> list backup by backup;

List of Backup Sets
===================
```

```
BS Key   Type  LV  Size  Device Type  Elapsed Time  Completion Time
------   ----  --  ----  -----------  ------------  ---------------
558      Full  610M        DISK         00:03:35      15-MAR-04
         BP Key: 561   Status: AVAILABLE  Compressed: NO  Tag:
                                                  TAG20040315T221256
         Piece Name:  /OraFlash/ORD/backupset/2004_03_15/
                          o1_mf_nnndf_TAG20040315T221256_05dzp9nz_bkp
   List of Datafiles in backup set 558
     File  LV   Type   Ckp SCN   Ckp Time   Name
     ----  --   ----   -------   --------   ------------------------------
      1         Full   1061186   15-MAR-04  /u05/oradata/ord/system01.dbf
      2         Full   1061186   15-MAR-04  /u05/oradata/ord/undotbs01.dbf
      3         Full   1061186   15-MAR-04  /u05/oradata/ord/sysaux01.dbf
      4         Full   1061186   15-MAR-04  /u05/oradata/ord/users01.dbf
      5         Full   1061186   15-MAR-04  /u05/oradata/ord/example01.dbf


BS Key   Type   LV   Size   Device Type  Elapsed Time  Completion Time
------   ----   --   -----  -----------  ------------  ---------------
559             Full  0      DISK         00:00:02      15-MAR-04
         BP Key: 562   Status: AVAILABLE  Compressed: NO  Tag:
                                                  TAG20040315T221256
         Piece Name:  /OraFlash/ORD/backupset/2004_03_15/
                          o1_mf_nnsnf_TAG20040315T221256_05dzxg62_bkp
   SPFILE Included: Modification time: 14-MAR-04


BS Key   Type   LV   Size   Device Type  Elapsed Time  Completion Time
------   -- -   -----  ----  -----------  ------------  ---------------
560      Full   2M    DISK         00:00:03      15-MAR-04
         BP Key: 563   Status: AVAILABLE  Compressed: NO  Tag:
                                                  TAG20040315T221655
         Piece Name:  /OraFlash/ORD/autobackup/2004_03_15/
                          o1_mf_s_520899415_05dzxsnn_.bkp
   Controlfile Included: Ckp SCN: 1061328      Ckp time: 15-MAR-04
   SPFILE Included: Modification time: 14-MAR-04

RMAN>
```

This full backup can be used in conjunction with the archived redo logs (stored by default in the **/OraFlash** directory) to recover the database to any point in time up to the last committed transaction.

Figure 13-5 shows the same backup configured using OEM.

Displaying the contents of the catalog is just as easy in OEM. Figure 13-6 shows results equivalent to the **list backup by backup** command.

The **list** and **report** commands are covered in more detail later in this chapter.

Tablespace

After adding a tablespace to the database, performing an immediate backup of the tablespace will shorten the time it will take to restore the tablespace later in the event of media failure. In addition, you might back up individual tablespaces in a database that is too large to back up all at once; again, creating a backupset or image copy of a tablespace at frequent intervals will

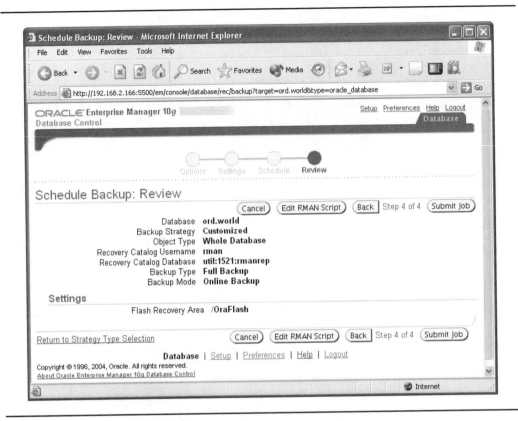

FIGURE 13-5. *Configure backup job with OEM*

reduce the amount of redo that would need to be applied to an older backup of the tablespace in the event of media failure. For example, in an environment with three large tablespaces—USERS, USERS2, and USERS3—along with the default tablespaces SYSTEM and SYSAUX, you might back up the SYSTEM and SYSAUX tablespaces on Sunday, USERS on Monday, USERS2 on Wednesday, and USERS3 on Friday. Failures of any media containing datafiles from one of these tablespaces will use a tablespace backup that is no more than a week old plus the intervening archived and online redo log files for recovery.

In our next example, we're adding a tablespace to the **ord** database to support order entry:

```
SQL> create tablespace oe_trans
  2     datafile '/u09/oradata/ord/oe_trans01.dbf'
  3     size 10m autoextend on next 5m;
Tablespace created.
```

From an RMAN session, we will back up the tablespace along with the control file. In this case, it's critical that we back up the control file because it contains the definition for the new tablespace.

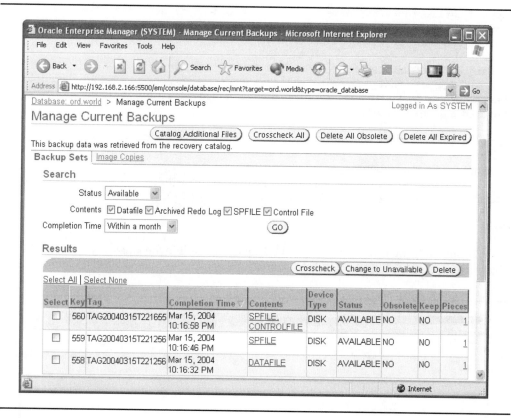

FIGURE 13-6.   *Display backupset information with OEM*

```
RMAN> report schema;

Report of database schema
File   K-bytes    Tablespace    RB segs    Datafile Name
----   -------    ----------    -------    -------------------------------
1      460800     SYSTEM        YES        /u05/oradata/ord/system01.dbf
2       25600     UNDOTBS1      YES        /u05/oradata/ord/undotbs01.dbf
3      307200     SYSAUX        NO         /u05/oradata/ord/sysaux01.dbf
4        5120     USERS         NO         /u05/oradata/ord/users01.dbf
5      153600     EXAMPLE       NO         /u05/oradata/ord/example01.dbf
6       10240     OE_TRANS      NO         /u09/oradata/ord/oe_trans01.dbf

RMAN> backup as backupset tablespace oe_trans;

Starting backup at 19-MAR-04
allocated channel: ORA_DISK_1
channel ORA_DISK_1: sid=271 devtype=DISK
channel ORA_DISK_1: starting full datafile backupset
channel ORA_DISK_1: specifying datafile(s) in backupset
```

```
input datafile fno=00006 name=/u09/oradata/ord/oe_trans01.dbf
channel ORA_DISK_1: starting piece 1 at 19-MAR-04
channel ORA_DISK_1: finished piece 1 at 19-MAR-04
piece
   handle=/OraFlash/ORD/backupset/2004_03_19/
          o1_mf_nnndf_TAG20040319T100418_056jctm_.bkp comment=NONE
channel ORA_DISK_1: backup set complete, elapsed time: 00:00:16
Finished backup at 19-MAR-04

Starting Control File and SPFILE Autobackup at 19-MAR-04
piece
   handle=/OraFlash/ORD/autobackup/2004_03_19/
          o1_mf_s_521201078_05p6js8r_.bkp comment=NONE
Finished Control File and SPFILE Autobackup at 19-MAR-04

RMAN>
```

In Figure 13-7, you can see the new RMAN backup records in the repository—one for the tablespace (recorded as a single datafile backupset) and one for the controlfile/SPFILE autobackup.

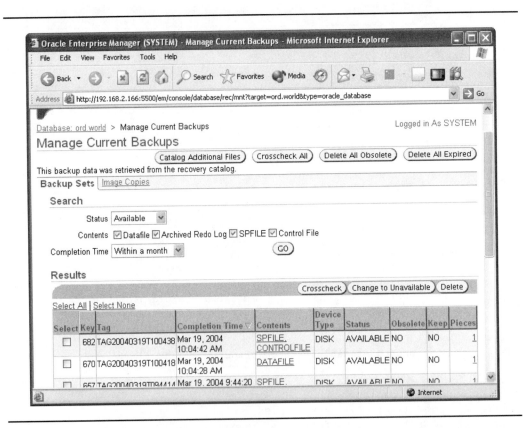

FIGURE 13-7.   *Tablespace backup files in OEM*

Datafiles

Individual datafiles can be backed up as easily as we can back up a tablespace. If it's impractical to back up an entire tablespace within an RMAN session, you can back up individual datafiles within the tablespace over a period of days, and the archived redo log files will take care of the rest during a recovery operation.

```
RMAN> backup as backupset datafile
2>        '/u09/oradata/ord/oe_trans01.dbf';
```

Image Copies

Up until this point, we have been using backupset backups; in contrast, image copies make bit-for-bit copies of the specified tablespace or entire database. There are a couple of distinct advantages for using RMAN to perform image copy backups: First, the backup is automatically recorded in the RMAN repository. Second, all blocks are checked for corruption as they are read and copied to the backup destination. Another side benefit to making image copies is that the copies can be used "as is" outside of RMAN if, for some reason, a recovery operation must occur outside of RMAN.

In the example that follows, we make another backup of the **oe_trans** tablespace, this time as an image copy:

```
RMAN> backup as copy tablespace oe_trans;

Starting backup at 19-MAR-04
using channel ORA_DISK_1
channel ORA_DISK_1: starting datafile copy
input datafile fno=00006 name=/u09/oradata/ord/oe_trans01.dbf
output filename=/OraFlash/ORD/datafile/o1_mf_oe_trans_05qn2bpz_.dbf
        tag=TAG20040319T230202 recid=2 stamp=521247723
channel ORA_DISK_1: datafile copy complete, elapsed time: 00:00:01
Finished backup at 19-MAR-04

Starting Control File and SPFILE Autobackup at 19-MAR-04
piece handle=/OraFlash/ORD/autobackup/2004_03_19/
        o1_mf_s_521247724_05qn2fbj_.bkp comment=NONE
Finished Control File and SPFILE Autobackup at 19-MAR-04

RMAN>
```

Image copies can only be created with DISK device types. In Figure 13-8, we perform the same backup with OEM.

Because we had earlier configured the default backup type to **compressed backupset**, we overrode the default value in an earlier setup screen for this backup.

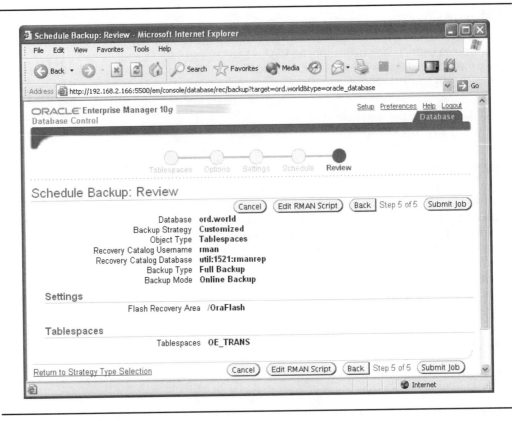

FIGURE 13-8. *Image copy backup of a tablespace using OEM*

Control File, SPFILE Backup

To back up the control file and SPFILE manually, use the following RMAN command:

```
RMAN> backup current controlfile spfile;

Starting backup at 19-MAR-04
allocated channel: ORA_DISK_1
channel ORA_DISK_1: sid=246 devtype=DISK
channel ORA_DISK_1: starting compressed full datafile backupset
channel ORA_DISK_1: specifying datafile(s) in backupset
including current controlfile in backupset
channel ORA_DISK_1: starting piece 1 at 19-MAR-04
channel ORA_DISK_1: finished piece 1 at 19-MAR-04
piece handle=/OraFlash/ORD/backupset/2004_03_19/
      o1_mf_ncnnf_TAG20040319T213310_05gvqd7_.bkp comment=NONE
channel ORA_DISK_1: backup set complete, elapsed time: 00:00:04
channel ORA_DISK_1: starting compressed full datafile backupset
```

```
channel ORA_DISK_1: specifying datafile(s) in backupset
including current SPFILE in backupset
channel ORA_DISK_1: starting piece 1 at 19-MAR-04
channel ORA_DISK_1: finished piece 1 at 19-MAR-04
piece handle=/OraFlash/ORD/backupset/2004_03_19/
        o1_mf_nnsnf_TAG20040319T213310_05gvxlb_.bkp comment=NONE
channel ORA_DISK_1: backup set complete, elapsed time: 00:00:05
Finished backup at 19-MAR-04
Starting Control File and SPFILE Autobackup at 19-MAR-04
piece handle=/OraFlash/ORD/autobackup/2004_03_19/
            o1_mf_s_521242402_05qgw3gl_.bkp comment=NONE
Finished Control File and SPFILE Autobackup at 19-MAR-04

RMAN>
```

Note that because we already had **autobackup** set to **on**, we actually performed two backups of the control file and the SPFILE. The second backup of the control file, however, has a record of the first control file and SPFILE backup.

Archived Redo Logs

Even when archived redo logs are sent to multiple destinations, including the Flash Recovery Area, due to the critical nature of the archived redo logs, we want to back up copies of the logs to tape. Once the backup is completed, we have the option to leave the logs in place, to delete only the logs that RMAN used for the backup, or delete all copies of the archived logs that were backed up to tape.

In the following example, we back up all the archived log files in the Flash Recovery Area and then remove them from disk:

```
RMAN> backup device type sbt archivelog all delete input;
```

If archived log files are being sent to multiple locations, then only one set of the archived redo log files are deleted. If we want all copies to be deleted, we use **delete all input** instead of **delete input**.

Backing up and deleting only older archived redo log files can be accomplished by specifying a date range in the **backup archivelog** command:

```
RMAN> backup device type sbt
2>        archivelog from time 'sysdate-30' until time 'sysdate-7'
3>        delete all input;
```

In the preceding example, all archived redo logs older than one week, going back for three weeks, are copied to tape and deleted from disk. In addition, you can specify a range using SCNs or log sequence numbers.

Incremental Backups

An alternative strategy to relying on full backups with archived redo logs is to use *incremental backups* along with archived redo logs for recovery. The initial incremental backup is known as a *level* 0 incremental backup. Each incremental backup after the initial incremental backup (also known as a *level 1* incremental backup) contains only changed blocks, and as a result takes less time and space. Incremental level 1 backups can either be *cumulative* or *differential*. A cumulative backup records all changed blocks since the initial incremental backup; a differential backup records all changed blocks since the last incremental backup, whether it was a level 0 or a level 1 incremental backup.

When a number of different types of backups exist in the catalog, such as image copies, tablespace backupsets, and incremental backups, RMAN will choose the best combination of backups to most efficiently recover and restore the database. The DBA still has the option to prevent RMAN from using a particular backup (for example, if the DBA thinks that a particular backup is corrupt and will be rejected by RMAN during the recovery operation).

The decision whether to use cumulative or differential backups is based partly on where you want to spend the CPU cycles, and how much disk space you have available. Using cumulative backups means that each incremental backup will become progressively larger and take longer until another level 0 incremental backup is performed, but during a restore and recover operation, only two backupsets will be required. On the other hand, differential backups only record the changes since the last backup, so each backupset might be smaller or larger than the previous one, with no overlap in data blocks backed up. However, a restore and recover operation may take longer if you have to restore from several backupsets instead of just two.

Following our example with the **ord** database, we find out that several files are outside of our retention policy of four days; in other words, files that need more than four days worth of archived redo logs to recover the database:

```
RMAN> report need backup;

RMAN retention policy will be applied to the command
RMAN retention policy is set to recovery window of 4 days
Report of files whose recovery needs more than 4 days of archived logs

File  Days  Name
----  ----  ----------------------------
1     5     /u05/oradata/ord/system01.dbf
2     5     /u05/oradata/ord/undotbs01.dbf
3     5     /u05/oradata/ord/sysaux01.dbf
4     5     /u05/oradata/ord/users01.dbf
5     5     /u05/oradata/ord/example01.dbf

RMAN>
```

To remedy this situation, we can do another full backup, or we can pursue an incremental backup policy, which might be easier to implement and maintain. To set up our incremental policy, we need to perform a level 0 incremental backup first:

```
RMAN> backup incremental level 0
2>      as compressed backupset database;

Starting backup at 20-MAR-04
allocated channel: ORA_DISK_1
channel ORA_DISK_1: sid=244 devtype=DISK
```

```
channel ORA_DISK_1: starting compressed incremental
                level 0 datafile backupset
channel ORA_DISK_1: specifying datafile(s) in backupset
input datafile fno=00001 name=/u05/oradata/ord/system01.dbf
input datafile fno=00003 name=/u05/oradata/ord/sysaux01.dbf
input datafile fno=00005 name=/u05/oradata/ord/example01.dbf
input datafile fno=00002 name=/u05/oradata/ord/undotbs01.dbf
input datafile fno=00006 name=/u09/oradata/ord/oe_trans01.dbf
input datafile fno=00004 name=/u05/oradata/ord/users01.dbf
channel ORA_DISK_1: starting piece 1 at 20-MAR-04
channel ORA_DISK_1: finished piece 1 at 20-MAR-04
piece handle=/OraFlash/ORD/backupset/2004_03_20/
                o1_mf_nnnd0_TAG20040320T153801_05gfwf1_.bkp comment=NONE
channel ORA_DISK_1: backup set complete, elapsed time: 00:02:47
Finished backup at 20-MAR-04

Starting Control File and SPFILE Autobackup at 20-MAR-04
piece handle=/OraFlash/ORD/autobackup/2004_03_20/
                o1_mf_s_521307651_05sgm5tv_.bkp comment=NONE
Finished Control File and SPFILE Autobackup at 20-MAR-04

RMAN>
```

At any point in the future after this level 0 backup, we can perform an incremental level 1 differential backup:

```
RMAN> backup as compressed backupset
2>        incremental level 1 database;
```

The default incremental backup type is differential; the keyword **differential** is neither needed nor allowed. However, to perform a cumulative backup, we add the **cumulative** keyword:

```
RMAN> backup as compressed backupset
2>        incremental level 1 cumulative database;
```

How much database activity is performed may also dictate whether you use cumulative or differential backups. In an OLTP environment with heavy insert and update activity, incremental backups may be more manageable in terms of disk space usage. For a data warehouse environment with infrequent changes, a differential backup policy may be more suitable. Compared to using redo log files, both types of incremental backups are far superior in terms of the time to recover a database. In any case, we have addressed RMAN's retention policy:

```
RMAN> report need backup;
```

```
starting full resync of recovery catalog
full resync complete
RMAN retention policy will be applied to the command
RMAN retention policy is set to recovery window of 4 days
```

```
Report of files whose recovery needs more than 4 days of archived logs
File    Days   Name
----    ----   --------------------------

RMAN>
```

Incrementally Updated Backups

An *incrementally updated* backup can potentially make a recover and restore operation even more efficient by rolling the changes from a level 1 incremental backup to a level 0 incremental image backup. If the incrementally updated backup is run on a daily basis, then any recovery operation would require at most the updated image copy, one incremental level 1 backup, and the most recent archived and online redo logs. The following example uses an RMAN script that can be scheduled to run at the same time every day to support an incrementally updated backup strategy:

```
run
{
    recover copy of database with tag 'incr_upd_img';
    backup incremental level 1
          for recover of copy with tag 'incr_upd_img' database;
}
```

The key part of both commands within the **run** script is the **recover copy** clause. Rather than doing a recovery of the actual database datafiles, we are recovering a *copy* of a database datafile by applying incremental backups. Using a *tag* with an RMAN backup allows us to apply the incremental backup to the correct image copy. Tags allow DBAs to easily refer to a specific backup for recovery or catalog cleanup operations; if the **backup** command does not provide a tag, one is automatically generated for the backupset and is unique within the backupsets for the target database.

The basics of standard recovery operations and RMAN scripting capabilities are covered later in this chapter.

The OEM backup wizards make it easy to automate an incrementally updated backup strategy. In the figures that follow, we'll cover the steps needed to configure this strategy within OEM.

In Figure 13-9, we're specifying the strategy for backing up our database.

The database is open, archivelog mode is enabled, and backups will follow the Oracle-suggested guidelines for a backup strategy. The other option in the pull-down menu is Customized. Figure 13-10 shows the next step in the backup configuration process: a summary of the database, the strategy selected, where the backups will be sent, the recovery catalog in use, and a brief explanation as to how the backup will be performed.

In Figure 13-11, we specify when the backups will start, and what time of day they will run. Although the backup job can run any time during the day, because we are performing a hot backup (the database is open and users can process transactions), we want to minimize the possible impact on query and DML response time by scheduling the job during a time period with low activity.

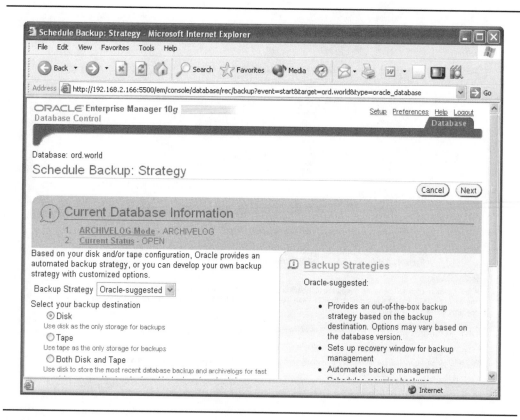

FIGURE 13-9. *OEM backup strategy selection*

Figure 13-12 gives us one more chance to review how the backup will be performed and where it will reside.

At the bottom of the browser window is the actual RMAN script that will be scheduled to run on a daily basis (see Figure 13-13). Coincidentally, it strongly resembles the RMAN script we presented earlier in this section.

Incremental Backup Block Change Tracking

Another way to improve the performance of incremental backups is to enable *block change tracking*. For a traditional incremental backup, RMAN must inspect every block of the tablespace or datafile to be backed up to see if the block has changed since the last backup. For a very large

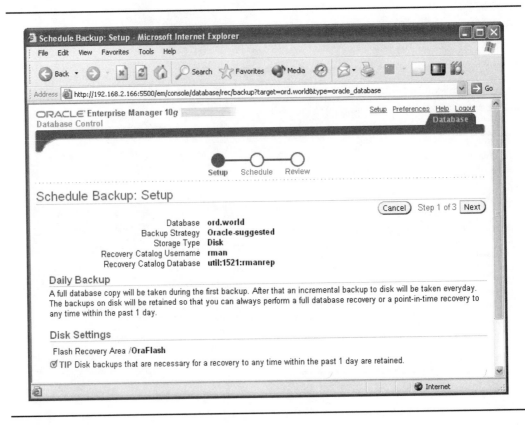

FIGURE 13-10. *OEM backup setup summary*

database, the time it takes to scan the blocks in the database can easily exceed the time it takes to perform the actual backup.

By enabling block change tracking, RMAN knows which blocks have changed by using a *change tracking file.* Although there is some slight overhead in space usage and maintenance of the tracking file every time a block is changed, the tradeoff is well worth it if frequent incremental backups are performed on the database. In the following example, we create a block change tracking file and enable block change tracking:

```
SQL> alter database enable block change tracking
  2      using file '/u06/oradata/ord/block_chg.dbf';

Database altered.

SQL> !ls -l /u06/oradata/ord/block_chg.dbf
-rw-r---   1 oracle   oinstall 11600384 Apr  8 21:47
                              /u06/oradata/ord/block_chg.dbf

SQL>
```

The next time a backup is performed, RMAN will only have to use the contents of the file /u06/oradata/ord/block_chg.dbf to determine which blocks need to be backed up. The space needed for the block change tracking file is approximately 1/250,000 the size of the database.

The dynamic performance view V$BLOCK_CHANGE_TRACKING contains the name and size of the block change tracking file as well as whether change tracking is enabled:

```
SQL> select filename, status, bytes from v$block_change_tracking;

FILENAME                            STATUS    BYTES
----------------------------------  -------   --------
/u06/oradata/ord/block_chg.dbf      ENABLED   11599872

SQL>
```

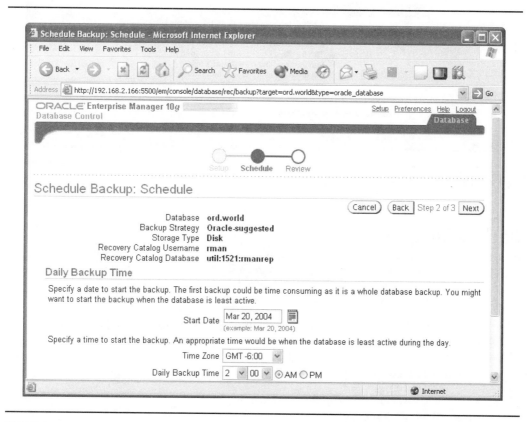

FIGURE 13-11. *OEM backup schedule*

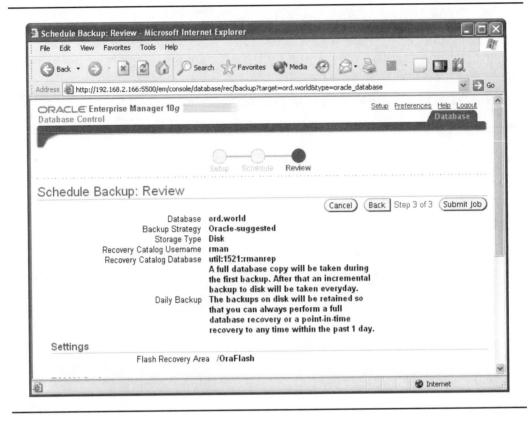

FIGURE 13-12. *OEM backup summary*

Backup Compression

As you learned earlier in this chapter, we can either configure backup compression as the default for backupsets or explicitly specify compression in an RMAN **backup** command:

```
RMAN> backup as compressed backupset database;
```

Comparing the size of the actual datafiles with the backupset, we can see just how much compression we can achieve for some additional CPU overhead:

```
[root@oltp root]# cd /OraFlash/ORD
[root@oltp ORD]# ls
archivelog   autobackup   backupset   datafile
[root@oltp ORD]# cd backupset
[root@oltp backupset]# ls
2004_03_15   2004_03_18   2004_03_19   2004_03_20
```

```
[root@oltp backupset]# cd *20
[root@oltp 2004_03_20]# ls -l
total 122172
-rw-r-----/ 1 oracle   oinstall 124977152 Mar 20 15:40
                       o1_mf_nnnd0_TAG20040320T153801_05sgfwf1_.bkp
[root@oltp 2004_03_20]# ls -l /u05/oradata/ord
total 981072
-rw-r-----/   1 oracle   oinstall 157294592 Mar 20 15:38 example01.dbf
-rw-r-----/   1 oracle   oinstall 314580992 Mar 20 15:38 sysaux01.dbf
-rw-r-----/   1 oracle   oinstall 482353152 Mar 20 15:38 system01.dbf
-rw-r-----/   1 oracle   oinstall 20979712 Mar 20 09:56 temp01.dbf
-rw-r-----/   1 oracle   oinstall 26222592 Mar 20 15:38 undotbs01.dbf
-rw-r-----/   1 oracle   oinstall  5251072 Mar 20 15:38 users01.dbf
[root@oltp 2004_03_20]#
```

The database files occupy just under 1GB on the file system; the compressed backupset from RMAN comes in under 125MB.

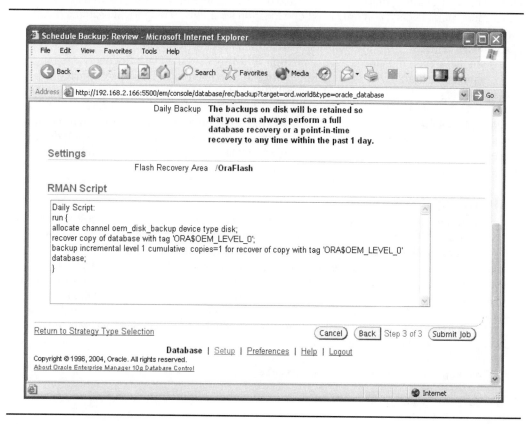

FIGURE 13-13. *OEM backup script*

Using a Flash Recovery Area

Earlier in this chapter, we covered the initialization parameters required to set up the Flash Recovery Area: DB_RECOVERY_FILE_DEST and DB_RECOVERY_FILE_DEST_SIZE. Both of these parameters are dynamic, allowing the DBA to change either the RMAN destination for backups or the amount of space allowed for backups in the Flash Recovery Area without restarting the instance.

To facilitate a completely disk-based recovery scenario, the Flash Recovery Area should be big enough for a copy of all datafiles, incremental backup files, online redo logs, archived redo logs not on tape, control file autobackups, and SPFILE backups. Using a larger or smaller recovery window or adjusting the redundancy policy will require an adjustment in the size of the Flash Recovery Area. If the Flash Recovery Area is limited in size due to disk space constraints, at a minimum there should be enough room to hold the archived log files that have not yet been copied to tape. The dynamic performance view V$RECOVERY_FILE_DEST displays information about the number of files in the Flash Recovery Area, how much space is currently being used, and the total amount of space available in the Flash Recovery Area.

The Flash Recovery Area automatically uses OMF. As part of Oracle 10g's simplified management structure, you do not need to explicitly set any of the LOG_ARCHIVE_DEST_*n* initialization parameters if you only need one location for archived redo log files; if the database is in **archivelog** mode, and a Flash Recovery Area is defined, then the initialization parameter LOG_ARCHIVE_DEST_10 is implicitly defined as the Flash Recovery Area.

As you have seen in many previous examples, RMAN uses the Flash Recovery Area in a very organized fashion—with separate directories for archived logs, backupsets, image copies, and automatic backups of the control file and SPFILE. In addition, each subdirectory is further subdivided by a datestamp, making it easy to find a backupset or image copy when the need arises.

Multiple databases can share the same Flash Recovery Area, even a primary and a standby database. Even with the same DB_NAME, as long as the DB_UNIQUE_NAME parameter is different, there will not be any conflicts. RMAN uses the DB_UNIQUE_NAME to distinguish backups between databases that use the same Flash Recovery Area.

Validating Backups

Having multiple image backups or enough archived redo log files to support a recovery window is of less value if there are problems with the live database files or control files. The RMAN command **backup validate database** will simulate a backup, checking for the existence of the specified files, ensuring that they are not corrupted. No backup files are created. This command would be useful in a scenario where you can check for problems with the database or archived redo logs proactively, giving you an opportunity to fix problems before the actual backup operation or for scheduling additional time overnight to repair problems found during the day.

In the following example, we will validate the entire database along with the archived redo logs:

```
RMAN> backup validate database archivelog all;

Starting backup at 21-MAR-04
allocated channel: ORA_DISK_1
channel ORA_DISK_1: sid=246 devtype=DISK
RMAN-00571: ============================================================
```

```
RMAN-00569: =============== ERROR MESSAGE STACK FOLLOWS ===============
RMAN-00571: ============================================================
RMAN-03002: failure of backup command at 03/21/2004 10:13:04
RMAN-06059: expected archived log not found,
            lost of archived log compromises recoverability
ORA-19625: error identifying file
/u01/app/oracle/flash_recovery_area/ORD/archivelog/2004_03_03/
          o1_mf_1_6_04fhy2t_.arc
ORA-27037: unable to obtain file status
Linux Error: 2: No such file or directory
Additional information: 3

RMAN>
```

The **backup validate** command has identified an archived redo log file that is no longer in the Flash Recovery Area. It may have been archived to tape outside of RMAN, or it may have been inadvertently deleted. Looking at the datestamp of the log file, we see that it is outside of our recovery window of four days, so it is not a critical file in terms of recoverability.

Synchronizing the Flash Recovery Area and the catalog with the **crosscheck** command is covered later in this chapter; once we have fixed the cross-reference problem we have just discovered, we can perform the rest of the validation:

```
RMAN> backup validate database archivelog all;

Starting backup at 21-MAR-04
using channel ORA_DISK_1
channel ORA_DISK_1: starting compressed archive log backupset
channel ORA_DISK_1: specifying archive log(s) in backup set
input archive log thread=1 sequence=207 recid=202 stamp=520901173
input archive log thread=1 sequence=208 recid=203 stamp=520905522
input archive log thread=1 sequence=209 recid=204 stamp=520905663
input archive log thread=1 sequence=210 recid=205 stamp=520905719
. . .
input archive log thread=1 sequence=316 recid=311 stamp=521364700
input archive log thread=1 sequence=317 recid=312 stamp=521370803
input archive log thread=1 sequence=318 recid=313 stamp=521373610
channel ORA_DISK_1: backup set complete, elapsed time: 00:01:30
channel ORA_DISK_1: starting compressed full datafile backupset
channel ORA_DISK_1: specifying datafile(s) in backupset
input datafile fno=00001 name=/u05/oradata/ord/system01.dbf
input datafile fno=00003 name=/u05/oradata/ord/sysaux01.dbf
input datafile fno=00005 name=/u05/oradata/ord/example01.dbf
input datafile fno=00002 name=/u05/oradata/ord/undotbs01.dbf
input datafile fno=00004 name=/u05/oradata/ord/users01.dbf
input datafile fno=00006 name=/u09/oradata/ord/oe_trans01.dbf
channel ORA_DISK_1: backup set complete, elapsed time: 00:01:46
Finished backup at 21-MAR-04

RMAN>
```

No errors were found during the validation; RMAN read every block of every archived redo log file and datafile to ensure that they were readable and had no corrupted blocks. However, no backups were actually written to a disk or tape channel.

Recovery Operations

Every good backup plan includes a disaster recovery plan so that we can retrieve the datafiles and logs from the backups and recover the database files. In this section, we'll review several different aspects of RMAN recovery operations.

RMAN can perform restore and recovery operations at various levels of granularity, and most of these operations can be performed while the database is open and available to users. We can recover individual blocks, tablespaces, datafiles, or even an entire database. In addition, RMAN has various methods of validating a restore operation without performing an actual recovery on the database datafiles.

Block Media Recovery

When there are only a small handful of blocks to recover in a database, RMAN can perform *block media recovery* rather than a full datafile recovery. Block media recovery minimizes redo log application time, and it drastically reduces the amount of I/O required to recover only the block or blocks in question. While block media recovery is in progress, the affected datafiles can remain online and available to users.

> **NOTE**
> *Block media recovery is only available from within the RMAN application.*

There are a number of ways in which block corruption is detected. During a read or write operation from an **insert** or **select** statement, Oracle may detect a block is corrupt, write an error in a user trace file, and abort the transaction. An RMAN **backup** or **backup validate** command can record corrupted blocks in the dynamic performance view V$DATABASE_BLOCK_CORRUPTION. In addition, the SQL commands **analyze table** and **analyze index** could uncover corrupted blocks.

To recover one or more data blocks, RMAN must know the datafile number and block number within the datafile. This information is available in a user trace file, as in the following example:

```
ORA-01578: ORACLE data block corrupted (file # 6, block # 403)
ORA-01110: data file 6: '/u09/oradata/ord/oe_trans01.dbf'
```

Alternatively, the block may appear in the view V$DATABASE_BLOCK_CORRUPTION after an RMAN **backup** command; the columns FILE# and BLOCK# provide the information needed to execute the **blockrecover** command. The column CORRUPTION_TYPE identifies the type of corruption in the block, such as FRACTURED, CHECKSUM, or CORRUPT. Fixing the block is easily accomplished in RMAN:

```
RMAN> blockrecover datafile 6 block 403;

Starting blockrecover at 21-MAR-04
```

```
using channel ORA_DISK_1

starting media recovery
media recovery complete

Finished blockrecover at 21-MAR-04

RMAN>
```

A corrupted block must be restored completely; in other words, all redo operations up to the latest SCN against the data block must be applied before the block can be considered usable again.

Restoring a Control File

In the rare event that you lose all copies of your control file, it is easy to restore the control file when a recovery catalog is used; start the instance with **nomount** (since we don't have a control file to read with **mount**) and issue the following RMAN command:

```
RMAN> restore controlfile;
```

If you are not using a recovery catalog, you can add the **from '<filename>'** clause to the command to specify where the latest control file exists:

```
RMAN> restore controlfile from '/u11/oradata/ord/bkup.ctl';
```

After restoring the control files, you must perform complete media recovery of your database and open the database with the **resetlogs** option. Complete media recovery can be performed using RMAN or the methods described in Chapter 12.

Restoring a Tablespace

If the disk containing the datafiles for a tablespace fails or becomes corrupted, recovery of the tablespace is possible while the database remains open and available. The exception to this is the SYSTEM tablespace. In our **ord** database, suppose the disk containing the datafiles for the USERS tablespace has crashed. After the first phone call from the users (which happened even before OEM notified us of the error), we can check the dynamic performance view V$DATAFILE_HEADER to see which datafiles need recovery:

```
SQL> select file#, status, error, tablespace_name, name
  2         from v$datafile_header;

  FILE#  STATUS  ERROR              TABLESPACE  NAME
  ----   ------  ----------------   ----------  -----------------------------
     1   ONLINE                     SYSTEM      /u05/oradata/ord/system01.dbf
     2   ONLINE                     UNDOTBS1    /u05/oradata/ord/undotbs01.dbf
     3   ONLINE                     SYSAUX      /u05/oradata/ord/sysaux01.dbf
     4   ONLINE  CANNOT OPEN FILE
     5   ONLINE                     EXAMPLE     /u05/oradata/ord/example01.dbf
     6   ONLINE                     OE_TRANS    /u09/oradata/ord/oe_trans01.dbf
```

```
   7 ONLINE  CANNOT OPEN FILE

7 rows selected.
```

After replacing the disk drive, we initiate an RMAN session and find out that file numbers 4 and 7 correspond to the USERS tablespace:

RMAN> **report schema;**

```
Report of database schema
File    K-bytes    Tablespace    RB segs    Datafile Name
----    -------    ----------    -------    --------------------
1       471040     SYSTEM        YES        /u05/oradata/ord/system01.dbf
2       25600      UNDOTBS1      YES        /u05/oradata/ord/undotbs01.dbf
3       307200     SYSAUX        NO         /u05/oradata/ord/sysaux01.dbf
4       10240      USERS         NO         /u05/oradata/ord/users01.dbf
5       153600     EXAMPLE       NO         /u05/oradata/ord/example01.dbf
6       10240      OE_TRANS      NO         /u09/oradata/ord/oe_trans01.dbf
7       5120       USERS         NO         /u05/oradata/ord/users02.dbf

RMAN>
```

To restore and recover the tablespace, we force the tablespace offline, restore and recover the tablespace, and bring it back online:

RMAN> **sql 'alter tablespace users offline immediate';**
```
sql statement: alter tablespace users offline immediate
```

RMAN> **restore tablespace users;**

```
Starting restore at 21-MAR-04
allocated channel: ORA_DISK_1
channel ORA_DISK_1: sid=241 devtype=DISK

channel ORA_DISK_1: starting datafile backupset restore
channel ORA_DISK_1: specifying datafile(s) to restore from backup set
restoring datafile 00004 to /u05/oradata/ord/users01.dbf
channel ORA_DISK_1: restored backup piece 1
piece handle=/OraFlash/ORD/backupset/2004_03_20/
     o1_mf_nnnd0_TAG20040320T153801_05gfwf1_.bkp tag=TAG20040320T153801
channel ORA_DISK_1: restore complete
channel ORA_DISK_1: starting datafile backupset restore
channel ORA_DISK_1: specifying datafile(s) to restore from backup set
restoring datafile 00007 to /u05/oradata/ord/users02.dbf
channel ORA_DISK_1: restored backup piece 1
piece handle=/OraFlash/ORD/backupset/2004_03_21/
     o1_mf_nnnd1_TAG20040321T115355_05ooogb_.bkp tag=TAG20040321T115355
channel ORA_DISK_1: restore complete
Finished restore at 21-MAR-04
```

```
RMAN> recover tablespace users;

Starting recover at 21-MAR-04
using channel ORA_DISK_1
channel ORA_DISK_1: starting incremental datafile backupset restore
channel ORA_DISK_1: specifying datafile(s) to restore from backup set
destination for restore of datafile 00004: /u05/oradata/ord/users01.dbf
channel ORA_DISK_1: restored backup piece 1
piece handle=/OraFlash/ORD/backupset/2004_03_20/
     o1_mf_nnnd1_TAG20040320T162357_05k3ysx_.bkp tag=TAG20040320T162357
channel ORA_DISK_1: restore complete
channel ORA_DISK_1: starting incremental datafile backupset restore
channel ORA_DISK_1: specifying datafile(s) to restore from backup set
destination for restore of datafile 00004: /u05/oradata/ord/users01.dbf
channel ORA_DISK_1: restored backup piece 1
piece handle=/OraFlash/ORD/backupset/2004_03_21/
        o1_mf_nnnd1_TAG20040321T115355_05ooogb_.bkp tag=TAG20040321T115355
channel ORA_DISK_1: restore complete

starting media recovery

archive log thread 1 sequence 320 is already on disk as file
    /OraFlash/ORD/archivelog/2004_03_21/o1_mf_1_320_05vp7k0m_.arc
archive log thread 1 sequence 321 is already on disk as file
    /OraFlash/ORD/archivelog/2004_03_21/o1_mf_1_321_05vpj1cq_.arc
archive log thread 1 sequence 322 is already on disk as file
    /OraFlash/ORD/archivelog/2004_03_21/o1_mf_1_322_05vtdg2x_.arc
archive log thread 1 sequence 323 is already on disk as file
    /OraFlash/ORD/archivelog/2004_03_21/o1_mf_1_323_05vzllqk_.arc
archive log filename=/OraFlash/ORD/archivelog/2004_03_21/
    o1_mf_1_320_05vp7k0m_.arc thread=1 sequence=320
archive log filename=/OraFlash/ORD/archivelog/2004_03_21/
    o1_mf_1_321_05vpj1cq_.arc
thread=1 sequence=321
media recovery complete
Finished recover at 21-MAR-04

RMAN> sql 'alter tablespace users online';

sql statement: alter tablespace users online

RMAN>
```

The **restore** command copied the latest image or backupset copy of the datafiles in the USERS tablespace to their original locations; the **recover** command applied redo from either redo log files or incremental backups to bring the objects in the tablespace back up to the latest SCN. Once the tablespace is back online, it is available for use again, without the loss of any committed transactions to tables in the tablespace.

Restoring a Datafile

Restoring a datafile is a very similar operation to restoring a tablespace. Once the missing or corrupted datafile is identified using the V$DATAFILE_HEADER view, the RMAN commands are very similar to the previous example; the tablespace is taken offline, the datafile(s) are restored and recovered, and the tablespace is brought back online. If only file number 7 was lost, the **recover** and **restore** commands are as simple as this:

```
RMAN> restore datafile 7;
RMAN> recover datafile 7;
```

Using OEM, the procedure is also very straightforward. In Figure 13-14, we configure the datafile restore by selecting the missing datafile (#7) in the USERS tablespace.

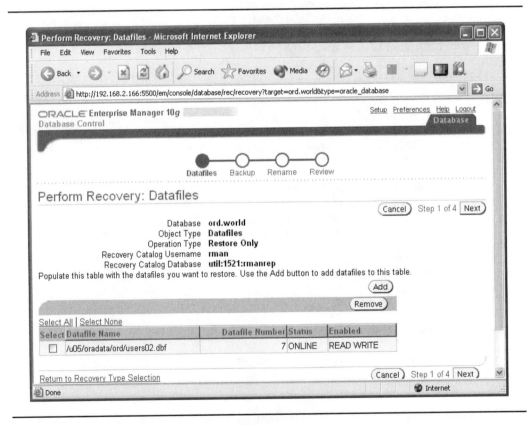

FIGURE 13-14. *Selecting the datafile to restore*

The screen in Figure 13-15 allows you to select which backup will be used to perform the restore operation. Unless you aware of corruption problems with the last backup, or the backup is not online with an older backup on disk, then using the most recent backup makes sense.

In Figure 13-16, we have the option to restore the datafile to an alternate location; in this case, we want to restore it to the original location. If the failed disk drive containing the datafile could not be repaired, we would specify an alternate location for the datafile.

Before the RMAN job is submitted, we have one more chance to review the configuration of the job. Figure 13-17 shows the actual RMAN commands that will be run to perform the requested operation.

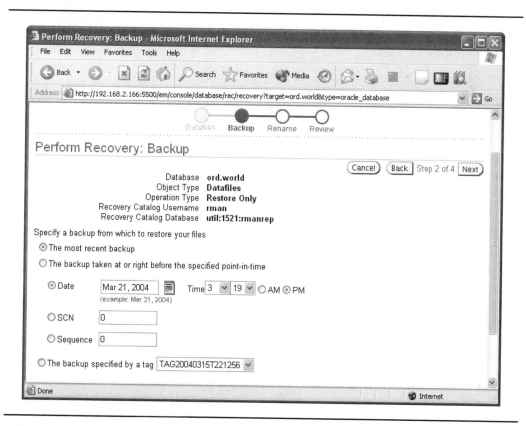

FIGURE 13-15. *Selecting the backup used for restore operation*

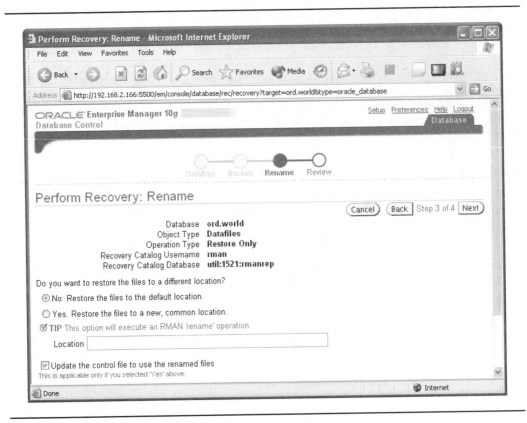

FIGURE 13-16. *Specifying a location for the restored datafile*

Restoring an Entire Database

Although the loss of an entire database is a serious and disastrous event, having a solid backup and recovery policy, as we've described previously in this chapter, can bring the database back up to the most recent committed transaction with a minimum of effort. In the following scenario, we have lost all datafiles. However, because we have multiplexed the control file and online redo log files on many different disks, we will have them available during the RMAN restore and recovery operation.

The entire restore and recovery operation can be performed within RMAN; first, we start up RMAN and open the database in **mount** mode:

```
[oracle@oltp oracle]$ rman target / catalog rman/rman001@rmanrep

Recovery Manager: Release 10.1.0.2.0 - Production
```

connected to target database (not started)
connected to recovery catalog database

RMAN> **startup mount**

Oracle instance started
database mounted
Total System Global Area   197132288 bytes
Fixed Size   778076 bytes
Variable Size   162537636 bytes
Database Buffers   33554432 bytes
Redo Buffers   262144 bytes
RMAN>

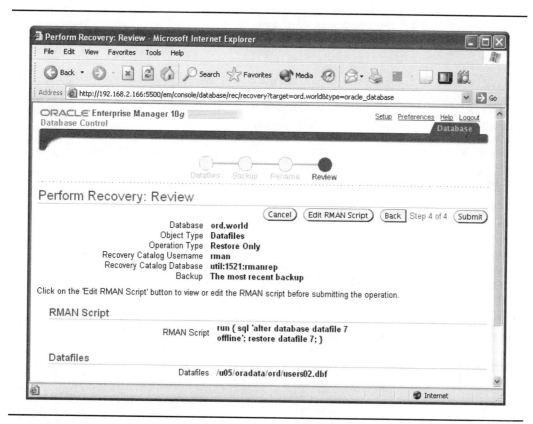

FIGURE 13-17.   *Review the restore options*

RMAN connects to the database and identifies it as being unavailable; this is the same as connecting to SQL*Plus and seeing the message "Connected to an idle instance." The next steps are to restore and recover the database:

```
RMAN> restore database;
Starting restore at 21-MAR-04
allocated channel: ORA_DISK_1
channel ORA_DISK_1: sid=270 devtype=DISK
channel ORA_DISK_1: starting datafile backupset restore
channel ORA_DISK_1: specifying datafile(s) to restore from backup set
restoring datafile 00001 to /u05/oradata/ord/system01.dbf
restoring datafile 00002 to /u05/oradata/ord/undotbs01.dbf
restoring datafile 00003 to /u05/oradata/ord/sysaux01.dbf
restoring datafile 00004 to /u05/oradata/ord/users01.dbf
restoring datafile 00005 to /u05/oradata/ord/example01.dbf
restoring datafile 00006 to /u09/oradata/ord/oe_trans01.dbf
channel ORA_DISK_1: restored backup piece 1
piece handle=/OraFlash/ORD/backupset/2004_03_20/
     o1_mf_nnnd0_TAG20040320T153801_05sgfwf1_.bkp tag=TAG20040320T153801
channel ORA_DISK_1: restore complete
channel ORA_DISK_1: starting datafile backupset restore
channel ORA_DISK_1: specifying datafile(s) to restore from backup set
restoring datafile 00007 to /u05/oradata/ord/users02.dbf
channel ORA_DISK_1: restored backup piece 1
piece handle=/OraFlash/ORD/backupset/2004_03_21/
     o1_mf_nnnd1_TAG20040321T115355_05vooogb_.bkp tag=TAG20040321T115355
channel ORA_DISK_1: restore complete
Finished restore at 21-MAR-04

RMAN> recover database;

Starting recover at 21-MAR-04
using channel ORA_DISK_1
channel ORA_DISK_1: starting incremental datafile backupset restore
channel ORA_DISK_1: specifying datafile(s) to restore from backup set
destination for restore of datafile 00001: /u05/oradata/ord/system01.dbf
destination for restore of datafile 00002: /u05/oradata/ord/undotbs01.dbf
destination for restore of datafile 00003: /u05/oradata/ord/sysaux01.dbf
destination for restore of datafile 00004: /u05/oradata/ord/users01.dbf
destination for restore of datafile 00005: /u05/oradata/ord/example01.dbf
destination for restore of datafile 00006: /u09/oradata/ord/oe_trans01.dbf
channel ORA_DISK_1: restored backup piece 1
piece handle=/OraFlash/ORD/backupset/2004_03_20/
     o1_mf_nnnd1_TAG20040320T162357_05sk3ysx_.bkp tag=TAG20040320T162357
channel ORA_DISK_1: restore complete
channel ORA_DISK_1: starting incremental datafile backupset restore
```

```
channel ORA_DISK_1: specifying datafile(s) to restore from backup set
destination for restore of datafile 00001: /u05/oradata/ord/system01.dbf
destination for restore of datafile 00002: /u05/oradata/ord/undotbs01.dbf
destination for restore of datafile 00003: /u05/oradata/ord/sysaux01.dbf
destination for restore of datafile 00004: /u05/oradata/ord/users01.dbf
destination for restore of datafile 00005: /u05/oradata/ord/example01.dbf
destination for restore of datafile 00006: /u09/oradata/ord/oe_trans01.dbf
channel ORA_DISK_1: restored backup piece 1

piece handle=/OraFlash/ORD/backupset/2004_03_21/
    o1_mf_nnnd1_TAG20040321T115355_05vooogb_.bkp tag=TAG20040321T115355
channel ORA_DISK_1: restore complete

starting media recovery

archive log thread 1 sequence 320 is already on disk as file
    /OraFlash/ORD/archivelog/2004_03_21/o1_mf_1_320_05vp7k0m_.arc
archive log thread 1 sequence 321 is already on disk as file
    /OraFlash/ORD/archivelog/2004_03_21/o1_mf_1_321_05vpj1cq_.arc
archive log thread 1 sequence 322 is already on disk as file
    /OraFlash/ORD/archivelog/2004_03_21/o1_mf_1_322_05vtdg2x_.arc
archive log thread 1 sequence 323 is already on disk as file
    /OraFlash/ORD/archivelog/2004_03_21/o1_mf_1_323_05vzllqk_.arc
archive log filename=/OraFlash/ORD/archivelog/2004_03_21/
    o1_mf_1_320_05vp7k0m_.arc thread=1 sequence=320
archive log filename=/OraFlash/ORD/archivelog/2004_03_21/
    o1_mf_1_321_05vpj1cq_.arc thread=1 sequence=321
media recovery complete
Finished recover at 21-MAR-04

RMAN> alter database open;
database opened
RMAN>
```

The database is now open and available for use. RMAN will pick the most efficient way to perform the requested operation, minimizing the number of files accessed or the number of disk I/Os to bring the database back to a consistent state in as short a time as possible. In the previous example, RMAN used image copies, incremental backups, and archived redo log files to recover the database.

During a recovery operation, RMAN may need to restore archived redo logs from tape; to limit the amount of disk space used during a recovery operation, the **recover** command used in the previous example could use the following options instead:

```
RMAN> recover database delete archivelog maxsize 2gb;
```

The parameter **delete archivelog** directs RMAN to remove archived log files from disk that were restored from tape for this recovery option; the **maxsize 2gb** parameter restricts the amount

of space that can be occupied by restored archived log files at any point in time to 2GB. In our
ord database, these two parameters are not needed; all archived log files needed to recover the
database are kept in the Flash Recover Area on disk to support the defined retention policy.

Validating Restore Operations

Earlier in this chapter, we validated the data blocks in the datafiles that we want to back up. In
this section, we'll take the opposite approach and instead validate the backups that we have
already made. We'll also find out from RMAN which backupsets, image copies, and archived
redo logs would be used in a recovery operation without actually performing the recovery.

RESTORE PREVIEW

The command **restore preview** will provide a list of the files that RMAN will use to perform
the requested operation; the preview will also indicate if a tape volume will be requested, for
example. No files are actually restored; only the recovery catalog is queried to determine which
files are needed. In the following example, we want to find out what RMAN will need if we
need to recover the USERS tablespace:

```
RMAN> restore tablespace users preview;

Starting restore at 21-MAR-04
using channel ORA_DISK_1

List of Backup Sets
===================

BS Key    Type    LV    Size    Device Type    Elapsed Time    Completion Time
------    ----    --    ----    -----------    ------------    ---------------
850       Incr    0     1M      DISK           00:02:42        20-MAR-04
          BP Key: 853    Status: AVAILABLE  Compressed: NO  Tag:
TAG20040320T153801
          Piece Name:
/OraFlash/ORD/backupset/2004_03_20/
    o1_mf_nnnd0_TAG20040320T153801_05sgfwf1_bkp
    List of Datafiles in backup set 850
    File    LV    Type    Ckp SCN    Ckp Time    Name
    ----    --    ----    -------    --------    ------------------------------
    4       0     Incr    1353755    20-MAR-04    /u05/oradata/ord/users01.dbf

BS Key    Type    LV    Size    Device Type    Elapsed Time    Completion Time
------    ----    --    ----    -----------    ------------    ---------------
1173      Incr    1     64K     DISK           00:02:03        21-MAR-04
          BP Key: 1176   Status: AVAILABLE  Compressed: NO  Tag:
                                                            TAG20040321T115355
          Piece Name:
/OraFlash/ORD/backupset/2004_03_21/
    o1_mf_nnnd1_TAG20040321T115355_05vooogb_.bkp
```

```
List of Datafiles in backup set 1173
  File   LV   Type   Ckp SCN   Ckp Time    Name
  ----   --   ----   -------   ---------   ----------------------------
   7     1    Incr   1409491   21-MAR-04   /u05/oradata/ord/users02.dbf
Finished restore at 21-MAR-04
RMAN>
```

For the restore operation, RMAN will need to use two backupsets—one for each datafile in the USERS tablespace. Archived redo log files will be used to bring the tablespace up to the current SCN.

If a restore operation needs to be performed immediately, and one of the files that RMAN will request to perform the operation is offsite, you can use the **change ... unavailable** command to mark a backupset as unavailable and then run the **restore tablespace ... preview** command again to see if RMAN can use disk-based backupsets to fulfill the request.

RESTORE VALIDATE

The **restore ... preview** command does not read the actual backupsets, only the catalog information; if we want to validate whether the backupsets themselves are readable and not corrupted, we use the **restore ... validate** command. As with most other RMAN commands, we can perform the validation for a datafile, a tablespace, or the entire database. In the following example, we'll perform a validation on the same backupsets that RMAN reported in the previous example for the USERS tablespace:

```
RMAN> restore tablespace users validate;

Starting restore at 21-MAR-04
using channel ORA_DISK_1

channel ORA_DISK_1: starting validation of datafile backupset
channel ORA_DISK_1: restored backup piece 1
piece
handle=/OraFlash/ORD/backupset/2004_03_20/
    o1_mf_nnnd0_TAG20040320T153801_05gfwf1_.bkp tag=TAG20040320T153801
channel ORA_DISK_1: validation complete
channel ORA_DISK_1: starting validation of datafile backupset
channel ORA_DISK_1: restored backup piece 1
piece
handle=/OraFlash/ORD/backupset/2004_03_21/
    o1_mf_nnnd1_TAG20040321T115355_05ooogb_.bkp tag=TAG20040321T115355
channel ORA_DISK_1: validation complete
Finished restore at 21-MAR-04

RMAN>
```

All blocks of both backupsets were read to ensure that they are usable for a restore operation for the USERS tablespace.

Point in Time Recovery

RMAN can be used to implement *point in time recovery,* or restoring and recovering a database up to a timestamp or SCN before the point at which a database failure occurred. As you found out in Chapter 12, a point in time recovery (PITR) may be useful for recovering from a user error where a table was dropped yesterday, but the error was not detected until today. Using PITR, we can recover the database to a point in time right before the table was dropped.

Using PITR has the disadvantage of losing all other changes to the database from the point at which the database was restored; this disadvantage needs to be weighed against the consequences of the dropped table. If both options are undesirable, then another method such as Flashback Table or tablespace point in time recovery (TSPITR) should be considered as an alternative for recovering from these types of user errors.

In Figure 13-18, we show how you can configure a TSPITR using OEM to restore the tablespace to March 21st, 2004 at 8:00 A.M., presumably right before the user error occurred. Note that we could alternatively specify an SCN or a log sequence number if we didn't know the precise date at which the event occurred.

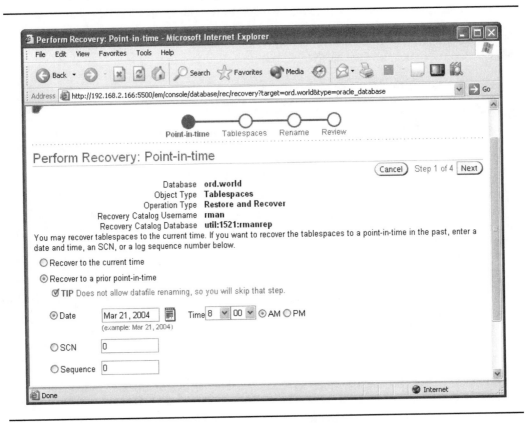

FIGURE 13-18. *Configuring point in time recovery with OEM*

Miscellaneous Operations

In the next few sections, we'll cover some of the other capabilities of RMAN, beyond the backup, restore, and recovery operations. We'll show how to record the existence of other backups made outside of the database and perform some catalog maintenance. We'll also give a couple more examples of the **list** and **report** commands.

Cataloging Other Backups

On occasion, we want the recovery catalog to include backups made outside of RMAN, such as image copies made with operating system commands:

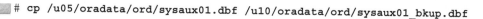

```
# cp /u05/oradata/ord/sysaux01.dbf /u10/oradata/ord/sysaux01_bkup.dbf
```

CAUTION
Image copies created with operating system commands must be performed either while the database is shut down or by using the **alter tablespace ... begin/end backup** *commands.*

Recording this image copy of the SYSAUX tablespace is easy in RMAN using the **catalog** command:

```
RMAN> catalog datafilecopy '/u10/oradata/ord/sysaux01_bkup.dbf';

cataloged datafile copy
datafile copy filename=/u10/oradata/ord/sysaux01_bkup.dbf
              recid=26 stamp=521415717

RMAN>
```

Now that the image copy is recorded in the RMAN repository, it may be considered for use in restore and recovery operations for the SYSAUX tablespace.

Catalog Maintenance

Earlier in this chapter, we discussed the use of the **backup validate** command to ensure that all the files that could be used in a backup operation were available, readable, and not corrupted. In that example, we found out that we had a mismatch between what the catalog reported and the archived redo logs on disk; some old archived redo logs were inadvertently removed from disk during a cleanup operation. In this section, we'll step through some of the maintenance operations we would need to perform to bring the catalog in synch with what actually exists on disk.

```
RMAN> backup validate database archivelog all;

Starting backup at 21-MAR-04
allocated channel: ORA_DISK_1
channel ORA_DISK_1: sid=246 devtype=DISK
```

```
RMAN-00571: ================================================================
RMAN-00569: =============== ERROR MESSAGE STACK FOLLOWS ===============
RMAN-00571: ================================================================
RMAN-03002: failure of backup command at 03/21/2004 10:13:04
RMAN-06059: expected archived log not found, lost of archived log
compromises recoverability
ORA-19625: error identifying file
/u01/app/oracle/flash_recovery_area/ORD/archivelog/2004_03_03/
     o1_mf_1_6_04f6hy2t_.arc
ORA-27037: unable to obtain file status
Linux Error: 2: No such file or directory
Additional information: 3
RMAN>
```

Our first attempt to fix the problem was to remove all obsolete files outside of our recovery window of four days, keeping an extra day's worth of logs, since we have plenty of space in the Flash Recovery Area.

```
RMAN> delete obsolete recovery window of 5 days;

using channel ORA_DISK_1
Deleting the following obsolete backups and copies:
Type           Key    Completion Time   Filename/Handle
----------     ---    ---------------   ---------------
Backup Set     559    15-MAR-04
  Backup Piece      562    15-MAR-04
                    /OraFlash/ORD/backupset/2004_03_15/
                    o1_mf_nnsnf_TAG20040315T221256_05dzxg62_.bkp
Archive Log         292    03-MAR-04
           /u01/app/oracle/flash_recovery_area/ORD/archivelog/2004_03_03/
                    o1_mf_1_6_04f6hy2t_.arc
Archive Log         293    03-MAR-04
           /u01/app/oracle/flash_recovery_area/ORD/archivelog/2004_03_03/
                    o1_mf_1_7_04f6xrp4_.arc
. . .
Archive Log         491    15-MAR-04
             /OraFlash/ORD/archivelog/2004_03_15/o1_mf_1_205_05ds6rqj_.arc
Archive Log         492    15-MAR-04
             /OraFlash/ORD/archivelog/2004_03_15/o1_mf_1_206_05dxmk83_.arc

Do you really want to delete the above objects (enter YES or NO)? yes
deleted backup piece
        backup piece handle=/OraFlash/ORD/backupset/2004_03_15/
    o1_mf_nnsnf_TAG20040315T221256_05dzxg62_.bkp recid=2 stamp=520899406
deleted archive log
archive log      filename=/OraFlash/ORD/archivelog/2004_03_14/
        o1_mf_1_180_059dscwh_.arc recid=175 stamp=520781518
deleted archive log
archive log filename=/OraFlash/ORD/archivelog/2004_03_14/
        o1_mf_1_181_059dshjx_.arc recid=176 stamp=520781519
. . .
archive log      filename=/OraFlash/ORD/archivelog/2004_03_15/
        o1_mf_1_206_05dxmk83_.arc recid=201 stamp=520897043
```

```
Deleted 28 objects

RMAN-06207: WARNING: 174 objects could not be deleted for DISK channel(s)
due
RMAN-06208:              to mismatched status.  Use CROSSCHECK command to fix
status
RMAN-06210: List of Mismatched objects
RMAN-06211: ==========================
RMAN-06212:   Object Type    Filename/Handle
RMAN-06213:   -----------    --------------------------------------
RMAN-06214: Archivelog
    /u01/app/oracle/flash_recovery_area/ORD/archivelog/2004_03_03/
        o1_mf_1_6_04f6hy2t_.arc
. . .
RMAN-06214: Archivelog
    /u01/app/oracle/flash_recovery_area/ORD/archivelog/2004_03_14/
        o1_mf_1_178_0593yl5x_.arc
RMAN-06214: Archivelog
    /OraFlash/ORD/archivelog/2004_03_14/o1_mf_1_179_059bch2k_.arc
RMAN>
```

Although we did remove a lot of the obsolete files from the Flash Recovery Area, the catalog and the contents of the disk were still not in synch; RMAN suggests that we use the **crosscheck** command to remedy the problem:

RMAN> **crosscheck archivelog all;**

```
released channel: ORA_DISK_1
allocated channel: ORA_DISK_1
channel ORA_DISK_1: sid=246 devtype=DISK
validation failed for archived log
archive log
    filename=/u01/app/oracle/flash_recovery_area/ORD/archivelog/2004_03_03/
        o1_mf_1_6_04f6hy2t_.arc recid=1 stamp=519857573
validation failed for archived log
. . .
archive log
    filename=/OraFlash/ORD/archivelog/2004_03_21/o1_mf_1_318_05vh0850_.arc
                recid=313 stamp=521373610
Crosschecked 286 objects

RMAN>
```

The missing archived redo logs are now marked as EXPIRED in the catalog, and they won't be considered when validating backups or for performing restore or recovery operations:

RMAN> **backup validate database archivelog all;**

```
Starting backup at 21-MAR-04
allocated channel: ORA_DISK_1
```

```
channel ORA_DISK_1: sid=252 devtype=DISK
channel ORA_DISK_1: starting compressed archive log backupset
channel ORA_DISK_1: specifying archive log(s) in backup set
input archive log thread=1 sequence=207 recid=202 stamp=520901173
input archive log thread=1 sequence=208 recid=203 stamp=520905522
input archive log thread=1 sequence=209 recid=204 stamp=520905663
. . .
input archive log thread=1 sequence=326 recid=321 stamp=521404606
input archive log thread=1 sequence=329 recid=324 stamp=521412412
channel ORA_DISK_1: backup set complete, elapsed time: 00:01:58
channel ORA_DISK_1: starting compressed full datafile backupset
channel ORA_DISK_1: specifying datafile(s) in backupset
input datafile fno=00001 name=/u05/oradata/ord/system01.dbf
input datafile fno=00003 name=/u05/oradata/ord/sysaux01.dbf
input datafile fno=00005 name=/u05/oradata/ord/example01.dbf
input datafile fno=00002 name=/u05/oradata/ord/undotbs01.dbf
input datafile fno=00004 name=/u05/oradata/ord/users01.dbf
input datafile fno=00006 name=/u09/oradata/ord/oe_trans01.dbf
input datafile fno=00007 name=/u05/oradata/ord/users02.dbf
channel ORA_DISK_1: backup set complete, elapsed time: 00:02:08
Finished backup at 21-MAR-04

RMAN>
```

All datafiles that RMAN could consider for a backup operation, including archived redo logs, are available and readable.

REPORT and LIST

All throughout this chapter, we've provided a number of examples of how to extract information from the recovery catalog, whether it resides in the target database control file or in a catalog database repository. We've used both the **list** and **report** commands. The primary difference between these commands is in their complexity: The **list** command displays information about backupsets and image copies in the repository as well as lists the contents of scripts stored in the repository catalog:

```
RMAN> list backup summary;
```

```
List of Backups
===============
```

Key	TY	LV	S	Device Type	Completion Time	#Pieces	#Copies	Compressed	Tag
558	B	F	A	DISK	15-MAR-04	1	1	NO	TAG20040315T221256
560	B	F	A	DISK	15-MAR-04	1	1	NO	TAG20040315T221655
657	B	F	A	DISK	19-MAR-04	1	1	NO	TAG20040319T094414
670	B	F	A	DISK	19-MAR-04	1	1	NO	TAG20040319T100418

. . .

```
1564  B  1  A  DISK      21-MAR-04        1        1      YES
                                                          TAG20040321T185604
1585  B  F  A  DISK      21-MAR-04        1        1      NO
                                                          TAG20040321T185806

RMAN>
```

In contrast, the **report** command performs a more detailed analysis of the information in the recovery catalog; as in one of our previous examples, we used **report** to identify which database files needed backups to comply with our retention policy. In the following example, we find out what the datafiles looked like back on 3/15/04, and then we query the current status of the datafiles:

```
RMAN> report schema at time='15-mar-04';

Report of database schema
File   K-bytes   Tablespace   RB segs   Datafile Name
----   -------   ----------   -------   --------------------------------
1      471040    SYSTEM       YES       /u05/oradata/ord/system01.dbf
2       25600    UNDOTBS1     YES       /u05/oradata/ord/undotbs01.dbf
3      307200    SYSAUX       YES       /u05/oradata/ord/sysaux01.dbf
4       10240    USERS        YES       /u05/oradata/ord/users01.dbf
5      153600    EXAMPLE      YES       /u05/oradata/ord/example01.dbf

RMAN> report schema;

Report of database schema
File   K-bytes   Tablespace   RB segs   Datafile Name
----   -------   ----------   -------   --------------------------------
1      471040    SYSTEM       YES       /u05/oradata/ord/system01.dbf
2       25600    UNDOTBS1     YES       /u05/oradata/ord/undotbs01.dbf
3      307200    SYSAUX       NO        /u05/oradata/ord/sysaux01.dbf
4       10240    USERS        NO        /u05/oradata/ord/users01.dbf
5      153600    EXAMPLE      NO        /u05/oradata/ord/example01.dbf
6       10240    OE_TRANS     NO        /u09/oradata/ord/oe_trans01.dbf
7        5120    USERS        NO        /u05/oradata/ord/users02.dbf

RMAN>
```

At some point between 3/15/04 and today, we created the tablespace OE_TRANS and added another datafile to the USERS tablespace.

CHAPTER
14

Oracle Data Guard

racle Data Guard provides a solution for high availability, enhanced performance, and automated failover. You can use Oracle Data Guard to create and maintain multiple standby databases for a primary database. The standby databases can be started in read-only mode to support reporting users, then returned to standby mode. Changes to the primary database can be automatically relayed from the primary database to the standby databases with a guarantee of no data lost in the process. The standby database servers can be physically separate from the primary server.

In this chapter, you will see how to administer an Oracle Data Guard environment, along with sample configuration files for a Data Guard environment.

Data Guard Architecture

In a Data Guard implementation, a database running in ARCHIVELOG mode is designated as the primary database for an application. One or more standby databases, accessible via Oracle Net, provide for failover capabilities. Data Guard automatically transmits redo information to the standby databases, where it is applied. As a result, the standby database is transactionally consistent. Depending on how you configure the redo application process, the standby databases may be in sync with the primary database or may lag behind it.

Figure 14-1 shows a standard Data Guard implementation.

The redo log data is transferred to the Standby Databases via Log Transport Services, as defined via your initialization parameter settings. Log Apply Services apply the redo information to the standby databases. A third set of services, Role Management Services, simplify the process of making Standby Databases serve as the primary database.

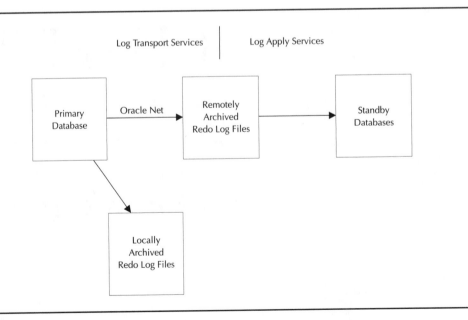

FIGURE 14-1. *Simple Data Guard configuration*

NOTE
The primary database can be a single instance or a multi-instance Real Application Clusters implementation.

Physical vs. Logical Standby Databases

Two types of standby databases are supported: physical standbys and logical standbys. A *physical standby* database has the same structures as the primary database. A *logical standby* database may have different internal structures (such as additional indexes used for reporting). You synchronize a logical standby database with the primary by transforming the redo data into SQL statements that are executed against the standby database.

Physical and logical standby databases serve different purposes. A physical standby database is a block-for-block copy of the primary database, so it can be used for database backups in place of the primary database. During disaster recovery, the physical standby looks exactly like the primary database it replaces.

A logical standby database, because it supports additional database structures, can more easily be used to support specific reporting requirements that would otherwise burden the primary database. Additionally, rolling upgrades of primary and standby databases can be performed with minimal downtime when logical standbys are used. The type of standby to use depends on your needs; many environments start out using physical standby databases for disaster recovery and then add in additional logical standby databases to support specific reporting and business requirements.

NOTE
The operating system and platform architecture on the primary and standby locations must be identical. The directory structures and operating system patch levels may differ, but you should minimize the differences to simplify administration and failover processes. If the standby is located on the same server as the primary, you must use a different directory structure for the two databases, and they cannot share an archive log directory.

Data Protection Modes

When you configure the primary and standby databases, you will need to determine the level of data loss that is acceptable to the business. In the primary database, you will define its archive log destination areas, and at least one of which will refer to the remote site used by the standby database. The ASYNC, SYNC, ARCH, LGWR, NOAFFIRM and AFFIRM attributes of the LOG_ARCHIVE_DEST_*n* parameter setting (see Table 14-1, later in this chapter) for the standby database will direct Oracle Data Guard to select among several modes of operation:

- In maximum protection (or "no data loss") mode, at least one standby location must be written to before a transaction commits in the primary database. The primary database shuts down if the standby database's log location is unavailable.

- In maximum availability mode, at least one standby location must be written to before a transaction commits in the primary database. If the standby location is not available, the primary database does not shut down. When the fault is corrected, the redo that has been generated since the fault is transported and applied to the standby databases.

■ In maximum performance mode (the default), transactions can commit before their redo information is sent to the standby locations. Commits in the primary database occur as soon as writes to the local online redo logs complete. The writes to the standby locations are handled by the ARCH process by default.

Once you have decided the type of standby and the data protection mode for your configuration, you can create your standby database.

LOG_ARCHIVE_DEST_*n* Parameter Attributes

As illustrated in the following sections, Oracle Data Guard configurations rely on a number of attributes within the LOG_ARCHIVE_DEST_*n* parameter. Table 14-1 summarizes the attributes available for this parameter. In almost all cases the attributes are paired; in some cases the second member of the pair simply serves to nullify the setting.

Attribute	Description
AFFIRM and NOAFFIRM	AFFIRM ensures all disk I/O to the archived redo log files or standby redo log files at the standby destination is performed synchronously and completes successfully before online redo log files on the primary database can be reused. AFFIRM is required to achieve no data loss.
	NOAFFIRM indicates all disk I/O to archived redo log files and standby redo log files is to be performed asynchronously; online redo log files on the primary database can be reused before the disk I/O on the standby destination completes.
ALTERNATE and NOALTERNATE	ALTERNATE specifies an alternate LOG_ARCHIVE_DEST_*n* destination to use when the original archiving destination fails.
ARCH and LGWR	ARCH, the default, specifies that the ARCH process is responsible for transmitting redo data to archival destinations. LGWR specifies that the LGWR process performs the log transport operations.
DB_UNIQUE_NAME and NODB_UNIQUE_NAME	DB_UNIQUE_NAME specifies the unique database name for the destination.
DELAY and NODELAY	DELAY specifies a time lag between archiving redo data on the standby site and applying the archived redo log file to the standby database; DELAY may be used to protect the standby database from corrupted or erroneous primary data. If neither DELAY nor NODELAY is specified, NODELAY is the default.
DEPENDENCY and NODEPENDENCY	DEPENDENCY allows you to transmit redo data to a destination that then shares its archived redo log files among multiple standby databases. You must use the REGISTER and SERVICE attributes when you create a DEPENDENCY.

TABLE 14-1.   *LOG_ARCHIVE_DEST_n Parameter Attributes*

Attribute	Description
LOCATION and SERVICE	Each destination *must* specify either the LOCATION or the SERVICE attribute to identify either a local disk directory (via LOCATION) or a remote database destination where Log Transport Services can transmit redo data (via SERVICE).
MANDATORY and OPTIONAL	If a destination is OPTIONAL, archiving to that destination may fail, yet the online redo log file is available for reuse and may be overwritten eventually. If the archival operation of a MANDATORY destination fails, online redo log files cannot be overwritten.
MAX_FAILURE and NOMAX_FAILURE	MAX_FAILURE specifies the maximum number of reopen attempts before the primary database permanently gives up on the standby database.
NET_TIMEOUT and NONET_TIMEOUT	NET_TIMEOUT specifies the number of seconds the log writer process on the primary system waits for status from the network server process before terminating the network connection. The default value is 180 seconds.
QUOTA_SIZE and NOQUOTA_SIZE	QUOTA_SIZE indicates the maximum number of 512-byte blocks of physical storage on a disk device that can be used by a local destination.
QUOTA_USED and NOQUOTA_USED	QUOTA_USED identifies the number of 512-byte blocks of data that were archived on a specified destination.
REGISTER and NOREGISTER	REGISTER indicates that the location of the archived redo log file is to be recorded at the corresponding destination.
REOPEN and NOREOPEN	REOPEN specifies the minimum number of seconds (the default is 300 seconds) before the archiver processes (ARC*n*) or the log writer process (LGWR) should try again to access a previously failed destination.
SYNC and ASYNC	SYNC and ASYNC specify that network I/O is to be done synchronously or asynchronously when using the log writer process (LGWR). The default is SYNC=PARALLEL, which should be used when there are multiple destinations with the SYNC attribute. All destinations should use the same value.
TEMPLATE and NOTEMPLATE	TEMPLATE defines a directory specification and format template for names of the archived redo log files or standby redo log files at the standby destination. You can specify these attributes in either the primary or standby initialization parameter file, but the attribute applies only to the database role that is archiving.

TABLE 14-1.   *LOG_ARCHIVE_DEST_n Parameter Attributes (continued)*

Attribute	Description
VALID_FOR	VALID_FOR identifies when Log Transport Services can transmit redo data to destinations based on the following factors: (1) whether the database is currently running in the primary or the standby role, and (2) whether online redo log files, standby redo log files, or both are currently being archived on the database at this destination. The default value for this attribute is VALID_FOR= (ALL_LOGFILES, ALL_ROLES). Other values include PRIMARY_ROLE, STANDBY_ROLE, ONLINE_LOGFILES, and STANDBY_LOGFILE.
VERIFY and NOVERIFY	VERIFY indicates an archiver process should verify the correctness of the contents of a completed archived redo log file. The default is NOVERIFY.

TABLE 14-1. *LOG_ARCHIVE_DEST_n Parameter Attributes (continued)*

Creating the Standby Database Configuration

You can use SQL*Plus, Oracle Enterprise Manager (OEM), or Data Guard–specific tools to configure and administer Data Guard configurations. The parameters you set will depend on the configuration you choose.

If the primary and standby databases are on the same server, you will need to set a value for the DB_UNIQUE_NAME parameter. Because the directory structures for the two databases will be different, you must either manually rename files or define values for the DB_FILE_NAME_CONVERT and LOG_FILE_NAME_CONVERT parameters in the standby database. You must set up unique service names for the primary and standby databases via the SERVICE_NAMES initialization parameter.

If the primary and standby databases are on separate servers, you can use the same directory structures for each, avoiding the need for the filename conversion parameters. If you use a different directory structure for the database files, you will need to define the values for the DB_FILE_NAME_CONVERT and LOG_FILE_NAME_CONVERT parameters in the standby database.

In physical standby databases, all the redo comes from the primary database. When physical standby databases are opened in read-only mode, no redo is generated. Oracle Data Guard does, however, use archived redo log files to support the replication of the data and SQL commands used to update the standby databases.

> **NOTE**
> *For each standby database, you should create a standby redo log file to store redo data received from the primary database.*

Preparing the Primary Database

On the primary database, make sure you have set values for the following parameters, which impact the transfer of the redo log data. The first five parameters, listed next, are standard for most databases; set REMOTE_LOGIN_PASSWORDFILE to EXCLUSIVE to support remote access by SYSDBA-privileged users.

DB_NAME	The database name. Use the same name for all standby databases and the primary database.
DB_UNIQUE_NAME	The unique name for the database. This value must be different for each standby database and must differ from the primary database.
SERVICE_NAMES	Service names for the databases; set separate service names for the primary and standby databases.
CONTROL_FILES	The location of the controlfiles.
REMOTE_LOGIN_PASSWORDFILE	Set to EXCLUSIVE or SHARED. Set the same password for SYS on both the primary and standby databases.

The LOG_ARCHIVE-related parameters, listed next, will configure how the Log Transport Services work:

LOG_ARCHIVE_CONFIG	Within the DB_CONFIG parameter, list the primary and standby databases.
LOG_ARCHIVE_DEST_1	The location of the primary database's archived redo log files.
LOG_ARCHIVE_DEST_2	The remote location used for the standby redo log files.
LOG_ARCHIVE_DEST_STATE_1	Set to ENABLE.
LOG_ARCHIVE_DEST_STATE_2	Set to ENABLE to enable log transport.
LOG_ARCHIVE_FORMAT	Specify the format for the archive log file's name.

For this example, assume that the primary database has a DB_UNIQUE_NAME value of 'headqtr' and the physical standby database has a DB_UNIQUE_NAME value of 'salesofc'. The SERVICE_NAMES values are the same as the DB_UNIQUE_NAME values.

The LOG_ARCHIVE_CONFIG parameter setting may resemble the following:

```
LOG_ARCHIVE_CONFIG='DG_CONFIG=(headqtr,salesofc)'
```

There are two LOG_ARCHIVE_DEST_n entries—one for the local copy of the archived redo log files, and a second for the remote copy that will be shipped to the physical standby database:

```
LOG_ARCHIVE_DEST_1=
  'LOCATION=/arch/headqtr/
   VALID_FOR=(ALL_LOGFILES,ALL_ROLES)
   DB_UNIQUE_NAME=headqtr'
LOG_ARCHIVE_DEST_2=
  'SERVICE=salesofc
   VALID_FOR=(ONLINE_LOGFILES,PRIMARY_ROLE)
   DB_UNIQUE_NAME=salesofc'
```

The LOG_ARCHIVE_DEST_1 parameter specifies the location of the archived redo log files for the primary database (as specified via the DB_UNIQUE_NAME parameter). The LOG_ARCHIVE_DEST_2 parameter gives the service name of the physical standby database as its location. For each of these destinations, the corresponding LOG_ARCHIVE_DEST_STATE_*n* parameter should have a value of 'ENABLE'.

The standby role–related parameters include the FAL (Fetch Archive Log) parameters used prior to Oracle Database 10*g* to resolve gaps in the range of archive logs copied to the standby databases:

FAL_SERVER	Specify the service name of the FAL server (typically the primary database).
FAL_CLIENT	Specify the service name of the FAL client (the standby database fetching the logs).
DB_FILE_NAME_CONVERT	If the primary and standby databases use differing directory structures, specify the pathname and filename location of the primary database datafiles, followed by the standby location.
LOG_FILE_NAME_CONVERT	If the primary and standby databases use differing directory structures, specify the pathname and filename location of the primary database log files, followed by the standby location.
STANDBY_FILE_MANAGEMENT	Set to AUTO.

Sample settings for these parameters are shown in the following listing:

```
FAL_SERVER=headqtr
FAL_CLIENT=salesofc
LOG_FILE_NAME_CONVERT=
'/arch/headqtr/','/arch/salesofc/','/arch1/headqtr/','/arch1/salesofc/'
STANDBY_FILE_MANAGEMENT=AUTO
```

If the primary database is not already in ARCHIVELOG mode, enable archiving by issuing the **alter database archivelog** command while the database is mounted but not open.

Once the log-related parameters have been set, you can begin the process of creating the standby database.

Step 1: Back Up the Primary Database's Datafiles
First, perform a physical backup of the primary database. Oracle recommends using the RMAN utility to back up the database; you can use the **duplicate** command within RMAN to automate the process of creating the standby database.

Step 2: Create a Controlfile for the Standby Database
In the primary database, issue the following command to generate a controlfile that will be used for the standby database:

```
alter database create standby controlfile as '/tmp/salesofc.ctl';
```

Note that you specify the directory and filename where you want the controlfile to be created. Also, do not use the same directory and controlfile name as you use for the primary database.

Step 3: Create an Initialization File for the Standby Database

In the primary database, create a parameter file from the server parameter file:

```
create pfile='/tmp/initsalesofc.ora' from spfile;
```

Edit this initialization file to set the proper values for the standby database. Set the standby database's values for the DB_UNIQUE_NAME, SERVICE_NAMES, CONTROL_FILES, DB_FILE_NAME_CONVERT, LOG_FILE_NAME_CONVERT, LOG_ARCHIVE_DEST_*n*, INSTANCE_NAME, FAL_SERVER, and FAL_CLIENT. The filename conversions should be the same as in the primary database—you want to convert the filenames from the primary database to the standby database format when the redo information is applied:

```
LOG_ARCHIVE_DEST_1=
'LOCATION=/arch/salesofc/
VALID_FOR=(ALL_LOGFILES,ALL_ROLES)
DB_UNIQUE_NAME=salesofc'
LOG_ARCHIVE_DEST_2=
'SERVICE=headqtr
VALID_FOR=(ONLINE_LOGFILES,PRIMARY_ROLE)
```

In the standby environment, the LOG_ARCHIVE_DEST_1 parameter points to its local archive log destination, and LOG_ARCHIVE_DEST_2 points to the primary database's service name. If the roles of the two databases are switched, the original primary database will be able to serve as the standby database. While the standby database is running in standby mode, the LOG_ARCHIVE_DEST_2 value will be ignored.

> **NOTE**
> *Set the COMPATIBLE parameter to the same value for both the primary and standby databases. To take advantage of the new features in Oracle 10g, set the COMPATIBLE value to 10.1.0 or higher. Once COMPATIBLE is set to 10.1.0, you cannot reset it to a lower value.*

Step 4: Copy the Database Files to the Standby Database Location

Copy the datafiles from Step 1, the controlfile from Step 2, and the standby initialization file from Step 3 to the standby database location. Put the files in the proper directories (as defined by the CONTROL_FILES, DB_FILE_NAME_CONVERT, and LOG_FILE_NAME_CONVERT parameters). Alternatively, use an RMAN backup of the primary database to create the standby database files.

Step 5: Configure the Standby Database Environment

At this point, the files are in place. You need to create the proper environment variables and services to allow an instance to access the files. For example, in a Windows environment you should use the ORADIM utility to create a new service, as shown in this example:

```
ORADIM -NEW -SID salesofc -INTPWD oracle -STARTMODE MANUAL
```

Next, create a password file for the standby database via the ORAPWD utility (see Chapter 2).

You then create the Oracle Net parameters and services needed to access the standby database. In the standby environment, create an Oracle Net listener service for the standby database. In the standby server's sqlnet.ora file, set the SQLNET.EXPIRE_TIME parameter to 1 to activate broken-connection detection after one minute. See Chapter 16 for further details on Oracle Net connections.

Next, create a service name entry for the standby database in the tnsnames.ora file and then distribute that update to both the standby and primary database servers.

Lastly, create a server parameter file via the **create spfile from pfile** command, passing the name and location of the standby parameter file as input to that command.

Step 6: Start the Standby Database

From within SQL*Plus, start the standby database in read-only mode, as shown in the following example:

```
startup open read only;
```

> **NOTE**
> *You can add new temporary files to the temporary tablespaces in the standby database. Adding temporary files will support sorting operations required for reporting activity within the standby database.*

Start the redo application process within the standby database via the following **alter database** command:

```
alter database recover managed standby database
    disconnect from session;
```

Step 7: Verify the Configuration

To test the configuration, go to the primary database and force a log switch to occur via the **alter system** command, as shown here:

```
alter system switch logfile;
```

The primary database's redo log data should then be copied to the standby location.

On the standby database, you can query the V$ARCHIVED_LOG view to see which archived logs have been applied to the database. As new logs are received from the primary database and applied to the standby, new rows will be added to the listing in V$ARCHIVED_LOG.

Creating Logical Standby Databases

Logical standby databases follow many of the same steps used to create physical standby databases. Because they rely on the reexecution of SQL commands, logical standby databases have greater restrictions on their use. If any of your tables in the primary database use the following datatypes, they will be skipped during the redo application process:

- BFILE
- ROWID

- UROWID
- User-defined datatype
- Object types
- REFs
- Varying arrays
- Nested tables
- XMLtype

Additionally, tables that use table compression and the schemas that are installed with the Oracle software are skipped during redo application. The DBA_LOGSTDBY_UNSUPPORTED view lists the objects that are not supported for logical standby databases. The DBA_LOGSTDBY_ SKIP view lists the schemas that will be skipped.

A logical standby database is not identical to the primary database. Each transaction that is executed in the logical standby database must be the logical equivalent of the transaction that was executed in the primary database. Therefore, you should make sure your tables have the proper constraints on them—primary keys, unique constraints, check constraints, and foreign keys—so the proper rows can be targeted for update in the logical standby database. You can query DBA_LOGSTDBY_NOT_UNIQUE to list tables that lack primary key or unique constraints in the primary database.

To create a logical standby database, follow the steps outlined in the remainder of this section.

Step 1: Create a Physical Standby Database
Following the steps in the prior section of this chapter, create a physical standby database.

Step 2: Enable Supplemental Logging
Supplemental logging on the primary database generates additional information in the redo log. That information is then used during the redo application process in the standby database to make sure the correct rows are affected by the generated SQL. To add primary key and unique index information to the redo data, issue the following command in the primary database:

```
alter database add supplemental log data
    (primary key, unique index) columns;
```

You can verify supplemental logging has been enabled by querying the Supplemenal_Log_ Data_PK and Supplemental_Log_Data_UI columns from the V$DATABASE view. The column values are YES/NO flags to indicate if logging has been enabled.

Step 3: Transition the Physical Standby to a Logical Standby
Physical standby databases operate in read-only mode; logical standby databases are open for writes and generate their own redo data. In the initialization file for the logical standby database, specify destinations for the logical standby database's redo data (LOG_ARCHIVE_DEST_1) and the incoming redo from the primary database (in this example, LOG_ARCHIVE_DEST_3 will be used to avoid conflicts with the earlier LOG_ARCHIVE_DEST_2 setting). You do not want a

logical standby database to have the LOG_ARCHIVE_DEST_2 destination enabled and pointing back to the primary database.

Shut down the logical standby database. In the primary database, create a logical standby controlfile, as shown in the following listing (be sure to use the **logical standby** clause of the **alter database** command):

```
alter database create logical standby controlfile
    as '/tmp/salesofc.ctl';
```

Copy that file to the standby database's server.

Step 4: Start the Logical Standby Database

Start up and mount the logical standby database, using its initialization parameter file. While the database is mounted, use the **alter database** command to prepare the database for redo application. Issue the following command in the mounted logical standby database:

```
alter database recover managed standby database;
```

Within the same session, activate the logical standby database:

```
alter database activate standby database;
```

Shut down the logical standby database, then start up and mount the database but do not open it.

Step 5: Set the New Database Name for the Logical Standby Database

Oracle provides a utility named DBNEWID to automate the process of changing the name of a logical standby database.

NOTE
You should run this utility only on the logical standby database.

The DBNEWID utility's executable is named "nid." While the logical standby database is mounted but not open, execute the following:

```
nid TARGET=sys/password@salesofc DBNAME=salesofc
```

The DBNEWID utility will display the operations it performs, including changing the internal database ID and the database name. When the utility completes, you must create a new password file via the ORAPWD utility.

To complete the database renaming steps, you must edit the initialization parameter file (modify DB_NAME) and then create a new server parameter file from that file (via the **create spfile from pfile** command). You can then start up and open the logical standby database, as shown in the following listing:

```
startup mount;
alter database open resetlogs;
```

Since the database has been renamed, you must reset the global name parameter via the **alter database** command, as shown in the following example:

```
alter database rename global_name to salesofc;
```

If you are expecting to generate large sorts within the logical standby database, you can create additional temporary files for its temporary tablespaces.

Step 6: Start the Redo Application Process

Within the logical standby database, you can now start the redo application process:

```
alter database start logical standby apply;
```

To see the logs that have been received and applied to the logical standby database, query the DBA_LOGSTDBY_LOG view. You can query the V$LOGSTDBY view to see the activity log of the logical standby redo application process. The logical standby database is now available for use.

Using Real-time Apply

By default, redo data is not applied to a standby database until the standby redo log file is archived. When you use the real-time apply feature, redo data is applied to the standby database as it is received, reducing the time lag between the databases and potentially shortening the time required to fail over to the standby database.

To enable real-time apply in a physical standby database, execute the following command in the standby database:

```
alter database recover managed standby database
using current logfile;
```

For a logical standby database, the command to use is

```
alter database start logical standby apply immediate;
```

The Recovery_Mode column of the V$ARCHIVE_DEST_STATUS view will have a value of 'MANAGED REAL-TIME APPLY' if real-time apply has been enabled.

As shown earlier in this chapter, you can enable the redo application on a physical standby database via the command:

```
alter database recover managed standby database
    disconnect from session;
```

The **disconnect from session** clause allows the command to run in the background after you disconnect from your Oracle session. When you start a foreground session and issue the same command without the **disconnect from session** clause, control is not returned to the command prompt until the recovery is cancelled by another session. To stop the redo application in a physical standby database—whether in a background session or a foreground session—use the following command:

```
alter database recover managed standby database cancel;
```

For a logical standby database, the command to stop the Log Apply Services is

```
alter database stop logical standby apply;
```

Managing Gaps in Archive Log Sequences

If the standby database has not received one or more archived logs generated by the primary database, it does not have a full record of the transactions in the primary database. Oracle Data Guard detects the gap in the archive log sequence automatically; it resolves the problem by copying the missing sequence of log files to the standby destination. Prior to Oracle 10g, the FAL (Fetch Archive Log) client and server were used to resolve gaps from the primary database.

To determine if there is a gap in your physical standby database, query the V$ARCHIVE_GAP view. For each gap, that view will report the lowest and highest log sequence number of the set of logs that are missing from the standby database. If there is some reason why Oracle Data Guard has not been able to copy the logs, you can copy the files manually to your physical standby database environment and register them using the **alter database register logfile** *filename* command; then you can start the redo apply process. After the logs have been applied, check the V$ARCHIVE_GAP view again to see if there is another gap to resolve.

Managing Roles—Switchovers and Failovers

Each database that participates in a Data Guard configuration has a role—it is either a primary database or a standby database. At some point, those roles may need to change. For example, if there is a hardware failure on the primary database's server, you may fail over to the standby database. Depending on your configuration choices, there may be some loss of data during a failover.

A second type of role change is called a *switchover*. This occurs when the primary database switches roles with a standby database, and the standby becomes the new primary database. During a switchover, there should be no data lost. Switchovers and failovers require manual intervention by a database administrator.

Switchovers

Switchovers are planned role changes, usually to allow for maintenance activities to be performed on the primary database server. A standby database is chosen to act as the new primary database, the switchover occurs, and applications now write their data to the new primary database. At some later point in time you can switch the databases back to their original roles.

NOTE
*You can perform switchovers with either a logical standby database
or a physical standby database; the physical standby database is the
preferred option.*

What if you have defined multiple standby databases? When one of the physical standby databases becomes the new primary database, the other standby databases must be able to receive their redo log data from the new primary database. In that configuration, you must define the LOG_ARCHIVE_DEST_*n* parameters to allow those standby sites to receive data from the new primary database location.

NOTE
*Verify that the database that will become the new primary database is
running in ARCHIVELOG mode.*

In the following sections, you will see the steps required to perform a switchover to a standby database. The standby database should be actively applying redo log data prior to the switchover, as this will minimize the time required to complete the switchover.

Switchovers to Physical Standby Databases

Switchovers are initiated on the primary database and completed on the standby database. In this section, you will see the steps for performing a switchover to a physical standby database.

Begin by verifying that the primary database is capable of performing a switchover. Query V$DATABASE for the value of the Switchover_Status column:

```
select Switchover_Status from V$DATABASE;
```

If the Switchover_Status column's value is anything other than TO STANDBY, it is not possible to perform the switchover (usually due to a configuration or hardware issue). If the column's value is SESSIONS ACTIVE, you should terminate active user sessions. Valid values for the Switchover_ Status column are shown in Table 14-2.

From within the primary database, you can initiate its transition to the physical standby database role with the following command:

```
alter database commit to switchover to physical standby;
```

As part of executing this command, Oracle will back up the current primary database's controlfile to a trace file. At this point, you should shut down the primary database and mount it:

```
shutdown immediate;
startup mount;
```

The primary database is prepared for the switchover; you should now go to the physical standby database that will serve as the new primary database.

Switchover_Status Value	Description
NOT ALLOWED	The current database is not a primary database with standby databases.
PREPARING DICTIONARY	This logical standby database is sending its redo data to a primary database and other standby databases to prepare for the switchover.
PREPARING SWITCHOVER	Used by logical standby configurations while redo data is being accepted for the switchover.
RECOVERY NEEDED	This standby database has not received the switchover request.
SESSIONS ACTIVE	There are active SQL sessions in the primary database; they must be disconnected before continuing.
SWITCHOVER PENDING	Valid for standby databases in which the primary database switchover request has been received but not processed.
SWITCHOVER LATENT	The switchover did not complete and went back to the primary database.
TO LOGICAL STANDBY	This primary database has received a complete dictionary from a logical standby database.
TO PRIMARY	This standby database can switch over to a primary database.
TO STANDBY	This primary database can switch over to a standby database.

TABLE 14-2. *Switchover_Status Values*

In the physical standby database, check the switchover status in the V$DATABASE view; its status should be TO PRIMARY (see Table 14-2). You can now switch the physical standby database to the primary via the following command:

```
alter database commit to switchover to primary;
```

Shut down and start up the database, and it will complete its transition to the primary database role. After the database starts, force a log switch via the **alter system switch logfile** command and then start the redo apply services on the standby databases if they were not already running in the background.

Switchovers to Logical Standby Databases

Switchovers are initiated on the primary database and completed on the standby database. In this section, you will see the steps for performing a switchover to a logical standby database.

Begin by verifying that the primary database is capable of performing a switchover. Query V$DATABASE for the value of the Switchover_Status column:

```
select Switchover_Status from V$DATABASE;
```

For the switchover to complete, the status must be either TO STANDBY, TO LOGICAL STANDBY, or SESSIONS ACTIVE.

In the primary database, issue the following command to prepare the primary database for the switchover:

```
alter database prepare to switchover to logical standby;
```

In the logical standby database, issue the following command:

```
alter database prepare to switchover to primary;
```

At this point, the logical standby database will begin transmitting its redo data to the current primary database and to the other standby databases in the configuration. The redo data from the logical standby database is sent but is not applied at this point.

In the primary database, you must now verify that the dictionary data was received from the logical standby database. The Switchover_Status column value in V$DATABASE must read TO LOGICAL STANDBY in the primary database before you can continue to the next step. When that status value is shown in the primary database, switch the primary database to the logical standby role:

```
alter database commit to switchover to logical standby;
```

You do not need to shut down and restart the old primary database. You should now go back to the original logical standby database and verify its Switchover_Status value in V$DATABASE (it should be TO PRIMARY). You can then complete the switchover; in the original logical standby database, issue the following command:

```
alter database commit to switchover to primary;
```

The original logical standby database is now the primary database. In the new primary database, perform a log switch:

```
alter system archive log current;
```

In the new logical standby database (the old primary database), start the redo apply process:

```
alter database start logical standby apply;
```

The switchover is now complete.

Failovers to Physical Standby Databases

Failovers occur when the primary database can no longer be part of the primary database configuration. In this section, you will see the steps required to fail over a physical standby database to the role of the primary database in a Data Guard configuration.

In the standby database, you should first attempt to identify and resolve any gaps in the archived redo log files (see the "Managing Gaps in Archive Log Sequences" section, earlier in this chapter). You may need to manually copy and register logfiles for use by the standby database.

Within the standby database, you must then finish the recovery process. If you have configured the standby database to have standby redo log files, the command to execute is

```
alter database recover managed standby database finish;
```

If there are no standby redo log files, execute the following command:

```
alter database recover managed standby database finish
    skip standby logfile;
```

Once the standby recovery operation has completed, you can perform the switchover using the following command:

```
alter database commit to switchover to primary;
```

Shut down and restart the new primary database to complete the transition. The old primary database is no longer a part of the Data Guard configuration. If you want to re-create the old primary database and use it as a standby database, you must create it as a standby database following the steps provided earlier in this chapter.

Failovers to Logical Standby Databases

Failovers occur when the primary database can no longer be part of the primary database configuration. In this section, you will see the steps required to fail over a logical standby database to the role of the primary database in a Data Guard configuration.

In the standby database, you should first attempt to identify and resolve any gaps in the archived redo log files (see the "Managing Gaps in Archive Log Sequences" section, earlier in this chapter). You may need to manually copy and register logfiles for use by the standby database. Query the DBA_LOGSTDBY_LOG view for details on the logs remaining to be applied. If the redo apply process was not active on the logical standby database, start it using the following command:

```
alter database start logical standby apply nodelay finish;
```

Next, enable the remote locations for the redo log files that the logical standby database generates. You may need to update the logical standby database's settings of the LOG_ARCHIVE_DEST_STATE_*n* parameters so the other standby databases in the configuration will receive the redo generated from the original logical standby database. You can then activate the original logical standby database as the new primary database via the following commands:

```
alter database stop logical standby apply;
alter database activate logical standby database;
```

If there are other logical standby databases that are part of the Data Guard configuration, you may need to re-create them or use database links to add them to the new configuration. First, create a link in each of the databases that will act as a logical standby database to the new primary database. The **alter session disable guard** command allows you to bypass the Data Guard processes within your session. The database account used by the database link must have the SELECT_CATALOG_ROLE role:

```
alter session disable guard;
create database link salesofc
 connect to username identified by password using 'salesofc';
alter session enable guard;
```

You should verify the link by selecting from DBA_LOGSTDBY_PARAMETERS in the remote database (the new primary database).

In each logical standby database, you can now start the redo apply process based on the new primary database:

```
alter database start logical standby apply new primary salesofc;
```

Administering the Databases

In the following sections, you will see the steps required to perform standard maintenance actions on the databases that are part of the Data Guard configuration, including startup and shutdown operations.

Startup and Shutdown of Physical Standby Databases

When you start up a physical standby database, you should start the redo apply process. First, mount the database:

```
startup mount;
```

Next, start the redo apply process:

```
alter database recover managed standby database
    disconnect from session;
```

Use the **using current logfile** clause in place of the **disconnect from session** clause to start real-time apply.

To shut down the standby database, you should first stop the Log Apply Services. Query the V$MANAGED_STANDBY view; if Log Apply Services are listed there, cancel them using the following command:

```
alter database recover managed standby database cancel;
```

You can then shut down the database.

Opening Physical Standby Databases in Read-Only Mode

To make the physical standby database open for read operations, you should first cancel any log apply operations in the database:

```
alter database recover managed standby database cancel;
```

Next, open the database:

```
alter database open;
```

Managing Datafiles in Data Guard Environments

As noted earlier in this chapter, you should set the STANDBY_FILE_MANAGEMENT initialization parameter to AUTO. Setting this parameter simplifies the administration of the Data Guard environment, because files added to the primary environment can be automatically propagated to the standby databases. When this parameter is set to AUTO, any new datafiles created in the primary database are automatically created in the standby databases; when the parameter is set to MANUAL, you must manually create the new datafiles in the standby databases.

When STANDBY_FILE_MANAGEMENT is set to MANUAL, follow these steps to add a datafile to a tablespace:

1. Add the new datafile in the primary database.

2. Alter the datafile's tablespace so it is offline.

3. Copy the datafile to the standby location.

4. Alter the datafile's tablespace so it is once again online.

To add a new tablespace using manual file management, follow the same steps—create the tablespace, take the tablespace offline, copy its datafiles to the standby location, and then alter the tablespace so it is online. If you are using automatic file management, you only need to create the new tablespace in the primary database for it to be propagated to the standby databases.

To drop a tablespace, simply drop it in the primary database and force a log switch via the **alter system switch logfile** command. You can then drop the file at the operating system level in the primary and standby environments.

Changes to the names of datafiles are not propagated, even if you are using automatic file management. To rename a datafile in a Data Guard configuration, take the tablespace offline and rename the datafile at the operating system level on the primary server. Use the **alter tablespace rename datafile** command on the primary database to point to the new location of the datafile. Bring the tablespace back online with the **alter tablespace** *tablespace_name* **online** command. On the standby database, query the V$ARCHIVED_LOG view to verify all logs have been applied and then shut down the redo apply services:

```
alter database recover managed standby database cancel;
```

Shut down the standby database and rename the file on the standby server. Next, use the **startup mount** command to mount the standby database. With the database mounted but not opened, use the **alter database rename file** command to point to the new file location on the standby server. Finally, restart the redo apply process:

```
alter database recover managed standby database
    disconnect from session;
```

Performing DDL on a Logical Standby Database

As illustrated earlier in this chapter, you can temporarily disable Data Guard within a logical standby database. When you need to perform DDL operations (such as the creation of new indexes to improve query performance), you will follow the same basic steps:

1. Stop the application of redo on the logical standby database.

2. Disable Data Guard.

3. Execute the DDL commands.

4. Enable Data Guard.

5. Restart the redo apply process.

For example, to create a new index, start by turning off the Data Guard features:

```
alter database stop logical standby apply;
alter session disable guard;
```

At this point, you can perform your DDL operations. When you are done, reenable the Data Guard features:

```
alter session enable guard;
alter database start logical standby apply;
```

The logical standby database will then restart its redo apply process, while the index will be available to its query users.

CHAPTER
15

Miscellaneous High
Availability Features

n this chapter, you will see the implementation details for features that can significantly enhance the availability of your database applications. Some of these features, such as the LogMiner options, are enhancements of features available in earlier versions of Oracle. Others, such as the use of the recycle bin and the **flashback database** command, have been introduced in Oracle Database 10g. In this chapter, you will see how to use the following features to enhance the availability of your database:

- Flashback Table to un-drop tables or restore them to a prior state

- Flashback Database

- LogMiner

- Online object-reorganization options

The flashback table Command

The **flashback table** command restores an earlier state of a table in the event of human or application error. Oracle cannot restore a table to an earlier state across any DDL operations that change the structure of the table.

NOTE
*The database should be using Automatic Undo Management (AUM) for **flashback table to timestamp/SCN** to work. The ability to flash back to old data is limited by the amount of undo retained in the undo tablespace and the UNDO_RETENTION initialization parameter setting.*

You cannot roll back a **flashback table** statement. However, you can issue another **flashback table** statement and specify a time just prior to the current time.

NOTE
*Record the current System Change Number (SCN) before issuing a **flashback table to timestamp/SCN** command.*

Privileges Required

You must have either the FLASHBACK object privilege on the table or the FLASHBACK ANY TABLE system privilege. You must also have SELECT, INSERT, DELETE, and ALTER object privileges on the table. Row movement must be enabled for all tables in the flashback list. To flash back a table to before a **drop table** operation, you only need the privileges necessary to drop the table.

Recovering Dropped Tables

Consider the AUTHOR table:

```
describe AUTHOR

Name               Null?    Type
-----------------  -------- ----------------------------
AUTHORNAME         NOT NULL VARCHAR2(50)
COMMENTS                    VARCHAR2(100)
```

Now, assume that the table is dropped accidentally. This usually happens when a privileged user intends to drop a table in a development/test environment but is pointing to the production database when the command is executed.

```
drop table AUTHOR cascade constraints;

Table dropped.
```

How can the table be recovered? As of Oracle Database 10g, a dropped table does not fully disappear. Its blocks are still maintained in its tablespace, and it still counts against your space quota. You can see the dropped objects by querying the RECYCLEBIN data dictionary view. Note that the format for the Object_Name column may differ between versions:

```
select * from RECYCLEBIN;

OBJECT_NAME                         ORIGINAL_NAME                       OPERATION
-----------------  --------  ----------------------------------  ---------
TYPE                         TS_NAME                             CREATETIME
-----------------  --------  ----------------------------------  -------------------
DROPTIME                     DROPSCN PARTITION_NAME              CAN CAN
-----------------  --------  ----------------------------------  --- ---
  RELATED   BASE_OBJECT PURGE_OBJECT        SPACE
---------- ----------- ------------ ----------
RB$$48448$TABLE$0                   AUTHOR                              DROP
TABLE                        USERS                               2004-02-23:16:10:58
2004-02-25:14:30:23    720519                                        YES YES
   48448          48448        48448            8

RB$$48449$INDEX$0                   SYS_C004828                         DROP
INDEX                        USERS                               2004-02-23:16:10:58
2004-02-25:14:30:23    720516                                        NO YES
   48448          48448        48449            8
```

RECYCLEBIN is a public synonym for the USER_RECYCLEBIN data dictionary view, showing the recycle bin entries for the current user. DBAs can see all dropped objects via the DBA_RECYCLEBIN data dictionary view.

As shown in the preceding listing, Oracle has dropped the AUTHOR table and its associated primary key index. Although they have been dropped, they are still available for flashback. Note that the recycle bin listings show the SCN for the command used to drop the base object. In this example, the base table had an object ID value of 48448. Its primary key index had an object ID value of 48449. The index's recycle bin entry shows the object ID (48448) for its base object (the AUTHOR table) in the Base_Object column. The index cannot be recovered by itself (its Can_Undrop column value is 'NO', while the AUTHOR table's Can_Undrop value is 'YES').

You can use the **flashback table to before drop** command to recover the table from the recycle bin:

```
flashback table AUTHOR to before drop;

Flashback complete.
```

The table has been restored, along with its rows, indexes, and statistics.

What happens if you drop the AUTHOR table, re-create it, then drop it again? The recycle bin will contain both the tables. Each entry in the recycle bin will be identified via its SCN and the timestamp for the drop.

> **NOTE**
> *The **flashback table to before drop** command does not recover referential constraints.*

To purge old entries from the recycle bin, use the **purge** command. You can purge all your dropped objects, all dropped objects in the database (if you are a DBA), all objects in a specific tablespace, or all objects for a particular user in a specific tablespace. See the **purge** command in the Alphabetical Reference for the full syntax and command options.

You can use the **rename to** clause of the **flashback table** command to rename the table as you flash it back.

Flashing Back to SCN or Timestamp

You can use flashback queries to show the data as of a particular timestamp or SCN. The **as of timestamp** clause of the **select** command uses the data in the undo segments to show the rows as they existed at the specified time.

You can save the results of a flashback query in a separate table while the main table stays unaffected. You can also update the rows of a table based on the results of a flashback query. You can use the **flashback table** command to transform a table into its prior version—wiping out the changes that were made since the specified flashback point.

During a **flashback table** operation, Oracle acquires exclusive DML locks on all the tables specified. The command is executed in a single transaction across all tables; if any one of them fails, the entire statement fails. You can flash back a table to a specific SCN or timestamp.

> **NOTE**
> *The command **flashback table to scn** or **to timestamp** does not preserve RowID.*

The following **update** command attempts to update a single row in the AUTHOR table. However, the **where** clause is not specified; all rows are updated with the same comment, and the change is committed.

```
update AUTHOR
    set Comments = 'ILLUSTRATOR OF BOOKS FOR CHILDREN';

commit;
```

In this case, we know that almost the entire table has incorrect data, and we know the transaction that was executed incorrectly. To recover the correct data, we can flash back the database to a prior time and then apply any new commands needed to bring the data up to date.

First, let's make sure we know the current SCN in case we need to return to this point:

```
commit;

variable SCN_FLASH number;
execute :SCN_FLASH :=DBMS_FLASHBACK.GET_SYSTEM_CHANGE_NUMBER;

PL/SQL procedure successfully completed.

print SCN_FLASH

 SCN_FLASH
----------
    720880
```

Now, we'll flash back the table to a time just prior to the update. First, we must enable row movement for the table:

```
alter table AUTHOR enable row movement;

Table altered.
```

We can then flash back the table either to an SCN or to a timestamp:

```
flashback table AUTHOR to scn (720000)
```

You can use the **to timestamp** clause if you wish to specify a timestamp instead of an SCN. Here's an example:

```
flashback table AUTHOR to timestamp (systimestamp-5/1440);
```

NOTE
When a table is flashed back, its statistics are not flashed back. Indexes that exist on the table are reverted and reflect the state of the table at the flashback point. Indexes dropped since the flashback point are not restored. Indexes created since the flashback point will continue to exist and will be updated to reflect the older data.

The flashback database Command

The **flashback database** command returns the database to a past time or SCN, providing a fast alternative to performing incomplete database recovery. Following a **flashback database** operation, in order to have write access to the flashed back database, you must reopen it with an **alter database open resetlogs** command. You must have the SYSDBA system privilege in order to use the **flashback database** command.

> **NOTE**
> *The database must have been put in FLASHBACK mode with an **alter database flashback on** command. The database must be mounted in exclusive mode but not open when that command is executed.*

The syntax for the **flashback database** command is as follows:

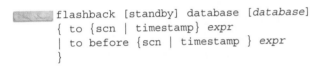

```
flashback [standby] database [database]
{ to {scn | timestamp} expr
| to before {scn | timestamp } expr
}
```

You can use either the **to scn** or **to timestamp** clause to set the point to which the entire database should be flashed back. You can flash back **to before** a critical point (such as a transaction that produced an unintended consequence for multiple tables). Use the ORA_ROWSCN pseudo-column to see the SCNs of transactions that most recently acted on rows.

If you have not already done so, you will need to shut down your database and enable flashback during the startup process:

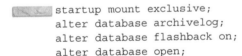

```
startup mount exclusive;
alter database archivelog;
alter database flashback on;
alter database open;
```

> **NOTE**
> *You must have enabled media recovery via the **alter database archivelog** command prior to executing the **alter database flashback on** command.*

Two initialization parameter settings control how much flashback data is retained in the database. The DB_FLASHBACK_RETENTION_TARGET initialization parameter sets the upper limit (in minutes) for how far back in time the database can be flashed back. The DB_RECOVERY_FILE_DEST initialization parameter sets the size of the Flash Recovery Area. Note that the **flashback table** command uses data already stored in the undo tablespace (it does not create additional entries), whereas the **flashback database** command relies on flashback logs stored in a Flash Recovery Area.

You can determine how far back you can flash back the database by querying the V$FLASHBACK_ DATABASE_LOG view. The amount of flashback data retained in the database is controlled by the initialization parameter and the size of the Flash Recovery Area. The following listing shows the available columns in V$FLASHBACK_DATABASE_LOG and sample contents:

```
desc V$FLASHBACK_DATABASE_LOG

Name                                       Null?    Type
----------------------------------------   -------- -------
OLDEST_FLASHBACK_SCN                                NUMBER
OLDEST_FLASHBACK_TIME                               DATE
RETENTION_TARGET                                   NUMBER
FLASHBACK_SIZE                                     NUMBER
ESTIMATED_FLASHBACK_SIZE                           NUMBER


select * from V$FLASHBACK_DATABASE_LOG;

OLDEST_FLASHBACK_SCN OLDEST_FL RETENTION_TARGET FLASHBACK_SIZE
-------------------- --------- ---------------- --------------
ESTIMATED_FLASHBACK_SIZE
------------------------
          722689 25-FEB-04             1440          8192000
             0
```

You can verify the database's flashback status by querying V$DATABASE; the Flashback_On column will have a value of 'YES' if the flashback has been enabled for the database:

```
select Current_SCN, Flashback_On from V$DATABASE;

CURRENT_SCN FLA
----------- ---
     723649 YES
```

With the database open for over an hour, verify that the flashback data is available and then flash it back—you will lose all transactions that occurred during that time:

```
shutdown;
startup mount exclusive;
flashback database to timestamp sysdate-1/24;
```

Note that the **flashback database** command requires that the database be mounted in exclusive mode, which will affect its participation in any RAC clusters (see Chapter 11).

When you execute the **flashback database** command, Oracle checks to make sure all required archived and online redo log files are available. If the logs are available, the online datafiles are reverted to the time or SCN specified.

If there is not enough data online in the archive logs and the flashback area, you will need to use traditional database recovery methods to recover the data. For example, you may need to use a file system recovery method followed by rolling the data forward.

Once the flashback has completed, you must open the database using the **resetlogs** option in order to have write access to the database:

```
alter database open resetlogs;
```

To turn off the flashback database option, execute the **alter database flashback off** command when the database is mounted but not open:

```
startup mount exclusive;
alter database flashback off;
alter database open;
```

You can use the flashback options to perform an array of actions—recovering old data, reverting a table to its earlier data, maintaining a history of changes on a row basis, and quickly restoring an entire database. All these actions are greatly simplified if the database has been configured to support AUM. Also, note that the **flashback database** command requires the modification of the database status. Although these requirements can present additional burdens to DBAs, the benefits involved in terms of the number of recoveries required and the speed with which those recoveries can be completed may be dramatic.

Using LogMiner

Oracle uses online redo log files to track every change that is made to user data and the data dictionary. The information stored in the redo log files is used to re-create the database, in part or in full, during recovery. To enable recovery of the database to a point in time after the database backup was made, you can maintain archived copies of the redo log files. The LogMiner utility provides a vital view into the modifications that have occurred within your database.

When you use LogMiner, you see both the changes that have been made (the SQL_*redo)* and the SQL you can use to reverse those changes (the SQL_*undo).* Thus, you can review the history of the database, without actually applying any redo logs, and obtain the code to reverse any problematic transactions. Using LogMiner, you can pinpoint the transaction under which corruption first occurred so that you can determine the correct point in time or System Change Number (SCN) to use as the endpoint for a database recovery.

If there were a small number of transactions that required rolling back, prior to LogMiner, you would have to restore the table to an earlier state and apply archived log files to bring the table forward to just before the corruption. When restoring the table and applying the archived log files, you would risk losing later transactions that you would like to retain. You can now use LogMiner to roll back only the transactions that are problematic without losing later, valid transactions.

LogMiner in its original form has had some limitations associated with its use. With the original approach, you could only review one log file at a time, and the interface to the tool was cumbersome to use. In Oracle9*i*, a major overhaul of the interface has been implemented, and the functionality has been greatly enhanced, including a LogMiner Viewer for use with the Oracle Enterprise Manager. Both the manual approach to using LogMiner and the OEM LogMiner Viewer are presented within this section.

How LogMiner Works

To run the LogMiner utility, you must have either EXECUTE privilege on the DMBS_LOGMNR package or the EXECUTE_CATALOG_ROLE role. LogMiner requires a data dictionary to fully translate the redo log file contents and translate internal object identifiers and datatypes to object names and external data formats. If a data dictionary is not available, LogMiner will return the data in hex format and the object information as internal object IDs.

You have three choices for obtaining a data dictionary for LogMiner use:

- Extract the data dictionary information to a flat file.

- Extract the data dictionary to redo log files.

- Use the online data dictionary from the current database.

The LogMiner analysis usually requires that the data dictionary in use was generated from the same database that generated the redo log files. However, if you are using a flat file format or are using the data dictionary from redo log files, you can analyze the redo log files either from the database on which LogMiner is running or from another database. If, however, you are using the online catalog from the current database, you can only analyze redo log files from the current database.

Since you can run LogMiner from one database against the redo log files in another database, the character sets used on both databases must match. The hardware platform must also match the one used when the redo log files were generated.

Extracting the Data Dictionary

One potential problem with extracting the data dictionary to a flat file is that while you are extracting the data dictionary, someone else could be issuing DDL statements. Therefore, the extracted data dictionary could be out of sync with the database. When you use a flat file to store the data dictionary, fewer system resources are required than when you use redo log files.

When you extract the data dictionary to redo log files, no DDL statements can be processed during the time in which the data dictionary is extracted. Therefore, the dictionary will be in sync with the database; the extraction is more resource intensive, but the extraction process is faster.

To extract the data dictionary to either a flat file or to redo log files, you use the procedure DBMS_LOGMNR_D.BUILD. The data dictionary file is placed in a directory. Therefore, you must have write permission for the directory in which the file will be placed. To define the location of the directory, use the initialization parameter UTL_FILE_DIR. For example, to specify the location D:\Oracle\Ora10\database as the location for the LogMiner output, you place the following entry in the parameter file:

```
UTL_FILE_DIR= D:\Oracle\Ora10\database
```

NOTE
*You cannot dynamically change the UTL_FILE_DIR parameter using the **alter system** command. You must modify the initialization file and then stop and restart the database.*

To execute the DBMS_LOGMNR_D.BUILD procedure, you must specify a filename for the dictionary, the directory pathname for the file, and whether you want the dictionary written to a flat file or redo log files. To extract the data dictionary to a flat file located in the directory G:\Oracle\Ora10\database with the filename mydb_dictionary, you issue the following command:

```
execute DBMS_LOGMNR_D.BUILD
('mydb_dictionary.ora',
'G:\Oracle\Ora10\database',
options=>DBMS_LOGMNR_D.STORE_IN_FLAT_FILE);
```

You can use DBMS_LOGMNR_D.STORE_IN_FLAT_FILE as the other option.

NOTE
Although the command is shown on several lines here, you must enter it on one continuous line; otherwise, you will receive error messages.

Once you have the dictionary stored in a flat file, you can copy it to another platform to run LogMiner. You may need to run dbmslmd.sql on the other database to establish the correct environment. The dbmslmd.sql file can be found in the $ORACLE_HOME\rdbms\admin directory on a Unix system.

Analyzing One or More Redo Log Files

To analyze redo log files using LogMiner, follow these steps:

1. Obtain a list of the available redo log files using V$LOGMNR_LOGS.

2. Start the LogMiner utility using the DBMS_LOGMNR.START_LOGMNR procedure. See Table 15-2, later in this section, for the START_LOGMNR parameters.

3. Query V$LOGMNR_CONTENTS to see the results.

4. Once you have finished viewing the redo logs, issue the following command to end the session:

   ```
   execute DBMS_LOGMNR.END_LOGMNR;
   ```

The available subprograms for the DBMS_LOGMNR package are described in Table 15-1. Table 15-2 shows the parameters for the START_LOGMNR procedure.

To create a list of the redo log files that are available for analysis, you run the procedure DBMS_LOGMNR.ADD_LOGFILE with the NEW option as follows:

```
execute DBMS_LOGMNR.ADD_LOGFILE(
LogFileName=> '/oracle/ora10/redo01.ora',
Options=> DBMS_LOGMNR.NEW);
execute DBMS_LOGMNR.ADD_LOGFILE(
LogFileName=> '/oracle/ora10/redo02.ora',
Options=> DBMS_LOGMNR.NEW);
```

Subprogram	Description
ADD_LOGFILE	Adds a file to the list of archive files to process
START_LOGMNR	Initializes the LogMiner utility
END_LOGMNR	Completes and ends a LogMiner session
MINE_VALUE (*function*)	Returns the undo or redo column value of the column name specified by the COLUMN_NAME parameter for any row returned from V$LOGMNR_CONTENT
COLUMN_PRESENT (*function*)	Determines if undo or redo column values exist for the column name specified by the COLUMN_NAME parameter for any row returned from V$LOGMNR_CONTENT
REMOVE_LOGFILE	Removes a log file from the list of log files to be processed by LogMiner

TABLE 15-1. *DBMS_LOGMNR Subprograms*

Options	Description
COMMITTED_DATA_ONLY	Only DMLs corresponding to committed transactions are returned if this option is set.
SKIP_CORRUPTION	Skips any corruption encountered in the redo log file during a select from V$LOGMNR_CONTENTS. This option works only if a block in the actual redo log file is corrupted and does not work if the corruption is in the header block.
DDL_DICT_TRACKING	Enables LogMiner to update the internal data dictionary if a DDL event occurs, to ensure that SQL_REDO and SQL_UNDO information is maintained and correct.
DICT_FROM_ONLINE_CATALOG	Instructs LogMiner to use the online data dictionary instead of a flat file or redo log file stored dictionary.
DICT_FROM_REDO_LOGS	Instructs LogMiner to use the data dictionary stored in one or more redo log files.
NO_SQL_DELIMITER	Instructs LogMiner to not place the SQL delimiter (;) at the end of reconstructed SQL statements.
NO_ROWID_IN_STMT	Instructs LogMiner not to include the ROWID clause in the reconstructed SQL statements.

TABLE 15-2. *Values for the START_LOGMNR Options*

Options	Description
PRINT_PRETTY_SQL	Instructs LogMiner to format the reconstructed SQL for ease of reading.
CONTINUOUS_MINE	Instructs LogMiner to automatically add redo log files to find the data of interest. Specify the starting SCN, date, or the first log to mine. LogMiner must be connected to the same database instance that is generating the redo log files.

TABLE 15-2. *Values for the START_LOGMNR Options* (continued)

You can specify the location of the data dictionary file as follows:

```
execute DBMS_LOGMNR.ADD_LOGFILE(
DictFileName=> '/oracle/ora10/dictionary.ora',
```

After you've told LogMiner the location of the data dictionary and added the redo log files, you can begin analyzing the redo log files using the DBMS_LOGMNR.START_LOGMNR package. For example, the following command analyzes log files over a range of times:

```
execute DBMS_LOGMNR.START_LOGMNR(
DictFileName => '/oracle/dictionary.ora',
StartTime => TO_DATE('01-JUNE-2001 12:31:00', DD-MON-YYYY HH:MI:SS')
EndTime => TO_DATE('01-JULY-2001 00:00:00', DD-MON-YYYY HH:MI:SS'));
```

> **NOTE**
> *Using the timestamp will not ensure ordering of the redo records. You must use the SCN numbers to ensure the order of the records.*

You can use the SCN values to filter data as follows:

```
execute DBMS_LOGMNR.START_LOGMNR(
DictFileName => '/oracle/dictionary.ora',
StartScn => 125,
EndScr => 300);
```

If you do not enter a start and end time or range of SCN numbers, the entire file is read for every **select** statement that you issue.

To look at the redo and undo code, you select the Sql_Redo and Sql_Undo columns as follows:

```
select Sql_Redo, Sql_Undo
  from V$LOGMNR_CONTENTS;
```

You can use the OEM Server Manager Console to launch the LogMiner Viewer to view redo and archived redo logs. To launch the LogMiner Viewer on a Windows platform, use the Start | Programs | Oracle_Home | Oracle Enterprise Manager Console option. Once you have connected to the OEM Server Console, select the database on which you want to run the LogMiner Viewer. Ensure that the database has been started.

To start the LogMiner Viewer, highlight the database and right-click. Move the cursor to the Related Tools option and then move to the LogMiner Viewer option. When the LogMiner Viewer Console screen is displayed, create an object query by either clicking the top icon in the icon panel or selecting Create Query from the Object pull-down menu. The LogMiner Viewer automatically looks for available archived redo log files from which to create a query. If there are no archived redo log files available, you receive an error message. You can create filtering options (by creating query criteria), see the beginning and ending SCN for each redo log file available, and choose the columns to display. The OEM LogMiner Viewer may simplify the process of sifting through the log file contents. Additionally, you can use the Grid Control screens to access and view the LogMiner output.

LogMiner Features Introduced in Oracle Database 10*g*

If you have used LogMiner with versions that preceded Oracle Database 10g, the following enhancements are now available to you:

As shown earlier in Table 15-1, DBMS_LOGMNR now has a REMOVE_LOGFILE procedure that removes files from the list to be analyzed. You should no longer use the REMOVEFILE option of the ADD_LOGFILE procedure.

You can use the NO_ROWID_IN_STMT option (refer back to Table 15-2) of START_LOGMNR to filter out the **rowid** clause from reconstructed SQL commands.

You can expand supplemental logging via the **alter database** command to include **foreign key** or **all** changes for rows. Using these settings will increase the amount of data written to the redo log files.

You can expand supplemental logging at the table level to track primary key, foreign key, unique index, and all changes. You can also use the **no log** option to prevent a column in a user-defined log group from being logged.

See the Oracle Utilities guide for further details on the use of LogMiner and its procedures.

Online Object Reorganizations

You can reorganize many database objects online. Options include the following:

- Creating indexes online

- Rebuilding indexes online

- Coalescing indexes online

- Rebuilding index-organized tables online

- Using the DBMS_REDEFINITION package to redefine a table online

In the following sections, you will see examples of each of these operations.

Creating Indexes Online

You can create and rebuild indexes while the base tables are accessible to end users. DDL operations are not allowed while the index is being built. To build an index online, use the **online** clause of the **create index command**, as shown in the following example:

```
create index AUTH$NAME on AUTHOR (AuthorName) online;
```

Rebuilding Indexes Online

When you use the **rebuild** clause of the **alter index** command, Oracle uses the existing index as the data source for the new index. As a result, you must have adequate space to store two copies of the index while the operation is taking place. You can use the **alter index rebuild** command to change the storage characteristics and tablespace assignment for an index.

To rebuild the index online, use the **rebuild online** clause of the **alter table** command, as shown in the following example:

```
alter index AUTH$NAME rebuild online;
```

Coalescing Indexes Online

You can coalesce an index to reclaim space within the index. When you coalesce an index, you cannot move it to another tablespace (as you can with a rebuild). Coalescing does not require storage space for multiple copies of the index, so it may be useful when you are attempting to reorganize an index in a space-constrained environment.

To coalesce an index, use the **coalesce** clause of the **alter index** command. All index coalesces are online operations. The following is a sample coalesce:

```
alter index AUTH$NAME coalesce;
```

Rebuilding Index-Organized Tables Online

You can use the **alter table ... move online** command to rebuild an index-organized table online. The overflow data segment, if present, is rebuilt if you specify the **overflow** keyword. For example, if BOOKSHELF is an index-organized table, you can rebuild it online via the following command:

```
alter table BOOKSHELF move online;
```

When using this command, you cannot perform parallel DML. Also, the move online option is only available for nonpartitioned index-organized tables.

Redefining Tables Online

You can change a table's definition while it is accessible by the application users. For example, you can partition a previously nonpartitioned table while it is being used—a significant capability for high-availability OLTP applications.

NOTE
You cannot perform online reorganizations for tables with no primary keys, for tables that have materialized views and materialized view logs defined on them, for materialized view container tables, for advanced queueing tables, or for IOT overflow tables.

The following example shows the steps involved in redefining a table online. First, verify that the table can be redefined. For this example, the CUSTOMER table will be created in the SCOTT schema and then redefined:

```
create table CUSTOMER
 (Name     VARCHAR2(25) primary key,
  Street   VARCHAR2(50),
  City     VARCHAR2(25),
  State    CHAR(2),
  Zip      NUMBER);
```

Next, verify that the table can be redefined by executing the CAN_REDEF_TABLE procedure of the DBMS_REDEFINITION package. Its input parameters are the username and the table name:

```
execute DBMS_REDEFINITION.CAN_REDEF_TABLE('SCOTT','CUSTOMER');
```

The table is a candidate for online redefinition if the procedure returns the message

```
PL/SQL procedure successfully completed.
```

If it returns an error, the table cannot be redefined online, and the error message will give the reason.

Next, create an interim table, in the same schema, with the desired attributes of the redefined table. For example, we can partition the CUSTOMER table (to simplify this example, the **tablespace** and **storage** clauses for the partitions are not shown):

```
create table CUSTOMER_INTERIM
 (Name     VARCHAR2(25) primary key,
  Street    VARCHAR2(50),
  City     VARCHAR2(25),
  State     CHAR(2),
  Zip      NUMBER)
partition by range (Name)
 (partition PART1  values less than ('L'),
  partition PART2  values less than (MAXVALUE))
 ;
```

You can now execute the START_REDEF_TABLE procedure of the DBMS_REDEFINITION package to start the redefinition process. Its input variables are the schema owner, the table to be redefined, the interim table name, and the column mapping (similar to the list of column names in a select query). If no column mapping is supplied, all the column names and definitions in the original table and the interim table must be the same.

```
execute DBMS_REDEFINITION.START_REDEF_TABLE -
  ('SCOTT','CUSTOMER','CUSTOMER_INTERIM');
```

Next, create any triggers, indexes, grants, or constraints required on the interim table. In this example, the primary key has already been defined on CUSTOMER_INTERIM; you could add the foreign keys, secondary indexes, and grants at this point in the redefinition process. Create the foreign keys disabled until the redefinition process is complete.

NOTE
To avoid that manual step, you can use the COPY_TABLE_ DEPENDENTS procedure to create all dependent objects on the interim table. Dependent objects supported via this method include triggers, indexes, grants, and constraints.

When the redefinition process completes, the indexes, triggers, constraints, and grants on the interim table will replace those on the original table. The disabled referential constraints on the interim table will be enabled at that point.

To finish the redefinition, execute the FINISH_REDEF_TABLE procedure of the DBMS_ REDEFINITION package. Its input parameters are the schema name, original table name, and interim table name:

```
execute DBMS_REDEFINITION.FINISH_REDEF_TABLE -
  ('SCOTT','CUSTOMER','CUSTOMER_INTERIM');
```

You can verify the redefinition by querying the data dictionary:

```
select Table_Name, High_Value
  from DBA_TAB_PARTITIONS
  where owner = 'SCOTT';


TABLE_NAME                     HIGH_VALUE
------------------------------ ------------------------
CUSTOMER                       MAXVALUE
CUSTOMER                       'L'
```

To abort the process after executing the START_REDEF_TABLE procedure, execute the ABORT_REDEF_TABLE procedure (the input parameters are the schema, original table name, and interim table name).

PART
IV

Networked Oracle

CHAPTER
16

Oracle Net

D istributing computing power across servers and sharing information across networks greatly enhances the value of the computing resources available. Instead of being a stand-alone server, the server becomes an entry point for intranets, the Internet, and associated websites.

Oracle's networking tool, Oracle Net, can be used to connect to distributed databases. Oracle Net facilitates the sharing of data between databases, even if those databases are on different types of servers running different operating systems and communications protocols. It also allows for client/server applications to be created; the server can then function primarily for database I/O while the application can be fielded to a middle-tier application server. Also, the data presentation requirements of an application can be moved to front-end client machines. In this chapter, you will see how to configure, administer, and tune Oracle Net and the Oracle Net Services.

The installation and configuration instructions for Oracle Net depend on the particular hardware, operating system, and communications software you are using. The material provided here will help you get the most out of your database networking, regardless of your configuration.

Overview of Oracle Net

Using Oracle Net distributes the workload associated with database applications. Because many database queries are performed via applications, a server-based application forces the server to support both the CPU requirements of the application and the I/O requirements of the database (see Figure 16-1*a*). Using a client/server configuration (also referred to as a *two-tier architecture*) allows this load to be distributed between two machines. The first, called the *client,* supports the application that initiates the request from the database. The back-end machine on which the database resides is called the *server.* The client bears the burden of presenting the data, whereas the database server is dedicated to supporting queries, not applications. This distribution of resource requirements is shown in Figure 16-1*b.*

When the client sends a database request to the server, the server receives and executes the SQL statement that is passed to it. The results of the SQL statement, plus any error conditions that are returned, are then sent back to the client. The client resources required have caused the client/server configuration to sometimes be dubbed *fat-client architecture.* Although workstation costs have dropped appreciably over recent years, the cost impact to a company can still be substantial.

The more common, cost-effective architecture used with Oracle Net is a *thin-client* configuration (also referred to as a *three-tier architecture*). The application code is housed and executed using Java scripts on a separate server from the database server. The client resource requirements become very low, and the cost is reduced dramatically. The application code becomes isolated from the database. Figure 16-2 shows the thin-client configuration.

The client connects to the application server. Once the client is validated, display management code is downloaded to the client in the form of Java applets. A database request is sent from the client through the application server to the database server; the database server then receives and executes the SQL statement that is passed to it. The results of the SQL statement, plus any error conditions that are returned, are then sent back to the client through the application server. In some versions of the three-tier architecture, some of the application processing is performed on the application server and the rest is performed on the database server. The advantage of a thin-client architecture is that you have low resource requirements and maintenance on the client side,

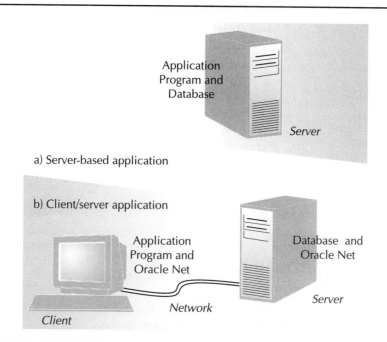

a) Server-based application

b) Client/server application

Application
Program and
Oracle Net

Database and
Oracle Net

Network

Client

Server

FIGURE 16-1.   *Client/server architecture*

medium resource requirements and central maintenance on the application server, and high resource but lower maintenance requirements on one or more back-end database servers.

In addition to client/server and thin-client implementations, *server/server* configurations are often needed. In this type of environment, databases on separate servers share data with each other. You can then physically isolate each server from every other server without logically isolating the servers. A typical implementation of this type involves corporate headquarters servers that communicate with departmental servers in various locations. Each server supports client applications, but it also has the ability to communicate with other servers in the network. This architecture is shown in Figure 16-3.

When one of the servers sends a database request to another server, the sending server acts like a client. The receiving server executes the SQL statement passed to it and returns the results plus error conditions to the sender.

When run on the clients and the servers, Oracle Net allows database requests made from one database (or application) to be passed to another database on a separate server. In most cases, machines can function both as clients and servers; the only exceptions are operating systems with single-user architectures, such as network appliances. In such cases, those machines can only function as clients.

The end result of an Oracle Net implementation is the ability to communicate with all databases that are accessible via the network. You can then create synonyms that give applications true network transparency: The user who submits the query will not know the location of the data that is used to resolve it. In this chapter, you will see the main configuration methods and files used to

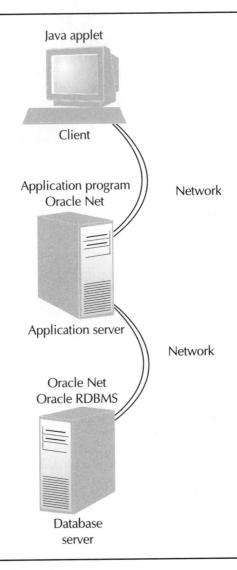

FIGURE 16-2. *Thin-client architecture*

manage interdatabase communications, along with usage examples. You will see more detailed examples of distributed database management in Chapter 18.

Each object in a database is uniquely identified by its owner and name. For example, there will only be one table named EMPLOYEE owned by the user HR; there cannot be two tables of the same name and type within the same schema.

Within distributed databases, two additional layers of object identification must be added. First, the name of the instance that accesses the database must be identified. Next, the name of

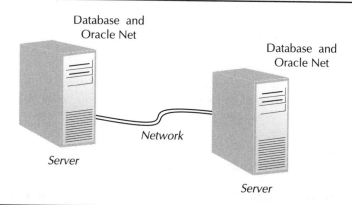

FIGURE 16-3. *Server/server architecture*

the server on which that instance resides must be identified. Putting together these four parts of the object's name—its server, its instance, its owner, and its name—results in a *global object name*. In order to access a remote table, you must know the table's global object name. DBAs and application administrators can set up access paths to automate the selection of all four parts of the global object name. In the following sections, you will see how to set up the access paths used by Oracle Net.

The foundation of Oracle Net is the Transparent Network Substrate (TNS), which resolves all server-level connectivity issues. Oracle Net relies on configuration files on the client and the server to manage the database connectivity. If the client and server use different communications protocols, the Oracle Connection Manager (described in a later section of this chapter) manages the connections. The combination of the Oracle Connection Manager and the TNS allows Oracle Net connections to be made independent of the operating system and communications protocol run by each server. Oracle Net also has the capability to send and receive data requests in an asynchronous manner; this allows it to support the shared server architecture.

Connect Descriptors

The server and instance portions of an object's global object name in Oracle Net are identified by means of a *connect descriptor*. A connect descriptor specifies the communications protocol, server name, and the instance's service name to use when performing the query. Because of the protocol-independence of Oracle Net, the descriptor also includes hardware connectivity information. The generic format for an Oracle Net connect descriptor is shown in the following example, which uses the TCP/IP protocol and specifies a connection to an instance named LOC on a server named HQ (note that the keywords are protocol specific):

```
(DESCRIPTION=
     (ADDRESS=
         (PROTOCOL=TCP)
         (HOST=HQ)
         (PORT=1521))
     (CONNECT DATA=
         (SERVICE_NAME=LOC)))
```

In this connect descriptor, the protocol is set to TCP/IP, the server (HOST) is set to HQ, and the port on that host that should be used for the connection is port 1521 (which is the Oracle registered port assignment for Oracle Net). The instance name is specified in a separate part of the descriptor as the SID assignment.

The structure for this descriptor is consistent across all protocols. Also, the descriptors can be automatically generated via the Net Configuration Assistant. As previously noted, the keywords used by the connect descriptors are protocol specific. The keywords to use and the values to give them are provided in the operating system–specific documentation for Oracle Net.

Service Names

Users are not expected to type in a connect descriptor each time they want to access remote data. Instead, the DBA can set up *service names* (or *aliases*), which refer to these connect descriptors. Service names are stored in a file called tnsnames.ora. This file should be copied to all servers on the database network. Every client and application server should have a copy of this file.

On the server, the tnsnames.ora file should be located in the directory specified by the TNS_ADMIN environment variable. The file is usually stored in a common directory, such as the $ORACLE_HOME/network/admin directory on Unix systems. For a Windows NT/2000 server or client, this would be in the \network\admin subdirectory under your Oracle software home directory.

A sample entry in the tnsnames.ora file is shown in the following listing. This example assigns a service name of LOC to the connect descriptor given earlier:

```
LOC =(DESCRIPTION=
    (ADDRESS=
        (PROTOCOL=TCP)
        (HOST=HQ)
        (PORT=1521))
    (CONNECT DATA=
        (SERVICE_NAME=LOC)))
```

A user wishing to connect to the LOC instance on the HQ server can now use the LOC service name, as shown in this example:

```
sqlplus hr/puffinstuff@LOC;
```

The @ sign tells the database to use the service name that follows it to determine which database to log into. If the username and password are correct for that database, a session is opened there and the user can begin using the database.

Service names create aliases for connect descriptors, so you do not need to give the service name the same name as the instance. For example, you could give the LOC instance the service name PROD or TEST, depending on its use within your environment. The use of synonyms to further enhance location transparency will be described in the "Using Database Links" section of this chapter.

Replacing tnsnames.ora with the Oracle Internet Directory

A *directory* is a specialized electronic database in which you store information about one or more objects. Your electronic mail address book is an example of a directory. Within each of your e-mail address entries is information about the contact's name, e-mail address, home and business addresses, and so on. You can use the address book to locate a specific person with whom you want to correspond.

Oracle provides an electronic database tool called the Oracle Internet Directory (OID) for use in resolving user, server, and database locations as well as password and other important information storage. As of Oracle9*i*, the emphasis moved from supporting many separate tnsnames.ora files on distributed machines to supporting one or more directories on centralized machines. See the section "Directory Naming with Oracle Internet Directory," later in this chapter, for more information about OID.

Listeners

Each database server on the network must contain a listener.ora file. The listener.ora file lists the names and addresses of all the listener processes on the machine and the instances they support. Listener processes receive connections from Oracle Net clients.

A listener.ora file has four parts:

- Header section

- Protocol address list

- Instance definitions

- Operational parameters

The listener.ora file is automatically generated by the Oracle Net Assistant tool. You can edit the resultant file as long as you follow its syntax rules. The following listing shows sample sections of a listener.ora file—an address definition and an instance definition:

```
LISTENER =
  (ADDRESS_LIST =
    (ADDRESS=
      (PROTOCOL=IPC)
      (KEY= loc.world)
    )
    (ADDRESS=
      (PROTOCOL=TCP)
      (HOST= HR)
      (PORT=1521)
    )
  )
SID_LIST_LISTENER =
  (SID_DESC =
    (GLOBAL_DBNAME = loc.world)
    (ORACLE_HOME = D:\oracle\ora10)
    (SID_NAME = loc)
  )
)
```

The first portion of this listing contains the protocol address list—one entry per instance. The protocol address list defines the protocol addresses on which a listener is accepting connections, including an interprocess calls (IPC) address-definition section. In this case, the listener is listening for connections to the service identified as loc.world as well as any requests coming from the HR machine on PORT 1521 using the TCP/IP protocol. The .world suffix is the default domain name for Oracle Net connections. As of Net8, the default domain name was changed to be a NULL string.

The second portion of the listing, beginning with the SID_LIST_LISTENER clause, identifies the global database name as defined in the init.ora file for that database, the Oracle software home directory for each instance the listener is servicing, and the instance name or SID. The GLOBAL_ DBNAME comprises the database name and database domain. The SID_LIST descriptor is retained for static database registration, backward compatibility with earlier versions, and for use by the Oracle Enterprise Manager. Databases dynamically register with the listener on database startup.

NOTE
*If you change the Oracle software home directory for an instance,
you need to change the listener.ora file for the server.*

Listener.ora Parameters

The listener.ora file supports a large number of parameters. The parameters should each be suffixed with the listener name. For example, the default listener name is LISTENER, so the LOG_FILE parameter is named LOG_FILE_LISTENER. The listener.ora parameters are listed in Table 16-1.

Parameter	Description
DESCRIPTION	Serves as a container for listener protocol addresses.
ADDRESS	Specifies a single listener protocol address. Embedded within a DESCRIPTION.
QUEUESIZE	Specifies the number of concurrent connection requests that the listener can accept on a TCP/IP or IPC listening endpoint.
RECV_BUF_SIZE	Specifies, in bytes, the buffer space for receive operations of sessions. Embedded within a DESCRIPTION.
SEND_BUF_SIZE	Specifies, in bytes, the buffer space for send operations of sessions. Embedded within a DESCRIPTION.
SID_LIST	Lists SID descriptions; configures service information for the listener; required for OEM, Oracle7, Oracle8 release 8.0, external procedure calls, and heterogeneous services.
SID_DESC	Specifies service information for a specific instance or service. Embedded within SID_LIST.
ENVS	Specifies environment variables for the listener to set prior to executing a dedicated server program or an executable specified via the PROGRAM parameter. Embedded within SID_DESC.
GLOBAL_DBNAME	Identifies the database service. Embedded within SID_DESC.
ORACLE_HOME	Specifies the Oracle software home directory for the service. Embedded within SID_DESC.

TABLE 16-1. *Listener.ora Parameters*

Parameter	Description
PROGRAM	Names the service executable program. Embedded within SID_DESC.
SID_NAME	Specifies the Oracle instance name for the service. Embedded within SID_DESC.
SDU	Specifies the session data unit (SDU) size for data packet transfers. Values are 512 to 32768 bytes. Embedded within SID_DESC.
ADMIN_RESTRICTIONS_*listener_name*	Disables run-time modification of listener parameters. Values are ON and OFF (the default).
INBOUND_CONNECT_TIMEOUT_*listener_name*	Specifies the time, in seconds, for the client to complete its connect request to the listener after the network connection has been established.
LOG_DIRECTORY_*listener_name*	Specifies the destination directory for the listener log file.
LOG_FILE_*listener_name*	Names the listener log file.
LOGGING_*listener_name*	Turns listener logging ON or OFF.
PASSWORDS_*listener_name*	Specifies an encrypted password for the listener process. The password can be generated via the Listener Control Utility (lsnrctl) or Oracle Net Manager.
SAVE_CONFIG_ON_STOP_*listener_name*	TRUE or FALSE parameter to specify whether runtime configuration changes are automatically saved to the listener.ora file.
SSL_CLIENT_AUTHENTICATION_*listener_name*	TRUE or FALSE parameter to specify whether a client is authenticated using SSL.
STARTUP_WAIT_TIME_*listener_name*	Deprecated; do not set.
TRACE_DIRECTORY_*listener_name*	Specifies the destination directory of the listener trace file.
TRACE_FILE_*listener_name*	Names the listener trace file.
TRACE_FILELEN_*listener_name*	Specifies the size, in KB, of the listener trace files.
TRACE_FILENO_*listener_name*	Sets the number of trace files to use for listener tracing; when this parameter is used with TRACE_FILELEN_*listener_name*, the files are used in cyclical fashion.
TRACE_LEVEL_*listener_name*	Enables tracing at specific levels. Values are OFF (the default), USER, ADMIN, and SUPPORT.
TRACE_TIMESTAMP_*listener_name*	Adds a timestamp to every trace event. Values are ON, OFF, TRUE, and FALSE.
WALLET_LOCATION	Specifies the location of certificates, keys, and trustpoints used by SSL for secure connections. For the WALLET_LOCATION parameter, you can specify the SOURCE, METHOD, METHOD_DATA, DIRECTORY, KEY, PROFILE, and INFILE subparameters.

TABLE 16-1. *Listener.ora Parameters* (continued)

You can modify the listener parameters after the listener has been started. If you use the SAVE_CONFIG_ON_STOP option, any changes you make to a running listener will be written to its listener.ora file. See examples of controlling the listener behavior later in this chapter.

Using the Oracle Net Configuration Assistant

The Oracle Net Configuration Assistant performs the initial network configuration steps after the Oracle software installation and automatically creates the default, basic configuration files. You can use the Oracle Net Manager tool to administer network services. The tools have graphical user interfaces for configuring the following elements:

- Listener
- Naming methods
- Local net service names
- Directory usage

Figure 16-4 shows the initial screen of the Oracle Net Configuration Assistant. As shown in Figure 16-4, "Listener configuration" is the default option.

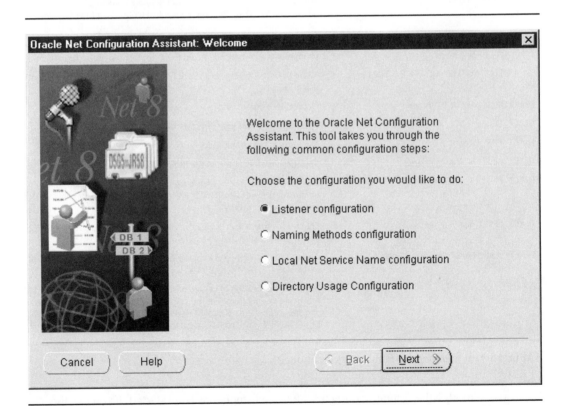

FIGURE 16-4. *Oracle Net Configuration Assistant: Welcome screen*

Configuring the Listener

Using the Oracle Net Configuration Assistant, you can configure a listener easily and quickly. When you select the Listener Configuration options, you are given the choice to add, reconfigure, delete, or rename a listener. After selecting the Add option, the first step is to select a listener name. Figure 16-5 shows the Listener Name screen with the default listener name, LISTENER, displayed.

After selecting a listener name, you must select a protocol. The default protocol selected is TCP. Figure 16-6 shows the protocol selection screen.

Once a protocol has been selected, you must designate a port number on which the new listener will listen. The default port number presented is 1521, but you are given the option to designate another port. The next three screens include a prompt to configure another listener, a request to indicate a listener you want to start, and a confirmation that the listener configuration is completed for this listener.

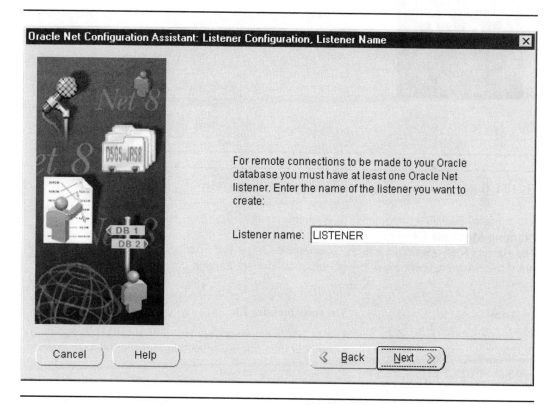

FIGURE 16-5.   *Listener Configuration, Listener Name screen*

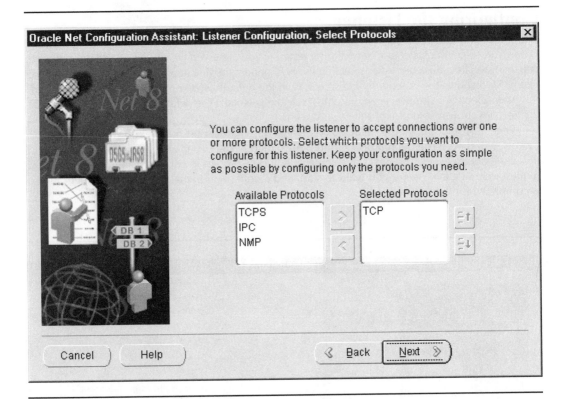

FIGURE 16-6. *Listener Configuration, Select Protocols screen*

Naming Methods Configuration

The Naming Methods Configuration option of the Oracle Net Configuration Assistant configures net service names. There are many options available for naming methods. A few of them are listed here:

Local	The tnsnames.ora File
Host Name	Uses a TCP naming service. You cannot use connection pooling or the Oracle Connection Manager with this option.
Sun NIS, DCE CDS, Directory	External naming services.

If you accept the Host Name option, you see an informational screen advising you that Host Name naming does not require any additional configuration "at this time." You are instructed that any time you add a database service in the future, you must make an entry in your TCP/IP host name resolution system.

Once you have selected the naming methods, the Oracle Net Configuration Assistant displays a confirmation screen.

Local Net Service Name Configuration

You can use the Oracle Net Configuration Assistant's Local Net Service Name configuration options to manage net service names. Five options are available for the Oracle Net Configuration Assistant's Local Net Service Name configuration tool:

- Add
- Reconfigure
- Delete
- Rename
- Test

For the Add option, you must first specify the database version you are going to access and the service name. Once you have entered the global service name or SID, you are prompted to enter the protocol. You must specify the machine name of the host and designate the listener port.

The next screen offers you the option to verify that the Oracle database you have specified can be successfully reached. You can choose to skip or perform the connection test. Once you have either chosen to test the connection, and it has completed successfully, or opted to skip the test, you are prompted to specify the net service name for the new net service. By default, the service name you entered earlier is used, but you can specify a different name if you so choose. Finally, you are notified that your new local net service name has been successfully created, and you are asked if you want to configure another one.

You can use the Reconfigure option to select and modify an existing net service name. You are prompted to select an existing net service name. The Database Version screen, the service name screen, and the Select Protocols screen are used as well as the TCP/IP Protocol screen. The option to test the database connection is offered as well as the net service name screen to enable you to rename the net service you are reconfiguring.

The Test option enables you to verify that your configuration information is correct, that the database specified can be reached, and that a successful connection can be made.

Directory Usage Configuration

A directory service provides a central repository of information for the network. The most common directory forms support the Lightweight Directory Access Protocol (LDAP). An LDAP server can provide the following features:

- Store net service names and their location resolution
- Provide global database links and aliases
- Act as a clearinghouse for configuration information for clients across the entire network
- Aid in configuring other clients
- Update client configuration files automatically
- House client information such as usernames and passwords

The Directory Usage Configuration option supports both Oracle Internet Directory and the Microsoft Active Directory. The actions that you can take are shown in Figure 16-7.

When you select the first option, "Select the directory server you want to use...," you are asked to select the type of directory you have: either OID or Microsoft Active Directory. If you select OID, you are prompted to supply the directory service location host name, port, and SSL port. By default, the port is 389 and the SSL port is 636. Once you have specified this information, the tool attempts to connect to your directory repository and verify that you have already established a schema and context. If you have not, you will receive an error message instructing you to do so. Figure 16-8 shows the schema error message, and Figure 16-9 shows the context error message.

From the second option, "Select the directory server you want to use, and configure the directory server for Oracle usage...," you receive the same initial prompts to select the directory type and enter the host name and ports. Once the information is verified, if your directory does not contain the required schema, you are given the opportunity to create the directory schema. You must have the appropriate privileges to perform this task. By default, the initial username with the appropriate privileges for schema creation for the Oracle Internet Directory is "cn=orcladmin," and the password is "welcome." You should change the password at your earliest opportunity.

The third and fourth options enable you to individually configure a schema and a context.

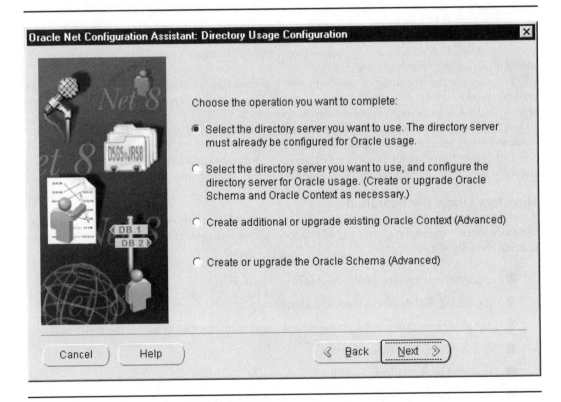

FIGURE 16-7. *Directory Usage Configuration*

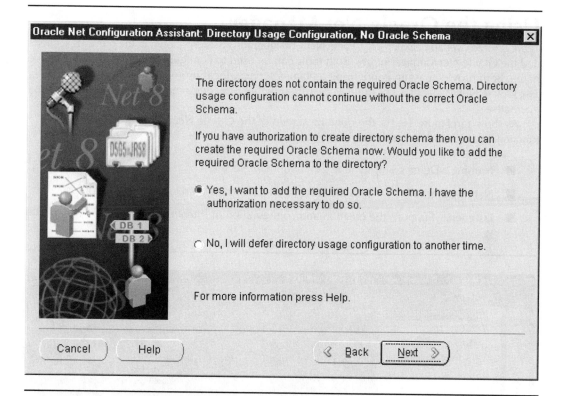

FIGURE 16-8. *Directory Usage Configuration, No Oracle Schema*

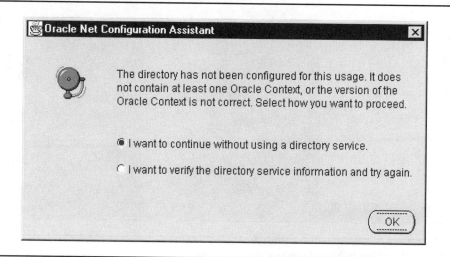

FIGURE 16-9. *"Directory service not configured" warning message*

Using the Oracle Net Manager

There is some overlap between the Oracle Net Configuration Assistant shown in the previous section and the Oracle Net Manager utility. Both tools can be used to configure a listener or a net service name. Both provide ease in configuring a Names service, local profile, and directory service. The Oracle Net Manager is not quite as user friendly but provides a more in-depth configuration alternative.

As shown in Figure 16-10, the opening screen of the Oracle Net Manager lists the basic functionality it provides, as follows:

- **Naming** Defines simple names to identify the location of a service

- **Naming Methods** Defines the way the simple names map to connect descriptors

- **Listeners** Supports the creation and configuration of listeners

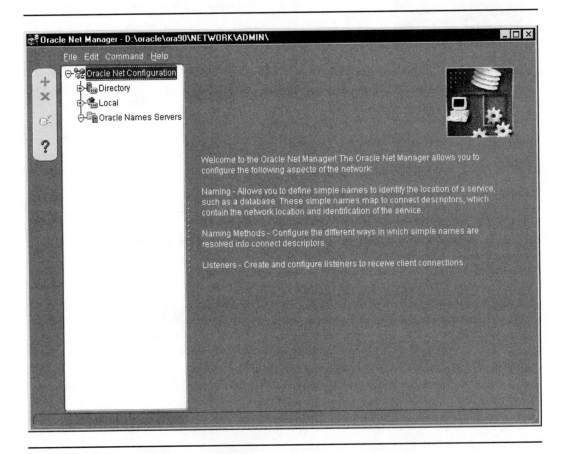

FIGURE 16-10. *Oracle Net Manager Console screen*

You can use Oracle Net Manager to manage your configuration files and test your connections. Options such as Oracle Advanced Security can be managed via the Oracle Net Manager. The Oracle Advanced Security option provides end-to-end encryption of data in a distributed environment. By default, your data will travel in clear text across the network unless you use Oracle's encryption or a hardware-based encryption.

You can create a new net service name for your tnsnames.ora file via the Oracle Net Service Names Wizard. Once you have specified a net service name, you are prompted to select the network protocol you want to use. The options are as follows:

- TCP/IP (Internet Protocol)

- TCP/IP with SSL (Secure Internet Protocol)

- Named Pipes (Microsoft Networking)

- IPC (Local Database)

The Oracle Net Manager will prompt you for each of the parameters required to establish a database connection and will modify your local tnsnames.ora file to reflect the information you provide. The information you will be prompted for is host, port number, service or SID name (depending on the Oracle version), and the connection type (either database default, shared server, or dedicated server). Finally, you are given the opportunity to test the new service name. You can also test existing net service names by selecting the net service name from the displayed list of services and then selecting the Test Connection option from the menu options.

When you test your connections, the Oracle Net Manager will attempt to log into the database using the default username, SCOTT, with the default password, TIGER, and will report the result of the connection attempt.

The simpler you keep your client and server configurations, and the closer you adhere to the default values, the simpler the management of your configuration files will be. The Oracle Net Manager simplifies your configuration file administration. One word of caution: If you are using your listener to listen for connections from the Internet through a firewall, be sure that you do not leave a listener listening on the default port, 1521, because a hole through your firewall can leave you open to potential remote listener reconfiguration. An unsecured listener using default values can enable a hacker to obtain database information that could compromise your site.

Starting the Listener Server Process

The listener process is controlled by the Listener Control utility, executed via the **lsnrctl** command. The options available for the **lsnrctl** command are described in the next section. To start the listener, use the command

```
lsnrctl start
```

This command will start the default listener (named LISTENER). If you wish to start a listener with a different name, include that listener's name as the second parameter in the **lsnrctl** command. For example, if you created a listener called MY_LSNR, you could start it via the following command:

```
lsnrctl start my_lsnr
```

In the next section you will find descriptions of the other parameters available for the Listener Control utility.

After starting a listener, you can check that it is running by using the **status** option of the Listener Control utility. The following command can be used to perform this check:

```
lsnrctl status
```

If the listener is named anything other than LISTENER in the listener.ora file, you must add the name of the listener to the status command. For example, if the listener is named MY_LSNR, the command is

```
lsnrctl status my_lsnr
```

The status output will show if the listener has been started and the services it is currently supporting, as defined by its listener.ora file. The listener parameter file and its log file location will be displayed.

If you wish to see the operating system–level processes that are involved, use the following command. This example uses the Unix **ps -ef** command to list the system's active processes. The **grep tnslsnr** command then eliminates those rows that do not contain the term "tnslsnr."

```
ps -ef | grep tnslsnr
```

Here's some sample output for this command:

```
oracle 4022   1 0 13:36:53 ?    0:00 /oracle/products/102/bin/tnslsnr
                  LISTENER -inherit
oracle 5469 2419 1 13:56:23 ttypc  0:00 grep tnslsnr
```

This output shows two processes: the listener process and the process that is checking for it. The first line of output is wrapped to the second line and may be truncated by the operating system.

Controlling the Listener Server Process

You can use the Listener Control utility, **lsnrctl**, to start, stop, and modify the listener process on the database server. Its command options are listed in Table 16-2. Each of these commands may be accompanied by a value; for all except the **set password** command, that value will be a listener name. If no listener name is specified, the default (LISTENER) will be used. Once within **lsnrctl**, you can change the listener being modified via the **set current_listener** command.

NOTE
*Options for **lsnrctl** may be introduced or removed with each new version of Oracle Net.*

You can enter the **lsnrctl** command by itself to enter the **lsnrctl** utility shell, from which all other commands can then be executed.

Command	Description
CHANGE_PASSWORD	Sets a new password for the listener. You will be prompted for the old password for the listener.
EXIT	Exits **lsnrctl**.
HELP	Displays a list of the **lsnrctl** command options. You can also see additional options via the **help set** and **help show** commands.
QUIT	Exits **lsnrctl**.
RELOAD	Allows you to modify the listener services after the listener has been started. It forces SQL*Net to read and use the most current listener.ora file.
SAVE_CONFIG	New as of Net8. Creates a backup of your existing listener.ora file and then updates your listener.ora file with parameters you have changed via **lsnrctl**.
SERVICES	Displays the services available, along with their connection history. It also lists whether each service is enabled for remote DBA or autologin access.
SET	Sets parameter values. Options include the following: **current_listener** changes the listener process whose parameters are being set or shown. displaymode changes the format and level of detail for the **services** and **status** commands. **inbound_connect_timeout** sets the time, in seconds, for the client to complete its connection to the listener before being timed out. **log_directory** sets the directory for the listener log file. **log_file** sets the name of the listener log file. **log_status** sets whether logging is ON or OFF. **password** sets the listener password. **raw_mode** changes the **displaymode** format to show all data; only use **raw_mode** in conjunction with Oracle Support. **save_config_on_stop** saves your configuration changes to your listener.ora file when you exit **lsnrctl**. **startup_waittime** sets the number of seconds the listener sleeps before responding to a **lsnrctl start** command. **trc_directory** sets the directory for the listener trace file. **trc_file** sets the name for the listener trace file. **trc_level** sets the trace level (ADMIN, USER, SUPPORT, or OFF). See **lsnrctl trace**.
SHOW	Shows current parameter settings. Options are the same as the **set** options with the sole omission of the **password** command.
SPAWN	Spawns a program that runs with an alias in the listener.ora file.
START	Starts the listener.
STATUS	Provides status information about the listener, including the time it was started, its parameter filename, its log file, and the services it supports. This can be used to query the status of a listener on a remote server.
STOP	Stops the listener.
TRACE	Sets the trace level of the listener to one of four choices: OFF, USER (limited tracing), ADMIN (high level of tracing), or SUPPORT (for ORACLE Support).
VERSION	Displays version information for the listener, TNS, and the protocol adapters.

TABLE 16-2. *Listener Control Utility Commands*

The command options listed in Table 16-2 give you a great deal of control over the listener process, as shown in the following examples. In most of these examples, the **lsnrctl** command is first entered by itself. This places the user in the **lsnrctl** utility (as indicated by the LSNRCTL prompt). The rest of the commands are entered from within this utility. The following examples show the use of the **lsnrctl** utility to stop, start, and generate diagnostic information about the listener.

To stop the listener:

```
lsnrctl
LSNRCTL> set password lsnr_password
LSNRCTL> stop
```

To list status information for the listener:

```
lsnrctl status
```

To list the status of a listener on another host, add a service name from that host as a parameter to the **status** command. The following example uses the HQ service name shown earlier in this chapter:

```
lsnrctl status hq
```

To list version information about the listener:

```
lsnrctl version
```

To list information about the services supported by the listener:

```
lsnrctl
LSNRCTL> set password lsnr_password
LSNRCTL> services
```

The Oracle Connection Manager

The Oracle Connection Manager portion of Oracle Net acts as a router used to establish database communication links between otherwise incompatible network protocols as well as to take advantage of multiplexing and access control.

The advantage of an Oracle Connection Manager is that all servers do not have to use the same communications protocol. Each server can use the communications protocol that is best suited to its environment and will still be able to transfer data back and forth with other databases. This communication takes place regardless of the communications protocols used on the remote servers; the Oracle Connection Manager takes care of the differences between the protocols. The protocols supported by Oracle Connection Manager are IPC, Named Pipes, SDP, TCP/IP, and TCP/IP with SSL.

You can use multiple access paths to handle different client requests. The Oracle Connection Managers will select the most appropriate path based on path availability and network load. The relative cost of each path is specified via the Network Manager utility when the Oracle Connection Managers are set up.

In an intranet environment, the Oracle Connection Manager can be used as a firewall for Oracle Net traffic. You can establish filtering rules to enable or disable specific client access using the Oracle Connection Manager. The filtering rules can be based on any of the following criteria:

- Destination host names or IP addresses for servers

- Destination database service name

- Source host names or IP addresses for clients

- Whether the client is using the Oracle Advanced Security option

The Oracle Connection Manager is used to enhance your firewall security by filtering out client access based on one or more aspects of the filtering rules you create. For example, you could specify that an IP address is to be refused access using the CMAN_RULES parameter within the cman.ora file.

The file sqlnet.ora may be used to specify additional diagnostics beyond the default diagnostics provided.

Using Connection Manager

Oracle Net uses the Connection Manager to support connections within homogenous networks, reducing the number of physical connections maintained by the database. Two main processes and a control utility are associated with the Connection Manager, as follows:

CMGW	The gateway process that acts as a hub for the Connection Manager
CMADMIN	A multithreaded process responsible for all administrative tasks and issues
CMCTL	A utility that enables basic management functions for Oracle Control Manager administration

The CMGW Process

The Connection Manager Gateway (CMGW) process registers itself with the CMADMIN process and listens for incoming connection requests. By default, this process listens on port 1630 using the TCP/IP protocol. The CMGW process initiates connection requests to listeners from clients and relays data between the client and server.

The CMADMIN Process

The multithreaded Connection Manager Administrative (CMADMIN) process performs many tasks and functions. The CMADMIN processes CMGW registrations and registers source route addressing information about the CMGW and listeners. The CMADMIN process is tasked with identifying all listener processes that support at least one database. Using Oracle Internet Directory, the CMADMIN performs the following tasks:

- Locates local servers

- Monitors registered listeners

- Maintains client address information

- Periodically updates the Connection Manager's cache of available services

The CMADMIN process handles source route information about the CMGW and listeners.

Configuring the Oracle Connection Manager

The cman.ora file, located by default in the $ORACLE_HOME/network/admin directory on a Unix system and in ORACLE_HOME\network\admin on a Windows system, contains the configuration parameters for the Oracle Connection Manager. The file contains protocol addresses of the listening gateway process, access control parameters, and profile or control parameters.

The complete set of cman.ora parameters is shown in Table 16-3.

Parameter	Description
ADDRESS	Specifies the protocol address (such as the protocol, the host, and the port) of the Connection Manager.
RULE	Specifies an access control rule list to filter incoming connections. Subparameters allow source and destination host names, IP addresses, and service names to be filtered.
PARAMETER_LIST	Specifies attribute values when overriding the default settings. The remainder of the parameters in this listing are subparameters within the PARAMETER_LIST setting.
ASO_AUTHENTICATION_FILTER	Specifies whether Oracle Advanced Security authentication settings must be used by the client. The default is OFF.
CONNECTION_STATISTICS	Specifies whether the SHOW_CONNECTIONS command displays connection statistics. The default is NO.
EVENT_GROUP	Specifies which event groups are logged. The default is none.
IDLE_TIMEOUT	Specifies the amount of time, in seconds, that an established connection can remain active without transmitting data. The default is 0.
INBOUND_CONNECT_TIMEOUT	Specifies, in seconds, how long the Oracle Connection Manager listener waits for a valid connection from a client or another instance of Oracle Connection Manager. The default is 0.
LOG_DIRECTORY	Specifies the destination directory for Oracle Connection Manager log files. The default is the /network/log subdirectory under the Oracle home directory.
LOG_LEVEL	Specifies the logging level (OFF, USER, ADMIN, or SUPPORT). The default is SUPPORT.
MAX_CMCTL_SESSIONS	Specifies the maximum number of concurrent local or remote sessions of the Oracle Connection Manager control utility allowable for a given instance. The default is 4.
MAX_CONNECTIONS	Specifies the maximum number of connections a gateway process can handle. The default is 256.
MAX_GATEWAY_PROCESSES	Specifies the maximum number of gateway processes that an instance of Oracle Connection Manager supports. The default is 16.
MIN_GATEWAY_PROCESSES	Specifies the minimum number of gateway processes that an instance of Oracle Connection Manager must support. The default is 2.

TABLE 16-3. *CMAN.ORA Parameters*

Parameter	Description
OUTBOUND_CONNECT_TIMEOUT	Specifies, in seconds, the length of time that the Oracle Connection Manager instance waits for a valid connection to be established with the database server or with another Oracle Connection Manager instance. The default is 0.
PASSWORD_*instance_name*	The encrypted instance password, if set.
REMOTE_ADMIN	Specifies whether remote access to an Oracle Connection Manager is allowed. The default is NO.
SESSION_TIMEOUT	Specify the maximum time, in seconds, allowed for a user session. The default is 0.
TRACE_DIRECTORY	Specifies the directory for the trace files. The default is the /network/trace subdirectory under the Oracle home directory.
TRACE_FILELEN	Specifies, in KB, the size of the trace file. The default is 0.
TRACE_FILENO	Specifies the number of trace files, used cyclically. The default is 0.
TRACE_LEVEL	Specifies the trace level (OFF, USER, ADMIN, or SUPPORT). The default is OFF.
TRACE_TIMESTAMP	Adds a timestamp to every trace event in the trace files. The default is OFF.

TABLE 16-3.   *CMAN.ORA Parameters* (continued)

The Connection Manager Control Utility (CMCTL)

The Connection Manager Control Utility provides administrative access to CMADMIN and CMGW. The Connection Manager is started via the **cmctl** command. The command syntax is

```
cmctl command process_type
```

The default startup command from an operating system prompt is

```
cmctl start cman
```

The commands are broken into four basic types:

- Operational commands such as **start**
- Modifier commands such as **set**
- Informational commands such as **show**
- Command utility operations such as **exit**

Using the parameter REMOTE_ADMIN, you can control, but not start, remote managers. Unlike the Listener utility discussed earlier in this chapter, you cannot interactively set a password for the Oracle Connection Manager. To set a password for this tool, you put a plain-text password in the cman.ora file. The available command options for the **cmctl** command are shown in Table 16-4.

Command	Description
ADMINISTER	Choose an instance of Oracle Connection Manager. The format is **administer –c** followed by the instance name, with an optional **using password** clause.
CLOSE CONNECTIONS	Terminate connections. You can specify the source, destination, service, state, and gateway process ID for the connections to terminate.
EXIT	Exit the Oracle Connection Manager Control utility.
HELP	List all CMCTL commands.
QUIT	Exit the Oracle Connection Manager Control utility.
RELOAD	Dynamically re-read parameters and rules from the cman.ora file.
RESUME GATEWAYS	Resume suspended gateway processes.
SAVE_PASSWORD	Save the current password to the cman.ora configuration parameter file.
SET	Display a list of parameters that can be modified within CMCTL. You can set values for aso_authentication_filter, connection_statistics, event, idle_timeout, inbound_connect_timeout, log_directory, log_level, outbound_connect_timeout, password, session_timeout, trace_directory, and trace_level.
SHOW	Display a list of parameters whose values can be displayed. You can show their values individually by specifically listing them after the SHOW command (for example, SHOW TRACE_LEVEL).
SHOW ALL	Display the values of all parameters and rules.
SHOW DEFAULTS	Display the default parameter settings.
SHOW EVENTS	Display the events.
SHOW GATEWAYS	Display the current status of specific gateway processes.
SHOW PARAMETERS	Display current parameter settings.
SHOW RULES	Display the current access control list.
SHOW SERVICES	Display information on the Oracle Connection Manager services, including gateway handlers and the number of connections.
SHOW STATUS	Display basic information about the instance and its current statistics.
SHOW VERSION	Display the current version and name of the CMCTL utility.
SHUTDOWN	Shut down specific gateway processes or the entire Oracle Connection Manager instance.
STARTUP	Start the Oracle Connection Manager.
SUSPEND GATEWAY	Prevent gateway processes from accepting new client connections.

TABLE 16-4. *CMCTL Command Options*

If the Connection Manager has been started, any client that has SOURCE_ROUTE set to YES in its tnsnames.ora file can use the Connection Manager. The Connection Manager reduces system resource requirements by maintaining logical connections while reusing physical connections.

Directory Naming with Oracle Internet Directory

Oracle Internet Directory facilitates support for LDAP-compliant directory servers for centralized network names resolution management in a distributed Oracle network. For localized management, you can still use the tnsnames.ora file.

The file ldap.ora, located in the $ORACLE_HOME/network/admin directory on a Unix system and in ORACLE_HOME\network\admin in a Windows environment, stores the configuration parameters to access a directory server. Oracle supports both the Oracle Internet Directory and Microsoft Active Directory.

To resolve a connect descriptor using a centralized directory server, the steps are as follows:

1. Oracle Net, on behalf of the client, contacts the directory server to obtain the resolution for the connect identifier to a connect descriptor.

2. The directory server takes the connect identifier, locates the associated connect descriptor, and returns the descriptor to Oracle Net.

3. Oracle Net uses the resolved descriptor to make the connection request to the correct listener.

The directory server uses a tree structure in which to store its data. Each node in the tree is an *entry*. A hierarchical structure of entries is used, called a *directory information tree (DIT)*, and each entry is identified by a unique *distinguished name (DN)* that tells the directory server exactly where the entry resides. DITs can be structured to use an existing Domain Name System (DNS), organizational or geographical lines, or Internet naming scheme.

Using a DIT that is organized along organizational lines, for example, the DN for the HR server could be this: (dn: cn=HR, cn=OracleContext, dc=us, dc=ourcompany, dc=com). The lowest component of a DN is placed at the leftmost location of the DIT and moved progressively up the tree. The following illustration shows the DIT for this example.

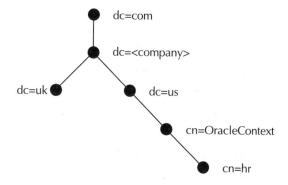

The commonly used LDAP attributes are

- **CommonName (cn)** Common name of an entry
- **Country (c)** Name of the country
- **Domain component (dc)** Domain component
- **Organization (o)** Name of organization
- **OrganizationalUnitName (ou)** Name of unit within the organization

NOTE
The value cn=OracleContext is a special entry in the directory server that supports directory-enabled features such as directory naming. The Oracle Context is created using the Oracle Net Configuration Assistant discussed earlier in this chapter.

Setting Up an Oracle Internet Directory

As detailed earlier, you can use the Oracle Net Configuration Assistant or the Oracle Net Manager to perform the initial configuration tasks. Once the directory schema and Oracle Context have been established, you can begin to register service names with the directory service using the Oracle Net Manager. The Oracle Context area is the root of the directory subtree where all information relevant to Oracle software is stored.

When the Oracle Context is installed, two entities are created: OracleDBCreators and OracleNetAdmins. The OracleDBCreators entity with a DN of (cn=OracleDBCreators, cn=OracleContext) is created. Any user who is a member of OracleDBCreators can register a database server entry or directory client entry using the Oracle Database Configuration Assistant. A user assigned as a member of OracleNetAdmins can create, modify, and delete net service names and modify Oracle Net attributes of database servers using the Oracle Net Manager. If you are a directory administrator, you can add users to these groups.

Clients who want to look up information in the directory must meet the following minimum requirements:

- They must be configured to use the directory server.
- They must be able to access the Oracle Net entries in the Oracle Context.
- They must have anonymous authentication with the directory server.

The clients can use the common names of database servers and net service entries to perform the lookups, or additional directory location information may be required in the connection string.

Using Easy Connect Naming

As of Oracle Database 10g, you can use the easy connect naming method to eliminate the need for service name files in a TCP/IP environment. Clients can connect to a database server by specifying the full connection information in their connect strings, in the format

```
connect username/password@[//]host[:port][/service_name]
```

The connection identifier elements are as follows:

Element	Description
//	Optional. Specify // for a URL.
Host	Required. Specify the host name or the IP address.
Port	Optional. Specify the port or use the default (1521).
service_name	Optional. Specify the service name. The default value is the host name of the database server.

For example, you can connect to the LOC service with this syntax:

```
connect username/password@hq:1521/loc
```

In order to use easy connect naming, you must have Oracle Net Services 10*g* software installed on your client. You must be using the TCP/IP protocol, and no features requiring a more advanced connect descriptor are supported.

For URL or JDBC connections, prefix the connect identifier with a double slash (//):

```
connect username/password@[//][host][:port][/service_name]
```

Easy connect naming is automatically configured at installation. In your sqlnet.ora file, make sure EZCONNECT is added to the list of values in the NAME.DIRECTORY_PATH parameter listing.

Using Database Links

You should create *database links* to support frequently used connections to remote databases. Database links specify the connect descriptor to be used for a connection, and they may also specify the username to connect to in the remote database.

A database link is typically used to create local objects (such as views or synonyms) that access remote databases via server/server communications. The local synonyms for remote objects provide location transparency to the local users. When a database link is referenced by a SQL statement, it opens a session in the remote database and executes the SQL statement there. The data is then returned, and the remote session may stay open in case it is needed again. Database links can be created as public links (by DBAs, making the links available to all users in the local database) or as private links.

The following example creates a private database link called HR_LINK:

```
create database link HR_LINK
connect to HR identified by PUFFINSTUFF
using 'loc';
```

The **create database link** command, as shown in this example, has three parameters:

- The name of the link (HR_LINK, in this example)
- The account to connect to

■ The service name

A public database link can be created by adding the keyword **public** to the **create database link** command, as shown in the following example:

```
create public database link HR_LINK
connect to HR identified by PUFFINSTUFF
using 'loc';
```

NOTE
Best practices for public database links would favor including the ***using*** *clause but not the* ***connect to*** *clause. You could then create a private database link with the same name that includes the* ***connect to*** *clause but not the* ***using*** *clause. Subsequent changes to the service name for the data would require re-creating only the public link, while the private links and the user passwords would be unchanged.*

If the LOC instance is moved to a different server, you can redirect the database links to LOC's new location simply by distributing a tnsnames.ora file that contains the modification or by revising the listing in the directory server. You can generate the revised entry for the tnsnames.ora file or directory server by using either the Oracle Net Configuration Assistant tool or the Oracle Net Manager, described previously in this chapter.

To use these links, simply add them as suffixes to the table names in commands. The following example creates a local view of a remote table, using the HR_LINK database link:

```
create view LOCAL_EMPLOYEE_VIEW
as
select * from EMPLOYEE@HR_LINK
where Office='ANNAPOLIS';
```

The **from** clause in this example refers to EMPLOYEE@HR_LINK. Because the HR_LINK database link specifies the server name, instance name, and owner name, the global object name for the table is known. If no account name had been specified, the user's account name would have been used instead. If HR_LINK was created without a **connect to** clause, the current username and password would be used to connect to the remote database.

In this example, a view was created in order to limit the records that users could retrieve. If no such restriction is necessary, a synonym can be used instead. This is shown in the following example:

```
create public synonym EMPLOYEE for EMPLOYEE@HR_LINK;
```

Local users who query the local public synonym EMPLOYEE will automatically have their queries redirected to the EMPLOYEE table in the LOC instance on the HQ server. Location transparency has thus been achieved.

By default, a single SQL statement can use up to four database links. This limit can be increased via the OPEN_LINKS parameter in the database's init.ora file.

Tuning Oracle Net

Tuning Oracle Net applications is fairly straightforward: Wherever possible, reduce the amount of data that is sent across the network, particularly for online transaction-processing applications. Also, reduce the number of times data is requested from the database. The basic procedures that should be applied include the following:

- The use of distributed objects, such as materialized views, to replicate static data to remote databases.

- The use of procedures to reduce the amount of data sent across the network. Rather than data being sent back and forth, only the procedure's error status is returned.

- The use of homogenous servers wherever possible to eliminate the need for connection managers.

- For OLTP applications only, the use of shared servers to support more clients with fewer processes.

The buffer size used by Oracle Net should take advantage of the packet sizes used by the network protocols (such as TCP/IP). If you send large packets of data across the network, the packets may be fragmented. Because each packet contains header information, reducing packet fragmentation reduces network traffic.

You can tune the size of the service layer buffer. The specification for the service layer data buffer is called SDU (Session Data Unit); if it is changed, this must be specified in your client and server configuration files. Oracle Net builds data into buffers the size of the SDU, so altering that size may improve your performance. The default size for the SDU is 2KB. If you will frequently be sending messages that are much larger than that, you can increase the SDU (up to a maximum of 32KB).

To configure the client to use a nondefault SDU, add the new SDU setting to the client configuration files. For the change to apply to all connections, add the following parameter to the sqlnet.ora file:

```
DEFAULT_SDU_SIZE=32767
```

For the change to apply to only specific service names, modify their entries in the tnsnames.ora file:

```
LOC =(DESCRIPTION=
    (SDU=32767)
    (ADDRESS=
        (PROTOCOL=TCP)
        (HOST=HQ)
        (PORT=1521))
    (CONNECT DATA=
        (SERVICE_NAME=LOC)))
```

On the database server, configure the default SDU setting in the sqlnet.ora file:

```
DEFAULT_SDU_SIZE=32767
```

For shared server processes, add the SDU setting to the DISPATCHERS setting in the instance initialization parameter file:

```
DISPATCHERS="(DESCRIPTION=(ADDRESS=(PROTOCOL=tcp))(SDU=32767))"
```

For dedicated server processes, edit the entries in the listener.ora file:

```
SID_LIST_listener_name=
  (SID_LIST=
  (SID_DESC=
(SDU=8192)
(SID_NAME=loc)))
```

Oracle Net Services provides support for the SDP protocol for Infiniband high-speed networks. Applications using SDP place most of the messaging burden on the network interface card, thus reducing the CPU requirements of the application. If you are using an Infiniband high-speed network (such as for communications among your application tiers), see the Oracle documentation for hardware and software configuration details.

Limiting Resource Usage

To limit the impact of unauthorized users on your system, you can reduce the duration for which resources can be held prior to authentication. The time-limiting parameters listed earlier in this chapter help to mitigate the performance problems caused by these unauthorized accesses. In the listener.ora file, set the INBOUND_CONNECT_TIMEOUT_*listener_name* parameter to terminate connections that are not authenticated by the listener within the specified time period. Failed connections will be logged to the listener log file. In the server-side sqlnet.ora file, set the SQLNET.INBOUND_CONNECT_TIMEOUT parameter to terminate connection attempts that cannot establish and authenticate connections within the specified interval. Set the server-side SQLNET.INBOUND_CONNECT_TIMEOUT parameter to a higher value than the INBOUND_CONNECT_TIMEOUT_*listener_name* parameter in the listener.ora file.

Debugging Connection Problems

Oracle Net connections require that a number of communication mechanisms be properly configured. The connections involve host-to-host communication, proper identification of services and databases, and proper configuration of the listener server processes. In the event of connection problems when using Oracle Net, it is important to eliminate as many of these components as possible.

Start by making sure that the host the connection is trying to reach is accessible via the network. This can be checked via the following command:

```
telnet host_name
```

If this command is successful, you will be prompted for a username and password on the remote host. If the **ping** command is available to you, you may use it instead. The following command will check to see if the remote host is available and will return a status message:

```
ping host_name
```

If the host is available on the network, the next step is to check if the listener is running. At the same time, you can check to see what parameters it is currently using; this is important if you are attempting a remote autologin access. The **lsnrctl status** command will provide this information:

```
lsnrctl status net_service_name
```

The **net_service_name** clause should refer to the name of a service on the remote server. If the **net_service_name** clause is not used, the command will return the status of the listener on the local server.

These two checks—of host availability and listener availability—will resolve over 95 percent of Oracle Net connection problems in server/server communications. The rest of the problems will result from difficulties with the database specification that is being used. These problems include invalid username/password combinations, down databases, and databases in need of recovery.

You can use the **tnsping** utility provided by Oracle to verify Oracle Net connectivity to a remote database listener. The **tnsping** utility has two parameters—the service name to connect to and the number of connections to attempt. The output from **tnsping** will include a listing showing the time required to connect to the remote database.

For example, to determine if the database identified by the HQ service name in your local tnsnames.ora file is accessible, use the following command:

```
tnsping HQ
```

To test ten consecutive connections to the HQ database, use this command:

```
tnsping HQ 10
```

In addition to **tnsping**, you can use the **trcroute** utility to discover the path a connection takes to a remote database. The **trcroute** utility reports on the TNS addresses of every node it travels through and reports any errors that occur. The command format is

```
trcroute net_service_name
```

In client/server communications, the same principles for debugging connection problems apply. First, verify that the remote host is accessible; most communications software for clients includes a **telnet** or **ping** command. If the remote host is not accessible, the problem may be on the client side. Verify that *other* clients are able to access the host on which the database resides. If they can, the problem is isolated to the client. If they cannot, the problem lies on the server side, and the server, its listener processes, and its databases should be checked.

CHAPTER
17

Managing Large
Databases

n Chapter 6, "Monitoring Space Usage," we talked about bigfile tablespaces and how they not only allow the total size of the database to be much larger than in previous versions of Oracle, but also ease administration by moving the maintenance point from the datafile to the tablespace.

In Chapter 4, "Physical Database Layouts and Storage Management," we presented an overview of Automatic Storage Management (ASM) and how it can ease administration, enhance performance, and improve availability. The DBA can add one or more disk volumes to a rapidly growing VLDB (Very Large Database) without bringing down the instance.

In this chapter, we'll revisit many of these database features, but with an emphasis on how they can be leveraged in a VLDB environment. Although these features surely provide benefits in all Oracle installations, they are especially useful in databases whose most heavily used resource is the amount of disk space allocated. First, we'll review the concepts behind bigfile tablespaces and delve more deeply into how they are constructed using a new ROWID format. We'll also show how transportable tablespaces are a distinct advantage in a VLDB environment because they bypass some of the export/import steps required in versions prior to Oracle9*i* to move the contents of a tablespace from one database to another. When tablespaces in a VLDB environment approach the exabyte size, both the extra space required for a traditional export and import operation and the time it takes to perform the export may become prohibitive. If you are using Oracle 10*g*, your tablespaces may even be transportable between different hardware and software platforms with minimal or no extra effort.

Next, we will review the various types of nontraditional (non-heap-based) tables that are often leveraged in a VLDB environment. Index organized tables (IOTs) combine the best features of a traditional table with the fast access of an index into one segment; we'll review some examples of how IOTs can now be partitioned in Oracle 10*g*. Global temporary tables dramatically reduce space usage in the undo tablespace and redo logs for recovery purposes because the table contents only persist for the duration of a transaction or a session. External tables make it easy to access data in a non-Oracle format as if the data was in a table; as of Oracle 10*g*, external tables can be created using Oracle Data Pump, covered at the end of this chapter. Finally, the amount of space occupied by a table can be dramatically reduced by using an internal compression algorithm when the rows are loaded using direct-path SQL*Loader and **create table as select** statements.

Table and index partitioning not only improves query performance but tremendously improves the manageability of tables in a VLDB environment by allowing you to perform maintenance operations on one partition while users may be accessing other partitions of the table. We will cover all the different types of partitioning schemes, including some of the new partitioning features in Oracle 10*g*: hash-partitioned global indexes, list-partitioned IOTs, and LOB support in all types of partitioned IOTs.

Bitmap indexes, available since Oracle 7.3, provide query benefits not only for tables with columns of low cardinality, but also for special indexes called *bitmap join indexes* that pre-join two or more tables on one or more columns. Oracle 10*g* removes one of the remaining obstacles for using bitmap indexes in a heavy, single-row insert, update, or delete environment: mitigating performance problems due to bitmap index fragmentation issues.

Oracle Data Pump, new to Oracle 10*g*, picks up where the traditional import and export functions leave off. One of many features supported by Oracle Data Pump performs export directly to another instance; in addition, most Data Pump operations occur on the server side instead of the client side.

Creating Tablespaces in a VLDB Environment

The considerations for creating tablespaces in a small database (terabyte range or smaller) also apply to VLDBs: Spread out I/O across multiple devices, use a logical volume manager (LVM) with RAID capabilities, or use ASM. In this section, we will present more detail and examples for bigfile tablespaces. Because a bigfile tablespace contains only one datafile, the ROWID format for objects stored in a bigfile tablespace is different, allowing for a tablespace size as large as 8 million terabytes, depending on the tablespace's block size.

Bigfile tablespaces are best suited for an environment that uses ASM, Oracle Managed Files (OMF), and Recovery Manager (RMAN) with a Flash Recovery Area. See Chapter 4, "Physical Database Layouts and Storage Management," for a detailed review of ASM; Chapter 13, "Using Recovery Manager (RMAN)," presents RMAN from a command-line and EM Database Control perspective and leverages the Flash Recovery Area for all backups. Finally, Chapter 6, "Monitoring Space Usage," describes OMF from a space-management perspective.

In the next few sections, we will present an in-depth look at creating a bigfile tablespace and specifying its characteristics; in addition, we will discuss the impact of bigfile tablespaces on both initialization parameters and data dictionary views. Finally, we will show you how the **dbverify** utility has been revised in Oracle 10*g* to allow you to analyze a single bigfile datafile using parallel processes.

Bigfile Tablespace Basics

Using bigfile tablespaces with a block size of 32K, a datafile can be as large as 128 terabytes, with a maximum database size of 8 exabytes (EB). In contrast, a database using only smallfile tablespaces can have a maximum datafile size of 128 gigabytes (GB) and therefore a maximum database size of 8 petabytes (PB). Because a bigfile tablespace can only have one datafile, you never need to decide whether to add a datafile or autoextend the single datafile for the tablespace. If you are using ASM and OMF, you won't even need to know the name of the single datafile.

Given that the maximum number of datafiles in a database on most platforms is 65,535, and the number of blocks in a bigfile tablespace datafile is 2^{32}, you can calculate the maximum amount of space (M) in a single Oracle database as the maximum number of datafiles (D) multiplied by the maximum number of blocks per datafile (F) multiplied by the tablespace block size (B):

$$M = D * F * B$$

Therefore, the maximum database size, given the maximum block size and the maximum number of datafiles, is

```
65,535 datafiles * 4,294,967,296 blocks per datafile * 32,768 block size =
9,223,231,299,366,420,480 = 8EB
```

For a smallfile tablespace, the number of blocks in a smallfile tablespace datafile is only 2^{22}. Therefore, our calculation yields

```
65,535 datafiles * 4,194,304 blocks per datafile * 32,768 block size =
9,007,061,815,787,520 = 8PB
```

In Table 17-1, you can see a comparison of maximum datafile sizes for smallfile tablespaces and bigfile tablespaces given the tablespace block size.

Creating and Modifying Bigfile Tablespaces

Here is an example of creating a bigfile tablespace in a non-ASM environment:

```
SQL> create bigfile tablespace dmarts
  2       datafile '/u05/oradata/dmarts.dbf' size 2500g
  3       autoextend on next 500g maxsize unlimited
  4       extent management local uniform size 50m
  5       segment space management auto;

Tablespace created.
```

In the example, you can see that **extent management** and **segment space management** are explicitly set, even though **auto** is the default for segment space management; bigfile tablespaces must be created as locally managed with automatic segment space management. Because the default allocation policy for bigfile tablespaces is **autoallocate**, you should change the allocation policy to **uniform**, as in the example with a large extent size, when the size of the tablespace is in the terabyte range and you know with some precision how large the table will be along with the growth pattern. As a rule of thumb, **autoallocate** is best for tablespaces whose table usage and growth patterns are indeterminate.

Even though the datafile for this bigfile tablespace is set to autoextend indefinitely, the disk volume where the datafile resides may be limited in space; when this occurs, the tablespace may need to be relocated to a different disk volume. Therefore, you can see the advantages of using ASM: You can easily add another disk volume to the disk group where the datafile resides, and Oracle will automatically redistribute the contents of the datafile and allow the tablespace to grow—all of this occurring while the database (and the tablespace itself) is available to users.

By default, tablespaces are created as smallfile tablespaces; you can specify the default tablespace type when the database is created or at any time with the **alter database** command, as in this example:

```
SQL> alter database set default bigfile tablespace;
Database altered.
```

Tablespace Block Size	Maximum Smallfile Datafile Size	Maximum Bigfile Datafile Size
2K	8GB	8TB
4K	16GB	16TB
8K	32GB	32TB
16K	64GB	64TB
32K	128GB	128TB

TABLE 17-1. *Maximum Tablespace Datafile Sizes*

Bigfile Tablespace ROWID Format

To facilitate the larger address space for bigfile tablespaces, a new extended ROWID format is used for rows of tables in bigfile tablespaces. First, we will review the ROWID format for smallfile tablespaces in previous versions of Oracle and for Oracle 10g. The format for a smallfile ROWID consists of four parts:

```
OOOOOO FFF BBBBBB RRR
```

Table 17-2 defines each part of a smallfile ROWID.

In contrast, a bigfile tablespace only has one datafile, and its relative datafile number is always 1024. Because the relative datafile number is fixed, it is not needed as part of the ROWID; as a result, the part of the ROWID used for the relative datafile number can be used to expand the size of the block number field. The concatenation of the smallfile relative datafile number (FFF) and the smallfile datablock number (BBBBBB) results in a new construct called an *encoded block number*. Therefore, the format for a bigfile ROWID consists of only three parts:

```
OOOOOO LLLLLLLLL RRR
```

Table 17-3 defines each part of a bigfile ROWID.

DBMS_ROWID and Bigfile Tablespaces

Because two different types of tablespaces can now coexist in the database along with their corresponding ROWID formats, some changes have occurred to the DBMS_ROWID package.

The names of the procedures in the DBMS_ROWID package are the same and operate as before, except for a new parameter, TS_TYPE_IN, which identifies the type of tablespace to which a particular row belongs: TS_TYPE_IN can be either BIGFILE or SMALLFILE.

For an example of extracting ROWIDs from a table in a bigfile tablespace, we have a table called OE.ARCH_ORDERS in a bigfile tablespace named USERS2:

```
SQL> select tablespace_name, bigfile from dba_tablespaces
  2        where tablespace_name = 'USERS2';

TABLESPACE_NAME                  BIG
------------------------------   ---
USERS2                           YES
```

Smallfile ROWID Component	Definition
OOOOOO	Data object number identifying the database segment (such as table, index, or materialized view)
FFF	Relative datafile number within the tablespace of the datafile that contains the row
BBBBBB	The datablock containing the row, relative to the datafile
RRR	Slot number, or row number, of the row inside a block

TABLE 17-2.   *Smallfile ROWID Format*

As with tables in smallfile tablespaces in previous versions of Oracle and Oracle 10g, you can use the pseudo-column ROWID to extract the entire ROWID, noting that the format of the ROWID is different for bigfile tables, even though the length of the ROWID stays the same. This query will also extract the block number in decimal format:

```
SQL> select rowid,
  2         dbms_rowid.rowid_block_number(rowid,'BIGFILE') blocknum,
  3         order_id, customer_id
  4  from oe.arch_orders
  5  where rownum < 11;

ROWID                  BLOCKNUM   ORDER_ID CUSTOMER_ID
------------------     ---------- ---------- -----------
AAANw4AAAAAAACsAAA         172       2458        101
AAANw4AAAAAAACsAAB         172       2397        102
AAANw4AAAAAAACsAAC         172       2454        103
AAANw4AAAAAAACsAAD         172       2354        104
AAANw4AAAAAAACsAAE         172       2358        105
AAANw4AAAAAAACsAAF         172       2381        106
AAANw4AAAAAAACsAAG         172       2440        107
AAANw4AAAAAAACsAAH         172       2357        108
AAANw4AAAAAAACsAAI         172       2394        109
AAANw4AAAAAAACsAAJ         172       2435        144

10 rows selected.
```

For the row with the ORDER_ID of 2358, the data object number is AAANw4, the encoded block number is AAAAAAACs, and the row number of the row, or slot, in the block is AAE; the translated decimal block number is 172.

NOTE
ROWIDs use base-64 encoding.

The other procedures in the DBMS_ROWID package that use the variable TS_TYPE_IN to specify the tablespace type are ROWID_INFO and ROWID_RELATIVE_FNO.

Bigfile ROWID Component	Definition
OOOOOO	Data object number identifying the database segment (such as table, index, or materialized view)
LLLLLLLLL	Encoded block number, relative to the tablespace and unique within the tablespace
RRR	Slot number, or row number, of the row inside a block

TABLE 17-3. *Bigfile ROWID Format*

ROWID_INFO Parameter	Description
ROWID_IN	ROWID to be described
TS_TYPE_IN	Tablespace type (SMALLFILE or BIGFILE)
ROWID_TYPE	Returns ROWID type (restricted or extended)
OBJECT_NUMBER	Returns data object number
RELATIVE_FNO	Returns relative file number
BLOCK_NUMBER	Returns block number in this file
ROW_NUMBER	Returns row number in this block

TABLE 17-4. *ROWID_INFO Parameters*

The procedure ROWID_INFO must be used in an anonymous or named procedure because it is not a function and returns five attributes of the specified ROWID. In Table 17-4 you can see the parameters of the ROWID_INFO procedure.

In the following example, we'll use an anonymous PL/SQL block to extract the values for OBJECT_NUMBER, RELATIVE_FNO, BLOCK_NUMBER, and ROW_NUMBER for a row in the table OE.ARCH_ORDERS:

```
variable object_number number
variable relative_fno number
variable block_number number
variable row_number number

declare
    oe_rownum     rowid;
    rowid_type    number;
begin
    select rowid into oe_rownum from oe.arch_orders
       where order_id = 2358 and rownum = 1;
    dbms_rowid.rowid_info (rowid_in => oe_rownum,
        ts_type_in => 'BIGFILE',
        rowid_type => rowid_type,
        object_number => :object_number,
        relative_fno => :relative_fno,
        block_number => :block_number,
        row_number => :row_number);
end;

PL/SQL procedure successfully completed.

SQL> print

OBJECT_NUMBER
-------------
        56376
```

```
RELATIVE_FNO
------------
        1024


BLOCK_NUMBER
------------
         172


ROW_NUMBER
----------
           4

SQL>
```

Note that the value for RELATIVE_FNO is always 1024 for a bigfile tablespace, and the BLOCK_NUMBER is 172, as you saw in the previous example that used the DBMS_ROWID.ROWID_BLOCK_NUMBER function.

Using DBVERIFY with Bigfile Tablespaces

The DBVERIFY utility, available since Oracle version 7.3, checks the logical integrity of an offline database. The files can only be datafiles; DBVERIFY cannot analyze online redo log files or archived redo log files. In previous versions of Oracle, DBVERIFY could analyze all of a tablespace's datafiles in parallel by spawning multiple DBVERIFY commands. However, because a bigfile tablespace has only one datafile, DBVERIFY has been enhanced to analyze parts of a bigfile tablespace's datafiles in parallel.

Using the **dbv** command at the Unix or Windows prompt, you can use two new parameters: START and END, representing the first and last block, respectively, of the file to analyze. As a result, you need to know how many blocks are in the bigfile tablespace's datafile; the dynamic performance view V$DATAFILE comes to the rescue, as you can see in the following example:

```
SQL> select file#, blocks, name from v$datafile;

     FILE#     BLOCKS NAME
---------- ---------- ------------------------------------------
         1      58880 /u05/oradata/ord/system01.dbf
         2      20480 /u05/oradata/ord/undotbs01.dbf
         3      42240 /u05/oradata/ord/sysaux01.dbf
         4       2720 /u05/oradata/ord/users01.dbf
         5      19200 /u09/oradata/ord/example01.dbf
         6       1280 /u09/oradata/ord/oe_trans01.dbf
         7        640 /u05/oradata/ord/users02.dbf
         8       1280 /u06/oradata/ord/logmnr_rep01.dbf
         9       2304 /u09/oradata/ord/big_users.dbf
        10        640 /u08/oradata/ord/idx01.dbf
        11        640 /u08/oradata/ord/idx02.dbf

11 rows selected.
```

In the next example, you will see how to analyze datafile #9, the datafile for the bigfile tablespace BIG_USERS. At the operating system command prompt, you can analyze the file with five parallel processes, each processing 500 blocks, except for the last one:

```
$ dbv file=/u09/oradata/ord/big_users.dbf start=1 end=500 &
[1] 6444
$ dbv file=/u09/oradata/ord/big_users.dbf start=501 end=1000 &
[2] 6457
$ dbv file=/u09/oradata/ord/big_users.dbf start=1001 end=1500 &
[2] 6466
$ dbv file=/u09/oradata/ord/big_users.dbf start=1501 end=2000 &
[2] 6469
$ dbv file=/u09/oradata/ord/big_users.dbf start=2001 &
[5] 6499
```

In the fifth command, we did not specify **end=**; if you do not specify **end=**, it is assumed that you will be analyzing the datafile from the starting point to the end of the file. All five of these commands run in parallel. The output from these commands looks similar to the following:

```
DBVERIFY: Release 10.1.0.2.0 -
          Production on Sat Aug 14 21:36:18 2004
Copyright (c) 1982, 2004, Oracle.  All rights reserved.

DBVERIFY - Verification starting :
          FILE = /u09/oradata/ord/big_users.dbf
DBVERIFY - Verification complete

Total Pages Examined        : 500
Total Pages Processed (Data) : 393
Total Pages Failing   (Data) : 0
Total Pages Processed (Index): 1
Total Pages Failing   (Index): 0
Total Pages Processed (Other): 18
Total Pages Processed (Seg)  : 0
Total Pages Failing   (Seg)  : 0
Total Pages Empty           : 88
Total Pages Marked Corrupt  : 0
Total Pages Influx          : 0
```

Bigfile Tablespace Initialization Parameter Considerations

Although there are no new initialization parameters specific to bigfile tablespaces, the values of one initialization parameter and a **create database** parameter can potentially be reduced because only one datafile is needed for each bigfile tablespace. The initialization parameter is DB_FILES and the **create database** parameter is MAXDATAFILES.

DB_FILES and Bigfile Tablespaces

As you already know, DB_FILES is the maximum number of datafiles that can be opened for this database. If you use bigfile tablespaces instead of smallfile tablespaces, the value of this parameter may be lower; as a result, because there are fewer datafiles to maintain, memory requirements are lower in the System Global Area (SGA).

MAXDATAFILES and Bigfile Tablespaces

When creating a new database or a new control file, you can use the MAXDATAFILES parameter to control the size of the control file section allocated to maintain information about datafiles. Using bigfile tablespaces, you can make the size of the control file and the space needed in the SGA for datafile information smaller; more importantly, the same value for MAXDATAFILES using bigfile tablespaces means that the total database size can be larger.

Bigfile Tablespace Data Dictionary Changes

The changes to data dictionary views due to bigfile tablespaces include a new row in DATABASE_PROPERTIES and a new column in DBA_TABLESPACES and USER_TABLESPACES.

DATABASE_PROPERTIES and Bigfile Tablespaces

The data dictionary view DATABASE_PROPERTIES, as the name implies, contains a number of characteristics about the database, such as the names of the default and permanent tablespaces and various NLS settings. Because of bigfile tablespaces, there is a new property in DATABASE_PROPERTIES called DEFAULT_TBS_TYPE that indicates the default tablespace type for the database if no type is specified in a **create tablespace** command. In the following example, you can find out the default new tablespace type:

```
SQL> select property_name, property_value, description
  2       from database_properties
  3  where property_name = 'DEFAULT_TBS_TYPE';

PROPERTY_NAME        PROPERTY_VALUE    DESCRIPTION
-----------------    ---------------   -----------------------
DEFAULT_TBS_TYPE     BIGFILE           Default tablespace type

1 row selected.
```

*_TABLESPACES, V$TABLESPACE, and Bigfile Tablespaces

The data dictionary views DBA_TABLESPACES and USER_TABLESPACES have a new column called BIGFILE. The value of this column is YES if the corresponding tablespace is a bigfile tablespace, as you saw in the query against DBA_TABLESPACES earlier in this chapter. The dynamic performance view V$TABLESPACE also contains this column.

Advanced Oracle Table Types

Many other table types provide benefits in a VLDB environment. Index organized tables, for example, eliminate the need for both a table and its corresponding index, replacing them with a single structure that looks like an index but contains data like a table. Global temporary tables create a common table definition available to all database users; in a VLDB, a global temporary table shared by thousands of users is preferable to each user creating their own definition of the table, potentially putting further space pressure on the data dictionary. External tables allow you to use text-based files outside of the database without actually storing the data in an Oracle table. Partitioned tables, as the name implies, store tables and indexes in separate partitions to keep the availability of the tables high while keeping maintenance time low. Finally, materialized views preaggregate query results from a view and store the query results in a local table; queries that use the materialized view may run significantly faster because the results from executing the view do not need to be re-created. We will cover all these table types to varying levels of detail in the following sections.

Index Organized Tables

You can store index and table data together in a table known as an *index organized table (IOT)*. Significant reductions in disk space are achieved with IOTs because the indexed columns are not stored twice (once in the table and once in the index); instead, they are stored once in the IOT along with any non-indexed columns. IOTs are suitable for tables where the primary access method is through the primary key, although creating indexes on other columns of the IOT is allowed to improve access by those columns.

In the following example, you will create an IOT with a two-part (composite) primary key:

```
create table oe.sales_summ_by_date
(    sales_date      date,
     dept_id         number,
     total_sales     number(18,2),
     constraint ssbd_pk primary key
         (sales_date, dept_id))
organization index tablespace prd04;
```

Each entry in the IOT contains a date, a department number, and a total sales amount for the day. All three of these columns are stored in each IOT row, but the IOT is built based on only the date and department number. Only one segment is used to store an IOT; if you build a secondary index on this IOT, a new segment is created.

Because the entire row in an IOT is stored as the index itself, there is no ROWID for each row; the primary key identifies the rows in an IOT. Instead, Oracle creates *logical ROWIDs* derived from the value of the primary key; the logical ROWID is used to support secondary indexes on the IOT.

No special syntax is required to use an IOT; although it is built and maintained much like an index, it appears as a table to any SQL **select** statement or other DML statements. Also, IOTs can be partitioned; information about partitioning IOTs is presented later in this chapter in the section "Partitioned Index Organized Tables."

Global Temporary Tables

Temporary tables have been available since Oracle8*i*. They are temporary in the sense of the data that is stored in the table, not in the definition of the table itself. The command **create global temporary table** creates a temporary table; all users who have permissions on the table itself can perform DML on a temporary table. However, each user sees their own and only their own data in the table. When a user truncates a temporary table, only the data that they inserted is removed from the table. Global temporary tables are useful in situations where a large number of users need a table to hold temporary data for their session or transaction, while only needing one definition of the table in the data dictionary. Global temporary tables have the added advantage of reducing the need for redo or undo space for the entries in the table in a recovery scenario. The entries in a global temporary table, by their nature, are not permanent and therefore do not need to be recovered during instance or media recovery.

There are two different flavors of temporary data in a temporary table: temporary for the duration of the transaction, and temporary for the duration of the session. The longevity of the temporary data is controlled by the **on commit** clause; **on commit delete rows** removes all rows from the temporary table when a **commit** or **rollback** is issued, and **on commit preserve rows** keeps the rows in the table beyond the transaction boundary. However, when the user's session is terminated, all of the user's rows in the temporary table are removed.

In the following example, you create a global temporary table to hold some intermediate totals for the duration of the transaction. Here is the SQL command to create the table:

```
SQL> create global temporary table subtotal_hrs
  2      (emp_id              number,
  3       proj_hrs            number)
  4   on commit delete rows;

Table created.
```

For the purposes of this example, you will create a permanent table that holds the total hours by employee by project for a given day. Here is the SQL command for the permanent table:

```
SQL> create table total_hours (emp_id number, wk_dt date, tot_hrs number);
```

In the following scenario, you will use the global temporary table to keep the intermediate results, and at the end of the transaction, store the totals in the TOTAL_HOURS table. Here is the sequence of commands:

```
SQL> insert into subtotal_hrs values (101, 20);
1 row created.

SQL> insert into subtotal_hrs values (101, 10);
1 row created.

SQL> insert into subtotal_hrs values (120, 15);
1 row created.

SQL> select * from subtotal_hrs;

    EMP_ID    PROJ_HRS
---------- ----------
       101          20
       101          10
       120          15

SQL> insert into total_hours
  2       select emp_id, sysdate, sum(proj_hrs) from subtotal_hrs
  3            group by emp_id;
2 rows created.

SQL> commit;
Commit complete.
```

```
SQL> select * from subtotal_hrs;
no rows selected

SQL> select * from total_hours;

    EMP_ID WK_DT         TOT_HRS
---------- --------- ----------
       101 19-AUG-04          30
       120 19-AUG-04          15

SQL>
```

Notice that after the **commit**, the rows are retained in TOTAL_HOURS because it is a permanent table, but are not retained in SUBTOTAL_HRS because it is a temporary table, and we specified **on commit delete rows** when we created the table.

NOTE
DDL can be performed on a global temporary table as long as there are no sessions currently inserting rows into the global temporary table.

There are a few other things to keep in mind when using temporary tables. Although you can create an index on a temporary table, the entries in the index are dropped along with the data rows, as with a regular table. Also, due to the temporary nature of the data in a temporary table, no recovery-related redo information is generated for DML on temporary tables; however, undo information is created in the undo tablespace and redo information to protect the undo. If all you do is insert and select from your global temporary tables, very little redo is generated. Because the table definition itself is not temporary, it persists between sessions until it is explicitly dropped.

External Tables

Sometimes you want to access data that resides outside of the database in a text format, but you want to use it as if it were a table in the database. Although you could use a utility such as SQL*Loader to load the table into the database, the data may be quite volatile or your user base's expertise might not include executing SQL*Loader at the Windows or Unix command line.

To address these needs, you can use *external tables,* which are read-only tables whose definition is stored within the database but whose data stays external to the database. There are a few drawbacks to using external tables: You cannot index external tables and you cannot execute **update**, **insert**, and **delete** statements against an external table. However, in a data warehouse environment where an external table is read in its entirety for a merge operation with an existing table, these drawbacks do not apply.

You might use an external table to gather employee suggestions in a web-based front end that does not have access to the production database; in this example, you will create an external table that references a text-based file containing two fields: the employee ID and the comment.

First, you must create a *directory object* to point to the operating system directory where the text file is stored. In this example, you will create the directory EMPL_COMMENT_DIR to reference a directory on the Unix file system, as follows:

```
SQL> create directory empl_comment_dir as
  2      '/u10/Employee_Comments';
Directory created.
```

The name of the text file in this directory is called empl_sugg.txt, and it looks like this:

```
$ cat empl_sugg.txt
101, The cafeteria serves lousy food.
138, We need a raise.
112, There are not enough bathrooms in Building 5.
138, I like the new benefits plan.
$
```

Because this text file has two fields, you will create the external table with two columns, the first being the employee number and the second being the text of the comments. Here is the **create table** command:

```
SQL> create table empl_sugg
  2      (employee_id     number,
  3       empl_comment    varchar2(250))
  4   organization external
  5      (type oracle_loader
  6       default directory empl_comment_dir
  7       access parameters
  8       (records delimited by newline
  9        fields terminated by ','
 10        (employee_id     char,
 11         empl_comment    char)
 12       )
 13       location('empl_sugg.txt')
 14      );
Table created.

SQL>
```

The first three lines of the command look like a standard **create table** command. The **organization external** clause specifies that this table's data is stored external to the database. Using the **oracle_loader** clause specifies the access driver to create and load an external table as read-only. The file specified in the **location** clause, empl_sugg.txt, is located in the Oracle directory **empl_comment_dir**, which you created earlier. The **access parameters** specify that each row of the table is on its own line in the text file and that the fields in the text file are separated by a comma.

NOTE
*Using an access driver of **oracle_datapump** instead of **oracle_loader** allows you to unload your data to an external table; other than this initial unload, the external table is accessible for read access only through the **oracle_datapump** access driver and has the same restrictions as an external table created with the **oracle_loader** access driver.*

Once the table is created, the data is immediately accessible in a **select** statement as if it had been loaded into a real table, as you can see in this example:

```
SQL> select * from empl_sugg;

EMPLOYEE_ID EMPL_COMMENT
----------- ----------------------------------------------------
        101  The cafeteria serves lousy food.
        138  We need a raise.
        112  There are not enough bathrooms in Building 5.
        138  I like the new benefits plan.

SQL>
```

Any changes made to the text file will automatically be available the next time you execute the **select** statement.

Partitioned Tables

In a VLDB environment, partitioned tables help to make the database more available and maintainable. A partitioned table is split up into more manageable pieces, called *partitions*, and can be further subdivided into *subpartitions*. The corresponding indexes on partitioned tables can be nonpartitioned, partitioned the same way as the table or partitioned differently from the table.

Partitioned tables can also improve the performance of the database: Each partition of a partitioned table can be accessed using parallel query. Multiple parallel execution servers can be assigned to different partitions of the table or to different index partitions.

For performance reasons, each partition of a table can and should reside in its own tablespace. Other attributes of a partition, such as storage characteristics, can differ; however, the column datatypes and constraints for each partition must be identical. In other words, attributes such as datatype and check constraints are at the table level, not the partition level. Other advantages of storing partitions of a partitioned table in separate tablespaces include the following:

- It reduces the possibility of data corruption in more than one partition if one tablespace is damaged.

- Each partition can be backed up and recovered independently.

- You have more control of partition-to-physical-device mapping to balance the I/O load (even in an ASM environment, with each partition in a different disk group).

Partitioning is transparent to applications, and no changes to SQL statements are required to take advantage of partitioning. However, in rare situations where specifying a partition would be advantageous, you can specify both the table name and partition name in a SQL statement. Examples of syntax using explicit partition names in a **select** statement are found later in this chapter in the section "Splitting, Adding, and Dropping Partitions."

Creating Partitioned Tables

Several methods of partitioning are available in the Oracle database, and some of these are new to Oracle 10g, such as list-partitioned index organized tables (IOTs). In the next few sections, we'll cover the basics of range partitioning, hash partitioning, list partitioning, composite range-hash partitioning, and composite range-list partitioning. We'll also show you how to selectively compress partitions within the table to save on I/O and disk space.

Using Range Partitioning   Range partitioning is used to map rows to partitions based on ranges of one or more columns in the table being partitioned. Also, the rows to be partitioned should be fairly evenly distributed among each partition, such as by months of the year or quarter. If the column being partitioned is skewed (for example, by population within each state code), another partitioning method may be more appropriate.

To use range partitioning, you must specify the following three criteria:

- Partitioning method (range)
- Partitioning column or columns
- Bounds for each partition

In the following example, you want to partition the catalog request table CAT_REQ by season, resulting in a total of four partitions per year:

```
create table cat_req
      (cat_req_num        number not null,
       cat_req_dt         date not null,
       cat_cd             number not null,
       cust_num           number null,
       req_nm             varchar2(50),
       req_addr1          varchar2(75),
       req_addr2          varchar2(75),
       req_addr3          varchar2(75))
   partition by range (cat_req_dt)
      (partition cat_req_spr_2004
            values less than (to_date('20040601','YYYYMMDD'))
            tablespace prd01,
       partition cat_req_sum_2004
            values less than (to_date('20040901','YYYYMMDD'))
            tablespace prd02,
       partition cat_req_fal_2004
            values less than (to_date('20041201','YYYYMMDD'))
            tablespace prd03,
       partition cat_req_win_2005
            values less than (maxvalue)
            tablespace prd04);
```

In the preceding example, the partitioning method is **range**, the partitioning column is REQ_DATE, and the **values less than** clause specifies the upper bound that corresponds to the dates for each season of the year: March through May (partition CAT_REQ_SPR_2004), June through August (partition CAT_REQ_SUM_2004), September through November (partition CAT_REQ_FAL_2004), and December through February (partition CAT_REQ_WIN_2005). Each partition is stored in its own tablespace—either PRD01, PRD02, PRD03, or PRD04.

You use **maxvalue** to catch *any* date values after 12/1/2004; if you had specified **to_date('20050301','YYYYMMDD')** as the upper bound for the fourth partition, then any attempt to insert rows with date values after 2/28/2005 would fail. On the other hand, *any* rows inserted with dates before 6/1/2004 would end up in partition CAT_REQ_SPR_2004, even rows with a catalog request date of 10/1/1963! This is one case where the front-end application may provide some assistance in data verification, both at the low end and the high end of the date range.

The data dictionary view DBA_TAB_PARTITIONS shows you the partition components of the CAT_REQ table, as you can see in the following query:

```
SQL> select table_owner, table_name,
  2          partition_name, tablespace_name
  3  from dba_tab_partitions
  4  where table_name = 'CAT_REQ';
```

TABLE_OWNER	TABLE_NAME	PARTITION_NAME	TABLESPACE_NAME
OE	CAT_REQ	CAT_REQ_FAL_2004	PRD03
OE	CAT_REQ	CAT_REQ_SPR_2004	PRD01
OE	CAT_REQ	CAT_REQ_SUM_2004	PRD02
OE	CAT_REQ	CAT_REQ_WIN_2005	PRD04

4 rows selected.

Finding out the dates used in the **values less than** clause when the partitioned table was created can be done in the same data dictionary view, as you can see in the following query:

```
SQL> select partition_name, high_value
  2       from dba_tab_partitions
  3  where table_name = 'CAT_REQ';
```

PARTITION_NAME	HIGH_VALUE
CAT_REQ_FAL_2004	TO_DATE(' 2004-12-01 00:00:00', 'SYYYY-MM-DD HH24:MI:SS', 'NLS_CALENDAR=GREGORIAN')
CAT_REQ_SPR_2004	TO_DATE(' 2004-06-01 00:00:00', 'SYYYY-MM-DD HH24:MI:SS', 'NLS_CALENDAR=GREGORIAN')
CAT_REQ_SUM_2004	TO_DATE(' 2004-09-01 00:00:00', 'SYYYY-MM-DD HH24:MI:SS', 'NLS_CALENDAR=GREGORIAN')
CAT_REQ_WIN_2005	MAXVALUE

4 rows selected.

In a similar fashion, you can use the data dictionary view DBA_PART_KEY_COLUMNS to find out the columns used to partition the table, as in the following example:

```
SQL> select owner, name, object_type, column_name,
  2          column_position from DBA_PART_KEY_COLUMNS
  3  where owner = 'OE' and name = 'CAT_REQ';
```

```
OWNER       NAME          OBJECT_TYPE      COLUMN_NAME       COL
---------   -------------   ---------------   ---------------   ---
OE          CAT_REQ       TABLE            CAT_REQ_DT        1

1 row selected.
```

We will show you how to modify the partitions of a partitioned table later in this chapter in the section "Managing Partitions."

Using Hash Partitioning   Hash partitioning is a good option if the distribution of your data does not easily fit into a range partitioning scheme or the number of rows in the table is unknown, but you otherwise want to take advantage of the benefits inherent in partitioned tables. Rows are evenly spread out to two or more partitions based on an internal hashing algorithm using the partition key as input. The more distinct the values are in the partitioning column, the better the distribution of rows across the partitions.

To use hash partitioning, you must specify the following three criteria:

■   Partitioning method (hash)

■   Partitioning column or columns

■   The number of partitions and a list of target tablespaces in which to store the partitions

For this example, you are creating a new customer table whose primary key is generated using a sequence. You want the new rows to be evenly distributed across four partitions; therefore, hash partitioning would be the best choice. Here is the SQL you use to create a hash-partitioned table:

```
create table oe.cust
       (cust_num        number not null primary key,
        ins_dt          date,
        first_nm        varchar2(25),
        last_nm         varchar2(35),
        mi              char(1),
        addr1           varchar2(40),
        addr2           varchar2(40),
        city            varchar2(40),
        state_cd        char(2),
        zip_cd          varchar2(10))
partition by hash (cust_num)
partitions 4
store in (prd01, prd02, prd03, prd04);
```

You do not necessarily have to specify the same number of partitions as tablespaces; if you specify more partitions than tablespaces, the tablespaces are reused for subsequent partitions in a round-robin fashion. If you specify fewer partitions than tablespaces, the extra tablespaces at the end of the tablespace list are ignored.

If you run the same queries that you ran for range partitioning, you may find some unexpected results, as you can see in this query:

```
SQL> select partition_name, tablespace_name, high_value
  2  from dba_tab_partitions
  3  where table_name = 'CUST';

PARTITION_NAME         TABLESPACE_NAME HIGH_VALUE
--------------------   --------------- --------------------
SYS_P1130              PRD01
SYS_P1131              PRD02
SYS_P1132              PRD03
SYS_P1133              PRD04

4 rows selected.
```

Because you are using hash partitioning, the HIGH_VALUE column is NULL.

Using List Partitioning   List partitioning gives you explicit control of how each value in the partitioning column maps to a partition by specifying discrete values from the partitioning column. Range partitioning is usually not suitable for discrete values that do not have a natural and consecutive range of values, such as state codes. Hash partitioning is not suitable for assigning discrete values to a particular partition because, by its nature, a hash partition may map several related discrete values into different partitions.

To use list partitioning, you must specify the following three criteria:

- Partitioning method (list)

- Partitioning column

- Partition names, with each partition associated with a discrete list of literal values that place it in the partition

NOTE
As of Oracle 10g, list partitioning can be used for tables with LOB columns.

In the following example, you will use list partitioning to record sales information for the data warehouse into three partitions based on sales region: the Midwest, the western seaboard, and the rest of the country. Here is the **create table** command:

```
create table oe.sales_by_region_by_day
       (state_cd          char(2),
        sales_dt          date,
        sales_amt         number(16,2))
partition by list (state_cd)
    (partition midwest values ('WI','IL','IA','IN','MN')
         tablespace prd01,
     partition westcoast values ('CA','OR','WA')
         tablespace prd02,
     partition other_states values (default)
         tablespace prd03);
```

Sales information for Wisconsin, Illinois, and the other Midwestern states will be stored in the **midwest** partition; California, Oregon, and Washington state will end up in the **westcoast** partition. Any other value for state code, such as **MI**, will end up in the **other_states** partition in tablespace PRD03.

Using Composite Range-Hash Partitioning   As the name implies, range-hash partitioning uses range partitioning to divide rows first using the range method and then subpartitioning the rows within each range using a hash method. Composite range-hash partitioning is good for historical data with the added benefit of increased manageability and data placement within a larger number of total partitions.

To use composite range-hash partitioning, you must specify the following criteria:

- Primary partitioning method (range)
- Range partitioning column(s)
- Partition names identifying the bounds of the partition
- Subpartitioning method (hash)
- Subpartitioning column(s)
- Number of subpartitions for each partition or subpartition name

In the following example, you will track house and garden tool rentals. Each tool is identified by a unique tool number; at any given time, only about 400 tools are available for rental, although there may be slightly more than 400 on a temporary basis. For each partition, we want to use hash partitioning for each of eight subpartitions, using the tool name in the hashing algorithm. The subpartitions will be spread out over four tablespaces: PRD01, PRD02, PRD03, and PRD04. Here is the **create table** command to create the range-hash partitioned table:

```
create table oe.tool_rentals
    (tool_num       number,
    tool_desc      varchar2(50),
    rental_rate    number(6,2))
partition by range (tool_num)
    subpartition by hash (tool_desc)
    subpartition template (subpartition s1 tablespace prd01,
                           subpartition s2 tablespace prd02,
                           subpartition s3 tablespace prd03,
                           subpartition s4 tablespace prd04,
                           subpartition s5 tablespace prd01,
                           subpartition s6 tablespace prd02,
                           subpartition s7 tablespace prd03,
                           subpartition s8 tablespace prd04)
    (partition tool_rentals_p1 values less than (101),
    partition tool_rentals_p2 values less than (201),
    partition tool_rentals_p3 values less than (301),
    partition tool_rentals_p4 values less than (maxvalue));
```

The range partitions are logical only; there are a total of 32 physical partitions, one for each combination of logical partition and subpartition in the template list. Note the **subpartition template** clause; the template is used for creating the subpartitions in every partition that doesn't have an explicit subpartition specification. It can be a real timesaver and reduce typing errors if the subpartitions are explicitly specified for each partition. Alternatively, you could specify the following clause, if you do not need the subpartitions explicitly named:

```
subpartitions 8 store in (prd01, prd02, prd03, prd04)
```

The physical partition information is available in DBA_TAB_SUBPARTITIONS, as for any partitioned table. Here is a query to find out the partition components of the TOOL_RENTALS table:

```
SQL> select table_name, partition_name, subpartition_name,
  2         tablespace_name
  3  from dba_tab_subpartitions
  4  where table_name = 'TOOL_RENTALS';
```

TABLE_NAME	PARTITION_NAME	SUBPARTITION_NAME	TABLESPACE
TOOL_RENTALS	TOOL_RENTALS_P1	TOOL_RENTALS_P1_S1	PRD01
TOOL_RENTALS	TOOL_RENTALS_P1	TOOL_RENTALS_P1_S2	PRD02
TOOL_RENTALS	TOOL_RENTALS_P1	TOOL_RENTALS_P1_S3	PRD03
TOOL_RENTALS	TOOL_RENTALS_P1	TOOL_RENTALS_P1_S4	PRD04
TOOL_RENTALS	TOOL_RENTALS_P1	TOOL_RENTALS_P1_S5	PRD01
TOOL_RENTALS	TOOL_RENTALS_P1	TOOL_RENTALS_P1_S6	PRD02
TOOL_RENTALS	TOOL_RENTALS_P1	TOOL_RENTALS_P1_S7	PRD03
TOOL_RENTALS	TOOL_RENTALS_P1	TOOL_RENTALS_P1_S8	PRD04
TOOL_RENTALS	TOOL_RENTALS_P2	TOOL_RENTALS_P2_S1	PRD01
TOOL_RENTALS	TOOL_RENTALS_P2	TOOL_RENTALS_P2_S2	PRD02
. . .			
TOOL_RENTALS	TOOL_RENTALS_P4	TOOL_RENTALS_P4_S8	PRD04

```
32 rows selected.
```

At the logical partition level, we still need to query DBA_TAB_PARTITIONS to obtain the range values, as you can see in the following query:

```
SQL> select table_name, partition_name,
  2         subpartition_count, high_value
  3  from dba_tab_partitions
  4  where table_name = 'TOOL_RENTALS';
```

TABLE_NAME	PARTITION_NAME	SUBPARTITION_COUNT	HIGH_VALUE
TOOL_RENTALS	TOOL_RENTALS_P1	8	101
TOOL_RENTALS	TOOL_RENTALS_P2	8	201
TOOL_RENTALS	TOOL_RENTALS_P3	8	301
TOOL_RENTALS	TOOL_RENTALS_P4	8	MAXVALUE

```
4 rows selected.
```

Also note that either the partition name or subpartition name can be specified to perform manual partition pruning, as in these two examples:

```
select * from oe.tool_rentals partition (tool_rentals_p1);
select * from oe.tool_rentals subpartition (tool_rentals_p3_s2);
```

In the first query, a total of eight subpartitions are searched, TOOL_RENTALS_P1_S1 through TOOL_RENTALS_P1_S8; in the second query, only one out of the 32 total subpartitions is searched.

Using Composite Range-List Partitioning   Similar to composite range-hash partitioning, composite range-list partitioning uses range partitioning to divide rows first using the range method and then subpartitioning the rows within each range using the list method. Composite range-list partitioning is good for historical data to place the data in each logical partition, further subdividing each logical partition using a discontinuous or discrete set of values.

NOTE
Range-list partitioning is new in Oracle 10g.

To use composite range-list partitioning, you must specify the following criteria:

- Primary partitioning method (range)

- Range partitioning column(s)

- Partition names identifying the bounds of the partition

- Subpartitioning method (list)

- Subpartitioning column

- Partition names, with each partition associated with a discrete list of literal values that place it in the partition

In the following example, we will expand on the previous "Sales by Region" list partitioning example and make the partitioned table more scalable by using the sales date for range partitioning, and we will use the state code for subpartitioning. Here is the **create table** command to accomplish this:

```
create table sales_by_region_by_quarter
    (state_cd          char(2),
     sales_dt          date,
     sales_amt         number(16,2))
partition by range (sales_dt)
    subpartition by list (state_cd)
        (partition q1_2004 values less than (to_date('20040401','YYYYMMDD'))
            (subpartition q1_2004_midwest values ('WI','IL','IA','IN','MN')
                tablespace prd01,
             subpartition q1_2004_westcoast values ('CA','OR','WA')
                tablespace prd02,
```

```
            subpartition q1_2004_other_states values (default)
                tablespace prd03
        ),
    partition q2_2004 values less than (to_date('20040701','YYYYMMDD'))
        (subpartition q2_2004_midwest values ('WI','IL','IA','IN','MN')
                tablespace prd01,
        subpartition q2_2004_westcoast values ('CA','OR','WA')
                tablespace prd02,
        subpartition q2_2004_other_states values (default)
                tablespace prd03
        ),
    partition q3_2004 values less than (to_date('20041001','YYYYMMDD'))
        (subpartition q3_2004_midwest values ('WI','IL','IA','IN','MN')
                tablespace prd01,
        subpartition q3_2004_westcoast values ('CA','OR','WA')
                tablespace prd02,
        subpartition q3_2004_other_states values (default)
                tablespace prd03
        ),
    partition q4_2004 values less than (maxvalue)
        (subpartition q4_2004_midwest values ('WI','IL','IA','IN','MN')
                tablespace prd01,
        subpartition q4_2004_westcoast values ('CA','OR','WA')
                tablespace prd02,
        subpartition q4_2004_other_states values (default)
                tablespace prd03
        )
    );
```

Each row stored in the table SALES_BY_REGION_BY_QUARTER is placed into one of 12 subpartitions, depending first on the sales date, which narrows the subpartition choice to three subpartitions. The value of the state code then determines which of the three subpartitions will be used to store the row. If a sales date falls beyond the end of 2004, it will still be placed in one of the subpartitions of Q4_2004 until you create a new partition and subpartitions for Q1_2005. Reorganizing partitioned tables is covered later in this chapter.

Compressed Partitioned Tables   Partitioned tables can be compressed just as nonpartitioned tables can; in addition, the partitions of a partitioned table can be selectively compressed. For example, you may only want to compress the older, less often accessed partitions of a partitioned table and leave the most recent partition uncompressed to minimize the CPU overhead for retrieval of recent data. In this example, you will create a new version of the CAT_REQ table you created earlier in this chapter, compressing the first two partitions only. Here is the SQL command:

```
create table cat_req_2
    (cat_req_num        number not null,
    cat_req_dt          date not null,
    cat_cd              number not null,
    cust_num            number null,
    req_nm              varchar2(50),
```

```
    req_addr1         varchar2(75),
    req_addr2         varchar2(75),
    req_addr3         varchar2(75))
partition by range (cat_req_dt)
    (partition cat_req_spr_2004
        values less than (to_date('20040601','YYYYMMDD'))
        tablespace prd01 compress,
    partition cat_req_sum_2004
        values less than (to_date('20040901','YYYYMMDD'))
        tablespace prd02 compress,
    partition cat_req_fal_2004
        values less than (to_date('20041201','YYYYMMDD'))
        tablespace prd03 nocompress,
    partition cat_req_win_2005
        values less than (maxvalue)
        tablespace prd04 nocompress);
```

You do not have to specify **nocompress** because it is the default. To find out which partitions are compressed, you can use the column COMPRESSION in the data dictionary table DBA_TAB_PARTITIONS, as you can see in the following example:

```
SQL> select table_name, partition_name, compression
  2      from dba_tab_partitions
  3    where table_name = 'CAT_REQ_2';

TABLE_NAME          PARTITION_NAME          COMPRESS
----------------    --------------------    --------
CAT_REQ_2           CAT_REQ_FAL_2004        DISABLED
CAT_REQ_2           CAT_REQ_SPR_2004        ENABLED
CAT_REQ_2           CAT_REQ_SUM_2004        ENABLED
CAT_REQ_2           CAT_REQ_WIN_2005        DISABLED

4 rows selected.
```

Indexing Partitions

Local indexes on partitions reflect the structure of the underlying table and in general are easier to maintain than nonpartitioned or global partitioned indexes. Local indexes are *equipartitioned* with the underlying partitioned table; in other words, it is partitioned on the same columns as the underlying table and therefore has the same number of partitions and the same partition bounds as the underlying table.

Global partitioned indexes are created irrespective of the partitioning scheme of the underlying table and can be partitioned using range partitioning or hash partitioning. In this section, first we'll show you how to create a local partitioned index; next, we'll show you how to create both range-partitioned and hash-partitioned global indexes. In addition, we'll show you how to save space in a partitioned index by using key compression.

Creating Local Partition Indexes   A local partitioned index is very easy to set up and maintain because the partitioning scheme is identical to the partitioning scheme of the base table. In other words, the number of partitions in the index is the same as the number of partitions and subpartitions in the table; in addition, for a row in a given partition or subpartition, the index entry is always stored in the corresponding index's partition or subpartition.

Figure 17-1 shows the relationship between a partitioned local index and a partitioned table. The number of partitions in the table is exactly the same as the number of partitions in the index.

In the following example, you will create a local index on the CUST table you created earlier in the chapter. Here is the SQL statement that retrieves the table partitions for the CUST table:

```
SQL> select partition_name, tablespace_name, high_value
  2  from dba_tab_partitions
  3  where table_name = 'CUST';

PARTITION_NAME          TABLESPACE_NAME HIGH_VALUE
--------------------    --------------- --------------------
SYS_P1130               PRD01
SYS_P1131               PRD02
SYS_P1132               PRD03
SYS_P1133               PRD04

4 rows selected.
```

The command for creating the local index on this table is very straightforward, as you can see in this example:

```
SQL> create index oe.cust_ins_dt_ix on oe.cust (ins_dt)
  2          local store in (idx_1, idx_2, idx_3, idx_4);
Index created.
```

The index partitions are stored in four tablespaces—IDX_1 through IDX_4—to further improve the performance of the table, because each index partition is stored in a tablespace separate from

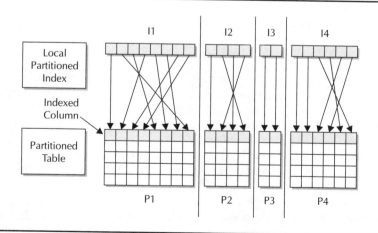

FIGURE 17-1.   *Local partitioned index on a partitioned table*

any of the table partitions. You can find out about the partitions for this index by querying DBA_
IND_PARTITIONS, as follows:

```
SQL> select partition_name, tablespace_name from dba_ind_partitions
  2         where index_name = 'CUST_INS_DT_IX';

PARTITION_NAME          TABLESPACE_NAME
--------------------    ---------------
SYS_P1130               IDX_1
SYS_P1131               IDX_2
SYS_P1132               IDX_3
SYS_P1133               IDX_4

4 rows selected.
```

Notice that the index partitions are automatically named the same as their corresponding table
partitions. One of the benefits of local indexes is that when you create a new table partition, the
corresponding index partition is built automatically; similarly, dropping a table partition automatically
drops the index partition without invalidating any other index partitions, as would be the case for
a global index.

Creating Range-Partitioned Global Indexes   Creating a range-partitioned global index involves
rules similar to those you use when creating range-partitioned tables. In a previous example, you
created a range-partitioned table called CAT_REQ that contained four partitions based on the
CAT_REQ_DT column. In this example, you will create a partitioned global index that will only
contain two partitions (in other words, *not* partitioned the same way as the corresponding table):

```
create index cat_req_dt_ix on oe.cat_req(cat_req_dt)
    global partition by range(cat_req_dt)
    (partition spr_sum_2004
      values less than (to_date('20040901','YYYYMMDD'))
          tablespace idx_4,
     partition fal_win_2004
      values less than (maxvalue)
          tablespace idx_8);
```

Note that you specify two tablespaces to store the partitions for the index that are different from
the tablespaces used to store the table partitions. If any DDL activity occurs on the underlying table,
global indexes are marked as UNUSABLE and need to be rebuilt. In the section "Managing Partitions"
later in this chapter, we will review the **update index** clause when you are performing partition
maintenance operations on partitioned indexes.

Figure 17-2 shows the relationship between a partitioned global index and a partitioned table.
The number of partitions in the table may or may not be the same as the number of partitions in the
index.

Creating Hash-Partitioned Global Indexes   As with range-partitioned global indexes, hash-
partitioned global index **create** statements share a syntax with hash-partitioned table **create**
statements. Hash-partitioned global indexes can improve performance in situations where a

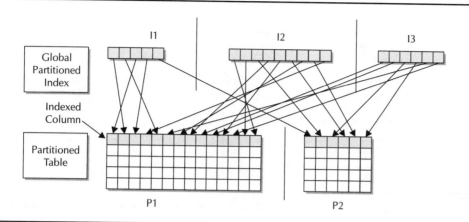

FIGURE 17-2. *Global partitioned index on a partitioned table*

small number of a nonpartitioned index's leaf blocks are experiencing high contention in an OLTP environment. Queries that use either an equality or IN operator in the WHERE clause can benefit significantly from a hash-partitioned global index.

NOTE
Hash-partitioned global indexes are new in Oracle 10g.

Building on our example using hash-partitioning for the table CUST, you can create a hash-partitioned global index on the ZIP_CD column:

```
create index oe.cust_zip_cd_ix on oe.cust(zip_cd)
  global partition by hash(zip_cd)
   (partition z1      tablespace idx_1,
    partition z2      tablespace idx_2,
    partition z3      tablespace idx_3,
    partition z4      tablespace idx_4,
    partition z5      tablespace idx_5,
    partition z6      tablespace idx_6,
    partition z7      tablespace idx_7,
    partition z8      tablespace idx_8);
```

Note that the table CUST is partitioned using the CUST_NUM column, and it places its four partitions in PRD01 through PRD04; this index partition uses the ZIP_CD column for the hashing function and stores its eight partitions in IDX_1 through IDX_8.

Creating Nonpartitioned Global Indexes   Creating a nonpartitioned global index is the same as creating a regular index on a nonpartitioned table; the syntax is identical. Figure 17-3 shows the relationship between a nonpartitioned global index and a partitioned table.

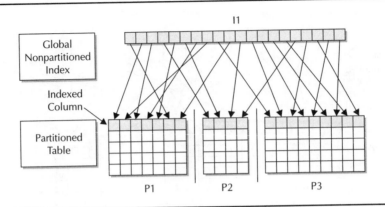

FIGURE 17-3. *Global nonpartitioned index on a partitioned table*

Using Key Compression on Partitioned Indexes   If your index is nonunique and has a large number of repeating values for the index key or keys, you can use key compression on the index just as you can with a traditional nonpartitioned index. When only the first instance of the index key is stored, both disk space and I/O is reduced. In the following example, you can see how easy it is to create a compressed partitioned index:

```
create index oe.cust_ins_dt_ix on oe.cust (ins_dt)
    compress local
    store in (idx_1, idx_2, idx_3, idx_4);
```

You can specify that a more active index partition not be compressed by using NOCOMPRESS, which may save a noticeable amount of CPU for recent index entries that are more frequently accessed than the others in the index.

Partitioned Index Organized Tables

Index organized tables (IOTs) can be partitioned using either the range, list, or hash partitioning method; creating partitioned index organized tables is syntactically similar to creating partitioned heap organized tables. In this section, we'll cover some of the notable differences in how partitioned IOTs are created and used.

For a partitioned IOT, the **organization index**, **including**, and **overflow** clauses are used as they are for standard IOTs. In the **partition** clause, you can specify the **overflow** clause as well as any other attributes of the overflow segment specific to a partition.

As of Oracle 10g, there is no longer the restriction that the set of partitioning columns must be a subset of the IOT's primary key columns; in addition, LIST partitioning is supported in addition to range and hash partitioning. In previous releases of Oracle, LOB columns were supported only in range-partitioned IOTs; as of Oracle 10g, they are supported in hash and list partitioning methods as well.

Managing Partitions

Fourteen maintenance operations can be performed on a partitioned table, including splitting a partition, merging partitions, and adding a new partition. These operations may or may not be available depending on the partitioning scheme used (range, hash, list, composite range/hash, or composite range/list). For composite partitions, these operations sometimes apply to both the partition and the subpartition, and sometimes to the subpartition only.

For partitioned indexes, there are seven different types of maintenance operations that vary depending on both the partitioning method (range, hash, list, or composite) as well as whether the index is a global or a local index. In addition, each type of partitioned index may support automatic updates when the partitioning scheme is changed, thus reducing the occurrences of unusable indexes.

In the next couple sections, we'll present a convenient chart for both partitioned tables and partitioned indexes that shows you what kinds of operations are allowed on which partition types. For some of the more common maintenance operations, we'll give you some examples of how they are used, extending some of the examples we have presented earlier in this chapter.

Maintaining Table Partitions   To maintain one or more table partitions or subpartitions, you use the **alter table** command just as you would on a nonpartitioned table. In Table 17-5 are the

Partition Operation	Range	Hash	List	Composite Range/ Hash	Composite Range/ List	Supports UPDATE INDEXES
Add a partition	ADD PARTITION	ADD PARTITION	ADD PARTITION	ADD PARTITION or MODIFY PARTITION <partition> ADD SUBPARTITION	ADD PARTITION or MODIFY PARTITION <partition> ADD SUBPARTITION	Yes
Coalesce a partition	N/A	COALESCE PARTITION	N/A	MODIFY PARTITION <partition> COALESCE SUBPARTITION	N/A	Yes
Drop a partition	DROP PARTITION	N/A	DROP PARTITION	DROP PARTITION	DROP [SUB]PARTITION	Yes
Exchange a partition	EXCHANGE PARTITION	EXCHANGE PARTITION	EXCHANGE PARTITION	EXCHANGE [SUB]PARTITION	EXCHANGE [SUB]PARTITION	Yes
Merge partitions	MERGE PARTITIONS	N/A	MERGE PARTITIONS	MERGE PARTITIONS	MERGE [SUB]PARTITIONS	Yes
Modify default attributes	MODIFY DEFAULT ATTRIBUTES	MODIFY DEFAULT ATTRIBUTES	MODIFY DEFAULT ATTRIBUTES	MODIFY DEFAULT ATTRIBUTES [FOR PARTITION]	MODIFY DEFAULT ATTRIBUTES [FOR PARTITION]	No
Modify real attributes	MODIFY PARTITION	MODIFY PARTITION	MODIFY PARTITION	MODIFY [SUB]PARTITION	MODIFY [SUB]PARTITION	No

TABLE 17-5.   *Maintenance Operations for Partitioned Tables*

Partition Operation	Range	Hash	List	Composite Range/ Hash	Composite Range/ List	Supports UPDATE INDEXES
Add values	N/A	N/A	MODIFY PARTITION ... ADD VALUES	N/A	MODIFY SUBPARTITION ... ADD VALUES	No
Drop values	N/A	N/A	MODIFY PARTITION ... DROP VALUES	N/A	MODIFY SUBPARTITION ... DROP VALUES	No
Modify a subpartition template	N/A	N/A	N/A	SET SUBPARTITION TEMPLATE	SET SUBPARTITION TEMPLATE	No
Move a partition	MOVE PARTITION	MOVE PARTITION	MOVE PARTITION	MOVE SUBPARTITION	MOVE SUBPARTITION	Yes
Rename a partition	RENAME PARTITION	RENAME PARTITION	RENAME PARTITION	RENAME [SUB]PARTITION	RENAME [SUB]PARTITION	No
Split a partition	SPLIT PARTITION	N/A	SPLIT PARTITION	SPLIT PARTITION	SPLIT [SUB]PARTITION	Yes
Truncate a partition	TRUNCATE PARTITION	TRUNCATE PARTITION	TRUNCATE PARTITION	TRUNCATE [SUB]PARTITION	TRUNCATE [SUB]PARTITION	Yes

TABLE 17-5. *Maintenance Operations for Partitioned Tables* (continued)

types of partitioned table operations and the keywords you would use to perform them for the five different types of partitioned tables (range, hash, list, composite range/hash, and composite range/list). The format of the **alter table** command is

```
alter table <tablename> <partition_operation> <partition_operation_options>;
```

Not all maintenance operations are available for every partition type, either because the operation would not make sense for the partition type or because Oracle does not yet support it yet!

In many cases, partitioned table maintenance operations invalidate the underlying index; while you can always rebuild the index manually, you can specify **update indexes** in the table partition maintenance command. Although the table maintenance operation will take longer, the most significant benefit of using **update indexes** is to keep the index available during the partition maintenance operation. The last column of Table 17-5 indicates whether the operation supports **update indexes**.

Splitting, Adding, and Dropping Partitions   In many environments, a "rolling window" partitioned table will contain the latest four quarters' worth of rows. When the new quarter starts, a new partition is created, and the oldest partition is archived and dropped. In the following example, you will split the last partition of the CAT_REQ table you created earlier in this chapter at a specific date and maintain the new partition with **maxvalue**, back up the oldest partition, and then drop the oldest partition. Here are the commands you can use:

```
SQL> alter table oe.cat_req split partition
  2      cat_req_win_2005 at (to_date('20050101','YYYYMMDD')) into
  3      (partition cat_req_win_2005 tablespace prd04,
  4       partition cat_req_spr_2005 tablespace prd01);
Table altered.

SQL> create table oe.arch_cat_req_spr_2004 as
  2      select * from oe.cat_req partition(cat_req_spr_2004);
Table created.

SQL> alter table oe.cat_req
  2      drop partition cat_req_spr_2004;
Table altered.
```

The data dictionary view DBA_TAB_PARTITIONS reflects the new partitioning scheme, as you can see in this example:

```
SQL> select partition_name, high_value
  2        from dba_tab_partitions
  3   where table_name = 'CAT_REQ';

PARTITION_NAME            HIGH_VALUE
------------------        -----------------------------------------
CAT_REQ_FAL_2004          TO_DATE(' 2004-12-01 00:00:00', 'SYYYY-M
                          M-DD HH24:MI:SS', 'NLS_CALENDAR=GREGORIA
                          N')

CAT_REQ_SUM_2004          TO_DATE(' 2004-09-01 00:00:00', 'SYYYY-M
                          M-DD HH24:MI:SS', 'NLS_CALENDAR=GREGORIA
                          N')

CAT_REQ_WIN_2005          TO_DATE(' 2005-01-01 00:00:00', 'SYYYY-M
                          M-DD HH24:MI:SS', 'NLS_CALENDAR=GREGORIA
                          N')

CAT_REQ_SPR_2005          MAXVALUE

4 rows selected.
```

Note that if you had dropped any partition other than the oldest partition, the next highest partition "takes up the slack" and contains any new rows that would have resided in the dropped partition; regardless of what partition is dropped, the rows in the partition are no longer in the partitioned table. To preserve the rows, you would use **merge partition** instead of **drop partition**.

Coalescing a Table Partition   You can coalesce a partition in a hash-partitioned table to redistribute the contents of the partition to the remaining partitions and reduce the number of partitions by one. For the new CUST table you created earlier in this chapter, you can do this in one easy step:

```
SQL> alter table oe.cust coalesce partition;
Table altered.
```

The number of partitions in CUST is now three instead of four:

```
SQL> select partition_name, tablespace_name
  2      from dba_tab_partitions
  3  where table_name = 'CUST';

PARTITION_NAME          TABLESPACE
--------------------    ----------
SYS_P1130               PRD01
SYS_P1131               PRD02
SYS_P1132               PRD03

3 rows selected.
```

Merging Two Table Partitions   You may find out through various Oracle advisors that one partition of a partitioned table is infrequently used or not used at all; in this situation, you may want to combine two partitions into a single partition to reduce your maintenance effort. In this example, you will combine the partitions MIDWEST and WESTCOAST in the partitioned table SALES_BY_REGION_BY_DAY into a single partition, MIDWESTCOAST:

```
SQL> alter table oe.sales_by_region_by_day
  2      merge partitions midwest, westcoast
  3      into partition midwestcoast tablespace prd04;
Table altered.
```

Looking at the data dictionary view DBA_TAB_PARTITIONS, you can see that the table now only has two partitions:

```
SQL> select table_name, partition_name, tablespace_name, high_value
  2      from dba_tab_partitions
  3  where table_owner = 'OE' and
  4          table_name = 'SALES_BY_REGION_BY_DAY';
```

TABLE_NAME	PARTITION_NAME	TABLESPACE	HIGH_VALUE
SALES_BY_REGION_BY_DAY	MIDWESTCOAST	PRD04	'WI', 'IL', 'IA', 'IN', 'MN', 'CA', 'OR', 'WA'
SALES_BY_REGION_BY_DAY	OTHER_STATES	PRD03	default

```
2 rows selected.
```

Maintaining Index Partitions   To maintain one or more index partitions or subpartitions, you use the **alter index** command just as you would on a nonpartitioned index. Table 17-6 lists the types of partitioned index operations and the keywords you would use to perform them for the different types of partitioned indexes (range, hash, list, and composite). The format of the **alter index** command is

```
alter index <indexname> <partition_operation> <partition_operation_options>;
```

As with table partition maintenance commands, not all operations are available for every index partition type. You should note that many of the index partition maintenance options do not apply to local index partitions. By its nature, a local index partition matches the partitioning scheme of the table and will change when you modify the table's partitioning scheme.

Partition Operation	Index Type	Range	Hash/List	Composite
Add a partition	Global	N/A	ADD PARTITION (hash)	N/A
	Local	N/A	N/A	N/A
Drop a partition	Global	DROP PARTITION	N/A	N/A
	Local	N/A	N/A	N/A
Modify default attributes	Global	MODIFY DEFAULT ATTRIBUTES	N/A	N/A
	Local	MODIFY DEFAULT ATTRIBUTES	MODIFY DEFAULT ATTRIBUTES	MODIFY DEFAULT ATTRIBUTES [FOR PARTITION]
Modify real attributes	Global	MODIFY PARTITION	N/A	N/A
	Local	MODIFY PARTITION	MODIFY PARTITION	MODIFY [SUB]PARTITION
Rebuild a partition	Global	REBUILD PARTITION	N/A	N/A
	Local	REBUILD PARTITION	REBUILD PARTITION	REBUILD SUBPARTITION
Rename a partition	Global	RENAME PARTITION	N/A	N/A
	Local	RENAME PARTITION	RENAME PARTITION	RENAME [SUB]PARTITION
Split a partition	Global	SPLIT PARTITION	N/A	N/A
	Local	N/A	N/A	N/A

TABLE 17-6.   *Maintenance Operations for Partitioned Indexes*

Splitting a Global Index Partition   Splitting a global index partition is much like splitting a table's partition. One particular global index partition may be a hotspot due to the index entries being stored in that particular partition; as with a table partition, you can split the index partition into two or more partitions. In the following example, you'll split one of the partitions of the global index OE.CAT_REQ_DT_IX into two partitions:

```
SQL> alter index oe.cat_req_dt_ix split partition
  2        fal_win_2004 at (to_date('20041201','YYYYMMDD')) into
  3          (partition fal_2004 tablespace idx_7,
  4            partition win_2005 tablespace idx_8);
Index altered.
```

The index entries for the FAL_WIN_2004 partition will now reside in two new partitions, FAL_2004 and WIN_2005.

Renaming a Local Index Partition   Most characteristics of a local index are updated automatically when the corresponding table partition is modified. However, a few operations still may need to be performed on a local index partition, such as rebuilding the partition or renaming a partition that was originally named with a default system-assigned name. In this example, you will rename the local index partitions in the index OE.CUST_INS_DT_IX using more meaningful names:

```
SQL> alter index oe.cust_ins_dt_ix
  2        rename partition sys_P1130 to cust_ins_dt_ix_P1;
Index altered.

SQL> alter index oe.cust_ins_dt_ix
  2        rename partition sys_P1131 to cust_ins_dt_ix_P2;
Index altered.

SQL> alter index oe.cust_ins_dt_ix
  2        rename partition sys_P1132 to cust_ins_dt_ix_P3;
Index altered.
```

Managing Partitions with EM Database Control
Creating and managing table and index partitions using EM Database Control saves you time and also the potential for errors. In the web pages displayed in the following figures, we'll show you the

steps required to create a partitioned table to support a new order-entry and quotation system. In Figure 17-4, on the Create Table page, you specify the table name, the schema where the table will reside, and the tablespace. You also specify the column names and their attributes.

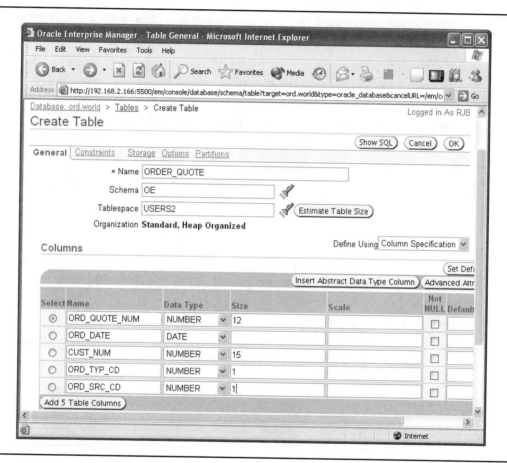

FIGURE 17-4. *EM Database Control Create Table page*

So far, we're only creating a standard heap-based table with no partitioning. However, when you click the Partitions tab, you can specify the partitioning method as shown in Figure 17-5.

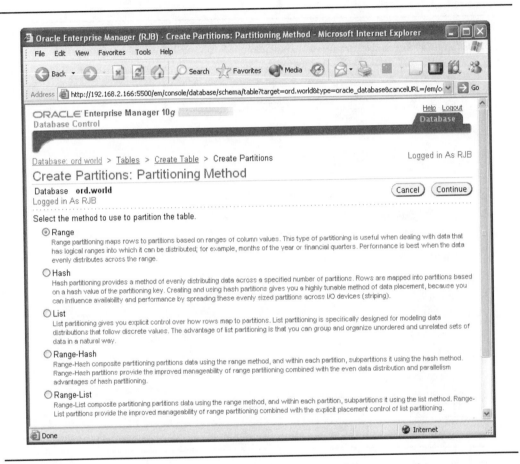

FIGURE 17-5. *EM Database Control Partitioning Method page*

For the ORDER_QUOTE table, you will choose range partitioning because you will use the ORD_DATE column to put each row into a specific partition. In Figure 17-6, on the Create Range

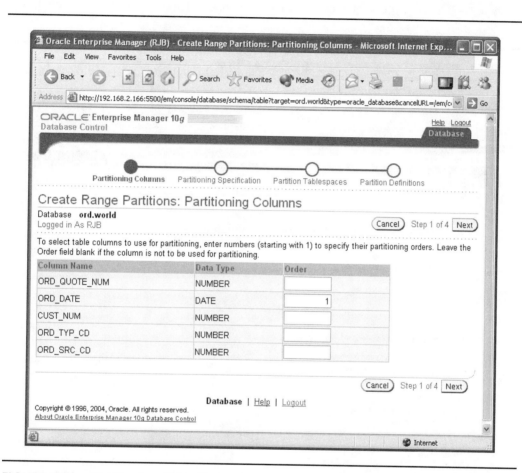

FIGURE 17-6. *EM Database Control Partitioning Columns page*

Partitions: Partitioning Columns page, you specify which columns to use for partitioning using the range method. In this case, you're only using one column, ORD_DATE.

After clicking the Next button, you proceed to the Partitioning Specification page, as presented in Figure 17-7. Initially, you want to create 12 partitions, one partition for each month of 2004. As

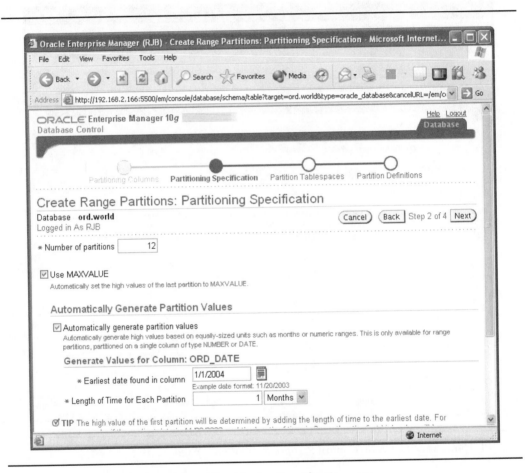

FIGURE 17-7. *EM Database Control Partitioning Specification page*

a result, you specify 12 for the number of partitions, 1/1/2004 as the starting date, and one month for each partition.

In Figure 17-8, you specify the tablespaces used to hold the partitions. In this case, you accept the default: the tablespace originally specified for the table before partitioning was specified. Another option on this page is to spread out the partitions among several tablespaces.

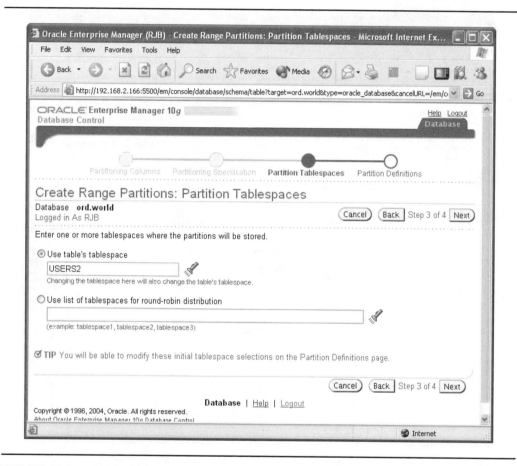

FIGURE 17-8. *EM Database Control Partition Tablespaces page*

After clicking the Next button, you see the Partition Definitions page in Figure 17-9, where the partition names, high values for each range, and tablespace are presented. Any changes to partition names or locations can be made on this page—for example, changing the name of each partition to include the high value for the partition key.

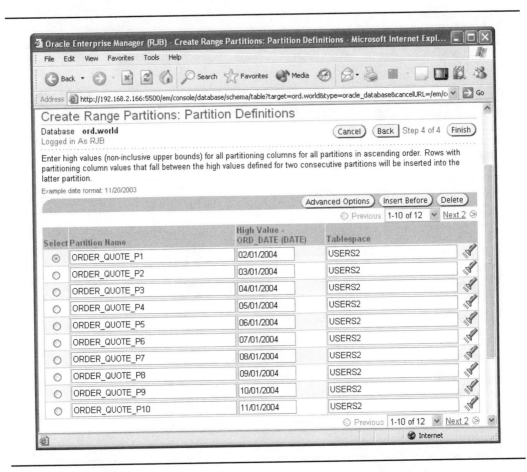

FIGURE 17-9.   *EM Database Control Partition Definitions page*

Clicking the Finish button brings you back to the Create Table page, as you can see in Figure 17-10. You have one more opportunity to change the characteristics of the partitioned table.

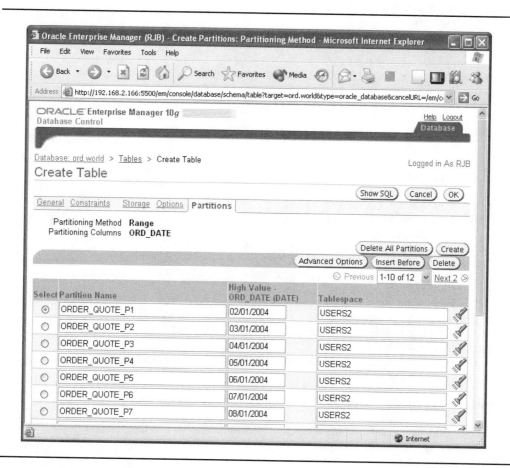

FIGURE 17-10. *EM Database Control Create Table summary*

This page also has a Show SQL button so you can see the SQL command that will be run to create the partitioned table. Here is the SQL command:

```
CREATE TABLE "OE"."ORDER_QUOTE"
        ("ORD_QUOTE_NUM" NUMBER(12),
         "ORD_DATE" DATE,
         "CUST_NUM" NUMBER(15),
         "ORD_TYP_CD" NUMBER(1),
         "ORD_SRC_CD" NUMBER(1))
TABLESPACE "USERS2" PARTITION BY RANGE ("ORD_DATE")
   (PARTITION "ORDER_QUOTE_P1"
       VALUES LESS THAN (TO_DATE('2/1/2004','MM/DD/YYYY')),
     PARTITION "ORDER_QUOTE_P2"
       VALUES LESS THAN (TO_DATE('3/1/2004','MM/DD/YYYY')),
     PARTITION "ORDER_QUOTE_P3"
       VALUES LESS THAN (TO_DATE('4/1/2004','MM/DD/YYYY')),
     PARTITION "ORDER_QUOTE_P4"
       VALUES LESS THAN (TO_DATE('5/1/2004','MM/DD/YYYY')),
     PARTITION "ORDER_QUOTE_P5"
       VALUES LESS THAN (TO_DATE('6/1/2004','MM/DD/YYYY')),
     PARTITION "ORDER_QUOTE_P6"
       VALUES LESS THAN (TO_DATE('7/1/2004','MM/DD/YYYY')),
     PARTITION "ORDER_QUOTE_P7"
       VALUES LESS THAN (TO_DATE('8/1/2004','MM/DD/YYYY')),
     PARTITION "ORDER_QUOTE_P8"
       VALUES LESS THAN (TO_DATE('9/1/2004','MM/DD/YYYY')),
     PARTITION "ORDER_QUOTE_P9"
       VALUES LESS THAN (TO_DATE('10/1/2004','MM/DD/YYYY')),
     PARTITION "ORDER_QUOTE_P10"
       VALUES LESS THAN (TO_DATE('11/1/2004','MM/DD/YYYY')),
     PARTITION "ORDER_QUOTE_P11"
       VALUES LESS THAN (TO_DATE('12/1/2004','MM/DD/YYYY')),
     PARTITION "ORDER_QUOTE_P12" VALUES LESS THAN (MAXVALUE));
```

Clicking the Create button runs the SQL command and confirms that the partitioned table has been created, as you can see in Figure 17-11.

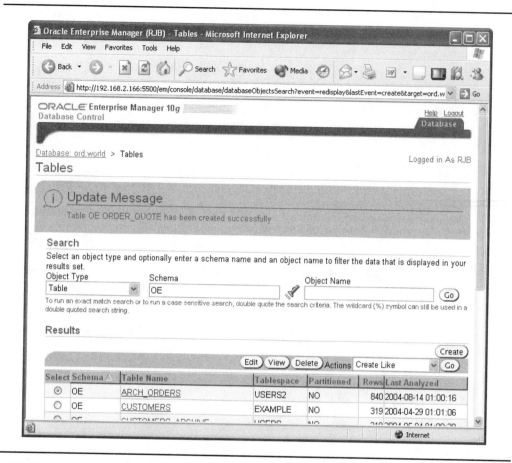

FIGURE 17-11. *EM Database Control create partition confirmation*

Editing the characteristics of a partitioned table is just as easy as creating the partitioned table in the first place. As shown in Figure 17-12, on the Edit Table: OE.ORDER_QUOTE page you select the Partitions tab and select the partition ORDER_QUOTE_P4 to change its characteristics.

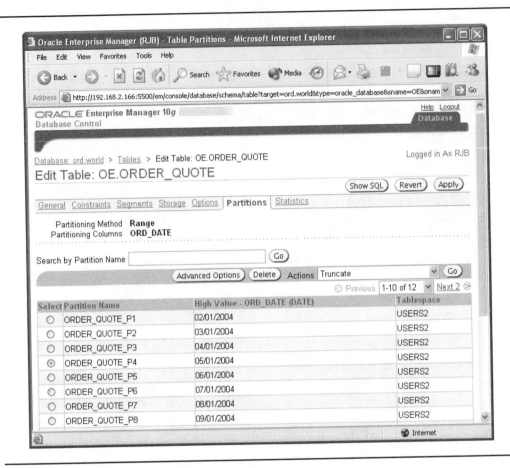

FIGURE 17-12. *EM Database Control Edit Table: OE.ORDER_QUOTE page*

When you select a partition (in this case, ORDER_QUOTE_P4) and click Advanced Options, you have the ability to change the partition's characteristics as you would for a nonpartitioned heap-based table. In Figure 17-13, you change the compression option for this partition only; when

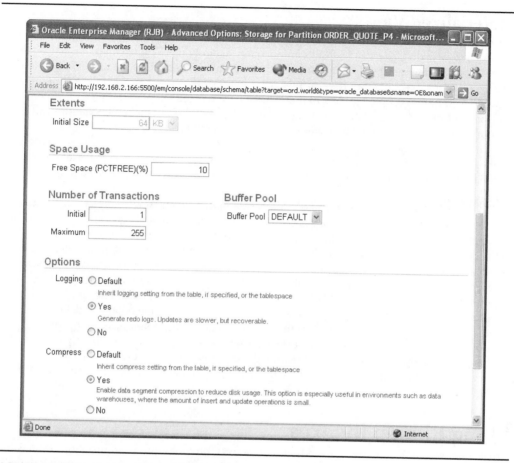

FIGURE 17-13.   *EM Database Control partition storage advanced options*

rows are inserted during a direct path insert, the rows in this segment are compressed to save space with only a slight increase in overhead to uncompress the rows when they are retrieved.

Materialized Views

Another type of table, called a *materialized view,* shares the characteristics of a table and a view. It is like a view in that it derives its results from a query against one or more tables; it is like a table in that it persists the result set of a view in a segment. Materialized views are useful in both OLTP and DSS systems. Frequent user queries against operational data may be able to use materialized views instead of the repeated joining of many highly normalized tables, and in a data warehouse environment the historical data can be aggregated ahead of time to make DSS queries run in a fraction of the time it would take to aggregate the data "on the fly."

The data in a materialized view can be refreshed on demand or incrementally, depending on the business need. Depending on the complexity of the view's underlying SQL statement, the materialized view can be quickly brought up to date with incremental changes via a *materialized view log.*

To create a materialized view, you use the **create materialized view** command; the syntax for this command is similar to creating a standard view. Because a materialized view stores the result of a query, you can also specify storage parameters for the view as if you were creating a table. In the **create materialized view** command, you also specify how the view will be refreshed. The materialized view can be refreshed either on demand or whenever one of the base tables changes. Also, you can force a materialized view to use materialized view logs for an incremental update, or you can force a complete rebuild of the materialized view when a refresh occurs.

Materialized views can automatically be used by the optimizer if the optimizer determines that a particular materialized view already has the results of a query that a user has submitted; the user does not even have to know that their query is using the materialized view directly instead of the base tables. However, to use query rewrite, the user must have the QUERY REWRITE system privilege and you have to set the value of the initialization parameter QUERY_REWRITE_ENABLED to TRUE.

Using Bitmap Indexes

An alternative to B*Tree indexes, called *bitmap indexes,* provides query optimization benefits in environments that frequently perform joins on columns with low cardinality. In this section, we'll review the basics of bitmap indexes, create a bitmap index, and show how bitmap indexes can be created ahead of time against columns in two or more tables.

Understanding Bitmap Indexes

A bitmap index is extremely useful in a VLDB environment when the column being indexed has a very low number of possible values, such as gender, where the possible values are usually 'M' and 'F'. A *bitmap index* uses a string of binary ones and zeros to represent the existence or nonexistence of a particular column value. Using bitmap indexes makes multiple AND and OR operations against several table columns very efficient in a query. Bitmap indexes are common in data warehouse and other VLDB environments where many low-cardinality columns exist, DML commands are done in bulk, and the query conditions frequently use columns with bitmap indexes.

The space requirements for a bitmap index are low as long as the cardinality is low; for example, a bitmap index on the GENDER column of the EMPLOYEES table would contain two bitmaps with a length equal to the number of rows in the table. If the EMPLOYEES table had 15 rows, the bitmaps for the GENDER column might look like the following:

```
GENDER_BM_IX:
    F: 1 1 0 1 1 1 0 0 0 1 0 1 1 1 0
    M: 0 0 1 0 0 0 1 1 1 0 1 0 0 0 1
```

As you can see, the size of the bitmap index is directly proportional to the cardinality of the column being indexed. A bitmap index on the LAST_NAME column of the employee table would be significantly larger, and many of the benefits of a bitmap index in this case might be outweighed by the space consumed by the index! Although there are exceptions to every rule, the cardinality can be up to ten percent of the rows and bitmap indexes will still perform well; in other words, a table with 1,000 rows and 100 distinct values in a particular column will still most likely benefit from a bitmap index.

NOTE
The Oracle optimizer dynamically converts bitmap index entries to ROWIDs during query processing. This allows the optimizer to use bitmap indexes with B*Tree indexes on columns that have many distinct values.

Previous to Oracle 10g, the performance of a bitmap would often deteriorate over time with frequent DML activity against the table containing the bitmap index. To take advantage of the improvements to the internal structure of bitmap indexes, you must set the COMPATIBLE initialization parameter to 10.0.0.0 or greater. Bitmap indexes that performed poorly before the COMPATIBLE parameter was adjusted should be rebuilt; bitmap indexes that performed adequately before the COMPATIBLE parameter was changed will perform better after the change. Any new bitmap indexes created after the COMPATIBLE parameter is adjusted will take advantage of all improvements.

Using Bitmap Indexes

Bitmap indexes are easy to create; the syntax is identical to that for creating any other index, with the addition of the BITMAP keyword. In the following example, you will add a GENDER column to the EMPLOYEES table and then create a bitmap index on it:

```
SQL> alter table hr.employees
  2      add (gender    char(1));
Table altered.

SQL> create bitmap index
  2      hr.gender_bm_ix on hr.employees(gender);
Index created.
```

Using Bitmap Join Indexes

As of Oracle9i, you can create an enhanced type of bitmap index called a *bitmap join index*. A bitmap join index is a bitmap index representing the join between two or more tables. For each value of a column in the first table of the join, the bitmap join index stores the ROWIDs of the corresponding rows in the other tables with the same value as the column in the first table. Bitmap join indexes are an alternative to materialized views that contain a join condition; the storage required for storing the related ROWIDs can be significantly lower than storing the result of the view itself.

In this example, you find out that the HR department is frequently joining the EMPLOYEES and DEPARTMENTS table on the DEPARTMENT_ID column. As an alternative to creating a materialized view, you decide to create a bitmap join index. Here is the SQL command to create the bitmap join index:

```
SQL> create bitmap index
  2         hr.emp_dept_bj_ix on hr.employees(hr.departments.department_id)
  3  from hr.employees, hr.departments
  4  where hr.employees.department_id = hr.departments.department_id;
Index created.
```

There are a few restrictions on bitmap join indexes:

- Only one of the tables in the bitmap join index can be updated concurrently by different transactions when the bitmap join index is being used.

- No table can appear more than once in the join.

- Bitmap join indexes cannot be created on an IOT or a temporary table.

- A bitmap join index cannot be created with the UNIQUE attribute.

- The join column(s) used for the index must be the primary key or have a unique constraint in the table being joined to the table with the bitmap index.

Oracle Data Pump

Oracle Data Pump, new to Oracle 10*g*, provides similar functionality to the original export (**exp**) and import (**imp**) utilities, but the infrastructure for Data Pump Export and Import is more server-centric. In fact, the original **exp** and **imp** utilities should only be used if you must import a dump set from a previous version of Oracle into an Oracle 10*g* database, or if you must export a dump set from an Oracle 10*g* database to be imported into a previous version of Oracle.

The new command-line clients, **expdp** and **impdp**, use the package DBMS_METADATA to extract the object definitions from the data dictionary as XML or DDL or use the package DBMS_DATAPUMP to perform the transfer of both metadata and data from one database to another. All Data Pump Export and Import processing is done on the server instead of the client, which requires directory objects on the source and target databases.

Here are a few of the other enhancements and features over the original **exp** and **imp** utilities:

- The job that exports or imports can control the number of parallel threads used for the job.

- The ability to restart a Data Pump job if the job fails or is stopped.

- Support for export and import over the network without using dump file sets.

- The ability to attach and detach from a running job by a client process.

- Space estimation capabilities, without actually performing the export.

- Specifying the database version of objects to be exported or imported.

- Support for fine-grained filtering of metadata as well as data filtering on a table-by-table basis.

We will also cover transportable tablespaces using the features of Data Pump and the package DBMS_FILE_TRANSFER to create and move a tablespace dump set to another database.

Data Pump Export

Data Pump Export, or just *Export,* unloads data and metadata into a set of operating system files called a *dump file set.* The dump file set is only readable by Data Pump Import. The dump file set consists of one or more disk files containing the metadata, data, and control information, and it's written in a proprietary binary format. You use **expdp** at the operating system command line to start Export.

Export can unload data in a number of different modes, depending on what types of objects you are exporting, from a single table to the entire database. The supported modes are Full Export, Schema, Table, Tablespace, and Transportable Tablespace.

Full Export Mode

A full export uses the **full** parameter to the **expdp** command. The entire database is unloaded; you must have the EXP_FULL_DATABASE role to export the entire database.

Schema Mode

You export one or more schemas with the **schemas** parameter in **expdp**; this is the default. If you have the EXP_FULL_DATABASE role, you can export any schema; otherwise, you can export only your own schema.

Table Mode

The table mode of **expdp** exports a specified set of tables; you use the **tables** parameter with **expdp**. If you have the EXP_FULL_DATABASE role, you can export tables in any schema; otherwise, you can only export tables in your own schema.

Tablespace Mode

You must have the EXP_FULL_DATABASE role to export an entire tablespace. Tablespace mode is essentially shorthand for exporting all tables within one or more specified tablespaces. Any dependent objects of tables that reside in the specified tablespaces are exported even if they reside in another tablespace. You use the **tablespaces** parameter with the **expdp** command to specify one or more tablespaces to export.

Transportable Tablespace Mode

Transporting a tablespace exports only the metadata for the objects within one or more tablespaces; unlike tablespace mode, the objects within the tablespace must be completely self-contained. You use the **transport_tablespaces** parameter on the **expdp** command line to specify the tablespaces. Once you create the dump set with the metadata, you copy the datafiles for the tablespace(s) to be transported to the destination server to be "plugged in" to the target database using **impdp**. Later in this chapter, in the section "Using Transportable Tablespaces," you will see how to transport a tablespace from one database to another using directory objects, **expdp**, and **impdp**. As with many of the other modes, transportable tablespace mode requires you to have the EXP_FULL_DATABASE role.

Data Pump Import

Data Pump Import, or just *Import,* loads an export dump file set created with Data Pump Export into a target system. Import is initiated at the operating system command line by using the **impdp** command.

The modes available for Import match the modes in Export: Full Import, Schema, Table, Tablespace, and Transportable Tablespace.

Full Import Mode

A full import uses the **full** parameter on the **impdp** command line. When you perform a full import, the entire dump file set (or the entire database, when performing a network import without a dump file set) is loaded into the target. You must have the IMP_FULL_DATABASE role if you're importing another database directly or if the dump file set was exported using the EXP_FULL_DATABASE role.

Schema Mode

You use the **schemas** parameter with **impdp** to import the objects in your own schema or, if you have the IMP_FULL_DATABASE role, any number of schemas in the dump file set.

Table Mode

To import specific tables from a dump file set that contains either a full, schema, tablespace, or table-only export operation, use the **tables** parameter with **impdp**. The source can also be another database. If the tables you are importing are not in your schema, you must have the IMP_FULL_DATABASE role.

Tablespace Mode

The parameter **tablespaces** is used at the **impdp** command line to import one or more tablespaces into the current database. The source for the tablespace import can be a tablespace export, a full database export, a schema export, a table-mode export, or another database.

Transportable Tablespace Mode

Using the **transport_tablespaces** parameter, you import the metadata from a transportable tablespace export dump file set or another database. The **transport_datafiles** parameter references the location where the datafiles for the transported tablespace are located.

Using Transportable Tablespaces

Transportable tablespaces make it easy to move large volumes of data between databases a tablespace at a time; Oracle 10g provides a number of enhancements to transportable tablespaces, making it easier to move data between databases that reside on different hardware and software platforms. Data Pump Export and Import play key roles in transporting a tablespace between databases.

In the following scenario, you will use **expdp** and **impdp** along with DBMS_FILE_TRANSFER to copy the INET_AUDIT tablespace from the **ord** database to the **rmanrep** database. Here are the high-level steps:

1. Set up the directories on the source and target databases for the dump file sets and the tablespace datafiles (one-time setup).

2. Check for tablespace self-consistency with DBMS_TTS.TRANSPORT_SET_CHECK.

3. Use **expdp** to create the metadata for the INET_AUDIT tablespace.

4. Use DBMS_FILE_TRANSFER to copy the dump file set(s) and datafile(s) to the target database.

5. On the target database, use **impdp** to "plug in" the tablespace.

Set Up Directory Objects

On the source database, **ord**, you need to create the directory objects that will hold the dump file set as well as a directory object that points to the location where the datafile for the INET_AUDIT tablespace is stored. Here are the SQL commands on the **ord** database:

```
SQL> create directory src_dpump_dir as '/u02/dumpset';
Directory created.
SQL> create directory src_dbf_dir as '/u04/oradata/ord';
Directory created.
```

On the destination database, **rmanrep**, you will execute similar commands, as you can see here:

```
SQL> create directory dest_dpump_dir as '/u03/dumpset';
Directory created.
SQL> create directory dest_dbf_dir as '/u03/oradata/ord';
Directory created.
```

These directory objects are persistent, and you may use these in the future for other Data Pump or file-transfer operations.

Check for Tablespace Self-Consistency

Before transporting the INET_AUDIT tablespace, you should check to make sure that all objects in the tablespace are self-contained with the procedure DBMS_TTS.TRANSPORT_SET_CHECK, as follows:

```
SQL> exec dbms_tts.transport_set_check('inet_audit', TRUE);
PL/SQL procedure successfully completed.
SQL> select * from transport_set_violations;
no rows selected
```

Not finding any rows in TRANSPORT_SET_VIOLATIONS means that the tablespace has no external dependent objects. This view is re-created every time you run DBMS_TTS.TRANSPORT_SET_CHECK.

Use expdp to Create Metadata
On the **ord** database, you will execute the **expdp** command to export the metadata associated with the INET_AUDIT tablespace after making the INET_AUDIT tablespace read-only:

```
SQL> alter tablespace inet_audit read only;
Tablespace altered.
```

To run **expdp**, you open an operating system command prompt and perform the metadata export as follows:

```
$ expdp system/manager dumpfile=expdat.dmp
        directory=src_dpump_dir transport_tablespaces=inet_audit

Export: Release 10.1.0.2.0 -
        Production on Sunday, 22 August, 2004 14:18

Copyright (c) 2003, Oracle.  All rights reserved.

Connected to: Oracle Database 10g Enterprise Edition
        Release 10.1.0.2.0 - Production
With the Partitioning, OLAP and Data Mining options
Starting "SYSTEM"."SYS_EXPORT_TRANSPORTABLE_01":
        system/******** dumpfile=expdat.dmp
        directory=src_dpump_dir transport_tablespaces=inet_audit
Processing object type TRANSPORTABLE_EXPORT/PLUGTS_BLK
Processing object type TRANSPORTABLE_EXPORT/TABLE
Processing object type TRANSPORTABLE_EXPORT/TTE_POSTINST/PLUGTS_BLK
Master table "SYSTEM"."SYS_EXPORT_TRANSPORTABLE_01"
        successfully loaded/unloaded
******************************************************************
Dump file set for SYSTEM.SYS_EXPORT_TRANSPORTABLE_01 is:
  /u02/dumpset/expdat.dmp
Job "SYSTEM"."SYS_EXPORT_TRANSPORTABLE_01"
        successfully completed at 14:19

$
```

Use DBMS_FILE_TRANSFER to Copy Files
In this step, you will copy the file /u02/dumpset/expdat.dmp and the tablespace's datafile to the remote database using DBMS_FILE_TRANSFER, as follows:

```
SQL> execute dbms_file_transfer.put_file(
  2      'src_dpump_dir', 'expdat.dmp',
  3      'dest_dpump_dir', 'expdat.dmp', 'rmanrep');
PL/SQL procedure successfully completed.
```

```
SQL> execute dbms_file_transfer.put_file(
  2        'src_dbf_dir', 'ORD/datafile/o1_mf_inet_audit_01kqy57o_.dbf',
  3        'dest_dbf_dir', 'inet_audit.dbf', 'rmanrep');
PL/SQL procedure successfully completed.
```

Because the tablespace was created using OMF, you will have to use the value of DB_FILE_
CREATE_DEST and some detective work, or use the dynamic performance views V$DATAFILE and
V$TABLESPACE, to track down the actual subdirectory and datafile name on the host operating
system.

Use impdp to Import Metadata

In the final step, you will run **impdp** on the target database to read the metadatafile and "plug in"
the tablespace datafile. Here is the output from this operation:

```
$ impdp system/manager directory=dest_dpump_dir
      dumpfile=expdat.dmp
      transport_datafiles=/u03/oradata/inet_audit.dbf

Import: Release 10.1.0.2.0 - Production on
      Sunday, 22 August, 2004 14:41
Copyright (c) 2003, Oracle.  All rights reserved.

Connected to: Oracle Database 10g Enterprise Edition
      Release 10.1.0.2.0 - Production
With the Partitioning, OLAP and Data Mining options
Master table "SYSTEM"."SYS_IMPORT_TRANSPORTABLE_01"
      successfully loaded/unloaded
Starting "SYSTEM"."SYS_IMPORT_TRANSPORTABLE_01":
  system/******** directory=dest_dpump_dir
  dumpfile=expdat.dmp
  transport_datafiles=/u03/oradata/inet_audit.dbf
Processing object type TRANSPORTABLE_EXPORT/PLUGTS_BLK
Processing object type TRANSPORTABLE_EXPORT/TABLE
Processing object type TRANSPORTABLE_EXPORT/TTE_POSTINST/PLUGTS_BLK
Job "SYSTEM"."SYS_IMPORT_TRANSPORTABLE_01"
      successfully completed at 14:41
$ sqlplus / as sysdba
. . .
SQL> select * from v$tablespace;
      TS# NAME                                  INC BIG FLA
---------- ------------------------------------- --- --- ---
        0 SYSTEM                                 YES NO  YES
        1 UNDOTBS1                               YES NO  YES
        2 SYSAUX                                 YES NO  YES
        4 USERS                                  YES NO  YES
        3 TEMP                                   YES NO  YES
        6 EXAMPLE                                YES NO  YES
```

```
        7 RMAN                          YES NO  YES
        8 INET_AUDIT                    YES YES YES
8 rows selected.

SQL> alter tablespace inet_audit read write;
Tablespace altered.
```

Note that you must change the tablespace from READ ONLY to READ WRITE; when
a tablespace is transported to another database, by default it is online but read-only.

CHAPTER
18

Managing Distributed
Databases

I n a distributed environment, databases on separate servers (hosts) may be accessed during a single transaction or query. Each server can be physically isolated without being logically isolated from the other servers.

A typical distributed database implementation involves corporate headquarters servers that replicate data to departmental servers in various locations. Each database supports local client applications and also has the ability to communicate with other databases in the network. This architecture is shown in Figure 18-1.

When one of the servers sends a database request to another server, the sending server acts like a client. The receiving server executes the SQL statement that is passed to it and returns the results plus error conditions to the sender.

Oracle Net allows this architecture to become reality. Run on all the servers involved, Oracle Net allows database requests made from one database (or application) to be passed to another database on a separate server. With this functionality, you can communicate with all the databases that are accessible via your network. You can then create synonyms that give applications true network transparency; the user who submits a query will not know the location of the data that is used to resolve it.

You can configure Oracle to support multimaster replication (in which all databases involved own the data and can serve as the source for data propagation) or single-master replication (in which only one database owns the data). When designing a replication configuration, you should try to restrict the ownership of data as much as possible. As the number of sources for propagation increases, the potential for errors to occur increases, as does the potential administration workload. In the following sections, you will see examples of the different replication capabilities available, followed by management techniques.

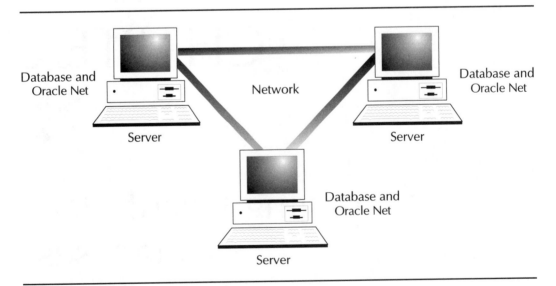

FIGURE 18-1. *Server/server architecture*

Remote Queries

To query a remote database, you must create a database link in the database in which the query will originate. The database link specifies the service name for the remote database and may also specify the username to connect to in the remote database. When a database link is referenced by a SQL statement, Oracle opens a session in the remote database, executes the SQL statement there, and returns the data. You can create database links as public links (created by DBAs, making the links available to all users in the local database) or as private links.

The following example creates a public database link called HR_LINK:

```
create public database link HR_LINK
connect to HR identified by PUFFINSTUFF
using 'hq';
```

The **create database link** command shown in this example has several parameters:

- The optional keyword **public**, which allows DBAs to create links for all users in a database. An additional optional keyword, **shared**, is described later in this chapter.

- The name of the link (HR_LINK, in this example).

- The account to connect to. You can configure the database link to use the local username and password in the remote database. This link connects to a fixed username in the remote database.

- The service name (hq, in this example).

To use the newly created link, simply add it as a suffix to table names in commands. The following example queries a remote table by using the HR_LINK database link:

```
select * from EMPLOYEE@HR_LINK
  where Office='ANNAPOLIS';
```

When you execute this query, Oracle will establish a session via the HR_LINK database link and query the EMPLOYEE table in that database. The **where** clause will be applied to the EMPLOYEE rows, and the matching records will be returned. The execution of the query is shown graphically in Figure 18-2.

The **from** clause in this example refers to EMPLOYEE@HR_LINK. Because the HR_LINK database link specifies the server name, instance name, and owner name, the full name of the table is known. If no account name had been specified in the database link, the user's account name and password in the local database would have been used during an attempt to log into the remote database.

The management of database links is described in the "Managing Distributed Data" section, later in this chapter.

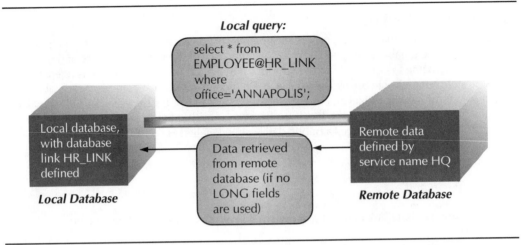

FIGURE 18-2. *Sample remote query*

Remote Data Manipulation: Two-Phase Commit

To support data manipulation across multiple databases, Oracle relies on *Two-Phase Commit (2PC)*. 2PC allows groups of transactions across several nodes to be treated as a unit; either the transactions all **commit** or they all get rolled back. A set of distributed transactions is shown in Figure 18-3.

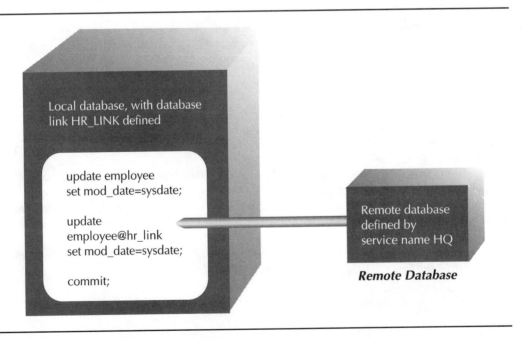

FIGURE 18-3. *Sample distributed transaction*

In that figure, two **update** transactions are performed. The first **update** goes against a local table (EMPLOYEE); the second, against a remote table (EMPLOYEE@HR_LINK). After the two transactions are performed, a single **commit** is then executed. If either transaction cannot **commit**, both transactions will be rolled back.

Distributed transactions yield two important benefits: databases on other servers can be updated, and those transactions can be grouped together with others in a logical unit. This second benefit occurs because of the database's use of 2PC. Here are its two phases:

- **The prepare phase**   An initiating node called the *global coordinator* notifies all sites involved in the transaction to be ready either to **commit** or to roll back the transaction.

- **The commit phase**   If there is no problem with the prepare phase, all sites **commit** their transactions. If a network or node failure occurs, all sites roll back their transactions.

The use of 2PC is transparent to the users. If the node that initiates the transaction forgets about the transaction, a third phase, the forget phase, is performed. The detailed management of distributed transactions is discussed in the "Managing Distributed Transactions" section, later in this chapter.

Dynamic Data Replication

To improve the performance of queries that use data from remote databases, you may wish to replicate that data on the local server. There are several options for accomplishing this, depending on which Oracle features you are using.

You can use *database triggers* to replicate data from one table into another. For example, after every **insert** into a table, a trigger may fire to insert that same record into another table—and that table may be in a remote database. Thus, you can use triggers to enforce data replication in simple configurations. If the types of transactions against the base table cannot be controlled, the trigger code needed to perform the replication will be unacceptably complicated.

When using Oracle's distributed features, you can use *materialized views* to replicate data between databases. You do not have to replicate an entire table or limit yourself to data from just one table. When replicating a single table, you may use a **where** clause to restrict which records are replicated, and you may perform **group by** operations on the data. You can also join the table with other tables and replicate the result of the queries.

NOTE
You cannot use materialized views to replicate data using LONG, LONG RAW, or user-defined datatypes.

The data in the local materialized view of the remote table(s) will need to be refreshed. You can specify the refresh interval for the materialized view, and the database will automatically take care of the replication procedures. In many cases, the database can use a *materialized view log* to send over only transaction data; otherwise, the database will perform complete refreshes on the local materialized view. The dynamic replication of data via materialized views is shown in Figure 18-4.

You can use Data Guard to create and manage a standby database whose content is updated as the primary database's data changes. The standby database can be used as a read-only database

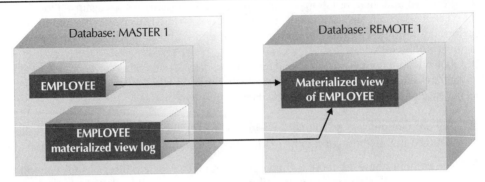

(a) *A simple materialized view; materialized view logs can be used.*

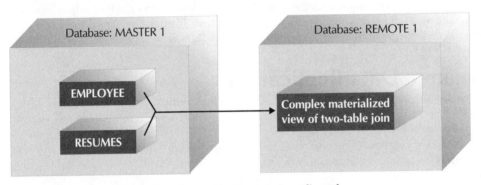

(b) *A complex materialized view; the result of the join is replicated.*

FIGURE 18-4. *Replication with materialized views*

to support reporting requirements and then returned to its status as a standby database. See Chapter 14 for details on the use and management of standby databases.

Managing Distributed Data

Before you can worry about managing transactions against remote databases, you have to get the data there and make it globally accessible to other databases. The following sections describe the requisite management tasks: enforcing location transparency and managing the database links, triggers, and materialized views.

NOTE
The examples in this chapter assume that you are using tnsnames.ora files for your database service name resolution.

The Infrastructure: Enforcing Location Transparency

To properly design your distributed databases for long-term use, you must start by making the physical location of the data transparent to the application. The name of a table within a database is unique within the schema that owns it. However, a remote database may have an account with the same name, which may own a table with the same name.

Within distributed databases, two additional layers of object identification must be added. First, the name of the instance that accesses the database must be identified. Next, the name of the host on which that instance resides must be identified. Putting together these four parts of the object's name—its host, its instance, its owner, and its name—results in a *global object name*. To access a remote table, you must know that table's global object name.

The goal of location transparency is to make the first three parts of the global object name—the host, the instance, and the schema—transparent to the user. The first three parts of the global object name are all specified via database links, so any effort at achieving location transparency should start there. First, consider a typical database link:

```
create public database link HR_LINK
connect to HR identified by PUFFINSTUFF
using 'hq';
```

NOTE
If the GLOBAL_NAMES initialization parameter is set to TRUE, the database link name must be the same as the global name of the remote database.

By using a service name (hq), the host and instance names are kept transparent. They are translated into their actual values via the local host's tnsnames.ora file. A partial entry in this file, for this service name, is shown in the following listing:

```
HQ =(DESCRIPTION=
        (ADDRESS=
                (PROTOCOL=TCP)
                (HOST=HQ)
                (PORT=1521))
        (CONNECT DATA=
                (SERVICE_NAME=LOC)))
```

The two lines in bold in this listing fill in the two missing pieces of the global object name: When the HQ service name is used, the host name is HQ and the instance name is LOC. This tnsnames.ora file shows the parameters for the TCP/IP protocol; other protocols may use different keywords, but their usage is the same. The tnsnames.ora entries provide transparency for the server and instance names.

The HR_LINK database link created via the code given earlier in this section will provide transparency for the first two parts of the global object name. But what if the data moves from the HR schema, or the HR account's password changes? The database link would have to be dropped and re-created. The same would be true if account-level security was required; you may need to create and maintain multiple database links.

To resolve the transparency of the schema portion of the global object name, you can modify the database link syntax. Consider the database link in the following listing:

```
create public database link HR_LINK
connect to current_user
using 'hq';
```

This database link uses the **connect to current_user** clause. It will use what is known as a *connected user connection*. The earlier example was a *fixed user connection*. An example of this link being used is shown here:

```
select * from EMPLOYEE@HR_LINK;
```

When HR_LINK is used, the database will resolve the global object name in the following manner:

1. It will search the local tnsnames.ora file to determine the proper host name, port, and instance name.

2. It will check the database link for a **connect to** specification. If the **connect to current_ user** clause is found, it will attempt to connect to the specified database using the *connected user*'s username and password.

3. It will search the **from** clause of the query for the object name.

Connected user links are often used to access tables whose rows can be restricted based on the username that is accessing the tables. For example, if the remote database had a table named HR.EMPLOYEE, and every employee was allowed to see his or her own record, then a database link with a specific connection, such as

```
create public database link HR_LINK
connect to HR identified by PUFFINSTUFF
using 'hq';
```

would log in as the HR account (the owner of the table). If this specific connection is used, you cannot restrict the user's view of the records on the remote host. However, if a connected user link is used, and a view is created on the remote host using the User pseudocolumn, then only that user's data would be returned from the remote host. A sample database link and view of this type is shown in the following listing:

```
REM  In the local database:
REM
create public database link HR_LINK
connect to current_user
using 'hq';

create view REMOTE_EMP
as select * from EMPLOYEE@HR_LINK
where Ename=User;
```

The User pseudocolumn's value is the current Oracle username. If you query the REMOTE_ EMP view, you are using the HR_LINK database link. Because that link uses a default connection, your username and password will be used to connect to the hq service name's database. You will therefore retrieve only those records from EMPLOYEE@HR_LINK for which your username is equal to the value of the Ename column in that table.

Either way, the data being retrieved can be restricted. The difference is that when a connected user link is used, the data can be restricted based on the username in the remote database; if a fixed connection is used, the data can be restricted after it has been returned to the local database. The connected user link reduces the amount of network traffic needed to resolve the query and adds an additional level of location transparency to the data.

NOTE
If you are using the Virtual Private Database features of the Oracle Database, you can restrict access to rows and columns without maintaining views for this purpose. See Chapter 10 for details on Virtual Private Database options.

Connected user database links raise a different set of maintenance issues. The tnsnames.ora files must be synchronized across the servers, and the username/password combinations in multiple databases must be synchronized. These issues are addressed in the next sections.

Database Domains

A *domain name service* allows hosts within a network to be hierarchically organized. Each node within the organization is called a *domain,* and each domain is labeled by its function. These functions may include COM for companies and EDU for schools. Each domain may have many subdomains. Therefore, each host will be given a unique name within the network; its name contains information about how it fits into the network hierarchy. Host names within a network typically have up to four parts; the leftmost portion of the name is the host's name, and the rest of the name shows the domain to which the host belongs.

For example, a host may be named HQ.MYCORP.COM. In this example, the host is named HQ and identified as being part of the MYCORP subdomain of the COM domain.

The domain structure is significant for two reasons. First, the host name is part of the global object name. Second, Oracle allows you to specify the DNS version of the host name in database link names, simplifying the management of distributed database connections.

To use DNS names in database links, you first need to add two parameters to your initialization file for the database. The first of these, DB_NAME, may already be there; it should be set to the instance name. The second parameter, DB_DOMAIN, is set to the DNS name of the database's host. DB_DOMAIN specifies the network domain in which the host resides. If a database named LOC is created on the HQ.MYCORP.COM server, its entries will be

```
DB_NAME = loc
DB_DOMAIN = hq.mycorp.com
```

To enable the usage of the database domain name, you must set the GLOBAL_NAMES parameter to TRUE in your parameter file, as shown in the following example:

```
GLOBAL_NAMES = true
```

NOTE
GLOBAL_NAMES is set to FALSE by default in Oracle Database 10g.

Once you have set these parameters, the database must be shut down and restarted using this parameter file for the settings to take effect.

NOTE
If you set GLOBAL_NAMES to TRUE, all your database link names must follow the rules described in this section.

When you use this method of creating global database names, the names of the database links that are created are the same as the databases to which they point. Therefore, a database link that points to the LOC database listed earlier would be named LOC.HQ.MYCORP.COM. This is shown in the following listing:

```
CREATE PUBLIC DATABASE LINK loc.hq.mycorp.com
USING 'service name';
```

Oracle may append the local database's DB_DOMAIN value to the name of the database link. For example, if the database was within the HQ.MYCORP.COM domain and the database link was named LOC, the database link name, when used, would be automatically expanded to LOC.HQ.MYCORP.COM.

Using global database names establishes a link between the database name, database domain, and database link names. This, in turn, may make it easier to identify and manage database links. For example, you can create a public database link (with no connect string, as shown in the preceding example) in each database that points to every other database. Users within a database no longer need to guess at the proper database link to use; if they know the global database name, they know the database link name. If a table is moved from one database to another, or if a database is moved from one host to another, it is easy to determine which of the old database links must be dropped and re-created. Using global database names is part of migrating from stand-alone databases to true networks of databases.

Using Shared Database Links

If you use the Multithreaded Server option for your database connections and your application will employ many concurrent database link connections, you may benefit from using *shared database links*. A shared database link uses shared server connections to support the database link connections. If you have multiple concurrent database link accesses into a remote database, you can use shared database links to reduce the number of server connections required.

To create a shared database link, use the **shared** keyword of the **create database link** command. As shown in the following listing, you will also need to specify a schema and password for the remote database:

```
create shared database link HR_LINK_SHARED
connect to current_user
authenticated by HR identified by puffinstuff
using 'hq';
```

The HR_LINK_SHARED database link uses the connected user's username and password when accessing the 'hq' database, as specified via the **connect to current_user** clause. In order to prevent unauthorized attempts to use the shared link, shared links require the **authenticated by** clause. In this example, the account used for authentication is an application account, but you can also use an empty schema for authentication. The authentication account must have the CREATE SESSION system privilege. During usage of the HR_LINK_SHARED link, connection attempts will include authentication against the HR link account.

NOTE
The authentication username and password are visible to users with access to the SYS.LINK$ table.

If you change the password on the authentication account, you will need to drop and re-create each database link that references it. To simplify maintenance, create an account that is only used for authentication of shared database link connections. The account should have only the CREATE SESSION system privilege, and it should not have any privileges on any of the application tables.

If your application uses database links infrequently, you should use traditional database links without the **shared** clause. Without the **shared** clause, each database link connection requires a separate connection to the remote database.

Managing Database Links

You can retrieve information about public database links via the DBA_DB_LINKS data dictionary view. You can view private database links via the USER_DB_LINKS data dictionary view. Whenever possible, separate your users among databases by application so that they may all share the same public database links. As a side benefit, these users will usually also be able to share public grants and synonyms.

The columns of the DBA_DB_LINKS data dictionary view are listed in the following table. The password for the link to use is not viewable via DBA_DB_LINKS; it is stored unencrypted in the SYS.LINK$ table.

Column Name	Description
OWNER	The owner of the database link
DB_LINK	The name of the database link (such as HR_LINK in this chapter's examples)
USERNAME	The name of the account to use to open a session in the remote database, if a specific connection is used
HOST	The connect string that will be used to connect to the remote database
CREATED	A timestamp that marks the creation date for the database link

NOTE
The number of database links that can be used by a single query is limited by the OPEN_LINKS parameter in the database's initialization file. Its default value is 4.

The managerial tasks involved for database links depend on the level to which you have implemented location transparency in your databases. In the best-case scenario, connected user links are used along with service names or aliases. In that scenario, the only requirements for successful maintenance are that the tnsnames.ora file be consistent across hosts and that user account/password combinations be maintained globally.

Synchronizing account/password combinations across databases may be difficult, but there are several alternatives. First, you may force all changes to user account passwords to go through a central authority. This central authority would have the responsibility for updating the password for the account in all databases in the network—a time-consuming task, but a valuable one.

Second, you may audit user password changes made via the **alter user** command by auditing the usage of that command (see Chapter 10). If a user's password changes in one database, it must be changed on all databases available in the network that are accessed via connected user links.

If any part of the global object name—such as a username—is embedded in the database link, a change affecting that part of the global object name requires that the database link be dropped and re-created. For example, if the HR user's password were changed, the HR_LINK database link with a specific connection defined earlier would be dropped with

```
drop database link HR_LINK;
```

and the link would then be re-created, using the new account password:

```
create public database link HR_LINK
connect to HR identified by NEWPASSWORD
using 'hq';
```

You cannot create a database link in another user's account. If you attempt to create a database link in SCOTT's account, as shown here,

```
create database link SCOTT.HR_LINK
connect to HR identified by PUFFINSTUFF
using 'hq';
```

then Oracle will not create the HR_LINK database link in SCOTT's account. Instead, Oracle will create a database link named SCOTT.HR_LINK in the account that executed the **create database link** command. To create private database links, you must be logged into the database in the account that will own the link.

NOTE
To see which links are presently in use in your database, query V$DBLINK.

Managing Database Triggers

If your data replication needs require synchronized changes in multiple databases, you can use database triggers to replicate data from one table into another. Database triggers are executed when specific actions happen. Triggers can be executed for each row of a transaction, for an entire transaction as a unit, or when system-wide events occur. When dealing with data replication, you will usually be concerned with triggers affecting each row of data.

Before creating a replication-related trigger, you must create a database link for the trigger to use. In this case, the link is created in the database that *owns* the data, accessible to the owner of the table being replicated:

```
create public database link TRIGGER_LINK
connect to current_user
using 'remote1';
```

This link, named TRIGGER_LINK, uses a service name (remote1) to specify the connection to a remote database. The link will attempt to log into the remote1 database using the same username and password as the account that calls the link.

The trigger shown in the following listing uses this link. The trigger is fired after every row is inserted into the EMPLOYEE table. Because the trigger executes after the row has been inserted, the row's data has already been validated in the local database. The trigger inserts the same row into a remote table with the same structure, using the TRIGGER_LINK database link just defined. The remote table must already exist.

```
create trigger COPY_DATA
after insert on EMPLOYEE
for each row
begin
        insert into EMPLOYEE@TRIGGER_LINK
        values
        (:new.Empno, :new.Ename, :new.Deptno,
        :new.Salary, :new.Birth_Date, :new.Soc_Sec_Num);
end;
/
```

This trigger uses the **new** keyword to reference the values from the row that was just inserted into the local EMPLOYEE table.

> **NOTE**
> *If you use trigger-based replication, your trigger code must account for potential error conditions at the remote site, such as duplicate key values, space-management problems, or a shutdown database.*

To list information about triggers, use the DBA_TRIGGERS data dictionary view. The following query will list the "header" information about the trigger—its type, the statement that calls it, and the table on which it calls. This example shows the header information for the COPY_DATA trigger just created:

```
select Trigger_Type,
        Triggering_Event,
        Table_Name
  from DBA_TRIGGERS
where Trigger_Name = 'COPY_DATA';
```

Sample output from this query is shown here:

```
TYPE                TRIGGERING_EVENT        TABLE_NAME
----------------    --------------------    ------------
AFTER EACH ROW      INSERT                  EMPLOYEE
```

You can query the text of the trigger from DBA_TRIGGERS, as shown in the following listing:

```
set long 1000
select Trigger_Body
  from DBA_TRIGGERS
 where Trigger_Name = 'COPY_DATA';
```

Sample output from this query is shown here:

```
TRIGGER_BODY
--------------------------------------------------------
begin
     insert into EMPLOYEE@TRIGGER_LINK
     values
     (:new.Empno, :new.Ename, :new.Deptno,
     :new.Salary, :new.Birth_Date, :new.Soc_Sec_Num);
end;
```

It is theoretically possible to create a trigger to replicate all possible permutations of data-manipulation actions on the local database, but this quickly becomes difficult to manage. For a complex environment, you should consider the use of materialized views or manual data copies. For the limited circumstances described earlier, triggers are a very easy solution to implement.

NOTE
If you use triggers for your data replication, the success of a transaction in the master database is dependent on the success of the remote transaction.

Managing Materialized Views

You can use materialized views to aggregate, pre-join, or replicate data. In an enterprise database environment, data generally flows from an online transaction-processing database into a data warehouse. Normally the data is prestaged, cleansed, or otherwise processed and then moved into the data warehouse. From there, the data may be fielded to other databases or data marts.

You can use materialized views to precompute and store aggregate information within a database, to dynamically replicate data between distributed databases, and synchronize data updates within replicated environments. In replication environments, materialized views enable local access to data that would normally have to be accessed remotely. A materialized view may be based on another materialized view.

In large databases, materialized views help to improve the performance of queries that involve aggregates (including sum, count, average, variance, standard deviation, minimum, and maximum) or table joins. Oracle's query optimizer will automatically recognize that the materialized view could be used to satisfy the query—a feature known as *query rewrite*.

NOTE
For best results, make sure the statistics on the materialized view are kept current.

You can use initialization parameters to configure the optimizer to automatically rewrite queries to use the materialized views whenever possible. Because materialized views are transparent to SQL applications, they can be dropped or created without impacting the execution code. You can create a partitioned materialized view and you can base materialized views on partitioned tables.

Unlike regular views, materialized views store data and take up physical space in your database. Materialized views are populated with data generated from their base queries, and they are refreshed on demand or on a scheduled basis. Therefore, whenever the data accessed by the base query changes, the materialized views should be refreshed to reflect the data changes. The data refresh frequency depends on how much data latency your business can tolerate in the processes supported by the materialized views. You'll see how to establish your refresh rate later in this chapter.

The materialized view will create several objects in the database. The user creating the materialized view must have the CREATE MATERIALIZED VIEW, CREATE TABLE, and CREATE VIEW privileges as well as the SELECT privilege on any tables that are referenced but are owned by another schema. If the materialized view is going to be created in another schema, the user creating the materialized view must have the CREATE ANY MATERIALIZED VIEW privilege and the SELECT privilege to the tables that are referenced in the materialized view if the tables are owned by another schema. To enable query rewrite on a materialized view that references tables within another schema, the user enabling query rewrite must have the GLOBAL QUERY REWRITE privilege or be explicitly granted the QUERY REWRITE privilege on any referenced table within another schema. The user must also have the UNLIMITED TABLESPACE privilege. Materialized views can be created in the local database, and pull data from the remote master database or materialized views can reside on the same database server on which the data is located.

If you plan to use the query rewrite feature, you must put the following entry in your initialization parameter file:

```
QUERY_REWRITE_ENABLED=TRUE
```

NOTE
If the OPTIMIZER_FEATURES_ENABLED parameter is set to 10.0.0 or higher, then QUERY_REWRITE_ENABLED defaults to TRUE.

A second parameter, QUERY_REWRITE_INTEGRITY, sets the degree to which Oracle must enforce query rewriting. At the safest level, Oracle does not use query rewrite transformations that rely on unenforced relationships. The valid values for QUERY_REWRITE_INTEGRITY are ENFORCED (Oracle enforces and guarantees consistency and integrity), TRUSTED (query rewrite is supported for declared relationships), and STALE_TOLERATED (query rewrite is supported even if the materialized views are inconsistent with their underlying data). By default, QUERY_REWRITE_INTEGRITY is set to ENFORCED.

Materialized View Decisions

Before you can create a materialized view, you must make several decisions, including:

- Whether the materialized view is to be populated with data during creation or after
- How often the materialized view is to be refreshed
- What type of refreshes to perform
- Whether to maintain a materialized view log or not

You can either have data loaded to the materialized view upon its creation using the **build immediate** command option of the **create materialized view** command or you can precreate the materialized view but not populate it until the first time it is used by declaring **build deferred**. The advantage of populating the view on creation is that the data will be available immediately when you make the materialized view available. However, if the materialized view is not going to be used for some time and the data changes fairly rapidly, the data could become stale before the view is used. If you wait to have the materialized view populated, the view will not be populated with data until the package DBMS_MVIEW.REFRESH is executed, and your user must wait for the view to populate before any data is returned, thus producing a performance degradation. If a view already exists and you want to convert it to a materialized view, you can use the **prebuilt** command option.

You must decide how much stale data is tolerable based on your company's needs. You can base your decision on how frequently the data changes in the table on which the materialized view is based. If your management does not have to have up-to-the-minute information on which to base decisions, you might only need to refresh your materialized view once an hour or once a day. If it is critical for the data to be absolutely accurate at all times, you may need to perform fast refreshes every five minutes throughout the day and night.

There are four forms of refresh: Complete, Fast, Force, and Never. In a Fast refresh, materialized view logs are used to track the data changes that have occurred within the table since the last refresh. Only changed information is populated back to the materialized view, on a periodic basis, based on the refresh criteria you have established. The materialized view log is maintained in the same database and schema as the master table for the materialized view. Because the Fast refresh just applies changes made since the last refresh, the time taken to perform the refresh should generally be very short.

In a Complete refresh, the data within the materialized view is completely replaced each time the refresh is run. The time required to perform a Complete refresh of the materialized view can be substantial. You can either have the refresh performed each time transactions are committed on the master table (**refresh on commit**) or only when the DBMS_MVIEW.REFRESH procedure is run (**refresh on demand**).

When you specify Force refresh, the refresh process first evaluates whether or not a Fast refresh can be run. If it can't, a Complete refresh will be performed. If you specify Never as the refresh option, the materialized view will not be refreshed.

If you do not have a materialized view log created and populated, only Complete refreshes can be executed.

Creating a Materialized View

A sample command used to create the materialized view is shown in the following listing. In this example, the materialized view is given a name (STORE_DEPT_SAL_MV) and its storage parameters are specified as well as its refresh interval and the time at which it will be populated with data. In this case, the materialized view is told to use the Complete refresh option and to not populate the data until the DBMS_MVIEW.REFRESH procedure is run. Query rewrite is enabled. The materialized view's base query is then given.

```
create materialized view STORE_DEPT_SAL_MV
tablespace MVIEWS
build deferred
refresh complete
enable query rewrite
as
select d.DNAME, sum(SAL) as tot_sum
  from DEPT d, EMP e
 where d.DEPTNO = e.DEPTNO
group sby d.DNAME;
```

> **NOTE**
> *A materialized view query cannot reference tables or views owned by the user SYS.*

The following listing shows another example of a materialized view creation, using **refresh fast on commit**. To support fast refreshes when commits occur, you will need to create a materialized view log on the base table. See "Managing Materialized View Logs" later in this chapter for details.

```
create materialized view STORE_DEPT_SAL_MV
tablespace MYMVIEWS
parallel
build immediate
refresh fast on commit
enable query rewrite
as
select d.DNAME, sum(SAL) as tot_sum
  from DEPT d, EMP e
 where d.DEPTNO = e.DEPTNO
group by d.DNAME;
```

In this example, the same base query is used, but the materialized view is created with a fast refresh to be performed every time a transaction is committed in the master table. This materialized view will be populated with data on creation, and the inserted information will be loaded in parallel. Query rewrite is enabled.

> **NOTE**
> *The Fast refresh option will not be used unless a materialized view log is created on the base table for the materialized view. Oracle can perform Fast refreshes of joined tables in materialized views.*

For both of these examples, the materialized view uses the default storage parameters for its tablespace. You can alter the materialized view's storage parameters via the **alter materialized view** command, as shown in the following example:

```
alter materialized view STORE_DEPT_SAL_MV pctfree 5;
```

The two most frequently used operations against a materialized view are query execution and Fast refresh. Each of these actions requires different resources and has different performance requirements. You may index the base table of the materialized view—for example, adding an index to improve query performance. If you have a materialized view that only uses join conditions and Fast refresh, indexes on the primary key columns may improve the Fast refresh operations. If your materialized view uses both joins and aggregates and is fast refreshable, as shown in the last example, an index is automatically created for the view unless you specify **using no index** in the **create materialized view** command.

To drop a materialized view, use the **drop materialized view** command:

```
drop materialized view STORE_DEPT_SAL_MV;
```

Using DBMS_MVIEW and DBMS_ADVISOR

There are multiple supplied packages you can use to manage and evaluate your materialized views, including DBMS_MVIEW, DBMS_ADVISOR, and DBMS_DIMENSION.

The DBMS_MVIEW package subprograms are shown in Table 18-1.

The DBMS_MVIEW package is used to perform management actions such as evaluating, registering, or refreshing a materialized view.

To refresh a single materialized view, use DBMS_MVIEW.REFRESH. Its two main parameters are the name of the materialized view to be refreshed and the method to use. For the method, you can specify 'c' for a Complete refresh, 'f' for Fast refresh, and '?' for Force. Here's an example:

```
execute DBMS_MVIEW.REFRESH('store_dept_sal_mv','c');
```

If you are refreshing multiple materialized views via a single execution of DBMS_MVIEW.REFRESH, list the names of all the materialized views in the first parameter and their matching refresh methods in the second parameter, as shown here:

```
execute DBMS_MVIEW.REFRESH('mv1,mv2,mv3','cfc');
```

In this example, the materialized view named MV2 will be refreshed via a Fast refresh, whereas the others will use a Complete refresh.

You can use a separate procedure in the DBMS_MVIEW package to refresh all the materialized views that are scheduled to be automatically refreshed. This procedure, named REFRESH_ALL, will refresh each materialized view separately. It does not accept any parameters. The following listing shows an example of its execution:

```
execute DBMS_MVIEW.REFRESH_ALL;
```

Because the materialized views will be refreshed via REFRESH_ALL consecutively, they are not all refreshed at the same time. Therefore, a database or server failure during the execution of

Subprogram	Description
BEGIN_TABLE_REORGANIZATION	A process to preserve the data needed for a materialized view refresh is performed, used prior to reorganizing the master table.
END_TABLE_REORGANIZATION	Ensures that the materialized view master table is in the proper state and that the master table is valid, at the end of a master table reorganization.
ESTIMATE_MVIEW_SIZE	Estimates the size of a materialized view, in bytes and rows.
EXPLAIN_MVIEW	Explains what is possible with an existing or proposed materialized view. (Is it fast refreshable? is query rewrite available?)
EXPLAIN_REWRITE	Explains why a query failed to rewrite, or which materialized views will be used if it rewrites.
I_AM_A_REFRESH	The value of the I_AM_REFRESH package state is returned, called during replication.
PMARKER	Used for Partition Change Tracking. Returns a partition marker from a RowID.
PURGE_DIRECT_LOAD_LOG	Used with data warehousing, this subprogram purges rows from the direct loader log after they are no longer needed by a materialized view.
PURGE_LOG	Purges rows from the materialized view log.
PURGE_MVIEW_FROM_LOG	Purges rows from the materialized view log.
REFRESH	Refreshes one or more materialized views that are not members of the same refresh group.
REFRESH_ALL_MVIEWS	Refreshes all materialized views that do not reflect changes to their master table or master materialized view.
REFRESH_DEPENDENT	Refreshes all table-based materialized views that depend on either a specified master table or master materialized view. The list can contain one or more master tables or master materialized views.
REGISTER_MVIEW	Enables an individual materialized view's administration.
UNREGISTER_MVIEW	Used to unregister a materialized view at a master site or master materialized view site.

TABLE 18-1.   *DBMS_MVIEW Subprograms*

this procedure may cause the local materialized views to be out of sync with each other. If that happens, simply rerun this procedure after the database has been recovered. As an alternative, you can create refresh groups, as described in the next section.

Using the SQL Access Advisor

As of Oracle Database 10*g*, you can use the SQL Access Advisor to generate recommendations for the creation and indexing of materialized views. The SQL Access Advisor may recommend specific indexes (and types of indexes) to improve the performance of joins and other queries.

The SQL Access Advisor may also generate recommendations for altering a materialized view so it supports query rewrite or Fast refreshes. You can execute the SQL Access Advisor from within Oracle Enterprise Manager or via executions of the DBMS_ADVISOR package.

NOTE
For best results from the DBMS_ADVISOR package, you should gather statistics about all tables, indexes, and join columns prior to generating recommendations.

To use the SQL Access Advisor, either from Oracle Enterprise Manager or via DBMS_ADVISOR, you follow four steps:

1. Create a task.

2. Define the workload.

3. Generate recommendations.

4. View and implement recommendations.

You can create a task in one of two ways: by executing the DBMS_ADVISOR.CREATE_TASK procedure or by using the DBMS_ADVISOR.QUICK_TUNE procedure (as shown in the next section).

The workload consists of one or more SQL statements plus the statistics and attributes that relate to the statement. The workload may include all SQL statements for an application. The SQL Access Advisor ranks the entries in the workload according to statistics and business importance. The workload is created using the DBMS_ADVISOR.CREATE_SQLWKLD procedure. To associate a workload with a parent Advisor task, use the DBMS_ADVISOR.ADD_SQLWKLD_REF procedure. If a workload is not provided, the SQL Access Advisor can generate and use a hypothetical workload based on the dimensions defined in your schema.

Once a task exists and a workload is associated with the task, you can generate recommendations via the DBMS_ADVISOR.EXECUTE_TASK procedure. The SQL Access Advisor will consider the workload and the system statistics and will attempt to generate recommendations for tuning the application. You can see the recommendations by executing the DBMS_ADVISOR.GET_TASK_ SCRIPT function or via data dictionary views. Each recommendation can be viewed via USER_ ADVISOR_RECOMMENDATIONS (there are "ALL" and "DBA" versions of this view available as well). To relate recommendations to a SQL statement, you will need to use the USER_ADVISOR_ SQLA_WK_STMTS view and USER_ADVISOR_ACTIONS.

When you execute the GET_TASK_SCRIPT procedure, Oracle generates an executable SQL file that will contain the commands needed to create, alter, or drop the recommended objects. You should review the generated script prior to executing it, particularly noting the tablespace specifications. Later in this chapter, you will see how to use the QUICK_TUNE procedure to simplify the tuning advisor process for a single command.

To tune a single SQL statement, use the QUICK_TUNE procedure of the DBMS_ADVISOR package. QUICK_TUNE has two input parameters—a task name and a SQL statement. Using QUICK_TUNE shields the user from the steps involved in creating workloads and tasks via DBMS_ADVISOR.

For example, the following procedure call evaluates a query:

```
execute DBMS_ADVISOR.QUICK_TUNE(DBMS_ADVISOR.SQLACCESS_ADVISOR, -
        'MV_TUNE','SELECT PUBLISHER FROM BOOKSHELF');
```

NOTE
The user executing this command needs the ADVISOR system privilege.

The recommendations generated by QUICK_TUNE can be viewed via USER_ADVISOR_ ACTIONS, but they are easier to read if you use the DBMS_ADVISOR procedures to generate a script file. The recommendation is that a materialized view be created to support the query. Because only one SQL statement was provided, this recommendation is given in isolation and does not consider any other aspects of the database or application.

You can use the CREATE_FILE procedure to automate the generation of a file containing the scripts needed to implement the recommendations. First, create a directory object to hold the file:

```
create directory scripts as 'e:\scripts';
grant read on directory scripts to public;
grant write on directory scripts to public;
```

Next, execute the CREATE_FILE procedure. It has three input variables—the script (generated via GET_TASK_SCRIPT, to which you pass the name of the task), the output directory, and the name of the file to be created:

```
execute DBMS_ADVISOR.CREATE_FILE(DBMS_ADVISOR.GET_TASK_SCRIPT('MV_TUNE'),-
'SCRIPTS','MV_TUNE.sql');
```

The MV_TUNE.sql file created by the CREATE_FILE procedure will contain commands similar to those shown in the following listing. Depending on the specific version of Oracle, the recommendations may differ.

```
Rem   Username:          PRACTICE
Rem   Task:              MV_TUNE
Rem

set feedback 1
set linesize 80
set trimspool on
set tab off
set pagesize 60

whenever sqlerror CONTINUE

CREATE MATERIALIZED VIEW "PRACTICE"."MV$$_021F0001"
    REFRESH FORCE WITH ROWID
    ENABLE QUERY REWRITE
    AS SELECT PRACTICE.BOOKSHELF.ROWID C1,
"PRACTICE"."BOOKSHELF"."PUBLISHER" M1
FROM PRACTICE.BOOKSHELF;
```

```
begin
  dbms_stats.gather_table_stats('"PRACTICE"',
'"MV$$_021F0001"',NULL,dbms_stats.auto_sample_size);
end;
/

whenever sqlerror EXIT SQL.SQLCODE

begin
dbms_advisor.mark_recommendation('MV_TUNE',1,'IMPLEMENTED');
end;
/
```

The MARK_RECOMMENDATION procedure allows you to annotate the recommendation so that it can be skipped during subsequent script generations. Valid actions for MARK_RECOMMENDATION include ACCEPT, IGNORE, IMPLEMENTED, and REJECT.

You can use the TUNE_MVIEW procedure of the DBMS_ADVISOR package to generate recommendations for the reconfiguration of your materialized views. TUNE_MVIEW generates two sets of output results—for the creation of new materialized views and for the removal of previously created materialized views. The end result should be a set of materialized views that can be Fast refreshed, replacing materialized views that cannot be Fast refreshed.

You can view the TUNE_MVIEW output via the USER_TUNE_MVIEW data dictionary view, or you can generate its scripts via the GET_TASK_SCRIPT and CREATE_FILE procedures shown in the previous listings.

The supplied programs for the DBMS_ADVISOR package are shown in Table 18-2.

Subprocedure	Description
ADD_SQLWKLD_REF	Add a workload reference to an Advisor task.
ADD_SQLWKLD_STATEMENT	Add a single statement to a workload.
CANCEL_TASK	Cancel a currently executing task operation.
CREATE_FILE	Create an external file from a PL/SQL CLOB variable.
CREATE_OBJECT	Create a new task object.
CREATE_SQLWKLD	Create a new workload object.
CREATE_TASK	Create a new Advisor task in the repository.
DELETE_SQLWKLD	Delete an entire workload object.
DELETE_SQLWKLD_REF	Delete an entire workload object.
DELETE_SQLWKLD_STATEMENT	Delete one or more statements from a workload.
DELETE_TASK	Delete the specified task from the repository.

TABLE 18-2. *DBMS_ADVISOR Subprograms*

Subprocedure	Description
EXECUTE_TASK	Execute the specified task.
GET_REC_ATTRIBUTES	Retrieve specific recommendation attributes from a task.
GET_TASK_SCRIPT	Create and return an executable SQL script of the Advisor recommendations.
IMPORT_SQLWKLD_SCHEMA	Import data into a workload from the current SQL cache
IMPORT_SQLWKLD_SQLCACHE	Import data into a workload from the current SQL cache.
IMPORT_SQLWKLD_STS	Import data into a workload from a SQL Tuning Set.
IMPORT_SQLWKLD_SUMADV	Import data into a workload from the current SQL cache.
IMPORT_SQLWKLD_USER	Import data into a workload from the current SQL cache.
INTERRUPT_TASK	Stop a currently executing task, ending its operations as it would at a normal exit.
MARK_RECOMMENDATION	Set the annotation status for a particular recommendation.
QUICK_TUNE	Perform an analysis on a single SQL statement.
RESET_TASK	Reset a task to its initial state.
SET_DEFAULT_SQLWKLD_PARAMETER	Import data into a workload from schema evidence.
SET_DEFAULT_TASK_PARAMETER	Modify a default task parameter.
SET_SQLWKLD_PARAMETER	Set the value of a workload parameter.
SET_TASK_PARAMETER	Set the specified task parameter value.
TUNE_MVIEW	Show how to decompose a materialized view into two or more materialized views or to restate the materialized view in a way that is more advantageous for Fast refresh and query rewrite.
UPDATE_OBJECT	Update a task object.
UPDATE_REC_ATTRIBUTES	Update an existing recommendation for the specified task.
UPDATE_SQLWKLD_ATTRIBUTES	Update a workload object.
UPDATE_SQLWKLD_STATEMENT	Update one or more SQL statements in a workload.
UPDATE_TASK_ATTRIBUTES	Update a task's attributes.

TABLE 18-2. *DBMS_ADVISOR Subprograms* (continued)

An additional package, DBMS_DIMENSION, provides two procedures:

DESCRIBE_DIMENSION   Show the definition of the input dimension, including owner, name, levels, hierarchies, and attributes.

VALIDATE DIMENSION   Verify that the relationships specified in a dimension are correct.

You can use the DBMS_DIMENSION package to validate and display the structure of your dimensions.

Enforcing Referential Integrity Among Materialized Views

The referential integrity between two related tables, both of which have simple materialized views based on them, may not be enforced in their materialized views. If the tables are refreshed at different times, or if transactions are occurring on the master tables during the refresh, it is possible for the materialized views of those tables to not reflect the referential integrity of the master tables.

If, for example, EMPLOYEE and DEPT are related to each other via a primary key/foreign key relationship, then simple materialized views of these tables may contain violations of this relationship, including foreign keys without matching primary keys. In this example, that could mean employees in the EMPLOYEE materialized view with DEPTNO values that do not exist in the DEPT materialized view.

This problem has a number of potential solutions. First, time the refreshes to occur when the master tables are not in use. Second, perform the refreshes manually (see the following section for information on this) immediately after locking the master tables or quiescing the database. Third, you may join the tables in the materialized view, creating a complex materialized view that will be based on the master tables (which will be properly related to each other). Fourth, you can force the materialized view updates to occur when transactions are committed in the primary database.

Using refresh groups provides another solution to the referential integrity problem. You can collect related materialized views into *refresh groups*. The purpose of a refresh group is to coordinate the refresh schedules of its members. Materialized views whose master tables have relationships with other master tables are good candidates for membership in refresh groups. Coordinating the refresh schedules of the materialized views will maintain the master tables' referential integrity in the materialized views as well. If refresh groups are not used, the data in the materialized views may be inconsistent with regard to the master tables' referential integrity.

Manipulation of refresh groups is performed via the DBMS_REFRESH package. The procedures within that package are MAKE, ADD, SUBTRACT, CHANGE, DESTROY, and REFRESH, as shown in the following examples. Information about existing refresh groups can be queried from the USER_REFRESH and USER_REFRESH_CHILDREN data dictionary views.

NOTE
Materialized views that belong to a refresh group do not have to belong to the same schema, but they do have to be all stored within the same database.

Create a refresh group by executing the MAKE procedure in the DBMS_REFRESH package, whose structure is shown in the following listing:

```
DBMS_REFRESH.MAKE
      (name IN VARCHAR2,
       list IN VARCHAR2, |
        tab IN DBMS_UTILITY.UNCL_ARRAY,
       next_date IN DATE,
       interval IN VARCHAR2,
       implicit_destroy IN BOOLEAN := FALSE,
       lax IN BOOLEAN := FALSE,
       job IN BINARY INTEGER := 0,
       rollback_seg IN VARCHAR2 := NULL,
       push_deferred_rpc IN BOOLEAN := TRUE,
       refresh_after_errors IN BOOLEAN := FALSE,
       purge_option IN BINARY_INTEGER := NULL,
       parallelism IN BINARY_INTEGER := NULL,
       heap_size IN BINARY_INTEGER := NULL);
```

All but the first four of the parameters for this procedure have default values that are usually acceptable. The *list* and *tab* parameters are mutually exclusive. You can use the following command to create a refresh group for materialized views named LOCAL_EMP and LOCAL_DEPT:

```
execute DBMS_REFRESH.MAKE
      (name => 'emp_group', -
       list => 'local_emp, local_dept', -
       next_date => SysDate, -
       interval => 'SysDate+7');
```

NOTE
The list *parameter, which is the second parameter in the listing, has a single quote at its beginning and at its end, with none between. In this example, two materialized views—LOCAL_EMP and LOCAL_DEPT— are passed to the procedure via a single parameter.*

The preceding command will create a refresh group named EMP_GROUP, with two materialized views as its members. The refresh group name is enclosed in single quotes, as is the *list* of members—but not each member.

If the refresh group is going to contain a materialized view that is already a member of another refresh group (for example, during a move of a materialized view from an old refresh group to a newly created refresh group), you must set the *lax* parameter to TRUE. A materialized view can only belong to one refresh group at a time.

To add materialized views to an existing refresh group, use the ADD procedure of the DBMS_REFRESH package, whose structure is

```
DBMS_REFRESH.ADD
      (name IN VARCHAR2,
       list IN VARCHAR2, |
        tab IN DBMS_UTILITY.UNCL_ARRAY,
       lax IN BOOLEAN := FALSE);
```

As with the MAKE procedure, the ADD procedure's *lax* parameter does not have to be specified unless a materialized view is being moved between two refresh groups. When this procedure is executed with the *lax* parameter set to TRUE, the materialized view is moved to the new refresh group and is automatically deleted from the old refresh group.

To remove materialized views from an existing refresh group, use the SUBTRACT procedure of the DBMS_REFRESH package, as in the following example:

```
DBMS_REFRESH.SUBTRACT
(name IN VARCHAR2,
 list IN VARCHAR2, |
  tab IN DBMS_UTILITY.UNCL_ARRAY,
 lax IN BOOLEAN := FALSE);
```

As with the MAKE and ADD procedures, a single materialized view or a list of materialized views (separated by commas) may serve as input to the SUBTRACT procedure. You can alter the refresh schedule for a refresh group via the CHANGE procedure of the DBMS_REFRESH package:

```
DBMS_REFRESH.CHANGE
(name IN VARCHAR2,
 next_date IN DATE := NULL,
 interval IN VARCHAR2 := NULL,
 implicit_destroy IN BOOLEAN := NULL,
 rollback_seg IN VARCHAR2 := NULL,
 push_deferred_rpc IN BOOLEAN := NULL,
 refresh_after_errors IN BOOLEAN := NULL,
 purge_option IN BINARY_INTEGER := NULL,
 parallelism IN BINARY_INTEGER := NULL,
 heap_size IN BINARY_INTEGER := NULL);
```

The *next_date* parameter is analogous to the **start with** clause in the **create materialized view** command. The *interval* parameter is analogous to the **next** clause in the **create materialized view** command. For example, to change the EMP_GROUP's schedule so that it will be replicated every three days, you can execute the following command (which specifies a NULL value for the *next_date* parameter, leaving that value unchanged):

```
execute DBMS_REFRESH.CHANGE
(name => 'emp_group',
 next_date => null,
 interval => 'SysDate+3');
```

After this command is executed, the refresh cycle for the EMP_GROUP refresh group will be changed to every three days.

NOTE
Refresh operations on refresh groups may take longer than comparable materialized view refreshes. Group refreshes may also require significant undo segment space to maintain data consistency during the refresh.

You may manually refresh a refresh group via the REFRESH procedure of the DBMS_REFRESH package. The REFRESH procedure accepts the name of the refresh group as its only parameter. The command shown here will refresh the refresh group named EMP_GROUP:

```
execute DBMS_REFRESH.REFRESH('emp_group');
```

To delete a refresh group, use the DESTROY procedure of the DBMS_REFRESH package, as shown in the following example. Its only parameter is the name of the refresh group.

```
execute DBMS_REFRESH.DESTROY(name => 'emp_group');
```

You may also implicitly destroy the refresh group. If you set the *implicit_destroy* parameter to TRUE when you create the group with the MAKE procedure, the refresh group will be deleted (destroyed) when its last member is removed from the group (usually via the SUBTRACT procedure).

NOTE
For performance statistics related to materialized view refreshes, query V$MVREFRESH.

Managing Materialized View Logs

A *materialized view log* is a table that maintains a record of modifications to the master table in a materialized view. It is stored in the same database as the master table and is only used by simple materialized views. The data in the materialized view log is used during Fast refreshes. If you are going to use Fast refreshes, create the materialized view log before creating the materialized view.

To create a materialized view log, you must be able to create an AFTER ROW trigger on the table, so you need CREATE TRIGGER and CREATE TABLE privileges. You cannot specify a name for the materialized view log.

Because the materialized view log is a table, it has the full set of table storage clauses available to it. The following example shows the creation of a materialized view log on a table named EMPLOYEE:

```
create materialized view log on EMPLOYEE
tablespace DATA_2;
```

The **pctfree** value for the materialized view log can be set very low, and the **pctused** value should be set very high; specify values for these parameters or use a tablespace whose storage parameters reflect these needs. The size of the materialized view log depends on the number of changes that will be processed during each refresh. The more frequently all the materialized views that reference the master table are refreshed, the less space is needed for the log.

You can modify the storage parameters for the materialized view log via the **alter materialized view log** command. When using this command, specify the name of the master table. An example of altering the EMPLOYEE table's materialized view log is shown in the following listing:

```
alter materialized view log EMPLOYEE
pctfree 10;
```

To drop a materialized view log, use the **drop materialized view log** command, as shown in the following example:

```
drop materialized view log on EMPLOYEE;
```

This command will drop the materialized view log and its associated objects from the database.

Purging the Materialized View Log

The materialized view log contains transient data; records are inserted into the log, used during refreshes, and then deleted. You should encourage reuse of the log's blocks by setting a high value for **pctused** when creating the log.

If multiple materialized views use the same master table, they share the same materialized view log. If one of the materialized views is not refreshed for a long period, the materialized view log may never delete any of its records. As a result, the space requirements of the materialized view log will grow.

To reduce the space used by log entries, you can use the PURGE_LOG procedure of the DBMS_MVIEW package. PURGE_LOG takes three parameters: the name of the master table, a *num* variable, and a DELETE flag. The *num* variable specifies the number of least recently refreshed materialized views whose rows will be removed from the materialized view log. For example, if you have three materialized views that use the materialized view log and one of them has not been refreshed for a very long time, you would use a *num* value of 1.

The following listing shows an example of the PURGE_LOG procedure. In this example, the EMPLOYEE table's materialized view log will be purged of the entries required by the least recently used materialized view:

```
execute DBMS_MVIEW.PURGE_LOG
(master => 'EMPLOYEE',
    num => 1,
    flag => 'DELETE');
```

To further support maintenance efforts, Oracle provides two materialized view–specific options for the **truncate** command. If you want to truncate the master table without losing its materialized view log entries, you can enter the command

```
truncate table EMPLOYEE preserve materialized view log;
```

If the EMPLOYEE table's materialized views are based on primary key values (the default behavior), the materialized view log values will still be valid following an export/import of the EMPLOYEE table. However, if the EMPLOYEE table's materialized views are based on RowID values, the materialized view log would be invalid following an export/import of the base table (because different RowIDs may be assigned during the import). In that case, you should truncate the materialized view log when you truncate the base table. Here's an example:

```
truncate table EMPLOYEE purge materialized view log;
```

What Kind of Refreshes Can Be Performed?

To see what kind of refresh and rewrite capabilities are possible for your materialized views, you can query the MV_CAPABILITIES_TABLE table. The capabilities may change between versions, so you should reevaluate your refresh capabilities following Oracle software upgrades. To create this table, execute the utlxmv.sql script located in the /rdbms/admin directory under the Oracle software home directory.

The columns of MV_CAPABILITIES TABLE are shown here:

```
desc MV_CAPABILITIES_TABLE
```

Name	Null?	Type
STATEMENT_ID		VARCHAR2(30)
MVOWNER		VARCHAR2(30)
MVNAME		VARCHAR2(30)
CAPABILITY_NAME		VARCHAR2(30)
POSSIBLE		CHAR(1)
RELATED_TEXT		VARCHAR2(2000)
RELATED_NUM		NUMBER
MSGNO		NUMBER(38)
MSGTXT		VARCHAR2(2000)
SEQ		NUMBER

To populate the MV_CAPABILITIES_TABLE table, execute the DBMS_MVIEW.EXPLAIN_MVIEW procedure, using the name of the materialized view as the input value, as shown in the following example:

```
execute DBMS_MVIEW.EXPLAIN_MVIEW('local_category_count');
```

The utlxmv.sql script provides guidance on the interpretation of the column values, as shown in the following listing:

```
CREATE TABLE MV_CAPABILITIES_TABLE
    (STATEMENT_ID      VARCHAR(30),  -- Client-supplied unique statement identifier
    MVOWNER           VARCHAR(30),  -- NULL for SELECT based EXPLAIN_MVIEW
    MVNAME            VARCHAR(30),  -- NULL for SELECT based EXPLAIN_MVIEW
    CAPABILITY_NAME   VARCHAR(30),  -- A descriptive name of the particular
                                    -- capability:
                                    -- REWRITE
                                    --   Can do at least full text match
                                    --   rewrite
                                    -- REWRITE_PARTIAL_TEXT_MATCH
                                    --   Can do at least full and partial
                                    --   text match rewrite
                                    -- REWRITE_GENERAL
                                    --   Can do all forms of rewrite
                                    -- REFRESH
                                    --   Can do at least complete refresh
                                    -- REFRESH_FROM_LOG_AFTER_INSERT
                                    --   Can do fast refresh from an mv log
```

```
                                         --    or change capture table at least
                                         --    when update operations are
                                         --    restricted to INSERT
                                         -- REFRESH_FROM_LOG_AFTER_ANY
                                         --    can do fast refresh from an mv log
                                         --    or change capture table after any
                                         --    combination of updates
                                         -- PCT
                                         --    Can do Enhanced Update Tracking on
                                         --    the table named in the RELATED_NAME
                                         --    column.  EUT is needed for fast
                                         --    refresh after partitioned
                                         --    maintenance operations on the table
                                         --     named in the RELATED_NAME column
                                         --     and to do non-stale tolerated
                                         --     rewrite when the mv is partially
                                         --     stale with respect to the table
                                         --     named in the RELATED_NAME column.
                                         --     EUT can also sometimes enable fast
                                         --     refresh of updates to the table
                                         --     named in the RELATED_NAME column
                                         --     when fast refresh from an mv log
                                         --     or change capture table is not
                                         --     possible.
  POSSIBLE            CHARACTER(1),  -- T = capability is possible
                                     -- F = capability is not possible
  RELATED_TEXT        VARCHAR(2000),-- Owner.table.column, alias name, etc.
                                     -- related to this message.  The
                                     -- specific meaning of this column
                                     -- depends on the MSGNO column.  See
                                     -- the documentation for
                                      -- DBMS_MVIEW.EXPLAIN_MVIEW() for details
  RELATED_NUM         NUMBER,        -- When there is a numeric value
                                     -- associated with a row, it goes here.
                                     -- The specific meaning of this column
                                     -- depends on the MSGNO column.  See
                                     -- the documentation for
                                     -- DBMS_MVIEW.EXPLAIN_MVIEW() for details
  MSGNO               INTEGER,       -- When available, QSM message #
                                     -- explaining why not possible or more
                                     -- details when enabled.
  MSGTXT              VARCHAR(2000),-- Text associated with MSGNO.
  SEQ                 NUMBER);       -- Useful in ORDER BY clause when
                                     -- selecting from this table.
```

Once the EXPLAIN_MVIEW procedure has been executed, you can query MV_CAPABILITIES_ TABLE to determine your options:

```
select Capability_Name, Msgtxt
  from MV_CAPABILITIES_TABLE
 where Msgtxt is not null;
```

For the LOCAL_BOOKSHELF materialized view, the query returns the following:

```
CAPABILITY_NAME
------------------------------
MSGTXT
------------------------------------------------------------
PCT_TABLE
relation is not a partitioned table

REFRESH_FAST_AFTER_INSERT
the detail table does not have a materialized view log

REFRESH_FAST_AFTER_ONETAB_DML
see the reason why REFRESH_FAST_AFTER_INSERT is disabled

REFRESH_FAST_AFTER_ANY_DML
see the reason why REFRESH_FAST_AFTER_ONETAB_DML is disabled

REFRESH_FAST_PCT
PCT is not possible on any of the detail tables in the
materialized view

REWRITE_FULL_TEXT_MATCH
query rewrite is disabled on the materialized view

REWRITE_PARTIAL_TEXT_MATCH
query rewrite is disabled on the materialized view

REWRITE_GENERAL
query rewrite is disabled on the materialized view

REWRITE_PCT
general rewrite is not possible or PCT is not possible on
any of the detail tables

PCT_TABLE_REWRITE
relation is not a partitioned table

10 rows selected.
```

Because the **query rewrite** clause was not specified during the creation of the materialized view, the query rewrite capabilities are disabled for LOCAL_BOOKSHELF. Fast refresh capabilities are not supported because the base table does not have a materialized view log. If you change your materialized view or its base table, you should regenerate the data in MV_CAPABILITIES_TABLE to see the new capabilities.

As shown in the preceding listing, the LOCAL_BOOKSHELF materialized view cannot use a Fast refresh because its base table does not have a materialized view log. Here are some other constraints that will limit your ability to use Fast refreshes:

- The materialized view must not contain references to nonrepeating expressions such as SysDate and RowNum.

- The materialized view must not contain references to RAW or LONG RAW datatypes.

■ For materialized views based on joins, RowIDs from all tables in the **from** list must be part of the **select** list.

■ If there are outer joins, all the joins must be connected by **and**s, the **where** clause must have no selections, and unique constraints must exist on the join columns of the inner join table.

■ For materialized views based on aggregates, the materialized view logs must contain all columns from the referenced tables, must specify the **rowid** and **including new values** clauses, and must specify the **sequence** clause.

See the *Data Warehousing Guide* for additional restrictions related to Fast refreshes of complex aggregates.

> **NOTE**
> *You can specify an **order by** clause in the **create materialized view** command. The **order by** clause will only affect the initial creation of the materialized view; it will not affect any refreshes.*

Using Materialized Views to Alter Query Execution Paths

For a large database, a materialized view may offer several performance benefits. You can use materialized views to influence the optimizer to change the execution paths for queries. This feature, called *query rewrite*, enables the optimizer to use a materialized view in place of the table queried by the materialized view, even if the materialized view is not named in the query. For example, if you have a large SALES table, you may create a materialized view that sums the SALES data by region. If a user queries the SALES table for the sum of the SALES data for a region, Oracle can redirect that query to use your materialized view in place of the SALES table. As a result, you can reduce the number of accesses against your largest tables, thus improving the system performance. Further, because the data in the materialized view is already grouped by region, summarization does not have to be performed at the time the query is issued.

> **NOTE**
> *You must specify **enable query rewrite** in the materialized view definition for the view to be used as part of a query rewrite operation.*

To use the query rewrite capability effectively, you should create a dimension that defines the hierarchies within the table's data. To execute the **create dimension** command, you will need to have been granted the CREATE DIMENSION system privilege. Countries are part of continents, so you can create tables and dimensions to support this hierarchy:

```
create dimension GEOGRAPHY
      level COUNTRY_ID      is COUNTRY.Country
      level CONTINENT_id    is CONTINENT.Continent
      hierarchy COUNTRY_ROLLUP (
         COUNTRY_ID            child of
         CONTINENT_ID
      join key COUNTRY.Continent references CONTINENT_id);
```

To enable a materialized view for query rewrite, you must place all the master tables for the materialized view in the materialized view's schema, and you must have the QUERY REWRITE system privilege. If the view and the tables are in separate schemas, you must have the GLOBAL QUERY REWRITE system privilege. In general, you should create materialized views in the same schema as the tables on which they are based; otherwise, you will need to manage the permissions and grants required to create and maintain the materialized views.

NOTE
You can enable or disable query rewrite at the SQL statement level via the REWRITE and NOREWRITE hints. When using the REWRITE hint, you can specify materialized views for the optimizer to consider.

NOTE
Query rewrite decisions are based on the costs of the different execution paths, so your statistics should be kept up to date.

For query rewrite to be possible, you must set the following initialization parameters:

- OPTIMIZER_MODE = ALL_ROWS or FIRST_ROWS
- QUERY_REWRITE_ENABLED = TRUE
- QUERY_REWRITE_INTEGRITY = STALE_TOLERATED, TRUSTED, or ENFORCED

By default, QUERY_REWRITE_INTEGRITY is set to ENFORCED; in this mode all constraints must be validated. The optimizer only uses fresh data from the materialized views and only uses those relationships that are based on ENABLED VALIDATED primary, unique, or foreign key constraints. In TRUSTED mode, the optimizer trusts that the data in the materialized view is fresh and the relationships declared in dimensions and constraints are correct. In STALE_TOLERATED mode, the optimizer uses materialized views that are valid but contain stale data as well as those that contain fresh data.

If you set QUERY_REWRITE_ENABLED to FORCE, the optimizer will rewrite queries to use materialized views even when the estimated query cost of the original query is lower.

If query rewrite occurs, the explain plan for the query will list the materialized view as one of the objects accessed, along with an operation listed as "MAT_VIEW REWRITE ACCESS." You can use the DBMS_MVIEW.EXPLAIN_REWRITE procedure to see if rewrite is possible for a query and which materialized views would be involved. If the query cannot be rewritten, the procedure will document the reasons.

EXPLAIN_REWRITE takes three input parameters—the query, a materialized view name, and a statement identifier—and can store its output in a table. Oracle provides the **create table** command for the output table in a script named utlxrw.sql in the /rdbms/admin directory under the Oracle software home directory. The utlxrw.sql script creates a table named REWRITE_TABLE.

You can query REWRITE_TABLE for the original cost, rewritten cost, and the optimizer's decision. The Message column will display the reasons for the optimizer's decision.

If you have used the **build deferred** option of the **create materialized view** or **alter materialized view** command, the query rewrite feature will not be enabled until after the first time the materialized view is refreshed.

NOTE
If bind variables have been used within the query, the optimizer will not rewrite it even though query rewrite has been enabled.

See the *Data Warehousing Guide* for further details and constraints related to query rewrite.

Managing Distributed Transactions

A single logical unit of work may include transactions against multiple databases. For example, a **commit** may be executed after two tables in separate databases have been updated. Oracle will transparently maintain the integrity between the two databases by ensuring that all the transactions involved either **commit** or roll back as a group. This is accomplished automatically via Oracle's Two-Phase Commit (2PC) mechanism.

The first phase of the 2PC is the prepare phase. In this phase, each node involved in a transaction prepares the data that it will need to either **commit** or roll back the data. Once prepared, a node is said to be "in doubt." The nodes notify the initiating node for the transaction (known as the *global coordinator)* of their status.

Once all nodes are prepared, the transaction enters the commit phase, and all nodes are instructed to **commit** their portion of the logical transaction. The databases all **commit** the data at the same logical time, preserving the integrity of the distributed data.

Resolving In-Doubt Transactions

Transactions against stand-alone databases may fail due to problems with the database server; for example, there may be a media failure. Working with distributed databases increases the number of potential failure causes during a set of related transactions.

When a distributed transaction is pending, an entry for that transaction will appear in the DBA_2PC_PENDING data dictionary view. When the transaction completes, its DBA_2PC_PENDING record is removed. If the transaction is pending, but is not able to complete, its record stays in DBA_2PC_PENDING.

The RECO (Recoverer) background process periodically checks the DBA_2PC_PENDING view for distributed transactions that failed to complete. Using the information there, the RECO process on a node will automatically attempt to recover the local portion of an in-doubt transaction. It then attempts to establish connections to any other databases involved in the transaction and resolves the distributed portions of the transaction. The related rows in the DBA_2PC_PENDING view in each database are then removed.

NOTE
*You can enable and disable the RECO process via the **enable distributed recovery** and **disable distributed recovery** clauses of the **alter system** command.*

The recovery of distributed transactions is performed automatically by the RECO process. You can manually recover the local portions of a distributed transaction, but this will usually result in inconsistent data between the distributed databases. If a local recovery is performed, the remote data will be out of sync.

To minimize the number of distributed recoveries necessary, you can influence the way that the distributed transaction is processed. The transaction processing is influenced via the use of *commit point strength* to tell the database how to structure the transaction.

Commit Point Strength

Each set of distributed transactions may reference multiple hosts and databases. Of those, one host and database can normally be singled out as being the most reliable, or as owning the most critical data. This database is known as the *commit point site*. If data is committed there, it should be committed for all databases. If the transaction against the commit point site fails, the transactions against the other nodes are rolled back. The commit point site also stores information about the status of the distributed transaction.

The commit point site will be selected by Oracle based on each database's *commit point strength*. This is set via the initialization file, as shown in the following example:

```
COMMIT_POINT_STRENGTH=100
```

The values for the COMMIT_POINT_STRENGTH parameter are set on a relative scale, not on an absolute scale. In the preceding example, the value is set to 100. If another database has a commit point strength of 200, that database would be the commit point site for a distributed transaction involving those two databases. The COMMIT_POINT_STRENGTH value cannot exceed 255.

Because the scale is relative, you should set up a site-specific scale. Set the commit point on your most reliable database to 200. Then, grade the other servers and databases relative to the most reliable database. If, for example, another database is only 80 percent as reliable as the most reliable database, assign it a commit point strength of 160 (80 percent of 200). Fixing a single database at a definite point (in this case, 200) allows the rest of the databases to be graded on an even scale. This scale should result in the proper commit point site being used for each transaction.

Monitoring Distributed Databases

Several key environmental performance measures must be taken into account for databases:

- The performance of the host
- The distribution of I/O across disks and controllers
- The usage of available memory

For distributed databases, you must also consider the following:

- The capacity of the network and its hardware
- The load on the network segments
- The usage of different physical access paths between hosts

None of these can be measured from within the database. The focus of monitoring efforts for distributed databases shifts from being database-centric to network-centric. The database becomes one part of the monitored environment, rather than the only part that is checked.

You still need to monitor those aspects of the database that are critical to its success—such as the free space in tablespaces. However, the *performance* of distributed databases cannot be measured except as part of the performance of the network that supports them. Therefore, all performance-related tests, such as stress tests, must be coordinated with the network management staff. That staff may also be able to verify the effectiveness of your attempts to reduce the database load on the network.

The performance of the individual hosts can usually be monitored via a network monitoring package. This monitoring is performed in a top-down fashion—from network to host to database. Use the monitoring system described in Chapter 6 as an extension to the network and host monitors.

Tuning Distributed Databases

When you're tuning a stand-alone database, the goal is to reduce the amount of time it takes to find data. As described in Chapter 8, you can use a number of database structures and options to increase the likelihood that the data will be found in memory or in the first place that the database looks.

When working with distributed databases, you have an additional consideration. Because data is now not only being found but also being shipped across the network, the performance of a query is made up of the performance of these two steps. You must therefore consider the ways in which data is being transferred across the network, with a goal of reducing the network traffic.

A simple way to reduce network traffic is to replicate data from one node to another. You can do this manually (via the SQL*Plus **copy** command), or it can be done automatically by the database (via materialized views). Replicating data improves the performance of queries against remote databases by bringing the data across the network once—usually during a slow period on the local host. Local queries can use the local copy of the data, eliminating the network traffic that would otherwise be required.

Let's consider a simple task—selecting a value from a sequence. A company has created a distributed application in which a new sequence value is generated for each row. However, the sequence is local, whereas the insert is being performed in a far distant database. Because the trigger that generates the sequence value is executed for each row, each insert generates a remote operation to generate the next sequence value.

The impact of this design is apparent when a session's trace file is examined:

```
SELECT NEWID_SEQ.NEXTVAL
FROM
 DUAL
```

call	count	cpu	elapsed	disk	query	current	rows
Parse	1	0.01	0.13	0	0	0	0
Execute	53	0.01	0.01	0	0	0	0
Fetch	53	0.06	6.34	0	159	0	53
total	107	0.09	6.50	0	159	0	53

```
Misses in library cache during parse: 0
Optimizer goal: CHOOSE
```

```
Rows      Execution Plan
-------   ---------------------------------------------------------
      0   SELECT STATEMENT    GOAL: CHOOSE
      0    SEQUENCE (REMOTE)
      0     TABLE ACCESS (FULL) OF 'DUAL'

Elapsed times include waiting on following events:
  Event waited on                             Times   Max. Wait  Total Waited
  --------------------------------------      Waited  ---------  ------------
  SQL*Net message to dblink                       53       0.00          0.00
  SQL*Net message from dblink                     53       0.13          6.29
```

In this case, the query is very simple—it selects the next value of the sequence from DUAL. But the sequence is remote (as seen in the execution plan), so the time required to fetch the values is 6.29 seconds for 53 rows, out of a total of 6.50 seconds. To tune the application, you either need to reduce the number of trips (such as by performing batch operations instead of row-by-row operations) or eliminate the remote architecture component of the **insert**. If the remote object (the sequence) and the local object (the DUAL table) can be brought together, the wait times associated with the remote operations can be eliminated.

Two problems commonly arise with replicated solutions: First, the local data may become out of sync with the remote data. This is a standard problem with derived data; it limits the usefulness of this option to tables whose data is fairly static. Even if a simple materialized view is used with a materialized view log, the data will not be refreshed continuously—only when scheduled.

The second problem with the replicated data solution is that the copy of the table may not be able to pass updates back to the master table. That is, if a read-only materialized is used to make a local copy of a remote table, the snapshot cannot be updated. If you are using materialized views, you can use updateable materialized views to send changes back to the master site, or you can use writeable materialized views to support local ownership of data.

Any updates that must be processed against replicas must also be performed against the master tables. If the table is frequently updated, then replicating the data will not improve your performance unless you are using Oracle's multimaster replication options. When there is multisite ownership of data, users can make changes in any database designated as an owner of the data. The management of Oracle's multimaster replication is very involved and requires creating a database environment (with database links and so on) specifically designed to support multidirectional replication of data. See the Oracle replication documentation for details on implementing a multimaster environment.

The performance of the refreshes generally won't concern your users. What may concern them is the validity and timeliness of the data. If the remote tables are frequently modified and are of considerable size, you are almost forced to use simple materialized views with materialized view logs to keep the data current. Performing complete refreshes in the middle of a workday is generally unacceptable. Therefore, it is the *frequency* of the refreshes rather than the size of them that determines which type of materialized view will better serve the users. After all, users are most concerned about the performance of the system while they are using it; refreshes performed late at night do not directly affect them. If the tables need to be frequently synchronized, use simple materialized views with materialized view logs.

As was noted previously in this chapter, you may index the underlying tables that are created by the materialized view in the local database. Indexing should also help to improve query performance, at the expense of slowing down the refreshes.

Another means of reducing network traffic, via remote procedure calls, is described in Chapter 8. That chapter also includes information on tuning SQL and the application design. If the database was properly structured, tuning the way the application processes data will yield the most significant performance improvements.

APPENDIX
A

Password Verify
Function

This appendix contains an abbreviated version of the password verify function referenced in Chapter 10. The complete script can be found in the directory $ORACLE_HOME/rdbms/admin/utlpwdmg.sql.

```
Rem
Rem $Header: utlpwdmg.sql 31-aug-2000.11:00:47 nireland Exp $
Rem
Rem utlpwdmg.sql
Rem
Rem  Copyright (c) Oracle Corporation 1996, 2000. All Rights Reserved.
Rem
Rem     NAME
Rem        utlpwdmg.sql - script for Default Password Resource Limits
Rem
Rem     DESCRIPTION
Rem        This is a script for enabling the password management features
Rem        by setting the default password resource limits.


CREATE OR REPLACE FUNCTION verify_function
(username varchar2,
  password varchar2,
  old_password varchar2)
  RETURN boolean IS
   n boolean;
   m integer;
   differ integer;
   isdigit boolean;
   ischar  boolean;
   ispunct boolean;
   digitarray varchar2(20);
   punctarray varchar2(25);
   chararray varchar2(52);

BEGIN
   digitarray:= '0123456789';
   chararray:= 'abcdefghijklmnopqrstuvwxyzABCDEFGHIJKLMNOPQRSTUVWXYZ';
   punctarray:='!"#$%&()``*+,-/:;<=>?_';

   -- Check if the password is same as the username
   IF NLS_LOWER(password) = NLS_LOWER(username) THEN
     raise_application_error(-20001, 'Password same as or similar to user');
   END IF;

   -- Check for the minimum length of the password
   IF length(password) < 4 THEN
       raise_application_error(-20002, 'Password length less than 4');
```

```
   END IF;

-- Check if the password is too simple. A dictionary of words may be
-- maintained and a check may be made so as not to allow the words
-- that are too simple for the password.
IF NLS_LOWER(password) IN ('welcome', 'database', 'account',
        'user', 'password', 'oracle', 'computer', 'abcd') THEN
    raise_application_error(-20002, 'Password too simple');
END IF;

-- Check if the password contains at least one letter, one digit and one
-- punctuation mark.
-- 1. Check for the digit
isdigit:=FALSE;
m := length(password);
FOR i IN 1..10 LOOP
    FOR j IN 1..m LOOP
        IF substr(password,j,1) = substr(digitarray,i,1) THEN
            isdigit:=TRUE;
             GOTO findchar;
        END IF;
    END LOOP;
END LOOP;
IF isdigit = FALSE THEN

    raise_application_error(-20003, 'Password should contain
            at least one digit, one character and one punctuation');
END IF;
-- 2. Check for the character
<<findchar>>
ischar:=FALSE;
FOR i IN 1..length(chararray) LOOP
    FOR j IN 1..m LOOP
        IF substr(password,j,1) = substr(chararray,i,1) THEN
            ischar:=TRUE;
             GOTO findpunct;
        END IF;
    END LOOP;
END LOOP;
IF ischar = FALSE THEN
    raise_application_error(-20003, 'Password should contain at least one
                digit, one character and one punctuation');
END IF;
-- 3. Check for the punctuation
<<findpunct>>
ispunct:=FALSE;
FOR i IN 1..length(punctarray) LOOP
    FOR j IN 1..m LOOP
        IF substr(password,j,1) = substr(punctarray,i,1) THEN
            ispunct:=TRUE;
```

```
            GOTO endsearch;
        END IF;
    END LOOP;
END LOOP;
IF ispunct = FALSE THEN
    raise_application_error(-20003, 'Password should contain at least one
                digit, one character and one punctuation');
END IF;

<<endsearch>>
-- Check if the password differs from the previous password
-- by at least 3 letters
IF old_password IS NOT NULL THEN
  differ := length(old_password) - length(password);

  IF abs(differ) < 3 THEN
    IF length(password) < length(old_password) THEN
      m := length(password);
    ELSE
      m := length(old_password);
    END IF;

    differ := abs(differ);
    FOR i IN 1..m LOOP
      IF substr(password,i,1) != substr(old_password,i,1) THEN
        differ := differ + 1;
      END IF;
    END LOOP;

    IF differ < 3 THEN
      raise_application_error(-20004, 'Password should differ by at
      least 3 characters');
    END IF;
  END IF;
END IF;
-- Everything is fine; return TRUE ;
RETURN(TRUE);
END;
```

Index

C

D

E

M

N

O

T

V

W

INTERNATIONAL CONTACT INFORMATION

AUSTRALIA
McGraw-Hill Book Company
Australia Pty. Ltd.
TEL +61-2-9900-1800
FAX +61-2-9878-8881
http://www.mcgraw-hill.com.au
books-it_sydney@mcgraw-hill.com

CANADA
McGraw-Hill Ryerson Ltd.
TEL +905-430-5000
FAX +905-430-5020
http://www.mcgraw-hill.ca

GREECE, MIDDLE EAST, & AFRICA
(Excluding South Africa)
McGraw-Hill Hellas
TEL +30-210-6560-990
TEL +30-210-6560-993
TEL +30-210-6560-994
FAX +30-210-6545-525

MEXICO (Also serving Latin America)
McGraw-Hill Interamericana Editores
S.A. de C.V.
TEL +525-1500-5108
FAX +525-117-1589
http://www.mcgraw-hill.com.mx
carlos_ruiz@mcgraw-hill.com

SINGAPORE (Serving Asia)
McGraw-Hill Book Company
TEL +65-6863-1580
FAX +65-6862-3354
http://www.mcgraw-hill.com.sg
mghasia@mcgraw-hill.com

SOUTH AFRICA
McGraw-Hill South Africa
TEL +27-11-622-7512
FAX +27-11-622-9045
robyn_swanepoel@mcgraw-hill.com

SPAIN
McGraw-Hill/
Interamericana de España, S.A.U.
TEL +34-91-180-3000
FAX +34-91-372-8513
http://www.mcgraw-hill.es
professional@mcgraw-hill.es

UNITED KINGDOM, NORTHERN,
EASTERN, & CENTRAL EUROPE
McGraw-Hill Education Europe
TEL +44-1-628-502500
FAX +44-1-628-770224
http://www.mcgraw-hill.co.uk
emea_queries@mcgraw-hill.com

ALL OTHER INQUIRIES Contact:
McGraw-Hill/Osborne
TEL +1-510-420-7700
FAX +1-510-420-7703
http://www.osborne.com
omg_international@mcgraw-hill.com

GET YOUR FREE SUBSCRIPTION TO ORACLE MAGAZINE

Oracle Magazine is essential gear for today's information technology professionals. Stay informed and increase your productivity with every issue of *Oracle Magazine*. Inside each free bimonthly issue you'll get:

IF THERE ARE OTHER ORACLE USERS AT YOUR LOCATION WHO WOULD LIKE TO RECEIVE THEIR OWN SUBSCRIPTION TO ORACLE MAGAZINE, PLEASE PHOTOCOPY THIS FORM AND PASS IT ALONG.

- Up-to-date information on Oracle Database, Oracle Application Server, Web development, enterprise grid computing, database technology, and business trends
- Third-party vendor news and announcements
- Technical articles on Oracle and partner products, technologies, and operating environments
- Development and administration tips
- Real-world customer stories

Three easy ways to subscribe:

① Web
Visit our Web site at otn.oracle.com/oraclemagazine. You'll find a subscription form there, plus much more!

② Fax
Complete the questionnaire on the back of this card and fax the questionnaire side only to +1.847.763.9638.

③ Mail
Complete the questionnaire on the back of this card and mail it to P.O. Box 1263, Skokie, IL 60076-8263

ORACLE®

FREE SUBSCRIPTION

○ **Yes, please send me a FREE subscription to *Oracle Magazine*.**
To receive a free subscription to *Oracle Magazine*, you must fill out the entire card, sign it, and date it (incomplete cards cannot be processed or acknowledged). You can also fax your application to +1.847.763.9638.
Or subscribe at our Web site at otn.oracle.com/oraclemagazine

○ **NO**

○ From time to time, Oracle Publishing allows our partners exclusive access to our e-mail addresses for special promotions and announcements. To be included in this program, please check this circle.

○ Oracle Publishing allows sharing of our mailing list with selected third parties. If you prefer your mailing address not to be included in this program, please check here. If at any time you would like to be removed from this mailing list, please contact Customer Service at +1.847.647.9630 or send an e-mail to oracle@halldata.com.

signature (required)   date

X

name   title

company   e-mail address

street/p.o. box

city/state/zip or postal code   telephone

country   fax

YOU MUST ANSWER ALL TEN QUESTIONS BELOW.

① WHAT IS THE PRIMARY BUSINESS ACTIVITY OF YOUR FIRM AT THIS LOCATION? (check one only)
- ☐ 01 Aerospace and Defense Manufacturing
- ☐ 02 Application Service Provider
- ☐ 03 Automotive Manufacturing
- ☐ 04 Chemicals, Oil and Gas
- ☐ 05 Communications and Media
- ☐ 06 Construction/Engineering
- ☐ 07 Consumer Sector/Consumer Packaged Goods
- ☐ 08 Education
- ☐ 09 Financial Services/Insurance
- ☐ 10 Government (civil)
- ☐ 11 Government (military)
- ☐ 12 Healthcare
- ☐ 13 High Technology Manufacturing, OEM
- ☐ 14 Integrated Software Vendor
- ☐ 15 Life Sciences (Biotech, Pharmaceuticals)
- ☐ 16 Mining
- ☐ 17 Retail/Wholesale/Distribution
- ☐ 18 Systems Integrator, VAR/VAD
- ☐ 19 Telecommunications
- ☐ 20 Travel and Transportation
- ☐ 21 Utilities (electric, gas, sanitation, water)
- ☐ 98 Other Business and Services

② WHICH OF THE FOLLOWING BEST DESCRIBES YOUR PRIMARY JOB FUNCTION? (check one only)
Corporate Management/Staff
- ☐ 01 Executive Management (President, Chair, CEO, CFO, Owner, Partner, Principal)
- ☐ 02 Finance/Administrative Management (VP/Director/ Manager/Controller, Purchasing, Administration)
- ☐ 03 Sales/Marketing Management (VP/Director/Manager)
- ☐ 04 Computer Systems/Operations Management (CIO/VP/Director/ Manager MIS, Operations)
IS/IT Staff
- ☐ 05 Systems Development/ Programming Management
- ☐ 06 Systems Development/ Programming Staff
- ☐ 07 Consulting
- ☐ 08 DBA/Systems Administrator
- ☐ 09 Education/Training
- ☐ 10 Technical Support Director/Manager
- ☐ 11 Other Technical Management/Staff
- ☐ 98 Other

③ WHAT IS YOUR CURRENT PRIMARY OPERATING PLATFORM? (select all that apply)
- ☐ 01 Digital Equipment UNIX
- ☐ 02 Digital Equipment VAX VMS
- ☐ 03 HP UNIX
- ☐ 04 IBM AIX
- ☐ 05 IBM UNIX
- ☐ 06 Java
- ☐ 07 Linux
- ☐ 08 Macintosh
- ☐ 09 MS-DOS
- ☐ 10 MVS
- ☐ 11 NetWare
- ☐ 12 Network Computing
- ☐ 13 OpenVMS
- ☐ 14 SCO UNIX
- ☐ 15 Sequent DYNIX/ptx
- ☐ 16 Sun Solaris/SunOS
- ☐ 17 SVR4
- ☐ 18 UnixWare
- ☐ 19 Windows
- ☐ 20 Windows NT
- ☐ 21 Other UNIX
- ☐ 98 Other
- 99 ☐ None of the above

④ DO YOU EVALUATE, SPECIFY, RECOMMEND, OR AUTHORIZE THE PURCHASE OF ANY OF THE FOLLOWING? (check all that apply)
- ☐ 01 Hardware
- ☐ 02 Software
- ☐ 03 Application Development Tools
- ☐ 04 Database Products
- ☐ 05 Internet or Intranet Products
- 99 ☐ None of the above

⑤ IN YOUR JOB, DO YOU USE OR PLAN TO PURCHASE ANY OF THE FOLLOWING PRODUCTS? (check all that apply)
Software
- ☐ 01 Business Graphics
- ☐ 02 CAD/CAE/CAM
- ☐ 03 CASE
- ☐ 04 Communications
- ☐ 05 Database Management
- ☐ 06 File Management
- ☐ 07 Finance
- ☐ 08 Java
- ☐ 09 Materials Resource Planning
- ☐ 10 Multimedia Authoring
- ☐ 11 Networking
- ☐ 12 Office Automation
- ☐ 13 Order Entry/Inventory Control
- ☐ 14 Programming
- ☐ 15 Project Management
- ☐ 16 Scientific and Engineering
- ☐ 17 Spreadsheets
- ☐ 18 Systems Management
- ☐ 19 Workflow

Hardware
- ☐ 20 Macintosh
- ☐ 21 Mainframe
- ☐ 22 Massively Parallel Processing
- ☐ 23 Minicomputer
- ☐ 24 PC
- ☐ 25 Network Computer
- ☐ 26 Symmetric Multiprocessing
- ☐ 27 Workstation
Peripherals
- ☐ 28 Bridges/Routers/Hubs/Gateways
- ☐ 29 CD-ROM Drives
- ☐ 30 Disk Drives/Subsystems
- ☐ 31 Modems
- ☐ 32 Tape Drives/Subsystems
- ☐ 33 Video Boards/Multimedia
Services
- ☐ 34 Application Service Provider
- ☐ 35 Consulting
- ☐ 36 Education/Training
- ☐ 37 Maintenance
- ☐ 38 Online Database Services
- ☐ 39 Support
- ☐ 40 Technology-Based Training
- ☐ 98 Other
- 99 ☐ None of the above

⑥ WHAT ORACLE PRODUCTS ARE IN USE AT YOUR SITE? (check all that apply)
Oracle E-Business Suite
- ☐ 01 Oracle Marketing
- ☐ 02 Oracle Sales
- ☐ 03 Oracle Order Fulfillment
- ☐ 04 Oracle Supply Chain Management
- ☐ 05 Oracle Procurement
- ☐ 06 Oracle Manufacturing
- ☐ 07 Oracle Maintenance Management
- ☐ 08 Oracle Service
- ☐ 09 Oracle Contracts
- ☐ 10 Oracle Projects
- ☐ 11 Oracle Financials
- ☐ 12 Oracle Human Resources
- ☐ 13 Oracle Interaction Center
- ☐ 14 Oracle Communications/Utilities (modules)
- ☐ 15 Oracle Public Sector/University (modules)
- ☐ 16 Oracle Financial Services (modules)
Server/Software
- ☐ 17 Oracle9i
- ☐ 18 Oracle9i Lite
- ☐ 19 Oracle8i
- ☐ 20 Other Oracle database
- ☐ 21 Oracle9i Application Server
- ☐ 22 Oracle9i Application Server Wireless
- ☐ 23 Oracle Small Business Suite

Tools
- ☐ 24 Oracle Developer Suite
- ☐ 25 Oracle Discoverer
- ☐ 26 Oracle JDeveloper
- ☐ 27 Oracle Migration Workbench
- ☐ 28 Oracle9i AS Portal
- ☐ 29 Oracle Warehouse Builder
Oracle Services
- ☐ 30 Oracle Outsourcing
- ☐ 31 Oracle Consulting
- ☐ 32 Oracle Education
- ☐ 33 Oracle Support
- ☐ 98 Other
- 99 ☐ None of the above

⑦ WHAT OTHER DATABASE PRODUCTS ARE IN USE AT YOUR SITE? (check all that apply)
- ☐ 01 Access
- ☐ 02 Baan
- ☐ 03 dbase
- ☐ 04 Gupta
- ☐ 05 IBM DB2
- ☐ 06 Informix
- ☐ 07 Ingres
- ☐ 08 Microsoft Access
- ☐ 09 Microsoft SQL Server
- ☐ 10 PeopleSoft
- ☐ 11 Progress
- ☐ 12 SAP
- ☐ 13 Sybase
- ☐ 14 VSAM
- ☐ 98 Other
- 99 ☐ None of the above

⑧ WHAT OTHER APPLICATION SERVER PRODUCTS ARE IN USE AT YOUR SITE? (check all that apply)
- ☐ 01 BEA
- ☐ 02 IBM
- ☐ 03 Sybase
- ☐ 04 Sun
- ☐ 05 Other

⑨ DURING THE NEXT 12 MONTHS, HOW MUCH DO YOU ANTICIPATE YOUR ORGANIZATION WILL SPEND ON COMPUTER HARDWARE, SOFTWARE, PERIPHERALS, AND SERVICES FOR YOUR LOCATION? (check only one)
- ☐ 01 Less than $10,000
- ☐ 02 $10,000 to $49,999
- ☐ 03 $50,000 to $99,999
- ☐ 04 $100,000 to $499,999
- ☐ 05 $500,000 to $999,999
- ☐ 06 $1,000,000 and over

⑩ WHAT IS YOUR COMPANY'S YEARLY SALES REVENUE? (please choose one)
- ☐ 01 $500, 000, 000 and above
- ☐ 02 $100, 000, 000 to $500, 000, 000
- ☐ 03 $50, 000, 000 to $100, 000, 000
- ☐ 04 $5, 000, 000 to $50, 000, 000
- ☐ 05 $1, 000, 000 to $5, 000, 000

100103